Managing Your
Personal Finances

• FIFTH EDITION •

JOAN S. RYAN
M.B.A., Ph.D., C.M.A.

Business Department Chair
Clackamas Community College
Oregon City, Oregon

THOMSON
™
SOUTH-WESTERN

Australia · Canada · Mexico · Singapore · Spain · United Kingdom · United States

THOMSON

SOUTH-WESTERN

Managing Your Personal Finances, 5th Edition
Joan S. Ryan

VP/Editorial Director:
Jack W. Calhoun

VP/Editor-in-Chief:
Karen Schmohe

Acquisitions Editor:
Marilyn Hornsby

Project Manager:
Carol Sturzenberger

Consulting Editor:
Cinci Stowell

Senior Marketing Manager:
Nancy Long

Production Editor:
Martha Conway

Manager of Technology, Editorial:
Liz Prigge

Technology Project Editor:
Scott Hamilton

Web Coordinator:
Ed Stubenrauch

Manufacturing Coordinator:
Kevin Kluck

Production House:
Navta Associates, Inc.

Art Director:
Stacy Jenkins Shirley

Cover and Internal Designer:
Grannan Graphic Design, Ltd.

Cover Images:
© Masterfile

Photo Permissions Manager:
Darren Wright

Printer:
RR Donnelley
Willard, Ohio

ASIA (including India)
Thomson Learning
5 Shenton Way
#01-01 UIC Building
Singapore 068808

AUSTRALIA/NEW ZEALAND
Thomson Learning
Australia
102 Dodds Street
Southbank, Victoria 3006
Australia

CANADA
Thomson Nelson
1120 Birchmount Road
Toronto, Ontario
M1K 5G4
Canada

UK/EUROPE/MIDDLE
EAST/AFRICA
Thomson Learning
High Holborn House
50/51 Bedford Row
London WC1R 4LR
United Kingdom

Don't Settle for the Status Quo

Financial Math Review

Learn all about basic math topics within the context of daily financial exchanges. *Financial Math Review* covers arithmetic, fractions, statistics, ratios, and proportions. Students can relate to the real world examples as they improve their knowledge and skills and prepare for algebra instruction. Students learn math skills that prepare them for standardized testing and allow them to become smart shoppers, valued employees, and informed taxpayers.

Text   0-538-44021-X

Investing in Your Future 2E

Start students on the path to dollars and sense. Use NAIC's respected Stock Selection Guide process to teach smart saving, investing, and planning. Students learn how to analyze the value of stocks and mutual funds. Company Profiles introduce every chapter and the lesson-plan approach makes material easy to comprehend.

Text   0-538-43881-9
Module (ExamView, Instructor's Resource CD, Video,
   Annotated Instructor's Edition)   0-538-43885-1

Banking Systems

Explore the principles and practices of banking and credit in the United States. This exciting new text guides users through an overview of financial services, mortgage lending, negotiable instruments, employment, security and ethics, and money and interest. Appropriate for the National Academy Foundation's Academy of Finance courses.

Text   0-538-44089-9
Module (ExamView, Instructor's Resource CD, Video,
   Annotated Instructor's Edition)   0-538-44094-5

Fundamentals of Insurance

Explore health and property insurance, insurance rates, claims procedures, careers in insurance, and annuities. The extensive use of hands-on activities helps students understand the importance of insurance and how it affects them today and through their retirement years. Appropriate for the National Academy Foundation's (NAF's) Academy of Finance courses.

Text   0-538-43201-2
Module (ExamView, Instructor's Resource CD, Video,
   Annotated Instructor's Edition)   0-538-43248-9

Family Financial Management 7E

This hands-on, money management simulation is presented in an extended family setting, presenting situations from young adult to preparing for retirement. Students calculate net worth, plan monthly budgets, complete banking transactions, pay utility bills, perform credit transactions, make housing payments, and reconcile monthly bank statements. Spreadsheet files allow students to use commercial software to work with budgets and financial statements.

Envelope Simulation   0-538-43804-5
Data CD (Windows/Macintosh)   0-538-43842-8

Instructor Support and Other Materials Available

Join us on the Internet
South-Western – http://www.swlearning.com
Thomson – http://www.thomsonlearning.com

THOMSON
———— ✶ ————™
SOUTH-WESTERN

HOW TO USE THIS BOOK

Engage Student Interest

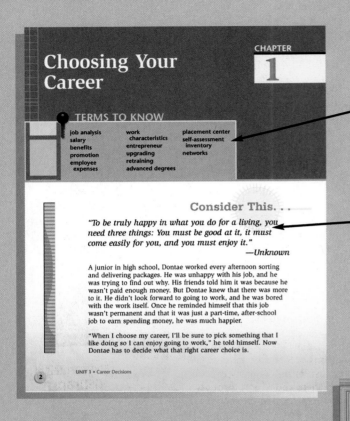

Terms to Know are vocabulary words defined within the chapter.

Consider This presents a story that's tailored to the chapter's contents. By reading the story, you'll have an overview of the chapter's main topics.

Lessons make the text easy to use in all classroom environments.

Goals are clearly stated learning objectives. Each goal represents a section of the chapter.

Issues in Your World **is a full-page feature that will extend your knowledge by acquainting you with real-world issues.**

Issues in Your World

Being a Lifelong Learner

Graduating from high school or its equivalent is a major milestone. It is the first step toward securing your financial future. You may choose additional or specialized training, an apprenticeship program, an associate's degree, a bachelor's degree, or beyond. Regardless of the highest level of formal education you attain, your opportunities for learning will continue throughout your life.

Lifelong learning means actively seeking new knowledge, skills, and experiences that will add to your professional and personal growth throughout your life. Upgrading your skills will do the following:

* Keep you marketable, both in your current job and in future jobs.
* Enhance your resume, showing you are interested and actively pursuing new skills, talents, or enrichment.
* Empower you to change directions when you feel it is time to move on, try new things, or pursue a different path.
* Open new opportunities for growth and fulfillment.

Your choices are virtually unlimited! You can learn a new hobby, improve and maintain your health, polish your leadership skills, discover new opportunities you would never have considered, meet new people who will become your friends, or get involved in community service. Lifelong learning will provide you with a versatility that will allow you to explore new directions, discover hidden talents and interests, and enrich your life.

Lifelong learning will keep you active—mentally as well as physically—as you find new paths to explore and add to your base of knowledge. When times change, you'll be ready!

Think Critically

1. Is there something you'd like to explore that is not your major career objective, such as playing an instrument, learning a new sport, making something, or learning a new skill?
2. How has lifelong learning been a significant part of the life of someone you know?
3. Why would a prospective employer be impressed with an applicant who was involved in community activities?

CHAPTER 1 • Choosing Your Career

15

unit **1**

PROJECT

Career Development: Planning and Leading a Meeting

A **Project** ends each unit. It's an opportunity for you to apply and extend your knowledge.

UNIT 1 PROJECT

108

Special Features Enhance Learning

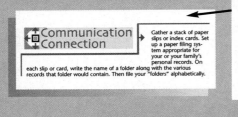

Communication Connection offers speaking and writing activities related to the chapter content.

Career Focus presents information on a career related to the chapter's topics.

Career Focus ⟶

Specialists involved in resolving disputes must be highly experienced and knowledgeable. Mediators advise labor and management to prevent and, when necessary, resolve disputes over labor agreements or other labor relations issues. Arbitrators, sometimes called referees, decide disputes that bind both labor and management to specific terms and conditions of labor contracts. A strong background in industrial relations and law is highly desirable for mediators and arbitrators. In fact, many people in these specialties are lawyers.

For more information, refer to the *Occupational Outlook Handbook* at www.bls.gov or search the Internet using such key words as "careers," "jobs," "mediator," and "arbitrator."

Global View supplies international connections relevant to personal finance topics.

VIEWPOINTS

Review the mutual fund risk/return pyramid shown in Figure 14-1, noting the range from lower risk/lower return potential through higher risk/higher return potential.

Think Critically: How would you describe your level of risk tolerance? Would you be willing to undertake higher risks for the potential of higher returns?

Viewpoints provides an opportunity for you to think critically about issues that have no clear-cut answers.

Math Minute — The Rule of 72

The Rule of 72 is a rule of thumb or approximation technique. You can use it to estimate either the number of years or rate of return needed to double your money.

If you want to find the number of years, divide 72 by the rate of return.

Example: You are earning 10% on your money. How long will it take to double your money?

Answer: 72 divided by 10 = 7.2 years

If you want to find the rate of return, divide 72 by the number of years in which you want your money to double.

Example: You have $5,000 and want to double it in 6 years. What rate must your investment earn to achieve $10,000 in 6 years?

Answer: 72 divided by 6 = 12%. At 12% your money will double in 6 years.

Math Minute presents review and practice in basic math skills linked to chapter topics.

Net Nuggets points you to Web sites that will help you learn more about the chapter's content.

 Net Nuggets

For many families, the greatest financial worry is whether they will be able to afford a college education for their children. Savingforcollege.com provides information and resources concerning qualified tuition programs, known as "529 plans." These plans are education savings plans operated by state or educational institutions, designed to help families set aside funds for future college costs. Check out the site at www.savingforcollege.com.

Review and Assessment

Check Your Understanding contains end-of-lesson activities to review terms and concepts.

✅ **Check Your Understanding**

1. What are some sources of financial information useful for making investment decisions?
2. Why should beginning investors choose safe investments?
3. Why is investing in stock considered more risky than investing in savings bonds?

Chapter Assessment gives you the opportunity to tie your learning together. *Summary* is a bulleted list of chapter concepts for quick review. *Review Terms* helps you acquire a vocabulary of personal finance terms. *Review Facts and Ideas* tests your recall of the chapter's main points. *Apply Your Knowledge* and *Solve Problems and Explore Issues* challenge you to dig deeper into issues.

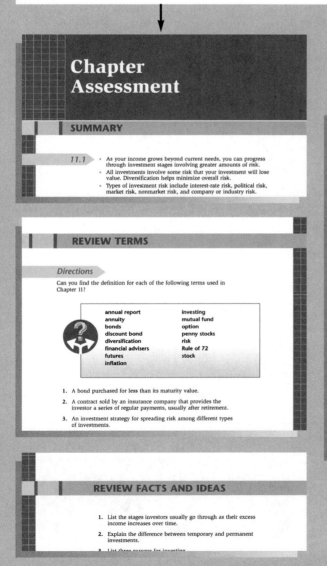

Chapter Assessment

SUMMARY

11.1
- As your income grows beyond current needs, you can progress through investment stages involving greater amounts of risk.
- All investments involve some risk that your investment will lose value. Diversification helps minimize overall risk.
- Types of investment risk include interest-rate risk, political risk, market risk, nonmarket risk, and company or industry risk.

REVIEW TERMS

Directions

Can you find the definition for each of the following terms used in Chapter 11?

annual report	investing
annuity	mutual fund
bonds	option
discount bond	penny stocks
diversification	risk
financial advisers	Rule of 72
futures	stock
inflation	

1. A bond purchased for less than its maturity value.
2. A contract sold by an insurance company that provides the investor a series of regular payments, usually after retirement.
3. An investment strategy for spreading risk among different types of investments.

REVIEW FACTS AND IDEAS

1. List the stages investors usually go through as their excess income increases over time.
2. Explain the difference between temporary and permanent investments.
3. List three reasons for investing.

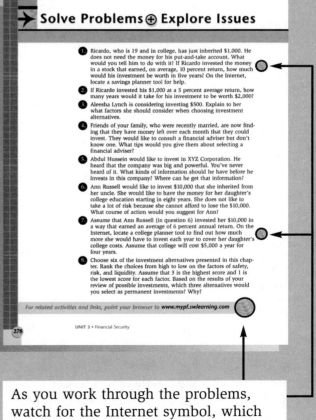

Solve Problems ⊕ Explore Issues

1. Ricardo, who is 19 and in college, has just inherited $1,000. He does not need the money for his put-and-take account. What would you tell him to do with it? If Ricardo invested the money in a stock that earned, on average, 10 percent return, how much would his investment be worth in five years? On the Internet, locate a savings planner tool for help.

2. If Ricardo invested his $1,000 at a 5 percent average return, how many years would it take for his investment to be worth $2,000?

3. Aleesha Lynch is considering investing $500. Explain to her what factors she should consider when choosing investment alternatives.

4. Friends of your family, who were recently married, are now finding that they have money left over each month that they could invest. They would like to consult a financial adviser but don't know one. What tips would you give them about selecting a financial adviser?

5. Abdul Hussein would like to invest in XYZ Corporation. He heard that the company was big and powerful. You've never heard of it. What kinds of information should he have before he invests in this company? Where can he get that information?

6. Ann Russell would like to invest $10,000 that she inherited from her uncle. She would like to have the money for her daughter's college education starting in eight years. She does not like to take a lot of risk because she cannot afford to lose the $10,000. What course of action would you suggest for Ann?

7. Assume that Ann Russell (in question 6) invested her $10,000 in a way that earned an average of 6 percent annual return. On the Internet, locate a college planner tool to find out how much more she would have to invest each year to cover her daughter's college costs. Assume that college will cost $5,000 a year for four years.

8. Choose six of the investment alternatives presented in this chapter. Rank the choices from high to low on the factors of safety, risk, and liquidity. Assume that 3 is the highest score and 1 is the lowest score for each factor. Based on the results of your review of possible investments, which three alternatives would you select as permanent investments? Why?

For related activities and links, point your browser to www.mypf.swlearning.com

As you work through the problems, watch for the Internet symbol, which will direct you to the World Wide Web.

TO THE STUDENT

Welcome to the exciting world of personal finance! This textbook focuses on your role as a citizen, student, family member, consumer, and active participant in the business world. The intent of *Managing Your Personal Finances* is to inform you of your various financial responsibilities and to provide you with opportunities for self-awareness, expression, and satisfaction in a highly technical and competitive society.

- Would you like to learn ways to maximize your earnings potential?
- Do you need to develop strategies for managing your financial resources?
- Are you interested in exploring skills for the wise use of credit?
- Do you want to gain insight into the different ways of investing your money?

This book will help you investigate many important areas of interest that will enhance your financial security. You will also better understand your own wants, needs, and values, and how these affect personal financial decisions. Understanding the concepts presented in this text will enable you to make wise decisions that will help your financial future and make you a more effective consumer.

To help you learn about personal finance, this text has a number of special highlights.

Terms to Know are vocabulary words that are printed in bold and defined within the chapter.

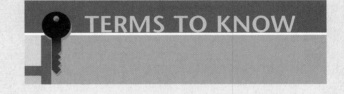

TERMS TO KNOW

Consider This presents a story that's tailored to the chapter's contents. By reading the story, you'll have an overview of the chapter's main topics.

Consider This. . .

Goals are clearly stated learning objectives that begin each lesson and offer an overview of the information you'll study.

Goals

Issues in Your World is a full-page feature that will extend your knowledge by acquainting you with real-world issues. Critical thinking questions help you go deeper into the topics.

Issues in Your World

Throughout the book, certain features will help you relate chapter concepts as they apply to the real world of personal finance. These include Communication Connection, Career Focus, Viewpoints, Net Nuggets, Global View, and Math Minute.

At the end of each lesson, Check Your Understanding contains activities to help you review terms and concepts you've learned.

Chapter Assessment gives you the opportunity to tie your learning together. *Summary* is a bulleted list of chapter concepts for quick review. *Review Terms* helps you acquire a vocabulary of personal finance terms. *Review Facts and Ideas* tests your recall of the chapter's main points. *Apply Your Knowledge* and *Solve Problems and Explore Issues* challenge you to dig deeper into issues. As you work through the problems, watch for the Internet symbol, which will direct you to the World Wide Web.

A Project ends each unit. It's an opportunity for you to apply and extend your knowledge about personal finance with exercises relevant to your own life.

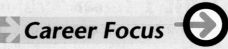

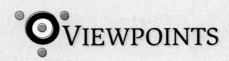

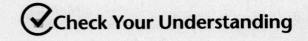

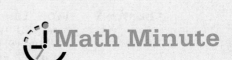

REVIEWERS

Anna D'Amelio
LaFollette High School
Madison, WI

Mike Bacsa
Miami Sunset Senior High School
Miami, FL

Lance Garvin
Pike High School
Indianapolis, IN

Lynn M. Hericks
Oak Hills High School
Cincinnati, OH

Steve Jostworth
Sycamore High School
Cincinnati, OH

Fran Loos
Taylorsville High School
Salt Lake City, UT

Melodi McGuire
Oshkosh West High School
Oshkosh, WI

Roxann M. Schneder
Milford High School
Milford, OH

Contents

Contents

Career Decisions

CHAPTERS

Project: **Career Development**

Unit 1 prepares you to analyze choices and develop the tools to get and keep temporary, part-time, or full-time employment, now or in the future. This unit is based on the concept that making wise career decisions is crucial to future financial planning.

The chapters describe career options and how to cope with changes that will affect your choices. You will learn why people work, how to begin career planning, and where to find up-to-date information. You also will find out how to compete with other applicants in getting a job. Then you will explore how to adapt to and keep the job—important skills that lead to good work relations and work history.

Choosing Your Career

TERMS TO KNOW

job analysis
salary
benefits
promotion
employee
  expenses

work
  characteristics
entrepreneur
upgrading
retraining
advanced degrees

placement center
self-assessment
  inventory
networks

Consider This. . .

"To be truly happy in what you do for a living, you need three things: You must be good at it, it must come easily for you, and you must enjoy it."

—Unknown

A junior in high school, Dontae worked every afternoon sorting and delivering packages. He was unhappy with his job, and he was trying to find out why. His friends told him it was because he wasn't paid enough money. But Dontae knew that there was more to it. He didn't look forward to going to work, and he was bored with the work itself. Once he reminded himself that this job wasn't permanent and that it was just a part-time, after-school job to earn spending money, he was much happier.

"When I choose my career, I'll be sure to pick something that I like doing so I can enjoy going to work," he told himself. Now Dontae has to decide what that right career choice is.

Considering Careers

Goals
- Discuss career and job trends, and describe sources of job information.
- Complete a job analysis, listing the positive and negative features of potential career choices.

▶ CAREERS OF THE FUTURE

Work enables us to earn a living. It provides money to buy food, clothing, shelter, and other important things, such as education and medical care. Your career path will likely look much different from that of past generations. New products and services, together with global competition and the computerized work environment, have changed the expectations and needs of business. You will probably retrain, upgrade, or change jobs several times during your working life. Some of you will choose the exciting path of self-employment.

Why is it likely that you will retrain, upgrade, or change jobs several times during your working life?

Technology creates better and faster ways of getting things done. In today's global economy, businesses must seek ways to improve quality, increase output, and lower costs. To stay in business, companies must offer products that meet diverse and changing needs of customers near and far. The Internet has opened a worldwide market to businesses of all sizes. Businesses may have a physical (brick–and–mortar) building, but most also have an Internet presence. Many companies do business only through the Internet. No matter what career path you choose, technology will affect the way you work.

Major Occupational Groups

Many of today's growing occupations focus on the collection, use, and distribution of information. Computers and the Internet are key tools for gathering, transmitting, and storing information. Skills required to succeed in today's jobs are changing as often as the jobs themselves! One of the highest paying career groups is the *professions*, where knowledge is the key job skill. For professionals (such as doctors, lawyers, and accountants), much of the job involves creating, processing, storing, and retrieving information. As computer technology and the Internet continue to evolve, many new professional careers will emerge. For example, people who gather and sell information provide a valuable service to all career fields.

Service jobs are a large and increasing sector of the market. They also are dominated by technology and information needs that determine what will be produced and how it will be made available to customers. Service employees use highly sophisticated information storage and retrieval devices, from point-of-sale computers to optical scanners for inventory management.

This extraordinary transformation of occupations has been variously labeled the "electronic era," "global village," "technological revolution," and "information age." All of these terms refer to technology and the rapid increase of knowledge that affect virtually all career choices today.

Job Titles and Descriptions

Careful research into descriptions of potential careers will help you make good career choices. Several U.S. government publications, available online and in most libraries, provide detailed job descriptions:

- *Dictionary of Occupational Titles (DOT)*, available online as O*NET (http://online.onetcenter.org)

- *Occupational Outlook Handbook (OOH)* (http://www.bls.gov/oco)

- *Monthly Labor Review* (http://stats.bls.gov/opub/mlr/mlrhome.htm)

*O*NET* is the *DOT* in the form of an online searchable database. At the *O*NET* site, you can search the database in several ways. You can look for occupations by entering keywords or selecting from a list of job families. Or, you can enter your skills into a checklist to search for occupations that match the skills you have. Figure 1-1 shows a portion of the "Tasks" in an *O*NET* job summary. As you can see, *O*NET* also provides links to knowledge, skills, and other information about this job.

The *Occupational Outlook Handbook* provides in-depth job descriptions and information about job opportunities nationwide. Figure 1-2 illustrates the kinds of information you will find in the *Handbook*.

Additional statistics and graphic information are available in the *Monthly Labor Review*. Articles in this publication provide current information about specific *occupation clusters* (groups of similar occupations) across the nation.

You can continue your research with the subject headings in your library's catalog, as well as magazine indexes such as the *Business Periodicals Index* and the *Readers' Guide to Periodical Literature*. Libraries typically provide Internet access and online research assistance. Online career sites, such as Monster.com, often provide career advice and information about different jobs.

figure **1-1**

o·net OnLine

Occupational Information Network
O·NET OnLine

| Related Links | OnLine Help | | Find Occupations | Skills Search | Crosswalk |

Partially updated 2003

Summary Report for:
21-1014.00 - Mental Health Counselors

Counsel with emphasis on prevention. Work with individuals and groups to promote optimum mental health. May help individuals deal with addictions and substance abuse; family, parenting, and marital problems; suicide; stress management; problems with self-esteem; and issues associated with aging and mental and emotional health.

This same data is also presented with one or two similar occupations within O*NET. Data specific to this occupation will be collected in the future.

Tasks | Knowledge | Skills | Abilities | Work Activities | Work Context | Job Zone | Interests | Work Values | Related Occupations | Wages & Employment

Tasks

- Act as client advocates in order to coordinate required services or to resolve emergency problems in crisis situations.
- Collaborate with other staff members to perform clinical assessments and develop treatment plans.
- Collect information about clients through interviews, observation, and tests.
- Counsel clients and patients, individually and in group sessions, to assist in overcoming dependencies, adjusting to life, and making changes.
- Develop and implement treatment plans based on clinical experience and knowledge.
- Discuss with individual patients their plans for life after leaving therapy.
- Encourage clients to express their feelings and discuss what is happening in their lives, and help them to develop insight into themselves and their relationships.
- Evaluate clients' physical or mental condition based on review of client information.

Source: Excerpted from *O*NET* Online, U.S. Department of Labor, *Dictionary of Occupational Titles*, 5th Edition, http://online.onetcenter.org/report?r=0&id=1247, accessed March 27, 2004.

▶ JOB ANALYSIS

A job analysis, such as the one in Figure 1-3, can help you identify types of work that would be a good fit for you. A **job analysis** is an evaluation of the positive and negative attributes of a given career choice. Gaining the skills you need for a career costs money. You may have to attend college or a training program. By taking the time now to identify a career that is right for you, you won't have to spend additional money later to change direction.

Preparing for a career is worth the cost. Your salary depends on the skills, experience, and education you bring to the job. These factors are under your control. Your salary also depends on the supply and demand for workers in that field. While you cannot control these factors, you can try to select a career in which the demand for workers is expected to grow. You can get this information from the Job Outlook section of the *OOH*.

What are some of the positive features that your chosen career will provide you?

©GETTY IMAGES/PHOTODISC

Positive Features of Employment

Your chosen career will provide you with many positive features. The most important is usually the **salary**, which is the amount of monthly or annual pay that you will earn for your labor. You should also

Computer Software Engineers

Significant Points
• Computer software engineers are projected to be one of the fastest growing occupations over the 2002–12 period.
• Highly favorable opportunities are expected for college graduates with at least a bachelor's degree in computer engineering or computer science and with practical work experience.

Nature of the Work
Computer software engineers apply computer science, engineering, and mathematical analysis to the design, development, testing, and evaluation of the software that enables computers to perform their many applications.

Working Conditions
Computer software engineers normally work in well-lighted and comfortable offices or computer laboratories in which computer equipment is located. Most software engineers work at least 40 hours a week; however, due to the project-oriented nature of the work, they also may have to work evenings or weekends to meet deadlines or solve unexpected technical problems.

Employment
Computer software engineers held about 675,000 jobs in 2002. About 394,000 were computer applications software engineers, and about 281,000 were computer systems software engineers.

Training, Other Qualifications, and Advancement
Most employers prefer to hire persons who have at least a bachelor's degree and broad knowledge of, and experience with, a variety of computer systems and technologies. Usual degree concentrations for applications software engineers are computer science or software engineering; for systems software engineers, usual concentrations are computer science or computer information systems.

Job Outlook
Computer software engineers are projected to be one of the fastest growing occupations from 2002 to 2012. Rapid employment growth in the computer systems design and related services industry, which employs the greatest number of computer software engineers, should result in highly favorable opportunities for those college graduates with at least a bachelor's degree in computer engineering or computer science and experience with computers.

Earnings
Median annual earnings of computer applications software engineers who worked full time in 2002 were about $70,900. Median annual earnings in the industries employing the largest numbers of computer applications software engineers in 2002 were:

Software publishers $76,450
Navigational, measuring, electromedical, and control instruments manufacturing 75,890
Computer systems design and related services 71,890
Architectural, engineering, and related services 70,090
Management of companies and enterprises 67,260

OOH ONET Codes
15-1031.00, 15-1032.00

Source: Abridged from the U.S. Department of Labor, *Occupational Outlook Handbook*, 2004–2005, http://stats.bls.gov/oco/oxos267.htm

consider whether there are scheduled salary increases after a month, six months, or a year. Some companies offer frequent evaluations, merit raises, bonuses, and pay schedules that allow you to advance.

figure **1-3**

JOB ANALYSIS

Job title: _____   Beginning salary: _____

Skills required: _____

Education required: _____

Experience required: _____

Positive Features: **Negative Features:**

Benefits: Employee expenses:

_____   _____
_____   _____
_____   _____
_____   _____
_____   _____
_____   _____

Promotion opportunities: Work requirements:

_____   _____
_____   _____
_____   _____
_____   _____
_____   _____
_____   _____

Other considerations*:   Other considerations*:

_____   _____
_____   _____
_____   _____
_____   _____
_____   _____
_____   _____

*Such as travel, expense accounts, bonuses, working hours, training programs, etc.

Benefits are also important. **Benefits** are company-provided supplements to salaries, such as sick pay, vacation time, profit-sharing plans, and health insurance, as discussed in Chapter 6.

Another important feature is the opportunity for **promotion**—the ability to advance, to accept more responsibilities, and eventually to work your way up to higher positions. Promotions give you recognition for your achievements, higher pay, and more challenging work.

For example, a retail clerk will want to work for a company in which advancement to store manager is possible.

You may also want to consider commuting distance and parking, company stability in the community, work hours and flexibility, and personnel policies. It's important to examine all features of a field of work and specific jobs so you will have some idea where the career path may lead you. You should evaluate both rewards and additional investments you may need to make. These investments can include retraining and upgrading, moving to a new location, and advanced education or specialized skill development, such as learning new computer programs, new electronic equipment, or new industry-specific technology.

Negative Features of Employment

Every job also has negative features. Try to see these negatives as challenges that go along with the positive aspects of employment.

Employee expenses include any costs paid by the employee that are not reimbursed by the employer (for example, uniforms or other special clothing and its cleaning, maintenance, and replacement). Although such expenses may be tax deductible, they can be very costly and can make the job less attractive. It is important to carefully balance employee expenses against benefits in a prospective job.

Work characteristics are the daily activities at work. They might include indoor versus outdoor work, working alone or with people, job pressures, time between breaks, supervisory relationships, number of employees with whom you will work, time spent at a computer terminal, and company rules and policies. Because you will do this work for eight or more hours a day in a full-time job, it is important to match work characteristics to your own preferences.

 VIEWPOINTS

Outsourcing has become a significant method for businesses to cut costs. Rather than hire internal employees to do certain work, businesses contract with other companies or individuals to provide the service for a flat fee or hourly rate. In some cases, American companies are hiring workers outside the United States to do the same job that American workers used to do. This is possible because of technology. When you call for service, your call may be answered by someone in India who is trained to answer your questions.

Think Critically: Do you think that, in the long run (20 years from now), having these jobs sent overseas will benefit American workers? Explain.

Entrepreneurship

Many people would like to own their own business and be their own boss. An **entrepreneur** is someone who organizes, manages, and assumes the risks of a business or enterprise. There are many opportunities for people to start their own business, continue a family business, or purchase an existing business or franchise. While long hours of work and dedication usually accompany such a move, rewards are also great because you can better control your own future.

To run your own business, you will need planning, training, advice, and financing. Small business management and entrepreneurship courses, information, and assistance are often available in high schools, community colleges, and through local business organizations such as Junior Achievement. Some local governments run incubator projects, in which they provide reduced-cost offices with financial support to get a small business on its feet. Small Business Assistance Centers provide ongoing training, education, and assistance. The Small Business Administration Web site is also a valuable resource. Visit the site at http:www.sba.gov.

©GETTY IMAGES/PHOTODISC

An entrepreneur assumes the risks of a business. Why might someone want to become an entrepreneur?

✓ Check Your Understanding

1. Why are terms such as "information age" and "electronic era" used to describe today's career environment?
2. What are some U.S. government publications you could use to research careers?
3. What are some positive features of employment? What are some negative features?
4. Why might a person want to be an entrepreneur?

The Challenge of Change

Goals
- Describe the techniques for coping with change.
- Explain changing career patterns in a world economy and the need for job networking.

▶ COPING WITH CHANGE

With rapidly advancing technologies, change is certain. There are three things you can do about change: accept it, reject it, or ignore it. If you accept change, you can help shape it. If you reject change, you will be run over by it because progress cannot be stopped. If you ignore change, you will be left behind. By rejecting or ignoring change, you will be frustrated, unemployed, or both. By reading, becoming a lifetime learner, taking classes, and completing a self-assessment, you can be aware of changes and make an action plan that will enable you to cope and reduce the stress of uncertainty.

Read Widely

A variety of resources follow national and international trends, from general technology to specific industries. Computer magazines or online technology news sources, such as CNET and *Wired* magazine, will keep you informed of technological advances. In addition, you need to read newspapers and magazines in order to keep up with what is going on in the United States and in the world.

Be a Lifetime Learner

Both at work and in your personal life, be interested in what is going on. Ask questions. Talk to people. Follow news and special events. Participate in community activities. Care about what is going on in your area and in the world. Joining professional and service organizations will also keep you informed of what's new in specific job areas. You can find out about workshops and seminars that will keep you aware of trends. This will help make you a more interesting person, and it is essential to your successful career development.

Take Classes

Sometimes technological advances require new skills that are too complex to learn by yourself, so actively seek new knowledge by taking classes. **Upgrading** means advancing to a higher level of skill to increase your usefulness to an employer. Many jobs, especially those affected by technological improvements, will require regular upgrading by employees. **Retraining** involves learning new and different skills so that an employee can retain the same level of employability. Community college and vocational training is geared as much to retraining displaced employees as to preparing employees for entry-level positions.

Many corporations offer technical courses to retrain their own employees. Those who volunteer and are eager to learn will position themselves for advancement. Other training is available through technical schools, vocational centers, job placement services, business colleges, and community colleges. Training over the Internet is becoming increasingly common. For many careers, applicants will need a college or technical degree and skills before they will be considered for employment.

Many young people are staying in college longer before entering the workforce. **Advanced degrees** are specialized, intensive programs (taken after the first college degree) that prepare students for higher level work responsibilities with more challenges and higher pay. An advanced degree may be a master's, a doctorate in a specialized field, or a professional degree in medicine, law, engineering, and so on. A master's degree often requires one year beyond the first college degree. A Ph.D. may require an additional three years after a master's degree. It is also possible to earn a Ph.D. without first obtaining a master's degree. This path usually takes longer (up to five years).

Complete a Self-Assessment

As you go through life, your needs and values will change. It is important to look inward to define what is important to you and then use this knowledge to plan your future. You should think about what you like doing, what you do well, and what skills and knowledge you want to enhance. Located at a high school, college, or technical training institute, a **placement center** offers advice and counseling to help you determine a career direction. Vocational, interest, and personal testing is often available through placement centers. You can compare your interests with those of successful people in various professions. A values clarification test will help you determine what is important to you both personally and professionally. You can find many self-assessment questionnaires at online career sites or by searching with the keyword "self-assessment."

©GETTY IMAGES/PHOTODISC

How could a self-assessment inventory help you prepare for a career?

Private career counselors are listed in the Yellow Pages. They offer their services for an hourly or fixed fee. A less expensive approach is to do your own research, using the sources listed in this chapter as well as in *The American Almanac of Jobs and Salaries*. This book evaluates job opportunities in many career fields and gives a full range of salaries for positions and levels. You can do industry research and look into major job categories (service, professional, and so on, as listed in Chapter 2).

Specific company research will help you determine which companies can offer you the best career opportunities. Check your library for sources such as *Standard & Poor's Register of Corporations, Directors, and Executives—United States and Canada* or *The 100 Best Companies to Work for in America*. In these publications you can read about major American companies and why they are successful. You might also want to visit company Web sites and read their descriptions of themselves. Finally, you can do field research. Talk to people working in careers that interest you. These informational interviews will show you strengths and weaknesses in some careers that you might not have anticipated. All this information is crucial in determining your needs and matching them to an appropriate career.

A **self-assessment inventory** lists your strong and weak points and gives you an idea of how to prepare for a career. As you improve your weak points, they become strengths in your inventory. Figure 1-4 is a self-assessment inventory that lists a typical young person's strengths, weaknesses, and plans for action. Completing a similar inventory based on your personal qualifications will help you determine areas that need work. You might ask another person to objectively assess your strengths and weaknesses. A different point of view can sometimes help clarify your self-assessment.

Net Nuggets

Many career assessment instruments can be found on the Internet. For example, Careerplanning.about.com contains articles about and tools for career planning and self-assessment, including inventories of values, interests, personality, and skills.

Strengths	Weaknesses	Plan of Action
Education: High school diploma, including business courses	*Education:* Weak in basic office skills	Take extra classes in office procedures, business communication, and basic computer applications.
Experience: Internship in office—part-time summer job as administrative assistant; volunteer at church	*Experience:* Need experience using database programs	Look for part-time job that involves using computer database applications.
Aptitudes and Abilities: Good hand-eye coordination; work well with people	*Aptitudes and Abilities:* Poor public speaker	Practice speaking in small groups; lead a class at church; attend more social functions.
Appearance: Neat and clean	*Appearance:* Wardrobe needs more professional work clothes	Start buying clothes that are appropriate for work.

► CHANGING CAREER OPPORTUNITIES

Career planning is changing as never before. A career choice may not be a permanent decision but is often subject to rapid, unpredictable change. To understand how the job market will be affected, let's examine some of the major changes sweeping the country and the world.

Long-Term Planning

Businesses must continually reinvent themselves to meet changing market needs. Individuals also must look to long-term planning to protect themselves from the effects of rapidly changing technology. You must embrace change and adapt to it. Your career plans should span several decades and be broad, diversified, and open to future opportunities and challenges.

A World Economy

Our nation is part of a worldwide, interdependent economy. How does this affect our job market?

We are part of a worldwide, interdependent economy. The Internet has helped to open the world market to companies of all sizes. To survive, American companies must find ways to compete successfully with businesses all over the world. Competition will likely intensify for new markets in *developing countries*. Developing countries are nations that currently have little industry and a low standard of living. These places represent opportunities for international businesses to invest.

The 20 fastest growing economies of the early 2000s were all in developing nations, including the oil-exporting countries, South Korea, India, Singapore, the Dominican Republic, Taiwan, Mexico, and Brazil. NAFTA, the North American Free Trade Agreement, has opened doors for American businesses to move production facilities to Mexico and hire Mexican workers. This has cost thousands of jobs in the U.S. It is expected that in the future, because citizens in these countries have increased purchasing power, they will be able to buy our products, broadening the market for American goods.

Should we try to recapture our role as leader of a modern Industrial Revolution? Most experts say no. Instead, we should adapt and move forward in the area in which we are the leader—information—as we develop new technologies, jobs, and products for the future.

Networking

Networking is an effective way to obtain useful information. **Networks** are informal groups of people with common interests who interact for mutual assistance. Networking includes making phone calls, sharing lunch, and creating opportunities to share ideas with your group of acquaintances. To find a career, you will need to establish a network of contacts—people you know who have information you need. Through networking, you can get inside information without being an "insider."

You can begin now to create your network by making a master list of people you know through your parents, school and business acquaintances, and personal friends and associates. By communicating within your network, you will learn how to prepare for a job, where the openings are, and how to pursue them.

⊘ Check Your Understanding

1. What steps can you take to deal with change and reduce uncertainty?
2. Why must individuals consider long-term planning, a world economy, and networking when making career plans?

Issues in Your World

Being a Lifelong Learner

Graduating from high school or its equivalent is a major milestone. It is the first step toward securing your financial future. You may choose additional or specialized training, an apprenticeship program, an associate's degree, a bachelor's degree, or beyond. Regardless of the highest level of formal education you attain, your opportunities for learning will continue throughout your life.

Lifelong learning means actively seeking new knowledge, skills, and experiences that will add to your professional and personal growth throughout your life. Upgrading your skills will do the following:

- Keep you marketable, both in your current job and in future jobs.
- Enhance your resume, showing you are interested and actively pursuing new skills, talents, or enrichment.
- Empower you to change directions when you feel it is time to move on, try new things, or pursue a different path.
- Open new opportunities for growth and fulfillment.

Your choices are virtually unlimited! You can learn a new hobby, improve and maintain your health, polish your leadership skills, discover new opportunities you would never have considered, meet new people who will become your friends, or get involved in community service. Lifelong learning will provide you with a versatility that will allow you to explore new directions, discover hidden talents and interests, and enrich your life.

Lifelong learning will keep you active—mentally as well as physically—as you find new paths to explore and add to your base of knowledge. When times change, you'll be ready!

Think Critically

1. Is there something you'd like to explore that is not your major career objective, such as playing an instrument, learning a new sport, making something, or learning a new skill?
2. How has lifelong learning been a significant part of the life of someone you know?
3. Why would a prospective employer be impressed with an applicant who was involved in community activities?

Chapter Assessment

SUMMARY

1.1
* Careers of the future will be based on technology and information management.
* Careers will change rapidly in requirements and skills.
* Service jobs will continue to grow.
* Businesses will depend more on the gathering and use of information.
* Evaluate positive features of a job, such as salary, benefits, promotions, and fulfillment.
* Evaluate negative features of a job, such as employee expenses, job pressures, and stress.
* Consider owning your own business.

1.2
* Read widely and be a lifetime learner.
* Take classes for upgrading and retraining.
* Consider earning an advanced degree.
* Complete a self-assessment inventory to learn your strengths and weaknesses.
* Make career planning a long-term strategy.
* Recognize that you are part of a worldwide, interdependent economy.
* Develop a network of contacts.

Directions

Can you find the definition for each of the following terms used in Chapter 1?

advanced degrees	promotion
benefits	retraining
placement center	salary
employee expenses	self-assessment inventory
entrepreneur	upgrading
job analysis	work characteristics
networks	

1. An evaluation of the positive and negative attributes of a given career choice.

2. One who organizes, manages, and assumes the risks of a business or enterprise.

3. A source of career counseling available at high schools, colleges, or technical training institutes.

4. Informal groups of people with common interests who interact for mutual assistance.

5. The amount of monthly or annual pay.

6. The daily activities at work, such as indoor or outdoor work, or working alone or with people.

7. Expenses paid by employees and not reimbursed by employers.

8. The opportunity to advance, accept more responsibility, and work your way up to higher positions.

9. Company-provided supplements to salaries, such as sick pay and vacation time.

10. Specialized, intensive educational programs taken after the first college degree.

11. Advancing to a higher level of skill.

12. Learning new and different skills in order to remain employable at the same level.

13. A listing of strong points, weak points, and plans for action.

REVIEW FACTS AND IDEAS

1. What do most occupations focus on today?

2. What is one of the highest paying career groups today?

3. List three publications of the U.S. government that will assist you with career choices.

4. Describe the types of information that would be listed on a job analysis.

5. List some employee expenses that you might expect to pay in your first career choice.

6. What are the three things you can do about change?

7. List four ways you can keep up with new technologies and stay prepared for tomorrow's career choices.

8. How much education do you need in order to earn an advanced degree?

9. List some major changes that are sweeping the country and the world.

10. What is meant by a world economy?

11. List some developing countries that have made great economic gains.

APPLY YOUR KNOWLEDGE

1. Describe some new technology that has been introduced in the past few years.

2. Describe some technological advance made just a year or two ago that is now obsolete.

3. What is the role of information in many of today's careers?

4. What are some positive features of employment that you have observed in the work of your parents or others?

5. What are some negative features of employment that you have observed in the work of your parents or others?

6. What types of independent research can you do to determine the type of work you want and the company you want to work for?

7. Describe ways you can keep in touch with what is going on in the world technologically.

8. Why is long-term planning necessary for individuals as well as for businesses?

9. How has world interdependence changed our lives as Americans?

Solve Problems ⊕ Explore Issues

1. Look up three career choices in the *Dictionary of Occupational Titles*. Summarize your findings in one paragraph about each choice. Look up the same three occupations in the *Occupational Outlook Handbook* and add a second paragraph about each. If you have Internet access, use the online versions of these publications.

2. From a current issue of *Monthly Labor Review* or from the online version of this publication, summarize an article about an industry or employment trend.

3. From the February 2004 issue (Vol. 127, No. 2) of the *Monthly Labor Review* in print or online, write a paragraph reviewing the article entitled "The U.S. Economy in 2012: Signs of Growth."

4. Complete a job analysis, using the form in Figure 1-3 as a guide, for three different occupations. To get this information, consult one of the sources listed in this chapter, or interview someone working in each occupation field. List your source(s) of information on the job analysis form.

5. Explain to a friend why it is necessary to be aware of what is happening technologically in the world. Give suggestions as to what she or he can do to keep up with changes.

6. Pick a large company you think you would like to work for in the future. Do some research to learn more about the company. (Suggestion: Check Standard & Poor's *The 100 Best Companies to Work for in America*. Also, look up the company's Web site and read the company's description of itself.) Summarize your findings in one or two paragraphs.

7. Develop a networking plan—a list of all your possible communication sources—and add to it each time you make a contact. List contacts you plan to set up, people you would like to meet, and places you would like to visit.

8. Choose three career choices that might interest you, from different career fields. Use print or online resources to find typical salaries for each career. Write a paragraph explaining why salaries differ among these career choices.

For related activities and links, point your browser to **www.mypf.swlearning.com**

Planning Your Career

TERMS TO KNOW

identity	interests	contact
values	personality	work history
lifestyle	goal	
aptitude	experience	

Consider This. . .

"To be happy in your work life, you must be able to work as if you don't have to."

—*Dr. Alfred Mukakis*

Rosa was energetic and outgoing. She enjoyed being around other people and helping them. She often volunteered in a retirement center, and it made her happy to support others in doing things they couldn't do by themselves. Rosa was strong and physically fit but not especially interested in athletics. She hoped to find a career that would allow her to use her natural talents and help others at the same time.

"I think I'd like to be a physical therapist," she told her high school counselor. "What steps should I take now, while I'm still in high school, to help me decide if this career is really right for me? If the career is a good fit for me, then what I can do to get there as quickly as possible?"

Finding a Good Career Fit

Goals
- **List reasons why people work and factors that affect career choices.**
- **Identify and describe good career planning techniques.**

▶ WHY PEOPLE WORK

What are some reasons why people work?

People work to meet their needs, wants, and goals. Working also provides a sense of purpose—such as helping others and making a difference in the world. You can gain this sense of purpose at the same time you earn a living and provide for life's necessities.

People also work to gain a sense of **identity**—of who they are. Because work is typically the central activity of a person's life, it often becomes a *way* of life, strongly linked to that person's identity. When you finish school, your identity will probably be based on your career or what you do with your time. Most people who are happy with their work lives are also productive and responsible members of the community in which they live.

▶ FACTORS AFFECTING CAREER CHOICE

Because your career will affect nearly every part of your life, your choice of career is very important. Many factors will affect your decision. Among them are your values and lifestyle, aptitudes and interests, and personal qualities.

Values and Lifestyle

Values are the ideals in life that are important to you. Values are based on life experiences as well as perceptions and beliefs. Each person chooses what he or she believes to be true, meaningful, and important. Your values are shaped by those of your family, social and cultural groups, and religion. They are also influenced by the media and society as a whole. Ultimately, you must establish your own value system.

Global View

A study conducted in the mid-1990s found that a significant problem for female German scientists was societal pressure on working mothers to take care of their children. Men in laboratory management positions were reluctant to make allowances for working mothers with young children. As a result, these women found it difficult to keep up with the 12-hour days and weekend work that is typical in German laboratories.

Think Critically: Should the German government do anything in order to help female scientists raise children and achieve meaningful careers? What could the laboratories do?

Lifestyle is the way people choose to live their lives, based on the values they have chosen. Your lifestyle is evident from the clothes you wear and the things you buy, use, do, say, and enjoy. A career is an important part of most people's lifestyle. Your career establishes not only the way you spend a large part of your time but also your level of income. For example, if you seek a lavish lifestyle, you will need a high-income job to achieve that lifestyle. To get a high-paying job, you must pursue higher levels of education. It's important for you to understand the connection between your lifestyle choices and the commitments required of you to achieve those goals.

Aptitudes and Interests

An **aptitude** is a natural physical or mental ability that allows you to do certain tasks well. For example, you may have an aptitude for working with numbers. If so, a career that requires calculations, such as engineering, might be a good fit for you. Aptitude tests can help you identify your natural abilities, so that you can focus your career search on jobs that use those aptitudes.

Your career search should also consider your **interests**—the things you like to do. By examining the types of activities you enjoy, you can choose a career that involves tasks you will find interesting and satisfying. For example, if you enjoy being with people, you will likely prefer a job working with others, such as sales or a helping profession, to one that involves working alone. Use Figure 2-1 to help identify your interests.

©GETTY IMAGES/PHOTODISC

What is the difference between values and lifestyle?

figure 2-1

TYPES OF WORK ACTIVITIES

Which of these work activities appeal to you?

analyzing and recording	physically inactive work
creating and designing	presenting or speaking
following directions	repetitive tasks
helping others	self-motivated work
indoor work	thinking work
managing people and resources	variety of tasks
manual work	working alone
outdoor work	working on a computer
physically active work	working with machines

The Internet offers a number of questionnaires to help job seekers identify their interests. Use keywords such as "interest test" to search for these questionnaires. They are fun to fill out. Plus, they may reveal something about you that will help you find a good career fit.

Personal Qualities

Your **personality** is made up of the many individual qualities that make you unique. Personal qualities include such things as your intelligence, creativity, sense of humor, and general attitude. Most jobs require a particular set of personal qualities. For example, a person who represents a company to potential customers needs an outgoing, friendly personality. A job that involves working alone at a computer needs someone with a more introverted personality. You will be happiest in a job that fits your personality. Which qualities listed in Figure 2-2 describe you?

► CAREER PLANNING

Planning for your future career is an important task. Consider the total time spent working: 8 hours a day, 5 days a week, 50 weeks a year totals 2,000 hours each year. If you work the average career span of 43 years (from age 22 to age 65), you will have spent 86,000 hours on the job! Because your work will likely take so much of your time, you will need to plan your career carefully.

Steps in Career Planning

Effective career planning involves careful investigation and analysis—a process that you should start now and revisit throughout your work life.

PERSONAL QUALITIES

figure **2-2**

1. I am ambitious and willing to work hard to reach high goals.
2. I prefer a low-stress work environment.
3. I am happiest working alone.
4. I enjoy working with a group to achieve goals.
5. I am friendly and outgoing.
6. I am shy, and meeting new people is hard for me.
7. I like to lead group activities.
8. I am more of a follower than a leader.
9. I am a high-energy person who must be constantly on the move.
10. I enjoy sitting quietly and reading for long periods of time.
11. I like my activities to vary a lot.
12. I am most comfortable when I follow a regular routine.

The steps in career planning are self-analysis, research, a plan of action, and re-evaluation.

1. *Self-Analysis.* Using resources available from schools, employment offices, testing services, and online, explore personal factors that relate to your career choice.

   a. Determine your wants and needs.

   b. Determine your values and desired lifestyle.

   c. Assess your aptitudes and interests and determine how they match job tasks.

   d. Analyze your personal qualities and the kinds of job tasks that best suit your personality.

2. *Research.* Based on a good self-analysis, determine the careers that best suit your interests and aptitudes and will help you meet your lifestyle goals.

   a. Seek information in books, magazines, Web sites, and other resources available from libraries, counseling centers, online resources, and employment offices.

   b. Compare your interests, aptitudes, and personal qualities to job descriptions and requirements. Most careers can fit into one of the classifications shown in Figure 2-3. In which cluster does the job of your choice fit? What training do you need to qualify for this job?

   c. Talk to people in the fields of work you find interesting.

   d. Observe occupations, spend time learning about jobs and companies, and seek part-time work to get direct experience. Sometimes job shadowing (following someone through his or

▶ figure 2-3

Job Classification	Description of Environment	Training/Education	Working Hours	Beginning Salary/Wages	Examples
Office and Administrative Support	Work in office setting; contact with people and equipment; computer use and organizational skills	High school diploma plus specialized training in software, computer use; two-year degree preferred	40 hours/week, normal business hours	Urban: $12-15/hour, $1,800 to $2,000 per month	Computer operator, desktop publisher, record clerk, office clerk, administrative assistant
Professional and Related	Specialized knowledge and skill; often stressful, high levels of responsibility	4+ years of college plus specialized training or education that may include many years of graduate work	40+ hours/week, often including overtime	Urban: $40,000 to $65,000 per year	Engineers, architects, teachers, artists, doctors, entertainers, scientists, technicians, lawyers, economists
Installation and Transportation	Specialized skills, special clothing, use of tools, equipment, machinery	High school diploma plus specialized training, licensing, or technical certification	40 hours/week plus overtime when required	Urban: $12-$18/hour, $2,000 to $2,500 per month	Machine repair, mechanic, traffic controller, public transportation operator
Sales and Related	Communication and persuasion skills; represents company and self	High school diploma plus training; license often required; college degree often preferred	Varied; sometimes seasonal	Base salary and/or commission, averages $3,000 per month	Real estate broker, insurance agent, retail sales, cashiers, clerks, travel agents
Service	Works around and with people serving needs of customers, clients, or guests	None to specialized vocational or two-year college degree; four-year degrees desired	Varied, split shifts or other, as needed	Minimum wage plus tips or salary based on experience and skills, $1,500 to $4,000 per month	Therapists, chefs, animal and child care workers, recreation, police, fire, security, maintenance
Management, Business, and Financial	Supervision of operations and others, decision making and leadership	Bachelor's degree plus experience; master's degree or other certification often desired	40+ hours/week	Urban: $2,500 to $5,000 per month, depending on qualifications	Managers, accountants, administrators, executives, analysts, adjustors
Construction, Farming, and Related	Assembly or manual work, physical fitness and strength required	Apprenticeship or vocational skill training; specialized degrees desired	40 hours/week plus overtime	$15 to $25/hour and higher for more skills	Carpenters, masons, electricians, roofers
Production and Related	Noisy and often hazardous areas utilizing specialized tasks	High school diploma preferred; individual and team skills by product; rotating tasks	40 hours/week plus overtime	$12-16/hour	Assembly workers, machinists, binders, lab technicians
Armed Forces	Defense, discipline, and training; must follow orders; must meet minimum service requirements	High school diploma usually required	Daily, depending on commitment	$25,000 plus all expenses, rises by rank	Armed forces services in Army, Navy, Marines, Air Force, as well as special forces

her workday) will give you real insight into the daily activities and requirements of a career.

3. *Plan of Action.* After you have done some job research, develop a plan of action that will eventually bring you to your career goals.

   a. Use good job search techniques. Get organized, make a plan, follow through, and don't give up.

   b. Develop necessary skills by taking courses (traditional or online) and gaining exposure to the field in which you want to pursue a career.

   c. Seek a part-time or volunteer job to gain experience in your area of choice.

   d. Evaluate your choices over time. People change and so do jobs. If you discover you are following the wrong career path, change your direction before you stay on it too long.

4. *Re-evaluation.* Because the world changes rapidly, we all need to prepare ourselves to meet the challenges ahead. You may wish to prepare for career changes in order to take advantage of new opportunities. About every five years, think about what you will be doing and where you would like to be in the next five years.

What are the steps involved in career planning?

The Importance of Goals

A **goal** is a desired end toward which efforts are directed. Goals provide a sense of direction and purpose in life. There are three types of goals: short-term, intermediate, and long-term.

A *short-term goal* is one you expect to reach in a few days or weeks. A short-term goal could be to achieve at least a B on next week's math test. You know you must plan time to study soon to meet your goal.

Intermediate goals are those you wish to accomplish in the next few months or years. Some examples are graduation from high school, a vacation trip, or plans for summer employment.

Long-term goals are those you wish to achieve in five to ten years or longer. They might include a college degree, career, marriage, or family.

If goals are to be meaningful, they should be defined and written down, to become a part of your life. Many people find a checklist a handy way to help them reach their goals. Figure 2-4 shows a typical goal checklist. Use it as a guide to create your own checklist.

figure 2-4

GOAL CHECKLIST

GOAL CHECKLIST
Week of ___Oct. 1___

Accomplished

Short-term goals (today/this week)
1. Buy birthday gift for mom.   _____
2. Get haircut (Saturday).   _____
3. See counselor about chemistry class.   _____

Intermediate goals (next month/year)
1. Get a C or better in chemistry class.   _____
2. Prepare for SAT test (test in May).   _____
3. Finish term report (due December 14).   _____
4. Complete college admission forms (by January 15).   _____

Long-term goals (future)
1. Graduate from college.   _____
2. Begin full-time job.   _____
3. Buy a car.   _____

Role of Experience

Experience is the knowledge and skills acquired from working in a career field. As you gain experience in a field, you become more valuable to an employer. Most employers give wage increases that reflect the increased value of an employee's experience. When you change career fields, however, you no longer have the advantage of experience. You may need to accept a lower wage as you work to gain experience in your new career field.

✅Check Your Understanding

1. If your job does not help you achieve your personal goals, what will likely happen?
2. How can taking an aptitude test help your career planning?
3. How can job shadowing help you evaluate a career option?
4. Why is it important to re-evaluate your career choices occasionally?

Issues in Your World

Help Wanted

The following is a typical ad from a newspaper's Help Wanted section. It poses a dilemma for many young people today. How can you have education *and* experience? If no one will hire you, how can you ever get that "experience"?

WANTED: Web site manager. Must have course work in HTML programming, graphic design, and platform management. Degree preferred. Two years of sales experience required. Starting salary $36,000 plus benefits.

There are a number of ways you can meet this employer's requirements of both education and experience. As you complete your formal education, you can prepare for your future career in the following ways:

1. *Cooperative Work Experience.* A job after class, part-time, evenings, and weekends while you are in school will add valuable experience and will give you insight into the work environment you will experience.
2. *Summer Work.* During the summers, you could work at a job that sounds exciting or interesting to you. To do this, try:
   a. *Temporary Work.* While the position is only temporary, it gives you valuable insight and work experience.
   b. *Volunteer Work.* As a volunteer worker, you may be giving up pay, but you will gain important skills and be able to observe working conditions.
   c. *Community Service.* Get involved in the community by serving on committees, working on clean-up projects, or serving food in a homeless shelter. These activities give you general work experience and tell a prospective employer about your character.
3. *Internship.* An internship is an on-the-job training experience that usually pays only your cost of getting to work and any extra expenses you incur. You receive training and exposure to the job requirements.

Think Critically
1. Does the career you want require experience for an entry-level position?
2. What are some specific ways you can gather experience for this career at the same time you are completing your formal education?

Finding Career Opportunities

Goals
- **List sources of job opportunity information.**
- **Itemize and explain good job search techniques.**
- **Formulate a personal plan of action to get the job you want.**

▶ SOURCES OF JOB OPPORTUNITY INFORMATION

You can find out about job opportunities in a number of ways: word of mouth from personal contacts; school counseling and placement services; periodicals, books, and other publications; public and private employment agencies; newspaper, telephone book, and private job listings; and online.

Contacts

Many job openings are never advertised. They are filled from within the company, or by people outside who have been privately informed of the opening by a contact within the company. A **contact** is someone you know, such as relatives, friends, members of groups to which you belong, and former employers. Contacts can provide you with inside information on job openings. Therefore, the more people you know, the better your chances of hearing about a job opening.

If you are seeking a job in a field in which you have no contacts, try to get to know people who can tell you about openings. If, for example, you want to work at a bank, you should meet people who work in banks. You can do this through acquaintances and friends in business, professional organizations, and community activities, and through school-sponsored visits, job shadowing, job fairs, or other activities.

How could you find out about job openings that aren't advertised?

©GETTY IMAGES/PHOTODISC

School Counseling and Placement Services

Many schools have programs to assist students in preparing for careers, making career choices, and securing part- or full-time work. One such program is the cooperative work experience, or supervised field experience. In this type of program, students receive high school credits for on-the-job experience that directly relates to classroom studies in a chosen career field. Students placed in work situations are given grades on their work and are paid minimum wage for their efforts. Employers receive tax credits for the wages they pay the students during training.

School counselors and teachers are also good sources of job opportunity information. They often know about specific job openings and are asked by employers to recommend students for them. If you are interested in an office job, you should talk to counselors and business teachers as you complete business courses.

Placement centers help students find employment. The services are usually offered free of charge. Placement centers post job openings at the school and provide information to qualified students so they can apply. They also keep a placement folder on each student that contains school records, including attendance, academic, and disciplinary records. When employers ask for information about a student, they receive copies of information from the student's placement folder. If your school has a placement center, examine your folder and have teachers and other adults write recommendations to put in it. You should also see that all school records are in the folder. Be sure to check at your school to see what other types of assistance are available.

Public and Private Employment Agencies

All major cities have public and private employment agencies. Their business is to help you find a job for which you are prepared and help employers locate the best applicants for job openings. Private employment agencies may or may not charge a fee for their services. Such fees vary from agency to agency, so you should compare prices before you sign with one. Some of these agencies charge a fee to the employer. Others charge the prospective employee when a job is found, and still others divide the fee between the employer and the hired employee.

Your state employment office does not charge a fee because it is a government agency. There you can also obtain information about government job-training assistance programs, YES (Youth Employment Services), Youth Corps, Civil Service (state and federal), and apprenticeship boards, as well as other government employment programs that exist from time to time. You may qualify for one or more of these types of work programs.

Newspaper, Yellow Pages, and Private Job Listings

The Help Wanted ads in the classified section of your local newspaper list job openings in your area. The ads give brief descriptions of the positions, often with salary ranges. Watch these ads closely and respond quickly when a new job enters the market. Both employers and employment agencies advertise job openings to attract qualified applicants.

The Yellow Pages is an alphabetically arranged subject listing of businesses advertising their services. If you are looking for a job in a certain field, determine the subject heading under which that type of work might be classified. You will find under that heading a list of companies that may be offering jobs in your field. You may want to send your resume by mail or e-mail to all those listed, asking to be considered for the next opening.

Many companies, government offices, and schools place job opening announcements on bulletin boards, circulate them within the company, and post them in other locations. Checking in these places may give you the inside information you need to apply for a position when it opens.

Online Job Information

Searching the Internet using keywords related to your field will provide many new sources of job information. Some Web sites are specifically designed to help people find jobs. These sites list job openings and offer assistance with applying for jobs. Many allow you to post your resume for employers to see and even apply for a job online. Some job sites—such as www.cooljobs.com, hotjobs.yahoo.com, www.monster.com, www.careerbuilder.com, and www.resumeblaster.com—help people find jobs in many fields. Others, such as www.guru.com and www.techies.com, are more specialized.

Companies often list their job openings on their own Web site. Find the sites of companies you would like to work for. Read the information the companies supply about themselves. Then follow the links to their list of openings. The site will tell you how to apply.

Professional associations often allow job seekers to post resumes and browse their database of job openings. For example, if you have trained for a career as a paralegal, you can post your resume and search for job openings at the National Paralegal Association Web site. Professional associations usually include job openings in their print publications as well.

Communication Connection

With a friend or classmate, role play contacting a human resources person or hiring manager about an interesting job advertised in the newspaper or from an online job resource. What questions would you ask about the prospective position and the company? How would you express your interest and your qualifications?

▶ JOB SEARCH TECHNIQUES

Finding and getting the right job takes hard work, careful planning, and often a great deal of time. Nevertheless, a careful search can land you a job you will enjoy for many years. Dissatisfaction leads to frequent job changing, which may damage your employment chances in the future. Your **work history** is a record of the jobs you have held and how long you stayed with each employer. Employers will evaluate your work history when you apply for a job. If it shows someone who changes jobs too frequently, potential employers may think hiring you is too risky.

The job search techniques described in the rest of this section will help you find and get the right job.

Get Organized

After you decide what kind of job you want, the first step toward getting that job is to get organized. Prepare a checklist of things to do and check them off as you complete them.

1. Assemble all the information you will need about the type of work you want to do.
2. List prospective companies for which you would like to work.
3. Gather your sources of information and research job descriptions, skills and aptitudes needed, and other job requirements.
4. Make lists of personal contacts, places to go, and people to see.
5. Prepare a current resume and a letter of application (discussed in Chapter 3).
6. Ask previous employers, teachers, or others to write letters of recommendation for you. Also, ask them if you may use their names as references for employment purposes.
7. Update your placement folder at school.

Make a Plan

A plan is important to the success of your job search because it keeps you organized, shows what you have done, and indicates what you need to do in the immediate future. A good plan lists all your goals and shows a time frame for getting them done. As you accomplish each step or goal, check it off. Your plan might look similar to Figure 2-5.

©GETTY IMAGES/PHOTODISC

How could your work history affect your chances of getting a job?

figure 2-5

PLAN TO GET A JOB

Job Leads:
State employment office
Help wanted ads (newspaper)
School placement office
Marketing teacher
Search online

Contacts:
Aunt Jessica (knows manager at Target)

Time Line—Week 1

Day 1:
Prepare resume and letter of application.
Check help wanted ads in newspaper.
Make a list of local stores from Yellow
   Pages.
Check store Web sites for job openings.

Day 2:
Send two application letters or e-mails.
Get two personal references.
Call Aunt Jessica to set a lunch date to talk.

Follow Up

After you have contacted a potential employer by letter or by filling out
an application for a job opening, or after you have interviewed with a
human resource manager, it is important that you check back from
time to time. You want these people to know you are still interested in
the job. At this time, ask when they expect to make their decision.

Don't Give Up

Before you get a good job, you will probably not get several other jobs
for which you applied. Remain courteous and upbeat, and keep checking back for openings. Try all your job leads. Be prepared, so that if
you are called for an interview on short notice—even on the same
day—you can go. Continually check the want ads for new openings.
Check with your contacts frequently. Although a good job search may
take several weeks or months, the effort will pay off.

✓ Check Your Understanding

1. How do companies fill jobs without advertising?
2. What can your contacts do for you?
3. How can the Internet help your job search?

Chapter Assessment

SUMMARY

2.1

* Do a self-analysis to identify your values, lifestyle, aptitudes, interests, and personal qualities.
* Research careers that best fit the characteristics revealed in your self-analysis.
* Make a plan to reach your career goals and re-evaluate your choices from time to time.
* Create a checklist of your short-term, intermediate, and long-term goals, and check them off as you accomplish them.
* Look for ways to gain experience in your chosen field.

2.2

* Search for job opportunity information through your contacts, placement services, newspaper ads and private job listings, the Yellow Pages, employment agencies, and online company and job sites.
* For a successful job search, get organized, make a plan, follow up, and don't give up.

REVIEW TERMS

Directions

Can you find the definition for each of the following terms used in Chapter 2?

aptitude   interests
contact   lifestyle
experience   personality
goal   values
identity   work history

1. The things in your life that are important to you.

2. A natural physical or mental ability.

3. Individual qualities that make you unique.

4. A person you know who can give you inside information about a job.

5. The record of jobs you have held.

6. A sense of who you are.

7. The way you choose to live your life, based on your values.

8. An end toward which efforts are directed.

9. Knowledge, skills, and practice gained from working in a career field.

10. The things you like to do.

1. Why do people work?

2. What is your identity at this time in your life? (You probably have more than one.)

3. What factors affect career choices?

4. Define "values." List three of your parents' values and three of your own.

5. What is an aptitude? Why is it important to know what your aptitudes are?

6. What are personal qualities? List three of yours.

7. What are the four major steps in good career planning?

8. Why do people need to set goals in life?

9. What are (a) short-term, (b) intermediate, and (c) long-term goals?

10. List five sources of job opportunity information.

11. How can you establish personal contacts within a business where you don't know anyone?

12. What types of placement services are available at your school?

13. Why should you check with different private employment agencies before signing up with one of them?

14. Where can you find job opportunity information online?

15. Why is a plan important to the success of your job search?

1. From Figure 2-1, list the activities that appeal to you. Then identify several occupations that offer these types of activities.

2. Describe your desired lifestyle in 10 years. Develop a plan of action to get a job that will support your desired lifestyle.

3. Using Figure 2-4 as an example, prepare a checklist of your short-term, intermediate, and long-term goals. At the end of one week, check to see what you have accomplished.

4. Cut these types of want ads from the classified section of your local newspaper: three ads by private employers, three ads by private employment agencies, one ad for someone to make a cash investment, one ad for someone in a sales position (to work on commission rather than for a salary), and one ad that gives the beginning salary in a dollar amount.

5. Using your telephone book, list five private employment agencies, their addresses, and their phone numbers. Also list the address and phone number of the state employment office. With your instructor's permission, call one of the private agencies and ask a counselor the fee for a job that will pay approximately $2,000 a month, and ask who would pay the fee.

6. Find the Web site of a major national company that has job openings listed. Briefly describe the available jobs. Then find the company's description of its business. Make a list of key information about the company you found there.

7. Using a search engine on your computer, type in key words such as "job" and "career." Write a one-page paper on your findings of current Internet resources to help you plan your career.

8. Write a paragraph describing your work history. It can be current or what you would like it to be in 10 years.

9. Using Figure 2-5 as an example, prepare a plan to get yourself a job using a one-week timetable. List your job leads, your contacts (or potential contacts), and a daily plan to accomplish several things each day.

Solve Problems ⊕ Explore Issues

1. Lacey Jones has decided that her long-term goal in life is to become an astronaut. She is now a sophomore in high school and hasn't done any planning. Lacey's grades are average. She is active, outgoing, and bright. What can Lacey do now, in the next few years, and beyond to prepare herself for a career as an astronaut?

2. With Figure 2-3 as a guide, use a separate sheet of paper to classify each of the following job titles into one of the job classifications. You may have to do some research to determine types of activities performed, skills and education required, working hours, and beginning pay. Next to each occupation, indicate whether or not you would be interested in the job. Next to the job classification, indicate whether or not you would be interested in this type of career.

a. Webmaster	j. physical therapist
b. court reporter	k. computer programmer
c. sheet-metal worker	l. radio announcer
d. technical writer	m. singer
e. building custodian	n. infantry officer
f. underwriter	o. administrative assistant
g. mechanical engineer	p. FBI special agent
h. sonar operator	q. tailor
i. cosmetologist	r. graphic designer

3. Meng Vann wants to work in marketing for a large company. What types of online resources could Meng use to find openings in the field of marketing? Go to three online sources. Find one job opening in marketing listed at each source. Make a list of the sources you used and describe the job opening you found at each source.

4. Parnell Rigsby would like to work as a merchandising manager for a large department store. He has all the qualifications, education, and skills necessary, but he doesn't know anyone in any large stores. Also, most openings are filled before he even knows they exist. What can Parnell do to find out about job openings in a large department store?

5. Moesha is a sophomore in high school. She plans to use the placement service of her high school to help get a part-time job in her senior year. What should Moesha do between now and her senior year to be sure her placement folder is ready when she is ready to find a job?

6. Carlos Diaz has worked part-time after school for the past two years. He worked for two weeks as a cook, but rarely got to work on time and was fired. He worked for two months as a busboy but quit because he didn't get enough tips. Carlos also worked for three weeks as a janitor but was laid off. Finally, he worked for four months as a plumber's assistant but quit because the work hurt his back. What is Carlos's record of job changes called? What does it say to potential employers? Would you hire Carlos?

For related activities and links, point your browser to **www.mypf.swlearning.com**

Getting the Job

application letter
return address
letter address
salutation
body

complimentary
 close
resume
references
scannable resume

reference letter
employment
 application
job interview
thank-you letter

Consider This. . .

Midori planned to get the right part-time job while she finished high school and prepared to go to college. Rather than waiting until spring when there would be far more competition, she decided to get the job in March and be all set when summer arrived. She had three interviews coming up, and she needed to mail or e-mail her resume before her appointments. She also wanted to draft an application letter to which she would attach her resume.

"Getting a job can be a job in itself," Midori told her mother. "I need to have all my materials in order. I'm really glad I have two reference letters ready to go. The good part is I'll get valuable experience for my resume. But for now, this isn't easy. In fact, it's pretty challenging."

Getting an Interview

Goals
- **Describe and prepare an application letter.**
- **List guidelines for and prepare a resume and scannable resume.**
- **Describe the reference letter and explain why it is useful to job applicants.**

▶ THE APPLICATION LETTER

©GETTY IMAGES/PHOTODISC

To apply for a job opening, or to inform a prospective employer of your interest in a future job opening, you need to mail or e-mail an application letter, together with a resume. The **application letter**, or cover letter, introduces you to the potential employer and gives you a chance to "sell" your qualifications. The application letter is really a sales letter. It is often your first contact with a new employer, and it is important to make a good impression.

Contents of an Application Letter

An application letter should be specific, interesting, and direct. The first paragraph should identify the purpose of the letter—why you are writing. Be *specific*. Tell the employer what job you want. If you know of an opening, tell the employer how you learned about it.

Why is an application letter really a "sales" letter?

The middle paragraph or paragraphs should give reasons why you are a good choice for the job. Use full sentences that explain your key qualifications—those that best fit the job. Express interest in the company as well. Briefly describe experiences, classes, or skills that relate to the job. Your tone should be enthusiastic and your writing style conversational. You should be able to "hear yourself talking" throughout the letter.

The closing paragraph should wrap up the letter in a friendly yet assertive manner. Be *direct*. Ask for an interview. For example, give the employer your telephone number and indicate a good time to call. In a friendly manner, make it clear that you are available for an interview.

Preparing an Application Letter

Generally, when you send an application letter by mail, use white, standard-size (8½ × 11-inch) paper of good quality. Choose a mailing envelope of the same color and quality. Your printer should make clear, crisp copies.

Figure 3-1 on page 44 shows an application letter using a typical font (or type style) called Times Roman. The size is 12 point, which makes it easy to read. You may use a different font and size if you want, but don't get too fancy. Your letter should look professional.

Along with your application letter, enclose a resume. You may also want to include a copy of your transcripts (school grade records), a reference letter, and other items specified in the job announcement. Be sure to refer to all enclosed items in the body of your letter. Then list them at the end of the letter in a separate notation.

Parts of an Application Letter

An application letter should contain five basic parts. As you can see from Figure 3-2 (page 45), they are the return address, letter address, salutation, body, and complimentary close.

RETURN ADDRESS

The **return address** is the first thing to appear at the top of the letter. It contains your complete mailing address and the date. If you have an e-mail address, add it below your city, state, and ZIP Code. Depending on the length of your letter, you may add blank lines above the return address to center the letter on the paper.

LETTER ADDRESS

The **letter address**, also called the inside address, contains the name and address of the person or company to whom you are writing. Find out the person's name and title, so you can address the letter directly to him or her. If you can't find out the person's name or you don't know whether the person is male or female, use the simplified letter format shown in Figure 3-3 (page 46).

SALUTATION

The **salutation** is the greeting that begins your letter. The person's name or other form of address (such as "Department Manager") may be followed by a colon or by nothing at all. "Dear Ms. Correa" is an example of a salutation. Avoid addressing application letters "To Whom It May Concern." The simplified format has no salutation. Instead, it has a subject line. This makes the letter less personal but avoids choosing a title, such as Mr., Ms., Mrs., Miss, or Dr., when you don't know which is appropriate.

 figure **3-1**   **APPLICATION LETTER, MODIFIED BLOCK STYLE**

234 Maple Street
Eugene, OR 97401-4321
tadams@stargaze.net

June 15, 20--

Ms. Marcia Hosteger, Owner
The Music Emporium
P.O. Box 8264
Eugene, OR 97405-8264

Dear Ms. Hosteger:

I would like to apply for your company's next opening in an office staff position.

I have prepared for this type of work and would appreciate the opportunity to visit with you about what I have to offer your company. As you can see from my resume, I have counter experience as well as accounting, clerical, and telephone skills. My course work in high school was in business and management, and I plan to continue my education as I work part-time for the next several years.

I am available for full-time work for the summer and part-time for the school year. I plan to continue my studies in business management, and my long-term goals include a permanent position in management that leads to increasing challenge and responsibility.

You can reach me at (503) 555-2000 after 3 p.m. daily. I am available to interview at your convenience. I look forward to discussing possible present or future employment with your company.

Sincerely,

Terrell B. Adams

Terrell B. Adams

Enclosure: resume

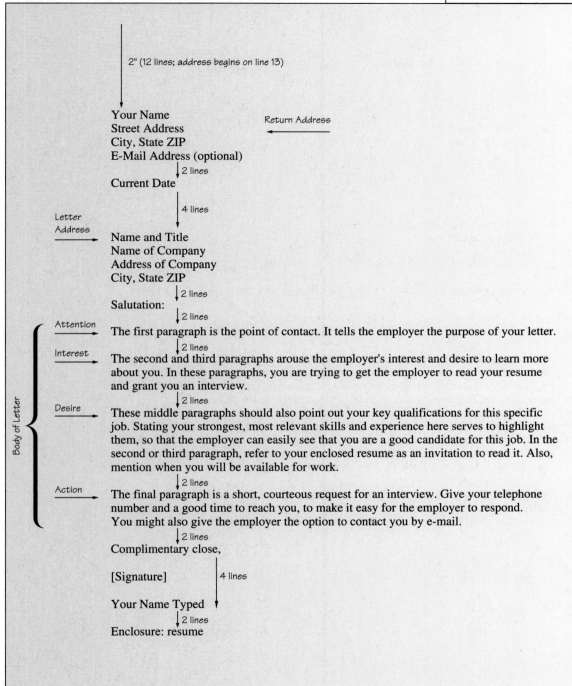

2" (12 lines; address begins on line 13)

Your Name   Return Address
Street Address
City, State ZIP
E-Mail Address (optional)
↓ 2 lines
Current Date

↓ 4 lines

Letter Address →

Name and Title
Name of Company
Address of Company
City, State ZIP
↓ 2 lines
Salutation:
↓ 2 lines

Attention → The first paragraph is the point of contact. It tells the employer the purpose of your letter.
↓ 2 lines
Interest → The second and third paragraphs arouse the employer's interest and desire to learn more about you. In these paragraphs, you are trying to get the employer to read your resume and grant you an interview.
↓ 2 lines
Desire → These middle paragraphs should also point out your key qualifications for this specific job. Stating your strongest, most relevant skills and experience here serves to highlight them, so that the employer can easily see that you are a good candidate for this job. In the second or third paragraph, refer to your enclosed resume as an invitation to read it. Also, mention when you will be available for work.
↓ 2 lines
Action → The final paragraph is a short, courteous request for an interview. Give your telephone number and a good time to reach you, to make it easy for the employer to respond. You might also give the employer the option to contact you by e-mail.
↓ 2 lines
Complimentary close,

[Signature] | 4 lines

Your Name Typed
↓ 2 lines
Enclosure: resume

Body of Letter

 figure **3-3**

SIMPLIFIED APPLICATION LETTER

2" (12 lines; address begins on line 13)

234 Maple Street
Eugene, OR 97401-4321
tadams@stargaze.net

↓ 2 lines

June 15, 20--

↓ 4 lines

Human Resource Manager
Excel Wholesale Company
818 Magnet
Eugene, OR 97401-0011

↓ 2 lines   (All caps)

POSITION POSTING OF JUNE 11, 20--, NO. 41826, ACCOUNTING CLERK

↓ 2 lines

Please consider me an applicant for the position posting referred to above.

↓ 2 lines

As you can see from my resume, I have completed the course work required to qualify
for an entry-level accounting clerk position. Also, I have worked for six months in a clerk
position where I learned about serving customers, keeping cash records, recording
purchases, and answering a multi-line telephone during busy hours.

↓ 2 lines

My long-term goal is to be a manager. I would like to work in a challenging job with
increasing responsibilities that use my business and accounting skills. I am available for
part-time employment now. In the fall, I plan to attend the community college part-time
to continue my studies in business and accounting.

↓ 2 lines

I am available for an interview at your convenience. Please call me at (503) 555-2000 to
discuss current or future employment opportunities with your company. If you prefer, you
can contact me by e-mail at tadams@stargaze.net. I look forward to hearing from you.

↓ 4 lines

Terrell B. Adams

TERRELL B. ADAMS (All caps)

↓ 2 lines

Enclosure: resume

BODY

The **body** is the message section of the letter. As you can see in Figure 3-2, the body contains four basic parts and should be three or four paragraphs long. These paragraphs should attract the employer's *attention*, inspire the employer's *interest* in learning more about you, create the employer's *desire* to read your resume, and request that the employer take *action* in the form of an interview. These parts of the body are often referred to as AIDA—attention, interest, desire, and action.

COMPLIMENTARY CLOSE

The **complimentary close** is a courteous phrase used to end a letter. Phrases commonly used in business are "Sincerely" and "Cordially," followed by a comma. Your typed name should appear four lines below the complimentary close to allow space for your signature. The simplified format does not include the complimentary close but goes directly to your name. Below your typed name are notations for enclosures that accompany the letter.

Preparing an E-Mail Application Letter

With e-mail, what you see on your screen is not necessarily how your message will appear on your receiver's screen. The receiver's software may not accept special formatting. Therefore, set your e-mail to Plain Text, as shown in Figure 3-4 on page 48. Place everything at the left margin. Use no special formatting or tabs.

Prepare your application letter in your e-mail message window. Your message will be dated automatically, so you need not type the date. Put the title of the job you are seeking in the Subject line. If possible, include a qualification that will catch the employer's attention. For example, the applicant in Figure 3-4 included years of experience in the subject line. Keep it short, however!

Start your message with the salutation. Omit the inside address and move your return address to the bottom of the message, below your name.

The body of your message should contain the same content as any other application letter. End the message with a complimentary close and your typed name, along with your mailing address, e-mail address, and phone number. Send your resume as an e-mail attachment. You need not include an enclosure notation since the attachment will show automatically.

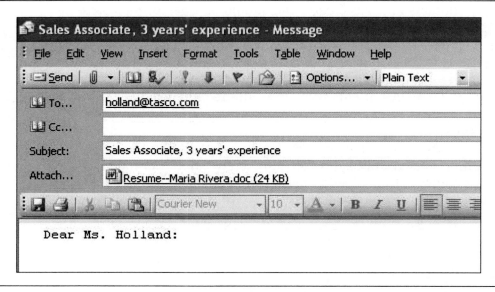

figure **3-4**

**PART OF AN E-MAIL APPLICATION
LETTER IN PLAIN TEXT**

Sales Associate, 3 years' experience - Message

File   Edit   View   Insert   Format   Tools   Table   Window   Help

Send | 📎 ▾ | 🗐 ⧨ | ! | ⬇ | ⚑ | 🖄 | Options... ▾ | Plain Text ▾

To...   holland@tasco.com

Cc...

Subject: Sales Associate, 3 years' experience

Attach...   📄Resume--Maria Rivera.doc (24 KB)

💾 🖨 | ✂ 📋 📋 | Courier New ▾ | 10 ▾ | A ▾ | B *I* U | ▤ ▤ ▤

  Dear Ms. Holland:

▶ THE RESUME

The **resume** is often called a personal data sheet, biographical summary, professional profile, or vita. It describes your work experience, education, abilities, interests, and other information that may be of interest to an employer. The resume tells the employer neatly and concisely who you are, what you can do, and your special interests. Always have an up-to-date resume ready for potential employers. Figure 3-5 shows a commonly used resume style. For more examples, go to www.monster.com and look for resume samples in the Advice section.

General Guidelines for a Resume

There are no set rules for preparing a resume. You should choose the style that best presents you to an employer. However, here are some helpful guidelines:

1. Early in your career, keep your resume to one page by carefully arranging the information you choose to include. Employers are busy people. They want a quick overview of you—not a lot of words to read. If you don't have enough information to fill a page, center what you have vertically on the page to make it attractive. After you have more education and work experience to summarize, your resume may extend to a second page. Resumes for professional applicants with publications and extensive work experience may run several pages.

figure **3-5** ◀ ◀

TERRELL B. ADAMS
234 Maple Street
Eugene, OR 97401-4321
(503) 555-2000
tadams@stargaze.net

CAREER OBJECTIVE

Office or accounting clerk position with challenge, responsibility, and opportunity for advancement to administrative assistant.

EDUCATION

2001-2005   Madison High School, Eugene, Oregon (GPA 3.00)
             Major Course of Study: Business and Accounting

Relevant Course Work: **Relevant Skills:**

Word Processing   Accounting I and II   Typing (70 wpm)
Computer Applications   Marketing I and II   Word processing and
Business Math   Business Law   spreadsheet software

Extracurricular Activities:

Member: National Honor Society, 2002-2005
Member: Future Business Leaders of America, 2003-2005
Competitor at regional skills event in area of accounting

EXPERIENCE

Accounting Clerk, Video Image Plus, Springfield, Oregon (six months)
        Cooperative work experience position through Madison High School.
                Duties included answering telephone, preparing statements, serving customers, keeping cash records, recording purchases, and filing.

Office Assistant, Madison High School, Eugene, Oregon (one year)
                Work in the front office included helping new students get to classes, answering the telephone, running errands, typing forms, and calling parents.

Newspaper Carrier, Register-Guard, Eugene, Oregon (two years)
                Delivered morning newspapers in one route for one year, and on two routes for one year. Duties included keeping good records, collecting from customers, sorting and doing inserts, making special deliveries, and substituting for others.

REFERENCES

Provided on request.

2. Include all information pertinent to the job for which you are applying. An employer wants to know that you are interested in the specific job opening. Rather than prepare a "generic" resume to fit all possible openings, use key words from a job posting or ad to show that your skills match that particular job.

3. Carefully choose fonts, bold, italic, boxes, spacing and other tools to arrange your information in a way that is attractive yet professional-looking and easy to read. Place the most important items in the upper third of the page.

4. Proofread thoroughly. Remember, your computer's spell check catches only misspelled words. It will not catch errors such as "then" instead of "than." Your resume must have no errors.

5. For hard copies, use a high-resolution printer and good quality 8½ × 11-inch paper. Avoid bright colors, odd sizes, and paper with stains or discolorations.

Parts of the Resume

A simple resume should include personal contact information, a career objective (optional), education, experience, additional qualifications or special items of interest (if applicable), and references. You may arrange your resume according to personal preference. However, generally you should show your most favorable section first. For example, if your work experience relates to the open job more closely than your education does, list experience ahead of education. Following is a discussion of the basic parts of a resume.

PERSONAL INFORMATION
This section usually appears first on the resume and includes your name, address, telephone number, and e-mail address. You may also wish to include a cell phone or pager number where the employer can reach you. Include your area code. Omit information such as age, gender, marital status, number of dependents, and ethnic background.

CAREER OBJECTIVE
The career objective is an optional statement. As your resume gets fuller, you may wish to omit it. If used, make it a short, assertive statement indicating your career goal. For example, your goal might be to rise to a particular position. Make the statement forward-looking, interesting, and specific. This statement helps the employer see how your plans could benefit the company. It also reveals your enthusiasm for the job. Avoid weak and unimpressive statements such as "any type of work in the office."

EDUCATION

List all high school and post-high school institutions you have attended, starting with the most recent. You may include major areas of study, grade point average, extracurricular activities, scholastic honors, specific courses that apply to the job opening, or any other pertinent facts that you think will create a favorable impression. For example, extracurricular activities tell an employer that you are a well-rounded person and that you possess different abilities and interests. Offices held in school organizations show the employer that you have leadership capability.

EXPERIENCE

List jobs, paid and unpaid, that you have held, including assisting at school functions, working as a teacher's aide, and any part- or full-time summer or vacation jobs (such as camp counselor). You may write this section in paragraph or outline form. Include information such as name and address of employer, job title, work duties, employment dates or length of time employed, and specific achievements while with this employer. Emphasize tasks you performed that relate directly to the open position.

Why is work experience an important part of the resume?

ADDITIONAL QUALIFICATIONS

You may have additional skills to bring to a potential employer's attention. For example, you may list special equipment you have learned to operate, software you can use, or foreign languages you know. You can also list awards you have received. All of these things give an employer a fuller picture of you.

REFERENCES

References are people who have known you for at least one year and can provide information about your skills, character, and achievements. References should be over age 18 and not related to you. The best types of references include teachers, advisors, current and former employers, and adults in business. Be sure to ask permission before listing people on your resume. If you choose not to list references on your resume, state "references available upon request." Then have names, addresses, telephone numbers, and e-mail addresses ready for employers who ask for them.

What kind of people could you ask for letters of reference?

Scannable Resumes

Some employers use scanners and special software to search for key words and phrases that match the skills required in their job descriptions. They can scan hard copy as well as electronic resumes. The scan determines which resumes will be considered further and which will not.

A **scannable resume** is a resume that has been designed for easy reading by a scanner and contains key words from the applicant's career field. To make the scanner's cut, describe your qualifications using key words from your field. For example, a publisher looking for an editor might scan for key words such as English or journalism degree, writing, editing, and copyediting. To make your resume easy for the scanner, use the following formatting:

- A simple, standard font, such as Times Roman or Arial

- Type size of 11 or 12 point for the body of the resume

- Headings no larger than 14 point bold or caps

  Avoid the following:

- Fancy fonts, italic, underlines, condensed type, shading, shadows, and white type on a black background

- Multiple columns

- Horizontal or vertical lines, boxes, and graphics

Net Nuggets

Jobweb.com contains an extensive section on writing resumes and cover letters, as well as interviewing. You can view sample resumes, learn 10 steps to a successful interview, and even take an online quiz that tests your interviewing skills. Check out this Web site at www.jobweb.com and follow the Resumes and Interview link for a variety of options on these topics.

REFERENCE LETTERS

A **reference letter** is a statement attesting to your character, abilities, and experience, written by someone who can be relied upon to give a sincere report. When you ask people to write a reference letter for you, be sure to give them enough time to prepare it. It is also helpful to give them a copy of your current resume or a short summary of your accomplishments and background. The letter should be on company letterhead stationery. A sample reference letter for another applicant is shown in Figure 3-6 on page 54.

When you receive the reference letter, make photocopies to give to employers along with your resume and application letter. Keep the original for your files, because you may need to make additional copies for other job applications.

✓ Check Your Understanding

1. List the parts of an application letter.
2. Why should you use the Plain Text setting when preparing an e-mail application letter?
3. What information is contained in a resume? List the parts of a resume.
4. Name three people who would be good references to list on your resume or who would write a reference letter for you.

figure **3-6**

REFERENCE LETTER

FARWEST TRUCK CENTER

402 First Street, NW
Eugene, OR 97402-2143

June 4, 20--

To Whom It May Concern:

RE: TayVon Shaw

I have known TayVon Shaw as an employee for one and a half years. TayVon began working for Farwest as a work-study student in the cooperative education program at his high school. He proved to be such a good employee that, at the end of the school year, we kept TayVon as a full-time summer worker. He now works for us part-time after school and on weekends.

TayVon is a fine young man. I have found him to be honest and sincere. He is always on time and is genuinely eager to do a good job. TayVon gets along well with other employees and customers. He has filled in for vacationing office employees and has been able to assume additional responsibilities very quickly.

Without hesitation I can recommend TayVon to you as a fine person and an outstanding employee. He will, I am sure, be an asset to any company for which he works.

If you have any further questions, please do not hesitate to call me.

Sincerely,

Harriet Chen

Harriet Chen
Manager

Issues in Your World

Whether you want to leave your job to look for better pay, growth opportunities, more satisfying work, or for some other reason, you should keep several important things in mind:

1. Find a new job before quitting your old job. Then you can conduct your job search carefully, not hastily.

2. Before leaving your current job, establish good relations with both co-workers and managers who will be helpful references for you. Employers usually check the backgrounds of people they consider hiring.

3. Don't talk negatively about your old job, boss, or company in job interviews. Be positive and talk about the future. Don't emphasize how important money is to you. To give the impression that your only concern is to make lots of money would be a mistake.

4. In your current job you may have many opportunities to learn about openings in other companies, especially competitors. Proceed with caution as you discuss with these potential employers possible jobs, your current job, or other factors affecting your decision. It is important to maintain confidentiality and good relations in your current position both before and after you leave.

5. Don't burn your bridges. You never know; in the future, you may want to go back to work for a previous employer. Also, people at your previous company know people in other companies. If you leave on bad term, word of your bad reputation may travel to other potential employers.

Changing jobs to move your career forward is accepted practice. But take care to set a good track record as you change jobs.

Think Critically

1. Suppose you are on your own and supporting yourself. One day your boss makes you angry, so you quit your job without having another one lined up. How would you feel as you interview for new jobs? What mistakes might you make under these circumstances?

2. Talk to someone who has changed jobs within the same field. Why did that person change jobs? Did the change accomplish his or her goal?

Applying, Interviewing, and Following Up

Goals
- Describe and fill out an employment application form.
- Discuss how to prepare for a job interview.
- Describe and prepare a thank-you letter.

▶ THE APPLICATION FORM

When you apply for a job opening, you will have to complete an **employment application**, like the one shown in Figure 3-7. When possible, ask to take the application form with you. If you must do it on the spot, use a good pen and fill it out completely. Some companies have a link to their application at their Web site. You may be able to download the form, fill it out on your computer, and submit it electronically. When completing an employment application, follow these steps:

1. Print neatly using a black or dark blue pen that does not skip or blot. Keep your responses within the space provided. Your printing must be easy to read and clear.

2. Fill in all the blanks. When you cannot answer a question, write "N/A" (for "not applicable") or use a line (——) to indicate to the employer that you have not skipped or ignored the question.

3. Be truthful. Give complete answers. Do not abbreviate unless the meaning of the abbreviation is clear.

4. Have with you all information that might be requested on the application form, such as telephone numbers, dates of employment, addresses of references, and work permit number. Calling later with the rest of the needed information inconveniences the employer and makes you look unprepared. Avoid giving confidential data, such as your social security number, until you have secured employment.

5. Whether you are completing the form by hand or by computer, proofread carefully!

How is an employment application different from an application letter?

EMPLOYMENT APPLICATION

figure **3-7**

EMPLOYMENT APPLICATION

Date: *7/15/20–*   Job you are applying for: *Clerk/Office Assistant*   ☐ Full Time   ☒ Part Time

Social Security Number: *Provided at employment*

First Name: *Terrell*   Middle Initial: *B.*   Last Name: *Adams*

Mailing Address: *234 Maple Street*   City: *Eugene*   State: *OR*   Zip: *97401*

Home Phone: *(503) 555-2000*   Work Phone: (   )

Have you worked for this company before?   ☐ Yes ☒ No   **From:**   **To:**   **What location?**

Your name at that time: –   Position when you left: –

If you are under 18, give your birthdate: _–_ / _–_ / _–_ and work permit number (if applicable): –

Date available for work: *7/15/20–*

Please indicate the hours that you are available to work on each of these days.

(Hours)	SUNDAY	MONDAY	TUESDAY	WEDNESDAY	THURSDAY	FRIDAY	SATURDAY
From	8	1	1	1	1	1	8
To	8	8	8	8	8	8	8

START WITH CURRENT OR LAST EMPLOYER—INCLUDE MONTH AND YEAR IN DATES

FROM	COMPANY		POSITION HELD	
Mo. 9 Yr. 04	*Video Image Plus*		*Accounting Clerk*	BEGINNING PAY *Min. Wage*
TO	STREET and NUMBER	CITY and STATE		ENDING
Mo. 2 Yr. 05	*1121 West 18th Springfield, OR 97477*			PAY *Min. Wage*
SUPERVISOR'S NAME *Jewel Clark*	TITLE *CWE Coordinator*	REASON FOR LEAVING *end of program*		

FROM	COMPANY		POSITION HELD	
Mo. 9 Yr. 03	*Madison High School*		*Office Assistant*	BEGINNING PAY *Volunteer*
TO	STREET and NUMBER	CITY and STATE		ENDING
Mo. 6 Yr. 04	*Eugene, OR 97401*			PAY *Volunteer*
SUPERVISOR'S NAME *Andy Williamson*	TITLE *Office Manager*	REASON FOR LEAVING *end of year*		

FROM	COMPANY		POSITION HELD	
Mo. 6 Yr. 99	*Register Guard*		*Newspaper Carrier*	BEGINNING PAY *Commission*
TO	STREET and NUMBER	CITY and STATE		ENDING
Mo. 9 Yr. 01	*Eugene, OR 97401*			PAY *Commission*
SUPERVISOR'S NAME *Mary Adamson*	TITLE *Supervisor*	REASON FOR LEAVING *to go to school*		

MAY WE CONTACT YOUR PRESENT EMPLOYER?   ☒ Yes   ☐ No

SCHOOL NAME	ADDRESS	FROM	TO	DEGREE/DIPLOMA
HIGH SCHOOL				DIPLOMA ☒ Yes ☐ No
Madison High School	*Eugene, OR 97401*	2001	2005	TYPE:
BUSINESS/VOCATION SCHOOL				DIPLOMA ☐ Yes ☐ No
				TYPE:
COMMUNITY COLLEGE/UNIVERSITY				DIPLOMA ☐ Yes ☐ No
				TYPE:
UNDERGRADUATE COURSEWORK EMPHASIS				CUM GPA
GRADUATE COURSEWORK EMPHASIS				CUM GPA

I understand that any offer of employment is conditioned upon the satisfactory completion of this verification process and that the complany will hire only those individuals who are legally authorized to work in the United States and who present acceptable proof of their lawful employment status and identity.

Terrell B. Adams
SIGN HERE

7 / 15 / 20–
DATE

CHAPTER 3 • Getting the Job

► THE JOB INTERVIEW

A **job interview** is a face-to-face meeting with a potential employer to discuss your job qualifications. During the job interview, the employer will have your completed application, together with your resume, application letter, and reference letter(s). The interviewer may question you about statements you made on any of these documents or about any other job-related matters. Therefore, you should spend at least as much time preparing for the interview as you did in getting the interview.

Preparing for the Interview

Review your resume so that all your qualifications will be fresh in your mind. Be prepared to answer open-ended questions such as "Tell me about yourself," "Why do you want to work for us?" or "What would you like to be doing in five years?" Your responses show how well you organize your thoughts, speak, and think under pressure. Avoid rambling, talking about unrelated topics, or speaking negatively of others. Emphasize your skills, achievements, and career plans. Prepare a list of likely questions. Then rehearse how you will answer them.

It is also important to learn something about your potential employer. Think of questions you might ask the interviewer about the company and about the position for which you are applying. Find out what the company makes or sells, where its branches are, how rapidly it has grown, and what its prospects are for the future. This kind of information can be obtained from such sources as these:

Why should you spend time preparing for an interview?

1. The Yellow Pages may have an advertisement that lists the company's products or services.

2. Visit the company's Web site and read about its products, history, financial performance, and other data.

3. Ask for information from an acquaintance who works for the company.

4. Review the company's annual reports, available online at the company Web site. Annual reports describe the company and its financial resources.

5. Find articles in current magazines and newspapers, including online publications, which discuss the company's economic health or plans for expansion.

Making a Good First Impression

Since it may affect your whole future, the interview is an important moment in your life. Prepare for it carefully. Discussed below are some ways to make a favorable impression.

1. *Arrive on Time.* Better yet, arrive five to ten minutes early so you have time to check your appearance and compose yourself. Never be late to an interview. The interviewer will consider your tardiness an indication of your expected job performance. Time your travel route before the day of the interview. Then allow extra time for traffic and parking.

2. *Dress Appropriately.* If you are seeking work in a bank, dress like those already employed at the bank. Whatever you wear, be neat and clean. Don't overuse jewelry, perfume, after-shave, or make-up. Be conservative in dress, hairstyle, and appearance. Look like you already have the job you are now applying for.

3. *Go Alone.* Don't bring along a friend or relative.

4. *Be Prepared.* Bring copies of your resume, reference letters, and school transcripts. All should be neat, up-to-date, and accurate. Take a pad of paper and two good pens, articles you have found about the company, and other information you may need. Bring your papers in a briefcase or some type of carrying folder to keep them neat and organized.

5. *Appear Poised and Self-Confident.* It's normal to be nervous, but don't let your emotions control you. It's important to appear relaxed and comfortable. Maintain good eye contact with the interviewer. Don't chew gum, smoke, or display nervous habits. An occasional smile shows you are relaxed and feel good about yourself. Avoid chattering to fill quiet times. Allow the interviewer to lead the discussion.

6. *Be Courteous.* Even if you are asked to wait, respond with courtesy and understanding. Convey an attitude of composure and congeniality. Use "please" and "thank you."

7. *Think Before You Answer Each Question.* Take a moment to organize your thoughts before answering. Be polite, accurate, and honest. Use correct grammar. Be especially careful of verb tenses. Say "yes" rather than "yeah." Avoid slang and informal speech. Speak slowly and clearly.

8. *Emphasize Your Strong Points.* Talk about your most relevant school subjects, grades, attendance, skills, work experience, activities, and goals in a positive manner. Negative comments reflect badly on you.

9. *Be Enthusiastic and Interested in the Company and the Job.* Show that you are energetic and able to do what is asked with a willing

attitude. Let the interviewer know that you are interested in the company, in the job, in your future, and in what's going on in the world. Look for nonverbal and other cues from the interviewer. Listen carefully and try to understand the company's needs.

When the interview is over, thank the interviewer for his or her time. Say you will check back later. Then do so. Leave a copy of your resume, reference letters, and other information with the interviewer, if he or she does not already have them. Exit with a smile and a comment such as "I look forward to hearing from you."

 ## Career Focus

Recruiters are human resource specialists. Maintaining contacts within a community, they may travel extensively, often to college campuses, to search for promising job applicants. Recruiters screen, interview, and sometimes test applicants. They also may check references and make job offers. Recruiters must be thoroughly familiar with the hiring company and its personnel policies in order to explain wages, working conditions, and promotional opportunities to prospective employees. They must be knowledgeable about equal employment opportunity and affirmative action guidelines and laws.

For more information, refer to the *Occupational Outlook Handbook* at www.bls.gov or search the Internet using such key words as "careers," "human resources," and "recruiter."

THE THANK-YOU LETTER

After the interview, the employer will have various candidates from which to choose. Your follow-up may help you stand out from the crowd. This contact reminds the employer of who you are and could improve your chance of getting the job. A **thank-you letter**, such as Figure 3-8 is a follow-up tool to remind the interviewer of your qualifications and desire to work for the company.

Basic Guidelines for the Thank-You Letter

Follow the same format and guidelines that you used in preparing your application letter. You may want to enclose an additional reference or other information that may help convince the interviewer to hire you. Remember to address the interviewer by name. If more than one person interviewed you during your visit, write a brief letter to each person.

234 Maple Street
Eugene, OR 97401-4321
tadams@stargaze.net

June 25, 20--

Mr. R.B. Rivera, Manager
Magna Music Company
2345 Main Street
Eugene, OR 97401-0013

Dear Mr. Rivera:

Thank you for the time you spent with me during our interview yesterday afternoon. I enjoyed meeting you and having the opportunity to see how your company operates.

Your description of the data entry position sounded very interesting and challenging to me. As you know, I worked as an accounting clerk as part of my cooperative work experience. In that position, I gained skills in entering data into accounting spreadsheets. You can be assured that I will do my best on the job and will continue to improve my skills to be more valuable to your company in the future.

If there is any further information I can supply to you, please feel free to contact me. You can reach me in the evenings at (503) 555-2000, or anytime by e-mail at tadams@stargaze.net. I look forward to hearing from you.

Sincerely,

Terrell B. Adams

Terrell B. Adams

Body of the Letter

The first paragraph should remind the interviewer of your interview by making reference to it. A good way to begin is as follows: "Thank you for giving me the opportunity to speak with you on [date and time of interview] concerning . . ."

The second paragraph reminds the interviewer of your desire to work for the company. Take this opportunity to remind the interviewer of one or two of your key qualifications that best fit the open position.

The final paragraph should courteously express your eagerness to hear from the interviewer when he or she has reached a decision. Include your telephone number and good times to reach you. This paragraph should end on a positive note.

Keep your letter short and to the point, and make sure it is error-free. This final opportunity to represent yourself to the potential employer may make the difference that will get you the job.

✔Check Your Understanding

1. What are some important steps to remember when filling out an employment application?
2. List several things you should do to prepare for a job interview.
3. What are some ways to make a good first impression at a job interview?
4. What is the purpose of the thank-you letter?

Chapter Assessment

SUMMARY

3.1
* An application letter sent by mail should include a return address, letter address, salutation, body, and complimentary close.
* When you prepare an application letter in the body of an e-mail, use the Plain Text setting and avoid special formatting and tabs.
* The purpose of an application letter is to interest the employer in reading your resume and granting you an interview.
* A resume is a concise summary of your work experience, education, abilities, and interests.
* To make your resume easy for a scanner to read, avoid fancy fonts and formatting.
* Ask for a reference letter from past employers, co-workers, teachers, and adults in business who can vouch for your skills, character, and experience.

3.2
* Fill out employment application forms completely, accurately, and honestly.
* Prepare for an interview by reviewing your materials, researching the company, and rehearsing answers to questions you might be asked.
* Arrive at the interview on time, dress appropriately, go alone, and be courteous and enthusiastic.
* After an interview, follow up with a short thank-you letter that reminds the interviewer of your key qualifications and your interest in the job.

REVIEW TERMS

Directions

Can you find the definition for each of the following terms used in Chapter 3?

application letter	references
body	resume
complimentary close	return address
employment application	salutation
job interview	scannable resume
letter address	thank-you letter
reference letter	

1. The part of a letter that shows the writer's name, street address, city, state, ZIP Code, e-mail address (optional), and current date.

2. The greeting that begins a letter.

3. The part of a letter that shows the name and address of the person or company to whom you are writing.

4. A summary of personal information, education, experience, additional qualifications, and references of the job seeker.

5. The message section of a letter.

6. People over 18, not related to you, who have known you for at least one year and can report on your skills, character, and achievements.

7. A statement, in letter form, attesting to your character, abilities, and experience, written by someone who can be relied upon to give a sincere report.

8. A form you fill out when you apply for a job.

9. A face-to-face meeting with a potential employer to discuss your job qualifications.

10. A letter that introduces you to the potential employer and gives you a chance to "sell" your qualifications.

11. The phrase that courteously ends a letter.

12. A tool to remind the employer of your qualifications and interest in the job, written after the interview.

13. A resume that has been designed for easy reading by a scanner and contains key words from the applicant's career field.

REVIEW FACTS AND IDEAS

1. What is the purpose of an application letter? What action does the writer desire? What do the letters AIDA stand for?

2. What size of paper should you use for an application letter or a thank-you letter?

3. List and describe briefly the five basic parts of an application letter.

4. When would you use the simplified letter format for an application letter?

5. What is a resume? Describe the parts you will include in your own resume.

6. Why should you list extracurricular activities on your resume?

7. Which kinds of people should you use as references on your resume?

8. What should you do to make your resume scannable? What should you avoid?

9. List four guidelines for filling out an employment application.

10. What information should you include in the second paragraph of a thank-you letter?

1. Follow the instructions in the chapter to prepare an application letter to a company that you would like to work for.

2. Prepare your resume, using your own design. Include all information that applies to you, emphasizing your strong points. Format it to be scannable.

3. Visit Career Consulting Corner online at www.careercc.com or another Web site that offers resume advice. Write a paragraph about the resume tips you find there. Which tips do you plan to follow when you prepare your own resume?

4. Call, e-mail, or speak directly to each person listed on your resume as a reference (or anyone you would use when asked for references). Ask permission to use their names on your resume or for job interview purposes. Ask one person to write a reference letter for you.

5. Obtain and complete an employment application from a local business. Or, search company sites on the Internet for an application you can download and fill out.

6. Write a thank-you letter for a job interview. Assume you were interviewed by the person to whom you sent your application letter (see Question 1). You should know the interviewer's name now. Address the person by name and title.

Solve Problems ⊕ Explore Issues

1. Darlene Fry wants to work as a forest ranger when she graduates from college. At present, she knows of no openings, but she does know the address of the local Bureau of Land Management, which occasionally hires students during summers to help in the forest. Darlene takes science courses and does well. She is available to work all summer and could even work without pay if her living expenses were covered. Because you are Darlene's friend, you have offered to help her write an application letter. Make up a return address, letter address, salutation, body, and complimentary close. Use the sample application letters in the chapter as guides.

2. Armando Torres must provide a resume in order to answer an advertisement in the local newspaper. Write in outline form a summary of the basic rules of writing a resume. On another piece of paper, sketch a resume and label its parts. You do not need to insert fictional information—just describe what kinds of information Armando should use.

3. Desmonique tells you that she has a job interview tomorrow. She has never been on a job interview before, and she is very nervous. Desmonique asks you to point out to her what she should and should not do during her interview. On a piece of paper, make a list for Desmonique of at least five things she should be sure to do and five things she should avoid during her job interview.

4. Savath Rajady has just completed a job interview. Savath knows that his competition is tough, but believes he stands a good chance of getting the job because he is available to work right away, his grades are high, and he has taken three marketing courses. Would you advise him to write a follow-up (thank-you) letter? What might he say?

For related activities and links, point your browser to **www.mypf.swlearning.com**

Adapting to Work

TERMS TO KNOW

hearing
listening
sympathetic
  listening
critical listening
creative listening

horizontal
  communication
downward
  communication
upward
  communication
human relations

empathy
self-esteem
self-actualization
hygiene factors
motivators

Consider This. . .

Stage fright is a common fear experienced by people who perform for audiences. It refers to the anxiety felt by a person who is confronted with doing something he or she is not comfortable doing.

Hugh had to give a presentation to his marketing class. He remembered the important things he learned in a previous speech class—to relax, look directly at the audience, speak slowly, take deep breaths—but still he didn't feel comfortable. According to Hugh, "My dad says I have to get used to this sort of thing. He says I'll have to communicate at work every day. Sometimes it will be one-on-one, but at times I'll have to speak in front of a group. He says this class presentation will be good for me. Fine, but I'm still nervous. The good thing is that I get a little less nervous every time I do this."

Communicating in the Work Environment

Goals • Identify and describe effective communication strategies on the job.
• Discuss guidelines for effective human relations at work.

▶ EFFECTIVE COMMUNICATION AT WORK

Success on the job depends on good communication skills. Of all the job activities you perform in a day, 80 percent involve communication in one form or another. More than half of all job communication involves listening and speaking. Figure 4-1 illustrates the relative importance of each form of communication (listening, speaking, writing, and reading) during the average workday.

Listening

Hearing is the process of perceiving sound. It requires little thinking and very little effort. **Listening** is an active hearing process that requires concentration and effort. To be a good listener, look at the speaker and maintain eye contact. Ask questions and get involved in the conversation. Avoid interrupting or changing the subject. Control your emotions. Listen to what the speaker says, and then evaluate it with an open mind.

Sympathetic listening, often called "empathetic listening," is the ability to perceive from another person's point of view and to sense what the person is feeling. To listen with empathy, keep your attention on the speaker. Do not interrupt. Ask questions that lead the speaker to make further analysis. Avoid giving approval or disapproval. With sympathetic listening, don't give your own opinion unless it is asked for.

What is the difference between hearing and listening?

Critical listening is the ability to differentiate facts from opinion. When analyzing information about a product or service you are considering purchasing, use critical listening. For example, claims that a product is "the best buy" or "top quality" are useless. They are opinions,

figure 4-1   **COMMUNICATION ON THE JOB**

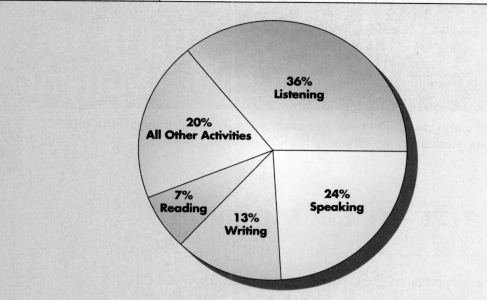

not facts. But when you hear factual information, such as "100 percent cotton" or "one-year guarantee," this is useful information.

Creative listening means listening with your mind open to new ideas. Group problem-solving techniques, such as brainstorming, require creative listening. In brainstorming, all ideas are recorded without judgment. Then, after the group exhausts all possibilities, they put the best ideas together to make a workable plan.

Speaking

At most workplaces, about a quarter of the average employee's time is spent in oral communication. Most of this is informal. People speak informally to:

1. Make contact with others.

2. Exchange information.

3. Influence others.

4. Solve problems.

At some times in your work life, you may need to give a formal speech. Formal speeches are prepared in advance and designed for a particular purpose. Common purposes for formal speeches are:

1. *To Inform.* In this type of presentation, your goal is to convey information to your audience in an understandable manner. You can give facts and then reach your conclusions (inductive reasoning), or give conclusions first followed by supporting facts (deductive reasoning).

2. *To Entertain.* The purpose of this type of speech is to get your audience to relax and enjoy themselves. Entertainment speech is difficult because it depends on the audience's reaction. For example, if the audience doesn't respond favorably, you may find it difficult to keep going.

3. *To Persuade.* This type of speech is designed to convince your audience to take some action or to believe something. To be convincing, you must use solid facts and statistics. You must appear to be honest and to believe in what you are saying. If you are not sincere, your audience will sense it.

To give your formal speech added style, use visual aids. For example, consider using video, computerized slide shows, audio recordings, display boards, flip charts, objects, models, or handouts. The setting, which includes lighting, room layout, seating, speaker's stand, and microphone, can also contribute to the positive acceptance of your speech.

Stage fright (nervousness) is a natural and common reaction. Many experienced speakers are tense before speaking. To control stage fright:

1. *Build Your Confidence.* Prepare in relatively non-threatening speaking situations. Talk before small groups, including friends and family. Take speech classes and observe other speakers.

2. *Be Well Prepared.* First, outline what you want to say. Then time yourself giving the speech on several occasions. Prepare an additional "comfort zone" of several minutes' worth of material in case your speech goes faster than you thought it would. Most people talk faster when they are nervous, so make allowances for this.

What are some things you can do to control stage fright while speaking formally?

3. *Practice Public Speaking.* Begin with short speeches and build to longer ones. Practice speaking slowly when expressing your thoughts. Keep your voice low-pitched, clear, and reasonably paced. Volunteer to speak to classes, clubs, and groups. Record your voice and evaluate its effectiveness.

Communication Flow in the Workplace

Workplace communication flows in several directions: horizontally, downward, and upward. **Horizontal communication** is communication among co-workers of equal rank. Most horizontal communication occurs informally in small groups, one-to-one, and by e-mail. Co-workers share information and solve problems together to complete their tasks. Horizontal communication also serves as the company "grapevine," transmitting rumors and office gossip.

Downward communication is communication that flows from higher to lower levels of the organization. Managers give employees job-related instructions, performance feedback, and company news. Employees also communicate with managers about work problems, policies, and suggestions for improving company practices. This communication flow from lower to higher levels of the organization is **upward communication**. The effectiveness of both downward and upward communication depends on building open, trusting relationships between managers and employees.

VIEWPOINTS

Downsizing has been defined as the elimination of part of the workforce, especially in business and government, in order to achieve a more efficient and cost-effective organization. Economic downturns and the resulting downsizing can create a tense workplace. Management insists that in order to remain competitive, jobs must be cut. Employees, particularly those with many years of service, believe their work and their loyalty are not important to management anymore.

Think Critically: Do you agree with the claims of each side? What point could you make to support each side? How does the state of the economy play a role in this issue?

E-Mail Communication

E-mail is the most common form of communication in business today. Messages between employees and managers are generally worded more formally than messages between employees of the same rank. However, the rules of good writing still apply. When you write an e-mail message, use good grammar and proofread before sending. Keep your messages concise.

E-mail has several advantages as a communication tool. It is fast. Messages go from one computer to another almost instantly. It is inexpensive. Messages can be sent all over the world without having to pay postage or long-distance charges. Messages can also be sent to many people at the same time. Finally, e-mail is easy to learn and use.

One disadvantage of e-mail arises from an advantage. E-mail is so easy that people tend to use it too much. Businesspeople often complain of information overload caused by e-mailboxes full of unnecessary messages. To be a good e-mail communicator at work, resist the temptation to send unnecessary messages, including jokes or office gossip.

Remember that e-mail is not private. Employers can monitor employees' e-mail. Even if you delete messages from your computer at work, they remain on servers. You may be fired for using e-mail or the Internet at work for non-business purposes.

▶ HUMAN RELATIONS AT WORK

Human relations is the art of getting along with others. To be truly competent in human relations, you need to have a good understanding of yourself and of others and a genuine concern for their needs and feelings. Here are some ways you can improve your relationships:

1. *Accept Differences.* Everyone is different. Accept others as they are, tolerate differences of opinion, and recognize that other ways of doing things may also be effective. Learn to disagree without being disagreeable.

2. *Treat Others as Individuals.* Take time to discover the individuality in others. Learn people's names and use them. Take an interest in what others are doing. Every person deserves respect as a human being.

3. *Empathize with Others.* **Empathy** is the ability to see others' points of view and understand their feelings. It does not mean you agree with them but rather that you understand what they are saying, feeling, or experiencing.

4. *Praise Others.* Be consistent in praising the achievements of others. Seek good things that are true and complimentary, and praise them freely. Avoid untrue or exaggerated claims that appear insincere.

©GETTY IMAGES/PHOTODISC

5. *Focus on Problems, not People.* When problems with someone occur, you will get cooperation by focusing on the problem rather than verbally attacking him or her personally. For example say, "The auditors would like a cost breakdown in your report," rather than, "You did a poor job on that report."

6. *Accept Responsibility.* Take responsibility for your actions. Don't blame others for your mistakes. Your co-workers and boss will respect your willingness to accept responsibility and say, "I messed up."

Why are human relations at work important?

7. *Avoid Dogmatic Statements.* A dogmatic statement asserts an opinion as if it were a fact. Present your opinions as possibilities rather than absolute truths.

8. *Treat Others as Equals.* Respect each person's contributions. Don't talk down to people by telling them what they should know or do. Allow others to make their own decisions without criticism.

9. *Trust Others.* People will live up to, or down to, your expectations. Think the best of others and expect the best. When they know you trust them, most people prove to be trustworthy.

10. *Control Your Emotions.* Withhold judgments, comments, and decisions until you gather enough information to evaluate the situation thoughtfully. Reacting emotionally may cloud your judgment, and you may later regret the emotional outburst.

✅ Check Your Understanding

1. Have you made presentations that have been uncomfortable for you? If so, what could you have done differently?
2. List situations in which you do sympathetic, critical, and creative listening.
3. What was your favorite presentation? What parts do you remember—in other words, what techniques did the speaker use effectively?

Lesson 4.2

Thriving in the Work Environment

Goals • Describe written and unwritten work rules.
• Discuss appropriate work attitudes and the problem of absenteeism.
• Discuss two theories of motivation and the results of job satisfaction.

▶ EMPLOYER EXPECTATIONS

Employers expect employees to behave in ways that will help meet the goals of the business. To inform employees of expected behavior, employers create work rules and policies. Employees who thrive in the workplace exceed these expectations.

Work Rules

Most businesses have written and unwritten work rules. *Unwritten work rules* often are commonly understood without being documented or verbally communicated. An informal dress code is one example. Observe how other employees dress. Then dress in a similar manner. An employer expects employees to know from common sense some of the work rules that apply to their jobs. Courtesy and teamwork are expected. Loyalty, a positive attitude, safety, punctuality, and good grooming are rules that are often unwritten and unspoken.

Written work rules are usually posted in employee work areas or included in an employee manual. These rules are generally written for the benefit and protection of all employees. Companies that deal with hazardous chemicals or potentially dangerous machinery enforce strict written safety rules. When everyone adheres to the rules, the work flows smoothly and safely, and everyone shares in the responsibilities. Figure 4-2 (page 76) is an example of work rules that might be posted in an employee break room.

Because the rules shown in Figure 4-2 are basic, employees who break them are subject to immediate discipline. When one employee is permitted to break the rules, others will see this and feel justified in doing the same thing. New employees should arrive early, leave on time, and never stay overtime on a break or sneak food into the work area. While these infractions are not acceptable in regular employees, they are tolerated even less in new employees.

Work Attitudes

Employees' work attitudes are important to employers because they affect morale, output (production), and public relations. Every employee in a company represents that company to the public. A good attitude makes a favorable impression. Good public relations are important to a company's future growth and profitability. To create a favorable impression:

■ Remember customers' names.

■ Make an unusual effort to help.

■ Demonstrate knowledge, enthusiasm, and interest in customers.

■ Display genuine concern for the quality of products and services.

■ Care about people and meeting their needs.

■ Listen sympathetically to customer complaints.

■ Take pride in yourself and your work.

 figure **4-2**

WORK RULES

COMPANY WORK RULES
Sanders Department Store

1. Work begins promptly at 8 a.m. or 2 p.m. and ends promptly at 5 p.m. or 10 p.m. These are our hours of operation, and the store must be covered.

2. No food, drink, or smoking is allowed in the store.

3. No smoking is permitted in the building. Outside smoking areas are provided at the south and north entrances. Please do not smoke within 15 feet of the doorway.

4. All employees will be clean and properly groomed at all times. Facial hair is permitted if it is well groomed. Use good judgment in what you wear.

5. When a worker is sick, he or she must call in by 7 a.m. for the day shift, or by 4 p.m. for the evening shift.

6. Vacations are taken according to seniority; no more than three employees may take vacations during the same week. All vacations must be arranged two weeks in advance.

Employers appreciate employees who "go the extra mile." This means doing more than required and doing it with a positive attitude.

Absenteeism

Absenteeism is a special kind of problem. How to deal with it depends on the reasons for the absence. One expert observed that of all absences:

■ 60 percent are due to serious or chronic illnesses, injuries, or family emergencies.

■ 20 percent are due to acute, short-term illnesses (such as the flu), work-related accidents, or personal problems.

■ 10 percent are due to a minor illness such as a cold, and to employees whose decision to report to work or not depends on their attitudes about their jobs.

■ 10 percent are due to a pretend illness so that the employee can enjoy a day off.

The absentees making up the last 20 percent are of greatest concern to businesses. Industrial psychologists call this "voluntary absence syndrome" and warn that these patterns can lead to serious emotional imbalance and disturbance in the absentees' lives.

Frequent absentees face consequences ranging from pay deductions and warnings to temporary layoffs, poor recommendations, lack of respect (from employers and fellow employees), and eventually to termination of employment. When employers do not take action, they are in effect giving their approval to the absences, thereby encouraging other employees to be absent often. The working employees resent having to do another employee's work when the employer takes no corrective action.

High rates of absenteeism cost companies thousands of dollars annually. The U.S. Department of Labor uses the formulas shown here in the Math Minute feature to compute the rate of absenteeism and the costs of absenteeism to a business. Most labor experts agree that an absentee rate of 2.0 is low, while a rate of 5.0 is high. In the Math Minute example, Bascom's Health Foods Market has an absentee rate of 2.08 percent. The company can conclude that its absenteeism is reasonable. However, Goldstein's has a rate of 4.69 percent. From this number, Goldstein's can see that it has a problem with absent employees and should search for causes and solutions.

Math Minute | Cost of Absenteeism

Bascom's Health Foods Market operates 24 hours a day, 365 days a year. Employees work three 8-hour shifts. In an average month, 12 employees work 30 days. On average, a total of 180 hours are missed from work per month (the equivalent of 7.5 days). The *rate of absenteeism* is determined as follows:

$$\text{Rate of Absenteeism} = \frac{\text{Absent Days per Month}}{\text{Work Days per Month} \times \text{Number of Employees}}$$

Using this formula, Bascom's absenteeism rate is 2.08%, or $7.5 \div (30 \times 12)$.

The following formula determines the *cost of absenteeism*:

Cost of Absenteeism = Annual lost time × Average wage rate × 2

The formula multiplies the cost of wages by 2 to include the costs of benefits paid to absent employees and the costs of paying temporary workers to replace the absent workers.

Bascom's average wage rate is $7.50 per hour. Using the formula, the cost of absenteeism is determined as follows:

Annual lost time = 180 hours per month × 12 months in a year = 2,160 hours
Cost = 2,160 hours × $7.50 = $16,200 wages paid to absent employees
$16,200 × 2 = $32,400 annual cost of absenteeism

Based on the preceding example, compute the absenteeism rate and annual cost in the following situation:

Goldstein's operates two 8-hour shifts a day. The company is open for business 24 days a month, with employees working two 8-hour shifts. Eight employees work 24 days per month. On average, a total of 144 hours are missed from work per month (the equivalent of 9 full days). The average wage rate is $12 per hour.

Solution: $9 \div (24 \times 8) = 4.69\%$ absenteeism rate
$144 \times 12 = 1{,}728$ hours lost annually
$1{,}728 \times \$12 = \$20{,}736$ wages paid to absent employees
$\$20{,}736 \times 2 = \$41{,}472$ annual cost of absenteeism

▶ MOTIVATION AND NEEDS

All human beings have some needs that are basic to survival and other needs that go beyond mere physical existence. Unfulfilled needs motivate people to work toward satisfying those needs. For example, hunger motivates a person to look for food.

Maslow's Hierarchy of Needs

Abraham Maslow, a psychologist, developed a human behavior model called the *hierarchy of needs*, as shown in Figure 4-3. Employment can help satisfy all five levels of needs. Levels 1 and 2 are things that are essential to physical survival: employees need pay that is adequate to provide food, clothing, and housing and sufficient job security to feel safe and comfortable. Until the job meets these basic needs, the employee will not be motivated to greater achievement. According to Maslow, in general, lower-level needs must be satisfied first. Once a need is met, the next higher one in the hierarchy begins to motivate the person's behavior. However, the progression is not so clear cut. Several needs may influence a person's behavior at the same time.

Every person needs fulfillment beyond physical requirements. Most businesses consider it the responsibility of management to provide opportunities for employees to meet their needs. In striving to satisfy higher-order needs, employees will likely achieve greater productivity, which will benefit the business.

Maslow's Level 3 is the need for "love" (acceptance) and the need to belong to a group: to have friends and to be valued as a member of the team. In the workplace, employees can meet this need through caring work relationships and through working and socializing with groups of co-workers.

figure **4-3**

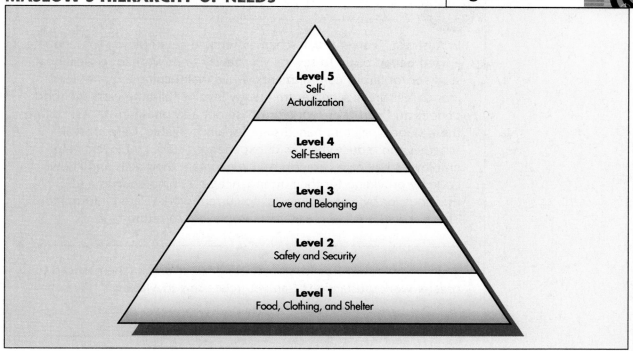

Level 4 is the need for **self-esteem**, or self-respect and recognition from others. When work is challenging and rewarding, employees feel good about their jobs and about themselves, and they want to do more. Workers trying to meet their need for self-esteem will be motivated by praise and recognition.

Level 5 is the need for **self-actualization**. This is the need to reach one's full potential, to grow, and to be creative. Workers can fulfill this need if they are able to do the work they choose, as they choose, and receive appropriate rewards for a job well done. To aid employees in achieving to their full potential, many managers challenge employees by providing greater decision-making responsibility and more complex work gradually as the employees become capable of handling it.

Herzberg's Two-Factor Theory

Frederick Herzberg studied employees to find out what satisfied and dissatisfied them about their jobs. From his research, he formulated his *two-factor theory*. Herzberg found that elements of a job that lead to job satisfaction or dissatisfaction fall into two groups: hygiene factors and motivators.

Hygiene factors are job elements that dissatisfy when absent but do not add to satisfaction when present. For example, pay, fringe benefits, and the workplace environment are hygiene factors. A clean,

Global View

In Australia, "career break schemes" enable an employee to negotiate a fixed period of up to several years away from work for educational study or for family commitments, while maintaining a guaranteed job. Career break schemes frequently involve full-time work for short periods and part-time work for phase-out and phase-in stages. During these stages, pay and benefits are usually available. Career break schemes can reduce the loss of experienced staff. Employers help employees having a career break to maintain their skills and knowledge by providing for their attendance at training courses and meetings, or by ensuring access to current work-related information. These activities make it easier for employees to return to work.

Think Critically: How might offering career break schemes lead to greater work satisfaction? Can you relate this to Maslow's Hierarchy of Needs?

roomy workspace will help maintain a level of satisfaction but will not increase motivation to work hard or increase satisfaction. However, a dirty, cramped workspace would decrease job satisfaction.

Motivators are job elements that increase job satisfaction. For example, challenging work, responsibility, recognition, achievement, and personal growth motivate workers to greater productivity and add to satisfaction in the job. Therefore, to motivate employees to achieve and to promote greater job satisfaction, employers must offer hygiene factors to avoid dissatisfaction plus provide motivators. For example, jobs need to be designed to meet employees' need for challenging, rewarding work.

Results of Job Satisfaction

When employees can meet their needs in their jobs, several positive outcomes benefit both the employees and the employer.

INCREASED PRODUCTIVITY

When employees are motivated, they are more productive. They use time wisely and produce more and higher quality work in less time. Increased productivity leads to higher profits for the employer and subsequent rewards for the employees—both tangible (raises, bonuses, or promotions) and intangible (praise and self-esteem).

SELF-ESTEEM AND SELF-ACTUALIZATION

To put forth your best effort, to win the praise of your employer and co-workers, to strive for new challenges—all are valid bases for career development and satisfaction. As you achieve these goals, you gain personal pride and enjoyment that are satisfying beyond the paycheck. Because you will probably work most of your adult life, why not strive to achieve to the best of your ability?

REWARDS AND OPPORTUNITIES

Employers often seek to motivate employees by using praise and pay as reinforcements for desirable results. Your rewards will vary: oral or written commendations; admiration and respect of others; pay raises (often called merit pay); increased opportunities for challenging work; and opportunities for advancement to higher-paying positions. You could become recognized as "one of the best in the field." This not only makes you valuable to your own employer, but it also makes you more employable in the future should you desire to move to another job. Achieving excellence in your work increases your opportunities and should be a part of your long-term career plans.

©GETTY IMAGES/PHOTODISC

How can job satisfaction benefit employees?

⊘Check Your Understanding

1. Why are work rules, both written and unwritten, important to employers and employees?
2. What are some things you can do to create a favorable impression with an employer?
3. How are motivators different from hygiene factors, according to Herzberg?

Issues in Your World

Work ethics or codes of conduct exist both formally and informally throughout corporate America. Companies are finding that employees, customers, and regulators are looking at their values, integrity, and sense of fairness in the workplace.

The Corporate Consensus on Values in the 21st Century concludes that "outstanding employees will only want to work for companies whose leadership they trust and values they respect." Many American companies, both large and small, are participating in integrity Web sites—places for customers and other stakeholders to go and examine values policies, from employee and customer privacy statements to workplace ethics enforcement. To attract and retain customers, stockholders, and financial partners, companies are becoming increasingly aware of the need for values, trust, and commitment.

Many employers are using a work ethics test for pre-employment screening. Why? To select the best workers, defined as people who adhere to high ethical principles. Work ethics for employees include giving the employer consistently high-quality work—a full day's work for a full day's pay.

When faced with an ethical dilemma at work, ask yourself these questions before taking action:

- Is it legal?
- Is it morally right?
- Who is affected?
- Would it cause harm?
- Would I be proud of doing it?
- What does it say about me?

Many ethical issues have no clear-cut right or wrong. How you choose to act depends on your values and moral standards. Each person must decide for himself/herself where to draw the line.

Think Critically

1. Describe a situation in which you believe a company acted unethically. How would these actions affect your decision to work for the company?

2. Describe a situation in which you faced an ethical dilemma. Are you comfortable with the choice you made? If an action is legal, does that make it ethical? Explain.

Chapter Assessment

SUMMARY

4.1

* Effective communication requires sympathetic, critical, and creative listening.
* People speak informally to make contact, exchange information, influence others, and solve problems.
* A formal speech may be designed to inform, entertain, or persuade. Practice can reduce stage fright.
* Workplace communication flows horizontally, upward, and downward.
* E-mail is fast and easy but not private.
* Good human relations require understanding and genuine concern for others.

4.2

* Most businesses have both written and unwritten work rules.
* A good work attitude creates a favorable impression on customers and your employer.
* Frequent absenteeism results in high costs to the absent employee as well as the company.
* Maslow's theory holds that people behave in ways that will meet their needs from lower to higher levels on a hierarchy.
* Herzberg's theory suggests that to motivate greater achievement, employers must offer both hygiene factors and motivators.
* Job satisfaction results in increased productivity for businesses and greater self-esteem and opportunities for employees.

REVIEW TERMS

Directions

Can you find the definitions for each of the following terms used in Chapter 4?

creative listening
critical listening
downward communication
empathy
hearing
horizontal communication
human relations

hygiene factors
listening
motivators
self-actualization
self-esteem
sympathetic listening
upward communication

1. Communication among employees of equal rank.

2. Active hearing that requires concentration and effort.

3. Communication that flows from higher to lower levels in an organization.

4. Job elements that dissatisfy when absent but do not add to satisfaction when present.

5. Job elements that increase job satisfaction.

6. A type of listening in which you differentiate fact from opinion.

7. Communication that flows from lower to higher levels in an organization.

8. Self-respect and recognition from others.

9. Getting along with others.

10. The type of listening in which you listen but offer no advice.

11. Listening with your mind open to new ideas.

12. Reaching your full potential, growing, and being creative.

13. The process of perceiving sound.

14. The ability to see others' points of view or understand their feelings.

1. On the job, which form of communication do employees engage in most? Least?

2. How is sympathetic listening different from critical and creative listening?

3. List four ways informal speaking is used on the job.

4. List three purposes of formal speeches.

5. List three things you can do about stage fright.

6. Distinguish among horizontal, upward, and downward communication.

7. Describe some advantages of e-mail as a business communication tool. Describe two disadvantages.

8. What is meant by good human relations?

9. List five techniques for maintaining effective human relations.

10. What is voluntary absence syndrome?

11. What are some effects of absenteeism on the absentee? On other employees? On the business?

12. List in order from bottom to top Maslow's five levels of needs.

13. List three hygiene factors and three potential motivators in a job.

14. What are three results of job satisfaction?

1. What are some things you can do to improve your listening skills?

2. Under what circumstances would you use sympathetic listening? Critical listening? Creative listening?

3. What type of speech or presentation did you hear recently (informational, entertaining, or persuasive)? Describe it.

4. Have you ever experienced stage fright? What did you do to reduce it?

5. Why are human relations important in any career or workplace?

6. Why is it important for a new employee to observe all unwritten and written work rules?

7. How might you benefit from excellent work performance?

8. Think about a job you have held or work you have done as part of a school or community group. What kinds of things motivated you to do your tasks well? Did these same things make the job more satisfying for you? What kinds of things made you less satisfied with the work?

Solve Problems ⊕ Explore Issues

1. Search the Internet using the keyword "emoticon." Write a brief explanation of what an emoticon is. Then print out or copy several emoticons to share with the class. Together with your classmates, discuss how emoticons can aid e-mail communication.

2. Use the questions below to interview employees about the need to get along with others at work. Then ask an employer the same questions.
   a. Do you feel that human relations are an important part of each job where you work?
   b. Does the employer (supervisor) feel that human relations are important?
   c. What types of company policies or unwritten rules are in place to ensure good human relations?

3. Selena works for a small delivery service and believes that she is underpaid. She tells her friends, "When I'm making deliveries, sometimes I stop for a pizza. Sometimes I even visit my boyfriend. Why should I knock myself out on what I earn?" What advice would you give Selena?

4. Make a list of unwritten rules that you observe in your home or your classroom. Compare your list to a friend's list to see the similarities and differences.

5. Use the formula given in the Math Minute to compute the rate of absenteeism and annual cost of absenteeism based on these facts:
   - Number of employees: 45
   - Number of workdays in an average month: 22
   - Workdays lost during an average month: 26
   - Work hours lost during an average month: 624
   - Average hourly wage: $8

6. Interview a person working full time and ask how the job helps to meet each level of needs on Maslow's hierarchy.

For related activities and links, point your browser to **www.mypf.swlearning.com**

Work Laws and Responsibilities

TERMS TO KNOW

Form W-4
allowances
exempt status
minors
Form W-2
Social Security Act
unemployment
 insurance

Fair Labor
 Standards Act
 (Wage and Hour
 Act)
minimum wage
workers'
 compensation
Family and Medical
 Leave Act

Equal Pay Act
Civil Rights Act of
 1964
Age Discrimination
 in Employment
 Act
Americans with
 Disabilities Act

Consider This. . .

Raequann worked part-time after school during high school, and full-time during the summers. She decided to stay with her job while attending college because the manager was willing to give her flexible hours. This enabled her to study and earn money to pay for college at the same time.

"I like my job because my employer deals with me fairly," Raequann told a friend. "I'm paid adequately, working conditions are good, and I like my supervisor. As a part-timer, I don't get a lot of benefits, but I'm able to attend classes for my degree. That flexibility makes me feel good about my job, and I'm motivated to give my best. It's a win-win situation. My employer wins because I'm loyal and serve the customers well. I win because I'm able to pursue my career goals and have a job that helps me pay for college expenses, too."

Work-Related Forms and Laws

Goals
- Discuss the purpose of various work-related forms.
- Explain provisions of major employment laws.

▶ REQUIRED WORK FORMS

When you get a job, the government will require a number of forms containing information about you. You will fill out some. Others, your employer will complete. If you are under age 16, you will need a social security card and work permit. Some forms, such as Forms W-2 and W-4, are part of the income tax process.

Form W-4

When you report to work, you will be asked to fill out a **Form W-4**, like the one in Figure 5-1. The information you put on this form determines the amount your employer will withhold from your paycheck for income taxes. The employer sends this money to the government as partial payment of your income taxes.

The form includes a simple worksheet to help you calculate your allowances. **Allowances** reduce the amount of tax withheld from your paycheck. The more allowances you claim, the less tax you will have withheld. However, claiming more allowances does not decrease the tax you will eventually owe. It only decreases the tax payments your employer makes for you from your paycheck during the year. If you have too little withheld, you will have a large tax bill to pay at the end of the year.

If you qualify, you may claim **exempt status**. This status applies only to people who will not earn enough that year to owe any federal income tax. Line 7 of the form in Figure 5-1 (page 90) shows the requirements to qualify. If you qualify, simply write the word *exempt* on Form W-4, as Marisa Clark has done in the figure. Then no money will be withheld from your paycheck for federal income taxes. The maximum amount of earnings allowable to qualify changes annually.

Form **W-4**	**Employee's Withholding Allowance Certificate**	OMB No. 1545-0010
Department of the Treasury Internal Revenue Service	▶ **Your employer must send a copy of this form to the IRS if: (a) you claim more than 10 allowances or (b) you claim "Exempt" and your wages are normally more than $200 per week.**	20—

1	Type or print your first name and middle initial	Last name		2	Your social security number
	Marisa M.	Clark			682 00 5896

Home address (number and street or rural route)	3	☒ Single ☐ Married ☐ Married, but withhold at higher Single rate.
685 West Circle Avenue		**Note:** *If married, but legally separated, or spouse is a nonresident alien, check the "Single" box.*

City or town, state, and ZIP code	4	If your last name differs from that shown on your social security card, check here. You must call 1-800-772-1213 for a new card. ▶ ☐
Cincinnati, OH 45227-6287		

5	Total number of allowances you are claiming (from line **H** above **or** from the applicable worksheet on page 2)	**5**	
6	Additional amount, if any, you want withheld from each paycheck	**6**	$
7	I claim exemption from withholding for 2004, and I certify that I meet **both** of the following conditions for exemption:		

• Last year I had a right to a refund of **all** Federal income tax withheld because I had **no** tax liability **and**
• This year I expect a refund of **all** Federal income tax withheld because I expect to have **no** tax liability.

If you meet both conditions, write "Exempt" here . . . . ▶ | **7** | Exempt

Under penalties of perjury, I certify that I am entitled to the number of withholding allowances claimed on this certificate, or I am entitled to claim exempt status.

Employee's signature
(Form is not valid
unless you sign it.) ▶ *Marisa M. Clark*   Date ▶ January 3, 20—

8	Employer's name and address (Employer: Complete lines 8 and 10 only if sending to the IRS.)	9	Office code (optional)	10	Employer identification number (EIN)

For Privacy Act and Paperwork Reduction Act Notice, see page 2.	Cat. No. 10220Q	Form **W-4** (2004)

Social Security Forms

Because workers in the United States must pay a social security tax from wages earned, all must have a social security number. Your social security number is your permanent work identification number. Employers withhold social security taxes from your pay and contribute matching amounts. The amounts you earn and the amounts contributed for social security throughout your work life are credited to your social security account number. When you become eligible, usually at retirement, benefits are paid to you monthly, based upon how much you have paid into your account.

If you don't already have a social security number and card, or if you have misplaced your card, you may get it replaced without charge. You can find the application and instructions for completing it online. Go to the Social Security Administration site (www.ssa.gov) and follow the links to the social security card page. You can complete and submit the application form online, or download it, fill it out, and mail it to the Social Security Administration.

Every few years, you should check to see that your earnings have been properly credited to your account. The Social Security Administration provides a form for you to complete for this purpose (see Figure 5-2). To request a statement online, go to the Social Security Administration site. Then follow the links to request a statement. Within 30 days you should receive a report that shows your income according to the Social Security Administration's records. There is no charge for this service. If you find any errors, report them immediately.

▶ figure **5-2**

Request for *Social Security Statement*

Form Approved
OMB No. 0960-0466   [   ] SP

☐ Please check this box if you want to get your *Statement* in Spanish instead of English.

Please print or type your answers. When you have completed the form, fold it and mail it to us. (If you prefer to send your request using the Internet, contact us at *www.socialsecurity.gov*)

1. Name shown on your Social Security card:

Marisa   M.
First Name   Middle Initial

Clark
Last Name Only

2. Your Social Security number as shown on your card:

[6][8][2] - [0][0] - [5][8][9][6]

3. Your date of birth (Mo.-Day-Yr.)

[0][8] - [2][1] - [1][9][8][5]

4. Other Social Security numbers you have used:

[ ][ ][ ] - [ ][ ] - [ ][ ][ ][ ]
[ ][ ][ ] - [ ][ ] - [ ][ ][ ][ ]

5. Your Sex: ☐ Male   ☒ Female

Form **SSA-7004-SM** (1-2003)   EF (01-2003)
Destroy prior editions

For items 6 and 8 show only earnings covered by Social Security. Do NOT include wages from state, local or federal government employment that are NOT covered for Social Security or that are covered ONLY by Medicare.

6. Show your actual earnings (wages and/or net self-employment income) for last year and your estimated earnings for this year.

A. Last year's actual earnings: *(Dollars Only)*

$ [ ][2] , [0][8][4] . [0][0]

B. This year's estimated earnings: *(Dollars Only)*

$ [ ][4] , [0][0][0] . [0][0]

7. Show the age at which you plan to stop working.

[6][5]

(Show only one age)

8. Below, show the average yearly amount (not your total future lifetime earnings) that you think you will earn between now and when you plan to stop working. Include performance or scheduled pay increases or bonuses, but not cost-of-living increases.

If you expect to earn significantly more or less in the future due to promotions, job changes, part-time work, or an absence from the work force, enter the amount that most closely reflects your future average yearly earnings.

If you don't expect any significant changes, show the same amount you are earning now (the amount in 6B).

Future average yearly earnings: *(Dollars Only)*

$ [ ][4] , [0][0][0] . [0][0]

9. Do you want us to send the *Statement:*
• To you? Enter your name and mailing address.
• To someone else (your accountant, pension plan, etc.)? Enter your name with "c/o" and the name and address of that person or organization.

Marisa M. Clark
"C/O" or Street Address (Include Apt. No., P.O. Box, Rural Route)

685 West Circle Avenue
Street Address

Cincinnati, OH 45227-6287
Street Address (If Foreign Address, enter City, Province, Postal Code)

U.S. City, State, Zip code (If Foreign Address, enter Name of Country only)

NOTICE:
I am asking for information about my own Social Security record or the record of a person I am authorized to represent. I declare under penalty of perjury that I have examined all the information on this form, and on any accompanying statements or forms, and it is true and correct to the best of my knowledge. I authorize you to use a contractor to send the *Social Security Statement* to the person and address in item 9.

▲ *Marisa M. Clark*

Please sign your name (Do Not Print)

1/9/—   (513)555-8684
Date   (Area Code)   Daytime Telephone No.

Work Permit Application

Many states require **minors**—people under the age of legal adult-hood—to obtain a work permit before they are allowed to work. You can obtain an application for a work permit from your state Department of Labor, a school counseling center, or work experience coordinator. There is usually no charge. You will have to provide your social security number and proof of age, and have your parent or legal guardian sign. Apply early to allow several weeks for processing.

Form W-2

Each company for which you worked during the year will give you a **Form W-2**, like the one shown in Figure 5-3. This form is a summary of the income you earned that year and all amounts the employer withheld for taxes. These amounts include federal, state, and local income taxes, and social security tax. Compare your W-2 to your pay-check stubs to be sure that the reported amounts are accurate. Your employer will also send a copy of your Form W-2 to the government.

The employer must provide you with a Form W-2 no later than January 31. This is true even if you worked only part of the year and were not working as of December 31. If you do not receive a W-2 from each employer you worked for during the year, contact the employer to get the W-2. You must file your W-2 forms with your tax return.

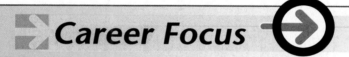

Career Focus

File clerks classify, store, retrieve, and update information generated by all types of organizations. A growing number of file clerks use imaging systems that scan paper files or film and store the material on optical disks; they may also use computerized retrieval systems. In many small offices, file clerks have additional responsibilities, such as entering data, performing word processing, sorting mail, and operating copying or fax machines. A high school diploma is the most common educational requirement. Familiarity or experience with computers and good interpersonal skills are becoming increasingly important to employers.

For more information, refer to the *Occupational Outlook Handbook* at www.bls.gov or search the Internet using such key words as "careers," "jobs," and "file clerk."

a Control number 22222	Void ☐	For Official Use Only OMB No. 1545-0008	

b Employer identification number 93-81256791	1 Wages, tips, other compensation $2,084.00	2 Federal income tax withheld
c Employer's name, address, and ZIP code Hanson Motors 85 Briar Street Cincinnati, OH 45230-5162	3 Social security wages $2,084.00	4 Social security tax withheld $129.21
	5 Medicare wages and tips $2,084.00	6 Medicare tax withheld $30.22
	7 Social security tips	8 Allocated tips
d Employee's social security number 682-00-5896	9 Advance EIC payment	10 Dependent care benefits
e Employee's first name and initial Last name	11 Nonqualified plans	12a See instructions for box 12
Marisa M. Clark 685 West Circle Avenue Cincinnati, OH 45227-6287	13 Statutory employee [X] Retirement plan ☐ Third-party sick pay ☐	12b
	14 Other	12c
		12d
f Employee's address and ZIP code		

15 State Employer's state ID number	16 State wages, tips, etc. $2,084.00	17 State income tax $14.04	18 Local wages, tips, etc. $2,084.00	19 Local income tax $41.60	20 Locality name Cincinnati

Form **W-2** Wage and Tax Statement   20—   Department of the Treasury—Internal Revenue Service

EMPLOYMENT LAWS

The federal government has enacted many laws to protect workers. The Department of Labor is responsible for enforcing labor laws that:

1. Provide unemployment, disability, and retirement insurance benefits.
2. Establish a minimum wage and regular working hours.
3. Help workers injured on the job.
4. Provide equal employment opportunities and prohibit discrimination.
5. Establish safe working conditions.

Laws covering minors specify:

1. Safety precautions and working conditions that are more extensive than for adults.
2. A maximum number of hours and times minors can work during the school year.
3. A work permit for those under age 16 in some states.

Employees who believe they have not received the protections required by law may turn to the government for *recourse*, or remedy. If you think you have a legitimate complaint, contact your state Department of Labor.

Social Security Act

The **Social Security Act**, passed in 1935, established a national social insurance program that provides federal aid for the elderly and for disabled workers. In 1965, the Medicare provision was added. It provides hospital and medical insurance for elderly retired workers. Originally known as OASDHI, social security provides these benefits: old age retirement income, survivorship income, disability income, and health insurance. Benefits received depend on the amount of contributions made. Self-employed workers pay their social security contributions when they pay their income tax. For employees in occupations covered by social security, contributions are mandatory. Social security (FICA) tax and Medicare (HI) tax are deducted from your pay and sent to the U.S. Treasury for proper crediting to your social security account.

Unemployment Compensation

The Social Security Act requires every state to have an **unemployment insurance** program. This insurance provides benefits to workers who lose their jobs through no fault of their own. After a waiting period, laid-off or terminated workers may collect a portion of their regular pay for a certain length of time. Premiums for unemployment insurance are usually paid by employers.

Each state has its own regulations for waiting periods, maximum benefits, and deadlines for filing claims. Usually, benefits are paid for a maximum of 26 weeks through the local state employment office. In most states, an unemployed worker must wait for at least one week before receiving benefits. To receive benefits, a worker must have been employed for a minimum period of time (6 months to one year, depending on the state) and for a minimum amount of earnings ($400 or more per month in most states). Workers fired for a good reason, such as poor performance, are usually not entitled to receive benefits.

Fair Labor Standards Act

Popularly known as the *Wage and Hour Act*, the **Fair Labor Standards Act** establishes a minimum wage. It also requires hourly workers to be paid "overtime wages" of 1½ times their hourly rate for hours worked beyond 40 per week. A **minimum wage** is the legally established lower limit on wages employers may pay. Tips are not considered wages, so they are not included in calculating the minimum wage. In 2004, the federal minimum wage was $5.15 an hour. Some states require employers to pay higher minimum wages than the federal government requires. To compare the minimum wages of different states, visit the U.S. Department of Labor site at www.dol.gov and follow links to minimum wage information. You can find more information about your state's labor laws at your state's Department of Labor Web site.

Workers' Compensation

Workers' compensation is an insurance program that pays benefits to workers and their families for injury, illness, or death that occurs as a result of the job. The employer is responsible for employee injuries and illnesses that are the result of employment, even though the employer may have done nothing to cause the injury or illness. Today all 50 states have workers' compensation laws. Employers pay the insurance premiums in most states. However, in some states, employees are required to pay all or part of the premium. Benefits include payments to doctors and hospitals, to the employee for temporary or permanent disability, and to survivors in the event of death.

Family and Medical Leave Act

The **Family and Medical Leave Act** (FMLA) of 1993 allows employees to take up to 12 weeks of unpaid leave in a 12-month period for certain medical and family situations. Some employers may choose to pay employees during some types of leave, such as sick leave, but they are not required by law to do so. Valid circumstances for unpaid leave under the FMLA are:

1. Birth and care of a newborn child, including adoption of a child.
2. Care of an immediate family member (spouse, child, or parent) with a serious health condition.
3. Medical leave when the employee is unable to work because of a serious health condition.

To find out more about FMLA, go to the Employment Standards Administration Web site at www.dol.gov/esa/welcome.html, and follow the links to FMLA.

Laws Against Discrimination in Employment

A number of laws protect workers from unfair treatment in the workplace. Here is a brief description of the most important of these laws:

1. **Equal Pay Act**: Prohibits unequal pay for men and women doing substantially similar work.
2. **Civil Rights Act of 1964**: Prohibits discrimination in hiring, training, and promotion on the basis of race, color, gender, religion, or national origin.

3. **Age Discrimination in Employment Act**: Prohibits discrimination in employment decisions against people age 40 and over.
4. **Americans with Disabilities Act**: Prohibits discrimination on the basis of physical or mental disabilities.

These laws are enforced by the Equal Employment Opportunity Commission (EEOC). Discrimination complaints can be filed with the EEOC.

What is the Americans with Disabilities Act?

✓Check Your Understanding

1. If you do not properly fill out the Form W-4 and thus claim too many allowances, what is likely to happen?
2. What should you do if you lose your social security card?
3. What law allows you to take unpaid leave when you have a new baby?

Lesson 5.2

Responsibilities on the Job

Goals
• Discuss employee responsibilities at work.
• Describe employer responsibilities to employees.

◤ EMPLOYEE RESPONSIBILITIES

To be successful as a new employee, you will have to meet a number of responsibilities. These include personal responsibilities to your employer, to other employees, and to customers.

Responsibilities to Employers

Your employer hires you and pays you at stated intervals. In return for this pay and other benefits, the employer expects certain things from you, as discussed on the following pages.

COMPETENT WORK

You should do your best to produce the highest quality finished product for your employer. The work needs to be *marketable*—that is, of such quality that the employer can sell it or use it to favorably represent the company. If, for example, you type an e-mail message to a client that has so many mistakes that it would make the company look incompetent or uncaring to the client, the message is not a marketable product. Also, when using an employer's property, you should be as thrifty as possible. You should conserve supplies and care for equipment with as much diligence as you would your own.

PUNCTUALITY

Arrive at work on time, take no more than the allotted time for breaks, and don't leave before quitting time. Being punctual means being ready to start working at the appointed time. For example, rather than arriving at 8 A.M. (starting time), you should be at your workstation at 8 A.M.

Why do you, as an employee, have a responsibility to be pleasant and easy to get along with?

PLEASANT ATTITUDE

On any job, it is important to be pleasant and easy to get along with. You should be willing to follow orders and accept feedback. Your employer also has the right to expect you to be courteous to customers, because you represent the company to others.

LOYALTY AND RESPECT

While working for a company, you should never spread rumors or gossip about your employer or job. As long as you are on the company "team," you are expected to be loyal. Loyalty includes showing respect to the employer and the company on and off the job.

DEPENDABILITY

When you say you will do something, follow through. The employer should be able to depend on you to do what you were hired to do. A person who is dependable has a good reputation and will be considered for increased responsibilities and promotions.

INITIATIVE

You should not have to be told everything to do. Employees who stand idle after completing a task are of little value to employers. You should show *initiative*. This means that you should recognize what needs to be done and do it without always having to be told.

INTEREST

It is important for you to show an interest in your job and your company. You should project an attitude of wanting to learn all you can and of giving all tasks your best effort. Being enthusiastic about your

job shows an employer your sincere interest in being a cooperative and productive worker.

SELF-EVALUATION

The ability to take criticism and to assess your own progress is important to you and your employer. You cannot improve your weak points unless you are willing to admit they exist and to work on them. Employers must evaluate employees' work to determine raises and promotions. Employees should be able to recognize their own strong points and limitations and do a realistic self-evaluation of their job performance.

Responsibilities to Other Employees

In addition to your responsibilities to your employer, you also have duties to your co-workers. These include the following obligations:

What are some of the responsibilities that employees have to their employers?

TEAMWORK

You are part of a team when you work with others in a company, and you need to do your share of the work. Employees must work cooperatively in order to produce a high-quality final product. When friction and personality conflicts occur, the productivity of the whole company decreases.

THOUGHTFULNESS

Be considerate of co-workers to promote a good work atmosphere for everyone, including customers. Having a pleasant attitude will result in a more enjoyable time for yourself and others. Personal problems and conflicts have no place at work.

LOYALTY

In addition to being loyal to your employer, you should be loyal to co-workers. This includes not spreading rumors about them. Gossiping leads to a breakdown of teamwork.

Responsibilities to Customers

As an employee, you represent the company. To the customer who walks in the front door, *you* are the company. Thus, your attitude toward a customer often will be the deciding factor in whether he or she continues to do business with your company. Therefore, remember that on behalf of your employer you have the responsibility to greet the customer with an attitude of helpfulness and courtesy.

HELPFULNESS

It is your responsibility to help customers find what they want or to do what is needed to make a sale. When customers contact you with a problem, you are responsible for solving the problem or finding another employee who can. An attitude of helpfulness reflects well on the company and is an important part of any job.

COURTESY AND RESPECT
Whether or not you like the customer, that customer actually pays your wages by keeping your employer in business. Without customers, the business could not exist. Therefore, your attitude toward customers should always be respectful and courteous, never hostile or unfriendly. Friendly, helpful employees build customer loyalty to the business.

On a sheet of paper, list several employee responsibilities toward a customer. What might a customer think about an employee if these responsibilities are not fulfilled? What might the customer think about the employee's company?

EMPLOYER RESPONSIBILITIES

Employers also have responsibilities to employees. Some responsibilities are required by law. Others are simply sensible practices for keeping employees happy and on the job. Failure to meet these responsibilities can result in a high employee turnover (with resulting high costs for finding and training new workers), increased premiums for unemployment insurance, and employer fines for unfair labor practices.

Adequate Supervision

Employees need proper supervision to do a good job. Good supervision includes providing appropriate instruction in the safe use of equipment, training new employees in their job tasks, helping employees solve problems on the job, and distributing information downward from management and upward to management.

Fair Human Resource Policies

Policies on hiring, firing, raises, advancement, and dispute resolution need to be fair and well defined. Employees should know clearly what is considered acceptable and unacceptable performance, what the standards are for advancements and raises, and what constitutes grounds for suspension or discharge.

Safe Working Conditions

All employees must be provided with safe equipment, a safe working environment, and adequate training for working under dangerous conditions. Special protective equipment and clothing and warning signs must be provided to employees working in hazardous situations. Laws governing working conditions for minors are stricter than those for adults in most industries.

Open Channels of Communication

Employers need to communicate with employees so that all employees have the opportunity to express concerns, ask questions, and make suggestions. Lack of open channels of communication can result in poor worker morale and low work output. Employees need to know they are an important part of the company and that their opinions are valuable.

Recognition of Achievement

Employers need to provide some form of reward for above-average performance. Merit pay raises, bonuses, and advancement opportunities encourage workers to do their best work. Employees also respond well to non-monetary rewards, such as providing extra time off or simply complimenting exceptional work in front of other employees. Recognizing achievement will motivate workers.

Compliance with Employment Laws

Employers must obey state and federal laws designed to protect workers from discrimination in employment on the basis of race, color, sex, national origin, religion, age, or disability. The employer is responsible for observing workers' rights. Failure to do so can result in severe penalties.

✓ Check Your Understanding

1. In a job you have had, what responsibilities did your employer expect from you?

2. What kinds of things do you expect from an employer in exchange for your hard work?

Sexual Harassment

A safe working environment also means one that is comfortable and free of unwanted conduct that interferes with work performance. *Sexual harassment* is any unwelcome advance, request for sexual favors, and other verbal or physical conduct that is offensive.

Workers are protected by the Equal Employment Opportunity Commission (EEOC) from these types of behaviors. Sexual harassment violates the Civil Rights Act of 1964, and employers have the responsibility to prevent it in the workplace. EEOC guidelines state that an employer is responsible for the actions of employees as well as non-employees on work premises.

Unfortunately, sexual harassment is widespread. Studies show that at least 50 percent of working women and 15 percent of working men have experienced sexual harassment on the job. Fortunately, steps are being taken to reduce this problem.

Until a decade ago, a victim's only recourse was to sue the offending person. Today, the EEOC investigates complaints. When it finds sexual harassment, the victim may receive a remedy such as back pay, a promotion, or reinstatement if he or she had been fired. When the victim's rights are not protected, the EEOC will sue the employer.

Many companies have policies to prevent sexual harassment. All employees are entitled to respect, courtesy, and tactful behavior. Abusing the dignity of anyone through ethnic, sexist, or racial slurs or other objectionable conduct is cause for disciplinary action. Objectionable conduct includes suggestive remarks, physical contact, and intimidation.

All employees should be aware of what sexual harassment is and how to avoid it. For example, employees who tell inappropriate jokes or engage in suggestive behavior, such as flirting, may find themselves in embarrassing situations. It is important to dress and act professionally at all times, so that you can truly say you did nothing to contribute to the situation.

Think Critically

1. What would you do if you were the target of inappropriate physical or verbal conduct on the job?
2. What are some things you can do to reduce your risk of sexual harassment?

Chapter Assessment

SUMMARY

5.1

* Form W-4 determines the amount your employer will withhold from your paycheck for taxes.
* Your contributions to social security throughout your work life determine the payments you will receive during retirement.
* If you are under age 16, you will likely need a work permit to hold a job.
* Form W-2 summarizes wages and amounts withheld for taxes that year.
* The Fair Labor Standards Act sets a minimum wage and overtime pay.
* Workers' compensation pays benefits for injury, illness, or death resulting from the job.
* The Family and Medical Leave Act allows employees to take unpaid leave for family and medical reasons.
* The Equal Pay Act, Civil Rights Act of 1964, Age Discrimination in Employment Act, and Americans with Disabilities Act protect employees from discrimination.

5.2

* Your responsibilities to your employer include competent work, a pleasant attitude, punctuality, loyalty, dependability, initiative, interest, and self-evaluation.
* Your responsibilities to your co-workers include teamwork, thoughtfulness, and loyalty.
* Your responsibilities to customers include helpfulness, courtesy, and respect.
* Your employer is responsible for giving you good supervision, safe working conditions, fair policies, open communications, rewards, and compliance with employment laws.

Directions

Can you find the definitions for each of the following terms used in Chapter 5?

Age Discrimination in Employment Act	Family and Medical Leave Act
allowances	Form W-2
Americans with Disabilities Act	Form W-4
Civil Rights Act of 1964	minimum wage
Equal Pay Act	minors
exempt status	Social Security Act
Fair Labor Standards Act (Wage and Hour Act)	unemployment insurance
	workers' compensation

1. The number that you calculate on Form W-4 that reduces the amount of tax withheld from your paycheck.

2. A summary of the income you earned that year and all amounts the employer withheld for taxes.

3. People under the age of legal adulthood.

4. The law that established a national insurance program that provides financial help for the elderly and for disabled workers.

5. A part of the Social Security Act that requires benefits to be paid to workers who lose their jobs through no fault of their own.

6. A form you fill out when you begin working that determines the amount your employer will withhold from your paycheck for income taxes.

7. Status that applies only to people who will not earn enough that year to owe any federal income tax.

8. Insurance program that pays benefits to workers and their families for injury, illness, or death that occurs as a result of the job.

9. The law that sets a minimum wage and an overtime rate for hours worked beyond 40 per week.

10. The lower limit on wages that employers can pay workers per hour.

11. The law that allows employees to take up to 12 weeks of unpaid leave for the birth or adoption of a child and for personal illness or the illness of an immediate family member.

12. The law that prohibits unequal pay for men and women doing substantially similar work.

13. The law that prohibits discrimination in hiring, training, and promotion on the basis of race, color, gender, religion, or national origin.

14. The law that prohibits discrimination in employment decisions against people age 40 and over.

15. The law that prohibits discrimination on the basis of physical or mental disabilities.

REVIEW FACTS AND IDEAS

1. What is the purpose of Form W-4?

2. Why do you need to have a social security number before you begin work?

3. Why should you request a social security statement?

4. Where can you obtain a work permit application?

5. What information is listed on Form W-2?

6. What should you do if your employer during the past year does not send you a Form W-2?

7. What benefits does the Social Security Act provide?

8. Who may receive unemployment insurance benefits?

9. How does the Fair Labor Standards Act protect employees?

10. Explain the provisions of the FMLA.

11. What laws protect people from employment-related discrimination?

12. List at least five responsibilities that you, as an employee, owe your employer.

13. List at least three responsibilities that you, as an employee, owe to your co-workers.

14. What responsibilities do you, as an employee, have to your employer's customers?

15. List and describe three responsibilities that your employer owes you as an employee.

APPLY YOUR KNOWLEDGE

1. Obtain a Form W-4 from the nearest office of the Internal Revenue Service or download one by going to the IRS Web site at www.irs.gov and following the links to forms and publications. Complete the W-4 form properly, claiming exempt status if you are entitled to do so.

2. Complete a Request for Social Security Statement online by going to the Social Security Administration site at www.ssa.gov and following the links to a statement request form.

3. Visit the Social Security Administration online at www.ssa.gov or look up the Social Security Act in an encyclopedia or historical reference book in your library. Obtain this information: (a) Why did the president at the time consider social security necessary? (b) Who was the president at the time? (c) Describe the history of benefits, deductions from paychecks, and purpose of social security.

4. Locate the Web site of your state Department of Labor. Check labor laws in your state. What is your state's minimum wage? Does your state require a work permit? If so, ask for a request form or download one and fill it out. (Your counseling center or work experience coordinator will probably have work permit forms also.)

5. Obtain from your state Department of Labor the provisions of state laws regarding employment of minors. Find out: (a) the maximum hours per week that can be worked, (b) latest hour in the evening that a minor can work, (c) whether a work permit is required for workers under 16, and (d) any other provisions to protect a minor working part- or full-time.

6. Research the history leading up to the Civil Rights Act of 1964. Write a two-page paper describing the controversy surrounding this law and how it eventually won passage.

7. On a piece of paper, list the responsibilities that employees have to their employers in the order you think most important. Then ask a working parent or other working person to list employee responsibilities in their order of importance. Compare the two lists. Then, if possible, ask an employer to list in order of importance the responsibilities that employees have to their employers.

8. A popular expression used in business today is "total customer satisfaction." What do you think this expression means?

9. What responsibilities do you think employers should have to employees besides the regular payment of wages earned? Ask a person who is working full-time the same question. Compare answers.

Solve Problems ⊕ Explore Issues

1. Your friend Benji thought that the amount of wages he received during the year was different from the amount listed on the W-2 he received from his employer. He asks you what to do. How would you reply?

2. Julia Reynolds worked for three employers last year. Now it's February 10 of the following year, and she has received Form W-2 from only two of those employers. She asks you what she should do about it. What would you tell her?

3. Because last year Miguel did not earn enough money at his part-time job to have to pay any federal taxes, his employer asked him if this year he would like to claim exempt status on his W-4. Explain to Miguel how he can claim to be exempt and what this means to him.

4. Ashley, age 14, has decided that she wants to work part-time this summer doing whatever kind of work she can find to earn money to buy clothes. Tell her what things she should do to prepare for work. Also tell her what forms she may have to complete when she begins work.

5. Gregory Schwab just received his Form W-2 from his employer and noticed that his social security number is wrong on the form. What should he do? What can happen if he does nothing?

6. Yang Li worked for over a year for the same employer but then was laid off because business was slow. She is looking for another job, but she needs income now to make her rent payment. You told Yang that she may be eligible for unemployment insurance payments. Explain how she could qualify and whom she should see to find out about unemployment benefits.

7. Drequon Farmer, who has a visual disability, applied for a position as an assistant credit manager at a local retail store. Brianna Holton, the store's human resource manager, tested Drequon's eyesight by having him read a chart written in small print. Drequon failed the test and, on that basis alone, was rejected for the position. Investigate the Americans with Disabilities Act and determine if Drequon's employment rights have been violated.

For related activities and links, point your browser to **www.mypf.swlearning.com**

PROJECT

Career Development: Planning and Leading a Meeting

This project is designed to develop leadership skills. If you've ever attended a meeting that failed—people were bored, there was no clear direction, or nothing was decided—you know why it is important to run effective meetings.

▶ PLANNING A SUCCESSFUL MEETING

If you are merely announcing information, an e-mail will do. The time to have a meeting is when you need input or opinions, when you want the group to make a decision that affects all of them, when you need a creative solution to a problem, or when you want everyone to hear important information at the same time. Here are some guidelines for planning a successful meeting:

1. Whenever possible, plan meetings to last no more than an hour. If the meeting must exceed an hour, provide drinks and a break. If it must last more than two hours, you also should provide food.

2. Make sure the meeting space is sufficient for participants to be comfortable. It must be large enough, have enough chairs, provide the right atmosphere, and include needed accessories, such as a flipchart, white board, or audio-visual equipment.

3. Give at least a week's notice, or preferably two, so people can plan their schedules to attend. Figure U1-1 (page 110) is a typical meeting notice.

4. Avoid calling a meeting late in the afternoon, unless you also have arranged a time of relaxation and entertainment. Friday afternoons are rarely a good time to schedule meetings.

5. Provide in advance an agenda of topics to be discussed, so that people can prepare their contributions and bring related information with them. Figure U1-2 (page 110) is a typical agenda.

6. Plan topics than can be completed in the scheduled time. Attention wanes when a meeting runs longer than participants expect.

 figure **U1-1**

MEETING NOTICE

The Teen Consumers Group will have its monthly meeting and will hear a presentation by Ms. Eva Diaz of the Better Business Bureau. Ms. Diaz will discuss Internet shopping.

Date: Thursday, February 15, 20--

Time: 3:00 p.m. to 4:30 p.m.

Place: Western High School Library

If you can't attend, please call LaMont Russell at 555-7825 or e-mail him at 1russell@omega.net.

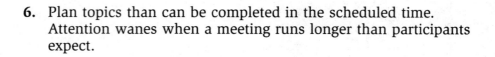 figure **U1-2**

AGENDA

Teen Consumers Group
February 15, 20--
3:00 p.m.

Facilitator—LaMont Russell
Note-Taker—Sun-Yi Wong

1. Opening comments—LaMont Russell
2. Report on next month's fund-raising car wash—Midori Tanaka
3. Report on consumer Web sites of interest—Barry Coogan
4. Presentation on Internet shopping—Ms. Eva Diaz, Better Business Bureau
5. Closing comments—LaMont Russell

► SETTING UP THE MEETING

A round table or circle is often a good way to encourage participation. Prepare and copy handouts before the meeting and have them waiting for people to arrive. Have extra paper and pencils available.

Set up and test your audio-visual tools ahead of time, such as computer presentation or video equipment, flipcharts, white boards, and markers. Make sure everything is ready to go when the meeting starts. Each participant should be able to see without obstruction. If you expect participants to write, make sure the table offers ample space.

Room ambiance is also important. If the room is too cold or too dark, group members will be unable to concentrate. If the room is too hot or bright, group members will be in a hurry to leave rather than to participate.

Make pre-arrangements to avoid meeting interruptions. For example, if refreshments will be served, arrange to have them delivered at a set time. You should stay with the meeting at all times rather than attend to details that you could have taken care of in advance.

► CONDUCTING A SUCCESSFUL MEETING

As the meeting leader, you are responsible for keeping the meeting moving and accomplishing its purpose. Here are some suggestions for keeping the meeting productive:

- Give a preview. Before you start the meeting, tell the participants what will happen, what will be expected from them, and what outcomes are desired.

- Make introductions. Unless everyone in the room already knows each other, have group members introduce themselves, or give a short introduction of each person yourself, briefly describing each person's role in the group.

- Assign someone to take notes and prepare the meeting summary. Figure U1-3 (page 113) shows a typical meeting summary.

- Keep the group focused on the purpose of the meeting. Some rambling is normal, but avoid getting sidetracked.

- If the purpose of the meeting is to generate ideas or come up with a creative solution to a problem, try *brainstorming*. With this technique, you present the topic or problem and ask participants to say their ideas out loud as they come to mind, no matter how wild the ideas. Do not judge the responses at this point. Just record them where participants can see them. The purpose of brainstorming is to allow a free flow of ideas. One person's wild idea may trigger a more workable idea from someone else. To encourage everyone to make suggestions, you could try going around the table, asking each person, in turn, for an idea, but allowing people to pass if they don't have one. Then keep going around the table until the group seems to have run out of ideas. Once all ideas are recorded, lead the group in discussing the ideas and selecting the best one to implement.

◆ No matter what your meeting format, keep everyone involved. Some people tend to be more reluctant to speak than others. To encourage their participation, use written feedback or ask directly for every person's opinion, allowing each person the same time to express his or her view. Everyone should feel safe and free to make contributions that will help accomplish the purpose of the meeting.

◆ To disarm disrupters, place time limits on comments. Acknowledge what they say with a comment such as "We hear you," and then move on to the next item or ask someone else to speak. Ask the group as a whole if they want to stop and address the issue at hand or deal with it at another time. When negativity creeps in, use humor to change the mood back to a positive tone. If you have known disrupters who will come prepared to sabotage the meeting, meet them head on by acknowledging their concern and setting a meeting time to deal with that issue specifically.

◆ Use consensus decision-making when possible. With consensus decisions, every person in the group agrees to and "buys into" the final outcome. This means negotiating until all participants feel they have been heard and each person is willing to accept the group's final decision. You will need to ask questions such as "What will it take to make you comfortable with our decision?" until everyone is satisfied that the best possible agreement has been reached.

◆ Wrap up the meeting with a summary of what the group decided and the next steps to be taken. People who have agreed to certain actions should be reminded of their commitments. Congratulate everyone for their hard work and contributions.

MEETING SUMMARY

Teen Consumers Group
February 15, 20--
3:00 p.m.

Attendees: Barry Coogan; Joel D'Aurizio; Cate Ewing; Deondra Holcomb; Danny Martinez; LaMont Russell; Midori Tanaka; Nancy Williams; Sun-Yi Wong; Mishelle Zambito

1. LaMont reminded the group that our picture for the school yearbook will be taken on Friday, February 23, in the lobby. Everyone should meet there at noon.
2. Midori handed out instructions for March's fund-raising car wash in the school parking lot. If you have questions, see her.
3. Barry provided a list of new Web sites that we should look at before our next meeting. Each group member will review one site and prepare a one-paragraph description. E-mail your information by March 10, to Barry at bcoogan@omega.net
4. Ms. Eva Diaz presented a helpful and informative discussion on the pros and cons of Internet shopping. She distributed some brochures from the Better Business Bureau and suggested that we contact the BBB if we experience problems.
5. LaMont closed the meeting with a reminder that the next meeting will take place on Thursday, March 15, at 3:00 p.m. in the Library. Last-minute details about the car wash will be discussed, and the reports on the consumer Web sites will be reviewed.

◤ AFTER THE MEETING

Soon after the meeting, distribute a copy of the meeting summary or *minutes* to each participant and to group members who could not attend. Include handouts for absent group members and reminders of subsequent actions to be taken and their timeframes. File the meeting summary for future reference. Include the names of all people who attended and the date of the meeting.

► FOLLOW-UP ASSIGNMENT

1. Ask someone you know who works in an office to arrange for you to observe a meeting. Take notes on the following issues and write a report for your class:

   a. Was an agenda distributed ahead of the meeting?

   b. Was the meeting room adequate? Was the audio-visual equipment set up and in working order at the start of the meeting? What elements of the physical environment could have been improved?

   c. What was the purpose of the meeting? Did the purpose seem clear to everyone?

   d. How well did the discussion stay focused on the purpose? What sidetracking occurred? How did the leader bring the discussion back to the purpose?

   e. How did the group go about accomplishing the meeting purpose? How did the leader help this process? How could the group process have been improved?

   f. Did everyone participate? How did the leader encourage participation? Were there disrupters? How did the leader handle disruptions? What could have been done to improve participation?

   g. What were the outcomes of the meeting? Did the meeting accomplish its purpose? Did everyone seem to agree with the decisions made and know their responsibilities for further action?

   h. Overall, how productive do you think the meeting was? Explain.

2. Using the issues listed in question 1, critique a meeting that you attend as a participating member. Summarize your findings in a report.

Money Management

CHAPTERS

Project: **Assessing Your Financial Health**

Unit 2 begins with an examination of your paycheck and benefits, trends in the workplace that affect your career, and opportunities for advancement. Then you will learn about preparing your income tax.

Next you will study financial management, beginning with preparing budgets and other financial records. You will also find out about informal and formal contracts that you enter into daily.

Finally, you will learn how to use a checking account, including writing checks, keeping a checkbook register, and reconciling your account. You will discover how to choose the right bank and services that meet your needs.

Pay, Benefits, and Working Conditions

TERMS TO KNOW

gross pay	incentive pay	labor union
overtime	vested	collective bargaining
deductions	flextime	seniority
net pay	compressed workweek	professional organization
self-employment tax	job rotation	lobbying
benefits	job sharing	

Consider This. . .

Ramon just got a job. When he was hired, his employer provided a packet containing all kinds of information, from union membership to sick pay. He will receive two weeks of paid vacation every year, after his first year of employment. The company allows 10 paid sick days per year. The company will grant a leave of absence in the case of pregnancy or death of a family member, and he is fully vested in the pension plan once he has been employed for five years. Also provided for employees is a full package of group health, dental, vision, and life insurance coverage. In addition, the company has a child care facility, altered workweeks, and job sharing.

"Wow, I'm sure glad I read that packet," Ramon said to himself. "There are a lot of things I need to understand."

Understanding Pay, Benefits, and Incentives

Goals
- **Compute payroll deductions and net pay.**
- **Identify optional and required employee benefits and recognize their value.**

▶ GROSS PAY, DEDUCTIONS, AND NET PAY

When you take a job, you agree to perform certain tasks in exchange for regular pay. **Gross pay** is the total amount you earn before any deductions are subtracted. If you work for an hourly wage, any overtime pay you earned during the pay period must be added to your regular pay to determine your gross pay.

Hourly Wages

Figure 6-1 shows a paycheck for M. J. Smith. As you can see, Ms. Smith works for $6.50 per hour. Her employer keeps a record of the hours she works. For this pay period, Ms. Smith worked 40 regular hours. To determine Ms. Smith's regular gross pay, multiply the pay rate by the number of hours:

$$\$6.50 \times 40 \text{ hours} = \$260.00$$

Overtime

Ms. Smith also worked some overtime during this pay period. **Overtime** is time worked beyond the regular hours. A standard workday is 8 continuous hours with scheduled breaks plus an unpaid lunch period. A standard workweek is 40 hours in a 5-day period of 8 hours each day. According to the Fair Labor Standards Act, employers must pay hourly workers for overtime at the rate of 1½ times the regular rate of pay. On Ms. Smith's paycheck stub, her regular rate of pay is $6.50 an hour. Her overtime rate is $9.75 an hour ($6.50 × 1.5). Her gross pay is computed as follows:

40 hours × $6.50 an hour (regular pay)	=	$260.00
5 hours × $9.75 an hour (overtime pay)	=	48.75
Gross pay	=	$308.75

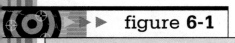

figure **6-1**

Marshall Manufacturing Co.

14 Ault Street El Paso, TX 79925-6457

88-0581 / 1120

PAYROLL CHECK

Co. Code	Department	File No.	Clock No. ID	Social Security No.			TO THE ORDER OF	Pay Date		Check No.
R&T	000108	43329	501 A	555	12	3344	M.J. SMITH	02	10 —	BELOW

PAY THIS AMOUNT	NET PAY
Two hundred thirty-four and 83/100 dollars	$234.83

M.J. SMITH
1133 ELM STREET
EL PASO, TX 79930-3264

**EL PASO BANK
EL PASO, TEXAS**

DISBURSING AGENT FOR ABOVE EMPLOYER

Jermaine Davis

AUTHORIZED SIGNATURE

⑈112005812⑈ 010450 001995⑈

Marshall Manufacturing Co.

14 Ault Street El Paso, TX 79925-6457

Co. Code	Department	File No.	Fed. Status	Name	Pay Period Ending		Pay Date	
R&T	000108	43329	501 A	SMITH, M.J.	02	10 —	02	10 —

Hours Units	Rate	Earnings	Type	Deduction	Type	Deduction	Type
40 00	6 50	260 00	REG	20 00	CR UN		
5 00	9 75	48 75	OT	11 00	H INS		
				2 50	UN DUES		
				3 80	ACC INS		

This Pay / YTD	Gross	Fed. With. Tax	OASD	Medicare	Other Deductions		Net Pay
This Pay	308 75	13 00	19 14	4 48	37 30		
YTD	1,852 50	78 00	114 84	26 88	223 80		234 83

Ms. Smith's gross pay appears under "Gross" at the bottom left of her paycheck stub. The letters "YTD" mean "year-to-date." The amounts on this line are cumulative totals up to this point in the year.

Salary

Perhaps you will work for a salary rather than an hourly wage. Salaried employees do not receive additional pay for overtime work. Therefore, your gross pay would be the same as your salary.

Your salary may be stated as an annual (yearly) amount. Thus, your employer will divide the annual salary into equal amounts to be paid each pay period. For example, suppose you agree to work for $24,000 a year. Your monthly gross pay will be $2,000 ($24,000 divided by 12 months in a year). If you are paid every two weeks, your gross pay per paycheck will be $923.08:

52 weeks in a year/2 weeks per pay period = 26 pay periods
$24,000/26 pay periods = $923.08 per paycheck

Notice that you will receive 26 paychecks using this method. If you were paid twice a month rather than every two weeks, you would receive only 24 paychecks (12 months in a year × 2 paychecks per month). In a later chapter, you will learn about budgeting when you receive paychecks weekly, biweekly (every two weeks), or monthly.

Deductions

Amounts subtracted from your gross pay are called **deductions**. Some deductions, such as social security tax and federal income tax, are required by law. Other deductions are optional and you may elect one or more of them. For example, you can have your employer automatically deduct an amount to deposit into your company-sponsored savings plan. As you can see in Figure 6-1, Ms. Smith has deductions for a credit union payment, health insurance, union dues, and accident insurance.

Employers are required to keep detailed records of wages earned and hours worked for inspection by the Department of Labor. With each paycheck, you will receive a detailed list of all deductions taken from your gross pay. Optional deductions may not be withheld without your written consent except by court order. This does not apply to taxes, social security, and other deductions required by law to be withheld from all paychecks.

©GETTY IMAGES/PHOTODISC

Net Pay

When all deductions are taken out of your gross pay, the amount left is your **net pay**. This is the amount of your paycheck, or the money you can actually spend. Net pay is often called "take-home pay" because it is the amount you can actually use as you wish. Stated mathematically:

Why would an employer track the number of hours an employee works?

Regular Wages or Salary + Overtime = Gross Pay
Gross Pay − Deductions = Net Pay

Figure 6-2 shows an employee withholding sheet. It lists weekly gross pay, deductions, and net pay. Save your withholding sheets or paycheck stubs that list the amounts withheld from your gross pay. You can use these to check the accuracy of the Form W-2 your employer gives you for your income tax return.

figure 6-2

EMPLOYEE WITHHOLDING SHEET

EMPLOYEE WITHHOLDING SHEET

Employee Name Shari Gregson   Social Security Number 898-40-7426

Pay Period: ☒ weekly   ☐ bimonthly   ☐ monthly

Number of allowances: 1   ☐ married   ☒ single

GROSS PAY

   1. Regular Wages: _40_ hours at $ _6.00_ /hr.   = $ 240.00

or

   2. Regular Salary: =

   3. Overtime: _4_ hours at $ _9.00_ /hr.   =   36.00

   GROSS PAY . . . .$ 276.00

REQUIRED DEDUCTIONS

   4. Federal Income Tax (use tax tables) . . . .$ 18.00

   5. State Income Tax (use tax tables) 16.00

   6. Social Security Tax (use 6.2% × gross pay, up to $87,900) 17.11

   7. Medicare Tax (use 1.45% × gross pay) 4.00

OTHER DEDUCTIONS

   8. Insurance . . . .

   9. Union Dues 3.00

  10. Credit Union 20.00

  11. Savings . . . .

  12. Retirement . . . .

  13. Charity . . . .

  14. Other: _____ . . . . _____

          _____ . . . . _____

     TOTAL DEDUCTIONS (total lines 4 through 14) . . . .$ 78.11

     NET PAY (subtract total deductions from gross pay) . . . .$ 197.89

Required deductions include federal, state, and local taxes, and social security and Medicare taxes. In Figure 6-1, the deductions for M. J. Smith appear at the bottom of the paycheck stub. "OASD" means "old age, survivors, and disability." This is the social security deduction.

The amounts to be withheld are determined from tax withholding tables. Figure 6-3 shows part of the weekly withholding table for the

Weekly payroll period (Oregon)

Amount of tax to be withheld

Wage		Number of Withholding Allowances																
		Two or Less						Three or More										
		Single			Married			Single or Married										
At Least	But Less Than	0	1	2	0	1	2	3	4	5	6	7	8	9	10	11	12	13	14
0 – 20		0	0	0	0	0	0	0	0	0	0	0	0	0	0	0	0	0	0
20 – 40		2	0	0	0	0	0	0	0	0	0	0	0	0	0	0	0	0	0
40 – 60		3	0	0	0	0	0	0	0	0	0	0	0	0	0	0	0	0	0
60 – 80		4	2	0	1	0	0	0	0	0	0	0	0	0	0	0	0	0	0
80 – 100		5	3	0	3	0	0	0	0	0	0	0	0	0	0	0	0	0	0
100 – 120		7	4	2	4	1	0	0	0	0	0	0	0	0	0	0	0	0	0
120 – 140		8	6	3	5	3	0	0	0	0	0	0	0	0	0	0	0	0	0
140 – 160		9	7	4	6	4	1	0	0	0	0	0	0	0	0	0	0	0	0
160 – 180		10	8	6	8	5	3	0	0	0	0	0	0	0	0	0	0	0	0
180 – 200		12	10	8	9	7	4	1	0	0	0	0	0	0	0	0	0	0	0
200 – 220		14	11	9	10	8	5	3	0	0	0	0	0	0	0	0	0	0	0
220 – 240		15	13	11	11	9	7	4	1	0	0	0	0	0	0	0	0	0	0
240 – 260		17	15	12	13	10	8	5	3	0	0	0	0	0	0	0	0	0	0
260 – 280		18	16	14	14	12	9	7	4	1	0	0	0	0	0	0	0	0	0
280 – 300		20	18	16	15	13	10	8	5	3	0	0	0	0	0	0	0	0	0
300 – 320		21	19	17	16	14	12	9	7	4	1	0	0	0	0	0	0	0	0
320 – 340		23	21	19	17	15	13	11	9	6	3	0	0	0	0	0	0	0	0
340 – 360		24	22	20	19	17	15	12	10	8	5	2	0	0	0	0	0	0	0
360 – 380		26	24	22	20	18	16	14	12	9	6	4	1	0	0	0	0	0	0
380 – 400		27	25	23	22	20	18	16	13	11	8	5	3	0	0	0	0	0	0
400		29	27		21	19		13			4			0					

state of Oregon. Figure 6-4 (page 124) shows part of the weekly federal withholding tax table. If you were paid monthly, you would use tax tables provided for a monthly pay period.

To determine the proper amount to withhold, first identify the appropriate withholding table for your pay period. For example, Shari Gregson in Figure 6-2 is being paid weekly, so you can use the weekly table in Figure 6-3 to find her state withholding. Move your finger down the left side of the table to the range that includes the employee's gross pay. Shari's gross pay of $276 falls in the table's range of $260–$280. Then run your finger to the right until you get to the proper number of allowances and marital status. Shari's form shows that she is single and claims 1 allowance. In Figure 6-3, the number that falls in the column for a single person with 1 allowance, making between $260 and $280, is $16. Notice that $16 shows in the state income tax line on Shari's withholding sheet.

figure 6-4

SINGLE Persons—WEEKLY Payroll Period

(For Wages Paid Through December 2004)

If the wages are—		And the number of withholding allowances claimed is—										
At least	But less than	0	1	2	3	4	5	6	7	8	9	10
		The amount of income tax to be withheld is—										
$0	$55	$0	$0	$0	$0	$0	$0	$0	$0	$0	$0	$0
55	60	1	0	0	0	0	0	0	0	0	0	0
60	65	1	0	0	0	0	0	0	0	0	0	0
65	70	2	0	0	0	0	0	0	0	0	0	0
70	75	2	0	0	0	0	0	0	0	0	0	0
75	80	3	0	0	0	0	0	0	0	0	0	0
80	85	3	0	0	0	0	0	0	0	0	0	0
85	90	4	0	0	0	0	0	0	0	0	0	0
90	95	4	0	0	0	0	0	0	0	0	0	0
95	100	5	0	0	0	0	0	0	0	0	0	0
100	105	5	0	0	0	0	0	0	0	0	0	0
105	110	6	0	0	0	0	0	0	0	0	0	0
110	115	6	0	0	0	0	0	0	0	0	0	0
115	120	7	1	0	0	0	0	0	0	0	0	0
120	125	7	1	0	0	0	0	0	0	0	0	0
125	130	8	2	0	0	0	0	0	0	0	0	0
130	135	8	2	0	0	0	0	0	0	0	0	0
135	140	9	3	0	0	0	0	0	0	0	0	0
140	145	9	3	0	0	0	0	0	0	0	0	0
145	150	10	4	0	0	0	0	0	0	0	0	0
150	155	10	4	0	0	0	0	0	0	0	0	0
155	160	11	5	0	0	0	0	0	0	0	0	0
160	165	11	5	0	0	0	0	0	0	0	0	0
165	170	12	6	0	0	0	0	0	0	0	0	0
170	175	12	6	0	0	0	0	0	0	0	0	0
175	180	13	7	1	0	0	0	0	0	0	0	0
180	185	13	7	1	0	0	0	0	0	0	0	0
185	190	14	8	2	0	0	0	0	0	0	0	0
190	195	14	8	2	0	0	0	0	0	0	0	0
195	200	15	9	3	0	0	0	0	0	0	0	0
200	210	16	9	3	0	0	0	0	0	0	0	0
210	220	18	10	4	0	0	0	0	0	0	0	0
220	230	19	11	5	0	0	0	0	0	0	0	0
230	240	21	12	6	1	0	0	0	0	0	0	0
240	250	22	13	7	2	0	0	0	0	0	0	0
250	260	24	15	8	3	0	0	0	0	0	0	0
260	270	25	16	9	4	0	0	0	0	0	0	0
270	280	27	18	10	5	0	0	0	0	0	0	0
280	290	28	19	11	6	0	0	0	0	0	0	0
290	300	30	21	12	7	1	0	0	0	0	0	0
300	310	31	22	13	8	2	0	0	0	0	0	0
310	320	33	24	15	9	3	0	0	0	0	0	0

Following the same process, you can find Shari's federal withholding from Figure 6-4. Try it. Did you find the number $18 in the table, as shown on Shari's withholding sheet for federal income tax?

The social security deduction is withheld at the standard rate of 6.2 percent of the first $87,900 (for 2004). The Medicare tax deduction is withheld at the rate of 1.45 percent of all pay earned. Employers must contribute matching amounts into each employee's Medicare and social security accounts. For example, Figure 6-2 shows Shari's Medicare tax withholding as $4 this week. As a result, Shari's employer will also contribute $4 into Shari's Medicare account. Congress periodically increases the withholding rate and maximum amount as needed to keep enough tax money coming in to pay social security benefits.

In addition to required deductions, the optional deductions an employee has authorized will be subtracted from gross pay to arrive at net pay. The most common of these deductions are insurance payments, union dues, credit union payments, savings deposits, retirement contributions, and charitable deductions.

 Global View

Article 7 of Mexico's Federal Labor Law requires employers to employ at least 90% Mexican workers in their enterprises. All technical and professional workers must be Mexican, unless there are no Mexican workers qualified in a particular specialty. In that case, the employer may employ foreign workers, but only to the extent of 10% of the labor force engaged in the specialty. The employer and the foreign workers are required to train the Mexican workers in the specialty. Article 7 is not applicable to company directors, administrators, and general managers.

Think Critically: Does Article 7 help or hinder development of the Mexican work force? What might be its impact on emigration from foreign countries to Mexico?

Self-Employed Requirements

People who are self-employed do not have employee deductions and withholdings. Instead, they must file estimated tax returns quarterly (four times during the year), with payments. To do this, self-employed people estimate the total amount they will owe in taxes for the coming year. They divide this number by 4 to determine the amount to pay with each quarterly return. The IRS credits each payment toward their tax obligation for the year.

Like other workers, self-employed people must pay social security tax and Medicare tax. However, since self-employed people are both employee and employer, they must pay both the employee and matching employer contributions to social security and Medicare. Thus, for social security tax, self-employed people pay 12.4% of gross income (6.2% $\times$ 2). For Medicare tax, they pay 2.9% (1.45% $\times$ 2). The total of 15.3% is called the **self-employment tax**. It is the total social security and Medicare tax, including employer-matching contributions, paid by people who work for themselves.

BENEFITS AND INCENTIVES

Many employers offer **benefits**, which are forms of employee compensation in addition to pay. Common benefits include health insurance, retirement savings plans, pension plans, paid sick leave and vacations, and profit sharing. Some of these benefits are required by law (such as unemployment compensation, workers' compensation, and matching social security and Medicare tax). Many employers also provide some of the optional (not required by law) benefits discussed below.

Profit Sharing

Profit sharing is a plan that allows employees to receive a portion of the company's profits at the end of the corporate year. The more money (profits) the company makes, the more the company has to share with employees. Most companies that provide profit sharing consider it **incentive pay**—money offered to encourage employees to strive for higher levels of performance. Employers offer profit sharing because it links part of employee compensation with company profit goals, giving employees an incentive to work harder and reduce waste.

Paid Vacations and Holidays

Most businesses provide full-time employees with a set amount of paid vacation time. This means that while you are on vacation, you are paid as usual. It is not uncommon to receive a week's paid vacation after a year of full-time employment, two weeks after two years, three weeks after five years' employment, and so on.

A benefit that you are likely to receive for any full-time job is paid time off for holidays. Paid holidays typically include Christmas, Thanksgiving, Fourth of July, Labor Day, and Memorial Day. Other holidays that many companies consider paid holidays are New Year's Day, Veterans Day, Martin Luther King Day, and Presidents Day. An employee required to work on a holiday is usually paid double or more than double the regular hourly rate of pay.

Employee Services

Employee services are the extras that companies offer in order to improve employee morale and working conditions. Many companies offer employee discounts on merchandise sold or made by the company. For example, if you work at a clothing store, you might be able to purchase clothing for a reduced price. Other services include social and recreational programs, free parking, tuition reimbursement for college courses, day-care centers, wellness programs, and counseling for employee problems.

Child Care

Child care is a major issue for working parents. Many companies provide on-site child-care facilities as well as coverage of child-care expenses as a part of employee benefit packages. Federal legislation is likely to change child care significantly in years to come, possibly offering affordable programs for children of working parents.

Sick Pay

Many businesses also provide an allowance of days each year for illness, with pay as usual. This benefit is usually available to full-time employees only. It is customary to receive three to ten days a year as "sick days" without deductions from pay.

Leaves of Absence

Some employers allow employees to temporarily leave their jobs (without pay) for certain reasons, such as having children or completing education, and return to their jobs at a later time. While a leave of absence may be unpaid, it has an important advantage: it gives job security and permits you to take time off for important events in your life. In addition to the Family and Medical Leave Act discussed in Chapter 5, employers sometimes allow personal leave (absences for personal reasons) so that employees can attend to important matters without calling in "sick" when they aren't sick.

Insurance

Most large companies provide group health insurance plans for all employees. A few plans are paid for almost entirely by the employer, as a part of employee compensation. Most plans require that employees pay for part of their own coverage, as well as to cover dependents (spouse and children). Insurance plans may include group health, dental, vision, and life insurance.

HEALTH INSURANCE

A typical health insurance plan has an employee-paid amount, or *deductible*. After the deductible has been reached, the plan pays 80 percent of most doctor bills and prescriptions and 100 percent of hospitalization charges and emergency bills. Traditional insurance plans generally will not cover routine physical examinations. As an alternative to a traditional plan, your employer may offer you a preferred-provider plan (PPO) or a health maintenance organization (HMO) plan. Health insurance will be discussed in Chapter 27.

LIFE INSURANCE

Many companies offer group life insurance. Life insurance pays a cash benefit to a designated person, called a *beneficiary*, when the insured person dies. The purpose of life insurance is to partially offset the income lost when a wage earner dies. When you leave your current employment, the group policy may not go with you. The employer may pay an amount each month for standard coverage for each employee. Employees who want additional coverage often can pay for it through payroll deductions. Life insurance is discussed in detail in Chapter 27.

DENTAL INSURANCE

Most dental plans provide a maximum benefit per year per family member. Orthodontia (braces) may not be covered. Routine exams and cleanings are often covered 100 percent, while most other services are covered at 80 percent of a predetermined fee range. If, for example, a dentist charges $110 for a filling, and the insurance plan pays a high of $80 for this service, the plan will pay 80 percent times $80, or $64. The patient must pay the remainder. In addition, non-routine work, such as crowns, bridges, or root canals, may be covered at a lesser rate, such as 50 percent. Dental insurance may have a small deductible, such as $50 per person per year.

What types of services are usually covered in insurance plans?

VISION INSURANCE

Vision insurance covers the cost of prescription lenses and eye examinations once every few years. As the employee gets older, more frequent exams may be allowed. Generally, frames are not covered, but sometimes coverage is available for contact lenses. Vision and dental insurance are explained further in Chapter 27.

Bonuses and Stock Options

Bonuses are incentive pay based on quality of work done, years of service, or company sales or profits. A factory manager may offer all workers a $100 year-end bonus as a reward for having no serious on-the-job accidents during the year. Holiday bonuses are often based on years of service. If a division of a company reaches a particular sales goal in a year, all top-level managers might receive a bonus equal to a percentage of their current salaries.

Stock-purchase options give employees (usually executives) the right to buy a set number of shares of the company's stock at a fixed price by a certain time. The employees gain as long as the stock price goes up. Many types of stock option plans exist.

Pension and Savings Plans

Some employers provide pension plans for retirement. Pension plans are completely funded by the employer. When an employee retires, he or she receives a monthly check. In some cases, an employee may withdraw funds early in part or in full, or retire early and begin collecting reduced benefits. Employees are fully **vested** (entitled to the full retirement account) after a specified period of time, such as five years.

Employer-sponsored savings plans, such as a 401(k) for private employers or a 403(b) for government employers, are also retirement plans. Employers do not bear the full cost of these plans, and as a result, many companies are switching from pensions to these savings plans. For the 401(k) or 403(b), the employee makes contributions to his or her own account. The employer may also (but is not required to) contribute money to the employee's account. Generally, withdrawing funds from savings plans before retirement will result in financial penalties, unless for certain reasons such as education, first-time home purchase, or medical expenses.

Travel Expenses

Companies that require employees to travel in the course of their work often provide a company car or a mileage allowance if employees use their own car. Generally, car insurance, gasoline, and repair and maintenance expenses for the company automobile are also provided. While out of town, employees receive a daily allowance, or have their motel, meals, and other travel expenses paid. In some cases, employees are expected to pay the costs of their travel and keep receipts as evidence of purchases so they can be reimbursed later.

Evaluating Employee Benefits

Many of these optional benefits are of great value to employees. Benefits generally are not currently taxable to employees (except bonuses and other benefits paid in cash), yet they provide valuable coverage and advantages. Generally, large companies provide more extensive optional benefits than do small companies.

In recent years, employee benefits have been expanded to meet the needs of different life situations. *Cafeteria-style* employee benefits are programs that allow workers to base their job benefits on personal needs. Flexibility in the selection of benefits has become quite common. For example, a married employee with children might opt for increased life and health insurance, while a single parent may choose child-care services.

✓ Check Your Understanding

1. What is included in gross pay?

2. If you are paid every two weeks, how many paychecks do you receive in a year?

3. How are employer-sponsored savings plans different from pension plans?

Lesson 6.2

Work Arrangements and Organizations

Goals
- **Explain several flexible job arrangements.**
- **Describe the role of unions and professional organizations in the workplace.**

▶ FLEXIBLE WORK ARRANGEMENTS

Many employers are responding to changing lifestyles and needs of their employees. By designing more flexible jobs, employers can reduce absenteeism, burnout, and turnover.

Altered Workweeks

Many firms have experimented with altered workweeks to get away from the standard eight-hours-a-day, five-days-a-week work schedule. Flextime is one work schedule alternative. Another is the compressed workweek.

Flexible schedules, or **flextime**, allow employees to choose their working hours within defined limits. Flextime plans generally require all employees to be present during a specified core time period. Employees can then choose the rest of their work hours around this core period. Employees negotiate their starting times, usually within a three- to four-hour period. This allows them to begin working as early as 6 A.M. or as late as 9 or 10 A.M. Even though starting times are flexible, most employers require employees to work a set number of hours per day. For example, a person arriving at 6 A.M. would be finished by 3 P.M. (having a one-hour unpaid lunch break), while a person arriving at 10 A.M. would be finished at 7 P.M. The core time period is a crucial time during the day when all employees must be working. This core period may be between 10 A.M. and 3 P.M., the peak hours for business activity.

Flextime is good for business because employees are responsible for working a full day regardless of when they arrive on the job. Employees experience greater job satisfaction because flextime helps them fulfill their personal needs. For example, employees who need to pick up children from school would find it convenient to be off at 3 P.M. Flextime also allows for the scheduling of medical or other appointments, and it reduces stress caused by the pressure of meeting strict work schedules.

A **compressed workweek** is a work schedule that fits the normal 40-hour workweek into less than five days. The typical compressed workweek is 10 hours a day for 4 days, followed by 3 days off. Some types of work are better suited to a compressed schedule than are others. For example, some kinds of strenuous physical or mental work are probably not suitable for a compressed workweek.

Job Rotation

Job rotation is a job design in which employees are trained to do more than one specialized task. Employees "rotate" from one task to another. Job rotation gives employees more variety in their work and allows them to use different skills. It reduces boredom and burnout, leading to greater job satisfaction. A major advantage of job rotation for both employer and employee is that information and ideas are freely exchanged among employees, so that everyone knows how to do each task. If one worker is absent, another can take over and keep the work flowing.

Job Sharing

Job sharing is a job design in which two people share one full-time position. They split the salary and benefits according to each person's contributions. Job sharing is especially attractive to people who want part-time work. By satisfying employees' needs for more personal time, job sharing reduces absenteeism and tardiness, lowers fatigue, and improves productivity.

Permanent Part-Time and Telecommuting

Many employees choose to work only part-time (16 to 25 hours a week). Companies can save on salary and benefits by hiring permanent part-time employees. Part-time work usually provides some benefits to the employee, such as job security, while allowing freedom to spend more time away from work. Parents with small children, older employees, and others may find that permanent part-time work best meets their needs.

Advances in technology make another flexible work arrangement possible: *telecommuting*. Telecommuters can work at home or on the road, and stay in contact with their manager and co-workers through e-mail, fax, and cell phone. Employees who telecommute often do computer-related work, such as data entry, Web design, information processing, or software development. Working at home is convenient and gives the worker flexibility. Telecommuting does not work well in jobs that require frequent face-to-face interaction among employees or that require employees to work together in one place to create a product.

▶ LABOR UNIONS AND PROFESSIONAL ORGANIZATIONS

Many jobs involve union membership or participation in a professional organization as a requirement of employment. Unions are groups of people joined together for a common purpose. A **labor union** is a group of people who work in the same or similar occupations, organized for the benefit of all employees in these occupations.

Functions of Unions

Labor unions have four major functions: (1) to recruit new members, (2) to engage in collective bargaining, (3) to support political candidates who are favorable to the union, and (4) to provide support services for members. Unions support their members by helping to keep them employed, negotiating wages and working conditions, providing credentials for job-seeking employees, and providing the education members need to obtain and keep jobs.

The main function of unions is **collective bargaining**, which is the process of negotiating the terms of employment for union members. Terms of the agreement are written into an employment contract. The contract usually specifies wages for each type of job, overtime rates, hours of work, and benefits. It also spells out a grievance procedure. A *grievance* is a formal complaint, by an employee or by the union, that management has violated some aspect of the contract.

Union contracts usually provide for **seniority** rights, a policy in which the last workers hired will be the first fired when jobs must be cut. So, when the company needs to reduce its workforce, it will lay off newer workers ahead of more experienced workers. Under this policy, the longer you work for the employer, the more job security you are entitled to. Seniority may be used to determine transfers, promotions, and vacation time according to most union contracts.

When the union and employer cannot agree on the terms of a new contract, the dispute can be mediated. Through *mediation*, a neutral third party (the *mediator* or *arbitrator*) helps the two parties reach a compromise. If they still cannot agree, the union may decide to *strike*, or refuse to work until an agreement is reached.

Career Focus

Specialists involved in resolving disputes must be highly experienced and knowledgeable. Mediators advise labor and management to prevent and, when necessary, resolve disputes over labor agreements or other labor relations issues. Arbitrators, sometimes called referees, decide disputes that bind both labor and management to specific terms and conditions of labor contracts. A strong background in industrial relations and law is highly desirable for mediators and arbitrators. In fact, many people in these specialties are lawyers.

For more information, refer to the *Occupational Outlook Handbook* at www.bls.gov or search the Internet using such key words as "careers," "jobs," "mediator," and "arbitrator."

Types of Unions

Unions are self-governing organizations that can be classified into three types: craft unions, industrial unions, and public-employee unions. Elected union leaders often work full time in their positions. Unions often employ their own lawyers, doctors, economists, educators, and public relations officials. Dues collected from members pay for the services of these professionals.

Membership in a *craft union* is limited to those who practice that craft or trade (for example, bricklayers, carpenters, or plasterers). Major craft unions exist in the building, printing, and maritime trades, and for railroad employees.

Members of *industrial unions* are skilled, semiskilled, or unskilled employees in a particular place, industry, or group of industries. Examples include the AFL-CIO, Teamsters, and United Auto Workers. Most of this country's basic industries (steel, automobiles, rubber, glass, machinery, mining) are heavily unionized.

Municipal, county, state, or federal employees such as firefighters, teachers, and police officers may organize *public-employee unions*. These unions are organized much like craft and industrial unions

©GETTY IMAGES/PHOTODISC

What kinds of employees are members of craft unions?

except that they generally do not hire outside officers. Members serve as union representatives and officers, sometimes with pay from union dues.

Professional Organizations

A **professional organization** is an organization of people in a particular occupation that requires considerable training and specialized skills. Professional organizations also collect dues from members and provide support services. Notable professional organizations include the American Bar Association for lawyers, the American Medical Association for doctors, and National Education Association for educators. In some cases, membership in a professional organization may be required. For example, to be licensed or "admitted to the bar," lawyers must pass rigorous tests administered by their state's bar association. Lawyers who commit serious misconduct may be "disbarred," which means they can no longer practice law.

©GETTY IMAGES/PHOTODISC

What role does a bar association play for lawyers?

Professional organizations establish and maintain professional standards and publish professional journals to help keep members up-to-date in their field. They often provide pension, retirement, and insurance benefits for members. Through **lobbying**, professional organizations try to influence public officials to take political action that benefits the profession. Because most doctors and lawyers are self-employed, their professional behavior is not regulated except through membership in these organizations. Professional organizations administer exams, accreditations, and admission requirements to maintain professional standards.

⊘Check Your Understanding

1. Which form of flexible work arrangement is most attractive to you? Why?

2. How do unions benefit their members?

3. What are some purposes of professional organizations?

Starting a Summer Business

It's the American dream—owning your own business and working for yourself. As a student in high school, you can also share a part of that dream by starting a summer business. You'll gain valuable experience, know what it's like to work independently, and maybe even pave the way for owning your own company in the future.

If a summer business sounds exciting to you, consider these questions:

1. Do you have a skill that you could offer to others such as light housekeeping, mowing lawns, or delivering newspapers?

2. Can you make and/or sell a product that others would be interested in buying—for example, flower planters, gift baskets, or crafts?

To start a summer business, here are some steps to take.

1. Get organized. Capture your business idea on paper. Write down what you wish to accomplish and how to finance it.

2. Talk with people who can help you get going. These people may be parents, relatives, friends, or others who can assist you with ideas, financing, or potential customers.

3. Decide how to advertise your business and find customers. Will you go door to door? Place an ad in the paper? Sometimes you have to spend money to make money. Can you save some money between now and summer to give you that needed cash?

4. Start small and build a solid customer base. When someone places trust in you and hires you to provide a product or service, do a great job. Your business will grow from word of mouth.

5. Keep good records. Keep track of money you spend, money you earn, and who owes you money.

6. Give good value to your customers. Provide a quality product or service and take pride in your work.

7. Keep a list of what went well and what went wrong. You can learn from your past experience.

Think Critically

1. Have you ever wanted to own your own small business? If so, what type of business would you like to have?

2. Do you know people who own their own business? If so, ask how they got started and what advice they have. If not, go into a small business and ask the owner to answer those questions for you.

Chapter Assessment

SUMMARY

6.1
* Gross pay includes your regular pay plus overtime wages earned during that pay period.
* Deductions (both required and voluntary) are subtracted from gross pay to determine net pay—the money you actually take home.
* Self-employed people pay both the employee and employer portions of social security and Medicare taxes.
* Benefits in addition to pay may include profit sharing, paid time off, employee services, insurance plans, bonuses, stock options, and retirement plans.
* Cafeteria-style plans allow employees to choose the benefits that best meet their needs.

6.2
* Flextime, a compressed workweek, job rotation, job sharing, permanent part-time jobs, and telecommuting offer employees flexibility.
* Labor unions—including craft unions, industrial unions, and public-employee unions—negotiate the terms of work contracts with employers on behalf of their members.
* Professional organizations serve people in highly skilled occupations. These organizations maintain standards and keep members current in their fields.

Directions

Can you find the definition for each of the following terms used in Chapter 6?

benefits
collective bargaining
compressed workweek
deductions
flextime
gross pay
incentive pay
job rotation
job sharing

labor union
lobbying
net pay
overtime
professional organization
self-employment tax
seniority
vested

1. Organization of people in a particular occupation that requires considerable training and specialized skills.

2. Trying to influence public officials to take political action that benefits a particular group.

3. Total pay before deductions are subtracted.

4. Pay remaining after deductions are subtracted.

5. Entitled to the full amount accumulated in a retirement plan.

6. A group of people in the same or similar occupations, organized for the benefit of all.

7. Amounts subtracted from gross pay.

8. A negotiation between unions and employers about terms of employment.

9. A workplace policy in which the last workers hired will be the first fired when jobs must be cut.

10. Money offered to encourage employees to strive for higher levels of performance.

11. A work schedule that allows employees to choose their working hours within defined limits.

12. A job design in which employees are trained to do more than one specialized task and move from one task to another.

13. A job design in which two people share one full-time position.

14. A work schedule that fits the normal 40-hour workweek into less than 5 days.

15. Forms of employee compensation in addition to pay.

16. Time worked beyond the regular 40-hour workweek.

17. Total social security and Medicare tax, including employer matching contributions, paid by people who work for themselves.

REVIEW FACTS AND IDEAS

1. How is gross pay different from net pay?

2. How much must an employer pay an hourly employee for hours worked beyond a regular workweek?

3. What is an important difference between employees who work for a salary and those who work for an hourly wage?

4. Give examples of required and voluntary payroll deductions.

5. How do self-employed people pay their income taxes during the year?

6. What is a leave of absence?

7. What is a core time period?

8. What is a major advantage of job rotation to employers?

9. What are the major functions of labor unions?

10. Describe the collective bargaining process.

11. Explain the principle of seniority.

12. How is mediation used in labor negotiations?

13. What are the three types of labor unions?

14. How are labor unions funded? (That is, who pays for the services they provide?)

15. How do professional organizations maintain professional standards?

APPLY YOUR KNOWLEDGE

1. Compute gross pay for these situations:
   a. Regular hours worked: 40
      Overtime hours worked: 5
      Regular rate of pay: $5.85 an hour
   b. Total hours worked: 43 (in 5 days)
      Regular rate of pay: $6.10 an hour
   c. Annual salary: $18,000
      Compute monthly gross pay.

2. Using the payroll tax withholding tables in Figures 6-3 and 6-4, find the state and federal withholding amounts for each of the following cases:
   a. For a single person, one allowance, who made $109 last week.
   b. For a single person, no allowances, who made $222 last week.
   c. For a single person, three allowances, who made $291 last week.

3. Go to the Internal Revenue Service Web site at www.irs.gov. Search "Forms and Publications" to locate this year's weekly withholding table for married persons. Then find the federal withholding amounts for each of the following cases:
   a. For a married person, two allowances, who made $642 last week.
   b. For a married person, six allowances, who made $444 last week.
   c. For a married person, three allowances, who made $523 last week.

4. Compute the following for a self-employed person who made $40,000 this year:
   a. Social security tax.
   b. Medicare tax.
   c. Self-employment tax.

5. Visit the Social Security Administration online at www.ssa.gov and look up the current-year social security changes. List the maximum taxable earnings for social security and for Medicare, and the current tax rate on earnings.

6. Visit the American Bar Association online at www.abanet.org and list or print out the goals of the association.

Solve Problems ⊕ Explore Issues

1. Trang Vu works for a weekly paycheck. She is single and claims no allowances. Last week she worked 5 days for a total of 44 hours. Her regular rate of pay is $6.40 an hour. In addition to withholding for federal income tax, state income tax (use Figures 6-3 and 6-4), Medicare, and social security, Trang also has insurance of $16 a week withheld and puts 6 percent of her gross pay into a retirement account. Compute her gross pay, deductions, and net pay.

2. D'Andre Johnson works for a weekly paycheck. He is single and claims one allowance. Last week he worked 5 days, for a total of 48 hours. His regular rate of pay is $5.80 an hour. In addition to required deductions, he also has $10 a week sent to his credit union account and gives $2 a week to United Fund (a charity). Compute his gross pay, deductions, and net pay.

3. Abigayle works for herself. She estimates that her gross income this year will be $44,000, and she will owe about $12,000 in federal income tax. How much should she pay when she files each quarterly tax return? How much social security tax will she owe for the year? How much Medicare tax will she owe for the year? What is the total amount of Abigayle's self-employment tax?

4. Marcus Zambito works for an annual salary and is paid every two weeks. His annual salary is $20,700. How much is his gross pay for each paycheck?

5. Keyondra makes an annual salary of $31,200. However, she gets paid every month. How much is her gross pay for each paycheck?

For related activities and links, point your browser to **www.mypf.swlearning.com**

Federal Income Tax

TERMS TO KNOW

revenue
progressive taxes
regressive taxes
proportional
 taxes
tax brackets
tax evasion

audit
exemption
gross income
child support
alimony
adjusted gross
 income

deductions
itemize
standard
 deduction
taxable income
tax credit

Consider This. . .

When Ichiro started his after-school part-time job last year, he filled out a Form W-4 declaring zero exemptions. At the end of the year, his employer sent him a Form W-2 listing the amounts that were withheld for taxes. Because Ichiro must now prepare his first tax return, he needs to pick up a tax form. He goes to the IRS Web site and downloads a copy of Form 1040EZ and its instructions.

"This is great," says Ichiro, as he completes the rough draft of his tax return. "I'm looking at a refund. I had a lot more withheld than I'll owe in taxes. Next year, I think I'll plan a little better. It's nice to have a refund, but it would be better to have the right amount withheld so I have full use of my money during the year. I could have earned interest on that money if I had put it away."

Lesson 7.1

Our Tax System

Goals
- Discuss the purpose of taxes and different types of taxes in the United States.
- Describe components of the U.S. tax system.

▶ TYPES OF TAXES

In a free enterprise system such as ours, the government collects money from citizens and businesses in the form of taxes. The government then spends this money, called **revenue**, according to priorities determined by Congress. The largest source of government revenue is income taxes. Other taxes providing government revenue include social security taxes, unemployment insurance taxes, inheritance and estate taxes, excise taxes, import duties, and personal property taxes.

A commonly accepted principle of tax fairness is that individuals with high incomes should pay more taxes than people with low incomes. This theory is called the *ability-to-pay principle*.

Progressive taxes are taxes that take a larger share of income as the amount of income grows. Federal income taxes are progressive. For example, someone with a low income may pay 15 percent of income as taxes. Someone with a high income may pay 28 percent for income taxes. Everyone who receives income from employment or any other source must pay income taxes.

Regressive taxes are taxes that take a smaller share of income as the amount of income grows. Sales taxes are regressive, because people with lower incomes pay a larger percentage of their income for sales taxes than do people with higher incomes. For example, your state may charge a 5 percent sales tax. If you buy an item worth $10, your tax would be 50 cents ($10 \times 0.05 = \$0.50$), and you would pay $10.50 for the item. For someone who earns $50 a week, this 50 cents represents 1 percent of income ($\$0.50/\$50 = .01 = 1\%$). For someone who earns $100 a week, this 50 cents represents only half a percent of income ($\$0.50/\$100 = .005 = .5\%$).

Almost all consumption taxes are regressive. Another type of tax on consumption is an *excise tax*. Excise taxes are sales taxes imposed on specific goods and services, such as gasoline, cigarettes, alcoholic beverages, air travel, and telephone service.

Proportional taxes, or *flat taxes*, are taxes for which the rate stays the same, regardless of income. Property taxes are proportional. For example, all people owning property in the same community pay the same tax rate, whether their property is worth $50,000 or $500,000.

On a local level, taxes provide services such as education, parks and playgrounds, roads, and police, fire, and health departments. On a national level, they provide salaries for Congress and funds for national defense, highways, wildlife refuges, welfare, foreign aid, and other services. Most of the services (local, state, and national) are provided for the general welfare of all citizens, although as an individual, you may not benefit from all of them directly.

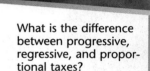

▶ COMPONENTS OF THE TAX SYSTEM

What is the difference between progressive, regressive, and proportional taxes?

Our tax system is complex. Both businesses and individuals pay income taxes and must file income tax returns each year. The basic components that allow the tax system to operate are the IRS, the country's power to tax income, and each taxpayer's willingness to pay his or her fair share.

The IRS

The Internal Revenue Service is an agency of the Department of the Treasury. It has headquarters in Washington, D.C., and seven regional offices throughout the country. Each regional office is a major data processing center that oversees at least 10 district and local offices. The main functions of the IRS are to collect income taxes and to enforce tax laws.

The IRS also provides services to taxpayers. In local offices, IRS employees assist taxpayers in finding information and forms. The IRS prints pamphlets to aid taxpayers in preparing their returns. It also furnishes tax information and instruction booklets free to schools and colleges. The IRS maintains a Web site at www.irs.gov, where citizens can get tax information, download tax forms, and even file their taxes electronically. Citizens can also obtain tax forms from their local IRS office and from many public libraries.

The Power to Tax

The power to levy taxes rests with Congress. The Constitution provides that "all bills for raising revenue shall originate in the House of Representatives." Proposals to increase or decrease taxes may come from the president, the Department of the Treasury, or a member of Congress representing the interests of a geographic area. The House Ways and Means Committee studies the proposals and makes recommendations to the full House. Revenue bills must pass a vote in both the House and the Senate and then be signed by the president before they become law.

Paying Your Fair Share

Our income tax system is graduated. This means that tax rates increase as taxable income increases. Tax rates apply to income ranges, or **tax brackets**. Currently, there are six tax brackets, ranging from 10 percent at the low end to 35 percent at the high end. For example, suppose that you earned $30,000 in a year. If the 25 percent tax bracket that year included incomes between $29,050 and $70,350, then your income would be taxed at the 25 percent rate. Congress increases the tax rates when needed to bring in more money to balance its budget. When the government spends more than it receives in revenue, it has a *deficit,* or shortage. It must then borrow money to pay its expenses.

Our income tax system is based on *voluntary compliance,* which means that all citizens are expected to prepare and file income tax returns. Taxes are due by April 15 of each year. Responsibility for filing a tax return and paying taxes due rests with the individual. Failure to do so can result in a penalty: interest charges on the taxes owed plus a fine and/or imprisonment. Willful failure to pay taxes is called **tax evasion**, which is a serious crime punishable by a fine or imprisonment or both.

©GETTY IMAGES/PHOTODISC

Our income tax system is based on *voluntary compliance.* What does this mean?

◉ VIEWPOINTS

A significant portion of local public school budgets is typically based upon taxes paid by property-owners who live within school districts. Elderly people, who often have fixed and limited incomes, may feel that they should not have to fund schools since they no longer have school-age children.

Think Critically: How do you feel about this point of view? Should elderly property owners be given a tax break or even be exempt from taxes that fund school districts?

An IRS Audit

Every year, the IRS calls thousands of taxpayers for an **audit**, or examination of their tax returns. Taxpayers being audited have three choices. First, they can represent themselves all the way to an appeal in Tax Court, if necessary. Second, they can give someone the power to take their place, as long as the designated person is a lawyer, certified public accountant, a member of the immediate family, or an enrolled agent (someone who is licensed to prepare tax returns). Third, they can bring anyone at all (tax preparer, attorney, or other representative) for support during the session. Most audit sessions involve nothing more than confirming supporting documentation. Therefore, most taxpayers can go alone unless the matter is unusually complicated.

A *correspondence audit* is much more common than an office audit, where the taxpayer sits down with the auditor to answer questions and produce records. In a correspondence audit, the IRS sends a letter, asking the taxpayer to respond to specific questions or produce evidence of deductions or other entries on the tax return. A *field audit* is similar, except that an IRS agent or local representative visits the taxpayer to verify information or ask specific questions.

✔ Check Your Understanding

1. What is the purpose of the Internal Revenue Service (IRS) within our income tax system?
2. Who has the power to levy taxes in the United States?
3. Explain why voluntary compliance is a vital component of our democracy.

Surviving an Audit

Every year, the IRS audits millions of American taxpayers. You may be one of them if you make math errors on your tax form or report income that does not match the income on your Form W-2. To avoid the audit, here are some helpful tips:

1. Check your math. Make sure all your additions and subtractions are correct. Many audits result from simple math errors.

2. Fill out the form neatly, so that it is easy to read. Using a tax software program helps you take advantage of all the credits and deductions you deserve and helps prevent errors.

3. Keep good records. Keep receipts for all deductions and credits you claim on your tax return.

4. File by April 15 to avoid penalties and interest.

Once you receive the audit notice, remember:

1. You have 30 days in which to respond. Get advice and help if needed, and respond to the notice within the time limit.

2. You can have a representative with you or in your place, such as a CPA, enrolled agent, or attorney.

3. Bring all of your receipts, forms, instructions, and other documentation with you to prove your case.

4. Learn more about audits and how to prepare from Publication 556 (available at www.irs.gov) and from other print or online resources.

5. The IRS can make mistakes, too. You have rights as a taxpayer (see Publication 1), and in many cases, the Tax Court rules in favor of the taxpayer.

6. Don't sign forms that take away your rights. Before you sign anything, be sure to get advice from a tax professional.

7. Stay calm and collected. Behave responsibly, return calls, ask questions, give reasonable explanations, and listen carefully.

After the audit is complete, you can appeal the auditor's decision if you feel you have good cause.

Think Critically

1. Do you know someone who has been audited by the IRS? Ask that person to share general information about the process.

2. What can you do to avoid an IRS audit?

Filing Tax Returns

Goals • **Define tax vocabulary.**
• **Prepare tax Forms 1040EZ and 1040A.**

▶ DEFINITIONS OF TERMS

You should prepare your tax forms with the idea of paying your fair share while taking advantage of the tax breaks legally available to you. Before you can understand how to prepare tax forms, you need a working knowledge of the tax vocabulary. The terms described in the following paragraphs appear on income tax returns, in IRS instruction booklets, and on forms and schedules you will use.

Filing Status

Select the filing status that best fits you from among these five choices:
1. Single person (not married)
2. Married person filing a joint return (even though only one spouse may have earned income)
3. Married person filing a separate return
4. "Head of household" (you may qualify as a head of household whether you are married or single if you meet certain conditions in providing a home for people dependent on you)
5. Qualifying widow(er) with a dependent child

Mark your filing status on the front of the tax form. The tax instruction booklet contains a more detailed description of these classifications. After you file your first tax return, each year thereafter you will automatically receive a tax booklet containing the necessary forms in the mail for use in preparing your tax returns.

©GETTY IMAGES/PHOTODISC

What are the five choices of filing status?

Exemptions

When figuring taxes, an **exemption** is an amount you may subtract from your income for each person who depends on your income to live. You would then not have to pay tax on this amount. Therefore, each exemption reduces your total tax. As a taxpayer you are automatically allowed one exemption for yourself unless someone else (such as a parent) claims you as a dependent on his or her return. If you are filing a joint return, you can take an exemption for your spouse.

A *dependent* is a person who lives with you and receives more than half his or her living expenses from you. Each exemption you claim on your income tax form excludes a certain amount of your income from being taxed. This amount increases each year according to the cost of living. Dependents include children, a spouse, elderly parents, or disabled relatives living with and depending on the taxpayer.

Gross Income

Gross income is all the taxable income you receive, including wages, tips, salaries, interest, dividends, unemployment compensation, alimony, workers' compensation benefits, and so forth. Scholarships and grants may be taxable for amounts used for expenses other than tuition and books. If you just take classes without pursuing a degree, more of the scholarship or grant money you receive will likely be taxable. Also, employer-reimbursed tuition is in most cases taxable. Certain types of income are not taxable and are not reported as income. These include child support, gifts, inheritances, life insurance benefits, and veterans' benefits.

You are also taxed on other forms of income, including winnings from gambling, bartering income, pensions and annuities, social security benefits, income from self-employment, rental income, royalties, estate and trust income, and income on sale of property.

WAGES, SALARIES, AND TIPS

This category on your Form W-2 includes all income you receive through employment. If you receive tips on your job, you must report your tips to your employer. Your employer then includes these earnings with your wages on your Form W-2.

INTEREST INCOME

Your interest income includes all taxable interest from banks, savings and loan associations, credit unions, series HH savings bonds, and so on. You should receive a Form 1099-INT for each investment that earned interest during the year. This form reports the amount of interest you earned from that investment.

DIVIDEND INCOME

Dividends are money, stock, or other property that corporations pay to stockholders in return for their investment. You will receive a Form 1099-DIV for each stock investment, listing the dividend income. According to the Jobs and Growth Tax Relief and Reconciliation Act of 2003, these dividends may be subject to a maximum 15% tax rate.

UNEMPLOYMENT COMPENSATION

If you receive any unemployment compensation during the year, you will receive a Form 1099-G, which shows the total you received. You must enter this amount as income on the tax return.

SOCIAL SECURITY BENEFITS

If you receive social security payments during the year, 85 percent of this money is taxable if your total income exceeds $25,000 for single taxpayers and $32,000 for married taxpayers filing jointly. You would receive a Form SSA-1099, listing the total paid for the year.

CHILD SUPPORT

Money paid to a former spouse for support of dependent children is called **child support**. This income is not taxable for the person receiving it, nor is it deductible for the person paying it.

ALIMONY

Money paid to support a former spouse is called **alimony**. It is taxable for the person receiving it and deductible for the person paying it.

Adjusted Gross Income

The law allows you to subtract some types of spending from gross income. You can "adjust" your income by subtracting such things as contributions to IRAs (which are retirement accounts you will learn about in Chapter 11). After these adjustments are subtracted from gross income, the result is **adjusted gross income**. These adjustments reduce your income that is subject to tax, and thus reduce your total tax. You will use your adjusted gross income as a basis for computing other deductions on your tax return.

Taxable Income

In Chapter 6, you learned that *deductions* are amounts subtracted from your gross pay to arrive at your take-home pay. On tax returns, **deductions** are expenses the law allows you to subtract from your adjusted gross income to determine your taxable income. Since your tax is based on your taxable income, anything that reduces taxable income also reduces your tax. To get the tax benefit from your deductions, you must list or **itemize** these allowable expenses on your tax return. To itemize deductions, you must use Schedule A and Form 1040. Common expenses you may deduct are medical and dental expenses beyond a specified amount, state and local income taxes and property taxes, home mortgage interest, gifts to charity, losses from theft or property damage, and moving expenses.

If you do not have many deductions, your tax may be less if you take the **standard deduction**. This is a stated amount that you may subtract from adjusted gross income instead of itemizing your deductions. Figure 7-1 shows the standard deduction in a recent year for most people, based on their filing status. If your individual deductions do not add up to the standard deduction, then you can reduce your total tax by taking the standard deduction rather than itemizing.

Once you have subtracted your standard deduction (or itemized deductions), you need to compute exemptions. You may deduct a stated amount for each exemption to arrive at your **taxable income**, which is the income on which you will pay tax. You can then determine your tax by looking up your taxable income on a tax table. The Math Minute feature shows the formula for determining your taxable income.

Math Minute — Calculating Income Tax

```
    Gross Income
  − Adjustments
  ─────────────────────────────
    Adjusted Gross Income
  − Standard Deduction or Itemized Deductions
  − Exemptions
  ─────────────────────────────
    Taxable Income
```

Look up taxable income in tax table to determine tax.

```
    Tax
  − Credits
  − Payments Made (Withholding)
  ─────────────────────────────
    Tax Owed or Refund Due
```

Tax Credits

After determining the tax you owe from the tax table, you may deduct any tax credits for which you qualify. A **tax credit** is an amount subtracted directly from the tax owed. It is different from a deduction. A deduction is subtracted from gross income. It reduces your tax by reducing the amount of income on which the tax is figured. A tax credit, on the other hand, reduces the tax itself. For example, if the tax table shows that your total tax is $1,000 and you can claim a tax credit of $100, then your tax drops to $900.

THE STANDARD DEDUCTION

figure 7-1

If your filing status is:	Your standard deduction is:
Single or married filing separately	$4,750
Married filing jointly	9,500
Head of household	7,000

A deduction of $100 would reduce your tax as well, but not by the full $100. A deduction reduces your tax by the amount of the deduction times your tax rate. If your tax rate is 20%, a $100 deduction reduces your tax by only $20 ($100 $\times$ 0.2).

The government allows tax credits for college tuition, for childcare to enable parents to work, and for lower income wage earners. The IRS publishes instructions outlining the requirements to qualify for each type of tax credit. The Math Minute shows how credits fit into the income tax calculation.

▶ PREPARING TO FILE

Once you have gathered your income and expense records, you can make a rough draft of your tax return. The tax booklet that accompanies the printed forms contains the instructions for completing the forms. A simple 1040EZ tax return may require only 15 minutes to prepare. The long Form 1040 may require most of a day after you have gathered all information. In addition to a federal tax return, you may have to file state and local income tax returns.

Who Must File?

You must file a tax return if you earned more than a certain amount specified by the government. In a recent year, a single person under age 65 had to file a tax return if he or she earned more than $7,800. If you earned less than the minimum, you may still have to file if you meet other qualifications outlined in the instructions. If you did not earn enough to owe taxes but you had taxes withheld from your paychecks, you must file a return to reclaim the taxes withheld. If you do not file, you will not get a refund.

When to File?

You must file no later than April 15 of the year after you earned income. If April 15 falls on a weekend or holiday, your tax return is due on the next weekday. If you file late, you will have to pay penalties and interest charges.

Which Form to Use?

Although there are nearly 400 federal tax forms, all taxpayers must use one of three basic forms when filing their return. You must decide whether to fill out a short form (1040A or 1040EZ) or to itemize your deductions using the long form (1040). Which form you choose will depend on the type and amount of your income, the number of your deductions, and the complexity of your tax situation.

In general, if your deductions add up to more than the standard deduction, your total tax will be lower if you use Form 1040 and itemize your deductions. Taxpayers who earn more than $50,000 in taxable income must use Form 1040. Those with taxable income less than $50,000 may use any of the three forms. If you have no deductions or credits, less than $1,500 in interest income, and no dependents, use Form 1040EZ, the easiest form. However, if you qualify for any credits and deductions listed on Form 1040A, use that form. If you have enough deductions to benefit from itemizing, use Form 1040.

Where to Begin?

During the year, save all receipts and proofs of payment for your itemized deductions. You will need these receipts to prove the accuracy of your tax return if you are audited. Save all employee withholding records, such as your paycheck stubs. By January 31 you should receive your Form W-2 from each of your employers. Compare it with your records to check for accuracy. Any discrepancy between the Form W-2 and your records should be reported immediately to the employer and corrected.

It is wise to prepare your tax return early—as soon as you receive your Form W-2 and any Forms 1099, which report other income you received. Gather all other necessary information, including instruction booklets and last year's tax return as a model for preparing this year's return. If you have a refund coming, the sooner you file, the sooner you will receive it.

Once you have gathered all your information, prepare both the short and the long form to determine whether you can save money by itemizing deductions.

Even if you hire a professional tax preparer, you are responsible for supplying accurate and complete information. Hiring a tax preparer will *not* guarantee that you are paying the correct amount. You must check the form before you sign it. If you discover an error after the return has been filed, you may file an amended return (Form 1040X) to make corrections.

Save copies of your tax returns, together with all supporting evidence (receipts) and Forms W-2 and Form 1099, for six years.

You can choose to file your return electronically through the IRS e-file program. Instructions for electronic filing appear on the IRS Web site at www.irs.gov/efile, as shown in Figure 7-2 (page 154). This Web site also allows you to pay electronically using a debit card or a credit card. If the government owes you a refund, you can have the refund transferred to your bank account electronically. If you file electronically, be sure to print a copy of the tax return for your records.

▶ PREPARING YOUR INCOME TAX RETURN

You must complete the tax return in ink or typed with no errors or omissions. The booklets provided by the IRS have line-by-line instructions that explain each section of the form.

Net Nuggets

Having trouble making sense of taxes? Check out the IRS Tax Tutorials geared toward students at www.irs.gov/app/understandingTaxes. You'll find answers to frequently asked questions on topics such as wage and tip income, withholding, deductions, self-employment, and filing your taxes electronically.

Tax Preparation Software

Most professional tax preparers use a tax preparation computer program. You can use tax preparation software to do your own taxes if you like. Good software provides all the necessary forms and leads you through the process of filling out the forms. Most tax software also provides tips and additional information to help you identify all the deductions and credits you are allowed. Search the Internet to find information about different brands of tax software. Software producers usually provide a feature tour at their Web site.

Form 1040EZ

You may use Form 1040EZ if you are single or married and claim no dependents. Your taxable income must be less than $50,000. Line-by-line instructions for filling out Form 1040EZ are given on the back of the form. Highlights of the instructions are described in the following paragraphs.

 Internal Revenue Service IRS.gov

DEPARTMENT OF THE TREASURY

Home | Accessibility | Tax Stats | About IRS | Careers | FOIA | The Newsroom | Site Map | Español | Help

Search IRS Site for:
[_____] GO
Advanced Search

Search Forms and Publications for:
[_____] GO
Tips for successful searching

Home > **e-file**

information for:
Individuals
Businesses
Charities & Non-Profits
Government Entities
Tax Professionals
Retirement Plans

resources
Compliance & Enforcement

Individual e-file Program Overview

How to e-file. It's as easy as 1-2-3 !

Step 1 - Get all your tax information together! - You'll save time and won't have to stop in the middle of preparing your return to find a missing document. Here's what you'll need :

- Social Security numbers for yourself, your spouse, and any dependents.
- W-2 forms from all employers are required for yourself and your spouse
- 1099 forms for Dividends, Retirement, or other income, or any 1099 forms with Income Tax Withholding.
- Receipts for expenses for Itemized Deductions (Schedule A).
- Receipts and records for other income or expenses.
- Bank Account numbers (for a fast refund, or to pay electronically).
- Complete information on what records you need, and how long to keep your records.

Step 2 - Choose the method of e-filing that works for you:

- **Tax Professional**
- **Personal Computer**
- **Free File**
- **TeleFile** - If using TeleFile, follow the instructions in your TeleFile booklet. Complete the worksheet, then call TeleFile. It's EZ!

Step 3 - e-file it!

Figure 7-3 shows Form W-2 for Roberto Flores. Figure 7-4 shows his completed Form 1040EZ tax return. Roberto is single and claims one exemption. His wages are found on the W-2. Roberto earned $134 in interest on his savings account. No one else can claim him as a dependent. Follow along on Roberto's Form 1040EZ as you read the instructions below.

STEP 1: NAME, ADDRESS, AND SOCIAL SECURITY NUMBER
Fill in your name, address, and social security number. If you have filed a tax return in previous years, the IRS will supply a printed name and address label for you for this year's return. Stick this self-adhesive label in this place on the form rather than write your information.

Check the "Yes" box if you want $3 to go to the Presidential Election Campaign Fund. This is a fund established by Congress so that taxpayers can share in the costs of election campaigns. The $3 contribution will not increase your tax or reduce your refund.

figure **7-3**

a Control number	22222	Void ☐	**For Official Use Only** OMB No. 1545-0008		

b Employer identification number 93-899348488		**1** Wages, tips, other compensation $14,720.00	**2** Federal income tax withheld $1,501.00

c Employer's name, address, and ZIP code Blanton School District T-31 23855 SW 85th Portland, OR 97215-4562	**3** Social security wages $14,720.00	**4** Social security tax withheld $912.64

5 Medicare wages and tips $14,720.00 | **6** Medicare tax withheld $213.44

7 Social security tips | **8** Allocated tips

d Employee's social security number 465-84-3894	**9** Advance EIC payment	**10** Dependent care benefits

e Employee's first name and initial	Last name	**11** Nonqualified plans	**12a** See instructions for box 12

Roberto J. Flores
285 SW 28th Street, #8
Portland, OR 97214-4562

13 Statutory employee ☐ Retirement plan ☐ Third-party sick pay ☐

12b

14 Other

12c

12d

f Employee's address and ZIP code

15 State	Employer's state ID number	**16** State wages, tips, etc.	**17** State income tax	**18** Local wages, tips, etc.	**19** Local income tax	**20** Locality name
OR	2384762	$14,720.00	$946.00			

Form **W-2** **Wage and Tax Statement** 20— Department of the Treasury—Internal Revenue Service

STEP 2: REPORT INCOME

First, enter your total wages, salaries, and tips, as shown on your W-2 form(s). On Roberto's Form W-2, you can see that he earned $14,720. He entered this amount on line 1 of his Form 1040EZ.

Second, enter interest earned on savings accounts and any unemployment compensation you may have received. Roberto Flores recorded the $134 of interest he earned on his savings. Add these income figures to the earnings shown in line 1. The result is your adjusted gross income, line 4.

Next, you must indicate if you are claimed as a dependent on another person's tax return. If so, you will lose most or all of the standard deduction. If not, you can enter the total standard deduction and personal exemption allowed on the 1040EZ ($7,800 at this writing). Subtract this amount from adjusted gross income to obtain your taxable income, line 6.

STEP 3: COMPUTE TAX

On line 7, enter the total federal tax withheld, as shown on your W-2 form(s). This is the amount of tax you have already paid. To find out the total tax you are required to pay, look up your taxable income in

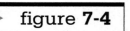 figure **7-4**   1040EZ TAX RETURN FOR ROBERTO FLORES

Form **1040EZ**	Department of the Treasuryó Internal Revenue Service **Income Tax Return for Single and Joint Filers With No Dependents** (99) **20—**	OMB No. 1545-0675

Label (See page 12.)
Use the IRS label. Otherwise, please print or type.

L A B E L   H E R E

Your first name and initial	Last name	Your social security number
Roberto J.	Flores	465 : 84 : 3894
If a joint return, spouse's first name and initial	Last name	Spouse's social security number

Home address (number and street). If you have a P.O. box, see page 12.
285 SW 28th Street   Apt. no. #8

City, town or post office, state, and ZIP code. If you have a foreign address, see page 12.
Portland, OR 97214-4562

▲ **Important!** ▲
You **must** enter your SSN(s) above.

Presidential Election Campaign (page 12) ▶

Note. Checking ì Yesî will not change your tax or reduce your refund.
Do you, or your spouse if a joint return, want $3 to go to this fund? . . . . . . ▶

	You		Spouse	
	☒Yes	☐No	☐Yes	☐No

Income

Attach Form(s) W-2 here.
Enclose, but do not attach, any payment.

1	Wages, salaries, and tips. This should be shown in box 1 of your Form(s) W-2. Attach your Form(s) W-2.	1	14,720 —
2	Taxable interest. If the total is over $1,500, you cannot use Form 1040EZ.	2	134 —
3	Unemployment compensation and Alaska Permanent Fund dividends (see page 14).	3	—
4	Add lines 1, 2, and 3. This is your **adjusted gross income.**	4	14,854 —

Note. You must check Yes or No.

5	Can your parents (or someone else) claim you on their return? **Yes.** ☐ Enter amount from worksheet on back. **No.** ☒ If **single,** enter $7,800. If **married filing jointly,** enter $15,600. See back for explanation.	5 7,800 —
6	Subtract line 5 from line 4. If line 5 is larger than line 4, enter -0-. This is your **taxable income.** ▶	6 7,054 —

Payments and tax

7	Federal income tax withheld from box 2 of your Form(s) W-2.	7 1,501 —
8	**Earned income credit (EIC).**	8
9	Add lines 7 and 8. These are your **total payments.** ▶	9 1,501 —
10	**Tax.** Use the amount on **line 6 above** to find your tax in the tax table on pages 24–28 of the booklet. Then, enter the tax from the table on this line.	10 708 —

Refund
Have it directly deposited! See page 19 and fill in 11b, 11c, and 11d.

11a	If line 9 is larger than line 10, subtract line 10 from line 9. This is your **refund.** ▶	11a 793 —
▶ b	Routing number 0 0 1 0 7 3 2 6 4 ▶ c Type: ☒ Checking ☐ Savings	
▶ d	Account number 4 1 1 2 0 3 6	

Amount you owe

12	If line 10 is larger than line 9, subtract line 9 from line 10. This is the **amount you owe.** For details on how to pay, see page 20. ▶	12

Third party designee

Do you want to allow another person to discuss this return with the IRS (see page 20)? ☐ **Yes.** Complete the following. ☐**No**

Designee's name ▶	Phone no. ▶ ( )	Personal identification number (PIN)

Sign here
Joint return? See page 11. Keep a copy for your records.

Under penalties of perjury, I declare that I have examined this return, and to the best of my knowledge and belief, it is true, correct, and accurately lists all amounts and sources of income I received during the tax year. Declaration of preparer (other than the taxpayer) is based on all information of which the preparer has any knowledge.

Your signature	Date	Your occupation	Daytime phone number
Roberto J. Flores	3/15/20—	mechanic	(555) 621-0052
Spouse's signature. If a joint return, **both** must sign.	Date	Spouse's occupation	

Paid preparer's use only

Preparer's signature ▶	Date	Check if self-employed ☐	Preparer's SSN or PTIN
Firm's name (or yours if self-employed), address, and ZIP code ▶		EIN Phone no. ( )	

For Disclosure, Privacy Act, and Paperwork Reduction Act Notice, see page 23.   Cat. No. 11329W   Form **1040EZ**

the tax table that comes with your return. It will look similar to the one in Figure 7-5. In the tax table in Figure 7-5, Roberto found that his taxable income of $7,054 fell within the range of $7,050–$7,100. In that row, he located his total tax liability of $708 in the "single" column.

STEP 4: REFUND OR AMOUNT OWED

If the amount of federal taxes withheld (the amount you already paid) is larger than your total tax (from the tax table), you will receive a refund. If you owe more tax than was withheld, you must pay the difference. Write your check to the United States Treasury and attach it to your return.

When Roberto subtracted his total tax of $708 from his taxes withheld of $1,501, the difference was $793. The amount of tax withheld was greater by $793 than the tax Roberto was required to pay, so he will receive a refund for that amount.

Roberto decided to have his refund deposited electronically into his checking account. His bank told him to look at the bottom of his checks. The first 9 numbers printed there are the routing number. The last 7 numbers are his account number. He entered these numbers in the Refund section of his tax form and checked the box for account type: Checking.

STEP 5: SIGN THE RETURN

Sign and date your tax return. Make sure your W-2 form(s) and check (if applicable) are attached to the completed return, and mail the return to the regional IRS office designated for your area.

Form 1040A

Individuals who earn less than $50,000 in taxable income can use Form 1040A. With Form 1040A, you can take deductions for individual retirement account (IRA) contributions and a tax credit for child-care expenses, if you qualify. Married people filing jointly with dependents may choose to file Form 1040A or Form 1040. Figures 7-6 and 7-7 show the Forms W-2 for Michael J. and Melissa B. Anderson. Figures 7-8A and 7-8B show their joint return using Form 1040A. Follow along on their Form 1040A as you read the instructions below.

STEP 1: NAME AND ADDRESS

Write the name, address, and social security number for each person filing the return. Michael and Melissa are filing a joint return, so they entered this information for both of them. If you receive a printed label from the IRS, use the label rather than write the information. Each person filing can elect to give or not give to the Presidential Election Campaign Fund.

figure 7-5

PART OF 1040EZ TAX TABLE

20— Tax Table

Example. Mr. Brown is single. His taxable income on line 6 of Form 1040EZ is $26,250. First, he finds the $26,250–26,300 income line. Next, he finds the "Single" column and reads down the column. The amount shown where the income line and filing status column meet → is $3,584. This is the tax amount he should enter on line 10 of Form 1040EZ.

At least	But less than	Single	Married filing jointly
26,200	26,250	3,576	3,219
26,250	26,300	(3,584)	3,226
26,300	26,350	3,591	3,234
26,350	26,400	3,599	3,241

If Form 1040EZ, line 6, is— / And you are—

At least	But less than	Single	Married filing jointly
0	5	0	0
5	15	1	1
15	25	2	2
25	50	4	4
50	75	6	6
75	100	9	9
100	125	11	11
125	150	14	14
150	175	16	16
175	200	19	19
200	225	21	21
225	250	24	24
250	275	26	26
275	300	29	29
300	325	31	31
325	350	34	34
350	375	36	36
375	400	39	39
400	425	41	41
425	450	44	44
450	475	46	46
475	500	49	49
500	525	51	51
525	550	54	54
550	575	56	56
575	600	59	59
600	625	61	61
625	650	64	64
650	675	66	66
675	700	69	69
700	725	71	71
725	750	74	74
750	775	76	76
775	800	79	79
800	825	81	81
825	850	84	84
850	875	86	86
875	900	89	89
900	925	91	91
925	950	94	94
950	975	96	96
975	1,000	99	99

1,000

At least	But less than	Single	Married filing jointly
1,000	1,025	101	101
1,025	1,050	104	104
1,050	1,075	106	106
1,075	1,100	109	109
1,100	1,125	111	111
1,125	1,150	114	114
1,150	1,175	116	116
1,175	1,200	119	119
1,200	1,225	121	121
1,225	1,250	124	124
1,250	1,275	126	126
1,275	1,300	129	129
1,300	1,325	131	131
1,325	1,350	134	134
1,350	1,375	136	136
1,375	1,400	139	139
1,400	1,425	141	141
1,425	1,450	144	144
1,450	1,475	146	146
1,475	1,500	149	149

At least	But less than	Single	Married filing jointly
1,500	1,525	151	151
1,525	1,550	154	154
1,550	1,575	156	156
1,575	1,600	159	159
1,600	1,625	161	161
1,625	1,650	164	164
1,650	1,675	166	166
1,675	1,700	169	169
1,700	1,725	171	171
1,725	1,750	174	174
1,750	1,775	176	176
1,775	1,800	179	179
1,800	1,825	181	181
1,825	1,850	184	184
1,850	1,875	186	186
1,875	1,900	189	189
1,900	1,925	191	191
1,925	1,950	194	194
1,950	1,975	196	196
1,975	2,000	199	199

2,000

At least	But less than	Single	Married filing jointly
2,000	2,025	201	201
2,025	2,050	204	204
2,050	2,075	206	206
2,075	2,100	209	209
2,100	2,125	211	211
2,125	2,150	214	214
2,150	2,175	216	216
2,175	2,200	219	219
2,200	2,225	221	221
2,225	2,250	224	224
2,250	2,275	226	226
2,275	2,300	229	229
2,300	2,325	231	231
2,325	2,350	234	234
2,350	2,375	236	236
2,375	2,400	239	239
2,400	2,425	241	241
2,425	2,450	244	244
2,450	2,475	246	246
2,475	2,500	249	249
2,500	2,525	251	251
2,525	2,550	254	254
2,550	2,575	256	256
2,575	2,600	259	259
2,600	2,625	261	261
2,625	2,650	264	264
2,650	2,675	266	266
2,675	2,700	269	269
2,700	2,725	271	271
2,725	2,750	274	274
2,750	2,775	276	276
2,775	2,800	279	279
2,800	2,825	281	281
2,825	2,850	284	284
2,850	2,875	286	286
2,875	2,900	289	289
2,900	2,925	291	291
2,925	2,950	294	294
2,950	2,975	296	296
2,975	3,000	299	299

3,000

At least	But less than	Single	Married filing jointly
3,000	3,050	303	303
3,050	3,100	308	308
3,100	3,150	313	313
3,150	3,200	318	318
3,200	3,250	323	323
3,250	3,300	328	328
3,300	3,350	333	333
3,350	3,400	338	338
3,400	3,450	343	343
3,450	3,500	348	348
3,500	3,550	353	353
3,550	3,600	358	358
3,600	3,650	363	363
3,650	3,700	368	368
3,700	3,750	373	373
3,750	3,800	378	378
3,800	3,850	383	383
3,850	3,900	388	388
3,900	3,950	393	393
3,950	4,000	398	398

4,000

At least	But less than	Single	Married filing jointly
4,000	4,050	403	403
4,050	4,100	408	408
4,100	4,150	413	413
4,150	4,200	418	418
4,200	4,250	423	423
4,250	4,300	428	428
4,300	4,350	433	433
4,350	4,400	438	438
4,400	4,450	443	443
4,450	4,500	448	448
4,500	4,550	453	453
4,550	4,600	458	458
4,600	4,650	463	463
4,650	4,700	468	468
4,700	4,750	473	473
4,750	4,800	478	478
4,800	4,850	483	483
4,850	4,900	488	488
4,900	4,950	493	493
4,950	5,000	498	498

5,000

At least	But less than	Single	Married filing jointly
5,000	5,050	503	503
5,050	5,100	508	508
5,100	5,150	513	513
5,150	5,200	518	518
5,200	5,250	523	523
5,250	5,300	528	528
5,300	5,350	533	533
5,350	5,400	538	538
5,400	5,450	543	543
5,450	5,500	548	548
5,500	5,550	553	553
5,550	5,600	558	558
5,600	5,650	563	563
5,650	5,700	568	568
5,700	5,750	573	573
5,750	5,800	578	578
5,800	5,850	583	583
5,850	5,900	588	588
5,900	5,950	593	593
5,950	6,000	598	598

6,000

At least	But less than	Single	Married filing jointly
6,000	6,050	603	603
6,050	6,100	608	608
6,100	6,150	613	613
6,150	6,200	618	618
6,200	6,250	623	623
6,250	6,300	628	628
6,300	6,350	633	633
6,350	6,400	638	638
6,400	6,450	643	643
6,450	6,500	648	648
6,500	6,550	653	653
6,550	6,600	658	658
6,600	6,650	663	663
6,650	6,700	668	668
6,700	6,750	673	673
6,750	6,800	678	678
6,800	6,850	683	683
6,850	6,900	688	688
6,900	6,950	693	693
6,950	7,000	698	698

7,000

At least	But less than	Single	Married filing jointly
7,000	7,050	703	703
7,050	7,100	708	708
7,100	7,150	713	713
7,150	7,200	719	718
7,200	7,250	726	723
7,250	7,300	734	728
7,300	7,350	741	733
7,350	7,400	749	738
7,400	7,450	756	743
7,450	7,500	764	748
7,500	7,550	771	753
7,550	7,600	779	758
7,600	7,650	786	763
7,650	7,700	794	768
7,700	7,750	801	773
7,750	7,800	809	778
7,800	7,850	816	783
7,850	7,900	824	788
7,900	7,950	831	793
7,950	8,000	839	798

8,000

At least	But less than	Single	Married filing jointly
8,000	8,050	846	803
8,050	8,100	854	808
8,100	8,150	861	813
8,150	8,200	869	818
8,200	8,250	876	823
8,250	8,300	884	828
8,300	8,350	891	833
8,350	8,400	899	838
8,400	8,450	906	843
8,450	8,500	914	848
8,500	8,550	921	853
8,550	8,600	929	858
8,600	8,650	936	863
8,650	8,700	944	868
8,700	8,750	951	873
8,750	8,800	959	878
8,800	8,850	966	883
8,850	8,900	974	888
8,900	8,950	981	893
8,950	9,000	989	898

FORM W-2 FOR MELISSA ANDERSON

figure **7-6** ◄

a Control number	22222	Void ☐	For Official Use Only OMB No. 1545-0008	

b Employer identification number 92-186848		**1** Wages, tips, other compensation $12,811.40	**2** Federal income tax withheld $611.00
c Employer's name, address, and ZIP code A&W Welding Supply 85 West Bensington Blvd. Chicago, IL 60615-2358		**3** Social security wages $12,811.40	**4** Social security tax withheld $794.31
		5 Medicare wages and tips $12,811.40	**6** Medicare tax withheld $185.77
		7 Social security tips	**8** Allocated tips
d Employee's social security number 411-86-3214		**9** Advance EIC payment	**10** Dependent care benefits
e Employee's first name and initial Last name		**11** Nonqualified plans	**12a** See instructions for box 12
Melissa B. Anderson 312 East 34th Street Chicago, IL 60604-5214		**13** Statutory employee ☐ Retirement plan ☐ Third-party sick pay ☐	**12b**
		14 Other	**12c**
			12d
f Employee's address and ZIP code			

15 State Employer's state ID number IL 33-261	**16** State wages, tips, etc. $12,811.40	**17** State income tax $820.00	**18** Local wages, tips, etc.	**19** Local income tax	**20** Locality name

Form **W-2** Wage and Tax Statement   20—   Department of the Treasury—Internal Revenue Service

FORM W-2 FOR MICHAEL ANDERSON

figure **7-7** ◄

a Control number	22222	Void ☐	For Official Use Only OMB No. 1545-0008	

b Employer identification number 91-4813141		**1** Wages, tips, other compensation $11,028.60	**2** Federal income tax withheld $591.00
c Employer's name, address, and ZIP code A Art Studios 48 East 11th Avenue Des Plaines, IL 60601-3132		**3** Social security wages $11,028.60	**4** Social security tax withheld $683.77
		5 Medicare wages and tips $11,028.60	**6** Medicare tax withheld $159.91
		7 Social security tips	**8** Allocated tips
d Employee's social security number 323-40-6128		**9** Advance EIC payment	**10** Dependent care benefits
e Employee's first name and initial Last name		**11** Nonqualified plans	**12a** See instructions for box 12
Michael J. Anderson 312 East 34th Street Chicago, IL 60604-5214		**13** Statutory employee ☐ Retirement plan ☐ Third-party sick pay ☐	**12b**
		14 Other	**12c**
			12d
f Employee's address and ZIP code			

15 State Employer's state ID number IL 226421	**16** State wages, tips, etc. $11,028.60	**17** State income tax $706.00	**18** Local wages, tips, etc.	**19** Local income tax	**20** Locality name

Form **W-2** Wage and Tax Statement   20—   Department of the Treasury—Internal Revenue Service

Form
1040A

Department of the Treasury—Internal Revenue Service
U.S. Individual Income Tax Return (99) **20—**   IRS Use Only—Do not write or staple in this space.

OMB No. 1545-0085

Label
(See page 19.)

Use the IRS label.
Otherwise, please print or type.

Your first name and initial: Melissa B.   Last name: Anderson

Your social security number
411 : 86 : 3214

If a joint return, spouse's first name and initial: Michael J.   Last name: Anderson

Spouse's social security number
323 : 40 : 6128

Home address (number and street). If you have a P.O. box, see page 20.
312 East 34th Street   Apt. no.

City, town or post office, state, and ZIP code. If you have a foreign address, see page 20.
Chicago, IL 60604-5214

▲ **Important!** ▲
You **must** enter your SSN(s) above.

Presidential Election Campaign
(See page 20.)

Note. Checking "Yes" will not change your tax or reduce your refund.
Do you, or your spouse if filing a joint return, want $3 to go to this fund? . . . ▶

	You	Spouse
	☒Yes ☐No	☒Yes ☐No

Filing status
Check only one box.

1 ☐ Single
2 ☒ Married filing jointly (even if only one had income)
3 ☐ Married filing separately. Enter spouse's SSN above and full name here. ▶
4 ☐ Head of household (with qualifying person). (See page 20.) If the qualifying person is a child but not your dependent, enter this child's name here. ▶
5 ☐ Qualifying widow(er) with dependent child (See page 21.)

Exemptions

6a ☒ **Yourself.** If your parent (or someone else) can claim you as a dependent on his or her tax return, **do not** check box 6a.
 b ☒ **Spouse**

If more than six dependents, see page 21.

c **Dependents:**

(1) First name Last name	(2) Dependent's social security number	(3) Dependent's relationship to you	(4) ✓if qualifying child for child tax credit (see page 23)
William Anderson	316 : 84 : 2915	son	☐
Diane Anderson	382 : 38 : 4814	daughter	☐
	: :		☐
	: :		☐
	: :		☐
	: :		☐

No. of boxes checked on 6a and 6b: **2**

No. of children on 6c who:
• lived with you: **2**
• did not live with you due to divorce or separation (see page 23)

Dependents on 6c not entered above

d Total number of exemptions claimed.

Add numbers on lines above: **4**

Income

Attach Form(s) W-2 here. Also attach Form(s) 1099-R if tax was withheld.

If you did not get a W-2, see page 24.

Enclose, but do not attach, any payment.

7	Wages, salaries, tips, etc. Attach Form(s) W-2.	7	23,840 —
8a	**Taxable** interest. Attach Schedule 1 if required.	8a	284 —
b	**Tax-exempt** interest. **Do not** include on line 8a. 8b		
9a	Ordinary dividends. Attach Schedule 1 if required.	9a	168 —
b	Qualified dividends (see page 25). 9b		
10a	Capital gain distributions (see page 25).	10a	—
b	Post-May 5 capital gain distributions (see page 25). 10b		
11a	IRA distributions. 11a	11b Taxable amount (see page 25).	11b —
12a	Pensions and annuities. 12a	12b Taxable amount (see page 26).	12b —
13	Unemployment compensation and Alaska Permanent Fund dividends.	13	—
14a	Social security benefits. 14a	14b Taxable amount (see page 28).	14b —
15	Add lines 7 through 14b (far right column). This is your **total income.** ▶	15	24,292 —

Adjusted gross income

16	Educator expenses (see page 28).	16	
17	IRA deduction (see page 28).	17	500 —
18	Student loan interest deduction (see page 31).	18	500 —
19	Tuition and fees deduction (see page 31).	19	
20	Add lines 16 through 19. These are your **total adjustments.**	20	1,000 —
21	Subtract line 20 from line 15. This is your **adjusted gross income.** ▶	21	23,292 —

figure **7-8B** ◄◄

Form 1040A (20—)   Page **2**

Tax, credits, and payments	**22**	Enter the amount from line 21 (adjusted gross income).	22	23,292 —

23a Check if: ☐ **You** were born before January 2, 1939, ☐ Blind **Total boxes**
       ☐ **Spouse** was born before January 2, 1939, ☐ Blind **checked** ► 23a [ ]

b If you are married filing separately and your spouse itemizes deductions, see page 32 and check here ► 23b ☐

Standard Deduction for—

24	Enter your **standard deduction** (see left margin).	24	9,500 —
25	Subtract line 24 from line 22. If line 24 is more than line 22, enter -0-.	25	13,792 —
26	Multiply $3,050 by the total number of exemptions claimed on line 6d.	26	12,200 —
27	Subtract line 26 from line 25. If line 26 is more than line 25, enter -0-. This is your **taxable income.** ► 27	27	1,592 —

• People who checked any box on line 23a or 23b **or** who can be claimed as a dependent, see page 32.

• All others:

Single or Married filing separately, $4,750

Married filing jointly or Qualifying widow(er), $9,500

Head of household, $7,000

28	**Tax,** including any alternative minimum tax (see page 33).	28	159 —
29	Credit for child and dependent care expenses. Attach Schedule 2.	29	
30	Credit for the elderly or the disabled. Attach Schedule 3.	30	
31	Education credits. Attach Form 8863.	31	
32	Retirement savings contributions credit. Attach Form 8880.	32	
33	Child tax credit (see page 37).	33	
34	Adoption credit. Attach Form 8839.	34	
35	Add lines 29 through 34. These are your **total credits.**	35	
36	Subtract line 35 from line 28. If line 35 is more than line 28, enter -0-.	36	
37	Advance earned income credit payments from Form(s) W-2.	37	
38	Add lines 36 and 37. This is your **total tax.** ► 38	38	159 —
39	Federal income tax withheld from Forms W-2 and 1099.	39	1,202 —
40	2003 estimated tax payments and amount applied from 2002 return.	40	

If you have a qualifying child, attach Schedule EIC.

41	**Earned income credit (EIC).**	41	
42	Additional child tax credit. Attach Form 8812.	42	
43	Add lines 39 through 42. These are your **total payments.** ► 43	43	1,202 —

Refund	**44**	If line 43 is more than line 38, subtract line 38 from line 43. This is the amount you **overpaid.**	44	1,043 —

Direct deposit? See page 50 and fill in 45b, 45c, and 45d.

45a Amount of line 44 you want **refunded to you.** ► 45a 1,043 —

► **b** Routing number [ ] ► **c** Type: ☐ Checking ☐ Savings

► **d** Account number [ ]

46 Amount of line 44 you want **applied to your 2004 estimated tax.** 46

Amount you owe	**47**	**Amount you owe.** Subtract line 43 from line 38. For details on how to pay, see page 51. ► 47	
	48	Estimated tax penalty (see page 52). 48	

Third party designee

Do you want to allow another person to discuss this return with the IRS (see page 52)? ☐ **Yes.** Complete the following. ☐ **No**

Designee's name	Phone no. ► ( )	Personal identification number (PIN) ► [ ]

Sign here

Joint return? See page 20.

Keep a copy for your records.

Under penalties of perjury, I declare that I have examined this return and accompanying schedules and statements, and to the best of my knowledge and belief, they are true, correct, and accurately list all amounts and sources of income I received during the tax year. Declaration of preparer (other than the taxpayer) is based on all information of which the preparer has any knowledge.

Your signature	Date	Your occupation	Daytime phone number
Melissa B. Anderson	4/15/20—	student/cashier	(555) 273-2211
Spouse's signature. If a joint return, **both** must sign.	Date	Spouse's occupation	
Michael J Anderson	4/15/20—	student/clerk	

Paid preparer's use only

Preparer's signature ►		Date	Check if self-employed ☐	Preparer's SSN or PTIN
Firm's name (or yours if self-employed), address, and ZIP code ►			EIN	
			Phone no. ( )	

STEP 2: FILING STATUS

In this section, you select your tax filing status. You must fill in your spouse's name and social security number if filing separately, names of dependents if head of household, and year spouse died, if filing as a widow(er).

STEP 3: EXEMPTIONS

In the Exemptions section, claim yourself and your spouse if you are filing jointly, and enter the names and social security numbers of your dependents. Total your exemptions on line 6d.

STEP 4: TOTAL INCOME

On line 7, enter wages, salaries, tips, and other income as shown on your Form W-2. The Andersons, filing jointly, entered the total earnings from their two Forms W-2.

You must also report taxable interest and dividend income. If you received over $1,500 in interest, you must list the name of each payer and the amount in Part I of Schedule 1 (see Figure 7-9). If you received more than $1,500 in dividends on your investments, you must list each payer and amount in Part II of Schedule 1. Then transfer the total interest and dividend amounts from Schedule 1 to lines 8a and 9a on Form 1040A. The Andersons did not earn more than $1,500 in interest or in dividends, so they did not use Schedule 1. However, they still had to report their amounts on Form 1040A.

If you received any tax-exempt interest, you would list it on line 8b, even though you would not have to pay tax on it. The rest of the Income section of Form 1040A requires you to report the taxable amount of any money received from IRAs, pensions, and social security benefits, as well as any unemployment compensation you received.

After listing income received from all sources, you would add them up to determine total income for line 15 of Form 1040A.

STEP 5: ADJUSTED GROSS INCOME

You can deduct contributions to an individual retirement account (IRA) and other expenses listed in this section of the form. Rules for eligibility are explained in the instruction booklet. If both you and your spouse are eligible, you would add both IRA contributions together and enter the total on line 17, as the Andersons have done in Figure 7-8A. You would then subtract the total from gross income to determine your adjusted gross income (line 21).

STEP 6: TAXABLE INCOME

Next you would compute your taxable income, as shown in Figure 7-8B. First, copy your adjusted gross income from the bottom of the first page of the form to the top of the second page. Then check if you or your spouse is 65 or older or blind or if you are married filing separately.

figure **7-9** ◄ ◄

Schedule 1
(Form 1040A)

Department of the Treasury—Internal Revenue Service

**Interest and Ordinary Dividends
for Form 1040A Filers**   (99)

20—

OMB No. 1545-0085

Name(s) shown on Form 1040A

Your social security number

Part I **Interest** (See back of schedule and the instructions for Form 1040A, line 8a.)	**Note.** If you received a Form 1099-INT, Form 1099-OID, or substitute statement from a brokerage firm, enter the firm's name and the total interest shown on that form.		
	1 List name of payer. If any interest is from a seller-financed mortgage and the buyer used the property as a personal residence, see back of schedule and list this interest first. Also, show that buyer's social security number and address.		Amount
		1	
	2 Add the amounts on line 1.	2	
	3 Excludable interest on series EE and I U.S. savings bonds issued after 1989. Attach Form 8815.	3	
	4 Subtract line 3 from line 2. Enter the result here and on Form 1040A, line 8a.	4	

Part II **Ordinary dividends** (See back of schedule and the instructions for Form 1040A, line 9a.)	**Note.** If you received a Form 1099-DIV or substitute statement from a brokerage firm, enter the firm's name and the ordinary dividends shown on that form.		
	5 List name of payer.		Amount
		5	
	6 Add the amounts on line 5. Enter the total here and on Form 1040A, line 9a.	6	

Then enter the standard deduction stated on the form for your filing status. In Figure 7-8B, the Andersons entered $9,500 because they are married filing jointly.

Subtract the standard deduction from adjusted gross income, and enter the result on line 25. Then multiply the number of exemptions claimed by the amount allowed for each exemption. Line 26 of the form shows the amount per exemption for this tax year as $3,050. On the first page of their form, the Andersons had claimed 4 exemptions, so they multiplied $3,050 by 4 to arrive at their $12,200 deduction. Subtract the result from adjusted gross income to determine taxable income for line 27.

STEP 7: TAX, CREDITS, AND PAYMENTS

For this section of Form 1040A, find your tax by looking up your taxable income in the tax table in your instruction booklet. Figure 7-10 shows a recent tax table for use with Form 1040A. The Andersons had a taxable income of $1,592. In Figure 7-10, this income falls in the range $1,575–$1,600. Reading across the row to the column marked "Married filing jointly," they found that their tax was $159. They entered this number in line 28 of their form.

In this section of the form, you may claim any credit due for child-care expenses. You would complete another form (Schedule 2) to determine the amount of the credit. After recording all credits for which you qualify, you would record the total in line 35. Then, subtract total credits from the tax in line 28 to determine total tax for line 38. The Andersons did not qualify for any credits, so their total tax in line 38 is the same as the tax shown in line 28.

Finally, enter the amount of federal income tax withheld, as shown on your Form W-2, which you will attach to the tax return. For the Andersons, the amount withheld was the total of the federal withholdings listed on their two Forms W-2. Their total was $1,202. If you qualify for the earned income credit (EIC), you would enter it in line 41. It would then be included as part of the total payments made in line 43.

STEP 8: REFUND OR AMOUNT OWED

If the total payments in line 43 exceed the total tax shown in line 38, the difference is your refund. But if you have more total tax than the amounts already paid, you owe taxes. You would record the amount you owe in line 47 and attach a check for that amount. The Andersons recorded their $1,043 refund on line 44. They recorded it again on line 45a to specify that they want the full amount refunded to them rather than applied to next year's taxes.

figure **7-10**

20—
Tax Table

Example. Mr. and Mrs. Green are filing a joint return. Their taxable income on Form 1040A, line 27, is $23,250. First, they find the $23,250–23,300 taxable income line. Next, they find the column for married filing jointly and read down the column. The amount shown where the taxable income line and filing status column meet is $2,776. This is the tax amount they should enter on Form 1040A, line 28.

Sample Table

At least	But less than	Single	Married filing jointly*	Married filing separately	Head of a household
			Your tax is—		
23,200	23,250	3,126	2,769	3,126	2,974
23,250	23,300	3,134	2,776	3,134	2,981
23,300	23,350	3,141	2,784	3,141	2,989
23,350	23,400	3,149	2,791	3,149	2,996

If Form 1040A, line 27, is— / And you are—

At least	But less than	Single	Married filing jointly*	Married filing separately	Head of a household
			Your tax is—		
0	5	0	0	0	0
5	15	1	1	1	1
15	25	2	2	2	2
25	50	4	4	4	4
50	75	6	6	6	6
75	100	9	9	9	9
100	125	11	11	11	11
125	150	14	14	14	14
150	175	16	16	16	16
175	200	19	19	19	19
200	225	21	21	21	21
225	250	24	24	24	24
250	275	26	26	26	26
275	300	29	29	29	29
300	325	31	31	31	31
325	350	34	34	34	34
350	375	36	36	36	36
375	400	39	39	39	39
400	425	41	41	41	41
425	450	44	44	44	44
450	475	46	46	46	46
475	500	49	49	49	49
500	525	51	51	51	51
525	550	54	54	54	54
550	575	56	56	56	56
575	600	59	59	59	59
600	625	61	61	61	61
625	650	64	64	64	64
650	675	66	66	66	66
675	700	69	69	69	69
700	725	71	71	71	71
725	750	74	74	74	74
750	775	76	76	76	76
775	800	79	79	79	79
800	825	81	81	81	81
825	850	84	84	84	84
850	875	86	86	86	86
875	900	89	89	89	89
900	925	91	91	91	91
925	950	94	94	94	94
950	975	96	96	96	96
975	1,000	99	99	99	99

1,000

At least	But less than	Single	Married filing jointly*	Married filing separately	Head of a household
1,000	1,025	101	101	101	101
1,025	1,050	104	104	104	104
1,050	1,075	106	106	106	106
1,075	1,100	109	109	109	109
1,100	1,125	111	111	111	111
1,125	1,150	114	114	114	114
1,150	1,175	116	116	116	116
1,175	1,200	119	119	119	119
1,200	1,225	121	121	121	121
1,225	1,250	124	124	124	124
1,250	1,275	126	126	126	126
1,275	1,300	129	129	129	129

If Form 1040A, line 27, is— / And you are—

At least	But less than	Single	Married filing jointly*	Married filing separately	Head of a household
			Your tax is—		
1,300	1,325	131	131	131	131
1,325	1,350	134	134	134	134
1,350	1,375	136	136	136	136
1,375	1,400	139	139	139	139
1,400	1,425	141	141	141	141
1,425	1,450	144	144	144	144
1,450	1,475	146	146	146	146
1,475	1,500	149	149	149	149
1,500	1,525	151	151	151	151
1,525	1,550	154	154	154	154
1,550	1,575	156	156	156	156
1,575	1,600	159	159	159	159
1,600	1,625	161	161	161	161
1,625	1,650	164	164	164	164
1,650	1,675	166	166	166	166
1,675	1,700	169	169	169	169
1,700	1,725	171	171	171	171
1,725	1,750	174	174	174	174
1,750	1,775	176	176	176	176
1,775	1,800	179	179	179	179
1,800	1,825	181	181	181	181
1,825	1,850	184	184	184	184
1,850	1,875	186	186	186	186
1,875	1,900	189	189	189	189
1,900	1,925	191	191	191	191
1,925	1,950	194	194	194	194
1,950	1,975	196	196	196	196
1,975	2,000	199	199	199	199

2,000

At least	But less than	Single	Married filing jointly*	Married filing separately	Head of a household
2,000	2,025	201	201	201	201
2,025	2,050	204	204	204	204
2,050	2,075	206	206	206	206
2,075	2,100	209	209	209	209
2,100	2,125	211	211	211	211
2,125	2,150	214	214	214	214
2,150	2,175	216	216	216	216
2,175	2,200	219	219	219	219
2,200	2,225	221	221	221	221
2,225	2,250	224	224	224	224
2,250	2,275	226	226	226	226
2,275	2,300	229	229	229	229
2,300	2,325	231	231	231	231
2,325	2,350	234	234	234	234
2,350	2,375	236	236	236	236
2,375	2,400	239	239	239	239
2,400	2,425	241	241	241	241
2,425	2,450	244	244	244	244
2,450	2,475	246	246	246	246
2,475	2,500	249	249	249	249
2,500	2,525	251	251	251	251
2,525	2,550	254	254	254	254
2,550	2,575	256	256	256	256
2,575	2,600	259	259	259	259
2,600	2,625	261	261	261	261
2,625	2,650	264	264	264	264
2,650	2,675	266	266	266	266
2,675	2,700	269	269	269	269

If Form 1040A, line 27, is— / And you are—

At least	But less than	Single	Married filing jointly*	Married filing separately	Head of a household
			Your tax is—		
2,700	2,725	271	271	271	271
2,725	2,750	274	274	274	274
2,750	2,775	276	276	276	276
2,775	2,800	279	279	279	279
2,800	2,825	281	281	281	281
2,825	2,850	284	284	284	284
2,850	2,875	286	286	286	286
2,875	2,900	289	289	289	289
2,900	2,925	291	291	291	291
2,925	2,950	294	294	294	294
2,950	2,975	296	296	296	296
2,975	3,000	299	299	299	299

3,000

At least	But less than	Single	Married filing jointly*	Married filing separately	Head of a household
3,000	3,050	303	303	303	303
3,050	3,100	308	308	308	308
3,100	3,150	313	313	313	313
3,150	3,200	318	318	318	318
3,200	3,250	323	323	323	323
3,250	3,300	328	328	328	328
3,300	3,350	333	333	333	333
3,350	3,400	338	338	338	338
3,400	3,450	343	343	343	343
3,450	3,500	348	348	348	348
3,500	3,550	353	353	353	353
3,550	3,600	358	358	358	358
3,600	3,650	363	363	363	363
3,650	3,700	368	368	368	368
3,700	3,750	373	373	373	373
3,750	3,800	378	378	378	378
3,800	3,850	383	383	383	383
3,850	3,900	388	388	388	388
3,900	3,950	393	393	393	393
3,950	4,000	398	398	398	398

4,000

At least	But less than	Single	Married filing jointly*	Married filing separately	Head of a household
4,000	4,050	403	403	403	403
4,050	4,100	408	408	408	408
4,100	4,150	413	413	413	413
4,150	4,200	418	418	418	418
4,200	4,250	423	423	423	423
4,250	4,300	428	428	428	428
4,300	4,350	433	433	433	433
4,350	4,400	438	438	438	438
4,400	4,450	443	443	443	443
4,450	4,500	448	448	448	448
4,500	4,550	453	453	453	453
4,550	4,600	458	458	458	458
4,600	4,650	463	463	463	463
4,650	4,700	468	468	468	468
4,700	4,750	473	473	473	473
4,750	4,800	478	478	478	478
4,800	4,850	483	483	483	483
4,850	4,900	488	488	488	488
4,900	4,950	493	493	493	493
4,950	5,000	498	498	498	498

(Continued on page 59)

* This column must also be used by a qualifying widow(er).

STEP 9: SIGNATURE

In this section, both spouses must sign and date the joint return, even though only one may have earned income. Anyone who was paid to prepare your tax return for you also must sign and date the return.

✓Check Your Understanding

1. Who is eligible to use Form 1040EZ to file their income taxes?

2. Who is eligible to use Form 1040A to file their income taxes?

3. Who is required to use Form 1040 to file their income taxes?

Chapter Assessment

7.1
* The government collects money, or revenue, from citizens and businesses to spend as specified by Congress.
* As income grows, progressive taxes take a larger share of income and regressive taxes take a smaller share.
* Proportional or flat taxes take the same percentage regardless of income.
* The IRS is the government agency in charge of collecting taxes, enforcing tax laws, and supplying information to help taxpayers prepare their tax returns.
* The income tax system is graduated. Different tax rates apply to different income ranges.

7.2
* Gross income consists of taxable income received from all sources.
* To determine taxable income, subtract adjustments, deductions, and exemptions from gross income.
* Tax deductions are subtracted from the income used to figure the tax. Tax credits are subtracted from the tax owed.
* File the short form, 1040EZ, if your income is less than $50,000 and you have no dependents.
* File Form 1040A if you do not have enough deductions to itemize and have less than $50,000 of income.
* If the amount withheld from your paychecks exceeds your total tax, you will receive a refund. If the amount withheld is less than your total tax, you must pay the difference when you file your tax return.

Directions

Can you find the definition for each of the following terms used in Chapter 7?

adjusted gross income	proportional taxes
alimony	regressive taxes
audit	revenue
child support	standard deduction
deductions	tax brackets
exemption	tax credit
gross income	tax evasion
itemize	taxable income
progressive taxes	

1. Money collected by the government through taxes.

2. Taxes that take a larger share of income as the amount of income grows.

3. Taxes for which the rate stays the same regardless of income; also called flat taxes.

4. Taxes that take a smaller share of income as the amount of income grows.

5. Stated amount taxpayers may subtract from adjusted gross income instead of itemizing their deductions.

6. Income ranges to which different tax rates apply.

7. Willful failure to pay taxes.

8. The process of listing allowable deductions on a tax return.

9. An amount taxpayers may subtract from their income for each person who depends on their income to live.

10. All the taxable income received during the year, including wages, tips, salaries, interest, dividends, alimony, and unemployment compensation.

11. Gross income minus allowed adjustments.

12. Money paid to a former spouse to support dependent children.

13. Money paid to support a former spouse.

14. Expenses the law allows taxpayers to subtract from their adjusted gross income to determine their taxable income.

15. Income on which you will pay tax.

16. An examination of a tax return by the IRS.

17. An amount subtracted directly from the tax owed.

REVIEW FACTS AND IDEAS

1. What is the United States government's largest source of revenue?

2. List five other taxes providing government revenue besides income taxes.

3. Describe the three basic types of taxes.

4. List three services provided by the IRS.

5. What is the purpose of the IRS?

6. List at least five services the government provides for all citizens from taxes collected.

7. Who has the ability to levy taxes on the citizens of the United States?

8. What is meant by a tax system based on voluntary compliance?

9. What can happen to you if you deliberately do not file your tax return and pay taxes due?

10. List five types of income that are taxable.

11. How is child support different from alimony in terms of taxation?

12. Explain the standard deduction and when you should itemize.

13. When must you file your federal income tax return? Why?

14. Under what circumstances would you file the long Form 1040 tax return?

15. Why should you file your tax return early when you expect a refund?

16. What should you do if you discover an error after you have filed your tax return?

17. If you file electronically, how do you pay the tax you owe?

18. If you check the "Yes" box on your return to contribute to the Presidential Election Campaign Fund, does it increase your taxes by $3?

APPLY YOUR KNOWLEDGE

1. Explain the need for taxes in this country. How does everyone benefit from taxes?

2. Explain how new federal taxes are imposed.

3. How does your filing status affect the amount of taxes you will pay?

4. How does the number of exemptions claimed affect the amount of taxes you will pay?

5. What are deductible expenses?

6. Which would reduce your income tax more—a $300 tax deduction or a $300 tax credit? Explain.

7. Search the Internet for a tax calculator. Some calculators figure the income taxes you would pay if our country had a flat tax. Others calculate taxes based on today's system and rates. If you have a job, enter numbers based on your earnings. Estimate any numbers you don't have. Then enter different income levels to see how the tax changes as income rises.

8. What must you do if you are married and wish to deduct charitable contributions on your tax return?

9. Visit www.irs.gov, follow the link to Forms and Publications, and download this year's Form 1040EZ and instruction booklet. Fill out the form using estimates if you don't know the real numbers for yourself. Use the tax tables in the booklet to find your tax obligation based on your estimates.

10. Many people believe that someday we will all file our income taxes electronically. Go to the IRS e-file site at www.irs.gov/efile and find out how to file taxes electronically. Write a one-page paper describing the process.

→ Solve Problems ⊕ Explore Issues

1. Acquire a copy of Form 1040EZ. Prepare a tax return for Tomeka Hunt. Use the tax table in Figure 7-5 and the following information:

   > Tomeka M. Hunt (social security number 541-33-9892)
   > 54 Center Street
   > San Francisco, CA 96214-3627

   Tomeka is a part-time engineer. She wants $3 to go to the Presidential Election Campaign Fund. She is single and claims only herself as an exemption. Tomeka's salary is $16,200, plus interest of $155. No one else claims her as a dependent, and she had $3,660 in federal taxes withheld.

2. Using Form 1040A and the tax table in Figure 7-10, calculate the total tax of Mack R. Rueoff, a part-time auto mechanic. Mack's gross income is $13,255. He has a $1,000 IRA deduction, claims the standard deduction, and had $350 in federal taxes withheld. He is single and is entitled to one exemption. Based on this information and the Figure 7-10 tax table, how much does Mack owe, or how much is his refund?

3. Using Form 1040A and the tax table in Figure 7-10, calculate the total tax of Yi Chang, a part-time teacher. Yi's wages totaled $12,201; interest income, $190; tax-exempt interest, $200. He has an IRA contribution of $500, claims the standard deduction, and had $520 in federal taxes withheld from his wages. He is married filing separately and claims only himself as an exemption. How much does Yi owe in taxes, or how much is his refund?

4. Acquire a copy of Form 1040A and Schedule 1 to prepare a joint tax return for Mell and Janis Saperstein.

Mell K. and Janis B. Saperstein
(SS#s 895-10-9008, 485-01-9089)
2450 West 18th Avenue
Dallas, TX 75201-7242

Mell is a construction worker, and Janis is a preschool teacher. They both want to contribute $3 to the Presidential Election Campaign Fund. Married, filing jointly, Mell and Janis have three dependent children who live with them: Mark J. Saperstein, social security number 354-58-6102; Julia C. Saperstein, social security number 300-92-7871; and Andrew H. Saperstein, social security number 291-61-4012. Mell and Janis each contributed $2,000 to IRAs. Mell's and Janis's combined incomes totaled $30,400. They had a total federal tax of $3,672 withheld. Mell and Janis had taxable interest income of $1,400: First National Bank, $300; interest on a private loan to J. Smith, $600; certificate of deposit at State Savings & Loan, $500. Tax-exempt interest income was $400. Dividend income amounted to $1,100: $411 from CDK stock, $621 from Investors' Mutual Fund, Inc., and $68 from I.P.Q. Manufacturing Co. Use the tax table in Figure 7-10.

*For related activities and links, point your browser to **www.mypf.swlearning.com***

Budgets and Financial Records

TERMS TO KNOW

disposable income	assets	negotiable instrument
financial plan	liabilities	co-signer
budget	net worth	warranty
fixed expenses	contract	spreadsheet
variable expenses	consideration	database

Consider This. . .

Rania has a part-time job, attends school six hours a day, and participates in two after-school sports. She no longer receives a monthly allowance from her parents. She pays for all of her own clothes, gas, insurance, and entertainment. Last year, she was able to save over $600.

"How do you do it?" asked her friend JoAnn. "I work more hours than you do, my parents pay for my clothes and most of my expenses, and I still don't have any money left over for entertainment. I didn't save a dime last year!"

"I have a budget," said Rania. "Every time I get paid, I put aside money for savings. I know how much I spend on everything I buy. Keeping a good record of income and expenses helps me plan better, so I don't run out of money. That doesn't mean I buy anything I want, but it does mean that I know how much I can spend, so I can stretch my money to cover as many things as possible."

Budgeting and Record Keeping

Goals
- **Describe and prepare personal budgets.**
- **Explain the purpose of record keeping.**
- **Prepare a net worth statement and a personal property inventory.**

▶ IMPORTANCE OF FINANCIAL PLANNING

Do you have unlimited resources to buy all the things you want? Some people do, but if you are like most Americans, to achieve financial success you will have to plan and work for it. Budgeting and maintaining financial records are a significant part of financial planning. They provide the road map to financial security. Budgeting is the first step.

Disposable income is the money you have left to spend or save after taxes have been paid. In order to use this income to your best advantage, you need a financial plan.

All the money you receive is spent, saved, or invested. You may spend it for things you need or want, save it for future needs, or invest it to earn more money. A **financial plan** is a set of goals for spending, saving, and investing the money you earn. Financial planning helps you:

What are some of the benefits of financial planning?

1. Determine and evaluate options for your money.
2. Prioritize your options so your money goes as far as possible.
3. Avoid careless and wasteful spending.
4. Organize your *financial resources* (sources of income) so you can achieve your financial goals.
5. Avoid money worries by planning your saving, spending, and borrowing to live within your income.

▶ PREPARING A BUDGET

The first step toward achieving your financial goals is to prepare a budget. A **budget** is a spending and saving plan based on your expected income and expenses. In a budget, money coming in (earnings plus borrowing) must equal money going out (spending plus saving). The budget must balance. A budget helps you plan your spending and saving so that you won't have to borrow money to meet your daily needs.

Figure 8-1 shows a high school student's budget for one month. This student expects to receive a total of $380 and plans to use the money for certain needs and wants and to save part of it as well. Notice that the total income equals the total of expenses plus savings. The budget balances.

Steps in Preparing a Budget

Follow these steps to prepare a budget:
1. Estimate your total expected income for a certain time period. Include all the money you expect to receive. You may wish to use a weekly, biweekly, or monthly budget—whichever best matches how often you expect to receive money.

SIMPLE BUDGET   figure 8-1 ◀◀ ◀ (◉)

BUDGET FOR SEPTEMBER

Income

Work (part-time)	$320.00
Allowances for household chores	20.00
Lunch money	40.00
Total income	$380.00

Expenses

Daily lunches	$ 80.00
Supplies	20.00
Snacks	40.00
Entertainment (movies and golfing)	140.00
Total expenses	$280.00

Savings

To Columbia County Credit Union	$100.00
Total expenses plus savings	$380.00

2. Decide how much of your income you want to save—to set aside for future needs. Most financial experts advise saving at least 10 percent of your disposable income each pay period. By saving at least this amount, you will have money to pay for future needs, both expected and unexpected.

3. Estimate your expenses, or money you will need for day-to-day purchases—for example, lunches, fees, personal care items, and clothing.

4. Balance your budget. If your expenses plus savings exceed your income, adjust your plan to make them match. Avoid spending more than you make. Use of credit limits future spending because you must pay off the loan with future income. To balance your budget, you may have to delay buying some items you want but don't need. Or, you may decide to save a little less this month. If you don't want to do either of these options, you'll have to find a way to bring in more money.

A Typical Monthly Budget

Figure 8-2 shows the monthly budget of Mike and Jennifer Harris. Mike and Jennifer have no children, and both are working. The Harrises estimated their expected income by adding together their two take-home incomes (paychecks), along with anticipated interest on savings and earnings on investments. They would like to save at least 10 percent every month, setting aside money for emergency savings, short-term savings, and long-term investments as shown.

Fixed expenses are costs you are obligated to pay at specific times, regardless of other events. You cannot change them without making a major revision in your lifestyle. For example, you must pay your rent or mortgage, utility bills, car loan, and insurance premiums when they are due, no matter what else is going on in your life. Most financial experts recommend that a family have fixed expenses of no more than 50 to 60 percent of take-home pay. However, this standard is difficult to achieve for young people just starting life on their own. But with time, pay raises, and careful budgeting, a family can achieve that goal.

Would vacation costs be considered fixed or variable expenses? Explain your answer.

©GETTY IMAGES/PHOTODISC

Variable expenses are costs that vary in amount and type, depending on events and the choices you make. For example, your grocery bill can be larger or smaller, depending on what you choose to buy. Other examples of variable expenses are costs for eating out, going to movies, and buying clothes.

BUDGET — Mike and Jennifer Harris

	Monthly	Yearly
Income		
Salary (Mike) after taxes	$ 1,600	$19,200
Salary (Jennifer) after taxes	1,800	21,600
Interest on savings	50	600
Earnings on investments	50	600
Total income	$ 3,500	$42,000
Expenses		
Fixed expenses:		
Rent	$ 1,000	$12,000
Utilities	150	1,800
Car payment	300	3,600
Insurance:		
Car	100	1,200
Life and Health	75	900
Total fixed expenses	$ 1,625	$19,500
Variable expenses:		
Telephone	$ 45	$ 540
Gasoline	150	1,800
Car repairs and maintenance	60	720
Cable television	40	480
Groceries	400	4,800
Clothing	200	2,400
Personal care:		
Dry cleaning, household	50	600
Drugs, cosmetics	50	600
Insurance deductibles and co-pays	50	600
Recreation and entertainment	100	1,200
Gifts, donations, miscellaneous	300	3,600
Total variable expenses	$ 1,445	$17,340
Total fixed and variable expenses	$ 3,070	$36,840
Cash surplus (total income minus total expenses)	$ 430	$ 5,160
Allocation of cash surplus:		
Emergency savings fund	$ 100	$ 1,200
Short-term savings	100	1,200
Long-term investments	230	2,760
Total savings and investments	$ 430	$ 5,160
Total expenses plus savings	$ 3,500	$42,000

▶ PERSONAL RECORDS

Good personal record keeping makes budgeting and long-range planning easier. Your records also form the basis for completing income tax returns, credit applications, and other financial forms. You should keep four types of personal records: income and expense records, a net worth statement, a personal property inventory, and tax records. Many people keep financial records on their computer, usually password-protected. As with any important files you keep electronically, always keep a current backup of your financial records.

Records of Income and Expenses

Your W-2 forms show the money earned and deductions taken from your paycheck during the year. The W-2 forms also state the amount of taxes and social security tax withheld. You may need the W-2 forms later when you want to collect benefits. Other records of income include statements from banks showing interest earned on savings and statements from investment companies listing dividends earned from stock or other investments. Expense items include receipts listing charitable contributions, medical bills, or work-related expenses. When you prepare your budgets and tax returns, these receipts and statements serve as documentation (proof) of income and expenses. Store these documents in a safe place for future reference.

©GETTY IMAGES/PHOTODISC

What are the different kinds of financial records you should keep?

Net Worth Statement

A *net worth statement*, such as that shown in Figure 8-3, is a list of items of value that a person owns, called **assets**; amounts of money owed to others, called **liabilities** or debts; and the difference between the two, known as **net worth**. If your assets are greater than your lia-

figure 8-3 ◄ ◄ (⊙)

NET WORTH STATEMENT
Nygen Phomn
January 1, 20--

ASSETS		LIABILITIES	
Checking account	$ 500	Loan on car	$1,800
Savings account	800	Loan from mother	100
Car value	3,000		
Personal property:		Total liabilities	$1,900
(inventory attached)	5,000		
Total assets	$9,300	**NET WORTH**	
		Assets minus liabilities	$7,400
		Total	$9,300

bilities, you are said to be *solvent,* or in a favorable financial position. But if your liabilities are greater than your assets (you owe more than you own), you are said to be *insolvent,* or in a poor financial position.

You will need your net worth information (lists of assets and liabilities) when you apply for a loan or credit. The bank or other financial institution will want you to be solvent and a good risk—a person who will likely pay back the loan. It also helps you keep track of how you spend your money and what you have to show for it at the end of the year.

Personal Property Inventory

A *personal property inventory,* such as the one shown in Figure 8-4, is a list of all valuable items you own, along with their purchase prices and approximate current values. Personal property includes anything of value inside your home—clothing, furniture, appliances, and so forth. A personal property inventory is useful in the event of fire, theft, or property damage. The inventory will help you list lost items and their value when you make an insurance claim.

As a further safeguard, photograph items of value, attach the photographs to the inventory, and keep this information in a safe deposit box or other secure place to use as evidence in the event the property is damaged, lost, or stolen. A personal property inventory also helps you see what you have to show for the money you have spent. Reviewing it will help you assess your spending patterns. As you buy new items and dispose of others, revise the inventory.

PERSONAL PROPERTY INVENTORY
Nygen Phomn
January 2, 20--

Item	Year Purchased	Purchase Price	Approximate Current Value
Sphinx XTL DVD Player with big-screen TV	2003	$3,200	$1,300
Bedroom furniture (bed, dresser, lamp, clock)	2001	2,000	1,200
Clothing, jewelry	-----	3,000	500
MBD motor bike	2000	1,800	1,000
CD collection, digital camera, scanner, CD burner	2001	2,000	1,000
		$12,000	$5,000

Tax Records

All taxpayers should keep copies of their tax records for at least three years after they file their tax return. Tax records include the return form, W-2 forms, and other receipts verifying income and expenses listed on each return. Keep your tax records in a safe place in case of an audit. The IRS has the legal right to audit your tax returns and supporting records for three years from the date of filing (longer if fraud or intentional wrongdoing on your part can be proved).

✔Check Your Understanding

1. What is the first step in budgeting?
2. How are fixed expenses different from variable expenses?
3. Why would you prepare a net worth statement?

Issues in Your World

Living Within Your Income

To be financially responsible, you must recognize that you are responsible for your own financial future.

A balanced personal budget is the first step to financial security. Living within your income means that you spend less than you make, and that you plan savings for future as well as current needs.

Setting financial goals is the next step to securing your financial future. You can't achieve future financial goals if you aren't paying your current bills on time.

It is easy to believe advertisements that stimulate demand. These emotional appeals are designed to get you to buy things you don't need in order to be more popular or to keep up with your friends. Ask yourself:

- Do I need it?
- Why am I buying it?
- How else could I spend the same money?
- How will buying it affect my financial goals?

Many people have a threshold of how much money they will spend without careful analysis and a family decision to spend the money. Whatever your limit, before spending a large sum or accepting a loan that will take a big bite from your future earnings, think through the decision carefully.

Living within your income is an important part of being happy. Regardless of the amount of your income, careful planning and budgeting can enhance your lifestyle and secure your future.

Think Critically

1. Make a list of things you'd like to have, along with the purchase price of each. Next to each item, indicate the cost. Read this list a week from now. Do you still want the same things? If so, what do you plan to do to buy one or more of them?

2. Do you know people who live within their income? If so, ask one of them to share how he or she does it.

3. Do you know people who live beyond their income? What do you observe about their stress, financial stability, and financial goals?

Legal Documents and Filing Systems

Goals
- Discuss the elements of legal contracts and your responsibilities regarding contracts.
- Describe negotiable instruments and warranties.
- Discuss ways to set up a filing system for personal records.

▶ CONTRACTS AND AGREEMENTS

A **contract** is a legally enforceable agreement between two or more parties. We all have many transactions in our daily lives that can be properly classified as legal contracts. Contracts are part of personal business situations, too. For example, if you buy a suit and you want it altered, the clerk fills out a ticket. The ticket lists the changes requested and the promised date of completion. This ticket is a contract between you and the store. The store agrees to make the alterations by the stated date and for the stated price, and you agree to pay the price.

Other common legal agreements are credit plans, mortgages, and rental agreements. When you sign up for a retail credit plan, the store agrees to give you products now in exchange for your regular payments over time. When you rent an apartment, the landlord agrees to let you live in the apartment, and you agree to pay the rent by a certain day each month. Each of these cases constitutes an express contract. *Express contracts* can be oral or written. What makes them *express* is that the parties have stated the terms of their agreement in words.

Figure 8-5 shows a credit application from a retail store. A credit application asks you to agree to certain conditions before opening an account. Attached to the application will be an explanation of finance charges and how they are computed. You will sign the application to show that you understand the finance charges and agree to pay them if your balance is not paid in full each month. Be sure you have read everything contained in the agreement before you sign it. If something is not clear, ask for an explanation so you can understand your rights and responsibilities before you enter into the contract.

In addition to written agreements, you take part in many unwritten agreements. When you ride a bicycle, you have made an *implied contract*. Whether you realize it or not, you have agreed to certain things by riding on public streets. For example, you agree to obey traffic laws,

CREDIT APPLICATION

CREDIT CARD APPLICATION
(Please print. Not valid unless signed below.)

Title (optional): Mr. ☒ Mrs. ☐ Ms. ☐ Other _____

First Name __Richard__ MI __J__ Last Name __Washington__

Street Address __45 Cleveland Avenue__ Apt. # _____

City __Portland__ State __OR__ Zip + 4 __97201-1072__

Home Phone __(513)555-0181__ Business Phone __(513)555-9213__ E-Mail _____

Soc. Sec. # __482-51-9384__ Est. Monthly Charges __$100.00__ # Cards Desired __1__

Former Address __-----__
(if less than 1 year at current address)

City _____ State _____ Zip + 4 _____

Mother's Maiden Name __Hawkins__ Years Employed __3__ Position __Payroll specialist__

Present Housing: Own ☐ Rent ☒ Live with Parents ☐

# of Dependents (exc. self) __1__ Student? Full ☒ Part ☐

Note: An applicant, though married, may apply for a separate Account in his or her own name. If your spouse will use this Account, please indicate his or her name, and social security number for credit reporting purposes.

First Name of Spouse __-----__ MI ____ Last _____ Soc. Sec. # _____

I HAVE READ AND AGREE TO BE BOUND BY THE TERMS OF THIS APPLICATION (INCLUDING THE ADDITIONAL APPLICATION PROVISIONS AND ACCOMPANYING FEDERAL AND STATE NOTICES AND SUMMARY OF CREDIT TERMS PRINTED TO THE RIGHT AND BACK).

I understand and agree that if I am approved for an Account, (i) the Central Credit Bank, N.A., Retail Installment Credit Agreement (the "Agreement") that I will receive with my credit card, will govern my Account, (ii) the Agreement is incorporated by reference into and made a part of the Application, and (iii) THE AGREEMENT INCLUDES AN ARBITRATION PROVISION THAT MAY SUBSTANTIALLY LIMIT MY RIGHTS IN THE EVENT OF A DISPUTE, INCLUDING MY RIGHT TO LITIGATE IN COURT OR HAVE A JURY TRIAL, DISCOVERY AND APPEAL RIGHTS, AND THE RIGHT TO PARTICIPATE AS A REPRESENTATIVE OR MEMBER OF A CLASS IN A CLASS ACTION. I MAY REQUEST THE COMMERCIAL ARBITRATION RULES OF THE AMERICAN ARBITRATION ASSOCIATION, WHICH SERVES AS ARBITRATION ADMINISTRATOR, BY CALLING 1-800-555-0155. I understand and agree that the Bank will first consider this application with respect to the credit card program described in this application. If for any reason, at the Bank's sole discretion, I do not qualify for this program, I request the Bank consider this application with respect to alternative credit card programs. My signature on this Application represents my signature on the Agreement.

NOTICE TO THE APPLICANT: (1) DO NOT SIGN THIS APPLICATION/AGREEMENT BEFORE YOU READ IT OR IF IT CONTAINS ANY BLANK SPACES. (2) YOU ARE ENTITLED TO A COMPLETELY FILLED IN COPY OF THE RETAIL INSTALLMENT CREDIT AGREEMENT

x _Richard J. Washington_ __3/11/--__
Signature of Card Applicant Date

CHAPTER 8 • Budgets and Financial Records

ride in a responsible manner, and observe the rights of other riders, pedestrians, and car drivers around you. A violation of one of these unwritten agreements can result in a traffic ticket and a fine.

Elements of an Enforceable Contract

To accomplish its purpose, a contract must be *binding*. That is, all who enter into the contract must be legally obligated to abide by its terms. Some contracts must be in writing and signed by everyone involved in order to be legally binding. Examples of contracts that must be written are contracts for the sale of real property (homes and land), contracts that cannot be fully performed in less than a year, contracts involving $500 and over, and contracts in which one person agrees to pay the debts of another.

To be legally binding, enforceable agreements, contracts must have all of the following elements:

1. Agreement
2. Consideration
3. Contractual capacity
4. Legality

AGREEMENT

A contract has legal agreement when a valid offer is made and accepted. Both the offer and acceptance must express a voluntary intent to be bound by the agreement. When one person makes an offer and another person changes any part of it, the second person is making a *counteroffer*. The counteroffer is a new offer and has to be accepted or rejected by the first person.

On the Internet, you may click on an "acceptance" of an offer. This *click-on acceptance* is considered a voluntary intent to be bound. If you do not intend to enter a binding agreement, or you accidentally hit the wrong button, notify the online seller immediately of your error (and lack of intent to be bound).

It is important that both parties to an agreement genuinely agree to the contract terms. Genuine agreement does not exist when there is a mistake, fraud (an intentional misrepresentation), duress (threats), or undue influence (having free will overcome by a person who has a special interest, such as a parent or guardian).

CONSIDERATION

The **consideration** is anything of value exchanged as part of a contract. Consideration may be in the form of an object of value, money, a promise, or a performed service. If one person is to receive something but gives nothing in return, the contract may not be enforceable. The idea behind consideration is that each party to the agreement receives something of value. When you buy a pair of shoes, you get the shoes and the store gets your money. The shoes and the money are items of consideration.

CONTRACTUAL CAPACITY

Contractual capacity refers to the competence (legal ability) of the parties to enter a contract. *Competent parties* are people who are legally capable of agreeing to a binding offer. Those who are unable to protect themselves because of mental deficiency or illness, or who are otherwise incapable of understanding the consequences of their actions, cannot be held to contracts. Minors have limited contractual capacity, which means that they may legally set aside contractual obligations. This privilege is allowed in order to protect minors from those who would take advantage of them. Married people under age 18 are considered competent to enter into contracts. All people 18 or older are considered legally competent unless they are declared incompetent by a court.

How does the element of consideration come into play when a person buys a house?

LEGALITY

To be legally enforceable, a contract must be lawful. A court will not require a person to perform an agreed-upon act if it is illegal. Without a lawful objective, the agreement has no binding effect on a person. Some contracts must have a special form in order to be legally enforceable. For example, a contract for sale of real estate would have to contain a specific legal description of the property. A deed to transfer title to property would have to be *notarized* (receive a seal that says the person signed the document of his or her free will).

Consumer Responsibilities in Agreements

As a consumer, you have the following responsibilities regarding the contracts and agreements you enter into:

1. Fill in all blank spaces or indicate N/A for items that are not applicable.
2. Write all terms clearly. Because interpretation may vary, vague phrases are often not enforceable.
3. Enter dates, amounts, and other numbers correctly and clearly.
4. Be sure the seller has supplied all relevant information, including rate of interest, total finance charges, cash payment price, and so on.
5. Understand all terms contained in the agreement. Do not sign it until you have read it. Your signature acknowledges that you have read and understood the contract.

6. Check that no changes have been made after you have signed it. Your initials at the bottom of each page will prevent substitution of pages.

7. Keep a copy of the agreement. Put it in a safe place for future use.

Although consumers are protected by numerous consumer protection laws, occasionally you may need legal services. But your best protection is to guard yourself in advance by understanding the agreements you enter into.

▶ NEGOTIABLE INSTRUMENTS

The word "negotiable" means legally collectible. A **negotiable instrument** is an unconditional written promise to pay a specified sum of money upon demand of the holder. The negotiable instruments most people use are checks (discussed in Chapter 9) and, to a lesser extent, promissory notes.

A promissory note, like the one shown in Figure 8-6, is a written promise to pay a certain sum of money to another person or to the holder of the note on a specified date. A promissory note is a legal document, and payment can be enforced by law.

The person who creates and signs the promissory note and agrees to pay it on a certain date is called the *maker*. The person to whom the note is made payable is known as the *payee*. A promissory note is normally used when borrowing a large sum of money from a financial institution.

▶ figure 8-6

PROMISSORY NOTE

PROMISSORY NOTE

$ 400.00   January 15   , 20 - -

I (we) ___Marilyn Huykamp_____ , jointly and severally,
do agree and promise to pay to __Emerald Furniture Co.__
the sum of ____Four hundred and 00/100_____ dollars
with interest at the rate of __9%__ from __January 15, 20--__, payable in
monthly installments of $ 69.67 beginning February 1 , 20 - -
and on a like day each month until paid in full, the last payment
due ___July 1_____ , 20 - -. Said payment shall include interest.
In the event of default, the maker hereof agrees to pay attorneys' fees and
court costs in collection of this note.

_Marilyn Huykamp_____
Maker

UNIT 2 • Money Management

186

In some cases, creditors (those extending credit) will require a co-signer with a good credit rating as additional security for repayment of a note. A **co-signer** is a person who promises to pay the note if the maker fails to pay. The co-signer's signature is also on a note. Young people and people who have not established a credit rating are often asked to provide a co-signer for their first loan. If someone asks you to co-sign a loan, do so only if you are sure the person is financially responsible. If that person fails to repay the debt, you will be legally responsible to repay it.

► WARRANTIES

A **warranty**, also called a *guarantee*, is a statement about a product's qualities or performance that the seller assures the buyer are true. If the product fails to live up to the standards specified, the warranty usually states what the seller will do as a remedy, such as return the purchase price or repair the product at no extra charge. The warranty may be in writing or assumed to exist by the nature of the product. However, a warranty is not a safeguard against a consumer's poor buying decision.

All products contain implied warranties, and some also have written guarantees stating responsibilities that the manufacturer agrees to. For example, all products carry the warranty of merchantability. This means that a product is supposed to do what it is made to do, whether or not standards are stated in writing. For example, a new tennis ball must bounce. If it does not bounce, you can return the defective ball, even if there is no written warranty.

Specific written warranties often guarantee that a product will perform to your satisfaction for a certain period of time. Many written warranties state that you may return a product for repair or replacement if it ceases to work because of a defect. However, warranties will not protect against normal wear and tear of the product.

Figure 8-7 illustrates a limited warranty that might accompany a home product. Read it carefully to determine what the manufacturer does and does not guarantee.

► FILING SYSTEMS FOR PERSONAL RECORDS

Keeping a good filing system for your personal records will help you organize, store, and retrieve needed information. An electronic filing system can be a convenient way to organize some records.

Limited Warranty ㄹ2 Y 845

This product is guaranteed for one year from the date of purchase to be free of mechanical and electrical defects in material and workmanship. The manufacturer's obligations hereunder are limited to repair of such defects during the warranty period, provided such product is returned to the address below within the warranty period.

This guarantee does not cover normal wear of parts or damages resulting from negligent use or mis-use of the product. In addition, this guarantee is void if the purchaser breaks the seal and disassembles, repairs, or alters the product in any way.

The warranty period begins on the date of purchase. The card below must be received by the manufacturer within 30 days of purchase or receipt of said merchandise. Fill out the card completely and return it to the address shown.

Owner's Name: _____
Address: _____
City, State, Zip: _____
E-Mail Address: _____
Date of Purchase: _____
Store Where Purchased: _____

Return to: ALCOVE ELECTRICAL, INC.
42 West Cabana
Arlington, VA 23445-2909

To register your warranty online, visit our Web site at www.alcoveelectrical.com.

Serial No.   ㄹ2 Y 845

Paper Filing System

A typical home filing system would include folders and labels and a file cabinet. Most households need folders for each category shown in Figure 8-8. You may have additional categories. Name your folders with a descriptive word or short phrase that tells you immediately what records it contains. File your folders alphabetically.

Communication Connection

Gather a stack of paper slips or index cards. Set up a paper filing system appropriate for your or your family's personal records. On each slip or card, write the name of a folder along with the various records that folder would contain. Then file your "folders" alphabetically.

figure **8-8**

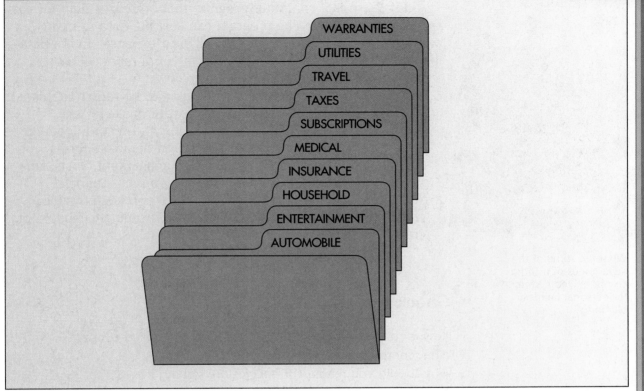

WARRANTIES
UTILITIES
TRAVEL
TAXES
SUBSCRIPTIONS
MEDICAL
INSURANCE
HOUSEHOLD
ENTERTAINMENT
AUTOMOBILE

Keep records and receipts in the appropriate folder. For example, in the "automobile" folder, you might want to keep track of oil changes, tune-ups, repairs, and other car expenses. Original copies of important documents such as insurance policies and wills should be kept in a safe deposit box. After you submit your tax return, file your receipts and tax records in your filing system.

Electronic Record Keeping

Many people invest in home computers and software for personal financial planning. The advantages of computerized systems include (1) ease of updating information, (2) ease of record storage and retrieval, and (3) speed of making new computations and comparisons.

Many software programs are available to consumers at reasonable prices. A **spreadsheet** is a computer program that organizes data in columns and rows and can perform calculations using the data. You can use a general-purpose spreadsheet program to maintain a list of your income and expenses. You can enter a formula that will add them up. When you enter a new expense, the formula will recalculate

@GETTY IMAGES/PHOTODISC

the new sum automatically. You can even design your own budget worksheet in a spreadsheet program.

A **database** is a computer program that organizes data for easy search and retrieval. The program can sort the data in many ways. For example, if you entered all your expenses into a database program, you could ask it to give you a report of all expenses associated with travel.

A general-purpose database program can be rather sophisticated. However, several available software packages are specially designed for financial planning and record keeping. These programs provide spreadsheet and database forms already set up for personal financial management. For example, Microsoft Money and Quicken are popular financial management programs designed to help you keep track of your income and expenses, keep an electronic checkbook, and create budgets.

What are some of the advantages of using a computerized system for personal financial planning?

✅ Check Your Understanding

1. How is an express contract different from an implied contract?
2. What contracts have you agreed to?
3. Why should you read a contract before signing it?

Chapter Assessment

SUMMARY

8.1

* A budget is a spending and saving plan based on expected income and expenses.
* To prepare a budget, you should estimate your income, set a savings goal, and estimate your expenses.
* If expenses plus savings exceed income, adjust your spending or saving to balance your budget, or find a new source of income.
* Keep four types of personal records: income and expense records, a net worth statement, a personal property inventory, and tax records.
* Net worth is the difference between assets (value of items owned) and liabilities (money owed).
* A personal property inventory serves as proof of value for insurance claims.

8.2

* Contracts are legally binding agreements. They can be express or implied.
* An enforceable agreement has offer and acceptance, consideration, contractual capacity, and legality.
* It is your responsibility to read and understand an agreement before you sign it.
* Negotiable instruments, such as checks and promissory notes, are promises to pay a specified sum to the holder.
* Good filing systems can be paper or electronic. Spreadsheet and database programs can facilitate budgeting and record keeping.

REVIEW TERMS

Directions

Can you find the definition for each of the following terms used in Chapter 8?

assets	fixed expenses
budget	liabilities
consideration	negotiable instrument
contract	net worth
co-signer	spreadsheet
database	variable expenses
disposable income	warranty
financial plan	

1. Costs you are obligated to pay at specific times, regardless of other events.

2. Costs that vary in amount and type, depending on events and the choices you make.

3. A legally enforceable agreement between two or more parties.

4. Anything of value exchanged as part of a contract.

5. Things of value that a person owns.

6. A person who promises to pay a note if the maker fails to pay.

7. A statement about a product's qualities or performance that the seller assures the buyer are true.

8. A set of goals for spending, saving, and investing your income.

9. A spending and saving plan based on your expected income and expenses.

10. Money that you owe to others, also known as debts.

11. An unconditional written promise to pay a specified sum of money upon demand of the holder.

12. A computer program that organizes data in columns and rows and can perform calculations using the data.

13. A computer program that organizes data for easy search and retrieval.

14. Money you have left to spend or save after taxes have been paid.

15. The difference between assets and liabilities.

REVIEW FACTS AND IDEAS

1. Why should you prepare a budget?

2. What are the four steps in preparing a budget?

3. What choices do you have if your initial budget doesn't balance?

4. If you had to reduce your spending to balance your budget, which would you try to reduce first: fixed or variable expenses? Why?

5. What four types of personal records should you prepare and keep in a safe place?

6. Besides for obtaining credit, what is another good reason for preparing a personal property inventory?

7. How is an implied contract different from an express contract?

8. Give three examples of contracts that must be in writing in order to be enforceable.

9. In order to be legally enforceable, contracts must contain what four elements?

10. List five consumer responsibilities when entering into a contract.

11. What is the most commonly used form of negotiable instrument?

12. Explain the concept of a filing system for personal records and list several file labels you would choose.

1. Using Figure 8-1 as a model, prepare a simple budget for yourself, listing expected income, savings, and expenses for a month. If your budget does not balance at first, make adjustments until it does. How much will you set aside for savings? Now assume that you can set aside this same amount each month. Locate a savings planner tool and calculate your total savings after 12 months, at 6 percent interest, starting with $0 savings.

2. How will your budget change in the next few years? What are your short-term and intermediate goals?

3. Using Figure 8-3 as a model, prepare a net worth statement. List your assets and liabilities. Compute your net worth. How can you use this information?

4. Using Figure 8-4 as a model, prepare a personal property inventory, listing items of personal property in your room at home. Why should you and your family keep a record such as this?

5. After examining the credit application in Figure 8-5, list the kinds of information requested by a retail store. Why do you think a store wants this type of information?

6. Following the example of Figure 8-6, handwrite a promissory note from you to John Doe, payable in one year of monthly payments, in the amount of $50 with interest at 11 percent and monthly payments of $4.63. Are you the maker or the payee? On the Internet, locate a notes and interest planner tool and calculate the amount of interest you would earn on this note.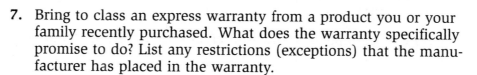

7. Bring to class an express warranty from a product you or your family recently purchased. What does the warranty specifically promise to do? List any restrictions (exceptions) that the manufacturer has placed in the warranty.

8. Search online for articles or reviews about financial planning software. Write a one-page description of what you could do with the software and what features make one software better than another.

Solve Problems ⊕ Explore Issues

1. Based on the following information, prepare a monthly and yearly budget for Antwan and Keyondra Harbour. Use Figure 8-2 as a model.

Average Income
Net paychecks total $1,800 monthly
Interest on savings = $50 monthly

Average Monthly Expenses

Rent payment	$400
Utilities	120
Gasoline	100
Insurance	150
Groceries	200
Clothing	100
Car payment	210
Car maintenance	50
Telephone	40
Entertainment and Recreation	200

Cash Surplus

Savings	To be Determined
Investment fund	60
Miscellaneous	120

2. Based on the following information, prepare a monthly and yearly budget for Elena Espinoza. Follow the style shown in Figure 8-2.

Average Income
Net monthly pay is $1,400

Average Monthly Expenses

Rent	$410
Insurance	60
Utilities	50
Gasoline	60
Clothing	60
Entertainment	100
Savings	120
Telephone	15
Car payment	150
Car repairs	20
Groceries	150
Personal care	50
Miscellaneous	155

3. Revise Elena's budget when she agrees to share her apartment with a friend. Some expenses can be shared equally. Assume the telephone expense increases to $30, utilities to $60, and insurance to $70. These expenses along with rent are shared equally. What will you have her do with the added funds?

4. Based on the following information, prepare a net worth statement for Sako Masuta. Follow Figure 8-3. Sako owns a car worth about $3,000 but owes $1,500 on it to the bank. He has $500 in savings and $100 in checking. His personal property totals $3,000, and he also owes $90 to his credit union.

5. Sako has 5 payments left to pay off the remaining $1,500 of his car loan. He is paying 8 percent interest. Locate a loan planner tool and determine his monthly payments.

6. Based on the following information, prepare a personal property inventory for Sako Masuta. Follow Figure 8-4.

Sako has these furnishings in his apartment:
- JWA CD stereo system, Model 252, SN 975923, bought last year for $600, presently worth $500
- Sofa, presently worth about $800
- Bright alarm clock, SN 630AM and Blare radio, Model 2602, SN 413T, bought four years ago, total worth about $100.

Sako also has the following personal items:
- Miscellaneous clothing and jewelry, presently worth about $800
- Quantex wristwatch, presently worth about $100
- Coin collection, valued last year at $600.

Sako has photographs of these items. (List a hypothetical purchase price for all items except the CD system in preparing your property inventory.)

For related activities and links, point your browser to **www.mypf.swlearning.com**

Checking Accounts and Other Banking Services

TERMS TO KNOW

- check
- demand deposit
- canceled check
- overdraft
- floating a check
- checkbook register
- reconciliation
- blank endorsement
- special endorsement
- restrictive endorsement
- certified check
- cashier's check
- stop payment order

Consider This. . .

Luisa works part-time after school and one weekend a month. She receives a paycheck once a week from her employer.

"I can't cash my paychecks," Luisa told her boyfriend, "unless my mom goes with me to her bank. They told me that I need my own account. They recommended a checking account that has a savings account attached to it. That way I can transfer the money I don't need each month into savings, where I can earn higher interest."

The bank told Luisa that her mother has to be a joint account holder with her until she reaches age 18. Then she can have her own private account. But for now, a joint account with her mother will allow Luisa to deposit her checks into her checking account and manage her own money.

Lesson 9.1

Checking Accounts

Goals
- Describe the purpose of a checking account.
- Discuss how to prepare banking forms.
- Be able to distinguish between different types of checking accounts.

▶ PURPOSE OF A CHECKING ACCOUNT

Financial institutions such as banks and credit unions offer a number of services. The first service you will likely want is a checking account. A *checking account* is an account that allows depositors to write checks to make payments. A **check** is a written order to a bank to pay the stated amount to the person or business (payee) named on it. A checking account is also called a **demand deposit**, because the money can be withdrawn at any time—that is, "on demand." Only you, the depositor, can write checks on the account. Financial institutions often charge a fee for checking services, or require depositors to keep a minimum balance in the account. In shopping for a checking account, you will find a wide variety of account types and fees.

Checks follow a process through the banking system. Your payee cashes your check. The bank that cashed the check returns it to your bank. To reimburse the payment, your bank withdraws the money from your account and sends it to the other bank. Your bank then stamps the back of your check, indicating that it has *cleared*, or successfully completed its trip through the system. A **canceled check** is a check that bears the bank's stamp, indicating that it has cleared. Because of this stamp, you can use your canceled checks as proof of purchase or of payment if a dispute arises. Your canceled checks should become part of your record keeping system.

A checking account offers several advantages:
1. It provides a convenient way to pay your bills.
2. Writing a check is often safer than using cash, especially when making major purchases in person, paying bills, or ordering merchandise through the mail.
3. A checking account has a built-in record keeping system that you can use to track expenses and create budgets.

4. As a checking account customer, you have access to other bank services, such as instant loans, online banking, and 24-hour access to your money through ATMs.

In exchange for the convenience of using a checking account, you must accept certain responsibilities. First, you must write checks carefully and keep an accurate record of checks written and deposits made. Second, you must verify the accuracy of the bank statement you receive each month. Third, you must keep canceled checks among your permanent records.

Some banks do not return cancelled checks. This is called "truncation." What is the disadvantage of having checks truncated?

In addition, you must maintain sufficient funds in your account to cover all the checks you write. A check written for more money than your account contains is called an **overdraft**. A financial institution receiving an overdraft usually stamps the check with the words "not sufficient funds" (NSF) and returns the check to the payee or the payee's institution. When an overdraft occurs and a check is returned, the check has "bounced." In addition, your bank will charge you a fee of $25 or more for each NSF check processed. When checks are returned, the institution notifies the account holder of its action.

You are **floating a check** when you realize your account contains insufficient funds, but you write a check anyway, hoping that a deposit will clear before the check is cashed. Floating a check is riskier in the computer age, because computers process checks very quickly. Purposely overdrawing your account by floating a check is illegal in most states. Writing NSF checks can result in a fine, imprisonment, or both.

◢ OPENING A CHECKING ACCOUNT

To open a checking account, you must fill out and sign a signature authorization form, such as the one shown in Figure 9-1 (page 200). The signature form provides an official signature that the bank can compare to the signature you write on your checks. This is done to verify that the checks were not forged. Most banks also require that you have an initial deposit of $50 or more.

In Figure 9-1, Ardys Johnson completed and signed the form. Additional space is allotted for a joint account holder. (Signature forms look different at various banks, but they contain the same basic information.) Ardys also listed her mother's maiden name for use in identification. Anyone forging Ardys's signature is not likely to know her mother's maiden name when questioned by a teller.

 figure **9-1**

SIGNATURE AUTHORIZATION FORM

FIRST INDEPENDENT MUTUAL SAVINGS BANK
CHECKING SIGNATURE VERIFICATION

Customer Name *Ardys Johnson*   Date *4/28/--*

Account No. *08 40 856*   Individual *X* Joint

Address *4250 West 18th Avenue*   Daytime Phone *555-8925*

City/State/ZIP *Chicago, IL 60601-2180*   Evening Phone *555-0100*

Social Security No. *482-81-8096*   Birthdate *11/20/80*

Occupation *Accountant*   How long? *2 years*

Employer *Cho and Jackson, Inc.*   Phone *555-8925*

Contact in cast of emergency:

  Harold Johnson   Phone *555-2322*

Relationship *father*

Mother's Maiden Name or other code word *Williams*

JOINT ACCOUNT HOLDER (if any):

Customer Name   Date

Account No.   Individual   Joint

Address   Daytime Phone

City/State/ZIP   Evening Phone

Social Security No.   Birthdate

Occupation   How long?

Employer   Phone

Contact in cast of emergency:

      Phone

Relationship

Mother's Maiden Name or other code word

SIGNATURES: *Ardys Johnson*   #1 Date *4/28/--*

_____   #2 Date _____

(Use second page if more signatures are needed.)

▶ PARTS OF A CHECK

A check consists of the following parts. Look at the lettered elements of the check in Figure 9-2 as you read their explanations below.
A *Check Number.* Checks are numbered for easy identification. In Figure 9-2, Check 581 has been pre-numbered by the bank.

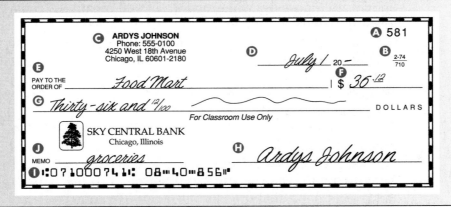

Ⓐ 581

Ⓒ **ARDYS JOHNSON**
Phone: 555-0100
4250 West 18th Avenue
Chicago, IL 60601-2180

Ⓓ July 1 20 —

Ⓑ 2-74
710

Ⓔ PAY TO THE
ORDER OF *Food Mart*

Ⓕ $ 36 12

Ⓖ *Thirty-six and 12/100* _____ DOLLARS

For Classroom Use Only

SKY CENTRAL BANK
Chicago, Illinois

Ⓙ MEMO *groceries*

Ⓗ *Ardys Johnson*

Ⓘ ⑆071000741⑆ 08⑈40⑈856⑈

Ⓑ *ABA Number.* The American Bankers Association (ABA) number appears in fraction form in the upper right corner of each check. The top half of the fraction identifies the location and district of the bank from which the check is drawn. The bottom half helps in routing the check to the specific area and bank on which it is drawn.

Ⓒ *Maker's Preprinted Name and Address.* The *maker,* or *drawer,* is the person authorized to write checks on the account. Ardys Johnson is the maker of the check in Figure 9-2. You should have your name and address printed on your checks. Some people also include their phone number. Businesses may be reluctant to accept a check unless it is preprinted with at least the name and address. To avoid identity theft, do not have your social security number printed on your checks.

Ⓓ *Date.* In this blank, fill in the date you write the check. Do not postdate checks. That is, do not write a future date in this blank. Banks will not cash a check before the date written on it, or they may charge a fee for holding the check until the date arrives. Also, banks may not honor checks over six months old.

Ⓔ *Payee.* The payee is the person or company to whom the check is made payable. Food Mart is the payee in Figure 9-2.

Ⓕ *Numeric Amount.* The numeric amount is the amount of dollars and cents being paid, written in figures. Write the amount neatly and clearly as close as possible to the dollar sign, with the dollars and cents clearly distinguished. Many people raise the cents above the line of writing, as shown in Figure 9-2, and insert a decimal point between the dollar and cent amounts.

Ⓖ *Written Amount.* The written amount shows the amount of dollars and cents being paid, written in words. The word "dollars" is preprinted at the end of the line. Write the word "and" to separate dollar amounts from cents; the word replaces the decimal point. When checks are written by computers, the "and" is usually omitted. Always begin writing at the far left of the line, leaving no space between words, and draw a wavy line from the cents to the word "dollars," as shown. In Figure 9-2, the fraction 12/100 means 12 cents, which is 12 hundredths of a dollar.

H *Signature.* Sign your check on the signature line. If the bank suspects the check is forged, the teller can compare the signature against the one on your signature authorization form.

I *Account and Routing Numbers.* The account number appears in bank coding at the bottom of each check. In Figure 9-2, 08 40 856 is Ardys's checking account number. The number 071000741 is the bank's identification code for the electronic sorting and routing of checks. As you learned in Chapter 7, you can write this routing number along with your account number on your tax return to have your tax refund deposited directly into your account.

J *Memo.* The memo line at the bottom left of each check provides a place to write the purpose of the check. You do not have to fill in this line. It is there for your convenience.

Banks sell inexpensive "stock" checks to customers. Those willing to pay more can buy checks with special designs or colors. You can also buy checks from a check-printing company. While these checks may be less expensive than those ordered through the bank, they are less secure because they are easier for imposters to alter or duplicate.

▶ USING YOUR CHECKING ACCOUNT

Checking accounts can help you manage your personal finances but only if you use them correctly. Careless or improper use of a checking account can result in financial loss. Here are some tips on using a checking account.

Writing Checks

When writing checks, be sure to do the following:

1. Always use a pen, preferably one with dark ink that does not skip or blot.

2. Write legibly. Keep numbers and letters clear and distinct, without any extra space before, between, or after them.

3. Sign your name exactly as it appears preprinted on the check and on the signature card you signed when you opened the account. If you opened your account under your full name, don't use a nickname when writing a check.

4. Avoid mistakes. When you make a mistake, *void* (cancel) the check and write a new one. To cancel a check, write the word

VOID in large letters across the face of the check. Save the voided check for your records.

5. Be certain you have deposited adequate funds in your account to cover each check you write. A check is a negotiable instrument. It represents your written promise to pay the stated amount to the payee when it is cashed.

©GETTY IMAGES/PHOTODISC

When writing a check, how should you sign your name?

Paying Bills Online

To pay bills online, you must first register at your bank's Web site. In that process, you establish your *personal identification number (PIN)* or password to gain entry into your account. Screen prompts will lead you to the bank's online bill payment page, such as the one shown in Figure 9-3 (page 204). After you set up your list of payees, you can pay bills each month by simply selecting the payee from the list and entering the payment amount. The bank will remove the money from your checking account and transfer it to the payee. When you pay a bill online, be sure to enter the payee and amount in your checkbook register, just as you would when you write a check.

Some banks do not actually make the online payments for several days. Usually the online bill payment page will show the date when the bill will actually be paid. Be sure to make your online payments early enough to allow for this lag time, so that your payments will arrive on time.

Some banks charge a monthly fee for online bill payment privileges. Some limit the number of bills you can pay online each month. Consider the fees and restrictions on online banking when you choose a bank.

Making Deposits

You must complete a form each time you want to deposit or withdraw money from your account. Figure 9-4 (page 205) illustrates a deposit slip. To prepare a deposit slip, follow these guidelines:

1. Insert the date of the transaction.

2. In the "cash" section, write in the amount of currency (paper money) and coin you are depositing.

3. If you are depositing any checks, write the amount of each check, together with the ABA check number (top part of fraction), in the "checks" section of the slip.

4. Total the currency, coin, and check amounts. Write this figure on the subtotal line.

CHAPTER 9 • Checking Accounts and Other Banking Services

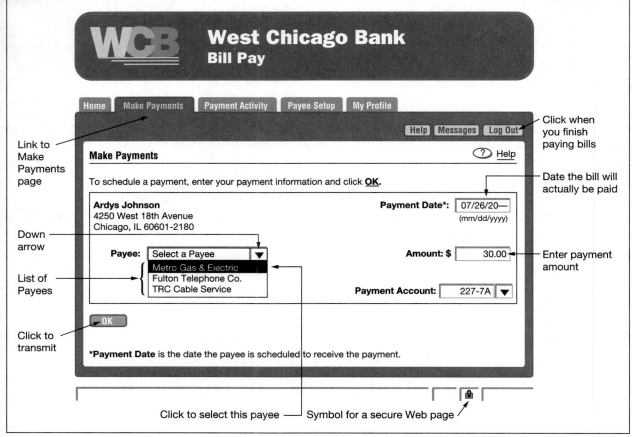
figure **9-3**

ONLINE BILL-PAYMENT PAGE

West Chicago Bank
Bill Pay

| Home | Make Payments | Payment Activity | Payee Setup | My Profile |

Help   Messages   Log Out

Click when you finish paying bills

Make Payments   (?) Help

To schedule a payment, enter your payment information and click **OK**.

Ardys Johnson   **Payment Date*:**   07/26/20—
4250 West 18th Avenue   (mm/dd/yyyy)
Chicago, IL 60601-2180

Date the bill will actually be paid

Link to Make Payments page

Down arrow

Payee: Select a Payee ▼   **Amount: $**   30.00

Metro Gas & Electric
Fulton Telephone Co.
TRC Cable Service

Enter payment amount

List of Payees

OK

Payment Account: 227-7A ▼

Click to transmit

***Payment Date** is the date the payee is scheduled to receive the payment.

Click to select this payee —— Symbol for a secure Web page

5. If you wish to receive some cash at the time of your deposit, fill in the desired amount on the "Less Cash Received" line.

6. Subtract the cash received from the subtotal, and write the final amount of the deposit on the "Net Deposit" line.

7. If you will receive cash, write your signature on the line above the words "Sign here for less cash in teller's presence" (this wording will vary). If you do not want cash back, leave this signature line blank.

8. The teller will give you either a copy of this deposit slip or a receipt. Keep the copy or receipt as proof of the amount of your deposit.

When writing deposit slips, carefully count the currency and coins you are depositing and recheck all addition and subtraction. Properly endorse all checks you deposit (see the discussion of endorsements on pages 208–210). Hand the deposit slip to the teller with the currency, coins, and checks. You can also make deposits at automated teller machines and at the night deposit box.

	DOLLARS	CENTS
CASH	20	50
CHECKS 2-51	200	00
SUBTOTAL	220	50
LESS CASH RECEIVED		
NET DEPOSIT	220	50

FOR DEPOSIT TO THE ACCOUNT OF

ARDYS JOHNSON
Phone: 555-0100
4250 West 18th Avenue
Chicago, IL 60601-2180

DATE _____ July 15 _____ 20 __

_____
SIGN HERE FOR LESS CASH IN TELLER'S PRESENCE

🌲 SKY CENTRAL BANK
Chicago, Illinois

2-74
710

BE SURE
EACH ITEM
IS PROPERLY
ENDORSED

⑈071000741⑈ 08⑈40⑈856⑈

CHECKS AND OTHER ITEMS ARE RECEIVED FOR DEPOSIT SUBJECT TO THE TERMS AND CONDITIONS OF THIS INSTITUTION'S COLLECTION AGREEMENT.

Using a Checkbook Register

A **checkbook register** is a booklet used to record checking account transactions. Figure 9-5 (page 206) shows a page from the checkbook register of Ardys Johnson. Through the use of her checkbook register, Ardys can keep track of all checks, online payments, fees, interest, and deposits for her account. Follow along in Figure 9-5 as your read the following guidelines for recording transactions in a checkbook register.

1. Record the current amount in your account at the top of the "Balance" column. When you fill a page in the checkbook register and turn to the next page, copy your account balance from the bottom of the previous page to the top of the new page.

2. As soon as you write a check, make an online payment, or make a deposit, record the transaction in your checkbook register. For online payments, you may wish to print a copy of the screen showing the completed transaction as proof that you made the payment.

3. Write the preprinted check number in the first column. If the transaction is not a check, make up a code to represent the kind of transaction, such as DEP for deposit, WD for withdrawal, ON for online transaction, SC for service charge, and INT for interest.

4. Write the month, day, and year of the transaction in the "Date" column.

5. Enter the name of the payee on the first line of the "Description" section. On the second line, write the purpose of the check or any description of the transaction you find useful.

6. If the transaction will reduce your balance, write the amount in the "Payment/Debit" column. Debit transactions include checks,

online bill payments, debit card purchases, withdrawals, check fees, and service charges. If the transaction will add to your balance, record the amount in the "Deposit/Credit" column. Credit transactions include deposits and interest earned on the account.

7. Some banks charge a fee for each check written. In this case, record the fee in the "Fee" column next to the check.

8. Add the amount of the check to the check fee, and record the result in the "Balance" column. For a deposit, simply repeat the amount in the "Balance" column.

9. If the amount is a debit transaction, subtract it from the previous balance. If the amount is a deposit or credit, add it to the previous balance. Write the new balance on the next line of the Balance column.

10. The column headed by a check mark is provided so that you can check off each transaction when it appears on your monthly bank statement. The check mark shows that the bank has cleared the transaction and it is no longer outstanding.

Always keep your checkbook register handy so you can write down the necessary information each time you make a transaction. If you don't record it promptly, you could forget a transaction and accidentally overdraw your account.

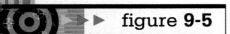 figure **9-5**

CHECKBOOK REGISTER

CHECK NO. OR TRANSACTION CODE	DATE	DESCRIPTION OF TRANSACTION	PAYMENT/ DEBIT(–)	FEE (–)	✓	DEPOSIT/ CREDIT (+)	BALANCE $800 00
581	7/1/--	Food Mart	$ 36 12	.20		$	36 32
		Groceries					763 68
DEP	7/15/--	Deposit Paycheck				220 50	220 50
							984 18
WD	7/16/--	ATM Withdrawal	20 00				20 00
							964 18
582	7/20/--	Bellvue Apts.	600 00	.20			600 20
		Rent					363 98
ON	7/22/--	Metro Gas & Electric	32 50				32 50
		Online Payment					331 48
SC	7/31/--	Monthly Account Fee		5.00			5 00
		July					326 48

Reconciling Your Checking Account

Financial institutions that offer checking accounts provide each customer with a monthly statement. This statement lists checks received and processed by the bank, plus all other withdrawals, deposits, service charges, and interest.

Most financial institutions return your canceled checks with your bank statement. Some, however, make copies of the processed checks and destroy the originals. If necessary, you can get copies of your canceled checks for a small fee.

The process of matching your checkbook register with the bank statement is known as **reconciliation**. The back of the bank statement is usually printed with a form to aid you in reconciling your account. Figure 9-6 represents both sides of a typical bank statement.

The left side of Figure 9-6 is a statement showing the bank's record of activity on Ardys Johnson's checking account. The statement lists all checks that have cleared as well as all withdrawals, online bill payments, and fees that the bank subtracted from Ardys's account. It also shows all deposits added to the balance that month. After subtracting all debit transactions and adding all deposits, the bank arrives at the ending, or current, balance for the account.

BANK ACCOUNT RECONCILIATION

figure **9-6** ◀

Bank Statement
SKY CENTRAL BANK

Ardys Johnson
4250 West 18th Avenue
Chicago, IL 60601-2180

Statement Date: July 31, 20—
Opening Balance: $820.20
Ending Balance: $926.68

Checks

Check No.	Date Paid	Amount
580	7/2/—	20.00
581	7/4/—	36.12

Debits and Withdrawals

Date	Amount	Description
7/16/—	20.00	ATM withdrawal
7/22/—	32.50	Online bill payment
7/31/—	.40	Check fee ($0.20 per check)
7/31/—	5.00	Monthly account fee

Deposits

Date	Amount	Description
7/15/—	220.50	Deposit

Account Reconciliation

1. Ending balance shown on the bank statement: _926.68_

2. Total of all credits and deposits made but not shown on statement: _0_

3. Total lines 1 and 2: _926.68_

4. List all checks, withdrawals, and debits made but not shown on statement:

Check No. or Transaction Code	Amount	
582	600	00
SC		20

5. Total of outstanding debit transactions: _600.20_

6. Subtract line 5 from line 3: (Result should match checkbook balance.) _326.48_

The balance your checkbook register shows will not always match the ending balance shown on the bank statement. A check does not appear on the statement until the payee has cashed it and the check completes its route through the banking system. Since you recorded the check and subtracted the amount from your balance when you wrote it, your balance will be lower than the bank's until the check clears and the bank removes the payment from your account. As you can see by comparing Ardys's checkbook register (Figure 9-5) to her bank statement (Figure 9-6), the ending balances do not match. When this occurs, you can check for errors by reconciling your account. Follow along on the right side of Figure 9-6 as Ardys reconciles her account:

1. Write the ending balance shown on the bank statement.
2. From your checkbook register, total any deposits you made that do not appear on the bank statement.
3. Add the ending bank balance to the outstanding deposits.
4. List all debit transactions from your checkbook register that do not appear on the statement. Debit transactions are any transactions that reduce your balance, including checks, online bill payments, withdrawals, and fees. Ardys listed check #582 and its check fee, since these did not appear on her statement.
5. Total all outstanding debit transactions.
6. Subtract the total debits from the previous total. The result should match the balance shown in your checkbook register.

If the balances do not match, check your addition and subtraction in the reconciliation process. Next, go through your checkbook register and check all addition and subtraction for the period covered by the statement. Finally, make certain that you have deducted service charges from and added any interest earned to your register balance. If you still cannot reconcile your account, ask the bank for help in discovering where the error lies. Usually you need to make an appointment for this. Be sure to take your checkbook, canceled checks, and bank statement with you. There normally is no charge for this service.

Do the reconciliation immediately upon receipt of the bank statement. This will allow you to report any problems to the bank as soon as possible. Occasionally the bank does make an error, which it will correct when you report the mistake.

▶ ENDORSING CHECKS

A check cannot be cashed until it has been endorsed. When two or more people are named as payees, all must endorse the check. To endorse a check, the payee named on the face of the check signs the back of the check in ink no more than one and one-half inches from the trailing edge, as shown here. There are three major types of endorsements: blank, special, and restrictive.

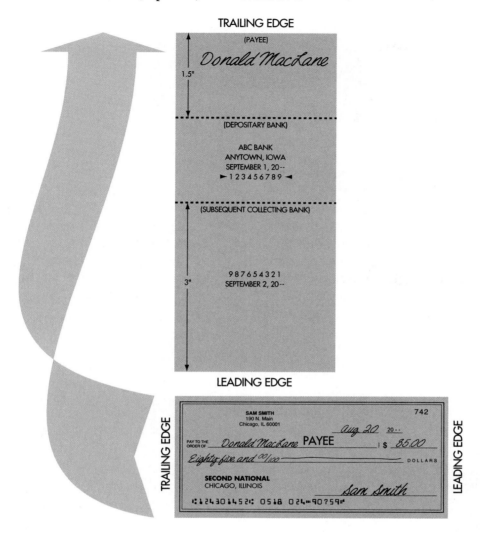

Blank Endorsement

A **blank endorsement** is the signature of the payee written exactly as his or her name appears on the front of the check.

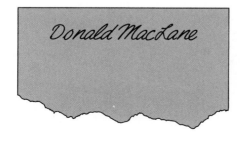

If Donald's name had been written incorrectly on the face of the check, he would correct the mistake by endorsing the check with the misspelled version first and then with the correct version of his name, as shown here.

Special Endorsement

A **special endorsement**, or an endorsement in full, is an endorsement that transfers the right to cash the check to someone else. It consists of the words "Pay to the order of [new payee's name]" and the signature of the original payee. In the following illustration, for example, Donald MacLane uses a check written to him to pay a debt owed to Diane Jones. By using a special endorsement, Donald avoids having to cash the check before repaying Diane.

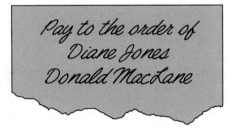

Restrictive Endorsement

A **restrictive endorsement** restricts or limits the use of a check. For example, a check endorsed with the words "For Deposit Only" above the payee's signature can be deposited only to the account specified. The restrictive endorsement is safer than the blank endorsement for use in mailing deposits, in night deposit systems, or in other circumstances that may result in loss of a check. If a check with a restrictive endorsement is lost, the finder cannot cash it.

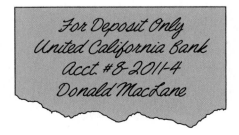

▶ TYPES OF CHECKING ACCOUNTS

Financial institutions offer many types of checking accounts. You should carefully study your options, because a wise choice can save you money. Most banks still offer free checking (no service fees) if you maintain a certain balance or agree to certain conditions (such as using ATMs rather than using teller services). Free checking is often available to senior citizens, nonprofit groups, and to others during special bank promotions, such as the opening of a new bank or branch.

 ## Career Focus

Financial managers direct bank branches and departments, resolve customers' problems, ensure that standards of service are maintained, and administer the institutions' operations and investments. They must keep updated on the rapidly growing selection of financial services and products. Financial managers perform data analysis and use it to offer senior managers ideas on how to maximize profits. A bachelor's degree in finance, accounting, or a related field is the minimum academic preparation, but many employers look for graduates with a master's degree.

For more information, refer to the *Occupational Outlook Handbook* at www.bls.gov or search the Internet using such key words as "careers," "jobs," and "banking."

Joint Accounts

Accounts can be either joint or individual. A *joint account* is opened by two or more people. Such an account is also called a *survivorship account* because any person who signs on the account has the right to the entire amount deposited. If one person using the account dies, the other (the survivor) then becomes the sole owner of the funds in the account. All of the checking accounts discussed in this chapter can be joint accounts.

When opening a joint account, you must decide if it will be an "or" account in contrast to an "and" account. If it is specified as an "or" account, any authorized account holder can write checks on the account. An "and" account with two owners, on the other hand, would require the signatures of both owners on checks.

Special Accounts

Most banks offer a special checking account to customers who have a small amount of activity in their accounts each month. Service fees are charged at a flat rate per month with an additional fee for each check written (for example, $3 per month plus 15 cents for each check cashed). Banks may charge service fees only when the number of checks written or deposits made in a month exceeds the set limit (such as more than 10 checks or 3 deposits in a given month). If you write only a few checks each month, this type of account might be right for you.

Another type of special account is one where you are assessed a small or no fee, but if you use banking services, such as making a deposit or withdrawal at a teller station, you agree to pay a fee for each service used. This type of account is good for people who have their paychecks deposited automatically by their employers and who use ATMs for withdrawals and other transactions.

Standard Accounts

A standard account usually has a set monthly service fee of between $5 and $12 but no per-check fee. Often, if you are able to maintain the average minimum balance the bank requires, you can avoid service fees entirely. Many banks give a package of services for this type of account, such as free traveler's checks, an ATM card, or a free safe deposit box. Some banks offer reduced interest rates on credit card balances to customers who also have checking, savings, and other accounts at their bank.

Interest-Bearing Accounts

Most financial institutions offer checking accounts that earn interest. With these accounts, your account balance must not fall below a minimum average set by the bank during any month. The minimum may be $500 or more.

How financial institutions determine the balance you must maintain to waive fees can make a big difference in the cost of an account. With the passage of the Truth-in-Savings Law in 1993, depositors must receive interest on their full balance every day. The *average-daily-balance method* triggers a fee or service charge only if the monthly average of each day's balance drops below a certain dollar amount.

Interest rates rise and fall with economic conditions. When overall interest rates drop, you may receive less than 1 percent. When overall interest rates rise, you might expect 5 percent or more. Keeping money in a low-interest account can cost you money in interest lost because you could have invested elsewhere. Yet, it also is useful in avoiding bank service charges.

Most credit unions offer *share accounts*. These are checking accounts with low (or no) average daily balance requirements and no service fees. If you are eligible for credit union membership, this type of account may be the least expensive and most convenient checking method for you. Credit unions and the types of services they offer will be discussed in Chapter 10.

✓Check Your Understanding

1. What is an overdraft? Why is it important to avoid overdrafts?
2. Why should you keep a checkbook register?
3. Why might you use a special endorsement?

Lesson 9.2

Other Banking Services

Goals
- **Describe various banking services.**
- **Identify services for which banks commonly charge fees.**

▶ OTHER BANKING SERVICES

A full-service bank is one that offers every possible kind of service, from checking accounts to credit cards, safe deposit boxes, loans, and automated tellers (ATMs). Other services commonly offered are online banking, telephone banking, certified checks, cashier's checks, money orders, and debit cards. Most banks offer FDIC (Federal Deposit Insurance Corporation) insurance, which protects the deposits of customers against loss up to $100,000 per account.

The Women's World Banking (WWB) network aims to have a major impact on expanding the economic assets, participation, and power of low-income women as entrepreneurs and economic agents by opening their access to finance, knowledge, and markets. At the end of 2002, the WWB in India had over 84,000 borrowers, all of whom were women in rural areas in the commerce and trade sectors. The average loan was approximately equivalent to $100.

Think Critically: Why would a bank make a loan for as little as $100? Does this make good business sense?

Guaranteed-Payment Checks

A **certified check** is a personal check that the bank guarantees or certifies to be good. Sometimes a payee might want you to get your personal check certified to reduce the risk of accepting your check in payment. For example, if you buy a used car from someone, the owner might want a certified check before allowing you to take the car.

To get a check certified, write your check in the normal manner. Then take it to your bank. A bank officer will immediately deduct the amount from your checking account, stamp the word "certified" on the check, and initial it. In effect, the bank puts a hold on that amount in your account so that the money will be there when the certified check is presented for payment. Most financial institutions charge the account holder for this service. Typically, the fee ranges from $2.50 to $5 per check.

A **cashier's check**, also called a *bank draft*, is a check written by a bank on its own funds. You can pay for a cashier's check through a withdrawal from your savings or checking account, or in cash. After receiving your payment, the teller makes out the cashier's check to your payee, and an officer of the bank signs it.

Cashier's checks are generally used when the payee requires a guaranteed payment but cash is not desirable. A cashier's check also might be requested instead of a personal check when the payee questions your credit standing or you do not have a credit history established. A cashier's check also can be used for transactions in which you wish to remain anonymous. The bank is listed as the maker of the check, and your identity need not be revealed. As with certified checks, many banks charge a fee for issuing cashier's checks.

Money Orders

Banks sell money orders to people who do not wish to use cash or do not have a checking account. A money order is like a check, except that it can never bounce. There is a charge for purchasing a money order. It can cost from 50 cents to $5 or more, depending on the size of the money order. You also can purchase money orders through the post office and local merchants.

Debit Cards

Debit cards allow immediate deductions from a checking account to pay for purchases. The debit card is presented at the time of purchase. When the merchant presents the debit card receipt to the bank, the amount of the purchase is immediately deducted from the customer's checking account and paid to the merchant. The debit card transaction is similar to writing a check to pay for purchases. The issuing bank may charge an annual fee for the card or a fee for each transaction. (Note: There is no credit extended to you when you are using a debit card.) Debit cards can also be used for cash withdrawals at ATMs.

Bank Credit Cards

You can apply to a full-service bank for a bank credit card such as VISA or MasterCard. If you meet the requirements, you can use the card instead of cash at any business that will accept it. Banks offering national credit cards usually charge both an annual fee for use of the card and interest on the unpaid account balance. The topics of credit and credit cards will be discussed in detail in Unit 4.

©GETTY IMAGES/PHOTODISC

What kinds of transactions can you make through ATMs?

Automated Teller Machines

Most banking transactions can now be made through electronic funds transfer (EFT). The main component of the EFT system is the automated teller machine (ATM). Using an ATM and an ATM (debit) card, you can make cash withdrawals from or check deposits to any of your accounts, make payments on loans, and pay bills. Using a VISA or MasterCard, you can receive a cash advance electronically. To use 24-hour ATMs, you must have a card that is electronically coded. You also must know your personal identification number (PIN), which usually is some combination of numbers and letters. For safety, memorize your personal identification number. Do not keep a written copy of it with your bank card.

Online and Telephone Banking

Most financial institutions offer online and telephone banking services to their customers. These services give you the ability to access your accounts from a computer or telephone, transfer money from one account to another, and pay bills by authorizing the bank to disburse money. You can find out your current balance, what checks have cleared, and which deposits have been entered. Online and telephone banking enable you to access your account anytime, day or night.

Stop Payment Orders

A **stop payment order** is a request that the bank not cash a specific check. The usual reason for stopping payment is that the check has been lost or stolen. By issuing a stop payment order, the check writer can safely write a new check, knowing that the original check cannot be cashed if it is presented to the bank. Most banks charge a fee (usually $20 or more) for stopping payment on a check. The stop payment is usually good for only 6 months. After that, the check will no longer be honored because checks over six months are not valid for cashing or depositing.

What items are commonly kept in safe deposit boxes?

Safe Deposit Boxes

Financial institutions offer safe deposit boxes for customers to store particularly valuable small items or documents. They charge a yearly fee based on the size of the box. Annual rental fees may range from $25–$100 or more. The customer is given two keys for the box. Documents commonly kept in a safe deposit box are birth certificates, marriage and death certificates, deeds and mortgages, and stocks and bonds. Jewelry, coin collections, and other small valuables also are commonly stored there. Keeping important documents and other items in a safe deposit box ensures that the items won't be stolen, lost, or destroyed. Documents that can be easily replaced with a duplicate need not be stored there.

When you rent a safe deposit box, you will fill out a signature card. Then each time you enter your safe deposit box, you must sign a form so that your signature can be compared to the one on file. This procedure prevents unlawful entry to your box by an unauthorized person.

Loans and Trusts

Financial institutions also make loans to finance the purchase of cars, homes, vacations, home improvements, and other items. Banks also can provide advice for estate planning and trusts. (You'll learn more about estates and trusts in Chapter 15.) In addition, banks can act as trustees of estates for minors and others. A *trustee* is a person or an institution that manages property for the benefit of someone else under a special agreement.

Financial Services

Many larger banks offer financial services such as purchasing or selling savings bonds and investment brokerage services to their depositors. You may buy and sell stocks and bonds through the brokerage service. The purchases and sales are "cleared" through your checking or savings accounts with the bank. Brokerage services will be discussed in Chapter 12. Many banks also purchase a block of bonds (debt obligations) that they allow their members and depositors to purchase. Generally there is no additional fee to buy or sell these securities (the fee is included in the purchase price). However, a minimum purchase such as $1,000 is often required.

▶ BANK FEES

Banks charge fees to their customers to help cover their operating costs. For example, when a bank grants you a loan, it charges you a loan fee. When the bank acts as a trustee, it charges a fee for this service. Banks also charge non-customers for services such as check cashing. If you want to cash a check at a bank where you do not have an account, the bank may charge you a fee or refuse to cash the check. Non-depositors pay for other services that may be free to depositors, such as traveler's checks and notary services.

Under the Truth-in-Savings Act (1993), checking advertised as "free" must carry no hidden charges or conditions. The bank or savings institution cannot charge regular maintenance or per-check fees or require balance minimums to avoid fees. However, it still may charge for a box of checks and for ATM transactions.

Banks make a lot of money from charging fees. Most charge for overdrafts, NSF checks, using tellers, balances that fall below the stated minimum, cashier's and certified checks, travelers' checks, use of other banks' ATMs, online bill payment, and monthly account servicing. The best way to avoid fees is to sign up for the kind of account that best fits your needs. For example, if you need to write a lot of checks each month, sign up for an account that does not charge a per-check fee. Some accounts charge a fee for using a teller. Only sign up for such an account if you can do almost all of your transactions by ATM. Shop around and find the account that is right for you. Be aware of the rules of your account, so that you don't violate them, resulting in high fees. If your account requires a minimum balance, plan enough cushion that your balance will not drop below that amount and incur the fee.

✅ Check Your Understanding

1. To withdraw money from your account using an ATM, what do you need besides an ATM card?

2. What would you put into a safe deposit box?

3. What fees does the Truth-in-Savings Act allow banks to charge on "free" checking accounts?

Issues in Your World

Shopping for the Right Bank

A checking account is a personal choice. Some people choose the bank closest to their home or work. Others choose the biggest bank or the one with the most ATMs. While all of these are good reasons, there are many other considerations in choosing your bank. Sometimes the best choice is a credit union where you can have the same services and possibly lower fees.

Finding the right bank can take a lot of time. All banks and services are not the same; they vary a great deal. A good way to start is to make a list of the features that are important to you. Rank them 1 to 10. For example, #1 may be a low interest rate on a VISA card; #2 may be a low minimum deposit for a free or interest-bearing account; and #3 may be low or no service fees. Arrange your features into a table, either on paper or in a word processor or spreadsheet. At the top, list the banks that you are considering. Your table might look like this:

	Bank 1	*Bank 2*	*Bank 3*
1. Free online bill payment			
2. Low/no minimum deposit			
3. Low/no service fee			
4. Telephone banking available			
5. Low-cost credit card available			
6. Conveniently located ATMs			

Fill in your table by inserting information you find out about the different banks. Then compare information to determine which bank overall provides the best services at the lowest costs for you.

Think Critically

1. Which is your favorite bank or credit union? Why?

2. What features do you think are the most important when choosing a financial institution for your checking account?

3. What would cause you to switch from one financial institution to another?

Chapter Assessment

SUMMARY

9.1
* A checking account is a safe, convenient way to pay bills, with a built-in record keeping system.
* To open a checking account, fill out a signature authorization form and make a deposit.
* To write a check, fill in the current date, name of the payee, and the amount in figures and words. Then sign the form.
* After setting up your online account, you can pay bills by selecting the payee and entering the amount.
* As soon as you make a checking transaction, record it in your checkbook register.
* Reconcile your bank statement with your register each month and correct any errors.
* To cash a check, you must endorse it with a blank, special, or restrictive endorsement.

9.2
* Certified checks and cashier's checks guarantee payment.
* If you don't have a checking account, you can buy a money order to use like a check.
* You can pay for purchases or make ATM transactions using a debit card.
* Online and telephone banking enable you to access your account 24 hours a day.
* To avoid high bank fees, choose the type of account that best fits your needs and follow the account rules.

REVIEW TERMS

Directions

Can you find the definition for each of the following terms used in Chapter 9?

blank endorsement	floating a check
canceled check	overdraft
cashier's check	reconciliation
certified check	restrictive endorsement
check	special endorsement
checkbook register	stop payment order
demand deposit	

1. A check written for more money than the writer's account contains.

2. A request that the bank not cash a specific check.

3. Comparing your checkbook register with the bank statement each month.

4. A check that bears the bank's stamp, indicating that it has cleared.

5. An endorsement that consists only of the payee's signature.

6. An endorsement, such as the words "For Deposit Only," that limits use of the check.

7. A booklet used for recording checking account transactions.

8. An endorsement that transfers the right to cash the check to someone else.

9. A personal check guaranteed by the bank to be good.

10. Money on deposit in a bank that can be withdrawn at any time.

11. A written order to a bank to pay a stated amount to the person or business named on it.

12. Intentionally writing a check on an account without sufficient funds in the hope of making a deposit before the check is cashed.

13. A check written by a bank on its own funds.

REVIEW FACTS AND IDEAS

1. Why is a checking account called a demand deposit?

2. What is a canceled check, and why is it important to the checking account owner?

3. Describe some reasons for having a checking account.

4. What responsibilities do checking account owners have when using their account?

5. Why would you be asked your mother's maiden name when opening a bank account?

6. Why should you record online bill payments in your checkbook register?

7. Why do you need to reconcile your checking account promptly when you receive the monthly bank statement?

8. List three types of endorsements and give a written example of each.

9. What is a joint checking account?

10. What types of checking accounts do financial institutions offer? Briefly describe each type.

11. How is a bank debit card different from a bank credit card?

12. What is the purpose of a PIN (personal identification number)?

13. List at least four banking services provided by financial institutions.

APPLY YOUR KNOWLEDGE

1. Write on plain paper the information needed for a signature authorization form, as shown in Figure 9-1.

2. Visit a bank Web site that offers online bill payment. Write a summary of the process for setting up your list of payees. Share your summary with the class.

UNIT 2 • Money Management

3. Using Figure 9-2 as an example and following the guidelines on pages 200–203, write these checks:
   a. Check No. 12 to Melvin Quigly for $34.44, written today.
   b. Check No. 322 to Save-Now Stores for $15.01, written today. The purpose of your check is to buy school supplies.
   c. Check No. 484 to M.A. Rosario for $91.10, written today.
   Note: Blank checks are available in the *Student Activity Guide.*

4. Using Figure 9-4 as an example and following the guidelines on pages 203–204, prepare these deposit slips:
   a. Today's date; currency $40.00; coins $1.44; Check No. 18-81 for $51.00; no cash received back with the deposit transaction.
   b. Today's date; Check No. 40-22 for $300.00 and Check No. 24-12 for $32.00; $20.00 cash received back with the deposit transaction.
   Note: Blank deposit slips are available in the *Student Activity Guide.*

5. Using Figure 9-6 as an example, determine your ending reconciled checkbook balance when all of the following six conditions exist:
   a. Your ending checkbook balance is $311.40 (before the service fee is deducted).
   b. You made an error, resulting in $30.00 less showing in your account than should be.
   c. The service fee is $6.00.
   d. The ending bank balance is $402.00.
   e. Outstanding deposits total $100.00.
   f. Outstanding checks total $166.60.

6. Determine your ending reconciled checkbook balance when all of the following six conditions exist:
   a. Your checkbook ending balance is $800.40 (before the service fee is deducted).
   b. The service fee is $3.00.
   c. The ending bank balance is $1,100.00.
   d. Outstanding deposits total $50.00.
   e. Outstanding checks total $352.60.

7. List the names, addresses, and telephone numbers of five financial institutions in your community, and list the services provided by each. What type of checking account might you choose? Why?

8. Visit three bank Web sites and compare the types of accounts and services they offer. Do all of them allow you to do your banking online?

1. Find the errors in the following check.

RICHARD McGUIRE Phone: 555-0109 2802 Saratoga Street Ogden, UT 79393-4081	518

June 1 20 -- $\frac{97\text{-}145}{1243}$

PAY TO THE ORDER OF ___ *Best Buys* ___ | $ ___ *35.00* ___

Thirty five and $^{00}/_{100}$ _____ DOLLARS

For Classroom Use Only

PEAK BANK AND TRUST
OGDEN, UTAH

MEMO _____ *Rick McGuire*

⑆124301452⑇ 0518 024⑈90759⑈

2. The deposit slip shown here was written to deposit the check in Question No. 1. Find the errors on the deposit slip.

DEPOSIT SLIP

BEST BUYS FOODS
Ogden, Utah

CURRENCY		
COIN		
1243	35	00

$\frac{24/12\text{-}7}{33}$

DATE *June 1* _____ 20 __

SIGN HERE FOR LESS CASH IN TELLER'S PRESENCE

STATE BANK OF
UTAH
Main Branch   Ogden, Utah

TOTAL FROM OTHER SIDE		
TOTAL	35	00
LESS CASH RECEIVED		
NET DEPOSIT	30	00

A hold for uncollected funds may be placed on checks or similar instruments you deposit. Any delay will not exceed the period of time permitted by law.

⑆123000 123⑇017 0 30123⑆   FOR CLASSROOM USE ONLY

RM 552 (0584)

3. Complete the bank reconciliation form shown here by first finishing the checkbook register on the next page, entering the service charge, and then computing balances. (Don't write in your textbook. Use another piece of paper.)

CHECK NO. OR TRANSACTION CODE	DATE	DESCRIPTION OF TRANSACTION	PAYMENT/ DEBIT(−)		FEE (−)	✓	DEPOSIT/ CREDIT (+)		BALANCE $ 100	00
101	3/1/--	Grocery Mart	$ 24	75			$		24	75
		Groceries							75	25
ON	3/3/--	Independent Phone Co.	13	00					13	00
		Online Payment								
DEP	3/5/--	ATM Deposit					30	00	30	00
102	3/8/--	Local High School	10	00					10	00
		Band Donation								
103	3/10/--	Alan's Bakery	3	80					3	80
		Bread								
104	3/15/--	Grocery Mart	18	20					18	20
		Groceries								
DEP	3/18/--	Deposit					42	00	42	00
105	3/20/--	Acme Hardware	4	18					4	18
		Hammer								

Bank Statement
HOMETOWN BANK

Statement Date: March 31, 20—
Opening Balance: $100.00
Ending Balance: $77.25

Checks

Check No.	Date Paid	Amount
101	3/4/—	24.75
102	3/11/—	10.00
103	3/11/—	3.80

Debits and Withdrawals

Date	Amount	Description
3/3/—	13.00	Online bill payment
3/31/—	1.20	Service charge

Deposits

Date	Amount	Description
3/5/—	30.00	ATM Deposit

Account Reconciliation

1. Ending balance shown on the bank statement: _____

2. Total of all credits and deposits made but not shown on statement: _____

3. Total lines 1 and 2: _____

4. List all checks, withdrawals, and debits made but not shown on statement:

Check No. or Transaction Code	Amount	

5. Total of outstanding debit transactions: _____

6. Subtract line 5 from line 3: _____
   (Result should match checkbook balance.)

For related activities and links, point your browser to ***www.mypf.swlearning.com***

PROJECT

Assessing Your Financial Health

OVERVIEW

This project is designed to help you begin the financial planning process. Here you will assess your financial health by carefully examining your present financial condition. By taking inventory of where you are now, you can begin to build a plan for the future.

▶ YOUR JOB

Let's begin with your job. The money you earn affects what you are able to purchase and save now as well as your future prospects for financial stability. Rate your current job in terms of your opportunities for advancement, the company's chances for survival, and job satisfaction. If you feel you are in a dead-end job, working for a weak or financially unstable company or in an obsolete industry, start looking for a more promising situation. On the other hand, if you like your work, and the future looks good for the company and the industry, then examine your opportunities for advancement. In addition, consider your own mental attitude, skills, and aptitudes for higher-level positions. If you aren't currently working or are in a dead-end job, get started by interviewing a person who has the type of job you'd like to have.

Remember that the pay you receive in any job is only part of what you get as an employee. You also should consider benefits, training received, and opportunities for making contacts that could be important in your career plans.

Worksheet 1 (Rate Your Job) is designed to help you assess your current job and any potential job you might consider. Complete Worksheet 1 provided in the *Student Activity Guide*. (For your reference, it also appears at the end of this project.) When you examine the scores, you will have a clearer picture of the direction you should pursue. The time to do career research is now, not when you've invested several years of your life in the wrong job, the wrong employer, or the wrong industry.

Worksheet 1 Scores: A score of 25 points is possible for each section. A score between 20 and 25 for any section indicates stability and good prospects for the future. A score between 15 and 20 indicates that you should examine the characteristics carefully before making long-term commitments. A score between 10 and 15 indicates that you should start looking for a new job, a new employer, or a new type of career soon. A score under 10 indicates that you are in a hopelessly dead-end job that has no future and should be viewed as only temporary.

▶ YOUR INCOME AND OUTGO (CASH FLOW)

Having completed the budgeting exercises in Chapter 8, you recognize the importance of keeping track of dollars that regularly flow through your hands. Worksheet 2 is a Cash Flow Statement that will help you identify where your money comes from and where it goes. In addition, it allows you to make projections for future income and outgo on a yearly basis. It's important to pinpoint your spending habits, analyze them, and take steps to improve your financial picture.

Examine your cash flow closely, looking for places where your income may be leaking away. Plugging the small leaks will help you build larger cash reserves and spend money more wisely. For example, think about three things you bought last year and later regretted. What is the total amount of money you could have saved? What other things could you have purchased?

Complete Worksheet 2, which is provided in the *Student Activity Guide*. (For your reference, it also appears at the end of this project.)

▶ YOUR NET WORTH

An assessment of where you stand begins with what you own and owe at the moment. Worksheet 3 is a Net Worth Analysis that is used for listing your assets and liabilities and making projections of where you would like to be at some future date (such as a month, a year, or five years).

The purpose of the net worth analysis is threefold: (1) to show you your strong and weak areas, (2) to help you plan for specific short-term changes, and (3) to allow you to project goals into the future based on those decisions.

Complete Worksheet 3 in the *Student Activity Guide*. (For your reference, it also appears at the end of this project.)

UNIT 2 PROJECT

► YOUR TAX LIABILITY (FOR EXTRA CREDIT)

Based on the income tax returns you prepared in Chapter 7, use Worksheet 4 (Tax Liability) to analyze your total tax and determine whether or not you can reduce your taxes through careful planning. Keep copies of your tax returns. Compare total tax by preparing Forms 1040EZ, 1040A, and the long Form 1040. Use the form that gives the greatest tax advantage (that is, the lowest amount of taxes). Then study tax booklets and other information to see where you can benefit from taking more deductions.

Complete Worksheet 4 (Tax Liability) in the *Student Activity Guide*. (For your reference, it also appears at the end of this project.)

WORKSHEET 1
Rate Your Job

Directions: Rate each of the following characteristics on a 1 to 5 point scale. A score of 5 means *always;* a score of 4 means *usually;* a score of 3 means *as often as needed;* a score of 2 means *sometimes;* a score of 1 means *never;* and a score of 0 means *not applicable.* If you do not have a job, complete this worksheet after doing research about your desired future job.

Your Score

1. You enjoy the work you do, and you look forward to going to work each day.   _____
2. You are willing to get extra training, education, or extra skills in order to be challenged.   _____
3. You seek additional responsibility and can do the job well.   _____
4. You like the work environment, and others recognize you as someone who will help and be a team player.   _____
5. You receive regular pay raises large enough to keep you ahead of inflation and support your desired lifestyle.   _____

Your total _____

Job Score

1. The product or service is in demand and prospects look good for the future.   _____
2. The industry is growing as a whole, with opportunities for advancement in other companies similar to yours.   _____
3. The product or service is inflation-resistant (rising prices don't greatly affect sales).   _____
4. Turnover among employees is generally low.   _____
5. Pay scale and fringe benefits compare well with other companies in the same field.   _____

Job total _____

Employer's Score

1. Your boss calls on you to handle tough assignments and gives you credit for your accomplishments.   _____
2. The boss regularly solicits your suggestions and follows them.   _____
3. The company promotes from within.   _____
4. The company has a large number of customers rather than just a few big ones.   _____
5. The company is well established and still growing.   _____

Employer's total _____

Total of all points _____

WORKSHEET 2
Cash Flow Statement

Directions: Keep a record of income and expenses for a month (you might want to do this for a year to build a budget base for the following year). In the first column, list each item you receive or spend in a month. In the second column, project your annual income or expense for each item. In the third column, check any items that need attention. In the fourth column, indicate how much (increase or decrease) each item should change monthly—what you'd like to accomplish. In the fifth column, indicate how much additional money you would save (or spend) annually by making the changes in the fourth column.

Example:	THIS MONTH	YEARLY TOTAL	NEED CHANGE	MONTHLY CHANGE	YEARLY EFFECT
Entertainment expense	$38.00	$456.00		$12.00	$144.00

	1	2	3	4	5
ITEM	THIS MONTH	YEARLY TOTAL	NEED CHANGE	MONTHLY CHANGE	YEARLY EFFECT
Income:					
Take-home pay	_____	_____	_____	_____	_____
Bonuses/gifts	_____	_____	_____	_____	_____
Interest income	_____	_____	_____	_____	_____
Other _____	_____	_____	_____	_____	_____
Totals	_____	_____	_____	_____	_____
Outgo:					
_____	_____	_____	_____	_____	_____
_____	_____	_____	_____	_____	_____
_____	_____	_____	_____	_____	_____
_____	_____	_____	_____	_____	_____
_____	_____	_____	_____	_____	_____
_____	_____	_____	_____	_____	_____
Savings	_____	_____	_____	_____	_____
Totals	_____	_____	_____	_____	_____

Analysis:
List ways you can cut expenses or increase income (such as by substituting activities, buying cheaper products, or working odd jobs in the summer).

WORKSHEET 3
Net Worth Analysis

Directions: Fill in the blanks below. In column 1, write in the market value of each item you possess or debt you owe. See Chapter 8 for definitions of terms (assets, liabilities, and net worth). In column 2, write in what each item will be worth in one year. In column 3, indicate the value of each item in five years. You can assume an item will increase it if gains in value over time (through interest or inflation) or if you add to or purchase an item from that category.

ITEM	1 TODAY'S BALANCE	2 ONE-YEAR PROJECTION	3 FIVE-YEAR PROJECTION
Assets:			
	$_____	$_____	$_____
Total assets	_____	_____	_____
Liabilities:			
Total liabilities	_____	_____	_____
Net worth	_____	_____	_____

Analysis: List major purchases that you wish to make and how you plan to pay for them.

WORKSHEET 4
Tax Liability

Directions: To complete this worksheet, first list your gross income, taxable income, tax before credits, and total tax for the last three years you have filed tax returns and paid income taxes. If you have not yet filed a tax return, use the projected gross income that you would receive in the entry-level position of your choice (used for Worksheet 1). Compute taxes owed on that amount (see Chapter 7). Then compute how much you could save in income taxes if you made changes as shown. Finally, list some of the tax deductions and credits available on the Form 1040 in the *Student Activity Guide* that you might use to decrease your tax liability.

YEAR	GROSS INCOME	ADJUSTED GROSS INCOME	TAXABLE INCOME	TAX (BEFORE CREDITS)	TOTAL TAX (AFTER CREDITS)
1. _____	_____	_____	_____	_____	_____
2. _____	_____	_____	_____	_____	_____
3. _____	_____	_____	_____	_____	_____

How would each of the above years' tax liabilities have changed *if* you could have had the following changes:

YEAR	CHANGE	TAX DECREASE
1	IRA deduction of $2,000	$_____
2	Child care credit of $500	$_____
3	One more exemption	$_____

Analysis:
Examine Schedule A of Form 1040 (itemized deductions) in the *Student Activity Guide.* Identify some deductions you might wish to take advantage of to reduce your tax liability.

Examine Form 1040 in the *Student Activity Guide* and list additional types of income, deductions, and credits that are required and/or permitted when this form is used.

unit 3

Financial Security

Project: **Assessing Your Financial Security**

U nit 3 starts with a basic explanation of saving, investing, investment alternatives, investment risks, and how to invest wisely. You will explore the types of stock. You will also look at bonds, mutual funds, real estate, precious metals, gems, and collectibles, as well as futures and options.

You'll end this unit learning about retirement and estate planning, wills, trusts, and the taxatio of your estate.

Saving for the Future

TERMS TO KNOW

discretionary
  income
principal
interest
compound
  interest

annual
  percentage yield
  (APY)
share account
securities
stockbroker

liquidity
certificate of
  deposit (CD)
maturity date
money market
  account

Consider This. . .

Hazem saves regularly from his allowance and the money he gets from relatives and friends for special occasions. He makes it a point to set aside some of what he receives, rather than spending all of it.

"For every dollar I save, Dad will contribute 10 cents to my savings," Hazem told his best friend. "That gives me a 10 percent return, in addition to the interest I earn on my savings account. Dad wants me to save money for the future. I'm going to college some day, and I want to minimize the amount of student loans I'll need. It may not seem like a lot of money each month, but every year my savings grow. This year, I'll have enough to get a CD at the bank. That way, I get a higher interest rate on money deposited. Sure, it's tempting to spend some of my savings on fun stuff, but I have to pay back the 10 percent to my dad on everything I take out. It's kind of like a tax on spending, isn't it?"

Savings Goals and Institutions

Goals
- Describe different purposes of saving.
- Explain how money grows through compounding interest.
- List and describe the financial institutions where you can save.

▶ WHY YOU SHOULD SAVE

The best reason to save some of your income as you earn it is to provide for future needs, both expected and unexpected. If you set nothing aside for these inevitable needs, you will constantly live on the edge of financial disaster. Let's begin by examining some reasons why you should start saving regularly.

Short-Term Needs

Often you will have short-term needs that require money beyond what you can cover with your current paycheck. You will have to pay for these things out of savings. Some of these needs you can anticipate. For those, you can plan the savings into your budget. Others you can't foresee, but you must have enough in savings to cover them anyway. Some short-term needs you might encounter include the following:

©GETTY IMAGES/PHOTODISC

1. Emergencies—such as unemployment, sickness, accident, or death in the family.

2. Vacations—short weekend trips or longer excursions.

3. Social events—weddings, family gatherings, or other potentially costly special occasions.

4. Major purchases—a car, major appliances, furniture, remodeling, or other expenses that become necessary as time goes by. Things do wear out and have to be replaced, repaired, or remodeled.

What are some short-term needs that could require you to save?

Long-Term Needs

While you need savings to meet emergencies and short-term needs, investing provides for long-term needs. Long-term needs can require a lot of money, such as for home ownership, education, and retirement. Saving money now will enable you to make larger purchases in the future, invest, and accumulate enough money for a secure retirement.

HOME OWNERSHIP

A downpayment on a house amounts to thousands of dollars. The larger the downpayment you can make, the smaller your monthly payments will be. Many people consider owning their own home a very important part of their future.

EDUCATION

Many high school graduates will borrow money, obtain grants and scholarships, or pay for their own post-secondary training. Education for one or both spouses may involve completing a bachelor's or master's degree, an advanced degree (such as law or medical), or mastering some special skill or trade through a vocational or apprenticeship program. Education is a long-term investment that pays off in higher income potential.

In addition, many couples begin a savings plan when children are born. Then when the time comes for college, they have money for their children's education.

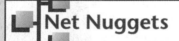 Net Nuggets

For many families, the greatest financial worry is whether they will be able to afford a college education for their children. Savingforcollege.com provides information and resources concerning qualified tuition programs, known as "529 plans." These plans are education savings plans operated by state or educational institutions, designed to help families set aside funds for future college costs. Check out the site at www.savingforcollege.com.

RETIREMENT

Social security was never designed to provide a comfortable retirement. It is meant to be a supplement to an individual's own savings. To have a financially secure retirement, you must begin to save regularly as early in life as you can.

INVESTING

After you have saved enough to cover daily expenses and emergencies, you can afford to invest your extra savings. Investing in stocks, bonds, mutual funds, real estate, and other investments can make your money grow faster than a savings account can. Because investments are often risky, you should make them in addition to—not instead of—regular savings. Types of investments will be described in later chapters.

Financial Security

Probably the best reason to save is the peace of mind that comes from knowing that when needs arise, you will have adequate money to pay for them now and into the future. The amount of money you save will vary according to several factors: (1) the amount of your **discretionary income**—what you have left over after you have paid your bills; (2) the importance you attach to savings; (3) your anticipated needs and wants; and (4) your will power, or ability to give up present spending in order to provide for your future.

▶ HOW YOUR MONEY GROWS

The amount of money deposited by a saver is called the **principal**. For use of the saver's money, the financial institution pays the saver money called **interest**. **Compound interest** is interest computed on the original principal plus accumulated interest. Figure 10-1 illustrates how interest is compounded annually. Notice how the interest earned increases each year because the saver is earning interest on the previous year's interest *as well as* on the initial deposit.

The more often interest is compounded, the greater your earnings. (See the Math Minute feature.) Figure 10-2 (page 240) illustrates what happens when 6 percent interest is compounded quarterly (every three months) and added to the principal before more interest is calculated. Notice that you will earn more interest with quarterly compounding than with annual compounding. Today, many financial institutions offer interest compounded each day savings are on deposit. They use computers to rapidly compute the compounding daily interest.

COMPOUNDING INTEREST ANNUALLY

figure 10-1 ◀◀ ◀ (◉)

Year	Beginning Balance	Interest Earned (5%)	Ending Balance
1	$100.00	$5.00	$105.00
2	105.00	5.25	110.25
3	110.25	5.51	115.76

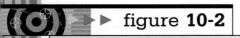 figure 10-2   COMPOUNDING INTEREST QUARTERLY

			Quarterly Interest				
Year	Beginning Balance	Rate	1	2	3	4	Ending Balance
1	$100.00	.015	$1.50	$1.52	$1.55	$1.57	$106.14
2	$106.14	.015	$1.59	$1.62	$1.64	$1.66	$112.65
3	$112.65	.015	$1.69	$1.72	$1.74	$1.77	$119.57

Quarterly Compounding
Annual Interest Rate = 6%

Earnings on savings can be measured by the *rate of return* or *yield*. *Yield* is the percentage of increase in the value of your savings due to earned interest. Because financial institutions compound interest in many ways, comparing yields can be difficult. To solve this problem, the law requires all financial institutions to tell consumers the **annual percentage yield (APY)** on their accounts. This is the actual interest rate the account pays per year, with compounding included. Because all financial institutions must calculate APY the same way, you can use APY to easily compare the yields on different accounts.

▶ WHERE YOU CAN SAVE

Most cities have commercial banks, savings banks, savings and loan associations, credit unions, and brokerage firms. Most of these institutions have greatly expanded their services in recent years, so the differences among them are becoming increasingly blurred. Interest rates vary among all savings institutions. No one type will always offer the best deal.

Commercial Banks

Commercial banks provide the widest variety of banking services of any financial institutions. Many people prefer to keep their checking and savings accounts in the same bank for ease in transferring funds and making deposits and withdrawals. Commercial banks offer many kinds of savings and checking accounts. Almost all commercial banks are insured by the Federal Deposit Insurance Corporation (FDIC). This insurance protects depositors from loss due to bank failure, up to $100,000 per account.

Math Minute

Compound interest means earning interest on principal, and then allowing the interest to remain on deposit so you will then earn interest on both your principal and your previous interest. Let's look at how this happens when interest is compounded quarterly for three years. To compute interest compounded quarterly, divide the annual interest rate by 4 to get the quarterly rate. For monthly compounding, divide the annual interest rate by 12. For interest compounded every 6 months (a half year), divide the annual rate by 2. Round all interest computations up if the remainder is .5 or greater.

Suppose you deposit $100 in a savings account that will pay you 6 percent per year, compounded quarterly. This means that for each quarter, you will receive ¼ of the yearly interest. Six percent divided by 4 is 1.5 percent each quarter. At the end of the first quarter, you will have earned $1.50 in interest, using the following computation:

$$\$100 \times .015 = \$1.50$$

At the beginning of the second quarter, you now have $101.50 in your account ($100 + the $1.50 interest). At the end of the second quarter, you will earn interest as follows:

$$\$101.50 \times .015 = \$1.52$$

At the beginning of the third quarter, you have $103.02 ($101.50 + the $1.52 interest). At the end of the third quarter, you will earn interest as follows:

$$\$103.02 \times .015 = \$1.55$$

At the beginning of the fourth quarter, you have $104.57 ($103.02 + the $1.55 interest). At the end of the fourth quarter (the end of the first year), you will earn interest as follows:

$$\$104.57 \times .015 = \$1.57$$

Your balance at the end of the first year is $106.14. You earned a total of $6.14 in interest for the year. At the end of Year 3, your balance is $119.57. That's a total interest of $19.57 on your original deposit of $100, as shown in Figure 10-2. Based on the previous example, compute your quarterly interest for three years if you deposit $500 at 8 percent, compounded quarterly.

Year	Beginning Balance	Rate	Quarterly Interest 1	2	3	4	Ending Balance
1	$500.00	____	$____	$____	$____	$____	$____
2	$____	____	$____	$____	$____	$____	$____
3	$____	____	$____	$____	$____	$____	$____

Solution:

Year	Beginning Balance	Rate	Quarterly Interest 1	2	3	4	Ending Balance
1	$500.00	.02	$10.00	$10.20	$10.40	$10.61	$541.21
2	$541.21	.02	$10.82	$11.04	$11.26	$11.49	$585.82
3	$585.82	.02	$11.72	$11.95	$12.19	$12.43	$634.11

Savings Banks

Savings banks are usually referred to as mutual savings banks. These financial institutions are few in number—about 500 of them in roughly a dozen states, mostly throughout New England and the Northeast—but substantial in size. Savings banks are insured by the FDIC. Two primary services offered by these institutions are savings accounts and loans on real property, including mortgages and home-improvement loans.

Savings and Loan Associations

Savings and loan associations (S&Ls) are organized primarily to lend money for home mortgages. S&Ls offer many of the services of commercial banks, including interest-bearing checking accounts and special savings plans. You may find a slightly higher interest rate on savings at an S&L. S&Ls are insured by the FDIC.

Why might people prefer to keep their checking and savings accounts in the same bank?

Credit Unions

Credit unions are not-for-profit organizations established by groups of employees in similar occupations who pool their money. To use a credit union, you must be a member of the employee group. Credit unions generally offer higher interest rates on savings and lower interest rates on loans. Their membership in the NCUA (National Credit Union Administration) provides insurance for depositors' accounts, up to $100,000.

Credit unions are owned by their members. A savings account at a credit union is usually called a **share account**. Credit union members save their money in the form of "shares," or part ownership in the credit union. From funds accumulated by these shares, the credit union makes loans to its members. Credit unions also offer IRAs (Individual Retirement Accounts) and other financial services to members, including savings and investing plans that may pay higher rates of return than other banking options.

Brokerage Firms

Brokerage firms buy and sell different types of securities. **Securities** are stocks and bonds issued by corporations or by the government. Stocks represent equity, or ownership. Bonds represent debt, or a loan. In other words, when you buy stock, you become an owner of the company. When you buy a bond, you are loaning money to the company or to the government. Investors buy and sell securities through a **stockbroker**, who works for the brokerage firm. As you will learn in a later chapter, you can buy stocks, bonds, and mutual funds directly, or you can buy them through brokerage firms.

UNIT 3 • Financial Security

✓ Check Your Understanding

1. Why do you need to start saving now to cover long-term needs?
2. Explain how compounding interest makes your savings grow.
3. How can you compare interest rates on accounts that compound differently?

Lesson 10.2

Savings Options, Features, and Plans

Goals
- Explain the features and purposes of different savings options.
- Discuss some factors that influence the selection of a savings plan.
- Explain at least two ways to save regularly.

▶ SAVINGS OPTIONS

Once you have decided to establish a savings program, you need to know about the different savings options available to you. You may want to deposit money in several types of accounts, because each can contribute to your overall plan in different ways.

Regular Savings Account

A regular savings account has a major advantage—high liquidity. **Liquidity** is the ability of an asset (a resource owned) to be converted into cash quickly without loss of value. A regular savings account is said to be very liquid because you can withdraw your money at any time without penalty. The tradeoff for high liquidity, however, is lower interest. A regular savings account generally pays the least amount of interest of the savings options.

Once you have opened the account, you are free to make withdrawals and deposits. Some financial institutions charge service fees when you make more than a maximum number of withdrawals in a certain period of time. Other institutions charge a monthly fee if your

Career Focus

Personal financial advisors use their knowledge of investments, tax laws, and insurance to recommend financial options to individuals in line with their short-term and long-term goals. Some of the issues that these advisors address are retirement and estate planning, funding for college, and general investment options. While most offer advice on a wide range of topics, some specialize in areas such as retirement and estate planning or risk management. A bachelor's degree in accounting, finance, economics, business, mathematics, or law provides good preparation for the occupation. Courses in investments, taxes, estate planning, and risk management also are helpful.

For more information, refer to the *Occupational Outlook Handbook* at www.bls.gov or search the Internet using such key words as "careers," "jobs," and "financial planning."

balance falls below a set minimum. In most cases, you will receive a debit or ATM card that goes with the account so that you can make withdrawals and deposits at ATMs. You can also check your balance and transfer money between your checking and savings accounts online and by telephone.

Certificate of Deposit

A **certificate of deposit (CD)**, or time deposit, is a deposit that earns a fixed interest rate for a specified length of time—for example, 5 percent for six months. A CD requires a minimum deposit. The interest rate on a CD is usually slightly higher than on regular savings accounts because CDs are less liquid. You must leave the money in the CD for the full time period. If you take out any part of your money early, you will pay an early withdrawal penalty. Generally, the penalty is in the form of substantially less interest earned on the CD.

A CD has a set **maturity date**—the date on which an investment becomes due for payment. Within a stated number days after the maturity date, your certificate will renew automatically. You may prefer to redeem it for cash or purchase a new certificate for a different time period. Financial institutions offer CDs that allow the interest to accumulate to maturity. Often you can choose to receive a check periodically for the interest earned or have the interest deposited in a separate regular account.

©GETTY IMAGES/PHOTODISC

Why is a regular savings account said to be very liquid?

Money Market Account

A **money market account** is a combination savings-investment plan in which money deposited is used to purchase safe, liquid securities. Brokerage firms as well as banks offer money market accounts. Money may be deposited or withdrawn from a money market account at any time without a fee. As a result, this account is quite liquid.

Money market accounts with brokerage firms are not insured. At banks, some money market accounts are insured by the FDIC. Others are not. However, even without insurance, money market accounts are generally considered safe because the securities backing these funds are very stable. Managers of these accounts frequently use the money to purchase short-term (one year or less) securities issued by the U.S. Treasury. Therefore, the chance of losing your money is very low.

Unlike regular savings accounts, the interest rates on money market accounts go up and down with the stock market. Banks and brokerage firms may change their rates on these accounts as much as weekly, or even more often. However, interest rates on money market accounts are typically higher than on regular savings accounts, and the rate changes are small. Usually money market accounts require a minimum balance, such as $500 or more. These accounts also may have restrictions on the number of checks you can write over a period of time and the minimum amount for which you can write each check.

▶ SELECTING A SAVINGS PLAN

There are important factors to consider in selecting a savings account and a savings institution. All savings or investment options involve a tradeoff between liquidity or safety and yield. The safer or more liquid an investment, the less earning potential it is likely to have. Use the following criteria in judging which savings options best meet your needs.

Liquidity

Liquidity (how quickly you can turn savings into cash when you want it) may be important to you. The need for liquidity will vary, based on your age, health, family situation, and overall wealth. For example, if you have little money left over after paying your bills, you may need to keep this money liquid so you can get it quickly, without penalty, if you face some emergency. In this case, a regular savings account or money market account would be best for you. CDs impose a penalty if you withdraw early, so you should choose this option when you don't expect to need the money before the maturity date.

©GETTY IMAGES/PHOTODISC

What are some important factors to consider when selecting a savings account and a savings institution?

Safety

You want your money to be safe from loss. Most financial institutions are insured by a government agency, the FDIC or NCUA. Accounts protected by insurance are safe for up to $100,000. You should be sure the financial institution of your choice has federal insurance to protect your deposit. Deposits in banks, no matter what type, are almost always safer than investments in the stock market.

Convenience

People often choose their financial institution because of convenience of location and the services offered. Interest rates on various savings accounts and certificates of deposit may vary only slightly. Fees charged are often very similar within a community.

Many banks have several branches within a limited geographic area, which makes your banking convenient. If a bank has only one branch located several miles from your home, the inconvenience of driving there might outweigh a slightly higher interest rate at this bank. A very large bank may have branches in other states, giving you banking privileges while out of town.

Many banks offer drive-up windows with expanded hours. Telephone and online banking make most savings plans very accessible. Branches are often located in grocery stores or residential areas. You may want to look for a bank that offers ATMs near your home or job, or at other locations you frequent, such as the local shopping mall.

Interest-Earning Potential (Yield)

You want to earn as much interest as you can on your deposit, while maintaining the degree of liquidity, safety, and convenience you want. Shop around for the best APY in your area for the type of account you want. Usually, the more liquid your deposit, the less interest it will earn. A regular account usually earns a low rate because you can maintain a low minimum balance and withdraw money as needed. CDs tie up your money for some length of time. In exchange for your commitment to leave this money with the bank for this time period, you will usually earn higher interest.

Fees and Restrictions

Different accounts and institutions have different rules. Before you open an account, be sure to understand the withdrawal restrictions, minimum balances, service charges, fees, and any other requirements. For example, some accounts charge a fee for using a human teller rather than making your transactions through an ATM. CDs exact a heavy cost in lost interest for withdrawing money before maturity.

Fees for use of an ATM can vary as well. Some banks may charge nothing to use their ATMs but charge a hefty fee for using another bank's ATM.

► SAVING REGULARLY

Everyone should have saving as a goal. In simplest terms, you can grow your savings only by spending less than you take in. It is important not just to save but to save regularly. Over time, and with compounding interest, your savings can grow into a substantial sum. Figure 10-3 illustrates the effect of compounding when you make regular deposits and earn interest on interest.

Obviously, no savings plan is effective unless you have the willpower to set aside money. The safe storage of funds for future use is a basic need of every individual. There are ways to make regular saving easier, including direct deposits and payroll deductions.

Direct Deposit

Both employers and financial institutions offer the direct deposit of paychecks into bank accounts. This service helps you because your money is available in your account faster. You can also have part or all of your direct deposit put into your savings account. Then you could transfer what you need to cover your bills into checking and save the rest. This way, you are truly paying yourself first. You can earmark the money you set aside for a vacation or some other special purpose.

Automatic Payroll Deductions

Having a certain amount withheld from your paycheck and deposited into a savings account is another method of "paying yourself." Contributions to savings are part of pre-authorized payment systems.

COMPOUNDING INTEREST AND MAKING ADDITIONAL DEPOSITS

figure 10-3 ◄

Year	Beginning Balance	Deposits	Interest Earned (5%)	Ending Balance
1	$ 0.00	$100.00	$ 5.00	$105.00
2	105.00	100.00	10.25	215.25
3	215.25	100.00	15.76	331.01
4	331.01	100.00	21.55	452.56

In this case, money is automatically deducted from your paycheck and deposited in your savings account.

You may authorize your employer to make automatic deductions from your paycheck each month. Many people participate in *payroll savings plans*, in which money is taken out of each paycheck and deposited in a bank or credit union or used to buy government savings bonds.

✓Check Your Understanding

1. Explain how a savings account is more liquid than a certificate of deposit.
2. To earn a higher interest rate, what tradeoff will you likely have to make?
3. In what way is the interest paid on a money market account different from interest paid on a regular savings account?

Saving to Keep Life Simple

Saving is often defined as deferred spending. In other words, you set money aside today so you can spend it in the future. But saving money can be more than providing for some future need. Saving itself can be a virtue.

Abraham Lincoln said, "Most people are about as happy as they make up their minds to be." But what is happiness? According to many philosophers, it is enjoying what you have, not wishing for more. Consider what some people learn well into their lives—that the accumulation of possessions does not bring happiness! By keeping your life simple, you don't get used to having more and more and keeping up with what everyone else is buying. This means not buying "things" that have to be protected and maintained. Instead, you can enjoy life without having to earn large sums of money to achieve some high standard of consumer spending.

In today's competitive marketplace, people frequently lose their jobs and must retrain and even find a new career. If you keep your life simple, you won't have a lot of payments to make. Then, if you lose your job, you will be less likely to lose your house, car, and other possessions. If you stay liquid, you can more easily move and start a new career and have money on hand to carry you through jobless periods.

Most people "buy things they don't need, with money they don't have, to impress people they don't like." Those you love and who care about you aren't impressed with how much money you spend or all the possessions you own. Wouldn't it be better to put money aside so that you can retire early, enjoy traveling, or live comfortably without the stress of keeping up with the rat race? Remember, even if you win the rat race, you're still a rat!

Think Critically
1. Do you buy things that you later wish you hadn't? If you had the money back, what would you do with it instead?
2. Do you know someone who is "happy" and at peace with his or her life? If so, describe the person's lifestyle.

Chapter Assessment

10.1
* Savings provide money for emergencies and for short-term needs.
* Start saving early to accumulate enough money for large future purchases and a secure retirement.
* Compounding, or interest earned on principal and previous interest, makes savings grow faster.
* To compare accounts with different compounding methods, simply compare annual percentage yields.
* Commercial banks, savings banks, savings and loan associations, credit unions, and brokerage firms offer a variety of accounts and services.

10.2
* Savings options include savings accounts, certificates of deposit, and money market accounts.
* Among the savings options, regular savings accounts usually pay the lowest interest because they offer the highest liquidity and safety.
* In selecting a savings plan, consider liquidity, safety, convenience, earning potential, fees, and restrictions.
* Saving regularly helps you meet your goals more quickly.
* Direct deposit and automatic payroll deductions are ways to force yourself to save.

Directions

Can you find the definition for each of the following terms used in Chapter 10?

annual percentage yield (APY)	maturity date
	money market account
certificate of deposit (CD)	principal
compound interest	securities
discretionary income	share account
interest	stockbroker
liquidity	

1. The ability of an asset to be converted into cash quickly without loss of value.

2. The date on which an investment becomes due for payment.

3. Money paid by a financial institution for the use of the saver's money.

4. A savings account at a credit union.

5. A sum of money in a savings account on which interest is earned.

6. Interest computed on the principal plus accumulated interest.

7. The amount of money left over after the bills are paid.

8. A person who buys and sells securities for investors.

9. A combination savings-investment plan in which the money deposited is used to purchase safe, liquid securities.

10. A deposit that earns a fixed interest rate for a specified length of time.

11. Stocks and bonds issued by corporations or by the government.

12. The actual interest rate an account pays per year, with compounding included.

REVIEW FACTS AND IDEAS

1. Explain several reasons why you should save.

2. List several short-term needs that you expect to have in the next few months or years.

3. List your long-term plans that will require money in the next five years or more.

4. What are some personal factors that help determine the amount of money you will save?

5. Why might people choose to save their money in a commercial bank when another type of financial institution offers a higher interest rate?

6. How is a credit union different from a savings and loan association?

7. How much is an account insured for by the FDIC?

8. Why does a regular savings account pay less interest than a certificate of deposit?

9. What types of penalties might you face for early withdrawal of all or part of your savings from (a) regular savings, (b) certificates of deposit, or (c) money market funds?

10. What things should you consider when choosing a financial institution for your savings?

11. Describe ways you can force yourself to save.

APPLY YOUR KNOWLEDGE

1. Describe advantages and disadvantages of spending now rather than saving for a future goal.

2. Give three examples of how saving money can improve your financial well being.

3. Write out your savings plans, listing your short-term and long-term goals and how you plan to achieve them. How much money will you have to save to meet them? On the Internet, locate a savings planner tool and calculate how much you would have to save each month to total the amount you need to meet your short-term goals. Assume you will be saving for five years and will earn 7 percent on your savings.

4. What does discretionary income have to do with saving?

5. If two savings accounts offered 5 percent interest, but one was compounded quarterly and the other was compounded daily, which account would have the higher APY? Why?

6. Select a situation—amount saved and yield—and show the difference between simple and compounded interest. Figure the annual interest earned over a five-year period. Calculate the compound interest manually or go to the Internet to find a savings planner tool. Then write a paragraph explaining the benefits of compound interest.

7. Search the Internet for a savings calculator. Plug in different numbers and note the results. For example, try a certain regular savings amount compounded annually, then quarterly, then monthly. Note the differences that occur because of the different compounding method. Then try different savings amounts using the same compounding method. How does saving just a little more each month affect your total savings in, say, 10 years? Then try different interest rates with the same savings amounts and compounding method. Write a page about the conclusions you drew from your research.

8. Collect advertisements offering various financial services. What factors would you consider before using these services and the financial institutions that offer them?

9. Visit a financial institution in your community and describe the following:
   a. types of savings accounts
   b. services available to depositors
   c. fees charged for services
   d. requirements, such as minimum deposits
   e. other enticements to get your business

10. Call a credit union in your area or find one online. Who can be a member of this credit union? What services does the credit union offer its members?

11. Norma Munoz is considering buying a certificate of deposit with the $500 she has in regular savings. Explain to her what factors she should consider when choosing a certificate of deposit.

12. Suppose you need to withdraw the money in a two-year CD before the certificate matures. Ask a local bank what the penalty is for withdrawing early from a two-year CD. What is the penalty for withdrawing all or part of your money from a regular savings account?

Solve Problems ⊕ Explore Issues

1. Compute the interest compounded for LaDoris Casey, assuming that she deposits $1,000 in a CD with interest compounded every six months at the rate of 8½ percent. The certificate matures in three years. Use this format on a separate sheet of paper:

Year	Beginning Balance	First-Half Interest	Second-Half Interest	Total Interest	Ending Balance
1	$1,000	_____	_____	_____	_____
2	_____	_____	_____	_____	_____
3	_____	_____	_____	_____	_____

2. Ada Hernandez wishes to save $100 a month. Her bank computes compound interest monthly. The current rate for a regular savings account is 5½ percent. Compute the ending balance in her account after one year. Use this format on a separate sheet of paper:

Month	Beginning Balance	+ Deposit	= Total	+ Interest	= Ending Balance
1	_____	_____	_____	_____	_____
2	_____	_____	_____	_____	_____
3	_____	_____	_____	_____	_____
4	_____	_____	_____	_____	_____
5	_____	_____	_____	_____	_____
6	_____	_____	_____	_____	_____
7	_____	_____	_____	_____	_____
8	_____	_____	_____	_____	_____
9	_____	_____	_____	_____	_____
10	_____	_____	_____	_____	_____
11	_____	_____	_____	_____	_____
12	_____	_____	_____	_____	_____

3. Compute the interest compounded quarterly on a deposit of $500 for three years at 8 percent APY. Use the following format on a separate sheet of paper:

		Interest					
Year	**Beginning Balance**	**First Quarter**	**Second Quarter**	**Third Quarter**	**Fourth Quarter**	**Total Interest**	**Ending Balance**
1	$500	_____	_____	_____	_____	_____	_____
2	_____	_____	_____	_____	_____	_____	_____
3	_____	_____	_____	_____	_____	_____	_____

4. Compute your total savings if you keep $1,000 in a regular savings account at 5¼ percent, compounded quarterly, for two years. Use this format on a separate sheet of paper:

		REGULAR SAVINGS ACCOUNT					
		Interest					
Year	**Beginning Balance**	**First Quarter**	**Second Quarter**	**Third Quarter**	**Fourth Quarter**	**Total Interest**	**Ending Balance**
1	$1,000	_____	_____	_____	_____	_____	_____
2	_____	_____	_____	_____	_____	_____	_____

For related activities and links, point your browser to **www.mypf.swlearning.com**

Investing for Your Future

TERMS TO KNOW

investing	financial advisers	annuity
inflation	annual report	stock
Rule of 72	bonds	futures
risk	discount bond	option
diversification	mutual fund	penny stocks

Consider This. . .

Soon-Yi has saved some money that she will use for college expenses in a few years. Right now, it's in her savings account, earning 1 percent a year.

"My parents say I can do better," Soon-Yi told her best friend. "If I invest the money, I could get 6 to 8 percent, or maybe even better. So I've been checking my options. You know what I've found so far? That risk is a big part of investing. If I'm willing to take a lot of risk, then I may be able to earn more money. But I also stand a chance of losing part or all of my money. So I have to decide what my goals are, weigh the tradeoffs, and make the best choice to meet my goals. This is interesting stuff, but it isn't as easy as it sounds."

Investing Fundamentals

Goals
- Describe the stages of investing and the relationship between risk and return.
- Discuss investment strategies, options, and sources of information.

▶ STAGES OF INVESTING

Your goals for saving and investing will be different, depending on your lifestyle, age, purposes for saving or investing, and income. Typically, as your income grows, you can progress through stages from temporary savings into different kinds of investing and greater amounts of risk.

Stage 1. Put-and-Take Account

When you first begin to earn a paycheck, your savings will be temporary. You will put your paycheck into an account and take money out as needed to pay your bills. This money is your *emergency fund*, or your "put-and-take" account. (See Figure 11-1, page 258.) The purpose of this money is to pay for your short-term needs with enough left over to cover unexpected expenses. For example, you would use this money to pay your rent and utility bills, buy food and clothes, and pay for unexpected expenses, such as car repairs. Then your next paychecks would replenish the fund for upcoming short-term expenses.

Many financial advisers recommend that you have three to six months' net pay set aside for this type of fund. Then, should a need arise, you won't dip into permanent, long-term investments to pay for temporary, short-term needs. Your main concern in saving these funds should be safety.

©GETTY IMAGES/PHOTODISC

If your car needed repairs, where would you likely get the money?

Stage 2. Beginning Investing

Investing is the use of savings to earn a financial return. The overall objective of investing is to earn money with money. As shown in Figure 11-1, investing really begins when you have "excess" savings beyond what you need for daily expenses and emergencies. You can then afford to make "permanent" investments in addition to "temporary put-and-take." Your initial investments should be conservative

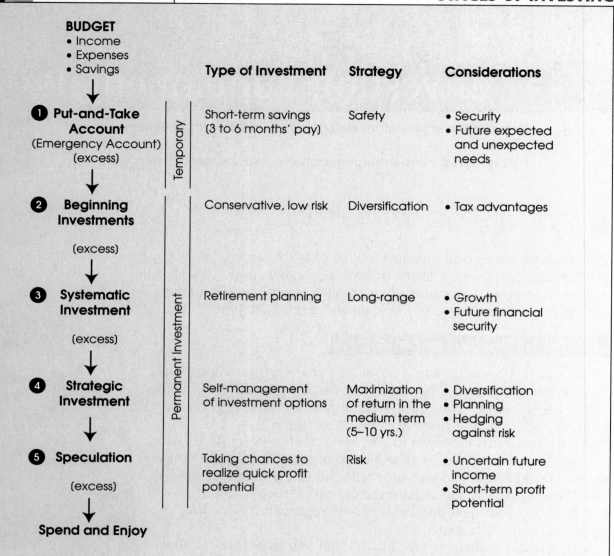

BUDGET
- Income
- Expenses
- Savings

	Type of Investment	Strategy	Considerations
❶ Put-and-Take Account (Emergency Account) (excess)	Short-term savings (3 to 6 months' pay)	Safety	• Security • Future expected and unexpected needs
❷ Beginning Investments (excess)	Conservative, low risk	Diversification	• Tax advantages
❸ Systematic Investment (excess)	Retirement planning	Long-range	• Growth • Future financial security
❹ Strategic Investment	Self-management of investment options	Maximization of return in the medium term (5–10 yrs.)	• Diversification • Planning • Hedging against risk
❺ Speculation (excess)	Taking chances to realize quick profit potential	Risk	• Uncertain future income • Short-term profit potential

Temporary — stages 1–2
Permanent Investment — stages 3–5

Spend and Enjoy

and low risk. At this stage, you don't have a lot of money to invest, so you don't want to risk losing it. Once you have established a safe cushion of investment, you can afford to make riskier (and potentially more profitable) investments. Typically, young workers in their 20s and early 30s begin investing when their budgets and spending are stable and their excess cash is increasing.

Stage 3. Systematic Investing

Once you are comfortable with your beginning investments, you can then enter a stage called *systematic investment*—investing on a regular and planned basis. You would regularly set aside a certain amount for investing each month, increasing the amount as your income grows. At this stage, your goals are long-range. You are investing for a financially secure future. This ability to contribute regular sums of money usually happens in your 30s and 40s, when earning potential is highest.

Stage 4. Strategic Investing

Strategic investing is the careful management of investment alternatives to maximize growth of your *portfolio* (collection of investments) over the next 5–10 years. For example, when the growth prospects for one investment seem to be declining, you would move your money into another investment where the prospects for growth seem greater. You would invest in different types of securities to try to maximize your returns.

Stage 5. Speculative Investing

When you are investing regularly in a broad collection of investments but you still have money available to take bigger risks, then you can choose to move into the final stage, called *speculation*. In this stage, you can make—or lose—a great deal of money in a short period of time. You must be aware of the risks and be prepared to lose the money you invest. Typically, odds are small that you will make a profit in a speculative investment, but when the speculation pays off, the profit can be great. Beginning investors should avoid speculation because they cannot take the loss that is likely to occur. Many investors never choose to speculate. Instead, they prefer to invest regularly over their lifetimes in solid securities with moderate risk.

▶ REASONS FOR INVESTING

Investing is a proven and powerful way to strengthen your financial position over time. It is more than just an option. It is an essential part of providing for present and future needs. It provides a source of income in addition to a paycheck as you invest successfully and make money on money.

Investing Helps Beat Inflation

Inflation is a rise in the general level of prices. Inflation reduces purchasing power over time. As prices rise, it takes more money to buy the same goods and services. Thus, investors seek investments for the long term that will grow faster than the inflation rate. For example, if the annual inflation rate is 4 percent, you will want your overall portfolio to yield a rate of return higher than 4 percent. During inflationary times, when prices are rising rapidly, you may not be able to earn a return that will keep pace with the inflation rate.

A quick way to evaluate an investment's rate of return is to use the **Rule of 72**. This is a technique for estimating the number of years required to double your money at a given rate of return. Simply divide the percentage rate of return into 72. For example, if an investment is yielding an average of 6 percent, it will take 12 years to double your money (72 divided by 6). You can also use the Rule of 72 to estimate the rate of return needed to double your money in a given number of years. (See the Math Minute.)

Math Minute
The Rule of 72

The Rule of 72 is a rule of thumb or approximation technique. You can use it to estimate either the number of years or rate of return needed to double your money.

If you want to find the number of years, divide 72 by the rate of return.

Example: You are earning 10% on your money. How long will it take to double your money?

Answer: 72 divided by 10 = 7.2 years

If you want to find the rate of return, divide 72 by the number of years in which you want your money to double.

Example: You have $5,000 and want to double it in 6 years. What rate must your investment earn to achieve $10,000 in 6 years?

Answer: 72 divided by 6 = 12%. At 12% your money will double in 6 years.

Global View

On January 1, 2002, euro banknotes and coins were introduced in 12 member states of the European Union. This was a significant part of the Union's overall objective of a common European market, with the aim of increasing economic prosperity and contributing to "an ever closer union among the peoples of Europe."

Think Critically: Some nations are members of the European Union but have chosen not to adopt the euro as their currency. What do you think might be reasons for this?

Investing Increases Wealth

Financial success grows from the assets that you build up over time. Investing helps you accumulate wealth faster than if you simply saved your excess cash in a savings account. Over the long run, investments earn higher profits than savings do. When you invest in stocks and bonds, you are participating in helping businesses make and sell new products and services. You will be rewarded with dividends and interest that will add to your personal wealth.

Investing Is Fun and Challenging

Investors make choices and hope to pick winners. Once you gain experience, you can have fun choosing investments, buying and selling when the time is right, and using your knowledge to plan for your financial security.

▶ RISK AND RETURN

Risk is the chance that an investment's value will decrease. All types of investing involve some degree of risk. The greater the risk you are willing to take, the greater the potential returns. A safe investment has little risk of loss. Some people are willing to take more risks than others. Those who are willing to accept a reasonable amount of risk will likely make considerably more in the long run than investors who are *risk averse* (afraid to make investments in which they might lose some or all of their investment). However, *risk-takers* (investors who like to take on a great deal of risk) could make a lot or lose a lot. The best plan for most investors is to plot a moderate course, somewhere between no risk and extreme risk, wherever they feel comfortable.

©GETTY IMAGES/PHOTODISC

Diversification

One way to minimize risk is through **diversification**, which involves spreading the risk among many types of investments. Rather than buying only one kind of investment, you should choose several types of investments, such as stocks, bonds, and real estate. Also, you should diversify among types of stocks. For example, you might select some low-risk stocks to balance others with greater risk. Diversification reduces overall risk because not all of your choices will perform poorly at the same time. If one choice does not do well, the others will likely make up some or all of the loss.

Is there any type of investing that does not involve some degree of risk?

Types of Risk

Short-term investments are generally less risky than long-term investments. You can predict much more accurately what will happen in a week, a month, or a year than you can in 10 or 20 years.

During inflationary times, there is *interest-rate risk* that the return on an investment will not keep pace with the inflation rate. Inflation makes your fixed-rate investments worth less because they are "locked in" at lower rates of interest. The value of a fixed-rate investment decreases when overall interest rates increase. The value increases when overall interest rates decrease. For example, if you own a security paying a fixed interest rate (say, 5 percent) and interest rates are increasing (more than 5 percent), your investment will be worth less over time.

Government actions that affect business conditions are the basis of *political risk*. Increased taxes and certain regulations, such as costly environmental controls that businesses are required to apply, can make some investments less attractive.

Market risk, which affects many types of investments at once, is caused by business declines or interest rate fluctuations. There is also *nonmarket risk*, which is risk unrelated to market trends. Nonmarket risk is entirely unpredictable and uncontrollable. For example, terrorism threats affect all investments in the short term. Because of the violent and unpredictable nature of such events, people change their behavior and seek ways to protect themselves. This causes markets to suffer as people sell their investments to hold more cash for personal security.

Company or *industry risk* is produced by events that affect only one company or industry. For example, if you invest in the candy industry, a nationwide trend toward dieting or the avoidance of sugar may adversely affect the value of your investment.

▶ INVESTMENT STRATEGIES

Many individuals never start an investment program because they think they don't have enough money. But even small sums of money grow over time. To achieve financial security, start investing as soon as you can and continue to invest over your lifetime. The suggestions that follow will help you make wise investment decisions.

Criteria for Choosing an Investment

Some investments increase in value at a rate higher than the rate of inflation. Some do not. Some investments provide for increases in value that do not show up as taxable income for many years. Others do not. Evaluate your investment options according to these factors:

1. Degree of safety (risk of loss)
2. Degree of liquidity (ability to get your money quickly)
3. Expected dividends or interest
4. Expected growth in value, preferably exceeding the inflation rate
5. Reasonable purchase price and fees
6. Tax benefits (saving or postponing tax liability)

No investment offers a high degree of all of these. Each investment choice represents a tradeoff. For example, in exchange for tax benefits, you would likely have to give up a high return and liquidity. However, you should choose investments that offer, for example, the highest degree of safety you can get for the expected return. A diversified portfolio of investments achieves a balance among these factors. It would include some safe but low-yield investments as well as some riskier, higher-growth choices plus some tax-deferred investments. These factors will be examined in the discussion of specific types of investments in Chapters 12–15.

Wise Investment Practices

People commonly make investment mistakes. Some mistakes are minor and can be corrected easily. Others cause serious financial damage. To avoid investment mistakes and maximize your investing returns, follow the investment practices described below.

DEFINE YOUR FINANCIAL GOALS

Clearly defined financial goals will help you to identify which investments to purchase. To be useful, investment goals must be specific and measurable. Set specific monetary targets. Identify how you plan to use the money and how soon you need to accomplish each goal.

GO SLOWLY

Before making investment decisions, gather the information you need to make a wise decision. Don't act on impulse. Some investment schemes are really hoaxes that capitalize on people's fears and greed. If it sounds too good to be true, it probably is. Take the time to obtain and analyze the needed information and make good choices.

FOLLOW THROUGH

Putting off plans and never taking action will lead to failure in meeting financial goals. Act on your important goals now. Don't wait for a future day that may not come. A common mistake is keeping too much money in the "put-and-take" account and not taking advantage of the higher rates of return of permanent investments.

KEEP GOOD RECORDS

To keep a clear view of your future needs and goals, keep good financial records. Your personal net worth statement, plus lists of insurance policies and investments, account balances and the location of bank accounts, and the contents and location of your safe deposit box are essential information. As you make investment choices, keep good records as well. Every year, update the account balance and compare it to other choices. Keep statements to verify your account balances and make transfers when needed. Unless you know where you have been and where you are now, it is difficult to plan where you are going.

SEEK GOOD INVESTMENT ADVICE

Don't be afraid to ask questions. In general, it is wise to seek competent advice from a trained professional before making any investment decision. To get this advice at low cost and without a commitment, consider attending an investment seminar. Here you can learn about products, costs, and risks—then decide what to do in your own home. You will learn more about sources of investment information in the next lesson.

KEEP INVESTMENT KNOWLEDGE CURRENT

Be aware of what is new in the financial market, what kinds of investments are currently good prospects, when to sell, and when to buy. The economy is a major consideration in making investment decisions. You need to understand how it works and what various economic indicators mean. Although you should seek advice before making a major investment move, it is your responsibility to know when to ask questions and to make the final decisions about your investments.

KNOW YOUR LIMITS

Understand your risk tolerance and the amount of money you can afford to risk, so you can maximize returns within your risk comfort zone. If you are uncomfortable taking large risks, then avoid them. The chance of making huge profits is not worth being stressed out by the risk.

✓Check Your Understanding

1. Why do you need an emergency fund before you start investing?
2. How does investing help you beat inflation?
3. What is diversification and what is its purpose?

Exploring Investment Options

Goals	• List and describe sources of financial information to make investment decisions.
	• List and define basic investment options, rated by risk.

▶ SOURCES OF FINANCIAL INFORMATION

Investment information can be found in print, online, and through other sources. When you want to evaluate investment options, you can find plenty of information to make an informed decision.

Newspapers

Most newspapers contain *financial pages*. Reading these pages daily will help you keep track of financial markets and obtain information needed to make wise investment decisions. *The Wall Street Journal* is a daily paper that provides detailed coverage of the business and financial world. *Barron's* is a weekly paper that also provides charts of trends, financial news, and technical analysis of financial data. Both of these publications offer online subscriptions as well as free articles and data available at their Web sites: http://public.wsj.com/home.html (*The Wall Street Journal*) and www.barrons.com (*Barron's*).

©GETTY IMAGES/PHOTODISC

What are some sources of investment information?

Investor Services and Newsletters

Companies called *investor services* provide extensive financial data to clients. Main resources are *Moody's Investors Service* (www.moodys.com), *Standard and Poor's Reports* (www.standardandpoors.com), and *Value Line* (www.valueline.com). These publications are found in public libraries and brokerage firms, as well as online. They contain precise current and historical financial data. Many investors subscribe to weekly or monthly investment newsletters, which give them the latest financial data and information.

Financial Magazines

A number of weekly and monthly magazines specialize in business and financial information. Most of them interpret financial data and give opinions and recommendations. Weekly magazines include *Business Week* (www.businessweek.com) and *Forbes* (www.forbes.com). Monthly magazines include *Money* (http://money.cnn.com), *Fortune* (www.fortune.com), *Kiplinger's Personal Finance* (www.kiplinger.com), and *The Economist* (www.economist.com). Once you have made your choices, these magazines will keep you current, so you can determine when it is time to buy, hold, or sell. All of these publications offer financial news and stock market performance data at their Web sites.

Brokers

Full-service brokers provide clients with analysis and opinions based on their judgments and the opinions of experts at the company they represent. However, you cannot expect a broker to pick winners for you every time. Almost all full-service brokerage firms provide monthly market letters giving advice on the purchase and sale of certain securities. Some well-known brokers include Merrill Lynch (www.ml.com), Fidelity Investments (www.fid-inv.com), and American Express (www.americanexpress.com).

Some people are well informed and know what they want to buy and sell. For these investors, a discount broker is adequate. *Discount brokers* buy and sell securities for clients at a reduced commission. A discount broker usually provides little or no investment advice to a client. A pioneer in the discount trading business is Charles Schwab (www.charlesschwab.com). Two other well-known online discount brokers are Ameritrade (www.ameritrade.com) and E*Trade (www.etrade.com). Also, because of the increasing popularity of inexpensive trading, many full-service brokers also offer discount trading at their Web sites.

Many banks, credit unions, and savings and loans have discount brokers available to customers who want to trade securities. In most cases, you will be required to have a checking or savings account at that institution. Money can be transferred from your account to pay for securities purchased, or deposited to your account to reflect securities sold. A bank, credit union, or savings and loan will also maintain a brokerage account for you and send you account statements showing the current value of your securities.

With most types of brokerage accounts, you can manage your account online. You can give buy and sell orders, transfer money among investment accounts, and track the progress of your investments either with your own software or with a platform supplied by the broker or bank.

Financial Advisers

Professional investment planners are called **financial advisers** or certified financial planners (CFPs). They are trained to give investment advice based on your goals, age, lifestyle, and other factors. The advisor will ask you to fill out confidential information showing assets, liabilities, net worth, income, and budget, as well as your financial goals. The adviser usually receives a fee for services rendered, although some receive fees when they sell you investment products (such as stocks, bonds, or life insurance policies). Generally, you will get better overall advice when the adviser does not stand to make a profit on the investment you choose to buy.

Annual Reports

An **annual report** is a summary of a corporation's financial results for the year and prospects for the future. The Securities and Exchange Commission (SEC) requires all corporations to prepare this report at the end of each year and send it to their stockholders. Investors can use the information contained in the report to evaluate the corporation as an investment prospect.

You can find annual reports online at the SEC Web site (www.sec.gov). Corporations often publish their financial performance data in the investor section of their Web sites. If you are interested in investing in a corporation, you can receive a copy of the annual report by writing the company or requesting it at the company Web site. Also, some large libraries keep copies of annual reports of major corporations.

Online Investor Education

In addition to the Web sites of print publications and brokers, the Internet offers many educational sites for new investors. Teenvestor (www.teenvestor.com) is dedicated to helping teens learn how to invest and manage their money. The Motley Fool (www.fool.com) offers money management tips in its personal finance section. Its "fool's school" presents investment basics in reader-friendly language. The National Association of Investors Corporation (www.better-investing.org) is a nonprofit site dedicated to investor education. This organization also helps investment clubs get started. These are just a few of the many educational sites available to investors online. A Web search using a search engine or a directory from a popular home page, such as Yahoo! (www.yahoo.com), will produce many more.

▶ INVESTMENT OPTIONS

Once you have established your emergency fund and have some additional money in savings, it's time to consider other investment alternatives. The following discussion groups different types of investments according to their degree of risk and expected return. In Chapters 12 through 15, you will explore each type of investment more thoroughly.

Low Risk/Low Return

For your first investments, you will likely want to consider fairly safe investments, even though their returns will be relatively low. Even as you grow as a sophisticated investor, however, you will probably continue to include some low-risk investments as part of your diversified portfolio.

CORPORATE AND MUNICIPAL BONDS

Bonds are debt obligations of corporations (*corporate bonds*) or state or local governments (*municipal bonds*). When a corporation or government body sells a bond to an investor, it is borrowing from the investor. When you buy a corporate bond as an investment, the corporation pays you a fixed amount of money (called interest) at a fixed interval (usually every six months). The corporation also must repay the principal (amount borrowed) at maturity. The maturity date of a bond is the date on which the borrowed money must be repaid. When you loan money to a government authority, such as a city, county, community college district, or utility district, you are also paid interest on your investment. Your principal is repaid when the bond matures. Typically, interest earned on government bonds is tax-free, giving the investor a tax advantage. Bonds are explained in detail in Chapter 13.

U.S. GOVERNMENT SAVINGS BONDS

When you buy a savings bond, you are lending money to the United States government. A *Series EE savings bond* is a **discount bond**, because you buy it for less than its maturity value. The purchase price of a Series EE bond is one half of its maturity value. For example, you would buy a $50 bond for $25 and a $100 bond for $50. At maturity, you receive the full value of the bond. The difference between the purchase price and the maturity value is the amount of interest earned. Generally, EE bonds mature in 10 years but can be extended for up to 30 years.

The interest accumulates every six months. You receive the interest at the time you cash in your bond. Interest earned on Series EE savings bonds is exempt from state and local taxes. It is not subject to federal taxation until the bonds are cashed in. These bonds earn a variable rate of interest and have a higher rate of return than regular savings accounts and some CDs.

A *Series HH savings bond* pays interest semiannually (every six months) and matures in 10 years. These bonds can be purchased only in exchange for maturing EE bonds. Series HH bonds may be redeemed at any time after being held for a minimum of six months.

A *Series I savings bond* is designed for investors wanting to protect against inflation and earn a guaranteed rate of return. With I bonds, interest is added to the bond monthly and is paid when the bond is cashed. I bonds are sold at face value (you pay $50 for a $50 bond) and they grow with inflation-indexed earnings for up to 30 years. In other words, the I bond pays a fixed rate combined with a semiannual inflation adjustment to help protect purchasing power.

You can buy savings bonds from commercial banks or through payroll deductions. Savings bond certificates should be stored in a safe deposit box.

If you are seeking safety, savings bonds are a good investment. They are also very liquid. You can hold them to maturity or cash them in anytime at a bank for their current value. Their interest is not subject to state or local taxes, only federal. Some savings bonds used to finance a college education are free of federal taxation as well. If savings bonds are lost, stolen, or destroyed, they can be replaced without cost.

TREASURY SECURITIES

U.S. Treasury bills (called *t-bills*) are available in denominations of $10,000 and then in increments of $5,000 more. A Treasury bill matures in one year or less. The bill is usually a three-month, six-month, or one-year government obligation.

Treasury notes are issued in units of $1,000 or $5,000. Maturities range from two years to ten years. Interest rates for Treasury notes are slightly higher than for Treasury bills.

Treasury bonds are issued in minimum units of $1,000 with maturities that range from 10 to 30 years. Interest rates for Treasury bonds are generally higher than interest rates for either t-bills or Treasury notes. Interest paid every six months is taxed by the federal government, but it is exempt from state and local income taxes.

Medium Risk/Medium Return

When you feel secure enough to take more risk and you have additional money to invest, you are ready to step up to the medium-risk range to increase your return. Some of these medium-risk options involve investing with companies that manage the investment.

STOCKS

Stock is a unit of ownership in a corporation. The owner of stock is called a *stockholder*. A stockholder receives a stock certificate, which is evidence of the ownership. When you are a stockholder, you will share in a corporation's profits, which are paid to you as dividends. If the company does well, you earn returns in two ways: in dividends and in the increased value of the stock you own.

Stocks generally carry more risk than choices with fixed interest, such as savings bonds, because a stockholder's earnings can go up or down, depending on the company's fortunes. Stocks in well-established companies are reasonably safe, while stocks in less-stable companies can be quite risky. However, a diversified portfolio of stocks of various risk levels can achieve a medium overall risk. You will learn more about investing in stocks in Chapter 12.

MUTUAL FUNDS

Suppose you have $500, which is not enough to buy a diversified portfolio of stocks. You can buy shares in a large, professionally managed group of investments called a **mutual fund**. A mutual fund pools the money of many investors and buys a large selection of securities that meet the fund's stated investment goals. Two major advantages of a mutual fund for investors are professional management and diversification. Since the fund invests in a wide variety of securities, it provides diversification that small investors could not otherwise achieve with their limited resources.

Although some mutual funds fall in the speculative category and others fall in the low-risk category, such as those that specialize in money market securities, most mutual funds fall somewhere in the broad medium range in terms of risk and return. You can further diversify your portfolio by investing in mutual funds with different objectives. For example, some funds buy securities in riskier small companies, hoping to earn a higher return. Others stick to well-established, safe companies to earn a lower but stable return. By investing money in both funds, you are diversifying your investments. If your riskier fund does not do well, your stable fund will limit your losses.

Mutual funds are the fastest-growing segment of the American financial services industry. You will learn more about mutual funds in Chapter 14.

ANNUITIES

An **annuity** is a contract sold by an insurance company that provides the investor with a series of regular payments, usually after retirement. Generally, you receive income monthly, with payments to continue as long as you live. You usually buy an annuity directly from a life insurance company. The interest on the principal, as well as the interest compounded on that interest, builds up free of current income tax. Taxes are deferred until you receive payments from your annuity. The payments from an annuity are normally used to supplement retirement income. The annuity is often described as the opposite of life insurance. It pays while you are alive; life insurance pays when you die.

REAL ESTATE

Many people like to invest in real estate—houses and land. While this type of investment usually represents a large and often non-liquid investment of cash, it has proven to be protection against inflation in most parts of the United States. In some areas, prices of homes have increased faster than the inflation rate. Real estate investments also have tax benefits. Certain costs associated with home ownership are deductible from gross income, and therefore they lower taxable income. For people who don't want to own real estate but want to invest in it, REITs (Real Estate Investment Trusts) are available. While investing in your own home carries little risk, investment in other types of real estate can be very risky. Chapter 14 presents a more in-depth explanation of real estate investing.

What are some advantages of investing in real estate?

High Risk/High Return

High risk/high return options involve considerable uncertainty. Returns can be high, but they can also be low, none at all, or a loss to principal (the amount of the original investment). If you are willing to take the risks involved with these choices, you stand to make high returns over time. But you also risk high losses if your investments prove to be poor performers.

FUTURES

Futures are contracts to buy and sell commodities or stocks for a specified price on a specified date in the future. The investor is betting that the price of the commodity or stock will be higher on that future date than it is at the time of the contract. Thus, trading in futures is very risky speculation. If prices fall, the investor loses. If prices rise, the investor stands to make a lot of money. This type of investment is not for beginners or for individuals who cannot afford to lose their investment.

OPTIONS

An **option** is the right, but not the obligation, to buy or sell a commodity or stock for a specified price within a specified time period. As with futures, the investor is betting that, during the option period, the price of the stock will rise. If it does, the investor can choose to buy it at the lower option price, resulting in an instant profit. Typically, options are short-term investment devices used by speculators to make a quick profit. They are risky and not for inexperienced investors.

PENNY STOCKS

Penny stocks are low-priced stocks of small companies that have no track record. The stock usually sells for under a dollar per share. The small companies often have low revenues and few assets to assure future growth. Dot-com (Internet) companies typically begin this way. Many of them fail, and the stock is worthless. Occasionally, a penny stock will be successful, and the investor will make a large windfall. Generally, penny stocks are highly risky.

COLLECTIBLES

Many people like to collect items such as coins, art, memorabilia, ceramics, or other items that are popular from time to time, such as Beanie Babies or baseball cards. If you collect an item that goes up in value rapidly, you can reap large rewards. If, however, you don't sell when your items are a hot commodity, they are likely to lose their value just as quickly, making them a risky investment. Collectors must be aware of the market and realize that their collections are subject to changing public tastes and can be difficult to sell.

Communication Connection

Talk with a relative or friend who has investments. What different types of investments does the person have? How would you describe the investments in terms of degrees of risk and expected returns? Write a one-page summary of your findings.

✔Check Your Understanding

1. What are some sources of financial information useful for making investment decisions?
2. Why should beginning investors choose safe investments?
3. Why is investing in stock considered more risky than investing in savings bonds?

Issues in Your World

Choosing the Right Financial Adviser

Selecting the right financial adviser can be tricky. The most important factor is *trust*. You must feel comfortable with your adviser, be willing to give him or her a complete picture of your finances and financial goals, and then follow his or her advice.

Many people begin their investing with a trusted family friend who is in the business of giving financial advice at a bank, brokerage firm, or other financial institution. Or, you may know someone who has worked with a particular adviser for several years and can recommend him or her. If so, your choice will be somewhat easier.

Some people consult with financial advisers at credit unions or through employee assistance plans. Others participate in group seminars offered by employers or professional organizations. In many cases, you can get good general advice about investment strategies that are effective for people with investment goals similar to yours.

The trick to finding and building a relationship of trust with a financial adviser involves taking the time to ask questions and discuss thoroughly your income, assets, liabilities, risk comfort level, and financial goals. Be sure to ask potential financial advisers about their training, background, and experience. Ask their philosophy of investing, fees (how they earn money), and investment strategies. You also should know how clients have done in the past with their investment recommendations. Ask for references. Good advisers will tell you about their past successes. You can also check up on the past performance of stockbrokers through the National Association of Securities Dealers. The association monitors complaints and actions taken against its members. Remember: If you don't feel comfortable with a prospective financial adviser, keep looking until you find one who you feel can help you achieve your investment goals.

Think Critically

1. If you needed financial advice, whom would you ask? Why?

2. What are the characteristics you would look for in a successful financial adviser? What would it take to build your trust?

3. Locate the names and addresses of three or more financial advisers in your area.

Chapter Assessment

SUMMARY

11.1

* As your income grows beyond current needs, you can progress through investment stages involving greater amounts of risk.
* All investments involve some risk that your investment will lose value. Diversification helps minimize overall risk.
* Types of investment risk include interest-rate risk, political risk, market risk, nonmarket risk, and company or industry risk.
* Evaluate investment options for their degree of safety, liquidity, dividends or interest, growth, cost, and tax benefits. All investments involve tradeoffs among these criteria.
* To make wise investments, define your goals, go slowly, keep good records, get good advice, keep your investment knowledge current, and know your limits.

11.2

* You can get investment information from print and online newspapers, investor newsletters, financial magazines, and annual reports as well as from brokers and financial advisors.
* Generally, the more risk you are willing to take, the more you stand to gain or lose from an investment.
* Low risk/low return investment options include corporate or government bonds and Treasury securities.
* Medium risk/medium return investments include stocks, mutual funds, annuities, and real estate.
* Futures, options, penny stocks, and collectibles carry a high risk of loss.

Directions

Can you find the definition for each of the following terms used in Chapter 11?

annual report	investing
annuity	mutual fund
bonds	option
discount bond	penny stocks
diversification	risk
financial advisers	Rule of 72
futures	stock
inflation	

1. A bond purchased for less than its maturity value.

2. A contract sold by an insurance company that provides the investor a series of regular payments, usually after retirement.

3. An investment strategy for spreading risk among different types of investments.

4. The use of savings to earn a financial return.

5. A rise in the general level of prices.

6. The chance that an investment's value will decrease.

7. An SEC-required summary of a corporation's financial results for the year and prospects for the future.

8. A unit of ownership in a corporation.

9. Professional investment planners who are trained to give investment advice.

10. An investment that represents the debt of a company or a government.

11. A professionally managed group of investments bought using a pool of money from many investors.

12. Contracts to buy and sell commodities or stocks for a specified price on a specified date in the future.

13. The right, but not the obligation, to buy or sell a commodity or stock for a specified price within a specified time period.

14. Low-priced stocks of small companies that have no track record.

15. Technique for estimating the number of years required to double your money at a given rate of return.

REVIEW FACTS AND IDEAS

1. List the stages investors usually go through as their excess income increases over time.

2. Explain the difference between temporary and permanent investments.

3. List three reasons for investing.

4. What can you use the Rule of 72 to estimate?

5. How does risk relate to potential return?

6. How does inflation affect an investment's return?

7. Identify criteria you can use to evaluate an investment.

8. What are seven wise investment practices?

9. Name at least six main sources of financial information.

10. What are advantages and disadvantages of investing through a discount broker rather than a full-service broker?

11. Where can you find investment information online?

12. Distinguish among t-bills, Treasury notes, and Treasury bonds.

13. Explain the difference between stocks and bonds.

14. What are some advantages of investing in mutual funds?

15. Why are futures and options risky investments?

1. Explain the put-and-take concept. Why is it important that money set aside remain a permanent investment? How will you personally design an investment plan? Will it include a put-and-take or emergency account? Explain.

2. Why is risk such an important consideration when investing? Write a paragraph explaining your comfort level with risk and how it will affect your investment decisions.

3. Explain why it is not possible for one investment to offer high levels of all the criteria for choosing an investment. Which criteria are most important to you?

4. Read the financial section of your local newspaper. Write a few paragraphs summarizing the type of information covered and its usefulness to you as an investor.

5. Visit a discount brokerage firm online to find out how to open an account. Summarize their requirements in a paragraph.

6. Visit a library and get a copy of a current annual report for a major corporation that does business in your state. Or, visit a large corporation online and go to its investor page to find its financial data. Outline the contents of the report or the online financial data and give a brief oral review of your findings to the class. Give your opinion of whether or not this corporation would be a good investment choice, and present reasons why you feel this way.

7. Using key words such as "investment," "stock," or some others you can think of, search the Internet for resources to help you make investing choices. List the names and URLs of three sites that you think would help you most. Briefly describe the types of investment information available at those sites.

8. Compare U.S. government savings bonds to mutual funds and collectibles in terms of risk and potential return. Explain why these investments are categorized as they are.

9. Consult a financial newspaper or magazine or search the Internet to find the current rate for each of the following securities:
   a. Series EE savings bonds
   b. one-year Treasury bills
   c. two-year Treasury notes
   d. thirty-year Treasury bonds

Solve Problems ⊕ Explore Issues

1. Ricardo, who is 19 and in college, has just inherited $1,000. He does not need the money for his put-and-take account. What would you tell him to do with it? If Ricardo invested the money in a stock that earned, on average, 10 percent return, how much would his investment be worth in five years? On the Internet, locate a savings planner tool for help.

2. If Ricardo invested his $1,000 at a 5 percent average return, how many years would it take for his investment to be worth $2,000?

3. Aleesha Lynch is considering investing $500. Explain to her what factors she should consider when choosing investment alternatives.

4. Friends of your family, who were recently married, are now finding that they have money left over each month that they could invest. They would like to consult a financial adviser but don't know one. What tips would you give them about selecting a financial adviser?

5. Abdul Hussein would like to invest in XYZ Corporation. He heard that the company was big and powerful. You've never heard of it. What kinds of information should he have before he invests in this company? Where can he get that information?

6. Ann Russell would like to invest $10,000 that she inherited from her uncle. She would like to have the money for her daughter's college education starting in eight years. She does not like to take a lot of risk because she cannot afford to lose the $10,000. What course of action would you suggest for Ann?

7. Assume that Ann Russell (in question 6) invested her $10,000 in a way that earned an average of 6 percent annual return. On the Internet, locate a college planner tool to find out how much more she would have to invest each year to cover her daughter's college costs. Assume that college will cost $5,000 a year for four years.

8. Choose six of the investment alternatives presented in this chapter. Rank the choices from high to low on the factors of safety, risk, and liquidity. Assume that 3 is the highest score and 1 is the lowest score for each factor. Based on the results of your review of possible investments, which three alternatives would you select as permanent investments? Why?

For related activities and links, point your browser to **www.mypf.swlearning.com**

Investing in Stocks

TERMS TO KNOW

stockholders	growth stocks	bear market
dividends	blue chip stocks	leverage
capital gain	par value	short selling
common stock	market value	stock split
proxy	earnings per	direct investment
preferred stock	share	dividend
income stocks	bull market	reinvestment

Consider This. . .

Jeff worked hard for the summer and managed to save $500 to invest. He decided he wanted to buy a stock and see what happened.

"I've been doing research about a medical research company, and I think it's on the verge of something big," he said to his discount broker in an e-mail. "I think the stock price is low now because the company isn't paying dividends. Instead, management is using company profits to develop new products. The president and management team are very strong. All the information I've gathered online suggests that the company is solid. I think this growth stock is worth the risk. Please buy me as many shares as my money will purchase."

Evaluating Stocks

Goals
- Describe the features of common and preferred stock.
- Discuss stock investing classifications.
- Explain how stock values are determined.
- Discuss factors that affect a stock's price.

▶ CHARACTERISTICS OF STOCK

Nearly 50 million people in the United States own stocks. There are more than 34,000 public corporations from which to choose. A *public corporation* is a company whose stock is traded openly on stock markets.

Stockholders, also known as *shareholders*, are the owners of the corporation. If the corporation does well, stockholders will profit in two ways. One is through dividends. **Dividends** are the part of the corporation's profits paid to stockholders. The other way stockholders profit when the corporation does well is through **capital gain**. This is an increase in the value of the stock above the price initially paid for it. For example, if you bought stock for $5 per share and the corporation thrived, its stock price might go up to $10 per share. If it did, you could sell it for a substantial profit. Part of the risk in owning stock, however, is that the price could also go down below the price initially paid for it, resulting in a *capital loss*. Also, a capital gain becomes profit only when you sell the stock. Until then, it is a profit only on paper.

Stockholders can lose all of their investment should the company fail. However, one advantage to owning stock is that stockholders can lose no more than their investment in the stock. The owner of a small business, on the other hand, can also lose personal assets when the business fails.

©GETTY IMAGES/PHOTODISC

Why is owning a stock risky?

Stocks are traded in round lots or odd lots. A *round lot* is 100 shares or multiples of 100 shares of a particular stock. An *odd lot* is fewer than 100 shares of a particular stock. Brokerage firms usually charge slightly higher per-share fees for trading in odd lots. Odd lots must be combined into round lots before they can be traded.

Common Stock

Common stock is a type of stock that pays a variable dividend and gives the holder voting rights. The *board of directors*, elected by stockholders to guide the corporation, decides the amount of the dividend each year. Common stockholders do not directly manage the corporation, but they may vote on major policy decisions, such as whether to issue additional stock, sell the company, or change the board of directors. Each share has the same voting power, so the more shares a stockholder owns, the greater the power to influence corporate policy.

Common stockholders may vote in person at the stockholders' meeting or by proxy. A **proxy** is a stockholder's written authorization to transfer his or her voting rights to someone else, usually a company manager. Most stockholders sign the proxy rather than attend the meetings.

Preferred Stock

Preferred stock is a type of stock that pays a fixed dividend and carries no voting rights. Preferred stockholders earn the stated dividend, regardless of how the company is doing, making preferred stock less risky than common stock. In the event the company fails, the preferred stockholder would be paid ahead of common stockholders. As with most investments, however, the tradeoff for less risk is lower return. Dividends on preferred stock may be lower than common stockholders would earn on a thriving corporation over time.

▶ CLASSIFYING STOCK INVESTMENTS

When evaluating common stock investments, investors often classify stocks into different categories. Common categories of stocks include income, growth, blue chip, defensive, and cyclical. Which category is best for you will depend on how much risk you are willing to assume for a chance to earn larger returns on your investments. Also, most investors buy stocks in several of these categories to diversify their risk.

Income versus Growth Stocks

Corporations can use their profits in two ways. They can distribute the profits to stockholders as dividends, or they can reinvest the profits in the business to help it grow. Stocks that have a consistent history of paying high dividends are known as **income stocks**. Investors choose income stocks in order to receive current income in the form of dividends. Preferred stocks pay the most certain and predictable dividends and are often the choice of retired people and others investing for income from dividends.

Corporations that pay high dividends put less profit back into the business. As a result, income stocks usually do not grow in value as quickly as growth stocks. **Growth stocks** are stocks in corporations that reinvest their profits into the business so that it can grow. These corporations may pay little or no dividends. Instead of current income, investors buy growth stocks for future capital gains. If the reinvested profits do make the business grow, the stock will be worth substantially more in the future, when the investor is ready to sell it. As a result, growth stocks are long-term investments. If the value of the stock increases, stockholders must decide whether to sell it at the higher price now or to continue to hold it, hoping that it will go up even more. When stockholders decide to sell, the difference between their original purchase price and the selling price they receive is their capital gain.

Less-Established versus Blue Chip Stocks

Stocks in young, often small corporations have higher overall risk than stocks of companies that have been successful for many years. These young companies may be on their way to becoming highly profitable. Or, they may be among the many small companies that fail every year. Because the future of these companies is so uncertain, their stocks are often inexpensive but risky.

Blue chip stocks are stocks of large, well-established corporations with a solid record of profitability. Most people have heard of these companies because their products and services have been around for decades. They are companies like IBM and Coca-Cola. Blue chip stocks are a conservative investment. Investors choose them for relatively safe, stable, but moderate returns.

Why are blue chip stocks a conservative investment?

Defensive versus Cyclical Stocks

A *defensive stock* is one that remains stable and pays dividends during an economic decline. Generally, companies in this category have a history of stable earnings. A defensive stock is not affected as much by the ups and downs of business cycles. Examples include utilities, drugs, food, and health care. In other words, the demand for these products remains fairly consistent regardless of economic conditions. Therefore, stocks in these industries protect the investor from sharp losses during bad economic times.

Cyclical stocks do well when the economy is stable or growing but often do poorly during *recessions*, when the economy slows down. Examples of cyclical stocks are travel-related companies such as airlines and resorts, manufacturing companies, and agriculture. For example, during a recession, many people lose their jobs or earn less than they would during good economic times. As a result, people have less money for luxuries, such as leisure travel, causing reduced profits for travel-related companies such as airlines and resorts. In response to this poor profit performance, the value of the stocks in these companies will likely decline.

▶ DETERMINING A STOCK'S WORTH

When you buy stock, you expect to hold it for a period of time and then sell it, hopefully for a profit. Whether or not you make a profit on the sale of your stock depends on how much someone else is willing to pay for it when you are ready to sell.

Stock Value

When you purchase stock, you may receive a stock certificate or have it held electronically. The certificate states the number of shares you own, the name of the company, the type of stock (common or preferred), and the par value. The **par value** is an assigned (and often arbitrary) dollar value.

Par value is an artificial number. It has nothing to do with a stock's **market value**, which is the price for which the stock is bought and sold in the marketplace. Market value reflects the price investors are willing to pay for the stock. How a company currently is doing, its track record, and how well it is expected to perform in the future determine market value.

Some stocks perform very well, yet their market value seems too low—or a "real bargain." These "undervalued" stocks are worth more than the price for which they are selling. Stocks that are undervalued make good bargains for investors, while creating a dangerous situation for businesses. With this condition, the corporation is vulnerable to a takeover by a large investor or company. The result is often loss of jobs for workers and a company that is broken into parts for sell-off. Takeovers may be unfavorable for employees but can be very favorable for stockholders, because the market value of the stock is likely to rise.

On the other hand, stocks can be "overvalued," which means they are selling at a price that is not justified by their earnings potential. This situation is very risky for the investor, because it is likely that the price of the stock will drop.

Stock prices go up and down constantly. The wider the price swings, the riskier the stock. That is, a stock that has a history of very high highs and very low lows is a riskier investment than a stock that goes up and down only moderately over time.

Stock Price

Several factors affect the price you will pay for a share of stock. These factors include the company's financial situation, current interest rates, the market for the company's products or services, and earnings per share.

1. *The Company.* When a company is performing well (meeting its current obligations and making a profit), the company's stock is attractive. Investors consider the company's earning power (its ability to continue to make a strong profit), as well as its debt obligations (how much the company owes). If the company seems to be in a good financial position, the stock price will continue rising.

2. *Interest Rates.* When interest rates are low, people who would normally put money in savings accounts and certificates of deposit look for more profitable places to invest their money. As interest rates rise, however, people tend to move their money to the safer investments. Generally, when interest rates fall below the current rate of inflation, people buy more stock, and stock prices rise.

3. *The Market.* The marketplace determines a company's ability to sell its product or service now and in the future. If the company is in a popular industry and its products or services are selling well, its stock price will rise. For example, when people are buying computers, software, and related items, companies in the high-tech industry are considered wise investments. If the demand for a particular product or service declines, the price of the stock will decrease.

4. *Earnings per Share.* **Earnings per share** are a corporation's after-tax earnings divided by the number of common stock shares outstanding, that is, shares in the hands of investors. For example, assume that in a given year, XYZ Corporation had after-tax earnings (net profit) of $1,000,000. It had 100,000 shares of common stock outstanding. Therefore, its earnings per share at that time were $10 ($1,000,000/100,000 = $10). Stockholders use earnings per share as a measure of a company's profitability.

Return on Investment

Because you can make money on stocks from dividends and from an increase in the price of the stock (capital gain), you should consider both when computing the return on your investment. Figure 12-1 shows the formula for computing a stock's *return on investment (ROI)*. Your ROI is the profit you earned on the stock as a percentage of the total cost of buying the stock. Your profit is the difference between what you paid for the stock and what you sold it for, plus any dividends you earned. To compute the total costs, add any commission you paid to the stockbroker to the purchase price of the stock. Then find the ROI percentage by dividing profit by cost.

✅ Check Your Understanding

1. In what two ways can you make money from owning stock?
2. How is an income stock different from a growth stock?
3. Why do stockholders want to know a corporation's earnings per share?

COMPUTING A STOCK'S RETURN ON INVESTMENT (ROI)

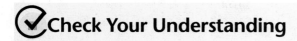

figure **12-1**

Computing a Stock's One-Year ROI

$$\frac{\text{Current Profit on Stock}}{\text{Purchase Price} + \text{Commission}} = \text{Return on Investment (ROI)}$$

Example: Current stock price: $40/share
Dividends received during the year: $1/share
Purchase price: $38/share
Discount brokerage fee: $19
Number of shares owned: 100

Computations:
Current profit: $40/share − $38/share = $2/share x 100 = $200 + dividends ($100) = total profits of $300.

$$\frac{\$300}{(100 \times \$38) + \$19} = \frac{\$300}{\$3,819} = 7.86\%$$

Buying and Selling Stock

Goals	• Describe the process for buying and selling securities.
	• Describe short- and long-term investment strategies when buying and selling stocks.
	• Explain how to read the stock listings and stock indexes.

▶ THE SECURITIES MARKET

The securities market consists of the channels through which you buy and sell securities (stocks and bonds). To purchase common or preferred stock, you need a trading agent. Your agent will buy or sell for you in a securities marketplace, which is either a securities exchange or the over-the-counter market.

Securities Exchanges

A *securities exchange* is a marketplace where brokers who are representing investors meet to buy and sell securities. The largest organized exchange in the United States is the New York Stock Exchange (NYSE). The smaller American Stock Exchange is also in New York City. Regional exchanges are located throughout the country. To have a stock listed with the NYSE or AMEX, a company must meet a minimum number of public shares and dollar market-value requirements.

In the New York Stock Exchange building, the trading floor (where stocks are bought and sold) is about two-thirds the size of a football field. Around the edge of the trading floor are booths with computer terminals that are open at both ends, with room inside for a dozen or more floor brokers. *Floor brokers* buy and sell stocks on the exchange. Only brokers who are members of the exchange may do business there.

Spaced at regular intervals around the trading floor are trading posts, which are horseshoe-shaped counters, each occupying about 100 square feet on the floor. Behind each counter are specialists—the brokers to the floor brokers. All buying and selling is done around trading posts. About 90 different stocks are assigned to each post. Post display units above each counter show which stocks are sold in each section, the last price of that stock, and whether that price represents an increase or a decrease from the previous price.

Orders received at a brokerage firm or discount brokerage are phoned or sent by computer to that firm's booth at the exchange. A message is printed out and is given to the floor broker to carry out. When the transaction is completed, the clerks for the brokers who bought and sold the stock report back to their respective brokerage firms. The buyer and seller can then be advised that the transaction has been concluded.

The exchange is a form of *auction market* where buyers and sellers are brought together to trade securities. Stock trading happens auction-style because in every transaction, stock is sold to the highest bidder (buyer) and bought from the lowest offeror (seller). Securities listed with the NYSE are traded only during official trading hours—9:30 a.m. to 4 p.m. New York time, Monday through Friday (except holidays).

Why is a securities exchange considered an auction market?

Career Focus

Securities brokers typically buy and sell stocks, bonds, mutual funds, and other financial services. They often provide advice to clients about possible investments. Typically, securities brokers have college degrees, an aptitude for numbers, and a keen interest in investing. In addition, most people in the industry are required to be licensed by the National Association of Securities Dealers (NASD) before they can sell securities or recommend specific investments.

For more information, refer to the *Occupational Outlook Handbook* at www.bls.gov or search the Internet using such key words as "careers," "jobs," and "brokers."

Over-the-Counter Market

When securities are bought and sold through brokers but not through a stock exchange, the transaction is over-the-counter (OTC). The *over-the-counter (OTC) market* is a network of brokers who buy and sell the securities of corporations that are not listed on a securities exchange. Brokers in the OTC market do not deal face-to-face. Their marketplace is as large as the number of desks with brokers at work that day. Trades with other brokers are completed by telephone, and a computerized system displays current price quotations on a terminal in a broker's office. Brokers operating in the OTC market use an electronic quotation system called NASDAQ. (The letters were originally an acronym for the National Association of Securities Dealers Automated Quotation System.) To be listed with NASDAQ, companies must have issued at least 100,000 shares of stock worth $1 million.

Net Nuggets

STOCK-TRAK provides a method to practice investment strategies, test theories, practice day trading, learn about the various markets, and compete against others. Students can play as a class or individually. The Individual Investment Simulation is open to anyone who wants to practice trading in the market. You start out with $100,000 in imaginary cash and buy and sell stocks, options, or futures for the next 12 weeks and see if you can outperform the market. Check out the web site at www.stocktrak.com.

Bull and Bear Markets

The stock market goes through cycles. For a period of time, stocks go up in value. Then the market corrects itself as people sell (to make a profit), and stock prices decrease. A **bull market** is a prolonged period of rising stock prices and a general feeling of investor optimism. Confidence about how the country is doing also serves to drive up stock prices.

A **bear market** is a prolonged period of falling stock prices and a general feeling of investor pessimism. It develops when investors become negative about the overall economy and start to sell stocks. In bear markets, stock prices may fall 20 percent or more. Bear markets are usually short and savage. The average bull market often lasts three to four times as long as a bear market.

Whether the stock market in general is bullish (on an upward trend in prices) or bearish (on a downward trend in prices) influences your decisions about when to buy stocks and which stocks to buy. To make a profit, you need to buy stock when the price is low and sell when the price is higher. However, nobody knows, including brokers, when a stock is at its lowest price or whether or not the price will rise. For this reason, you need to research individual stocks to judge which are most likely to earn a profit.

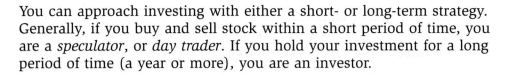

▶ INVESTING STRATEGIES

You can approach investing with either a short- or long-term strategy. Generally, if you buy and sell stock within a short period of time, you are a *speculator,* or *day trader*. If you hold your investment for a long period of time (a year or more), you are an investor.

Short-Term Techniques

When you buy and sell stocks for quick profits, you are "playing the stock market." The goal is to buy a stock that will soon increase in value. Then, when the price rises, you sell the stock. Many investors make short-term gains through processes called buying on margin and selling short.

BUY ON MARGIN

You can borrow money from your broker to buy stock if you open a margin account and sign a contract called a *margin agreement*. To establish a margin account, you must deposit a minimum of $2,000 in cash or eligible securities (securities your broker considers valuable collateral) with a broker. Let's assume you have $2,000 in your margin account. You want to buy 100 shares of XYZ Corporation at $20 per share ($2,000). You could use $1,000 from your margin account and borrow $1,000, with interest, from your broker. This strategy is called **leverage**—the use of borrowed money to buy securities. You use less of your own money and therefore can buy more stocks with less cash. You would still have $1,000 in your margin account to use toward another purchase on margin.

With a margin purchase, you are betting that the stock will increase in value. If it does, you sell the stock, repay the loan with interest and commission, and take your short-term profit. Figure 12-2 (page 290) shows how margin buying works.

Unfortunately, if the value of the stock does not increase, you will have to make up the difference. When the market value of a margined stock decreases to approximately one-half of the original purchase price, the investor will receive a margin call from the broker. After the margin call, the investor must pledge additional cash or securities to serve as collateral for the loan. If you don't have the cash, the stock is sold and the proceeds are used to pay the loan.

SELL SHORT

Short selling is selling stock borrowed from a broker that must be replaced at a later time. To sell short, you borrow a certain number of shares from the broker. You then sell the borrowed stock, knowing that you must buy it back later and return it to the broker. You are betting that the price will drop, so that you can buy it back at a lower

Buying on Margin

Example: You buy $2,000 worth of stock with $1,000 of your own money and $1,000 borrowed from your broker at 6% annual interest. The stock increases in value and you sell it after 60 days for $2,800. Your broker's commission to buy and sell is $200.

Computing Profit:

Interest cost: $1,000 borrowed × .06 annual interest × $\left(\dfrac{60 \text{ days}}{360 \text{ days in a year}}\right)$
= $10 interest on the 60-day loan

Costs: $1,000 purchase price + $1,000 amount borrowed
+ $10 interest + $200 commission = $2,210 total cost

Profit: $2,800 selling price − $2,210 cost = $590 total profit

Computing Return on Investment:

$$\dfrac{\$590 \text{ profit}}{\$2,210 \text{ cost}} = 26.7\% \text{ ROI}$$

price than you sold it for. However, if the stock price increases, you will lose money because you must replace the borrowed stock with stock purchased at a higher price. Figure 12-3 shows how selling short works. There is usually no broker fee for selling short. The broker receives a commission when the stock is bought and sold.

Long-Term Techniques

As you may already suspect, investing in the stock market for short-term gains can be extremely risky. You cannot beat the market all of the time, but you can make some healthy profits if you study and follow the market carefully. However, most financial consultants advise you to invest for the long term. Records have shown that, over a long time, stock investments have consistently beaten rates for savings accounts, CDs, and other conservative options.

BUY AND HOLD

Most investors consider stock purchases as long-term investments. All stocks go up and down, but over a number of years, the overall trend of non-speculative stocks is moderately up. Remember, a profit or loss occurs only when you sell the stock. If you "buy and hold" stocks for many years, you can ride out the down times. When you are ready to sell years later, most likely your stock will have gained value. In addition, many stocks pay dividends, so you are earning income while you hold the stock.

figure **12-3**

Selling Short

Example: You borrow 100 shares of stock of XYZ Corporation from your broker. You then sell 100 shares of XYZ at $28 per share and pay a $100 commission.

Income from sale = 100 shares x $28 per share – $100 commission
= $2,700 initial income

Two weeks later, the stock price drops to $22 per share. You buy 100 shares to return to the stockbroker and pay a $100 commission.

Cost of buying back the shares: 100 shares x $22 per share + $100 commission
= $2,300 cost

Profit from selling short: $2,700 income – $2,300 cost = $400 profit

Return on Investment: $\dfrac{\$400}{\$2,300}$ = 17.4% ROI

A stock split also can add to the value of the stock over time. A **stock split** is an increase in the number of outstanding shares of a company's stock. When a company increases its shares outstanding, it lowers the selling price in direct proportion. For example, if there were 1,000 shares outstanding with a market value of $60, then a 2:1 (two for one) stock split would result in 2,000 shares outstanding selling for $30. You will notice that the stock is still worth a total of $60,000. A stock split lowers the selling price of the stock, making the shares more affordable and encouraging investors to buy more. As investors buy more stock at the lower price, the share price often rises. If you held the stock before the split, then this price increase makes your stock worth more.

DOLLAR-COST AVERAGING

The *dollar-cost averaging* technique involves the systematic purchase of an equal dollar amount of the same stock at regular intervals. The result is usually a lower average cost per share. To calculate the average cost per share, divide the total amount invested by the total number of shares purchased, as shown in Figure 12-4 (page 292). In the figure, the investor purchased $100 worth of stock every quarter for one year. Over that time, the average price of the stock was $8. However, by investing at regular intervals over the time period, the investor's average cost per share was lower: $7.41.

Dollar-Cost Averaging

Quarterly investment amount		Share price ($)		Number of shares
$100	÷	10	=	10
$100	÷	7	=	14.29
$100	÷	5	=	20
$100	÷	10	=	10
$400		$32		54
Total $ invested				Total number of shares

Average share price = $8
$32 ÷ 4

Your average cost per share = $7.41
total $ invested ($400) ÷ total number of shares (54)

Ending value = $540
last share price ($10) × number of shares (54)

Investors use this technique so they don't have to worry about timing their investment purchases. A regular purchase over a year's time will usually average out to a reasonable price per share. With dollar-cost averaging, the investor makes a profit when the selling price per share is higher than the average cost per share.

DIRECT INVESTMENT

You can save money using **direct investment**, or buying stock directly from a corporation. By buying directly, you avoid brokerage and other purchasing fees. You may also be able to obtain shares at prices lower than on open exchanges. Direct investment is often available to existing stockholders who may have the privilege of buying additional shares at fixed prices that are at or below market value.

REINVESTING DIVIDENDS

You can also save money by reinvesting your dividends. **Dividend reinvestment** means using dividends previously earned on the stock to buy more shares. Buying stock this way avoids a broker fee and other costs of receiving cash dividends on the stock.

► READING THE STOCK LISTINGS

To make wise investments in the stock market, you will need to track the progress of your chosen investments to see how they are performing. Whether you are reading *The Wall Street Journal* or following your stocks online, you should see a listing similar to Figure 12-5 (page 294) of the stocks that are bought and sold on stock exchanges or over-the-counter. Follow along in Figure 12-5 as you read the following explanation of each column.

1. *Columns 1 and 2.* These columns show the highest and lowest price this stock sold for during the year. For the ExeB stock in Figure 12-5, the high for the last 52 weeks was 57.00 and the low was 32.00. This means the stock sold for $57 a share at one point (high) and $32 a share at another (low), though it may have sold for many prices in between during the year.

2. *Column 3.* This column lists stocks alphabetically by name. You will notice that stock names are abbreviated. This abbreviated name is called the stock's *ticker symbol.* You may see additional abbreviations, such as "pf" (which means "preferred stock"), beside the name of the stock. There will be a legend at the bottom of the page that explains what these abbreviations mean. For example, a small "s" means that the stock has recently split. When a stock splits, each share owned is traded for additional shares. A 2:1 split would double your shares. If you owned 10 shares worth $50 each, you would now own 20 shares worth $25 each.

3. *Column 4.* This column shows the cash dividend per share for the year, listed in dollars and cents. For the ExeB stock, 2.50 means that if you owned 100 shares of this company, you would have received a dividend of $250 for the year.

4. *Column 5.* Yld % stands for *percent yield*, or the percentage of the current price the dividends represent. In other words, divide the amount of annual dividends (Column 4) by the closing price (Column 10).

5. *Column 6.* The *P/E ratio* (price/earnings ratio) is the price of a share of stock divided by the corporation's earnings per share over the last 12 months. For example, if XYZ Corporation's stock is selling for $50 per share and XYZ's earnings per share are $10, the P/E ratio is 5 ($50/$10 = $5). The price/earnings ratio is a key factor that serious investors use to evaluate stock investments. A low P/E may indicate a solid investment, and a high P/E may indicate higher risk.

6. *Column 7.* This column shows sales in hundreds of shares from the previous day—how many round lots of stock were bought and sold. Multiply the number by 100 to get the number of shares.

7. *Columns 8, 9, and 10.* These columns show the highest, lowest, and closing price for this stock on the previous day. The closing price is the final price at the end of trading for the day.

8. *Column 11.* This column, called *net change,* compares the closing price today with the closing price of the day before. A minus means the price has gone down. A plus means the price has risen. Stocks that have a price change of more than 5 percent are in boldface.

Keeping track of your *stock portfolio* (or stock holdings) can be as simple as checking the closing prices periodically. Some people check their investments only once a year to see if they should make changes to their portfolio. Investors might buy additional shares, sell, or choose a different type of stock after checking their portfolios.

The stocks shown in Figure 12-6 have been tracked for 10 days straight. As you can see, some stocks have done better than others in terms of market value as of a certain date. But remember, this chart does not take into account dividends received or the appreciation in value since a stock was purchased. The stock progress chart is merely a device for monitoring changes in the closing prices of stocks.

Many financial Internet sites enable you to follow stock prices. Using a stock's ticker symbol, you can find the stock's price up to the minute. If you want stock quotes sent to your computer automatically, you can sign up for the service with your Internet service provider. Most will allow you to specify the stocks you want to follow. You can even buy and sell stocks online. Most major stockbrokers maintain Web sites that allow online transactions.

©GETTY IMAGES/PHOTODISC

What kinds of stock-related activities are available online?

figure **12-5**

READING THE STOCK LISTINGS

Reading Stock Listings

Excerpt from stock exchange listings:

| 52 wks | | | | | P/E | Sales | | | | Net |
High	Low	Stock	Div	Yld %	Ratio	100s	High	Low	Close	Chg.
1	2	3	4	5	6	7	8	9	10	11
58.75	44.00	Enger	2.20	4.8	12	109	46.38	45.50	46.00	– .50
45.00	23.00	Eng pf	2.25	8.9	10	25	26.25	24.00	25.38	+ .38
10.50	9.00	Entld	.10	1.0	3	8	10.13	9.50	10.00	----
24.00	16.00	Epsco	1.00	5.0	7	12	21.00	19.00	20.00	+ .88
6.38	4.00	Exlab	--	--	15	300z	5.75	5.12	5.50	----
57.00	32.00	ExeB	2.50	5.7	11	48	46.00	43.00	44.00	+1.00

figure 12-6 ◄

Stock Progress Chart

Stock Names	Closing Prices for 10 days										Total Change (+ or −)
	1	2	3	4	5	6	7	8	9	10	
1. Enger	28	28.12	29	28	27	28	28.50	29	29.50	30	+2
2. Glastn	38	40	41	41.50	--	40	39	38	38	38	0
3. Karbr pf	61	61.25	61.13	61	61.38	61	62	62.38	61	61.13	+.13
4. Maxln	50.13	49	50	50.25	51	51	51.13	52	52	53.50	+3.37
5. Totlmb	10	11	11.13	11.50	11	10.88	10	9	8	8.50	−1.50

Global View

Online trading in Japan has boomed over the last few years. Many companies entered the new territory when brokerage commissions were deregulated in October 1999. Online brokerage accounts have grown steadily. However, given the fact that a significant portion of active individual investors are older than 50, it is uncertain whether many will move to the Web.

Think Critically: Are you comfortable with the idea of online investing? How could an online broker make it easier or more attractive for older people to invest?

► STOCK INDEXES

A *stock index* is a benchmark that investors use to judge the performance of their investments. One widely followed stock index is the *Dow Jones Industrial Average*. Often called simply *the Dow*, it is an average of the price movements of 30 major stocks listed on the New York Stock Exchange. This average provides a general overview of what stock prices are doing in the stock market as a whole. Investors compare the price fluctuations of their stocks against this average to judge how well their stocks are performing compared to the overall stock market. Indexes for judging the performance of all kinds of stocks are available online and in print publications. Other commonly used indexes are the Standard & Poor's 500 and the NASDAQ Composite Index.

✓Check Your Understanding

1. What are two kinds of markets where securities are bought and sold?
2. Why is buying on margin risky?
3. How do you save money by reinvesting dividends?

Issues in Your World

Inflation is an increase in the general level of prices. Inflation is measured yearly to see how much prices are rising. The *consumer price index (CPI)* is the instrument most often used as a measure of rising prices. The CPI measures price changes for a "market basket" of goods and services typically purchased by consumers. Inflation is also evident in rising interest rates. Interest rates reflect the cost of lending and borrowing money. As prices increase, interest rates go up as well.

Some people get hurt by rapidly rising prices and interest rates. People who get hurt include:

1. *People on fixed incomes.* Many retired people live on a fixed monthly retirement check. When prices rise, their fixed income stays the same. Thus, they are unable to maintain the same standard of living in inflationary times.

2. *People with a lot of debt.* During inflationary times, interest rates are rising. Thus, creditors (lenders of money) can charge higher interest rates. This makes it hard for people with a lot of debt to pay off their loans. More of each month's payment goes toward interest rather than paying off the debt.

3. *People who have to borrow.* If you need to borrow money, you will pay higher interest rates in times of inflation. As a result, your monthly payments will be higher or you will have to make payments for a longer time to pay off the loan.

4. *People working as employees.* As an employee, you work for a salary or wage. You may get a yearly raise, but that comes much later. Price increases (inflation) hit immediately and you must make rapid changes in lifestyle. This lowers your standard of living as rapidly rising prices erode your purchasing power.

To prepare for periods of inflation, save so you will have resources during hard times. Then you can be a lender rather than a borrower.

Think Critically

1. Using the key word "inflation," do Internet research and compare interest rates and rising prices in the United States to those in other countries, such as Brazil, Mexico, or France. Look at the rates over a three or five year period of time.

2. Have you noticed goods or services you buy frequently increasing in price? How have prices of those goods or services affected your lifestyle?

Chapter Assessment

SUMMARY

12.1

* Stockholders profit through dividends and capital gains.
* Because preferred stock pays a fixed dividend, it is less risky than the company's common stock, but generally earns a lower return.
* Corporations can distribute profits to stockholders as dividends or reinvest it in the business.
* Blue chip stocks provide a relatively safe but moderate return.
* Defensive stocks remain relatively stable during good and bad economic times.
* Cyclical stocks do well when the economy is growing but do poorly during recessions.
* The par value printed on the stock certificate has nothing to do with the market value investors actually pay for the stock.
* Stock price depends on company performance, general level of interest rates, the market for the company's products, and the company's earnings per share.
* Both dividends and capital gains go into determining the ROI.

12.2

* You can buy and sell securities through a securities exchange (physical place) or over-the-counter (by phone or computer).
* Stock prices are rising during a bull market and falling during a bear market.
* Short-term investors are speculators who try to make a quick profit by buying on margin or selling short.
* Long-term strategies are buy and hold, dollar-cost averaging, direct investment, and reinvesting dividends.
* You can track your stock's progress by reading the stock listings in print publications and online.

Can you find the definition for each of the following terms used in Chapter 12?

> bear market   income stocks
> blue chip stocks   leverage
> bull market   market value
> capital gain   par value
> common stock   preferred stock
> direct investment   proxy
> dividend reinvestment   short selling
> dividends   stock split
> earnings per share   stockholders
> growth stocks

1. A type of stock that pays a variable dividend and gives the holder voting rights.

2. A stockholder's written authorization to transfer his or her voting rights to someone else, usually a company manager.

3. Stocks with a consistent history of paying high dividends.

4. An increase in the number of outstanding shares of a company's stock.

5. The price for which a stock is bought and sold in the marketplace.

6. The use of borrowed money to buy securities.

7. A prolonged period of rising stock prices and a general feeling of investor optimism.

8. The part of the corporation's profits paid to stockholders.

9. A type of stock that pays a fixed dividend and carries no voting rights.

10. Stocks in corporations that reinvest their profits into the business so the company can grow.

11. Stock of large, well-established corporations with a solid record of profitability.

12. An assigned (often arbitrary) dollar value printed on a stock certificate.

13. A prolonged period of falling stock prices and a general feeling of investor pessimism.

14. A corporation's after-tax earnings divided by the number of shares of common stock outstanding.

15. Buying stock directly from a corporation.

16. Selling stock borrowed from a broker that must be replaced at a later time.

17. Using dividends previously earned on the stock to buy more shares.

18. Owners of a corporation.

19. An increase in the value of the stock above the price initially paid for it.

REVIEW FACTS AND IDEAS

1. How would you earn a capital gain on your stock?

2. How is common stock different from preferred stock?

3. What type of investor should purchase income stocks? growth stocks?

4. Which involves the greatest risk—stocks of young businesses or blue chip stocks? Explain the differences between the two types of stocks.

5. Why are defensive stocks not subject to the usual ups and downs of business cycles?

6. Explain the relationship between par value and market value.

7. What causes stock prices to rise and fall? List four factors that affect stock prices.

8. Which is the largest stock exchange in the United States? How does a company get listed on this exchange?

9. Why would a stock be listed on the NASDAQ rather than the NYSE or American Stock Exchange?

10. What characterizes a bull market? a bear market?

11. Explain two short-term strategies for investing in stocks.

12. Explain four techniques for long-term investing.

13. Why do investors use dollar-cost averaging?

14. In stock listings, what do these symbols stand for: P/E, s, pf?

15. How do investors use stock indexes?

APPLY YOUR KNOWLEDGE

1. If you own 100 shares of common stock, which you purchased for $28 a share, and the company declares a cash dividend of $.88 for the quarter, how much will you receive in dividends?

2. Common stockholders take more risk but have a higher rate of return than preferred stockholders. Explain why.

3. Assume a company has issued the following stock:
   a. 2,000 shares of 5 percent preferred stock at $50 per share
   b. 18,000 shares of common stock at $22 per share

   A cash dividend of $1.30 per share is declared for common stock, after preferred stockholders have received their 5 percent dividend. Compute your total cash dividends for the year if you own:
   a. 100 shares of preferred stock.
   b. 100 shares of common stock.
   c. 50 shares of preferred stock and 50 shares of common stock.

4. If you had an extra $1,000 that you just inherited, which type of common stock investment would you choose? Explain why.

5. Investing in blue chip stocks is said to be a conservative choice. Can you list several well-known stocks that are considered blue

chip, besides the two mentioned in the text? (Hint: Read through the listing of stocks in the financial pages and mark the stocks you recognize. Or, look for listings online.)

6. Suppose you purchased 100 shares of stock in January for $48 a share. You received dividends of $1.25 per share on April 1 and July 1 and $.95 per share on September 1. You sold the stock in December for $50 a share. What would be the stock's return on investment for the year? Assume a broker commission of 3 percent on the purchase and sale of the stock.

7. Use the Internet or library resources to research the history of bull and bear markets. List the years and months when each type of market occurred during the 1980s and 1990s. Why is it important to understand bull and bear market trends?

8. You have $2,500 in cash in a margin account. You decide to buy stock on margin. You buy 50 shares of stock selling at $100 per share. Assume that the stock rises in value, and 30 days later you sell the stock for $110 a share. Interest on the amount borrowed is 7 percent. The commission on the purchase and sale is $150. What is the total return on investment?

9. You wish to sell short. You arrange to borrow from your broker 100 shares of stock in XYZ Corporation on January 2, 2001. You immediately sell 100 shares of XYZ at $60 per share. On April 1, 2001, you instruct your broker to purchase 100 shares of XYZ at $53 per share. You return 100 shares of XYZ stock to your broker. Assume the commission was $200. What is your return on investment for this transaction?

10. Suppose you decided to buy stock using dollar-cost averaging. You purchased $200 worth of stock every quarter for one year. You paid the following share prices. Quarter 1: $5; Quarter 2: $10; Quarter 3: $8; Quarter 4: $4. Using Figure 12-4 as a guide, calculate these values: (a) average share price; (b) your average cost per share; (c) ending value. Did you benefit from dollar-cost averaging? Explain.

11. Search the Web for investment advice. In no more than one page, summarize what the experts are saying about which stocks are hot right now and which are not. Do the experts seem to agree or disagree with each other? Some sites you might try are listed below:
    www.forbes.com
    www.moneycentral.msn.com
    www.fortune.com
    www.money.cnn.com
    www.kiplinger.com
    www.barrons.com

Solve Problems ⊕ Explore Issues

1. Your friend Jehan is considering investing in stocks. She has an extra $5,000 that she wants to invest. She won't need the money for five years, when she hopes to start medical school. Would you recommend common or preferred stock? Explain why.

2. Mr. and Mrs. Watanabe are in their late fifties and plan to retire within the next three to five years. They would like to put some of their money into the stock market because interest rates on savings accounts are low. Which of these options would you recommend to them? Give a brief reason for each choice.
   a. income or growth stocks?
   b. stocks of new small businesses or blue chip stocks?
   c. defensive or cyclical stocks?

3. Mykel's grandmother gave him a gift—10 shares of stock in a leading manufacturing company. In the upper right corner, the certificate states PAR VALUE, $10 per share. Mykel is confused. His grandmother told him that the closing price for the stock was $50 per share on the day he received the gift. Explain this difference.

4. Conchita Lopez bought a stock one year ago. Since then, she has received quarterly dividends of $.50 per share. Her 50 shares are now worth $35 each. She paid $29 per share, plus a commission of $180. What is her return? Would you advise her to keep or to sell the stock?

5. Alice and Peter have been married for less than a year. They are considering buying some stock to have a "nest egg" for their future children. Peter prefers to buy stock in a local company that is small and just getting started. Alice prefers to buy the stock of a well-known company that is listed on a major exchange. Discuss with them the pros and cons of each course of action.

6. Choose three stocks to follow for a week: one listed on the NYSE, one on the AMEX, and one on the NASDAQ. Pretend that you invested $1,000 in each stock. On the Internet, find the closing price for these stocks on the day you "purchased" them and at the end of every day for one week. Keep a table of the dates and closing prices. At the end of the week, make a graph of the closing prices for each day for all three stocks. Analyze your findings. Which stock price varied the most? Which had the highest high? The lowest low? Which had the most consistent upward trend? If you sold the stocks at the end of the last day, how much would you have gained or lost on each one?

Investing in Bonds

face valuea	municipal bond	zero-coupon
callable bond	revenue bond	bond
debenture	general	investment-grade
mortgage bond	obligation bond	bond
convertible bond	agency bond	junk bond

Consider This. . .

Cassandra is a conservative investor. She wants to be certain her principal is safe and that it will be available to her in two years when she needs it to start her business.

"I want to get a better return than I can get for a certificate of deposit," she told her investment advisor. "I'm thinking about investing my money in bonds. I read in the financial section of today's paper that there are some tax-free municipal bonds that are paying 5.5 percent. I'm also considering a high-grade corporate bond that pays 7 percent. While the rate is higher on the corporate bond, interest earnings are taxable. What would you advise?"

Characteristics of Bonds

Goals
- Discuss the features and types of corporate bonds.
- Calculate earnings and percentage yield on a corporate bond.
- Describe federal and municipal government securities bonds.

▶ CORPORATE BONDS

While a corporation may use both bonds and stocks to finance business activities, there are important distinctions between the two. First, bonds are loans (debt) that must be repaid at maturity. Stocks are shares of ownership (equity) in the corporation, not loans, so stocks do not need to be repaid. Second, corporations must make interest payments on their bonds. Corporations are not required to pay dividends on stocks. The board of directors decides whether or not to pay stock dividends.

Bondholders (those who invest in bonds) receive interest twice a year. When the bond matures on its *maturity date,* the principal is repaid. The most common bond maturity is 10 years. **Face value** is the amount the bondholder will be repaid at maturity. Face value is commonly $1,000. Face value is also referred to as *par value* because the face value is the dollar amount printed on the certificate.

Features of Corporate Bonds

©GETTY IMAGES/PHOTODISC

What are some differences between stocks and bonds?

Corporate bonds are sold on the open market through brokers, just like stocks. Prices asked for bonds appear daily in *The Wall Street Journal* and the financial pages of major newspapers. However, only a small fraction of the bonds issued are listed in the newspaper.

Bonds are "fixed-income investments." They pay a specified amount of interest on a regular schedule. A bond's interest does not go up and down, like stock dividends do. A bond's *interest rate* (also called "contract rate") is the percentage of face value that the bondholder will receive as interest each year. Usually, payments of half the annual interest are made twice a year. For example, a $1,000 bond might pay

5 percent, or $50 a year. The bondholder would receive two $25 payments during the year. Interest received on corporate bonds is taxable, and it is reported as ordinary income on your tax return.

The process for collecting the interest on your bond depends on whether it is a registered bond or a coupon bond. A *registered bond* is recorded in the owner's name by the issuing company. Interest checks for registered bonds are mailed semiannually, directly to the bondholder. A *coupon bond* (also called a *bearer bond*) is not registered by the issuing company. To collect interest on a coupon bond, bondholders must clip a coupon and then cash it in at a bank, following the procedures outlined by the issuer. Today, most bonds are registered.

A major disadvantage for individual investors is the cost of bonds. Very few corporate bonds are sold in units of less than $1,000. Bonds are commonly sold in $5,000 units.

A bond may be issued with a call provision. A **callable bond** is a bond that the issuer has the right to pay off (call back) before its maturity date. The date when a bond can be called is identified at the time it is offered for sale. For example, a 10-year bond issued in 2005 with a maturity date of 2015 may be callable in the year 2010. If interest rates fall, corporations may choose to call the bonds because they can re-issue them at a lower interest rate. Generally, it is cost-effective for corporations to pay the costs of calling and re-issuing when interest rates drop by 2 percent or more. Corporations usually agree *not* to call bonds for the first five years after issuance. When the corporation does exercise its right to call the bond, it generally pays the bondholders a small premium—an amount above the face value of the bond. A $1,000 bond may be called for $1,020.

Types of Corporate Bonds

For corporations, bonds are a primary way of raising money. The money raised pays for expansion, new technology, and long-term operating expenses. You can choose from three types of corporate bonds: debentures, mortgage bonds, and convertible bonds.

DEBENTURES

A **debenture** is a corporate bond that is not backed by collateral but only by the general credit standing of the corporation. The issuer does not pledge any specific assets to assure repayment of the loan. An investor relies on the full faith and credit of the issuer for repayment of the interest and principal. When issued by reliable corporations, debentures are usually relatively safe investments.

MORTGAGE BONDS

A **mortgage bond**, or *secured bond*, is a corporate bond backed by specific assets as collateral to assure repayment of the debt. If the corporation fails to repay the loan as agreed, the bondholder may claim the property used as security for the debt. The asset or collateral used for security is typically real estate.

CONVERTIBLE BONDS

A **convertible bond** is a corporate bond that the bondholder can choose to exchange for a specified number of shares of the corporation's common stock. If the bondholder converts to common stock, the corporation no longer must redeem the bond at maturity. Each bond is convertible into a certain number of common shares at a specific price per share. For example, say you purchase a $1,000 corporate bond convertible to 50 shares of the company's common stock. You can convert the bond to stock whenever the price of the company's common stock is $20 ($1,000/50 shares = $20) or higher. Assume the company's stock is selling for $22. In this situation, you would have an investment worth $1,100 on conversion ($22 × 50 shares = $1,100).

Earnings on Corporate Bonds

All bonds are issued with a stated face value and interest rate. Figure 13-1 shows interest payments on a $10,000, 10-year, 6 percent corporate bond. Let's assume that the bond was issued January 1, 2000, and interest payments are due June 30 and December 31 of each year. The maturity date of the bond is the date when the principal (face value) must be repaid in full. This 10-year bond would have a maturity date of January 1, 2010, or 10 years from the date of issue.

The return on the bond in Figure 13-1 is 6 percent per year. The yield is also 6 percent. In other words, there is no compounding. Half the annual amount of simple interest is paid every six months.

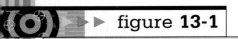 figure **13-1**

INTEREST PAYMENTS ON A TEN-YEAR, 6% CORPORATE BOND

Year	June 30 Interest	December 31 Interest
1	$300.00	$300.00
2	300.00	300.00
3	300.00	300.00
4	300.00	300.00
5	300.00	300.00
6	300.00	300.00
7	300.00	300.00
8	300.00	300.00
9	300.00	300.00
10	300.00	300.00

January 1, 2010: $10,000 principal is repaid

UNIT 3 • Financial Security

While the interest rate on your bond is fixed, the market price (what you could sell it for) can change. For example, a $10,000 bond may sell for more than $10,000 if interest rates are falling. People would be willing to pay more for the bond because it pays an interest rate higher than the current market rate. When bonds sell for more than their face value, they are selling at a *premium*. A $10,000 bond selling for $10,000 is at 100 percent of its face value, or "1." But if the bond sold for "104," it would have a premium of 4 percent. At 104, the market price would be $10,400:

$$\$10,000 \times .04 = \$400 \text{ premium}$$
$$\$10,000 + \$400 = \$10,400 \text{ market price}$$

In this case, the buyer's yield would be lower than 6 percent because the buyer had to pay more than face value to buy the bond.

Bonds also can sell below face value. Investors are not willing to pay face value for a bond yielding 6 percent when current interest rates are higher than 6% and rising. Therefore, the bond may have to be sold at a *discount*, or for an amount lower than face value, to attract buyers. If a bond sold for 96, it was sold at a 4 percent discount. The purchaser of the bond would pay only $9,600 for a $10,000 bond:

$$\$10,000 \times .04 = \$400 \text{ discount}$$
$$\$10,000 - \$400 = \$9,600 \text{ market price}$$

In this case, the buyer's yield would be higher than 6 percent because the buyer paid less than the face value for the bond.

Figure 13-2 shows how to compute the yield on bonds when they are issued at a premium or at a discount. Yield is not the same thing as the interest rate. In fact, yield may be higher or lower than the bond's stated interest rate, as you can see in Figure 13-2.

YIELD ON A 6% CORPORATE BOND PURCHASED AT A PREMIUM AND AT A DISCOUNT

figure 13-2

$$\frac{\text{Annual interest dollar amount}}{\text{Market price}} = \text{Yield}$$

	Annual Interest/Market Price = Yield	
If you buy the $10,000 bond at face value	$600/$10,000 =	6%
If you buy the bond at 104	$600/$10,400 =	5.8%
If you buy the bond at 96	$600/$9,600 =	6.3%

► GOVERNMENT BONDS

In addition to loaning money to corporations, you also can loan money to the government. Government bonds are issued by the federal as well as state and local governments. There are five major types of government bonds: municipal, general obligation, Treasury, savings, and federal agency bonds.

Municipal Bonds

A bond issued by state and local governments is called a **municipal bond**. The minimum investment in a municipal bond is usually $5,000, although brokers often ask for a multiple of this amount as a minimum investment. Municipal bonds, also known as "munis," can

be backed by specific projects, or by the general taxing authority of a governmental unit. For example, a **revenue bond** is a municipal bond issued to raise money for a public-works project. The revenues (income) generated by the project are used to pay the interest and repay the bonds at maturity. Major projects financed by revenue bonds include airports, hospitals, toll roads, and public housing facilities.

A **general obligation bond** (or GO) is a municipal bond backed by the power of the issuing state or local government to levy taxes to pay back the debt. For example, school districts issue bonds to finance construction of new buildings. A city may issue bonds to pay for a new police or administrative center. States may issue bonds to pay for a new college campus or a

Why might a state or local government issue a revenue bond?

new road system. A GO bond is repaid with the government's general revenue and borrowings. In contrast, a revenue bond is repaid from the revenue generated by the facility built with the borrowed funds. Cities pay off the bonds from city income and sales taxes collected, fees, fines, and other sources. Schools and colleges pay off the bonds from property taxes, tuition, fees, state funding, and other sources.

Municipal bonds generally pay a lower interest rate than corporate bonds. However, the interest is exempt from federal taxes (and sometime state taxes as well), so the effective rate is higher than the stated rate. As Figure 13-3 shows, the tax advantage of municipal bonds sometimes makes them a better deal than a corporate bond paying a higher interest rate. Figure 13-3 calculates net interest on both kinds of bonds for an investor in the 28 percent tax bracket.

figure 13-3 ◄◄

	Corporate Bond	Municipal Bond
Face Value (Principal)	$10,000	$10,000
Rate of Interest	6%	5%
Amount of Annual Interest	$ 600	$ 500
Tax on Interest Earned (28%)	168	0
Net Interest	$ 432	$ 500

VIEWPOINTS

You've decided to invest $5,000 in a bond. A friend advises you to avoid municipal bonds in favor of corporate bonds, stating that you'll get a higher interest rate with the latter type of bond. He claims that the interest rate is the most important consideration in choosing a bond.

Think Critically: Do you agree with this philosophy? What other factors should be considered when choosing between corporate and municipal bonds?

Savings Bonds and Treasury Securities

You can buy U.S. savings bonds from commercial banks, through payroll deduction, or directly from a Federal Reserve Bank. You can buy up to $15,000 worth of these bonds a year. Investors who buy Series EE bonds often hold them to maturity. These bonds are issued with maturity values that range from $50 to $10,000. You can postpone paying federal tax on the interest you earned on matured Series EE bonds by converting them to Series HH bonds.

Series I bonds are sold at face value and have fixed plus variable rates of return that increase as general interest rates rise. This helps protect you from the effects of rising prices (inflation).

Treasury securities (Treasury notes, bills, and bonds) are no longer issued as engraved certificates as are many stocks and corporate bonds. Instead, they are kept "electronically" and the investor receives a statement of account. Thus, these investments exist as bookkeeping entries in the records of the U.S. Treasury Department itself or in the records of commercial banks. Unlike corporate bonds, Treasury obligations are not rated, since the backing of the U.S. government makes them virtually risk-free. Treasury securities are exempt from state and local taxes and are usually *not* callable.

In addition to the U.S. Treasury, other federal agencies issue debt securities. Federal agencies that issue bonds include the Federal Home Loan Mortgage Corporation, Federal National Mortgage Association, Federal Land Bank, Federal Housing Administration, and the Tennessee Valley Authority. When you purchase an **agency bond**, you are loaning money to one of these agencies. Although agency issues are basically risk-free, they offer a slightly higher yield than securities issued by the Treasury. Both can be bought directly through banks or from brokers.

▶ ZERO-COUPON BONDS

A **zero-coupon bond** is a bond that is sold at a deep discount, makes no interest payments, and is redeemable for its face value at maturity. These bonds, whether issued by the U.S. government, corporations, or municipalities, are sold at as much as 50 to 75 percent below the face value of the bond. As the bond progresses toward maturity, it may *appreciate,* or increase in value. The bondholders make money by selling the bonds before maturity at a price higher than they paid for them. Or, they can hold the bonds to maturity and receive the face value.

With a zero-coupon bond, you must pay taxes on any interest earned each year (even though you don't actually receive it) until the bond is paid at maturity. Interest on zero-coupon municipal bonds, however, is not subject to taxation. Prices on zero-coupon bonds can fluctuate widely. Should you need to sell the bond before maturity, you may face a loss.

✅ Check Your Understanding

1. What is a callable bond? Does this feature make the bond more attractive to the investor?
2. Under what conditions would bonds sell at a premium?
3. What is a major advantage to government and municipal bonds?

Buying and Selling Bonds

Goals
- **Explain how to buy and sell bonds.**
- **Describe how to evaluate different grades of bonds.**
- **Explain how to read bond listings in financial publications.**

▶ HOW TO BUY AND SELL BONDS

Full-service brokers can assist you in purchasing all kinds of bonds. The broker will charge you a commission or a flat fee for this service. You also can use a discount broker to buy bonds. A *discount broker* charges a smaller fee or commission. You will receive no advice in your decisions to buy or sell. Full-service and discount brokerage firms are listed in the telephone book, and most can easily be found online. Also, many banks provide brokerage services.

You can buy savings bonds and Treasury securities through the Federal Reserve System. There are 12 Federal Reserve Banks and 25 regional branches spread across the nation. Check with your local financial institution to find the bank or branch closest to you. The Federal Reserve Bank will mail you an application form. You can send your check or money order with the application directly to the Federal Reserve. The Federal Reserve uses a system called *Treasury Direct* to record and store data about Treasury securities and their owners. You can even buy securities through Treasury Direct online at www.treasurydirect.gov. Interest (and principal when the bonds mature) is deposited directly into your bank account. Also, by using Treasury Direct, you can reinvest in Treasury securities automatically when existing securities mature. U.S. government securities also may be purchased through banks or brokers, but you will pay a commission.

You may wish to purchase savings bonds through payroll deductions. Some employers will withhold money from your paycheck and when your withholdings are sufficient, the bond will be purchased and sent to you. This process takes longer because your employer processes the money through a bank, which in turn purchases the bonds and returns them through your employer. It is often quicker to deal directly with a bank in your area.

©GETTY IMAGES/PHOTODISC

What are some ways in which you can buy Treasury securities?

You can buy municipal bonds through banks or brokers. In most states, you can set up a bank account to buy and sell municipal bonds. Generally, you are purchasing a bond from the inventory your bank has on hand. Banks buy large blocks of municipal bonds and make them available to their customers. There is a fee for this service, although it may be incorporated into the price of the bonds.

Most bond options require a minimum investment of $1,000. Only savings bonds can be purchased with small, regular payments. When you have a large sum of money to set aside, you can consider larger purchases of $5,000 or $10,000.

▶ EVALUATING BONDS

Investors can earn a return on bonds in three ways. First, bondholders earn interest for each day they own the bond. Second, they can redeem the bond for its face value at maturity. Third, bonds often appreciate in value, and bondholders may be able to sell the bond before maturity for a price higher than they paid for it.

Bonds are a safer investment than many other choices because they have a fixed interest rate and they represent a loan that the issuer must repay. Bonds play an important role in a diversified portfolio of investments. Bond prices tend to remain steadier than do stock prices. Also, bond prices tend to react in the opposite direction of stock prices. When stock prices are generally falling, bond prices tend to rise, and vice versa. As a result, bond investments can help offset the risk of the stocks in your portfolio.

To help investors evaluate the risk level of different bonds, independent rating services rate bonds according to their safety. Services such as Moody's (www.moodys.com) and Standard & Poor's (www.standardandpoors.com) base their ratings on the financial condition of the issuing corporation or municipality. The highest rating is AAA, or triple A. The lowest rating is a D. A D rating indicates that the bond is in *default*. This means that the issuer cannot meet the interest and/or principal payments. Because bonds are not insured, investors can lose their money if the corporation or municipality defaults.

Any bond with a rating of Baa or higher in Moody's, or BBB or higher in Standard & Poor's, is considered an **investment-grade bond**. These bonds are considered safe because the issuers are stable and dependable. For example, U.S. Treasury bonds provide maximum safety because these securities are backed by the federal government itself. Lowercase letters in a bond rating indicate more risk than capital letters. The letters stand for company stability, bond security, and general industry risk. Unfortunately, the higher the bond's rating, the lower the interest rate you will earn.

A **junk bond** is a bond that has a low rating, or no rating at all. Any bond with a rating of Ba/BB or lower is called a junk bond. Because of its low or no rating, this type of bond is highly speculative. Junk bonds have higher yields and at times appear to have reasonable levels of risk. However, in most cases, interest rates on junk bonds are high because they are high risk, since the companies issuing them are not financially sound. Carefully explore junk bonds before buying, and don't buy junk bonds at all if you can't afford to lose your investment.

► READING BOND LISTINGS

Only one factor has a real effect on bond prices—interest rates. When interest rates rise, the value of bonds decreases. The bonds are paying less in comparison to other fixed-rate investments. Conversely, when interest rates drop, fixed-rate bonds will become attractive because they are "locked in" at higher rates.

To track bond prices, you need to understand the bond price listings in the financial section of your newspaper. Not all local newspapers contain bond quotations, but *The Wall Street Journal* publishes complete information on bond transactions. Most portal sites such as www.yahoo.com or the user home page offered by Internet service providers enable users to track securities prices. Users can key in the names of the securities they wish to track, and the home page will display the updated prices each day.

Purchases and sales of corporate bonds are reported in tables similar to the one shown in Figure 13-4 (page 316). In bond quotations, prices are given as a percentage of face value, which is usually $1,000.

Name 1	Type/ Rating 2	Coup. 3	Mat. 4	3 P.M. Bid 5	Net Chg. 6	Yld 7
AK Steel	a/BB	9.125	12/06	98½	unch	9.46
Allied Waste	b/B+	10.00	8/09	102	unch	9.57
Am Std	a/BB+	7.375	2/08	98½	– 1¼	7.56
Chanclr	b/BB+	8.125	12/07	103	unch	7.36
Echostar	a/B	9.375	2/09	101¼	unch	9.52

1. *Column 1.* The first column lists the name of the bond, abbreviated.

2. *Column 2.* This column indicates the type of bond it is and its rating. The small letter "a" stands for a senior bond, a "b" stands for split coupon, a "c" stands for zero coupon bond, a "d" is an unsecured bond, and an "e" is a secured bond. The bond rating can range from AAA (highest) to C (junk bonds).

3. *Column 3.* This column shows the coupon rate of the bond (the guaranteed, fixed interest rate that will be paid annually on the bond). There may also be a volume column that lists the number of shares traded that day, in hundreds.

4. *Column 4.* This column shows the maturity date. A date of 12/06 means December, 2006.

5. *Column 5.* This column tells you what the final closing bid for the day was for this bond. It is similar to the closing price for stocks. For AK Steel, for example, the 3 p.m. price was 98 1/2.

6. *Column 6.* The net change column compares the last price paid for the bond today with that paid on the previous day. "Unch" means "unchanged"; the price has not changed from the previous day.

7. *Column 7.* The yield column states the current yield for the bond. The current yield is computed by dividing the bond's coupon rate by its average current market value (not its closing value). This yield figure varies as market interest conditions change, and thus the yield may be above or below the actual coupon rate.

✔Check Your Understanding

1. How can you purchase savings bonds?

2. How are bonds rated?

3. What factor affects bond prices?

Tax Strategies

When choosing investment options, investors must keep one important consideration in mind—taxability. Some investments are fully taxable while others are tax-free. There are numerous options in between. The choice of an investment might hinge on its tax status.

An investment is *tax-exempt* when there is no tax due, either now or in the future. Tax-exempt investments include municipal bonds sold by state and local governments. However, to be free from both federal and state taxes, you must live in the state where the bond is issued. For example, if you live in California, tax-free bonds in Oregon will be subject to state income taxes in California.

An investment is *tax-deferred* when income will be taxed at a later time. Tax-deferred investments include annuities, which will be discussed in Chapter 15. While earnings are credited to your account now, you do not pay taxes on the earnings until you withdraw them. At that time, your tax rate may be lower, so you will owe less tax.

Taxes also are deferred on assets that appreciate in value. *Capital gains*, the profits from the sale of assets such as stocks, bonds, or real estate, are not taxed until the asset is sold. For example, if shares of stock you own are currently worth more than you paid for them, you will owe no taxes on the gain until you sell the stock.

Income and deductions can be *shifted* by postponing them to the following tax year, or accelerating them forward into a current year, when they will do you more good. If your income is higher this year than usual, you can shift some deductions to help offset this increased income.

Taxes can be *avoided* by selling securities on which you lost money to offset gains on the sale of other securities. You can deduct losses to reduce capital gains on securities you sold at a profit. This strategy is not the same as *tax evasion*, which is the use of illegal actions to reduce your taxes.

Think Critically

1. Why is it important to consider tax consequences when choosing investment alternatives?

2. What type of investor would likely choose a tax-exempt investment? What type of investor would choose tax-deferred?

3. Why should you seek professional advice when shifting income and avoiding taxes?

Chapter Assessment

13.1

* Bonds are loans that the corporation or government body must repay at face value, with interest.
* Corporate bonds are a fixed-income investment. They pay a specified interest at regular intervals.
* A callable bond may be "called" (paid off) by the issuer before maturity.
* Debentures are unsecured bonds. Mortgage bonds are secured by a specific asset.
* Owners of convertible bonds can exchange their bonds for common stock if they wish.
* Bonds whose interest rates are higher than the current market rate will sell at a premium. Bonds whose interest rates are lower than the current market rate will sell at a discount.
* Government or municipal bonds generally are tax-free. General obligation municipal bonds are backed by the power of the issuing government unit to levy taxes.
* Zero-coupon bonds sell at a deep discount and make no interest payments. Holders make money by selling them at a profit before maturity or redeeming them at face value at maturity.

13.2

* You can buy bonds through a broker, discount broker, financial institution, or the Federal Reserve System.
* Investors can earn a return on bonds from interest, by redeeming the bonds for their face value at maturity, or by selling them before maturity for a price higher than they paid for them.
* Rating services rate bonds based on the financial condition of the issuing corporation or municipality. Investment-grade bonds have a rating of Baa or higher in Moody's or BBB or higher in Standard & Poor's. Junk bonds have a low rating or no rating.

* When interest rates rise, the values of bonds fall, because bonds are paying less in comparison to other fixed-rate investments. When interest rates drop, fixed-rate bonds become attractive because they are "locked in" at higher rates.

* Bond listings in the financial section of the newspaper provide information about price fluctuations, yield, and maturity dates.

REVIEW TERMS

Directions

Can you find the definition for each of the following terms used in Chapter 13?

agency bond
callable bond
convertible bond
debenture
face value
general obligation bond

investment-grade bond
junk bond
mortgage bond
municipal bond
revenue bond
zero-coupon bond

1. A bond with a very low rating, or no rating at all.

2. A corporate bond that the bondholder can choose to exchange for a specified number of shares of the corporation's common stock.

3. A bond that the issuer has the right to pay off before its maturity date.

4. Debt security issued by federal agencies.

5. A bond that is sold at a deep discount, makes no interest payments, and is redeemable for its face value at maturity.

6. A corporate bond not backed by collateral but only by the general credit standing of the corporation.

7. A corporate bond backed by specific assets as collateral to assure repayment of the debt.

8. A municipal bond backed by the power of the issuing state or local government to levy taxes to pay off the loan.

9. A high-quality bond considered to be a safe investment.

10. A bond issued by a state or local government.

11. The amount the bondholder will receive when the bond is repaid at maturity.

12. A municipal bond issued to raise money for a public-works project and repaid by the income from the project.

REVIEW FACTS AND IDEAS

1. In what two main ways are bonds different from stocks?

2. How does a bondholder make money from investing in bonds?

3. Why would a corporation issue callable bonds?

4. How are debentures different from mortgage bonds?

5. How do state or local governments pay off the principal and interest of municipal bonds issued?

6. Why do municipal bonds pay lower interest rates than corporate bonds?

7. How do investors make money on zero-coupon bonds?

8. What is "Treasury Direct"?

9. Why should you be concerned about a bond's rating before you buy it?

10. Why would anyone buy junk bonds?

11. How do interest rates affect the price (value) of bonds?

APPLY YOUR KNOWLEDGE

1. Why might an investor choose to buy bonds rather than stocks?

2. As a bondholder, would your investment in a corporate bond be more secure than a stockholder's investment? Why or why not?

3. Why might you choose a secured bond rather than an unsecured bond?

4. You bought a $10,000, 6 percent corporate bond at face value that matures in five years. What would be your total earnings during that five-year period?

5. A new bond issue you are considering has a face value of $1,000, an interest rate of 5 percent, and a maturity date eight years away. The bond is currently selling at 104. What is the current yield? What amount of interest would you earn in that time period?

6. Explain why you might choose a municipal bond paying 5 percent over a corporate bond paying 7 percent.

7. You can buy a $1,000 face value zero-coupon bond for $600. The bond matures in 10 years. Describe the circumstances under which you would consider buying the bond.

8. When buying Treasury bonds, which would you choose: full-service broker, discount broker, or Treasury Direct? Why?

9. Visit Treasury Direct online at www.treasurydirect.gov and find the answers to these questions:
    a. What are STRIPS?
    b. What is the current national debt figure?
    c. How can you replace a lost, stolen, or destroyed savings bond?

10. Visit the Federal Reserve System online at www.federalreserve.gov, and go to the consumer information section. Read one of the consumer information articles that interests you. In no more than a page, summarize, in your own words, what you learned from the article.

11. You have the choice of buying a municipal bond with a rating of Aaa paying 4 percent or a corporate bond with a rating of Ba paying 8 percent. Which bond would be your choice, and why?

12. Three $1,000 bonds have the following closing prices: 95 3/8, 103 1/4, and 99. What are the prices of the bonds in dollar amounts?

1. Your friend Pedro has just inherited $10,000. He considers the stock market too risky. He wants to preserve the safety of the principal he invests. Explain to him why buying a bond would be a safer investment than buying a stock.

2. Pedro now asks you if he should consider a corporate bond. Explain to him how bond investing works, and the difference between the types of corporate bonds. What type of corporate bond would you recommend? Why?

3. Rita Allende has just purchased a $10,000, 7.5 percent corporate bond that will pay interest semiannually for the next eight years. Prepare a chart showing how much in interest she will receive for the next eight years (total interest payments are 16).

4. Ari Nasser has chosen to buy a 5.5 percent, $1,000 corporate bond. The bond currently sells for 104. Compute his current yield on the bond, and explain to him why it is not the same as the stated interest rate.

5. Tatsu Hamazaki is considering purchasing a $10,000 corporate bond yielding 9 percent. She also found that she could buy a municipal bond for 7 percent. Her federal income tax rate is 28 percent. Determine her net interest. Show your work.

6. Silverio has narrowed his choice of bond purchases to two issues: MelMac, a 7 percent corporate issue selling for 102, or BrgPort, a 5 percent municipal issue selling for 96. Compute the current yield of each bond and advise him about which bond to choose.

7. Jerry has a regular job and is considering using payroll deductions to pay for savings bonds. If he could set aside $10 per month, how long would it take to buy a $500 EE bond? Explain to him how savings bonds work.

8. Tawana is considering buying some junk bonds. She has some money set aside to use for speculation. She is willing to take the risk. Investigate how these bonds work. Then explain to her what junk bonds are.

9. Anoosha has $10,000 to invest. She is considering buying high-quality corporate bonds because interest rates on bonds are somewhat higher than on CDs. She has rejected stocks because of the risk involved. Anoosha feels that interest rates are going to continue to rise but, in the meantime, she needs a relatively safe place for her money. Explain to Anoosha how bond prices are affected by interest rates. Is she making the right decision? Explain.

10. Choose a corporate bond listed on the New York Bond Exchange. Use Moody's Industrial Manuals (available at many public libraries) or Moody's online at www.moodys.com to answer the following questions about this bond issue.
   a. What is Moody's rating for the issue?
   b. What is the purpose of the issue?
   c. Does the issue have a call provision?
   d. What collateral, if any, has been pledged as security for the issue?
   e. Based on the information studied, would the bond be a good investment for you? Why or why not?

11. Using information from *The Wall Street Journal*, a local newspaper, or an online source, record the following data for three corporate bond issues you select. (Use a separate piece of paper.) Then briefly explain what each category of data means.

Source _____ Date _____

Stock Name	Current Yield	Volume	Close Price (or 3 p.m. Bid)
_____	_____	_____	_____
_____	_____	_____	_____
_____	_____	_____	_____

Investing in Mutual Funds, Real Estate, and Other Choices

TERMS TO KNOW

growth fund
income fund
growth and
  income fund
balanced fund
money market
  fund
global fund

index fund
prospectus
front-end load
back-end load
no-load fund
real estate
duplex
condominium

real estate
  investment trust
  (REIT)
participation
  certificate
mortgage
depreciation

Consider This...

Alonzo works 20 hours a week, lives at home, and can save $100 a month. He doesn't have a large lump sum to invest, but he's sure that he can set aside this amount permanently.

Alonzo told his adviser, "I've thought about several kinds of investments. I researched several mutual funds online, and I think I'm ready to buy shares in a fund that specializes in growth stocks. The one I'm most interested in has averaged 12 percent annual return over the last 15 years. That's good considering the ups and downs of the stock market. An important benefit I'll have is the ability to check my account daily if I want, by logging onto the fund's Web site. I can transfer my money from one fund to another electronically if I see that this would be a wise thing to do. And, once I buy in, I'm guaranteed to be able to keep buying shares of the fund, even if the fund is closed to new investors later on."

Investing in Mutual Funds

Goals
- Explain what mutual funds are and their advantages.
- Discuss different types of mutual funds.
- Describe how to evaluate mutual funds.

▶ WHAT ARE MUTUAL FUNDS?

A *mutual fund* is a professionally managed group of investments bought using a pool of money from many investors. Individuals buy shares in the mutual fund. The fund managers use this pooled money to buy stocks, bonds, and other securities. The kinds of securities they buy depends on the fund's stated investment objectives. For example, some mutual funds specialize in aggressive growth stocks. Others specialize in more conservative investments, such as bonds or money-market securities.

Most mutual fund companies offer a *family of funds*, which is a variety of funds covering a whole range of investment objectives. You can choose the family member that best matches your own objectives. You are allowed to move back and forth among the company's funds. You can purchase one type of fund (such as a stock fund) and later switch to another (such as a bond fund), all within the same family of funds.

Professional managers buy and sell according to their interpretation of market conditions, trends, and other factors. Fund managers research individual stocks and bonds and try to select good investments for their fund's investors. All fund investors share in any profits made by the mutual fund. They receive profits as dividends and as capital gains, both of which may be reinvested in the fund or distributed to investors as cash payments. The capital gains come from the profits made when the managers sell some of the fund's securities for more than they paid for them.

For most funds, you will have to make an initial purchase of $500 to $3,000 or more. Once you buy into a fund, you can make additional purchases as often as you like. Many people make regular purchases of $50 to $100 a month. To take money out of your fund, you may be able to simply call the company and place an order to sell your shares, or make your request online at the company Web site.

◢ ADVANTAGES OF MUTUAL FUNDS

Investors often choose mutual funds for the convenience of professional management. You don't have to worry about following stock and bond markets or looking for hot new investments. Professionals are doing the work for you.

Also, your investment is liquid. You can get your money quickly if you need it, though there is some risk of loss if the fund's price is low when you choose to sell.

When you invest in mutual funds, you are diversifying because mutual funds purchase a variety of stocks and bonds. When you have enough money to invest in more than one fund, you can further diversify by buying shares in funds with different investment objectives. In the same way that you would diversify individual stock purchases, you can buy some shares in riskier, aggressive mutual funds and limit the risk by also purchasing shares in more conservative funds.

Another advantage of mutual funds is that you need not have a lot of money to invest. Many funds require only a small minimum investment. Also, through pooling your money with other investors in the fund, you can own, for example, part of a $10,000 government bond without having $10,000 to buy the whole bond yourself.

Why is professional management an advantage of investing in mutual funds?

©GETTY IMAGES/PHOTODISC

◢ MUTUAL FUND RISK/RETURN CATEGORIES

Individual funds within a family have different investment goals and risk levels. In their publications and on their Web sites, investment companies describe the investment goal and level of risk for each fund in their family of funds. You should choose funds that match your investment goals and risk tolerance. As with any investment, the greater the potential return, the higher the risk. Figure 14-1 shows the general risk/return profiles for general categories of mutual funds.

Growth Funds

A **growth fund** is a mutual fund whose investment goal is to buy stocks that will increase in value over time. To do this, the fund's managers select stocks in companies that reinvest their profit in the company rather than distribute it to investors as dividends. Investors

MUTUAL FUND RISK/RETURN PYRAMID

figure 14-1

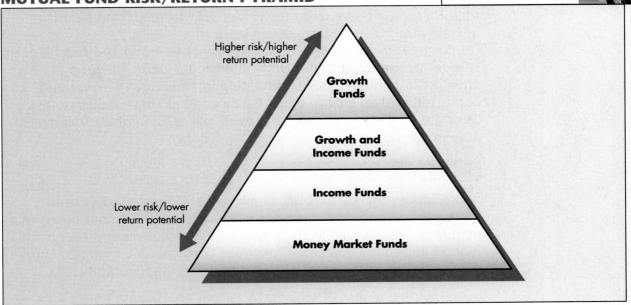

Higher risk/higher return potential

Growth Funds

Growth and Income Funds

Income Funds

Money Market Funds

Lower risk/lower return potential

in growth funds earn their return through capital gains rather than through dividends. An *aggressive growth fund* invests in stock of new or out-of-favor companies and industries that the fund managers think will achieve above-average increases in value. The philosophy behind aggressive growth funds is to accept high risk of loss in exchange for a chance to earn high returns. Other growth funds follow a less risky philosophy. They invest in more stable companies that the fund managers expect to increase in value but at a slower, steadier rate than the stocks of aggressive growth funds.

Income Funds

An **income fund** is a mutual fund whose investment goal is to buy bonds that produce current income in the form of interest. Investors in income funds are looking for income from their investments now rather than capital gains later. Income funds are considered to be of low-to-moderate risk and less risky than growth funds. Some income funds specialize in tax-exempt bonds. Their goal is to provide tax-free income for investors. Tax-exempt bond funds appeal to investors in high income tax brackets.

Growth and Income Funds

A **growth and income fund** is a mutual fund whose investment goal is to earn returns from both dividends and capital gains. Managers of these funds try to select stocks that pay dividends as well as achieve some increase in market value over time. The risk level of this type of fund is moderate—between the riskier growth funds and less risky income funds, as you can see in Figure 14-1.

Like growth and income funds, the goal of a **balanced fund** is to earn returns from current income and capital gains. However, it also attempts to minimize risk by investing in a mixture of stocks and bonds rather than stocks alone. Balanced funds have moderate risk. They are a little less risky than growth and income funds that invest only in stocks.

Money Market Funds

Like a money market account in a bank, a **money market fund** invests in safe, liquid securities, such as Treasury Bills and bonds that mature in three weeks to six months. These short maturities provide modest current income with little risk. The goal of any money market fund is the preservation of principal and very high liquidity.

VIEWPOINTS

Review the mutual fund risk/return pyramid shown in Figure 14-1, noting the range from lower risk/lower return potential through higher risk/higher return potential.

Think Critically: How would you describe your level of risk tolerance? Would you be willing to undertake higher risks for the potential of higher returns?

▶ MUTUAL FUNDS OF VARIOUS RISK CATEGORIES

Some types of mutual funds can fall in any risk/return category, depending on the types of securities they buy. Two types are global funds and index funds.

Global Funds

A **global fund** is a mutual fund that purchases international stocks and bonds as well as U.S. securities. Global funds fall into a variety of risk categories, depending on the investment objective of the individual fund. For example, a global fund can be very risky if its goal is to invest in aggressive growth international stocks. A global fund that invests in a conservative mix of international stocks and bonds would be less risky. However, global funds have risks that U.S. stock funds do not have. Fluctuations in currency exchange rates and political instability in other countries affect the value of global stocks. These uncertainties make global funds generally more risky than U.S. stock funds.

Index Funds

An *index* is an average of the price movements of certain selected securities. Investors use indexes as benchmarks for comparison to judge how well their investments are doing. An **index fund** is a mutual fund that tries to match the performance of a particular index by investing in the companies included in that index. For example, an index fund might invest in companies included in the Standard & Poor's 500 or the Dow Jones Industrial Average. The risk level of an index fund depends on the index it is tied to. Since the Dow includes only blue chip stocks, funds tied to this index would be relatively low risk. The NASDAQ Composite Index, on the other hand, averages stocks of some volatile high-tech companies. Funds tied to this index would be relatively risky.

▶ EVALUATING MUTUAL FUNDS

There are thousands of mutual funds covering the whole range of investment objectives and risk levels. To choose the mutual fund that is right for you, you must know your own investment objectives and risk tolerance. Do you want income from your investments now, or can you wait for capital gains in the future? Do you need a tax-free or tax-deferred investment to reduce your current income taxes? Are you comfortable with risking your investment for a chance at big returns, or do you prefer a safe but lower return? Once you know your own requirements, you can read about the objectives and risk profiles of different funds and find one that matches your requirements.

Net Asset Value

Unlike stocks, mutual fund prices are not determined by what people are willing to pay for them. They are determined by *net asset value (NAV)*. The NAV is the total value of a fund's investment portfolio minus its liabilities, divided by the number of outstanding shares of the fund:

$$NAV = \frac{\text{Value of Portfolio} - \text{Liabilities}}{\text{Number of Shares}}$$

For example, suppose the value of all stocks in a fund's portfolio is currently $100,000. The fund has $90,000 in liabilities and has sold 500 shares of its fund to investors. The price for one of its shares, or its net asset value, would be $20 at this time:

$$\frac{\$100,000 - \$90,000}{500} = \$20$$

Because the value of the portfolio changes as the stocks and other securities are traded throughout the day, the NAV is calculated at the end of each business day.

Although a mutual fund provides professional management, you should continually monitor your fund's performance. Some funds consistently outperform the average among those with the same objective and risk. For example, if you own an income fund, you should compare its performance to that of other income funds. When considering the purchase of a fund, always examine its prospectus, its costs and fees, and the published comparisons among funds of the same type.

The Prospectus

By law, investment companies must provide detailed information about their funds. A mutual fund company must provide a prospectus for each fund offered. The **prospectus** is a legal document that offers securities or mutual fund shares for sale. It must contain the terms, a summary of the fund's portfolio of investments, its objectives, and financial statements showing past performance. You can usually find this information on the investment company's Web site as well. Before choosing a mutual fund, read the prospectus carefully. Compare the fund's objectives with your own and compare its past performance with that of other funds you are considering.

Costs and Fees

If you buy a mutual fund through a broker, you will likely have to pay a sales fee, called a *load*. The broker's commission comes from this fee. A **front-end load** is a sales charge paid when you buy an investment. Sometimes you pay this fee on reinvested dividends as well. A **back-end load** is a sales charge paid when you sell an investment. Either way, loads can range from 2 to 8 percent of the value of the shares purchased.

In some cases, you can buy mutual funds directly from the investment companies. This kind of fund, called a **no-load fund**, does not charge a sales fee when you buy or sell because no salespeople are involved. You buy directly from the company by telephone, mail, or e-mail, or through the company's Web site.

Mutual funds make money by charging fees to their customers for the professional services provided. Funds often charge an annual management fee, which averages about 1 to 1½ percent of a fund's total assets. This charge is for the services of professional fund managers and for maintaining your account. The fund may also charge a *12b-1 fee* to defray the costs of marketing and distributing a mutual fund. These fees are part of the fund's *expense ratio* and are expressed as a percentage of assets deducted each year for fund expenses. Mutual funds publish their expense ratios with their fund descriptions. When you consider investing in mutual funds, compare expense ratios as part of your evaluation.

Print and Online Sources of Mutual Fund Information

@GETTY IMAGES/PHOTODISC

Financial publications, such as *Forbes*, *Fortune*, and *Money*, regularly review and rank mutual funds. They compare one-year, five-year, and ten-year performance of various funds with similar objectives. They also show the expense ratios of each one, so that you can compare. Occasionally, entire sections of business magazines are devoted to listing, describing, and ranking mutual funds.

You can also find a great deal of information online. For example, www.morningstar.com issues reports that compare mutual funds. You can also search by name for the sites of fund families, such as Vanguard, Fidelity, and Dreyfus. At their sites you can find detailed descriptions, including risk/return profiles, for all funds in their fund families. At Yahoo! Finance (http://finance.yahoo.com), you can search for fund information by their ticker symbols. Another good site for educational information on mutual funds is the Mutual Fund Investors Center at www.mfea.com.

If you were interested in a mutual fund, how might you get information about it?

 Check Your Understanding

1. Why might you choose a mutual fund over investing directly in stocks?
2. What is net asset value and how is it computed?

Issues in Your World

How to Read the Mutual Funds Listings

Mutual Fund Quotations

1	2	3	4	5	6	7	8
	Inv.		Offer	NAV	Total Return		
	Obj.	NAV	Price	Chg.	YTD	26wks	4yrs
Ables Fund:							
AciBt1A	GRO	9.63	10.11	...	0.0	−0.1	NA
BiClo	BND	1.51	NL	−.01	−2.9	−1.6	+8.9
CoxDli	SML	8.61	NL	+.01	+1.6	+1.5	+18.6
DrixLt	G&I	26.54	NL	−.07	+6.1	+4.0	+18.0
BB&B Fund:							
Globl B	WOR	6.25	6.25	−.03	−4.3	−4.3	+2.7
MtgLtd	MTG	2.80	2.80	+.02	−2.3	−1.4	−1.0

Column 1—The sponsoring mutual fund company's name is listed first. Its funds appear below in alphabetical order.

Column 2—The investment objective of the fund family is identified here. These companies offer investors a choice of growth (GRO), bond (BND), small company growth (SML), growth and income (G&I), global (WOR, for "world"), and mortgage (MTG) funds.

Column 3—NAV stands for *net asset value*. It is the dollar value of one share of the fund, based on closing quotes.

Column 4—The offer price reflects the net asset value plus sales commission, if any. An "NL" indicates a no-load fund.

Column 5—NAV change indicates the gain or loss in the price for a share of the fund, based on the previous NAV quotation.

Column 6—YTD stands for "year to date." It tells you how much this fund has gone up or down since January 1 of the current year.

Column 7—Total return, 26 weeks, shows the average earnings the fund has returned to investors in the last six months, stated as a percentage return on investment.

Column 8—Total return, 4 years, shows the average earnings the fund has returned to investors for the last four years, stated as a percentage return on investment.

Think Critically

1. Which of the mutual funds in the listing seems to be the best investment as compared to the other choices given? Why?

2. Why is it important to know the investment objective?

Lesson 14.2

Investing in Real Estate and Other Choices

Goals
- Describe direct and indirect real estate investments.
- Discuss some risks and responsibilities of owning rental property.
- Describe investments in precious metals, gems, and collectibles.
- Discuss the nature of futures and options markets.

▶ DIRECT REAL ESTATE INVESTMENTS

Real estate is land and any buildings on it. Real estate is often a good way to combat inflation, because it usually increases in value over the years, often at rates equal to or higher than inflation. However, real estate is one of the least liquid investments you can make. An investment can take months or even years to sell. Also, some real estate investments are speculative and can result in a substantial loss.

Commercial property is land and buildings that produce lease or rental income. Such property includes office buildings, stores, hotels, and duplexes and multi-unit apartments.

You can invest in real estate directly or indirectly. In direct investments, the investor holds legal title to the property.

Vacant Land

Vacant land, or unimproved property, is a speculative investment. Investors hold the property expecting it to go up substantially in value over time. Many people purchase a vacant lot with plans for building a house on it later, either when they can afford it or at retirement. In either case, you will likely have to pay cash for vacant land. Because it is considered speculative, banks are often unwilling to make loans on vacant land.

Single-Family Houses

You can purchase a single-family house and rent it to others. Because the property is not owner-occupied, you may find banks reluctant to make a mortgage loan for you to buy a house as rental property. As a condition for a loan, you may have to make a larger down payment or pay a higher interest rate. When a renter takes possession of your house, you still have responsibilities. For example, as the owner, you must maintain the premises in a livable condition. You must provide running water, electricity, sewer or septic hook-ups, and normal repairs and maintenance. If the roof leaks or a pipe breaks, it is your responsibility to fix it.

Duplexes, Apartments, and Condominiums

A **duplex** is a building with two separate living quarters. A duplex may be side-by-side living quarters with separate entrances, or it may be upper and lower floors of the building. The owner of a duplex has the same responsibilities to renters as the owner of a single-family home.

You can also buy and rent a triplex (three units), quad (four units), or building with many apartments. When investing in large tracts of real estate, most people join investment groups. By pooling your cash with that of other investors, you can afford to buy larger and more expensive pieces of property. For example, if you and three others formed a partnership to buy an eight-unit apartment building, each of you would have to pay only one fourth of the total costs of buying and maintaining the property.

A **condominium**, or *condo*, is an individually owned unit in an apartment-style complex with shared ownership of common areas. The owner of a condo owns the individual apartment as well as a proportional share of common areas, such as the lobby, yard, and hallways. Condo owners usually pay a monthly fee for the upkeep of the common areas, such as for mowing the lawn and maintaining a shared swimming pool. Condos are generally less expensive than single-family houses because they have less land and private areas, and they share roofs, walls, plumbing, and so on. Condos are particularly appealing to single people, young people, childless couples, and senior citizens because they have much lower maintenance requirements.

©GETTY IMAGES/PHOTODISC

Why might you want to join an investment group when purchasing large tracts of real estate?

Recreation and Retirement Property

Many people buy second homes for vacations or for their retirement years. Often the owners rent these properties to others during the times when they are not there, generating income for the owners. Of course, rented property will not be in brand-new condition when the owner retires to live there full time.

Recreation property includes beach and mountain cabins and even vacant land near vacation sites such as rivers, lakes, or an ocean. The owner can use and enjoy the property on weekends and during vacations, and at other times rent the property. However, absent owners must arrange for someone to take care of the property and manage the rental process. Real estate companies in popular vacation areas often provide these services for absent owners for a fee.

▶ INDIRECT REAL ESTATE INVESTMENTS

In indirect investments, investors appoint a trustee to hold legal title on behalf of all investors in a group. A *trustee* is an individual or institution that manages assets for someone else. Real estate syndicates, real estate investment trusts, and mortgage pools (in the form of participation certificates) are examples of indirect investments.

Real Estate Syndicates

A *real estate syndicate* (or *limited partnership*) is a group of investors who pool their money to buy high-priced real estate. This is a temporary association of individuals organized for the purpose of raising a large amount of capital. The organizer of the syndicate is called the general partner or syndicator. The people who contribute the capital are called limited partners.

In a real estate syndicate, the general partner forms a partnership and assumes unlimited liability for all the obligations of the partnership. The general partner then sells participation units to limited partners whose liability is restricted to the amount of their initial investment (perhaps $5,000 or $10,000). Limited liability is especially important in real estate partnerships because the mortgage acquired to purchase real estate often exceeds the net worth of the partners.

A real estate syndicate often owns several properties for diversification. The commercial properties acquired are usually professionally managed.

Real Estate Investment Trusts (REITs)

A **real estate investment trust (REIT)** is similar to a mutual fund. It is a corporation that pools the money of many individuals to invest in real estate. Like a mutual fund, the REIT makes all buy and sell decisions. You can buy and sell REIT shares at will. REITs trade on stock exchanges or over-the-counter. Like stocks, REIT shares fluctuate with market conditions, and dividends are paid when the real estate investments do well. There are many types of REITs, investing in everything from rental properties for monthly income to mortgages for long-term income. REITs are found in the financial section of the newspaper along with stock, bond, and mutual fund price quotations.

A **participation certificate** is an investment in a pool of mortgages that have been purchased by a government agency. Participation certificates are sold by federal agencies such as the Government National Mortgages Association ("Ginnie Mae"), the Federal Home Loan Mortgage Corporation ("Freddie Mac"), and the Federal National Mortgage Association ("Fannie Mae"). "Maes" and "Macs" are about as secure as Treasury securities. At one time, you needed $25,000 to invest in these certificates. However, many mutual funds invest entirely in them, making it possible to buy shares for as little as $1,000.

▶ OWNING AND MANAGING RENTAL PROPERTY

A **mortgage** is a loan to purchase real estate. When buying real estate, most people make a down payment and get a mortgage to pay the balance. Borrowing money to buy an investment is called *leverage*. A mortgage is a type of leverage. Only a small amount of the purchase price is your own money. For example, if you buy a duplex for $100,000 and make a down payment of $20,000 (a 20 percent down payment is usually required for rental property), you are borrowing $80,000 from the bank. As the property gains in value, the mortgage remains fixed. When you eventually sell the property, you keep the difference between the sales price and the mortgage. This difference is the *equity*, or ownership interest.

As your tenant makes rent payments, you make the mortgage payments to the bank. You would use the difference between the amount of rent and the mortgage payment to pay property taxes and the cost of upkeep on the property. If you have money left over after paying these expenses, you have a *positive cash flow*. If, however, you cannot collect enough rent to pay the mortgage, property taxes, repairs, and maintenance, then you have a *negative cash flow* and must make up the shortfall from your own pocket.

To manage your property, you can be a resident landlord or hire a resident landlord or property manager. A *resident landlord* lives at the rental site, takes care of all repairs and maintenance, collects the rent, and assures suitable living conditions. A

⌐⌐ Net Nuggets

Acting as a landlord can be a very complicated and time-consuming business. The landlord.com Web site provides free features and information for persons who own, manage, or control rental property. The site offers rental forms, management software, information on landlord/tenant law, a landlord discussion/knowledge exchange, and even advice on how to collect rent.

property manager collects rent, hires and pays people to make repairs and maintain the property, charges a fee for his or her services, and remits the difference to the owner of the property. Property managers do not live on site, but usually manage a large number of rental properties at the same time.

Depreciation is a decline in the value of property due to normal wear and tear. As the owner of rental property, you can deduct a depreciation expense on your taxes each year, reducing your taxable income. In addition, property taxes and other expenses of maintaining rental property are deductible. Thus, the expenses of ownership help to reduce the taxes you will have to pay on your rental income.

When you sell your property, you will have to pay taxes on the capital gain. But real estate can be difficult to sell. During slow economic times when people are not able to buy property, you may have to lower the price of your property substantially in order to sell.

You should also consider the risks of renting. Renters can damage or destroy your property to a degree far exceeding what a security deposit can pay for. When your units have vacancies, your rental income will decline, yet you still have to pay the mortgage and other expenses, thus cutting into your profits.

Real estate is also subject to zoning laws and other local use restrictions. Cities have laws that regulate what type of structure (single-family residence, apartment complex, office building, for example) that can be built in each area of the city. Before buying property, you should check the applicable zoning laws to make sure you will be allowed to use the property as you intend.

▶ INVESTING IN METALS, GEMS, AND COLLECTIBLES

Investments in this category are speculative. They can return large profits or losses when sold. In some cases, the enjoyment of having the investment will far exceed any resale value. Although not inexpensive, precious metals, gems, and collectibles are easy to purchase. However, they can be very difficult to sell in a hurry and do not provide any current income in the form of interest or dividends.

Gold, silver, and platinum are examples of *precious metals*. They are natural substances that people value. Prices of precious metals swing widely over time. These swings are what make investments in precious metals very risky.

You can buy gold and silver as coins, medallions, jewelry, and bullion. Storing precious metals safely may be a problem because of bulk and weight. Instead of storing your investment yourself, you can buy gold and silver in the form of a certificate stating how much you own of the metal being stored for you. You also can own gold indirectly by investing in gold-mining stocks or in mutual funds specializing in these stocks. Other metals in which you can invest include aluminum, tin, copper, lead, nickel, and zinc. Prices for metals can be found in the financial section of newspapers and online.

Gems are natural precious stones, such as diamonds, rubies, sapphires, and emeralds. Their prices are high and subject to drastic change. Precious metals and gems have their greatest value as jewelry. However, when you purchase jewelry at retail prices, you are paying markups of 50 to 500 percent or more. Prices must increase substantially in the world market before you can recover the cost and make a profit from reselling your jewelry.

©GETTY IMAGES/PHOTODISC

While it is easy to buy gems, it is difficult to resell them. Why is this?

The biggest disadvantage of investing in gems and precious metals is that the market to resell them is very small and unpredictable. No ready market exists. You must find an interested buyer.

Collections of valuable or rare items, from antiques to comic books, are called *collectibles*. They are valuable because they are old, no longer made, unusual, irreplaceable, or of historic importance. Coins are the most commonly collected items. Silver coins (rather than today's alloy coins) often are worth more than 20 times their face value.

People like to collect favorite items, from porcelain figures to hubcaps, and hope that someday their collection will be valuable. Collecting can be a satisfying hobby. Unfortunately, collectibles can be hard to sell. You may find it difficult to locate a buyer who is willing to pay you the value of your collection, even when the value is well known. If you want to collect, buy what you can enjoy through the years, knowing that the item may not result in a profit.

Communication Connection

Review the collectibles section(s) in your local newspaper's classified ads. What types of items are offered for sale? In contrast, what items are people looking for? Report back to your class, or prepare a one-page summary of your findings.

▶ INVESTING IN FINANCIAL INSTRUMENTS

Futures are contracts to buy and sell commodities or stocks for a specified price on a specified date in the future. Commodities include farm products, such as wheat, corn, and cattle, and metals such as gold and silver. Commodity prices are volatile because supply and demand for commodities are disrupted by all kinds of mostly unpredictable situations from political upheaval to the weather.

Commodities may be sold for cash (the local farmer's market) or traded in the futures market. For example, a farmer could sell a futures contract to deliver 5,000 bushels of wheat one year from today. The futures market was created for those who want to know in advance what they will be paid. Farmers enter the futures market only for protection against volatile prices. Futures contracts are like an insurance policy against changes in prices. In this case, the farmers know in advance what they will be paid for their wheat.

An *option* is the right, but not the obligation, to buy or sell a commodity or stock for a specified price within a specified time period. A *call option* is the right to buy 100 shares of stock at a set price by a certain expiration date. You can exercise the right at any time before the option expires. A *put option* is the right to sell stock at a fixed price until the expiration date. An investor who thinks a stock's price will increase during a short period of time may decide to purchase a call option. On the other hand, an investor who feels a stock's price will decrease during a short period of time may purchase a put option to safeguard the investment. Options are risky business and not for the inexperienced investor. Options also apply to the purchase and sale of futures contracts.

©GETTY IMAGES/PHOTODISC

Why are commodity prices unpredictable?

✅ Check Your Understanding

1. What are some advantages of owning real estate as an investment?
2. Why are collectibles risky investments?
3. Explain how futures contracts work.

Chapter Assessment

14.1

* Mutual funds use money pooled from many investors to buy securities that fit the fund's stated objectives.
* Investors choose mutual funds for the professional management, liquidity, diversification, and relatively small minimum investment required.
* Growth funds focus on stocks expected to earn future capital gains.
* Income funds invest in bonds to earn interest now rather than capital gains later.
* Growth and income funds and balanced funds seek current income and capital gains.
* Money market funds invest in safe, liquid securities.
* Global funds invest in international as well as U.S. securities.
* Index funds try to match the performance of a particular index.
* A mutual fund's price is determined by its net asset value, calculated as the total value of the fund's investments minus its liabilities, divided by the total number of shares.
* To evaluate a fund, examine the prospectus, fees, and published comparisons among funds of the same type.

14.2

* If you invest in real estate directly, you own legal title to it. If you invest indirectly, a trustee holds legal title on behalf of the investor group.
* Commercial property produces rental income that helps pay the mortgage.
* You can invest in real estate indirectly through real estate syndicates, REITs, or federal agency participation certificates.
* If your rental income exceeds your mortgage payment, property taxes, and upkeep expenses, then you have a positive cash flow.

If vacancies cause rental income to fall below expenses, you have a negative cash flow and must make up the difference.

* As the owner of rental property, you are responsible for maintaining it. However, you benefit from tax deductions for depreciation and expenses.

* Investments in precious metals, gems, futures contracts, and options are very risky and not for the novice investor.

* You can buy precious metals and store it yourself or buy a certificate of ownership of metals stored for you.

* Gems have their greatest value as jewelry, but the retail price has a huge markup and the resale market is small and unpredictable.

* Collectibles can be very profitable or worthless, depending on the changing tastes of consumers.

REVIEW TERMS

Directions

Can you find the definition for each of the following terms used in Chapter 14?

back-end load	index fund
balanced fund	money market fund
condominium	mortgage
depreciation	no-load fund
duplex	participation certificate
front-end load	prospectus
global fund	real estate
growth and income fund	real estate investment
growth fund	trust (REIT)
income fund	

1. A legal document that offers securities or mutual fund shares for sale.

2. A decline in the value of property due to normal wear and tear.

3. A mutual fund whose investment goal is to buy stocks that will increase in value over time.

4. A mutual fund that attempts to minimize risk by investing in a mixture of stocks and bonds that provide both current income and growth.

5. A sales charge paid when an individual buys an investment.

6. A mutual fund for which investors pay no sales fee.

7. A building with two separate living quarters.

8. A mutual fund whose investment goal is to buy bonds that produce current income in the form of dividends.

9. A mutual fund that purchases stocks and bonds from around the world as well as the United States.

10. A sales charge paid when an individual sells an investment.

11. An individually owned unit in an apartment-style complex with shared ownership of common areas.

12. Land and any buildings on it.

13. A mutual fund whose investment goal is to earn returns from both dividends and capital gains.

14. A loan to purchase real estate.

15. A mutual fund that tries to match the performance of a particular index by investing in the companies included in that index.

16. An investment in a pool of mortgages that have been purchased by a government agency.

17. A mutual fund that invests in safe, liquid securities.

18. A corporation that pools the money of many individuals to invest in real estate.

REVIEW FACTS AND IDEAS

1. What determines the kinds of securities a mutual fund manager will buy?

2. Give some advantages of buying mutual funds rather than individual stocks or bonds.

3. Identify and describe four broad risk/return categories of mutual funds.

4. What is the meaning of a mutual fund's NAV?

5. Explain the difference between a front- or back-end load fund and a no-load fund.

6. What kinds of comparisons among mutual funds can you find in print and online publications?

7. Describe three investments you could make that would earn rental income for you.

8. Why do many people join investment groups rather than purchase real estate individually?

9. As the owner of rental property, what responsibilities would you have toward your tenants?

10. How can vacancies in an apartment building you own affect you?

11. List some disadvantages of owning rental real estate.

12. Why are investments in precious metals, gems, and collectibles risky?

13. What are some advantages and disadvantages of collections as investments?

14. Why might farmers choose to sell their commodities on the futures market?

15. Explain the difference between put and call options.

APPLY YOUR KNOWLEDGE

1. Describe the type of investor (in terms of goals and risk tolerance) who would be interested in each of the following types of mutual funds:
   a. growth funds
   b. income funds
   c. municipal bond funds
   d. money market funds

2. Why should a new investor read the prospectus of a mutual fund carefully before purchasing the fund?

3. Why would a person choose a front- or back-end load fund over a no-load mutual fund?

4. Visit the Web site of an investment company that offers a family of mutual funds. For example, you could go to Vanguard Investments (www.vanguard.com) or Fidelity (www.fidelity.com). Select five of the company's funds that are very different from each other. From the information given, describe the investment objective and risk level for each of the five funds. Draw a graphic that visually represents risk level, going from least to most risky. On the graphic, write the name of the most risky fund you selected at the high-risk end and the least risky fund at the low-risk end. Then place the other three funds at their appropriate risk level between the two extremes. In a paragraph, summarize what you learned about mutual funds and risk from this activity.

5. Why would you wish to buy a piece of vacant land? Describe what your plans might be for the property in 10 or 20 years, including where you would buy such a lot and its potential uses.

6. Describe what it would be like to be a landlord (your responsibilities and duties) if you owned:
   a. A single-family house that you rented to a family.
   b. A second home on the beach that you rented to vacationers in the summer.
   c. An eight-unit apartment building where you were the on-site manager.

7. Describe investors who might buy a second home, such as a cabin in the woods. Why should they purchase the property now rather than in the future, when they plan to use it full time for retirement?

8. Explain how leverage applies to buying real estate. Why is it desirable to have a positive cash flow from real estate you own?

9. What is the meaning of the statement "Real estate is an illiquid investment"?

10. Price changes for precious metals can be very unpredictable. Why would anyone want to invest in these items?

11. Collections are fun to have and can sometimes gain in value over the years. Name some collectible items you have seen, collected, or read about that have increased substantially in value over the years. What would you like to collect?

12. The Internet has provided a new way for buyers and sellers of collectibles to find each other. Search the Internet for sites dealing with a collectible that interests you. How is this item bought and sold online? Is there an association or club for your collectible? If so, how does the site help collectors?

→ Solve Problems ⊕ Explore Issues

1. Trey and Kashara have been married for three years and have managed to save some money to invest. They have decided on mutual funds but don't want to take too much risk. Still, they would like to have some additional income, and yet sell the shares for a good profit in five to ten years. Suggest to them some types of mutual funds that might fit their investment goals and risk tolerance. Which type(s) of fund would you choose for them?

2. Obtain a prospectus for a specific mutual fund. You can write to an address provided in an ad in the financial pages of your newspaper or *The Wall Street Journal*, get one from a brokerage firm or financial counselor, or locate the information at an investment company's Web site. Read the prospectus or online information and report on your findings: objectives (goals) of the fund, risk profile, tax status (are investments taxable or tax-free?), and performance of the fund for the last year and the last five years.

3. Your friend Chuong has saved almost $10,000 for a down payment and has decided to buy a small, single-family house that he will fix up and rent. He figures he can get at least $800 a month in rental income. He also has the money to cover the cost of $2,000 to fix up the house. Explain to Chuong the concept of leverage and the need for a positive cash flow once the house is fixed and rented.

4. Daksha has decided to invest in real estate. She can't decide whether to buy a vacant lot for $25,000 or a one-fourth interest in a four-unit apartment building selling for $400,000. Explain to her the pros and cons of both of these alternatives.

5. Sonia and Nestor Medina will be retiring in less than 10 years. They are considering purchasing a house at the beach that they can use on weekends now and have as their home upon retirement. Explain to them the concept of buying recreation property and its potential as an investment.

6. Your grandmother has a wonderful collection of crystal, gold coins, diamond jewelry, and silver dating back to the early 19th century. When purchased, it cost very little, but today it could be worth a great deal of money. Explain to your grandmother, using a current issue of the newspaper or the Internet, what today's prices are for silver, gold, gems, and other valuables.

7. Your friend Mekhala wants to buy a ruby ring at a local jewelry store. She believes it will make an excellent investment for the future, and that she can always sell the ring and make a profit. Explain to her the pros and cons of this type of investment.

8. Buck is a very nervous person. He is worried that his money is not earning enough interest to keep up with inflation. He was reading about commodities and thinks it would be a great way to make some quick money. Explain to him the risks involved in trading commodities.

For related activities and links, point your browser to www.mypf.swlearning.com

Retirement and Estate Planning

TERMS TO KNOW

reverse mortgage	trust	Keogh plan
heirs	estate tax	defined-benefit plan
estate	inheritance tax	defined-contribution plan
estate planning	gift tax	
will	individual retirement account (IRA)	
codicil		
power of attorney		

Consider This. . .

"My grandparents say the time to think about retirement is when I get my first job," Susan told her co-workers. "But this isn't really my first job; it's just a part-time job while I go to school. When I get my first career-type job, then I'll start thinking about saving up for retirement."

"Your grandparents are right," replied Andrew. "I have a great-uncle who is getting social security benefits. He barely has enough money to buy his groceries and pay the rent. Every time prices go up, he gets all stressed out because, in his words, he 'won't get a pay increase to make up for it.' I'm already thinking about the time when I won't be able to work. I think it's important to have enough money to live comfortably."

Planning for Retirement

Goals
- Describe a person's or family's needs at retirement.
- List the features of wills, powers of attorney, trusts, and joint ownership.
- Discuss inheritance, estate, and gift taxes.

▶ DEFINING YOUR RETIREMENT NEEDS

When you get ready to retire, you will want to have enough financial resources to live comfortably. At that point, many people want to do the things they didn't have time for when they were working or raising families. To enjoy retirement, you must plan and save for it throughout your work life. Social security and a company pension may be insufficient to cover the cost of living. Inflation (increasing prices) will decrease the purchasing power of your retirement savings.

How Much Income Do You Need?

Many financial advisors tell clients that they will need between 60 and 80 percent of their before-retirement salary to live comfortably when they retire. This percentage may seem high. You may wonder how you can have that kind of income when you are no longer working. You can achieve a comfortable retirement only by limiting your current spending so that you can start saving now—at the beginning of your work life.

There will be times when you won't have much cash to set aside. You may be paying for a college education, children, cars, houses, furniture, and so on. But save regularly as much as you can without severely limiting your current lifestyle. Later in life, when you have fewer expenses, you can save even more. With regular saving and investing over many years, your nest egg can grow enough to meet your retirement needs.

Why must you save for retirement throughout your work life?

Keep the House or Move?

Once their children are adults, many couples choose to sell their family home and find something smaller and easier to maintain. Current tax law allows married couples to sell the house they have lived in at least two years without paying taxes on the profits up to $500,000. For single people, the tax-free profit limit is $250,000. Thus, you will have the opportunity to sell the family home and keep the proceeds. Other people choose to keep their house because it is paid off. Before moving, consider the negative aspects. Moving is expensive. Also, if you move far away, you will be leaving friends and community behind.

Equity in a house is the property's market value minus the amount of the mortgage not yet paid. As you make mortgage payments over the years, your equity in your home increases as the amount you owe decreases. However, equity is not income. It is money "tied up" in property. Some retirees need to turn their equity into current income. One way to do this is through a reverse mortgage.

A **reverse mortgage** is a loan against the equity in the borrower's home in which the lender makes tax-free monthly payments to the borrower. It works the opposite of a mortgage. Instead of making payments to the lender, the lender pays you. The loan amount must be repaid, with interest, when you sell your home, reach the end of the loan term, or die. For example, if you own a home worth $150,000 and your unpaid mortgage is $10,000, your equity is $140,000. With a reverse mortgage, the monthly payments to you will continue until they add up, together with interest, to the $140,000 equity. Once the loan is due, you may have to sell the home or get a regular mortgage to pay off the loan. If you die during the term of the loan, your heirs will have to pay it off. **Heirs** are people who receive property from someone who has died.

What Type of Investment Strategy?

Retired people view investments from a different perspective than when they were younger. Monthly income is often retirees' main goal for investments. For example, they may want to take dividends rather than reinvest them. Rather than saving for the future, investors at this stage are trying to preserve their financial position—that is, safeguard principal while earning a reasonable return. Fixed-income (low-risk) investments become a more practical choice. As people approach retirement, they often move some of their money out of growth stocks, which earn capital gains in the future, and into income stocks and bonds that produce dividends now. Many also move more of their investment into low-risk options, trading high-potential earnings for lower but more certain earnings.

How Much Insurance?

When you retire, your insurance needs also change. While your need for life insurance has diminished, your need for other types of insurance has increased.

For retired people, the crucial need for insurance falls in the area of health—being sure that an illness or injury will not wipe out a lifetime of saving and investing. When you qualify for *Medicare*, government-sponsored health insurance for the elderly, you may need supplemental insurance to cover expenses not covered by Medicare. The rapidly rising cost of prescription medications may be a major obstacle, along with extremely high payments for health insurance coverage. If there is an interim period between your retirement and Medicare coverage, you will have to pay for your own health insurance. Also, retired people may need coverage for long-term care in a nursing facility.

How Do You Beat Inflation?

The probable loss of buying power due to inflation is one reason that planning for retirement is so important. As you will recall, *inflation* is a general increase in prices. Because of inflation, the cost of living goes up over time. Price increases reduce buying power. If prices are increasing at 8 percent while your retirement income is increasing at only 3 or 4 percent, you'll have to cut out something from your budget, or dip into your principal to maintain your living standard. Therefore, budgeting must continue through retirement. Part-time work is often the choice of seniors who need more income to offset inflation or who simply enjoy working.

Net Nuggets

The retirement planning section of about.com contains a wide range of resources, including articles, tutorials, and calculators, on planning wisely and well for retirement. You can find information on lifestyles, financial and tax issues, where to live, and the potential impact of life events such as illness, divorce, or death. Visit the site at retireplan.about.com.

▶ ESTATE PLANNING TOOLS

An **estate** is all that a person owns, less debts owed, at the time of the person's death. When people die, their possessions pass to other people, either as directed by the person who died (called the *decedent*), or by the laws of the state in which the person died. The estate may be taxed by the federal and/or state governments. **Estate planning** is preparing a plan for transferring property during one's lifetime and at one's death. Your goals in estate planning should be to minimize taxes on the estate, to make known how you want your possessions distributed, and to provide for a smooth transfer of your possessions to your loved ones upon your death. Some tools of estate planning include wills, powers of attorney, trusts, and joint ownership of assets.

Wills

A **will** is a legal document that tells how you want your estate to be distributed after your death. In your will, you name an *executor*, a person to carry out the transfer of your estate when you die. Any person who is 18 or older and of sound mind can make a legally valid will. The person who makes the will is called the *testator*.

A *simple will* is a short document that lists the people you want to inherit and what you want each to receive. Simple wills take a short time to prepare, and they are fairly standard documents. If your estate is relatively uncomplicated, you can prepare a will yourself, using an inexpensive kit or software purchased online or at an office products or software store. Whether you use a lawyer or not, you will need witnesses to your signature. Usually the witnesses must be two people not mentioned in the will. They must be 18 or older, not related to you, and able to attest to your mental competency at the time you signed the will. An example of a simple will is shown in Figure 15-1 (page 352).

A *holographic will* is a will written in a person's own handwriting. A handwritten will is legally valid in 19 states and should be witnessed, like other wills. Because a handwritten will is often easier to contest (question), a typed will is recommended.

When people die without a will, they are said to be *intestate*. In that event, the person's property is distributed according to the laws of the state where the decedent died. By having a valid will, you can control who gets what, rather than allowing the state to make those decisions. Property reverts to the state when a person dies without heirs.

A person can make a will and later make small changes with a document called a **codicil**. The codicil lists the modifications and then reaffirms the rest of the original will document. A will cannot be legally amended by crossing out or adding words, or by removing or adding pages, or by making erasures. A codicil is drawn by an attorney and is executed and witnessed the same as a will.

Why is it important to prepare a will?

Power of Attorney

At some time in your life, you may become incapacitated and unable to make your own decisions. A **power of attorney** is a legal document

 **figure 15-1**

SIMPLE WILL

LAST WILL AND TESTAMENT OF ANTHONY JOHN HINTON

I, Anthony John Hinton, of the city of Dayton and state of Ohio, do make, publish, and declare this to be my Last Will and Testament in manner following:

FIRST: I direct that all of my just debts, funeral expenses, and the cost of administering my estate be paid by my personal representative hereinafter named.

SECOND: I give, devise, and bequeath to my beloved daughter, Carol Hinton Campbell, now residing in Englewood, New Jersey, that certain piece of real estate, with all improvements thereon, situated in the same city and at the corner of Hudson Avenue and Tenafly Road.

THIRD: All the remainder and residue of my property, real, personal, and mixed, I give to my beloved wife, Kimberly Sue Hinton, personal representative of this, my Last Will and Testament, and I direct that she not be required to give bond or security for the performance of her duties as such.

LASTLY: I hereby revoke any and all former wills by me made.

IN WITNESS WHEREOF, I have hereunto set my hand this tenth day of October, in the year two thousand --.

Anthony John Hinton
_____
Anthony John Hinton

We, the undersigned, certify that the foregoing instrument was, on the date thereof, signed and declared by Anthony John Hinton as his Last Will and Testament, in the presence of us who, in his presence and in the presence of each other, have, at his request, hereunto signed our names as witnesses of the execution thereof, this tenth day of October 20--; and we hereby certify that we believe the said Anthony John Hinton to be of sound mind and memory.

Vilbin Schaenbar	residing at	251 Wonderly Avenue Dayton, Ohio 45419-2521
Samuel Vance	residing at	3024 James Hill Road Kettering, Ohio 45429-2454
Irene Vasilhous	residing at	423 Goldengate Drive Centerville, Ohio 45459-2459

authorizing someone to act on your behalf. For example, if you become incapable of caring for yourself, the power of attorney gives your appointed person the power to use money from your savings to pay your bills and hire people to care for you. The power of attorney may be limited or general in time or in scope. A limited power of attorney may be good for 30 days or a year, or it may pertain to a particular transaction. A general power of attorney gives another person the right to act completely for you. When you give a power of attorney to another person, you give that person the power to do anything you could have done. Of course, you must fully trust the person to whom you give this legal right.

Figure 15-2 (page 354) shows a power of attorney form. You can hire a lawyer to write your power of attorney, or you can do your own, using a kit or software designed for creating legal documents. Many inexpensive programs are available online and in stores. Often software packages for writing wills, such as Quicken WillMaker and Kiplinger's WILLPower, also contain templates for creating powers of attorney and other common legal documents.

Trusts

A **trust** is a legal document in which an individual (the *trustor*) gives someone else (the *trustee*) control of property, for ultimate distribution to another person (the *beneficiary*). The trustee may be a financial institution or a person. A trust can exist during the lifetime of the trustor. This type of trust is called *inter vivos*, or a living trust. You simply transfer some property to a trustee, giving him or her instructions regarding its management and disposition while you are alive and after your death. The other type of trust is called a testamentary trust, or *trust will*. It takes effect upon the death of a trustor. Such a trust can be valuable if your beneficiaries are minor children or if you wish to avoid high taxes on your estate.

In order for money and property to be left to a minor child, the child must have a legal guardian who makes accountings of the child's property and money. Parents of small children typically create trust wills to provide for their children's education and living expenses. Then the balance of the estate is given to the children at some later age, such as 25 or 30, when all of them have reached adulthood.

The purpose of a trust is twofold. First, trusts provide for beneficiaries who might not be able to effectively manage assets for themselves. The trustee is held accountable for how money is spent and how the trust is administered. The trustee must file papers yearly with the court, reporting on how the trust is progressing. Also, the trustee typically receives a fee for these services. Second, a trust can minimize inheritance or estate taxes and avoid probate. *Probate* is a court-supervised process of paying your debts and distributing your property to

figure 15-2

POWER OF ATTORNEY

GENERAL POWER OF ATTORNEY

I, [YOUR FULL LEGAL NAME], residing at [YOUR FULL ADDRESS], hereby appoint
_____ of _____, as my Attorney-in-Fact ("Agent").

I hereby revoke any and all general powers of attorney that previously have been signed by me. However, the preceding sentence shall not have the effect of revoking any powers of attorney that are directly related to my health care that previously have been signed by me.

My Agent shall have full power and authority to act on my behalf. This power and authority shall authorize my Agent to manage and conduct all of my affairs and to exercise all of my legal rights and powers, including all rights and powers that I may acquire in the future. My Agent's powers shall include, but not be limited to, the power to:

1. Open, maintain or close bank accounts (including, but not limited to, checking accounts, savings accounts, and certificates of deposit), brokerage accounts, and other similar accounts with financial institutions.

2. Sell, exchange, buy, invest, or reinvest any assets or property owned by me. Such assets or property may include income producing or non-income producing assets and property.

3. Purchase and/or maintain insurance, including life insurance upon my life or the life of any other appropriate person.

4. Take any and all legal steps necessary to collect any amount or debt owed to me, or to settle any claim, whether made against me or asserted on my behalf against any other person or entity.

5. Enter into binding contracts on my behalf.

6. Exercise all stock rights on my behalf as my proxy, including all rights with respect to stocks, bonds, debentures, or other investments.

7. Maintain and/or operate any business that I may own.

~~~~~~

My Agent shall be entitled to reasonable compensation for any services provided as my Agent. My Agent shall be entitled to reimbursement of all reasonable expenses incurred in connection with this Power of Attorney.

My Agent shall provide an accounting for all funds handled and all acts performed as my Agent, if I so request or if such a request is made by any authorized personal representative or fiduciary acting on my behalf.

This Power of Attorney shall become effective immediately, and shall not be affected by my disability or lack of mental competence, except as may be provided otherwise by an applicable state statute. This is a Durable Power of Attorney. This Power of Attorney shall continue effective until my death. This Power of Attorney may be revoked by me at any time by providing written notice to my Agent.

Dated _____, 20-- at _____, _____.

[YOUR SIGNATURE]
_____
[YOUR FULL LEGAL NAME]

[WITNESS' SIGNATURE]   [WITNESS' SIGNATURE]
_____   _____
[WITNESS' FULL LEGAL NAME]   [WITNESS' FULL LEGAL NAME]

STATE OF _____, COUNTY OF _____, ss:

The foregoing instrument was acknowledged before me this _____ day of _____, 20-- by [YOUR FULL LEGAL NAME], who is personally known to me or who has produced _____ as identification.

_____
Signature of person taking acknowledgment

_____
Name typed, printed, or stamped

_____
Title or rank

_____
Serial number (if applicable)

your heirs upon your death. An attorney is required to complete the probate process. The estate pays the costs of probate before heirs receive any property. Property held in trust is not subject to probate. Therefore, the property can pass to beneficiaries quickly without a prolonged court proceeding and without the costs of probate.

Joint Ownership

There are several ways to hold title to property. By putting property in *joint ownership*, two or more people own an undivided interest in the property. Joint ownership of property between spouses is very common. Joint ownership also may exist between parents and children, other relatives, or any two or more people. If you and your spouse own property as *joint tenants with right of survivorship* (JTWROS), the ownership is split 50-50 for estate tax purposes. If one spouse dies, the surviving spouse automatically becomes the sole owner of the property. No legal action is necessary to transfer title. This form of ownership is commonly used for land, automobiles, residences, bank accounts, and securities. Joint tenancy is a convenient and automatic way to pass property. It is perhaps the most widely used property ownership arrangement.

Two or more people can own property without survivorship. As joint tenants without right of survivorship, when one person dies, his or her interest in the property passes to his or her heirs, not to the remaining owners.

When a person holds ownership singly, with no joint owner or named beneficiary, that asset becomes part of the person's estate upon death and will be distributed according to the terms of the will. Joint ownership is an effective way to avoid probate and inheritance taxes in some states.

▶ TAXATION OF ESTATES

Federal and state governments levy various types of taxes that must be considered in planning your estate. Three major taxes are estate, inheritance, and gift taxes.

Federal Estate Taxes

The federal government levies an **estate tax**, a tax on property transferred from deceased people to their heirs. An estate must be worth more than a certain amount ($3.5 million by 2009) to be subject to this tax. The federal estate tax is scheduled to be removed completely in 2010. The estate tax is paid from the assets of the estate, before anything can be distributed to heirs. An estate may have to sell property or investments in order to pay this tax.

State Death Taxes

Some states also levy death taxes in the form of estate tax, inheritance tax, and gift tax. The state **inheritance tax** is a tax on an heir who receives property from a deceased person's estate. The difference between an estate tax and an inheritance tax lies in who pays the tax. The estate tax is deducted from the value of the estate, but the heirs pay inheritance taxes on property received. The amount of tax is based on the value of the property in the estate. In states where inheritance taxes are imposed, laws vary widely as to the rate of taxation and the treatment of property to be taxed.

Federal Gift Taxes

Gifts are a popular way of distributing some property to loved ones before death to avoid estate and inheritance taxes. However, you would not want to give away property you need in order to live comfortably. One way to retain possession is to create a life estate. A *life estate* allows you to pass title to real property to a loved one but retain your right to live on the premises for as long as you live. This means that your children cannot evict you even after the property is in their names.

©GETTY IMAGES/PHOTODISC

A **gift tax** is a tax on a gift of money or property, to be paid by the giver, not the receiver, of the gift. You can give up to $11,000 per person per year without having to pay a gift tax. For gifts that exceed this amount, there is the unified gift tax credit, which basically allows a person to give away up to $1.5 million during their lifetime. Gifts to your spouse or to a charity are exempt from the gift tax. Also, gifts from a husband or a wife to a third party are considered as having been made in equal amounts by each spouse. Therefore, a husband and wife together may give as much as $22,000 per year to anyone, tax-free.

The timing of the gift also matters. Any gift given within three years of death is usually considered a "gift in contemplation of death." In this event, the estate still must pay taxes on the value of the gift, and the one receiving the cash or property would have to pay inheritance taxes.

What are some different taxes that will affect your estate planning?

Federal/State Income Taxes

When someone dies, income taxes must be paid on the income the decedent earned that year and on any income earned by the estate while its assets remain undistributed (such as interest or dividends). The executor or attorney representing the estate must file this tax return and pay the taxes from the estate before the estate can be distributed to heirs.

✅ Check Your Understanding

1. Why should you think about retirement when you are just beginning your work career?
2. Why is it important to have a will?
3. How does owning property jointly avoid probate?

Lesson 15.2

Saving for Retirement

Goals
- **Describe the features of retirement investment options.**
- **Explain basic benefits available through pension plans.**

▶ PERSONAL RETIREMENT ACCOUNTS

Personal retirement accounts are ways to set money aside for your later life. You can select from tax-sheltered plans, such as individual retirement accounts (IRAs), Keoghs, and simplified employee pensions (SEPs) for which you qualify, as well as annuities. You should also include some savings on which you have already paid taxes.

Individual Retirement Accounts (IRAs)

An **individual retirement account (IRA)** is a retirement savings plan that allows individuals to set aside up to $3,000 per year (or $6,000 for a married couple filing jointly) and delay paying tax on the earnings until they begin withdrawing it at age 59½ or later. People not covered by a pension plan at work may contribute the full amount per year, if they wish. Those who do participate in a pension plan at work can contribute to an IRA, but they may not be able to contribute the maximum, depending on their income.

With a *traditional IRA*, you can deduct your contribution each year from your taxable income. This allows you to delay paying the tax on that income and the earnings it accumulates in the account until you withdraw the money at retirement. At that time, your income will likely be lower than it was while you were working. As a result, you would be in a lower tax bracket and would pay less tax.

A *Roth IRA* is a type of IRA that taxes the contributions but not the money withdrawn at retirement. With a Roth IRA, you pay tax on your income before you put it into the account, but you never have to pay tax on the earnings the account accumulates over the years. In a traditional IRA, you would pay tax on the earnings as well as the contributions when you withdraw the money at retirement.

You cannot withdraw your money from an IRA before age 59½ without penalty. For early withdrawals, a 10 percent penalty is imposed on the amount withdrawn. This penalty can amount to a lot of money, so you should avoid withdrawing money early. In addition, the money you withdraw is subject to federal and state income taxes that year.

You can set up an *education IRA* if you have children under age 18. Contributions to an education IRA are not deductible. It is a trust created for the purpose of paying higher education expenses. Withdrawals for qualified expenses, such as tuition, books, fees, and supplies, are not taxable when withdrawn.

What is the value in contributing to a traditional IRA?

©GETTY IMAGES/PHOTODISC

Keogh Plans

A **Keogh plan** is a tax-deferred retirement savings plan available to self-employed individuals and their employees. Keogh contributions are restricted to $30,000 or 25 percent of earned income in any one year, whichever is less. Earned income is your net income after subtracting business expenses, including contributions to the plan for employees. Employees must be covered in the plan in a nondiscriminatory manner. Thus, if you contribute 15 percent of your earnings to the plan as an employer, you must contribute 15 percent of any employee's salary as well.

The amounts an employer contributes are fully tax deductible. Earnings on Keogh plans are also tax-deferred. Withdrawals cannot be made before age 59½ without penalty, and withdrawals must begin by age 70½. Keogh plans must be administered by a trustee, such as a financial institution.

Simplified Employee Pension (SEP) Plans

Simplified employee pension (SEP) plans were authorized by Congress to encourage smaller employers to establish employee pension plans with

IRAs as a funding method. Each employee sets up an IRA at a financial institution. Then the employer makes an annual tax-deductible contribution of up to 25 percent of the employee's salary or $40,000, whichever is less. Employees also can make contributions up to a $2,000 limit. Employee contributions to these plans are also tax-deductible.

Annuities

An *annuity* is an insurance company investment that provides a series of regular payments, usually after retirement. You can buy an annuity as your individual retirement account or as supplemental retirement income. An annuity can be bought with a single payment or with periodic payments. In recent years, *deferred annuities* have become popular because of the tax-free buildup of interest or dividends during the time the annuity contract remains in effect. Such annuities are often used by younger people to save money toward retirement.

Pre-Taxed Savings

Not all of your retirement savings should be in tax-deferred plans. Some should be savings and investments made with pre-taxed income (income on which you have already paid tax). Most financial advisors recommend that at least half of your retirement savings be pre-taxed. You will be able to withdraw these funds at any time, without tax consequences. Since there is no penalty for withdrawing these funds before retirement, you will have to restrain yourself from spending this part of your nest egg, so that it will be there for you when you retire.

▶ EMPLOYER-SPONSORED RETIREMENT PLANS

Another source of retirement income may be the pension plan offered by your company. With employer-sponsored plans, you and often your employer contribute to your tax-sheltered retirement savings. Contributions and earnings on employer-sponsored plans accumulate tax-free until you receive them.

Defined-Benefit Plans

Many larger companies provide defined-benefit plans for their employees. A defined-benefit plan, such as a pension, is a company-sponsored retirement plan in which employees receive, at normal retirement age, a specified monthly amount based on wages earned and number of years of service. The employer makes the entire contribution to the plan. To become *vested*, or entitled to the full amount in the plan, you must work for the company for a specified number of years. Employees who are vested but leave the company before retirement may withdraw the account balance in cash or "roll it over" (transfer it) to an IRA. In this situation, most people choose to roll the money into an IRA to delay paying taxes on it until retirement. If they take it as cash when they leave the company, they will have to pay tax on the full amount that year plus a 10 percent penalty if they are under age 59½.

Each pension plan has different rules and options. You should read the plan document to understand your choices.

If a company goes bankrupt or experiences serious financial difficulties, your plan may be protected by law. The Employee Retirement Income Security Act of 1974 (ERISA) sets minimum standards for pension plans in private industry and protects millions of workers from inadequately funded pension plans.

Defined-Contribution Plans

A **defined-contribution plan** is a company-sponsored retirement plan in which employees may choose to contribute part of their salary as a tax-deferred investment. The employer may or may not contribute to the employee's account as well. Each company's plan specifies the percentage of salary that an employee may contribute to his or her own account each year. The plan also specifies the amount the employer will contribute, if anything, but does not promise any particular benefit. When a plan participant retires or otherwise becomes eligible for benefits, the benefit is the total amount of money accumulated in the employee's account, including investment earnings on amounts put into the accounts. Two defined-contribution plans are 401(k) and 403(b) plans.

401(k) Plans

Employees of companies that operate for a profit may participate in 401(k) plans, if the company offers one. Under a *401(k) plan*, employees choose the percentage of salary they want to contribute to their account. The employer deducts this amount from their paychecks and puts it into the employees' individual accounts. This amount never becomes part of the employees' taxable income for the year, so they do not have to pay taxes on it until they withdraw the money at retirement. An investment company manages the accounts and invests the money. Usually employees may select the types of investments they want from among several options offered by the plan.

Frequently, employers match salary contributions by some percentage. For example, for every $1 of salary employees contribute to their account, the employer may add 50 cents (a 50 percent match). Companies usually set limits on how much they will match of an employee's salary contributed to a 401(k). Withdrawal restrictions and penalties apply when money is withdrawn early, except in the event of death, disability, or financial hardship. A 401(k) is usually an excellent investment for employees, particularly if the employer contributes. The employer's contribution is pure profit. In the example above, the 50 percent match is the same as making an immediate 50 percent return on your investment!

403(b) PLANS

Employees of government or not-for-profit businesses may participate in 403(b) plans. A *403(b) plan* is an account for employees of schools, tax-exempt organizations, and government units. While the rules may vary slightly, the 403(b) plan operates like a 401(k). These plans have been called tax-sheltered annuities (TSAs) because originally the law permitted only deferred annuities to be purchased by employees who were qualified under this section of the tax code.

Earnings are tax-deferred, and early withdrawal penalties apply. Should an employee leave this type of employer, the 403(b) funds can be rolled into an IRA.

▶ GOVERNMENT-SPONSORED PENSION PLANS

You may be entitled to government benefit checks—in the form of social security, military retirement, or veterans' benefits. Many state, county, and city governments operate retirement plans for their employees.

Social Security Benefits

When you retire, you will be eligible for social security benefits if you paid social security taxes during your lifetime. The amount of your benefit is based on your earnings and contributions to social security. Remember, these withholdings from your paychecks were matched by your employer(s). However, social security is designed as a safety net, or supplement to an individual's own retirement savings. It was never intended to fully support people in retirement. To retire comfortably, you must have accumulated your own nest egg apart from social security.

Can you rely on social security for full retirement support?

Each year you will receive a social security statement. This statement shows a record of the income on which you paid social security taxes and an estimate of the benefits you will receive at retirement. Some federal government employees and railroad employees are not covered by social security retirement benefits, although recent federal employees are now paying into social security.

Maximum social security retirement benefits are available at age 65 for many people. The government is raising the retirement age, so the age when you can receive the maximum benefits will likely be later than age 65. You can retire early, at age 62, and receive reduced benefits. If you were married for 10 years or more, you may be entitled to receive social security benefits based on your spouse's income, even if you are divorced.

Remember, too, most or all of social security retirement benefits are taxable if your total income from all sources exceeds amounts set from time to time. In addition, several states currently tax social security benefits as income.

Military Benefits

Retired military personnel receive pensions after 20 years of active duty in the U.S. armed forces. Pensions are payable in full regardless of other sources of income and are subject to income taxes. In addition, military retirees may have special privileges, such as the ability to purchase goods through military posts. These benefits can be very attractive, especially for people who retire from the military in their early 40s and continue working in different jobs for another 15 or 20 years.

The Veterans Administration provides regular pensions for many survivors of men and women who died while in the armed forces, and disability pensions for eligible veterans. In addition, veterans may be entitled to benefits ranging from low-interest mortgage loans to financing of a college education to low-rate car, life, or home insurance. Veterans should check to see what benefits are available—both now and at retirement.

Interview a relative or acquaintance who has retired. What kind of planning did the person do before retiring? What went according to plan? What unforeseen events or circumstances affected the plan? Write a one-page report of your findings.

✓Check Your Understanding

1. How is a traditional IRA different from a Roth IRA or an education IRA?

2. How is a 401(k) different from a 403(b)?

3. Who is eligible to collect social security retirement benefits?

Your Retirement Income

During your work life, you may set aside money in a retirement savings plan, such as a 401(k) or a 403(b). Money you set aside is *tax deferred*; that is, you do not have to pay income tax on it until you receive it and are able to spend it. Then you are taxed on it as ordinary income, at your tax rate when you are retired.

Tax-deferred investments provide a "tax shelter" benefit during your work years. They reduce your taxable income, and thus you pay less in taxes at that time. But when you retire and withdraw the money, you must claim it as income and pay taxes. Thus, retirement investments should consist of more than just tax-deferred options. Otherwise, all income received at retirement will be subject to tax.

Retirement income should provide enough money to pay your living expenses and other costs (such as medical care and prescriptions), as well as allow you to enjoy some travel and leisure activities. At least part of that income should be money set aside while you were working that will not be subject to tax (you paid taxes on it as you went along). Consider the following recommended income plan:

Source of Income	% of Total Retirement Income
Social security/government pensions (withheld from paychecks)	25%
401(k) or 403(b) savings plans during work years	25%
Employer-provided retirement accounts (you did not contribute to this)	15%
Private money you saved that was not tax deferred and will not be taxed at retirement	40%

With this plan, you depend on yourself more than on any other source. Income you set aside will be yours to take as you wish, without tax consequences. Because social security benefits become taxable after you earn a certain level of income, you should consider it as a part of the taxable portion of your retirement.

Think Critically
1. How much money will you need for a secure retirement? What is the ideal combination of savings for retirement to meet those needs?
2. Why is it important to set aside money that is not tax sheltered? How much of your retirement money should be tax sheltered?

Chapter Assessment

15.1

* Social security benefits alone will not provide a comfortable retirement. You must start building your nest egg now with regular saving and investing.
* The equity you build in your home can be a source of retirement income.
* As you near retirement, you may want to switch to less risky investments that emphasize current income over future capital gains.
* Plan your estate to minimize taxes, to make known how you want your possessions distributed after your death, and to provide a smooth transfer of your assets to your loved ones.
* A will specifies how to distribute your assets.
* A power of attorney empowers someone else to act on your behalf.
* Joint ownership with right of survivorship transfers property at death without the costs and time involved in probate.
* Estate tax is deducted from the value of the estate before it is distributed to the heirs. Inheritance tax is paid by the heirs on property received.

15.2

* A traditional IRA allows you to delay paying income tax on the contributions until you withdraw the money at retirement age.
* On a Roth IRA, you pay taxes on the contributions but pay no taxes on withdrawals at retirement.
* A Keogh plan is a tax-deferred plan for self-employed people.
* SEP plans are tax-deferred plans for employees of small businesses.
* An annuity is a tax-sheltered investment sold by insurance companies that provides regular payments after retirement.

- Under a defined-benefit plan, retired employees receive a specified amount based on wages earned and years of service.
- Defined-contribution plans allow employees to contribute part of their salary to tax-deferred investments. Employers may or may not contribute matching funds.
- You will be eligible for social security benefits at retirement if you paid social security taxes during your lifetime.

REVIEW TERMS

Directions

Can you find the definition for each of the following terms used in Chapter 15?

codicil
defined-benefit plan
defined-contribution plan
estate
estate planning
estate tax
gift tax
heirs

individual retirement
  account (IRA)
inheritance tax
Keogh plan
power of attorney
reverse mortgage
trust
will

1. All that a person owns, less debts owed, at the time of the person's death.

2. A company-sponsored retirement plan in which employees receive, at normal retirement age, a specified amount based on wages earned and number of years of service.

3. A loan against the equity in the borrower's home in which the lender makes tax-free monthly payments to the borrower.

4. A retirement savings plan that allows individuals to set aside up to $2,000 per year and delay paying tax on the earnings until they begin withdrawing it at age 59½ or later.

5. A legal document that tells how a decedent wishes his or her property to be distributed after death.

6. People who receive property from someone who has died.

7. A legal document that empowers a trustee to control property for ultimate distribution to a beneficiary.

8. A federal tax on property transferred from deceased people to their heirs.

9. A state tax on an heir who receives property from a deceased person's estate.

10. A tax-deferred retirement savings plan available to self-employed individuals.

11. A company-sponsored retirement plan in which employees may choose to contribute part of their salary as a tax-deferred investment.

12. Preparing a plan for transferring property during one's lifetime and at one's death.

13. A legal document that makes small changes to a will.

14. A legal document authorizing someone to act on your behalf.

15. A tax on a gift of money or property, to be paid by the giver, not the receiver, of the gift.

REVIEW FACTS AND IDEAS

1. About how much income will you need at retirement to live comfortably?

2. How might your housing needs change as you near retirement?

3. How can you turn the equity in your home into income?

4. How might your investment strategy change as you near retirement?

5. How might your insurance needs change at retirement?

6. What are the goals of estate planning?

7. Why do you need a will?

8. What is the difference between a simple will and a holographic will?

9. Why would you need a power of attorney?

10. What is the difference between an inter vivos trust and a testamentary trust?

11. What governmental unit levies inheritance taxes? Who pays them?

12. Why would a person give property to another person during his or her lifetime rather than wait to pass property by a will?

13. When do you pay income taxes on the amounts in a Roth IRA?

14. Who can establish a Keogh retirement plan?

15. Explain the tax-deductible features of IRAs, SEPs, and Keogh plans.

16. How is a 401(k) plan different from a 403(b) plan?

17. Why should retirees not rely entirely on social security benefits?

APPLY YOUR KNOWLEDGE

1. At what age would you like to retire? After how many years of work? Briefly describe your plans for retirement—for example, travel, leisure, and recreation.

2. Interview your colleagues and friends to get their views on retirement planning. Why are many young people who worry about the future often reluctant to plan for retirement?

3. Explain how you might invest your money to be sure your income keeps up with inflation. Assume that you will receive social security and pension benefits from an employer.

4. Search the Internet using the keywords "retirement calculator" and select a calculator. The calculator will require numbers such as salary and amount you plan to save each year. Make up reasonable numbers to plug in. Work through the calculator several times, changing only one number each time. Keep track of the numbers you use and the results, so you can compare. Write a one-page paper describing what you learned about saving for retirement from this exercise.

5. Visit www.nolo.com, and follow the links to estate planning. Select an article that interests you. Then write a paragraph summarizing the key points on that topic.

6. Read the will in Figure 15-1. In list form, summarize the key provisions of this will. What is the purpose of the three signatures at the bottom of the will?

7. Prepare a simple will for yourself, following Figure 15-1. What would happen to your property if you did not have a will?

8. If you had minor children, you might create a trust to provide for them if you died while they were still young. Explain why a trust fund is important for managing the financial needs of minors.

9. What are some advantages of owning property jointly with another person? Why would people own property as joint tenants with the right of survivorship?

10. Suppose you gave a $20,000 gift to a friend. Would you pay a gift tax on $20,000 if you were single? If so, how much of the gift amount would be taxed?

11. Visit the Roth IRA home page at www.rothira.com. From the information you find there, write a paragraph about Roth IRAs. Who would choose them and why?

12. Suppose your employer offers a 401(k) plan with a 50% match. How would contributing to this plan affect your current income? How would it affect your future income? Do you think participating in this plan is a good idea? Explain.

Solve Problems ⊕ Explore Issues

1. Mr. and Mrs. Shigeki are getting older. Their children are grown and through college. Their home is nearly paid off. In five more years, they both plan to retire. Explain to them how their investment strategies today should probably be different from when they still had children to support.

2. Mrs. Martinez is a widow. She has an employer-paid pension of $300 a month, together with social security benefits of $600 a month. She owns her home free and clear but has high medical bills. Explain to her how she can use her house equity to generate monthly income for her retirement years.

3. Lidia and Tomas own a new car jointly with right of survivorship. Can Lidia leave her share of the car to another person when she draws up her will? Why or why not?

4. Lashonda is self-employed. Every year, she has extra money she could save, but instead she spends it on trips and jewelry. She also pays high taxes because she earns considerable money from her business. Explain to her why she should strongly consider a Keogh plan for her retirement years.

5. Ian works and earns under $25,000 a year. He has never had an IRA because he thinks social security will be enough for retirement income. Explain to him how an IRA works, and why he should consider one.

6. Daymon has worked for over 45 years. He served in the military for 20 of those years. He is qualified to retire next year when he reaches age 65. Explain to him what type of benefits he might expect to receive.

7. On the Internet, locate a retirement planner tool, and use the following information: You are 21 years old and have no savings yet, but you have a good job and can start saving. You think you can retire comfortably at 65 on $30,000 a year, and plan to withdraw your savings until you are 85. On average, you think you can earn 8 percent on your savings. How much would you have to save each year to meet your savings goal? How much would you have to save each year if you didn't start until you were 35?

For related activities and links, point your browser to **www.mypf.swlearning.com**

Assessing Your Financial Security

At the end of Unit 2, you began financial planning with a project to carefully examine your financial position. Let's continue to build and protect your financial security through savings, investments, and retirement and estate planning.

▶ YOUR SAVINGS PLAN

Saving is often defined as postponed spending. The money you set aside today will allow you to make purchases later. A good financial plan begins first with setting aside a portion of your current income to provide for future needs.

In Chapter 10, you learned how to calculate interest on savings deposits. When money is set aside, it gains interest until some point in the future when it is withdrawn and spent. *Future value* is the final compounded value of a deposit or series of deposits. Using future value tables (which are built into financial calculators), you can determine how much money you need to set aside today in order to reach a future goal.

Figure U3-1 on page 372 shows the future value (compound sum) of an amount deposited at several interest rates and allowed to compound for a number of compounding periods. Rather than compute interest for each period and add it to the previous balance, you can use this table. For example, if you deposit $5,000 at 8 percent and leave it for five years, compounded semiannually, you would use the table as follows: 8 percent a year is 4 percent per compounding period (8 divided by 2). Five years, compounded semiannually, is 10 compounding periods (5 times 2). In the table, the factor for 4 percent and 10 periods is 1.48024. Multiply $5,000 times 1.48024, and the account total will be $7,401.20 after 5 years, at 8 percent interest, compounded semiannually.

When you make regular payments (rather than deposit a lump sum at irregular intervals) to your account, you can use another table to shortcut the calculations. Figure U3-2 on page 373 shows the future value (compound sum) of an annuity. (You will recall that an *annuity* is a sum of money set aside regularly, such as monthly, for the future.) Instead of calculating interest, adding a deposit, calculating interest, and so on, the table shown in Figure U3-2 simplifies the procedure. For example, say you deposit $1,000 per year for 12 years, earning 6 percent interest a year. In the table, the factor for 6 percent and 12 periods is 16.86994. Multiplying $1,000 times 16.86994, you get $16,869.94, which is the value of the deposits at the end of 12 years.

Using the two tables shown in Figures U3-1 and U3-2, complete Worksheet 1 (Future Values) in the *Student Activity Guide* (and illustrated here on page 378).

For your own personal savings plan, you should set aside a predetermined amount each month. Complete Worksheet 2 (Your Savings Plan) in the *Student Activity Guide* (and illustrated here on page 379). Then calculate the future values of money you can set aside.

figure U3-1

FUTURE VALUE (COMPOUND SUM) OF $1

Period	3%	4%	5%	6%	7%	8%	9%	10%	11%
1	1.03000	1.04000	1.05000	1.06000	1.07000	1.08000	1.09000	1.10000	1.11000
2	1.06090	1.08160	1.10250	1.12360	1.14990	1.16640	1.11810	1.21000	1.23210
3	1.09273	1.12486	1.15723	1.19102	1.22504	1.25971	1.29503	1.33100	1.36763
4	1.12551	1.16986	1.21551	1.26248	1.31080	1.36049	1.41158	1.46410	1.51807
5	1.15927	1.21665	1.27628	1.33823	1.40255	1.46933	1.53862	1.61051	1.68506
6	1.19405	1.26532	1.34010	1.41852	1.50073	1.58687	1.66710	1.77156	1.87042
7	1.22987	1.31593	1.40710	1.50363	1.60578	1.71382	1.82804	1.94872	2.07616
8	1.26677	1.36857	1.47746	1.59385	1.71819	1.85093	1.99256	2.14359	2.30454
9	1.30477	1.42331	1.55133	1.68948	1.83846	1.99901	2.17189	2.35795	2.55804
10	1.34392	1.48024	1.62890	1.79085	1.96715	2.15893	2.36736	2.59374	2.83942
11	1.38423	1.53945	1.71034	1.89830	2.10485	2.33164	2.58043	2.85312	3.15176
12	1.42576	1.60103	1.79586	2.01220	2.25219	2.51817	2.81266	3.13843	3.49845
13	1.46853	1.66507	1.88565	2.13203	2.40985	2.71962	3.06581	3.45227	3.88328
14	1.51259	1.73168	1.97993	2.26090	2.57853	2.93719	3.34173	3.79750	4.31044
15	1.55797	1.80094	2.07893	2.39656	2.75903	3.17217	3.64248	4.17725	4.78459
16	1.60471	1.87298	2.18288	2.54035	2.95216	3.42594	3.97031	4.59497	5.31089
17	1.65285	1.94790	2.29202	2.69377	3.15882	3.70002	4.32763	5.05447	5.89509
18	1.70243	2.02582	2.40662	2.54035	3.37993	3.99602	4.71712	5.55992	6.54355
19	1.75351	2.10685	2.52695	3.02560	3.61653	4.31570	5.14166	6.11591	7.26334
20	1.80611	2.19112	2.65330	3.20714	3.86968	4.66096	5.60441	6.72750	8.06231
25	2.09378	2.66584	3.38636	4.29187	5.42743	6.84848	8.62308	10.83471	13.58546
30	2.42726	3.24340	4.32194	5.74349	7.61226	10.06266	13.26768	17.44940	22.89230
35	2.81386	3.94609	5.51602	7.68608	10.67658	14.78534	20.41397	28.10244	38.57485
40	3.26204	4.80102	7.03999	10.28572	14.97446	21.72452	31.40942	45.25926	65.00087
45	3.78160	5.84118	8.98501	13.76461	21.00245	31.92045	48.32729	72.89048	109.53024
50	4.38391	7.10668	11.46740	18.42015	29.45703	46.90161	74.35752	117.39085	184.56483

FUTURE VALUE (COMPOUND SUM) OF AN ANNUITY (BASE VALUE $1)

Period	3%	4%	5%	6%	7%	8%	9%	10%	11%
					Percent				
1	1.00000	1.00000	1.00000	1.00000	1.00000	1.00000	1.00000	1.00000	1.00000
2	2.03000	2.04000	2.05000	2.06000	2.07000	2.08000	2.09000	2.10000	2.11000
3	3.09090	3.12160	3.15250	3.18360	3.21490	3.24640	3.27810	3.31000	3.34210
4	4.18363	4.24646	4.31013	4.37462	4.43994	4.50611	4.57313	4.64100	4.70973
5	5.30914	5.41632	5.52563	5.63709	5.75074	5.86660	5.98471	6.10510	6.22780
6	6.46841	6.63298	6.80191	6.97532	7.15329	7.33593	7.52334	7.71561	7.91286
7	7.66246	7.89829	8.14201	8.39384	8.65402	8.92280	9.20044	9.48717	9.78327
8	8.89234	9.21427	9.54911	9.89747	10.25980	10.63663	11.02847	11.43589	11.85943
9	10.15911	10.58280	11.02656	11.49132	11.97799	12.48756	13.02104	13.57948	14.16397
10	11.46388	12.00611	12.57789	13.18080	13.81645	14.48656	15.19293	15.93743	16.72201
11	12.80780	13.48635	14.20679	14.97164	15.79360	16.64549	17.56029	18.53117	19.56143
12	14.19203	15.02581	15.91713	16.86994	17.88845	18.97713	20.14072	21.38428	22.71319
13	15.61779	16.62684	17.71298	18.88214	20.14064	21.49530	22.95339	24.52271	26.21164
14	17.08632	18.29191	19.59863	21.10507	22.55049	24.21492	26.01919	27.97498	30.09492
15	18.59891	20.02359	21.57856	23.27597	25.12902	27.15211	29.36092	31.77248	34.40536
16	20.15688	21.82453	23.65749	25.67253	27.88805	30.32428	33.00340	35.94973	39.18995
17	21.76159	23.69751	25.84037	28.21288	30.84022	33.75023	36.97371	40.54470	44.50084
18	23.41444	25.64541	28.13239	30.90565	33.99903	37.45024	41.30134	45.59917	50.39594
19	25.11687	27.67123	30.53900	33.75999	37.37897	41.44626	46.01846	51.15909	56.93949
20	26.87037	29.77808	33.06595	36.78559	40.99549	45.76196	51.16012	57.27500	64.20283
25	36.45926	41.64591	47.72710	54.86451	63.24904	73.10594	84.70090	98.34706	114.41331
30	47.57542	56.08494	66.43885	79.05819	94.46077	113.28321	136.30754	164.49402	199.02088
35	60.46208	73.65223	90.32031	111.43478	138.23688	172.31680	215.71076	271.02437	341.58956
40	75.40126	95.02552	120.79977	154.76297	199.63511	259.05652	337.88245	442.59257	581.82607
45	92.71986	121.02939	159.70016	212.74351	285.74931	386.50562	525.85874	718.90484	986.63856
50	112.79687	152.66708	209.34800	290.33591	406.52893	573.77016	815.08356	1163.90853	1668.88115

▶ INVESTMENTS AND RISK

After you have provided for savings, you can then begin investing. The purpose of investing is to earn a higher return than you can earn on savings. In order to do this, you must take more risk. When choosing investments, it is important first to decide how much risk you are comfortable taking. For example, investing in riskier stocks may be profitable, but it may not be appropriate for people who get very nervous when the stock market goes down.

Worksheet 3, shown on page 380, is a Risk Aptitude Test for Investors that lets you assess your tolerance for risk when you are planning your investment strategy. If you find you are risk-averse, you should choose lower-risk investments to avoid the stress that accompanies high-risk investments. If, however, you are a risk-taker, then you can take maximum risks and enjoy the uncertainty. Most people fall somewhere between the two extremes. They must try to balance their investments to earn maximum return for the risk involved.

Complete Worksheet 3 (Risk Aptitude Test) in the *Student Activity Guide*. Write a paragraph summarizing what you discovered about your own tolerance for risk.

▶ INVESTMENT STRATEGY

An *investment strategy* is a plan that examines potential returns and rates investments according to desirability. To measure investment potential, two standards apply: the rate of inflation and the overall performance of the stock market. Inflation may be averaging 4 to 6 percent, and if your investment matches or exceeds that rate, you've done well. To estimate the return you're getting, follow the formula in Figure U3-3.

For example, let's say that four years ago you purchased 10 shares of stock at $35 each. The stock is now worth $38.50 a share. You have received dividends of $.50 per share for four years. Computation of the average rate of return is shown in Figure U3-4.

If inflation was less than 3.9 percent on the average during those four years, your investment was worthwhile. However, if the inflation rate was higher than your average return of 3.9 percent, you should sell that investment and buy something else.

Calculate the average gain per year and average rate of return on investments shown, and rank the investments in order of desirability on Worksheet 4 (Investment Analysis) in the *Student Activity Guide* (and illustrated here on page 381).

▶▶ **figure U3-3**

AVERAGE RATE OF RETURN FORMULA

Current market value of investment	$_____ A
minus price you paid for it	_____ B
Gain (+) or Loss (–)	$_____ C
plus dividends, interest, and other cash received	_____ D
Total Gain (+) or Loss (–)	$_____ E
Average yearly gain: *divide* by number of years you've owned it (divide E by number of years)	$_____ F
Average rate of return: *divide* average yearly gain (F) by original price (B)	_____ %G

Current value $38.50 × 10	$385.00 A
Original price 35.00 × 10	350.00 B
Gain (A − B)	$ 35.00 C
Dividends (.5 × 10 × 4)	20.00 D
Total gain	$ 55.00 E
Average yearly gain $55 ÷ 4	$ 13.75 F
Average rate of return $13.75 ÷ 350	3.9% G

▶ YOUR INVESTMENT PLAN

A good investment plan is to begin slowly, choosing low-risk, predictable, and stable options. Then, as your comfort level increases and you have more money to risk, expand into moderate and high-risk ventures with greater potential profits (and losses). Complete Worksheet 5 (Investment Plan) in the *Student Activity Guide* (and illustrated here on page 382). You may wish to refer to Chapters 12-14 to examine your options as you plan for future investments.

▶ YOUR RETIREMENT PLAN

The time to begin planning for retirement is now—at the beginning of your work career. Otherwise, unforeseen events may prevent you from implementing plans needed to provide a secure retirement. Because people are living longer and healthier lives, it is important for all of us to consider those post-working years. With adequate financial resources, retirement can offer activities and opportunities that are satisfying and enjoyable.

The most difficult part of retirement planning is estimating your post-retirement income and needs. Generally, living expenses decrease following retirement. Bureau of Labor statistics show that retired couples are able to maintain a similar standard of living with about half the spendable income needed by the average family of four. Some financial advisers recommend that retiring individuals have 60 to 80 percent of their take-home pay to maintain their pre-retirement lifestyle. The types of expenses will also change. Health care and food become major budget items while house payments generally disappear because mortgages are paid off. Other expenses, such as utilities and property taxes, do not change significantly.

Between today and the day you retire, inflation will likely continue to erode your purchasing power. However, your investments and savings should grow. Therefore, when planning for retirement needs, prepare a budget based on today's dollars, knowing that in the future, prices will be higher, but your savings and investments will also be higher to offset inflation.

To prepare for retirement, you can cut your costs and increase your income. Worksheet 6 (Retirement Plan) will help you determine how much of each you need to do. Complete Worksheet 6 in the *Student Activity Guide* (and illustrated here on page 383).

Social security payments probably will not be adequate to meet retirement expenses. Completing the retirement plan in Worksheet 6 should convince most people of the need to provide additional sources of income. Some of these will have a tax advantage; others will not. For example, IRA contributions that were deducted from gross income are now taxable when withdrawn. Therefore, when you withdraw money from an IRA or other tax-deferred accounts, such as a 401(k) or 403(b), you will pay income taxes on the full amount of principal and earnings. When computing the future monthly income to be derived from such sources, be sure to subtract the taxes (25 percent, for example).

▶ ESTATE PLANNING

You learned about estate planning in Chapter 15. But there are several other matters to consider that were not covered in the text. For example, when a person dies, loved ones left behind have many decisions to make and expenses to pay. The costs involved when a person dies can range from a few hundred dollars to several thousand dollars. These expenses include final medical and hospital charges, the funeral and a casket (or other desired arrangements), and burial.

By preparing instructions and making provisions for these costs in advance, you spare your loved ones the emotional decision-making process. Survivors who are grieving the loss of a loved one often are unprepared to make the many decisions involved in planning a funeral and burial. At such an emotional time, a family may incur excessive expenses neither they nor the estate can afford.

Traditional funeral services may be performed in a church or in a funeral home. The cost can be $1,500 to $5,000 or more, which includes cremation and urn or a casket, embalming, preparations, music, printed remembrances, and newspaper notices. All decisions about these matters must be made in a relatively short period of time.

Cremation is a process of reducing a body to ashes in a high-temperature oven. The ashes are placed in an urn that is presented to the family or placed in a grave or vault. Cremation is less expensive than casket burial, but there are special requirements. When a body is not cremated within a certain time span, usually two days, it must be embalmed or otherwise prepared for burial. These costs must be paid, even though cremation is later chosen.

Many funeral homes have prearranged plans available at guaranteed costs. Money for the funeral is placed into an account that is insured by the FDIC or NCUA and earns interest. Although the money is for the funeral, it can be withdrawn in an emergency. Written instructions will save the family from overspending at the time of death, minimize emotional and financial distress, and assure the family that the type and cost of the funeral is as desired by the loved one.

A typical letter of final instruction is shown as Figure U3-5. It outlines a person's wishes and helps others to implement them.

Prepare Worksheet 7 (Letter of Instruction), which is in the *Student Activity Guide*, to outline your wishes.

LETTER OF INSTRUCTION

figure **U3-5**

Date:_____

To my family,

This is a list of my last wishes and arrangements I have made which I hope will make decisions easier for you.

1. I wish to be cremated. I have prearranged services at the Bennet Funeral Home. These arrangements include the details of announcements, selection of urn, etc. I have prepaid these services, and the receipt is attached to this document.

2. I do not wish to be an organ donor. Please do not sign forms to indicate otherwise.

3. My Last Will and Testament is in my safe-deposit box at First Independent Bank, Main Branch, this city. A copy is also in my attorney's office (Anderson & Anderson, this city).

4. I have the following accounts and policies which should be included in my estate:

   Checking Account . . . . First Independent Bank
   Savings Account . . . . First Independent Bank
   Life Insurance Policy ($100,000) . . . New York Life
   Mortgage Insurance. . . . . Veterans Services

5. My safe-deposit box contains deeds to property I own, past tax returns, and lists of credit and charge accounts I hold.

_____
J. B. Adams

WORKSHEET 1
Future Values

Directions: For numbers 1–4, use Figure U3-1 to compute the value of each deposit at the rate given. For numbers 5–8, use Figure U3-2 to compute the value of each annuity at the given rate.

Future Value (Compound Sum) of $1

Deposit	Time	Annual Rate	Value
1. $5,000 Compounded quarterly	4 years	12%	$_____
2. $1,000 Compounded semiannually	10 years	6%	$_____
3. $7,500 Compounded annually	8 years	8%	$_____
4. $3,850 Compounded semiannually	2 years	8%	$_____

Future Value (Compound Sum) of an Annuity

Deposit	Time	Annual Rate	Value
5. $500/year	5 years	6%	$_____
6. $100/year	10 years	9%	$_____
7. $75/month ($900/yr)	2 years	8%	$_____
8. $250/year	10 years	5%	$_____

WORKSHEET 2
Your Savings Plan

Directions: In the spaces, project what you could save presently (either lump sum or monthly payment), and calculate the future value in 5, 10, and 20 years at the interest rate shown. Then project what you would like to be able to save (lump sum or monthly payment) in 5, 10, and 20 years.

Savings Amount	Interest Rates	Future Value
$_____ What you could set aside today	6% per year, compounded annually, in 5 years	$_____
	6% per year, compounded annually, in 10 years	$_____
	6% per year, compounded annually, in 20 years	$_____
$_____ What you want to be able to save 5 years from now	8% per year, compounded annually, in 10 years	$_____
	6% per year, compounded semi- annually, in 20 years	$_____
$_____ What you want to be able to save 10 years from now	5% per year, compounded annually, in 20 years	$_____
	6% per year, compounded semi- annually, in 5 years	$_____

Make a plan for the amount of money you will set aside now and in the future.

Directions: In the spaces below, write when you will set aside money, how much you will set aside and how often, your goal amount, and the future purpose of the amount saved.

Date	Amount Set Aside/How Often/Goal	Future Purpose of Saved Amount
_____	$_____/_____/_____	_____
_____	_____/_____/_____	_____
_____	_____/_____/_____	_____

WORKSHEET 3
Risk Aptitude Test

Directions: Answer the following questions, recording your answers in the spaces provided. Then compute your risk aptitude score as shown.

_____ 1. You have an extra $100 left over from your year-end bonus. Would you rather (a) put it all in savings, (b) spend some and save a little, (c) bet it on a lottery.

_____ 2. You are ready to buy a new car. Will it be a (a) small economy car, (b) conventional, standard car with a variety of options, (c) sports car emphasizing speed, style, or performance.

_____ 3. You have won a weekend trip of your choice. Will you (a) take cash instead, (b) go on a cruise or sightseeing trip, (c) fly to a mountain lodge for skiing.

_____ 4. You are considering a job offer. Which of these is most important to you? (a) job security (permanent employment), (b) higher salary with moderate security, (c) higher pay and less job security.

_____ 5. You are betting on a horse race. Which wager will you make? (a) bet on the favorite, even though winnings will be small, (b) select a horse with a good chance of winning and moderate payback if it does, (c) pick a long shot with high payback.

_____ 6. You have a mortgage on your home. Will you (a) make regular payments, paying off the loan on schedule, (b) repay the loan quicker than required so you can save interest, (c) refinance the loan and use the extra cash for other investments.

_____ 7. You are considering changing jobs. Which sounds best? (a) joining a well-established firm and doing similar work, (b) associating with a new company in a newly created position, (c) going into business for yourself.

_____ 8. You have a schedule conflict. The following three events are all scheduled for the same day and time. Which will you choose? (a) attending a seminar, (b) working on a committee, (c) giving a speech to a group of students.

_____ 9. Your dinner is "on the house." Which will you choose? (a) cold turkey sandwich and salad, (b) enchilada with hot peppers, (c) rare sirloin with fries.

_____10. You have a delayed flight and your plane will be four hours late. Will you (a) read a book and wait, (b) take in a short sightseeing trip, (c) book another flight.

Scoring: Give yourself 1 point for each question you marked (a); 3 points for each (b); and 5 points for each (c). Scores 40 and above indicate willingness to take risk (you are a risk taker); scores between 25 and 40 indicate a willingness to take moderate risk; and scores below 25 show high risk aversion. A score of 30 is average.

Analyzing Your Score:

Based on your score, what are some investments that have the amount of risk you are willing to take? (See Chapter 11.)

WORKSHEET 4
Investment Analysis

Directions: Calculate the average gain per year and average rate of return on investments shown, and rank the investments in order of desirability.

Asset Purchased	Original Price	Years Held	Current Value	Dividends or Interest Received	Avg. Gain/ Year	Avg. Rate Return	Rank
H&H Stock 25 shares	$14.00/sh	10	$16.00	$.30/share/ year	_____	_____	_____
Time CD	$5,000	5	$5,000	$1,055	_____	_____	_____
Mutual Funds 33 shares	$18.50/sh	7	$17.50	$.35/share/ year	_____	_____	_____
Gold 50 troy oz.	$325/oz.	3	$262/oz.	0	_____	_____	_____
ATZ Stock 50 shares	$29.50/sh	5	$35.50	$.50/share/ year	_____	_____	_____

WORKSHEET 5
Investment Plan

Directions: Complete the following worksheet by listing your investment and how much you expect to invest, how long you will keep the investment, and your potential return.

Investment Choice	Initial Cost	Time Kept	Expected Profit
Example: Time CD	$1,000	1 year	$80

Beginning Investments

1. _____
2. _____
3. _____

Systematic Investments

1. _____
2. _____
3. _____

Speculative Investments

1. _____
2. _____
3. _____

WORKSHEET 6
Retirement Plan

Directions: Fill in the amounts you project for each category in the spaces provided. In order to obtain realistic amounts, you may need to talk to a retired person or other person about projected benefits and costs.

1. Projected Income (monthly)

a. Anticipated benefits:
   Social security $_____
   Pensions   _____
   Annuities   _____
   Part-time work   _____
   Other   _____

b. Assets used for income:
   Savings accounts $_____
   IRAs   _____
   Investments   _____
   Other   _____

   Total projected
      monthly income $_____

   Projected − Projected =   Surplus
    Income   Costs   (Shortage)

   _____ − _____ = $_____

2. Projected Costs (monthly)

a. Fixed costs:
   Property taxes $_____
   Insurance premiums   _____
   Other   _____

b. Variable costs:
   Food $_____
   Utilities   _____
     Gas or oil   _____
     Electricity   _____
     Telephone   _____
   Household maintenance _____
   Transportation   _____
   Clothing and cleaning _____
   Personal care   _____
   Health care and medical _____
   Recreation/entertainment _____
   Miscellaneous   _____
   Other   _____

   Total projected expenses $_____

unit **4**

Credit Management

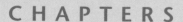
Project: **Managing Credit and Debt**

TRANSACTION RECORD

INS
HERE

nit 4 begins with a chapter that serves as a general introduction to what credit is and why it is important to you as a consumer in the American economy.

In Chapter 17, you will learn about credit bureaus, ratings, and reports, and your rights and responsibilities as a credit user. You will also discover many credit laws to protect consumers.

In Chapter 18, you will ties of consumer credit and explore ways to minimize

Finally, in Chapter 19, y credit problems and ways

Credit in America

TERMS TO KNOW

credit
capital
collateral
finance charge
line of credit

deferred billing
open-ended credit
annual percentage
 rate (APR)
closed-end credit

service credit
loan sharks
usury laws
pawnbroker

Consider This. . .

It was two days before the spring festival, and Promys still hadn't purchased the supplies she needed in order to make her costume. She had been saving her money for four months and was still $50 short of her goal.

"I'll just have to borrow the rest," she told her friends. "Otherwise, I won't be able to get the costume completed and that means I'll have let down the team. I really wanted to pay cash and not go into debt, but in this case, it can't be helped. Credit is serious because it's money I'll have to pay back in the future. I probably should have used credit a little sooner. Now I'll have to work all night in order to get this costume completed. I learned an important lesson. There's a time and a place for using credit."

What Is Credit?

Goals
- **Describe how credit developed in America.**
- **Define basic credit vocabulary.**
- **Discuss the advantages and disadvantages of using credit.**

▶ DEVELOPMENT OF CREDIT

When you borrow money or use a charge account to pay for purchases, you are taking advantage of the most commonly used method of purchase in the United States: credit. Over 80 percent of all purchases in the U.S. are made with credit rather than cash. **Credit** is money borrowed to buy something now, with the agreement to pay for it later.

In the Past

The need for credit arose in the United States when the country grew from a bartering and trading society to a currency exchange economy. During the 1800s, items were first manufactured for sale. People no longer produced everything exclusively for their own use. With their earnings, they bought the things they used to make themselves. Soon the need developed for sources of credit to help families meet their financial needs. Consumer credit had begun.

One of the earliest forms of credit was the account at the general store. Wage earners or farmers would pick up supplies and put the amount due "on account." When the borrowers received a paycheck or harvested the crop, they would pay their account in full, and the charging process would begin again. The store rarely charged interest. Credit was a convenience that store owners provided for customers they knew well and trusted. The customers paid off their accounts as soon as they could.

As the use of credit expanded, individual purchasing power also increased. Because credit increased people's ability to buy more goods and services, the American economy grew at a healthy pace. People bought luxuries as well as necessities with the help of credit, and the average American's standard of living rose. Businesses and consumers benefited from credit.

Between 1920 and 1990, buying on credit became the American way of life. No longer was credit saved for emergencies. Many different forms of credit developed to meet changing consumer needs and wants.

In the 1990s, record numbers of people declared bankruptcy. Overuse of credit cards was the main reason. With the economic prosperity of the decade, people were optimistic and willing to spend their income well into the future. But this overspending brought enormous credit debt.

Credit Today

Credit today is a way of life. Merchants encourage consumers to use credit to buy all kinds of goods and services. Banks and stores offer credit in the form of cards, loans, lines of credit, and all manner of short-term and long-term financing. Some transactions are difficult to make without a credit card, such as reserving a hotel room or making an online purchase. It's no longer "How can I get credit?" but "How can I wisely manage credit?" Unfortunately, credit trouble remains all too common as well.

©GETTY IMAGES/PHOTODISC

Why in recent years have so many people declared bankruptcy?

◢ THE VOCABULARY OF CREDIT

Certain terms are commonly used to describe credit, its availability, and its cost. When you borrow money or use credit, you are a *borrower* or *debtor*. The person or company who loans money or extends credit to you is the *creditor*.

To qualify for credit, you must have the ability to repay the loan. Having a job is important. Creditors may also expect you to have some capital. **Capital** is property you possess (such as bank accounts, investments, and other assets) that is worth more than your debts. Having capital tells the creditor that you have accumulated assets and are on your way to being a responsible citizen.

You will probably want to pay for large purchases with credit. For large sums, creditors often want more than just your promise to repay. They want collateral. **Collateral** is property pledged to assure repayment of a loan. If you do not make your loan payments, the creditor can seize the pledged property. For example, when you buy a car on credit, the car serves as collateral. If you do not repay the loan, the car can be *repossessed*. Ownership of the car would revert back to the lending institution.

Once you have completed the credit purchase, you owe money to the creditor. The *principal* (amount borrowed) plus interest for the time you have the loan is called the *balance due*. You generally will make monthly payments until you repay the balance due in full. The payments include both principal and interest, and with each payment, the amount you owe is reduced. The **finance charge** is the total dollar amount of all interest and fees you pay for the use of credit. It is the price you pay for the privilege of using someone else's money to buy goods and services now.

Credit statements usually specify a *minimum payment*. This is the least amount you may pay that month under your credit agreement, though you may pay more to further reduce your debt. All credit payments are due by a specific *due date*. Typically, you will be given 10 to 20 days from the date you receive a bill in which to pay. If you do not pay within the time allowed, you are likely to be charged a *late fee*, which is added to the balance due.

For particularly expensive purchases, you may have to sign an *installment agreement*, wherein you agree to make regular payments for a set period of time. At the end of that time, you will have repaid the entire debt. This is a type of *secured loan*, because the goods you purchased with the loan serve as collateral for the money loaned.

▶ ADVANTAGES AND DISADVANTAGES OF CONSUMER CREDIT

Some people use credit extensively while others pay cash as much as possible. Many people get into trouble each year by not using credit carefully. Credit can have several advantages for you, but you must not lose sight of its disadvantages.

Advantages of Credit

Used correctly, credit can greatly expand your purchasing potential and raise your standard of living. For example, credit allows you to purchase expensive items now that you do not currently have enough cash to buy, and then pay for them over time. As a result, you can enjoy items like furniture and a car earlier in your life than you otherwise could. Making your payments on time then helps you establish a good credit record that will help you get loans in the future.

Credit can also provide emergency funds. A sudden need for cash can be solved by a **line of credit**, which is a pre-established amount that can be borrowed on demand with no collateral. To establish a line of credit, you fill out the application with a lender. Lenders examine your income and financial position and approve an amount that they believe you can repay. With a line of credit, money is always available should you need it.

Credit is convenient. Credit customers often get better service when they make a purchase because they can withhold payment until a problem is resolved. Regular charge customers receive advance notices of sales and special offers not available to the public, such as deferred billing. **Deferred billing** is a service available to charge customers whereby purchases are not billed to the customer until later. For example, merchandise purchased in October might not be billed until January, with no payment due until February.

The proof of purchase provided by a charge slip is usually more descriptive than a cash register receipt and helps in making adjustments when merchandise is returned. Finally, carrying a credit card is safer than carrying large sums of cash.

©GETTY IMAGES/PHOTODISC

Disadvantages of Credit

Use of credit also has disadvantages. For instance, credit purchases may cost more than cash purchases. Merchants must pay the credit card company for using the card in transactions, and they often pass this cost on to customers in the form of higher prices. In addition, an item purchased on credit and paid for over time costs more because of finance charges. A finance charge of 18 percent a year is 1½ percent a month. On a $1,000 balance, the finance charge would be $15 a month. The larger your balance and the longer you take to pay it off, the greater the finance charges.

When you use credit, you tie up future income. You have committed to making payments, perhaps for several years. Over that time, those funds are not available to you for buying other products you may need. This situation can put a strain on your budget.

What are some advantages and disadvantages of consumer credit?

Buying on credit can lead to overspending. You can get into trouble with credit if you buy more than you can pay back comfortably. At the end of the month, when the bills come in, you may be surprised at how much you have really spent. Using credit too much can result in debts so high that you can never pay them off, and may even lead to bankruptcy.

Global View

Traditionally, consumers in Thailand preferred to use cash when purchasing goods and services. This conservative attitude toward cashless transactions hindered consumer credit expansion. As of 2002, it was estimated that only 10% of the Thai population owned a credit card. Major card issuers then began aggressive marketing campaigns and promotional offers to entice new customers. With extensive incentives for consumers and a low minimum income threshold for credit card eligibility, many issuers witnessed considerable growth in their customer numbers.

Think Critically: What consumer benefits as well as problems might result from the boom in credit card use in Thailand?

✓ Check Your Understanding

1. Compare the use of credit today to its use in this country's early years.
2. Why is it important to make credit payments by the due date?
3. For you, what is the greatest advantage and greatest disadvantage of credit?

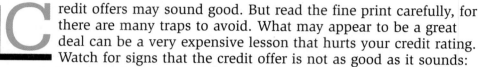

Issues in Your World

Credit Card Traps

Credit offers may sound good. But read the fine print carefully, for there are many traps to avoid. What may appear to be a great deal can be a very expensive lesson that hurts your credit rating. Watch for signs that the credit offer is not as good as it sounds:

1. *Low introductory rate.* Offers may be as low as 1% for a year. But the fine print may tell you that if you are late by even one day in making a payment, the rate will rise to 25–30% or more! This introductory rate may be subject to change without notice.

2. *Fixed percentage rate.* The offer may say the interest rate is fixed, which should mean that it will not go up. But the fine print may tell you that the fixed rate is subject to change without notice and that it can be "adjusted" (raised).

3. *Closed account rate.* You may see fine print that says "closed account rate." This is the rate you will be assessed if you close your account. These rates are often very high—25–30% or more! This tactic is used by credit card issuers to keep you from shopping around and closing your account when they raise their interest rate. You won't be able to "lock in" the lower rate you had previously agreed to pay.

4. *Late fees.* Most credit card issuers have late fees if you do not pay your account within the time specified. Often this timeframe is only 10–15 days. These late fees are bad enough. But if you read the fine print, you may discover that if your account is "late," the issuer will also raise your interest rate.

5. *Over-the-limit fees.* Card issuers will charge you a fee for exceeding your credit limit. This fee is added to your balance, and it will take even more money to pay the account down (remember, interest charges are increasing your balance daily). Fine print may tell you that if you go over the limit, your interest rate will increase.

To avoid being taken advantage of, read the credit offers carefully and compare them to offers by known lenders, such as your credit union or bank.

Think Critically

1. Look for a credit card offer in your mail. Then read the fine print. Make a list of all the potential "traps" you find.

2. Discuss credit offers with parents or others and ask their experience with credit offers. What did you learn?

Types and Sources of Credit

Goals
- List and describe the kinds of credit available.
- Describe and compare sources of credit.

▶ KINDS OF CREDIT

You will likely use several forms of credit throughout your life. Different types of credit are designed to meet different consumer needs.

Open-Ended Credit

Credit card accounts are open-ended forms of credit. **Open-ended credit** is an agreement to lend the borrower an amount up to a stated limit and to allow borrowing up to that limit again, whenever the balance falls below the limit. The borrower usually has a choice of repaying the entire balance within 30 days or repaying it over a number of months or years. Open-ended credit can be used again and again, as long as the balance owed does not exceed the limit.

OPEN 30-DAY ACCOUNTS

In an open *30-day credit agreement*, a consumer promises to pay the full balance owed each month. Travel-and-entertainment cards, such as American Express and Diner's Club, are examples of 30-day open-ended credit agreements. On all charges, the balance must be paid in full when the bill is received. There is no credit extended beyond the 30-day billing cycle. In some cases, the billing cycle may be less than 30 days. A 25-day billing period is common. These cards are widely accepted nationwide and overseas, usually have high or no credit limits, and provide instant purchasing power.

REVOLVING CREDIT ACCOUNTS

In a *revolving credit agreement*, a consumer has the option each month of paying in full or making payments at least as high as the stated minimum. The minimum payment is based on the amount of balance due. Most all-purpose credit cards, such as Visa, MasterCard, and Discover, are revolving credit agreements. Retail store cards, such as department store and gasoline company cards, are also based on revolving credit. Figure 16-1 shows a credit card statement for a revolving credit account.

CREDIT CARD TERMS

Credit card companies keep a record of transactions made on your account, and bill you at the end of each month for all purchases. If you pay off the total each month, you probably can avoid a finance charge. But remember—a credit card is a form of borrowing. It usually involves interest and other charges as well. Before selecting a credit card, learn which credit terms and conditions apply. Each affects the overall cost of the credit you will be using. Be sure to compare the following terms:

1. *Annual Percentage Rate.* The **annual percentage rate (APR)** is the cost of credit expressed as a yearly percentage. The Truth-in-Lending law requires lenders to include all loan costs in the APR. As a result, you can compare the APR of different lenders to find the best deal. The APR must be disclosed to you when you open the account and must be noted on each monthly bill you receive. Usually the APR is a variable rate, and it can be very high on credit cards.

2. *Free Period.* A free period—also called a *grace period*—allows you to avoid the interest charge by paying your current balance in full before the due date shown on your billing statement. If there is no free period of 10 to 25 days, the card issuer will impose an interest charge from the date you use your credit card or from the date each credit card transaction is posted to your account.

3. *Annual Fees.* Many credit card issuers charge an annual fee. The fee can range from $15 to $35 or more, and you must pay it whether or not you use the card.

4. *Transaction Fees and Late Fees.* A credit card also may involve other types of costs. For example, if you use an access check or pay by phone, or if you go over your limit or make your payment late, you are likely to be charged a fee.

5. *Method of Calculating the Finance Charge.* If your plan has no free period, or if you expect to pay for purchases over time, it is important to know how the card issuer will calculate your finance charge. This charge will vary, depending upon the method the card issuer used to figure your balance. The method used can make a difference, sometimes a big difference, in how much finance charge you will pay. Examples of how finance charges based on identical APRs can differ are explained in Chapter 18.

McAdams

Account Number	Payment Due Date	New Balance	Minimum Payment Due	Indicate Amount Paid
779 19 9171	05/24/--	$244.61	$20.00	

0 7 7 3 4 2 7 0 4 2 0 0 0 0 2 4 4 6 1 0 0 0 0 2 0 0 0 4   70

ADDRESS CHANGE

‖l‖ɪl‖l‖l‖ɪl‖ɪl‖l‖l‖l‖lɪɪɪɪl‖l‖ɪl‖l‖lɪɪɪɪl‖l‖ɪɪɪɪll

ELIZABETH SANCHEZ
3410 MAIN STREET
VANCOUVER WA 98684-0129

ADDRESS _____

CITY/STATE/ZIP _____

(AREA CODE) PHONE   5008440

Please return this portion
with your payment. Detach here ▼

- -

Account Number	779 19 9171

To avoid additional **FINANCE CHARGES** being applied to your current purchases on next month's statement, pay the new balance on this statement in full by the due date.

Page ☐1☐ of ☐1☐

Date	Store	Reference	Description	Charges	Payments Or Credits
3/28	021	108475936	SPECIAL CARE TREATMENT COSMETICS	60.00	
4/07	021	108476335	COSMETICS CLEANSERS, TONERS, MOISTURIZERS	80.00	
4/12	311	071070078	PAYMENT-THANK YOU		189.16
4/24	097		FINANCE CHARGE	4.61	

ANNIVERSARY TO DATE PURCHASES $1,853.39
ANNIVERSARY TO DATE DIVIDEND $5.96
YOU WILL EARN A 1% DIVIDEND ON MCADAMS PURCHASES
MADE PRIOR TO YOUR NEXT BILLING.
DIVIDEND WILL BE CREDITED ON YOUR JUNE 19-- STATEMENT.

Previous Balance	+ New Charges	– Payments Or Credits	Average Daily Balance (For Finance Charge Only)	+ FINANCE CHARGE (50¢ Minimum)	+ Late Payment Fee	= New Balance
289.16	140.00	189.16	307.19	4.61		244.61

Billing Date This Month	Payment Due Date	**PERIODIC RATE**	**ANNUAL PERCENTAGE RATE**	Credit Line	Amount Past Due	Minimum Payment Due
04/24/--	05/24/--	1.50	18.00	2,000		20.00

Payments or credits received after payment due date will appear on next month's statement. For customer service inquiries, please call 1-800-555-6200. **AMOUNTS DUE HEREUNDER MAY BE ASSIGNED. NOTICE: SEE REVERSE SIDE FOR IMPORTANT INFORMATION.**

McAdams

Closed-End Credit

To pay for very expensive items, such as cars, furniture, or major appliances, consumers often use closed-end credit. **Closed-end credit** is a loan for a specific amount that must be repaid, in full, including all finance charges, by a stated due date. Unlike open-end credit, closed-end agreements do not allow continuous borrowing or varying payment amounts. The borrower takes out a closed-end loan for a particular amount and then repays it with fixed payments, or *installments*, that include principal and interest. As a result, closed-end credit is sometimes called an *installment loan*.

The contract for closed-end credit tells, among other things, the amount loaned, the total finance charge, and the amount of each payment. Usually a down payment is required, and the product purchased with the loan becomes collateral to assure repayment.

©GETTY IMAGES/PHOTODISC

What kinds of businesses expect payment in full by a certain time limit?

Service Credit

Almost everyone uses some type of **service credit**, which is an agreement to have a service performed now and pay for it later. Your telephone and utility services are provided for a month in advance; then you are billed. Many businesses—including doctors, lawyers, hospitals, dry cleaners, and repair shops— extend service credit. Terms are set by individual businesses. Some of these creditors do not impose finance charges on unpaid account balances, but they do expect regular payments to be made until the bill is paid in full. Others, such as utility and telephone companies, expect payment in full within a time limit. However, they usually offer a budget plan as well, which allows you to average bills to get lower monthly payments.

► SOURCES OF CREDIT

Credit is a service consumers buy. As with other things you buy, it pays to shop around to get the best deal.

Retail Stores

Retail stores are stores that sell directly to consumers, such as department stores, restaurants, and most service businesses. Many retail stores offer their own credit cards. These cards are accepted only at those stores. Store credit customers often receive discounts, advance notice of sales, and other privileges not offered to cash customers. Most retail stores also accept credit cards issued by major credit card companies. Accepting credit cards helps retail stores attract customers, because people like to shop where they can buy on credit.

Credit Card Companies

You may receive credit offers directly from credit card issuers, such as Visa, MasterCard, American Express, and Discover. These all-purpose cards are generally accepted nationwide and even internationally. You can also get an all-purpose credit card through your financial institution or from various organizations. *Affinity cards* are credit cards sponsored by professional organizations, college alumni associations, and some members of the travel industry. An affinity card issuer often donates a portion of the annual fees or charges to the sponsoring organization, or qualifies you for free travel or other bonuses. Although these cards may show the name of the organization, they are actually issued and serviced by a credit card company.

When you have an all-purpose credit card, you have an automatic line of credit up to the limit of the card. A *cash advance* is money borrowed against the credit card limit. In other words, you are taking out a cash loan from your line of credit rather than making a purchase with it. You can access this money at a teller machine, at a customer service desk in your bank, or by writing an *access check* against the credit card account. Access checks look just like regular checks. They are supplied by the credit card company and, when written, are treated like a purchase. You must then pay back the cash advance in the same way that you pay for credit card purchases.

Banks and Credit Unions

In addition to offering credit cards, commercial banks and credit unions make closed-end loans to individuals and companies. They loan money to consumers for specific purchases, such as a home, car, or vacation. Interest on closed-end loans tends to be lower than on credit cards.

Credit unions make loans to their members only. Interest rates are generally lower than those charged by banks because credit unions are nonprofit and are organized for the benefit of members. Credit unions are more willing to make loans because the members who are borrowing also have a stake in the success of the credit union.

VIEWPOINTS

Some consumers are loyal to particular financial institutions, such as their banks, and obtain credit services from those institutions even if the rates and fees are higher than elsewhere. Other consumers shop around and may switch back and forth if they find better deals.

Think Critically: What advantages do you see to establishing an exclusive relationship with one financial institution? Are there disadvantages? What advantages are there to always shopping around? Are there disadvantages?

Finance Companies

Often called small loan companies, *finance companies* usually charge high interest rates for the use of their money. The reason for the high rates is that finance companies are willing to take risks that banks and credit unions will not take. In many cases, people who are turned down by banks and credit unions can get loans at finance companies. Finance companies are second only to banks in the volume of credit extended.

There are two types of finance companies. A *consumer finance company* makes mostly consumer loans to customers buying consumer durables. Consumer durables are items expected to last several years, such as an automobile, refrigerator, or stereo. (Non-durable goods, such as food products, are consumed in a few days or months.) Well-known consumer finance companies include Household Finance and Beneficial Finance.

The second type of company is the manufacturer-related *sales finance company* that makes loans through authorized representatives. For example, General Motors Acceptance Corporation (GMAC) finances General Motors automobile dealers and their customers. Both types of finance companies borrow money from banks and lend it to consumers at higher rates.

Finance companies take more risks than banks. Therefore, they must be more careful to protect their loans. If you do not make your payments when due, you can expect a call from someone at the finance company, who will ask for an explanation. The company will stay in constant contact with you until you make your payments as agreed. You can expect phone calls, letters, and even personal visits if you deviate even slightly from the agreed-upon payment schedule.

High interest rates are another form of protection for the finance company. The Uniform Small-Loan Law in most states permits loans of up to $5,000 and allows interest rates of up to 42 percent a year. The growth of finance companies is the result of efforts to eliminate **loan sharks**—unlicensed lenders who charge illegally high interest rates. Nevertheless, it is difficult to eliminate such practices, which take advantage of the poorest members of society who can least afford to pay.

Usury laws set maximum interest rates that may be charged for loans. In states where usury laws exist, finance companies charge the maximum. Where no usury laws exist, finance companies charge as much as the customer is willing to pay. When an emergency or other extreme need arises, consumers often feel forced to pay these higher rates to get the money they need.

Pawnbrokers

A **pawnbroker** is a legal business that makes high-interest loans based on the value of personal possessions pledged as collateral. Possessions that are readily salable (such as guns, cameras, jewelry, radios, TVs, and coins) are usually acceptable collateral. The customer brings in an item of value to be appraised. The pawnbroker then makes a loan for considerably less than the appraised value of the item. Some pawnshops give only 10 to 25 percent of the value of the article. Most give no more than 50 or 60 percent.

For example, if you have a ring appraised at $500, you could probably borrow between $50 and $250 with the ring as collateral. You would turn the ring over to the pawnbroker and receive a receipt and a certain length of time—from two weeks to six months—to redeem the ring by paying back the loan plus interest. If you do not pay back the loan and claim the ring, the pawnbroker will sell it in the pawnshop and keep the proceeds. Property taken in by a pawnbroker is considered collateral for the loan because it is something of value that may be sold if you fail to pay off the loan.

©GETTY IMAGES/PHOTODISC

What do pawnbrokers usually accept as collateral? Why?

Private Lenders

The most common source of cash loans is the private lender. Private lenders include your parents, other relatives, friends, and so on. Private lenders may or may not charge interest.

Other Sources of Consumer Credit

Life insurance policies can be used as an alternate source of consumer credit. As some life insurance policies build cash value, policyholders can borrow at low interest rates against the value of their policy. The loan does not have to be repaid, but interest will be charged; and the amount of the loan will reduce the value of the life insurance policy. (See the section on life insurance in Chapter 27.)

If you have a certificate of deposit with a financial institution, you can borrow money against the certificate. The certificate is used as collateral, and the interest rate charged is usually only 2 to 5 percent above the interest rate you are receiving on the certificate. If you cash in the certificate before maturity, you incur a penalty. If you borrow money using the certificate as collateral, you get a moderate rate of interest on the loan, and the certificate retains its full value.

✓Check Your Understanding

1. What is a revolving credit agreement?
2. Why should you get a bank loan rather than a loan from a finance company?

Chapter Assessment

SUMMARY

16.1
* Credit began here when the U.S. grew from a bartering society to a currency exchange economy and manufactured products became available.
* Early forms of credit were accounts at the general store, offered by store owners to customers they knew and trusted.
* Today, credit has become a way of life.
* To borrow, you must have sufficient capital and often collateral to pledge as security for the loan.
* For the privilege of using credit, you will pay a finance charge.
* Advantages of credit are the ability to buy now and pay later, a source of emergency funds, deferred billing, receipts as proof of purchase, and the safety of not having to carry a lot of cash.
* Disadvantages of credit are higher product prices, finance charges, decreased ability to spend in the future, and the tendency to overspend.

16.2
* Open-ended credit allows you to borrow again and again, up to your set limit.
* The finance charge is the total dollar cost of credit, including interest and fees.
* The annual percentage rate is the cost of credit expressed as a percentage.
* Closed-end credit is a loan for a specific amount that must be repaid, including finance charges, by a due date. Lenders generally require payment in monthly installments.
* Sources of credit include retail stores, credit card companies, banks, credit unions, finance companies, pawnbrokers, private lenders, and life insurance policies.
* Loan sharks are unlicensed lenders who charge illegally high rates and prey on people who can least afford to pay.
* Usury laws protect consumers from unfairly high interest rates.

Directions

Can you find the definition for each of the following terms used in Chapter 16?

annual percentage rate (APR)	finance charge
capital	line of credit
closed-end credit	loan sharks
collateral	open-ended credit
credit	pawnbroker
deferred billing	service credit
	usury laws

1. Money borrowed to buy something now, with the agreement to pay for it later.

2. An agreement to have a service performed now and pay for it later.

3. Laws setting maximum interest rates that may be charged for loans.

4. A legal business that makes high-interest loans based on the value of personal possessions pledged as collateral.

5. A pre-established amount that can be borrowed on demand with no collateral.

6. A service to credit customers whereby purchases are not billed for several months.

7. Unlicensed lenders who charge illegally high interest rates.

8. An agreement to lend the borrower an amount up to a stated limit and to allow borrowing up to that limit again, whenever the balance falls below the limit.

9. A loan for a specific amount that must be repaid, in full, including all finance charges, by a stated due date.

10. Property owned that is worth more than the owner's debt.

11. Property pledged to assure repayment of a loan.

12. Total dollar amount of all interest and fees you pay for the use of credit.

13. The cost of credit expressed as a yearly percentage.

REVIEW FACTS AND IDEAS

1. When credit first began in this country, did loans have high interest rates?

2. How has credit affected the American economy?

3. How does collateral help assure repayment of a loan?

4. List several advantages of using credit.

5. List several disadvantages of using credit.

6. What are two kinds of open-ended credit?

7. How is open-ended credit different from installment (closed-end) credit?

8. Identify common credit card terms and explain how each affects borrowing costs.

9. Why does the law require lenders to include all loan costs in the APR?

10. List seven major sources of credit for consumers.

11. Give three examples of service credit.

12. Why do credit unions offer lower interest rates on loans than do commercial banks?

13. How are consumer finance companies different from sales finance companies?

14. Why do finance companies charge high interest rates on their loans?

15. Explain how pawnbrokers work.

1. Give an example of a situation in which you would use collateral when making a purchase on credit.

2. How does your family make use of credit? Do you see credit use in your family as a good or bad thing? Explain your answer.

3. Do you think consumers are being unfair when they accept a "free ride" based on a "grace period" for credit cards? Give reasons for your answer.

4. Companies and organizations that offer credit cards compete for your credit card business by offering "low introductory rates." Search the Internet for offers of a special deal to new credit card customers. What is the "low introductory rate"? Now read the fine print. What would your rate be later, after the introductory period? At this regular rate, how much finance charge would you have to pay on a $1,000 balance each month? How much would the finance charge be if you maintained a $1,000 balance all year?

5. One major advantage of credit is that it helps consumers deal with emergencies. How does this advantage have special meaning where service credit is concerned?

6. If you were going into business for yourself, you would have to decide whether or not to accept credit cards from customers. Explain the points in favor of both positions.

7. Would it be possible to live without ever using coins, paper money, or checks? Explain how you might live on credit alone.

8. Does your state have usury laws? You can find out by consulting a current almanac or other references at your library or on the Internet. Identify some of the finance rates that states allow, including your state and neighboring states.

Solve Problems ⊕ Explore Issues

1. Suppose that your elderly neighbors have never used credit. When they were young, their families lost their life savings during bad economic times, and they have never trusted others enough to pay for anything except with cash. What types of problems can result from not using credit? What would be your advice to them, knowing that they have a good income from investments and have no need to buy on credit?

2. Interview three or four adults about credit. Ask them the following questions. Prepare a short report from what you learn.
  a. How do you feel about the use of credit?
  b. Do you use credit cards, such as store credit cards or all-purpose credit cards?
  c. Do you think the interest rates charged by stores and credit card companies on unpaid balances are reasonable?
  d. What are some typical interest rates that you have experienced?
  e. How would you advise a young person just starting out about credit?

3. Do you feel that the advantages of using credit outweigh the disadvantages? Write a paper of no more than one page, either defending the use of credit or explaining why it should be avoided.

4. A friend of yours wishes to buy a new car. She has picked one out at a local dealer but has only enough money to make a down payment. She asks your advice about where she can finance the balance of her loan for $10,000. What will you tell her? Explain.

5. Your cousin Tyler needs $100 immediately. He has a portable stereo worth at least $800 and wants to take it to a pawnbroker. Explain to him how much he can borrow against the stereo, and what will happen with pawnbroker credit.

*For related activities and links, point your browser to **www.mypf.swlearning.com***

Credit Records and Laws

TERMS TO KNOW

credit history	character	discrimination
credit bureau	capacity	debt collector
credit report	credit rating	

Consider This. . .

Vongsa is a full-time student and works part-time on weekends and during the summer. She has been able to save a little money and now, at age 16, she is learning to drive.

"I'd like to buy my own car," she told her friend Bang Chau. "That way I can drive myself to work. If I had my own car, I could work after school too, and I'd have a way to get to more school activities. As it is, I depend on my mom to get me everywhere. She also works, so the car isn't always available to take me places. To get a car, I'll have to get a loan. My mom says I'll be establishing credit, but because I don't have any credit already, she'll probably have to co-sign for me to get my first car loan."

Establishing Good Credit

Goals
- Discuss the importance and purpose of credit records.
- Describe the five Cs of credit.
- Explain how to get started using credit.

▶ CREDIT RECORDS

Before granting you credit, a *creditor* (a person or company that gives you credit) will ask about your past credit performance: Did you pay your bills on time? Did you pay your debts according to the loan agreement? How much total credit did you receive? How much do you owe now and how large are your payments? Your **credit history** is the complete record of your borrowing and repayment performance. This record will provide answers to these questions and thus help the creditor determine your ability to pay new debts.

Your Credit File

Every person who uses credit has a credit history on file at a credit bureau. A **credit bureau** is a company that gathers, stores, and sells credit information to business subscribers. Maintaining credit files is big business. Credit bureaus assemble and distribute detailed credit information concerning an estimated 150 million consumers. When you open a new credit account with a business, a credit clerk at the business keys into a computer the relevant information from your application, along with details about the initial credit transaction. Then each time you use credit or make a payment, the business records the transaction. Once a month, the business electronically transmits the accumulated data about your borrowing and repayments to one or more of the three big national credit bureaus listed in Figure 17-1 (page 408). The credit bureau enters the information into your file and stores it under your social security number for identification. Local and regional credit bureaus hook into the Big Three's computer networks, making everybody's files widely accessible.

TransUnion
P.O. Box 2000
Chester, PA 19022
(800) 888-4213
www.transunion.com

Experian
475 Anton Blvd
Costa Mesa, CA 92626
(714) 830-7000
www.experian.com

Equifax
P.O. Box 740241
Atlanta, GA 30374
(800) 685-1111
www.equifax.com

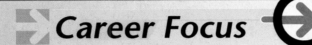

Career Focus

Bill and account collectors keep track of accounts that are overdue and attempt to collect payment on them. Some are employed by third-party collection agencies, while others work directly for the original creditors, such as department stores, hospitals, or banks. A high school education is typically the minimum requirement for these collectors. They generally receive training in telephone techniques, negotiation skills, and the laws governing the collection of debt. Collectors must pay attention to detail, be discreet, and be computer literate.

For more information, refer to the *Occupational Outlook Handbook* at www.bls.gov or search the Internet using such key words as "careers," "jobs," and "account collector."

Credit bureaus issue credit reports about consumers. A **credit report** is a written statement of a consumer's credit history, issued by a credit bureau to its business subscribers. You can order a copy of your credit report online at the credit bureau's Web site or by writing to the bureau. You should check your local telephone book for the names and addresses of credit bureaus in your area that also can provide a credit report about you. Ordinarily, a credit bureau will charge $5 to $15 to give you your credit file information. When you are denied credit, you can get a free credit report if you ask within 30 days of being denied.

How Information Is Gathered and Used

Credit bureaus gather information from businesses, called *subscribers*, who pay a monthly fee to the credit bureau. Each subscriber supplies information about its accounts with customers—names, addresses, credit balances, on-time payment record, and so forth. Credit bureaus also gather information from many other sources. Articles about consumers found in local newspapers are clipped and added to files. Public records are searched for information to add to a file. When someone applies to a business for credit, the business asks the credit bureau for the applicant's credit report. Information in the credit report is then used as the basis for granting or denying credit. Usually credit grantors (banks and retail businesses) and employers, landlords, and insurance companies have an interest in credit reports. Before entering into a financial agreement with someone, they want evidence that the person is financially responsible.

©GETTY IMAGES/PHOTODISC

Types of Information Stored

Any public information becomes part of your credit record. For example, if you fail to pay your property taxes, file for bankruptcy, file for a divorce, or apply for a marriage license, this information will appear in your credit record. Birth announcements published in newspapers, job promotions, lawsuits, and other visible activities are recorded. When you fill out a credit application, information requested such as occupation, length of employment, spouse's name and occupation, residence, length of occupancy, number of children and other dependents, and other related data is sent to the credit bureau by the subscriber.

Why might you want to order a copy of your credit report?

▶ CREDITWORTHINESS

Before potential creditors will grant credit to you, they must determine whether you are a good risk—that you are *creditworthy*. A person who is considered creditworthy usually meets five basic qualifications, called the five *C*s of credit: character, capacity, capital, conditions, and collateral.

1. *Character: Will you repay the debt?* **Character** is a responsible attitude toward living up to agreements, often judged on evidence in the person's credit history. If you have character, you pay your bills on time, and your credit history will show it. Creditors often use *stability* as a measure of character as well. For example, a person who has moved six times during the past year might not be considered a good credit risk.

2. *Capacity: Can you repay the debt?* The financial ability to repay a loan with present income is known as **capacity**. Before lending you money, creditors want to make certain that your income is sufficient to cover your current expenses each month plus the payments on the new loan.

3. *Capital: Is the creditor fully protected if you fail to repay? Capital* is property you possess that is worth more than your debts. In other words, when you add up all that you own (assets) and subtract all that you owe (liabilities), the difference (net worth or capital) should be sufficient to ensure payment of your debt.

4. *Conditions: What general economic conditions can affect your repayment of debt?* The state of the economy can affect your ability to repay. For example, if the economy is slowing and many people in your geographic area are losing their jobs, creditors may be less willing to loan to you. If you lose your job, you may not be able to meet your payments. Therefore, creditors want to know the following: How secure is your job? How secure is the firm you work for? How is the employment situation in your geographic location and in your occupation?

5. *Collateral: What assets back up your promise to pay? Collateral* is property pledged to assure repayment of a loan. Collateral protects creditors, making them more willing to lend to you. If you do not repay your debt as agreed, they can sell the collateral to collect on the debt.

▶ GETTING STARTED WITH CREDIT

Establishing a good credit record is a slow process. It can take several years of responsible money management to prove your creditworthiness.

Begin with a Savings Account

Open a savings account. Start at a financial institution that will not charge you a monthly fee when your savings account balance is small. Many banks allow minors to establish accounts with small balances and waive normal fees charged to other depositors. Also, choose a financial institution that has full services available as you prove yourself: checking accounts, loans, and credit cards. Each month or pay period, make a deposit to your savings account. Keep your account growing through regular saving.

Open a Checking Account

As soon as you have enough money in your savings account to allow you a little "cushion," open a checking account. This will provide a convenient method of paying your bills when you have credit accounts and will serve as a record-keeping system for your budget. Choose a checking plan that is the least expensive and most convenient for you. Then carefully manage your checking account. Do not write checks when your account contains insufficient funds to cover them. Bouncing checks will tarnish your creditworthiness. Record all your transactions immediately in your checkbook register and balance your checkbook as soon as you receive your statement. In this way, you will always know how much is in your account, so that you won't bounce a check accidentally.

Open a Store Credit Account

Your parent or guardian may need to serve as co-signer to help you open your first credit account. A *co-signer* is someone who promises to pay if the borrower fails to pay. Many stores will allow you to open a small account with a responsible adult as co-signer. Make small purchases on your new account and pay the bills promptly, using your checking account. Be sure to make your monthly payments on or before the due date. If you mail your payment, allow sufficient time for your payment to arrive before the due date. Never pay late!

©GETTY IMAGES/PHOTODISC

What kind of savings account should you open if you want to establish a good credit record?

Get a Small Loan

Take out a small loan from the financial institution where you have your savings and checking accounts. Use the money to buy something you really need. Then pay back the loan as agreed. Make early payments if possible. A six-month loan is sufficient. Again, you may need to rely on your parents or another adult with a good credit record to co-sign your first loan.

Apply for a Credit Card

With credit established for a couple of years, a part-time job, and a few credit references, you might now be eligible for a credit card, such as a VISA or MasterCard. Check the application carefully and ask about the income limit. If you do not make enough money to qualify for the card, do not apply until you do. It's safer to apply for a card with your bank or credit union. They will have brochures explaining the terms and conditions and you will be less likely to be hit with high interest rates or fees. Once you have your first credit card and you make the payments without fail, you will find it easy to obtain additional credit.

✅Check Your Understanding

1. How do credit bureaus gather information for your credit file?
2. What does "creditworthiness" mean?
3. Why is it important to make payments on time?

Teenage Credit

Many businesses are finding it financially rewarding to offer credit to teenagers. The logic is simple! Teenagers have a lot of money to spend, whether it is earned or supplied by parents. Because teenagers make many buying decisions, from clothing to automobiles, they are a market worth targeting.

Retail businesses that sell merchandise to teenagers are the first to admit that their teenage customers are important to them. By extending credit to teens, they are winning loyalty and at the same time helping teens get established with credit.

A typical teenage credit account might begin at age 16. The applicant (teenager) should have some steady source of income, whether it is from part-time, full-time, or summer jobs, or from parents. In most cases, the teenager needs permission from her or his parents. Permission is expressed in the form of a parent's signature as *co-signer* on the account. What this means to the parent is this: If the teenager fails to make the payments, the parent is responsible not only for the payments, but also for the entire balance owed.

Why would parents consider such a deal? Teenagers would be turned down if they asked for credit in their own name. A parent's signature on the credit application allows the credit grantor to rely on the parent's credit rating at first.

Typically, teen credit accounts also have a low credit limit, or maximum amount that they can spend on credit. However, even a $300 credit limit would allow a teenager to charge purchases, pay them off responsibly, and build a good credit record. By keeping the credit limit low, merchants and parents are assured that young people just beginning to use credit won't get carried away and get into debt trouble.

Think Critically

1. Do stores in your area extend credit to teenagers? If so, under what conditions?

2. Would you like to get established in credit early? How would you pay for purchases you make?

3. Pick several stores where you would like to have a credit account. Why did you choose these stores?

Lesson 17.2

Credit Ratings and Legal Protection

Goals
- **Describe credit ratings and a point system for determining creditworthiness.**
- **Outline the contents of a credit report.**
- **Discuss the protections provided by the major credit laws.**

▶ CREDIT RATINGS

Credit bureaus give each consumer a **credit rating**, which is a measure of creditworthiness based on an analysis of the consumer's financial history. Different bureaus use different rating systems, but a point system is common. In a *point system*, the bureau assigns points based on factors such as amount of current debt, number of late payments, number and types of open accounts, current employment, amount of income, and so on. Business subscribers then use these scores as part of their decision to grant or not grant credit. Your score is based on data provided to credit bureaus. If the data is wrong, so is your score.

Another rating system, which is accepted by many creditors, rates consumers according to how reliably they pay back money borrowed or charged. Credit bureaus merely supply credit files (names of customers, account balances, and payment records) to their subscribers, and the subscribers make their own rating decisions. Consumers may earn ratings such as excellent, good, fair, or poor.

To earn an *excellent credit rating*, sometimes called an *A Rating*, a customer must pay bills before the due date. If a payment is due on the fifth of the month, it must be received *before* the fifth. An excellent rating also means that the customer is well established (has used credit successfully for many years), has not missed any payments, and has made larger payments than the minimum amount required (paying off debts early).

To earn a *good credit rating*, which is designated a *B Rating*, a customer must pay bills on the due date or within a ten-day grace period. That is, if the payment is due on the first of the month, it must be received no later than the tenth of the month. (When a bill is paid within ten days of its due date, this is considered an automatic grace period.) A good customer pays around the due date, but never outside the grace period, and does not miss any payments.

A *fair credit rating* is earned by a customer who usually pays all bills within the grace period, but occasionally takes longer. Late charges are sometimes applied, but normally no reminder is needed. This person is often described as slow in paying but fairly dependable.

People with a *poor credit rating* are usually denied credit because their payments are not regular. They miss some monthly payments, and they must be reminded frequently. In many cases, they have failed entirely to pay back a debt, have filed for bankruptcy, or have otherwise shown that they are not a good credit risk.

▶ CREDIT REPORTS

Credit files are updated continuously, and information stays in the file for seven years. In bankruptcy cases, information stays in the file for 10 years. Credit reports legally may be requested for investigations of credit applications, employment applications, and insurance matters. Reports from different credit bureaus may be arranged differently, but they will contain sections similar to those shown in Figure 17-2. These sections are described below.

1. *Summary of Information.* This first section is a summary of negative and positive items. It tells the subscribers what to look for as they go through the information that follows. Negative items are those that could harm your ability to get credit. Accounts in good standing are those that are favorable to your credit.

2. *Public Record Information.* This section lists information found in public records. You would expect to find any lawsuits, judgments, bankruptcy, marriage, divorce, adoption, and other public information available to anyone who searches public records.

3. *Credit Information.* This section lists the credit accounts, including department stores, credit cards, and other loans, that have been reported to credit bureaus. It reports details such as each account's high and payment status.

4. *Account Detail.* This section shows the monthly balances of accounts. It also lists the credit limits that have been reported.

5. *Requests for Credit History.* This section lists every business that has sought information from your credit file—requests by potential employers, creditors, insurance companies, and others, along with requests that you may have made to inspect your credit records.

6. *Personal Information.* This section lists the personal information that you have given when applying for credit or that is available through public records. It includes your name and previous

What kind of credit information can be found in a credit report?

©GETTY IMAGES/PHOTODISC

UNIT 4 • Credit Management

figure **17-2**

PERSONAL CREDIT REPORT

Prepared for	*Report Date*	*Report Number*	**Summary of Information:**	
Jane Smith	June 1, 20--	108881	Potentially negative items:	
			Public records	2
			Accounts with creditors	2
			Accounts in good standing:	3

Public Record Information:

Source	Date Filed	Responsibility	Liability Amount	Comments
1. Jess County Courthouse	3/2003	Joint	$5,000	District Court complaint (defendant)
2. U.S. District Court	6/2000	Joint	$85,000	Bankruptcy discharged 11.97

Credit Information:

Source	Date Opened Last Report	Responsibility	Type/ Payment	High Amount	Status
3. Fidelity Bank (VISA)	6/1999	Individual	Revolv. $100 min.	$5,000	Late 2 pmts
4. CC & C Credit	10/2000	Individual	Install. $200/mo.	$8,500	Late charges-3
5. U.S. Finance Co.	3/2004	Joint	Install. $350/mo.	$18,000	Current

Account Detail:

Source	Date/Balance
6. U.S. Finance Co.	3/2004 $0 4/2004 $17,850 5/2004 $17,700 6/2004 $17,500 7/2004 $17,250 8/2004 $17,000
7. Merlo's Dept. Store	5/2003 $0 6/2003 $500 6/2003 $850 7/2003 $700 8/2003 $900 9/2003 $1,000 10/2003 $800 11/2003 $900 12/2003 $1,000 1/2004 $900 2/2004 $700 3/2004 $500 4/2004 $300 5/2004 $100 6/2004 $0

Between 5/2003 and 6/2004 your credit limit was $2,500.

Others Who Have Requested Your Credit History:
11/2003 Bill's Frame Shop (employment check)
2/2004   ABCD Mortgage Co. (related to real estate offer)
8/2004   Art's Motors (car loan application)

Requests Initiated by You:
5/2004   Credit report for denial of credit

Personal Information:
Names: Jane L. Smith
            Jane Louise Smith
            J. L. Smith

Social Security Number: 541-00-9999

Residences: 123 Main Street   Single-family house (owned)   4488 West Melody Lane   Condominium (rental)
                Clio, CA 90001   Brighton, NJ 02411

Date of Birth: 9.23.1961   *Driver's License Number*:   CA0948X23
Telephone Numbers: 503.444.3331
                            253.622.4441
Spouse's Name: John B. Smith
Employers: Cranston Bakery (Partner) $48,000 salary, reported 3/2/2004
                   4480 West Palm Beach
                   Clio, CA 90022

                   McGraw School District $37,000 salary, reported 2/1/1999
                   42 Maple Wood
                   Clinton, NY 00442

names, your contact information, whether you own or rent, your date of birth and driver's license number, your spouse's name, your employers and salaries with each one, and your social security number.

Global View

Visa International is developing payment technologies that will make it possible to make purchases over the Internet using mobile "e-devices." Visa has launched a global e-devices initiative to ensure that Visa customers will be able make payments with their Visa cards and access online financial resources anytime, anywhere using any Internet-capable device.

Think Critically: What benefits do you see with Visa's global e-device? What drawbacks?

◤ CREDIT LAWS

The government has passed a number of laws to protect consumers from unfair credit practices. Each law was intended to remove some of the problems and confusion surrounding the use of credit. Together, these laws set a standard for how individuals are to be treated in their daily credit dealings. Several of these laws are summarized on the following pages.

Consumer Credit Protection Act

The Consumer Credit Protection Act of 1968, known as the Truth-in-Lending Law, requires lenders to fully inform consumers about all costs of a credit purchase before an agreement is signed. Lenders must disclose the *finance charge*, which is the total dollar amount of all costs of the credit, including interest, service fees, and any other costs. Lenders must also state the *annual percentage rate (APR)*, the yearly percentage cost, calculated the same way by all lenders. Consumers can then use the APR to compare costs from different lenders. In addition, the law requires a grace period of three business days in which purchasers can change their mind about a credit agreement. The law also limits the consumer's liability to $50 after the consumer reports a credit card lost or stolen. There is no liability if the card is reported lost prior to its fraudulent use.

Fair Credit Reporting Act

If you are denied credit based on a credit report, inaccurate information in your file may be the cause. Under the Fair Credit Reporting Act, you have a right to know what is in your file and who has seen your file. A listing of requests made for your file for credit purposes in the last six months, and for employment purposes in the last two years, must be available to you. You may see your credit file at no charge within 30 days of a credit denial. A small fee may be charged in the event you want to see your file at any other time for any reason. You have the right to have inaccurate information investigated, corrected, and deleted from your file and have a new report furnished to creditors. Or, if the information is essentially correct, you can write your own statement giving your side of the story. Your statement must be added to the file.

Fair Credit Billing Act

Under the Fair Credit Billing Act, creditors must resolve billing errors within a specified period of time. A *statement* is an itemized bill showing charges, credits, and payments posted to your account during the billing period. Suppose your monthly statement showed purchases you did not make. Perhaps the company billed you for merchandise you ordered but did not receive. Creditors are required to have a written policy for correcting such errors.

If you believe your bill contains an error, act immediately. Do not write on the bill sent to you. On a separate piece of paper, write a letter explaining what you believe the problem to be. Write clearly and give a complete explanation of why you believe there is an error. Be specific about the amount in dispute, when you noticed the error, and any details relevant to the disputed amount. Figure 17-3 (page 418) shows an example of what you might say. Include your account number for identification and your contact information.

Your complaint must be in writing and mailed within 60 days after you receive the statement. The company must deal with the error or amount disputed in a reasonable manner and within a reasonable period of time. The creditor must acknowledge your complaint within 30 days. Within 90 days after receipt of your letter, the creditor must either correct the error or show why the bill is correct. Customers are still liable for amounts not disputed while the error dispute is being settled. Figure 17-4 (page 419) shows an example of one company's written policy for handling billing errors.

Equal Credit Opportunity Act

The Equal Credit Opportunity Act of 1975 was designed to prevent discrimination in the judgment of creditworthiness. **Discrimination** is

P.O. Box 4848
Milwaukee, WI 40412-4848
April 10, 20--

Melon Visa Bank
Customer Service Center
24 Chambers Street
New York, NY 02040-3112

RE: ACCOUNT # 4902 3818 4783 1783
      Disputed Amount: $289.00 Melvin's, 3/21/--

As stated in my telephone conversation with Melanie at your 800 number on April 9, 20--, I am hereby disputing the above charge.

Enclosed are copies of the invoice and other documentation for the purchase I made on March 21. I am disputing the amount listed because the service provided was unsatisfactory. I was charged $589, but within a week, the same operational problem occurred. I asked Melvin's to correct the problem, but they said it was not their responsibility and that they would charge me an additional $200 in parts and labor. As you can see, I then went to Barlow's, and they fixed the defective part for $300. Therefore, I believe that of the $589, which is the fair market value of the product, I should not have to pay more than $289 to Melvin's.

You can reach me at (201) 555-2372 on weekdays. My e-mail address is listed below. Please let me know if you need any further information.

Thank you,

Jackie B. Chen

JACKIE B. CHEN
Jackiebc@starnet.com

Enclosure

treating people differently based on prejudice rather than individual merit. There are many legitimate reasons for denying an applicant credit. Some reasons, however, are considered discriminatory. The act provides that:

1. Credit may not be denied solely because you are a woman, single, married, divorced, separated, or widowed.

2. Credit may not be denied specifically because of religion, national origin, race, color, or age (except as age may affect your ability to perform, or your ability to enter into contracts; for example, minors cannot be held liable for their contracts because they are not considered competent parties).

figure **17-4** ◄

IN CASE OF ERRORS OR INQUIRIES ABOUT YOUR BILL:

The Fair Credit Billing Act requires prompt resolution of errors. To preserve your rights, follow these steps:

1. Do not write on the bill. On a separate piece of paper, write a description as shown below. A telephone call will not preserve your rights.

   a. Your name and account number.
   b. Description of the error and your explanation of why you believe there is an error. Send copies of any receipts or supporting evidence you may have; do not send originals.
   c. The dollar amount of the suspected error.
   d. Other information that might be helpful in resolving the disputed amount.

2. Mail your letter as soon as possible. It must reach us within 60 days after you receive your bill.

3. We will acknowledge your letter within 30 days. Within 90 days of receiving your letter, we will correct the error or explain why we believe the bill is correct.

4. You will receive no collection letters or collection action regarding the amount in dispute; nor will it be reported to any credit bureau or collection agency.

5. You are still responsible for all other items on the bill and for the balance less the disputed amount.

6. You will not be charged a finance charge against the disputed amount, unless it is determined that there is not an error in the bill. In this event, you will be given the normal 25 days to pay your bill from the date the bill is determined to be correct.

3. Credit may not be denied because you receive public assistance (welfare), unemployment, social security, or retirement benefits.

4. Credit applications may be oral or written. However, a creditor is prohibited from asking certain questions, either orally or in writing, such as: Do you plan to have children? What is your ethnic origin? What church do you attend?

5. A creditor may not discourage you, in writing or orally, from applying for credit for any reason prohibited by the act (such as being divorced).

In addition to these prohibitions, the act states that creditors must notify you of any action taken on your credit application within 30 days of submission. If you are denied credit, the denial must be in writing and must list a specific reason for the denial. After a denial of credit, the creditor must keep for 25 months all information used to determine the denial and any written complaint from you regarding the denial. You have the right to appeal, and the creditor must give you the name and address of the federal agency that enforces compliance with the law.

Also, the act requires new accounts to reflect the fact that both husband and wife are responsible for payment. In this way, both spouses establish their own credit histories. Existing accounts should be changed to assure that the wife, as well as the husband, receives credit for the payment record.

©GETTY IMAGES/PHOTODISC

What law was designed to prevent discrimination in the judgment of credit-worthiness?

Fair Debt Collection Practices Act

The Fair Debt Collection Practices Act was designed to eliminate abusive collection practices by debt collectors. A **debt collector** is a person or company hired by a creditor to collect the overdue balance on an account. The fee charged by the debt collector is often half of the amount collected. The law prohibits use of threats, obscenities, and false and misleading statements to intimidate the consumer into paying. It also restricts the time and frequency of collection practices, such as telephone calls and contacts at place of employment. Debt collectors are required to verify the accuracy of the bill and give the consumer the opportunity to clarify and dispute it.

✓ Check Your Understanding

1. What are some things you can do to maintain a good credit rating?

2. What is the purpose of a credit report?

3. What should you do if you believe there is an error on your credit card statement?

Chapter Assessment

SUMMARY

17.1

* Your credit history is a complete record of your experience with credit.
* Credit bureaus collect information about consumers' credit transactions from businesses and prepare credit reports about individual consumers for their business subscribers.
* Businesses use a consumer's credit report to decide whether to grant credit.
* Businesses judge your creditworthiness based on the five Cs of credit: character, capacity, capital, conditions, and collateral.
* To start building a good credit history, follow these steps: open a savings account, open a checking account, open a store credit account, get a small loan, apply for a credit card.
* Make all payments on time or early. Never miss a payment.

17.2

* Many credit bureaus rate consumers' creditworthiness on a point system, assigning points based on debt, payment history, income, and other factors.
* Some businesses determine their own ratings based on credit histories supplied by the credit bureau.
* Credit reports give personal information about individual consumers, including information from public records, credit account details, and a list of requests to see the consumer's credit history.
* The Consumer Credit Protection Act (Truth-in-Lending Law) requires full disclosure of all costs of credit, including finance charge and APR.
* The Fair Credit Reporting Act gives you the right to inspect your credit file and to make changes or dispute information contained in the file.
* The Fair Credit Billing Act requires creditors to resolve billing errors within a reasonable time.

* The Equal Credit Opportunity Act prohibits discrimination in judgment of creditworthiness.
* The Fair Debt Collection Practices Act prohibits abusive collection practices by debt collectors.

REVIEW TERMS

Directions

Can you find the definition for each of the following terms used in Chapter 17?

capacity	credit rating
character	credit report
credit bureau	debt collector
credit history	discrimination

1. A person or company hired by a creditor to collect the overdue balance on an account.

2. A business that accumulates, stores, and sells credit information to business subscribers.

3. A responsible attitude toward living up to agreements, often judged on evidence in the person's credit history.

4. A written statement of a consumer's credit history, issued by a credit bureau to its business subscribers.

5. The financial ability to repay a loan with present income.

6. A complete record of a person's borrowing and repayment performance.

7. Treating people differently based on prejudice rather than individual merit.

8. A measure of creditworthiness based on an analysis of the consumer's financial history.

REVIEW FACTS AND IDEAS

1. What does a credit bureau do to earn money? Who pays for its services?

2. How do credit reports benefit lenders? How do they benefit borrowers?

3. What types of public records become a part of your credit record?

4. Why is it important to pay your bills when they are due rather than a few days late?

5. How could a negative credit report affect your financial future?

6. Why do creditors care about how long you have worked at your present job and about how many jobs you have had?

7. What kinds of entries on a credit report would indicate that the person has more debt than he or she can handle?

8. What are the five *C*s of credit?

9. List personal factors that creditors often consider.

10. What types of discrimination are unlawful in granting or denying credit?

11. What federal law protects consumers from unfair discrimination in credit?

12. Do you have a right to see your own credit file? Explain.

13. What is the purpose of the Truth-in-Lending Law?

14. What should you do if you are denied credit based on your credit file? What can you do if information in your credit file is basically correct but damaging to you as is?

15. What is the purpose of the Fair Credit Reporting Act?

16. What should you do if there is an error on your statement from a creditor?

APPLY YOUR KNOWLEDGE

1. With your instructor's permission, go to a local credit bureau and ask about the system the bureau uses for locating, storing, and using credit information. Write a one-page report describing the process. Be sure to include the credit rating system used and explain how customers are rated and by whom (the creditor or the credit bureau). Before visiting the credit bureau, prepare a list of questions to ask and call first to make an appointment.

2. Visit the Web site of one of the three major credit bureaus listed in Figure 17-1. In no more than one page, summarize what the bureau includes in its credit reports and outline the procedure you would have to follow to get a copy of your own report.

3. As a teenager, you would like to get started in establishing a good credit history. Based on your personal situation and the stores and banks in your area, prepare a plan that you might follow in getting started using credit.

4. What kinds of credit do you think you will be using in five years? How will you establish a good credit rating to be eligible for increasing credit limits and privileges?

5. You have filled out an application for credit at a local department store. The store has notified you that it cannot give you credit because you have a poor credit rating. What are your rights, and what are some things you should do? You have not paid late or missed any payments, and you have paid off previous debts as agreed. Suppose there is an error. What responsibilities does the credit bureau have to you?

6. Visit the Federal Reserve Board's Web site entitled "Consumer Handbook to Credit Protection Laws" at www.hsh.com/pamphlets/cons_handbook_credit.html. Summarize in a one-page, double-spaced report three consumer protection laws described there.

7. Describe what you must do if you believe a statement you receive from a creditor contains an error. Describe the process for error correction, including your responsibilities and time limits and the responsibilities and time limits of your creditor.

1. Obtain a credit application from a local merchant or national credit card company. On a separate piece of paper, list each question on the form in a column on the left. To the right of the column of questions, make another column. Indicate beside each question whether it is (a) a personal question, (b) a payment record question, (c) an employment stability question, or (d) an income question.

2. Your friend Lisa has just been turned down for credit. She works part-time and would like to buy on credit from a local department store. The department store stated lack of credit history as the reason for credit denial. Is there anything Lisa can do?

3. You have just received your monthly Visa bill. There is a charge on your bill of $42, but you have a receipt showing the amount should have been $24. You made the purchase at a local clothing store (you supply the name and address) one month ago. Write a letter to the bank that issued the Visa (choose a local bank) and explain the error.

4. Obtain a written error policy supplied by a local or national credit card company or other creditor. Companies that sell over the Internet should state their policy at their Web site. Compare the policy statement with Figure 17-4 and describe the similarities and differences.

5. Your friend DuWayne was denied credit, so he asked for a copy of his credit report from one of the national credit bureaus. On examination of the report, he discovered several errors. For example, the report showed a previous employer and account that he never had. It also showed a previous address in another state that was not correct. What can DuWayne do about this incorrect information?

6. Your neighbor recently purchased a refrigerator but was unable to continue making payments because he lost his job. In the last week he has had abusive telephone calls at home. A collector has come to your house looking for him and has made false and degrading comments about the neighbor's character. Your neighbor has volunteered to return the refrigerator, but the bill collector refuses and threatens him with public humiliation. What is your advice to your neighbor? What law protects him?

For related activities and links, point your browser to **www.mypf.swlearning.com**

Responsibilities and Costs of Credit

TERMS TO KNOW

garnishment
unused credit
rebate

fixed-rate loans
prime rate
simple interest

principal (loan)
down payment

Consider This. . .

Steve was well on his way to managing credit and taking the next steps, such as buying a house and making a commitment to long-term payments.

"I learned the hard way that all credit isn't created equal," he thought. "Some credit cards have annual fees, and others charge very high interest rates. I switched from credit accounts that didn't meet my needs. Now I have a group of cards and accounts that have no annual fees, low interest rates, and the kinds of rebates that benefit me. I keep my accounts paid off and use credit cards mainly for emergencies and convenience. It wasn't always so easy, though. When I wasn't careful, I ended up spending a lot of money impulsively that I could have used later to buy something I wanted more."

Using Credit Responsibly

Goals
- Describe the responsibilities of consumer credit.
- Discuss how to protect your credit card from fraud.
- Explain how you can reduce or avoid credit costs.

▶ RESPONSIBILITIES OF CONSUMER CREDIT

Once you have established credit, you have the responsibility to manage it carefully. Failure to take this responsibility seriously can result in having your credit limited or, in some cases, withdrawn. Because using credit is important to your financial future, you should be aware of your responsibilities to yourself and to creditors. In return, creditors have responsibilities to you, their customer.

Responsibilities to Yourself

As a credit user, you have a responsibility to yourself to use credit wisely and not get into debt beyond an amount you can comfortably repay. Never having enough money and always scrambling to make your next payment is a stressful way to live. If you can't meet your payments, a creditor may take you to court to have your wages garnished. **Garnishment** is a legal process that allows part of your paycheck to be withheld for payment of a debt. Your employer sends the amount directly to the creditor.

You are also responsible for checking out businesses before making credit purchases. Better Business Bureaus and Chambers of Commerce have information about businesses and complaints that have been filed against them.

You owe it to yourself to comparison shop. Don't buy on impulse. Check prices in various stores. Take the time to evaluate the product and your other options before buying. Be sure you are buying for the right reasons—because you have a need, rather than buying to impress people. Tying up future income should be done with careful planning to maximize your purchasing power.

Comparison shop for credit as well. Compare features, costs, and availability of credit and make wise choices. Become familiar with

©GETTY IMAGES/PHOTODISC

What responsibilities do you have to yourself as a credit user?

billing cycles, annual percentage rates, and any special charges related to each credit account. Learn about state and local laws regarding the use of credit.

Finally, as a credit user, you should have the right attitude about using credit. Enter into each transaction in good faith and with full expectation of meeting your obligations and upholding your good credit reputation.

Responsibilities to Creditors

When you open an account, you are entering into a relationship with a store, bank, or credit card company. You are pledging your honesty and sincerity in the use of credit.

You have the responsibility to limit your spending to amounts that you can repay according to the terms of the credit agreement. By signing a credit application, you agree to make all payments promptly, on or before the due date. In addition, you are responsible for reading and understanding the terms of all agreements, including finance charges, what to do in case of error, late fees, over-the-limit fees, and any other provisions of the agreement.

It is your responsibility to contact the creditor immediately when you find a problem with the bill or discover that the merchandise is defective. If an emergency prevents you from making a payment, you should contact the creditor to make arrangements to pay at a later date.

Creditors' Responsibilities to You

Creditors also have responsibilities to consumers to whom they grant credit. These responsibilities include the following:

1. Assisting consumers in making wise purchases by honestly representing goods and services, with all their advantages and disadvantages.

2. Informing customers about all rules and regulations (such as minimum payments and due dates), interest rates, credit policies, and fees.

3. Cooperating with established credit reporting agencies, making credit records available to the consumer, and promptly fixing mistakes in records when they occur.

4. Establishing and carrying out sound lending and credit policies that do not overburden or deceive customers. This includes setting reasonable guidelines for credit use to avoid extending additional credit to customers who cannot afford it.

5. Using reasonable methods of contacting customers who fail to meet their obligations and assisting them whenever possible with payment schedules and other means for solving credit problems.

PROTECTING YOURSELF FROM CREDIT CARD FRAUD

Credit card fraud costs businesses and consumers millions of dollars each year. The most common type of fraud is the illegal use of a lost or stolen credit card or of credit card information intercepted online. While the credit card holder's liability is limited to $50, the merchant is not protected from loss. Consequently, merchants often raise their prices to cover such losses.

Safeguarding Your Cards

It is your responsibility to protect your cards from unauthorized use. Here are some commonsense tips for doing so:

1. Sign your cards as soon as you receive them.

2. Carry only the cards you need.

3. Keep a list of your credit card numbers, their expiration dates, and the phone number and address of each card company in a safe place.

4. Notify creditors immediately by phone when your card is lost or stolen and follow up with a letter so that you have written evidence of the notification.

5. Watch your card during transactions and get it back as soon as you can.

6. Tear up any carbon or carbonless paper that contains account information.

7. Do not lend your card to anyone or leave it lying around.

8. Destroy expired cards by cutting them up.

9. Don't give credit card numbers and expiration dates by phone to people or businesses you don't know.

10. Keep your sales receipts and verify all charges on your credit card statements promptly. Use the procedure printed on your statement to question charges that you think are in error.

Protecting Your Cards Online

Buying on the Internet has opened new avenues for criminals to steal credit card information for illegal use. Software makers and online organizations are fighting back by constantly developing new ways to offer secure electronic transmission of customer information. There are some steps you can take as well to help protect your credit card and personal information during online transactions.

1. Deal only with companies online that you know and trust. If the retailer also has a physical "bricks-and-mortar" store, then it is

likely to be safer than an unknown merchant that exists only online.

2. When making an online transaction, always look for your browser's symbol that indicates a secure site before entering your personal information. For example, the Internet Explorer and Netscape browsers display a small closed-lock symbol on the bottom of your screen when you have entered a secure Web page. The symbol should appear whenever a Web site asks you to enter credit card and other personal information to make a purchase. Among other security measures, this symbol means that the information you enter will be *encrypted*, or put into code, before transmission. If you don't see the symbol, don't enter the information.

3. Legitimate online merchants clearly state their privacy policy, explaining how they use the information you provide and how they protect your privacy. Review the policy to make sure you are comfortable with it before dealing with that company.

4. Many sites offer assurance by displaying the seal of a nonprofit watchdog group, such as the Better Business Bureau or TRUSTe. Sites that follow the privacy principles set forth by these organizations are allowed to display their seal. This kind of oversight is not fully developed yet, so not all legitimate merchants display seals.

5. *Phishing* is a scam that uses online pop-up messages or e-mail to deceive you into disclosing personal information. "Phishers" send messages that appear to be from a business that you normally deal with, such as your Internet service provider. They ask you to verify your bank account number, password, credit card number, or other personal information. They may direct you to a Web site that looks like the real company site but isn't. Do not respond to e-mail requests for personal information or pop-up offers. Initiate all transactions yourself at sites you trust.

What are some ways in which you can protect your credit online?

◤ AVOIDING UNNECESSARY CREDIT COSTS

Credit can be helpful if you use it wisely. Before deciding whether to borrow money, ask yourself these three critical questions: Do I need credit? Can I afford credit? Can I qualify for credit? If you can answer "yes" to these questions, then follow these guidelines to minimize the cost of credit:

1. *Accept only the amount of credit that you need.* Although having credit available when you need it may seem comforting, unused credit can count against you. **Unused credit** is the remaining credit available to you—that is, your credit limit minus the amount you have already spent. For example, if the limit on your

credit card is $1,000 and you owe $200, your unused credit is $800. Other creditors may be reluctant to loan money to you because you could at any time charge the other $800, thereby reducing your ability to pay back another debt. Potential creditors, then, may view you as a bad risk because of your unused credit. Unused credit accounts are also temptations for you to use more credit than you need.

2. *Make more than the minimum payment.* Minimum payments result in maximum cost. They also mean remaining in debt for a very long time. For example, suppose you owe $5,000 on your credit card and make no additional credit purchases. Your rate is 18 percent, and you make the minimum payments (typically about 2 percent of the loan amount). It would take you nearly 33 years to pay off the loan. You would pay a total interest of about $12,000 for this $5,000 loan! If you put any additional purchases on your card during those 33 years, the cost would be even higher and the payoff time longer.

©GETTY IMAGES/PHOTODISC

3. *Do not increase credit spending when your income increases.* Instead of spending that extra income, put it into savings or invest it. Avoid the trap of increasing spending with each increase in your income. It is wiser to reduce existing debt or invest the additional income for future use.

Why is it a good idea to pay for small purchases with cash?

4. *Keep the number of credit cards to a minimum.* Most credit counselors recommend carrying no more than one or two credit cards. The more credit cards you have, the more temptation you have to make purchases. A major credit card, such as Visa or MasterCard, is good at most businesses, which eliminates the need for having numerous individual charge accounts.

5. *Pay cash for purchases under $25.* If you make yourself pay cash for small purchases, you won't be surprised with a big bill at the end of the month. Paying cash will help you realize how much you are spending. Consequently, you may buy less and only when you really need the item.

6. *Understand the cost of credit.* Think about how the finance charges, monthly payments, and length of time you will be committed to payments will affect your lifestyle. Consider how this commitment of future income to paying off debt might affect your budget in the months to come.

7. *Shop for loans.* The type and source of your loan will make a big difference in cost. Compare the cost of credit from three different sources. Plan your major purchases carefully. Never make such

decisions on the spur of the moment. Don't sit and figure costs in the lender's office. Go home, figure all costs, and consider the purchase carefully without the lender being present.

8. *Take advantage of rebate programs.* Many credit cards provide rebates or rewards. A **rebate** is a partial refund of an amount spent. For example, a credit card company might rebate a percentage of the amount you charged during a period of time. Some credit cards allow you to accumulate points that can be used for free hotel rooms, airline tickets, or car rentals. However, do not use cards just to get rebates! You could end up paying higher finance charges or accumulating more debt than you can comfortably repay.

VIEWPOINTS

Many credit card companies market their services aggressively to college students, offering free cards and other inducements. As a result, the number of college students with credit card debts has increased significantly over the past decade. Students may graduate owing thousands of dollars.

Think Critically: Do you think it should be so easy for students to obtain credit cards? What qualifications should students fulfill in order to get cards?

Check Your Understanding

1. List three responsibilities you have to your creditors.
2. List three responsibilities that creditors have to you.
3. List three things you can do to help avoid credit card fraud.

Maxing Out the Cards

Your credit cards are "maxed out" when there is no room left to charge. You cannot buy anything else on credit until you pay down the current balance. Maxing out is not a good idea. Here's why:

1. When you get really close to the top, it is very easy to "go over." Most credit card companies charge a fee for exceeding the card's credit limit. This fee may be $25 or more. Going over the limit also gives credit card issuers a reason to raise your interest rate.

2. In some cases, the credit card company will not honor charges that exceed the credit limit. It can be very embarrassing to try to use your credit card, only to have it rejected by the verification machine.

3. When your cards are maxed out, you are paying maximum interest and maximum monthly payments. At the same time, you cannot use the card because the balance is going down very slowly and a single charge might take the card over the top once again.

4. Having maxed-out credit cards does not look good on your credit report. It tells potential creditors that you are already overextended and unable to pay down existing debts.

5. With a maxed-out credit card, having the credit card offers no advantages. In other words, you cannot use it for current purchases. You must be very careful not to use it until you have created enough room for additional charges.

6. When you pay down your charges regularly, credit card companies will be more willing to raise your credit limit. But when the card is maxed out, the credit card company will not likely extend additional credit if you need it for a major purchase.

For all these reasons, avoid the practice of maxing out your cards.

Think Critically

1. How might maxing out your credit card affect your lifestyle?

2. If you were a creditor and someone with maxed-out cards asked you for a loan, would you grant it? Why or why not?

Analyzing and Computing Credit Costs

Goals
- **Explain why credit costs vary.**
- **Compute and explain simple interest and APR.**
- **Compare methods of computing finance charges on revolving credit.**

▶ WHY CREDIT COSTS VARY

Several factors determine how much you will pay for the use of credit. One important factor is the method used to compute finance charges, explained later in the chapter. Other important factors include the following:

1. *Source of credit.* Some lenders offer better credit plans than others.

2. *Amount financed and length of time.* The more money you borrow and the longer you take to pay it back, the more you will pay in finance charges.

3. *Ability to repay debt.* The greater your ability to repay and, consequently, the higher your creditworthiness, the better your chances of obtaining credit at reasonable rates.

4. *Type of credit selected.* Different credit plans impose different finance charges.

5. *Collateral.* When you buy an item that serves as collateral (security) for the loan, such as a home or car, you are taking out a *secured loan*. Secured loans generally have fixed interest rates that are lower than current variable rates charged on credit cards and open-ended credit. **Fixed-rate loans** are loans for which the interest rate does not change (up or down) over the life of the loan.

6. *Prime rate.* The interest rates charged for the use of credit are affected by the prime rate. The **prime rate** is the interest rate that banks offer to their best business customers, such as large corporations. Individuals pay more than prime-rate customers because the risk is greater to the lender. Generally, if the prime rate is 8 percent, consumers will pay 11 or 12 percent.

7. *Economic conditions.* Borrowers pay more for the use of credit during inflationary economic periods. When prices are rising

(inflation), then money is more in demand in order to buy higher-priced goods and services. Because people need to borrow more money, lenders can charge higher interest rates.

8. *The business's costs of providing credit.* Businesses pass along their costs for providing credit to consumers in the form of higher finance charges and higher product prices. These costs are related to delinquent accounts (overdue, but still collectible), bad debts (probably uncollectible), and bankruptcy. These debts add unpredictable and often uncontrollable costs to offering credit. Other costs of issuing credit include printing and mailing monthly statements, electronic authorization of credit charges, and salaries and facilities for a credit department.

Net Nuggets

Practical Money Skills is a Web site that provides financial information for students of all ages. Included are budget advice and resources; credit card facts and resources (including a cost of credit calculator that helps you understand the real costs of using a credit card); a banking tutor; games; and financial calculators. Go to www.practicalmoneyskills.com and use the "for students" link.

► COMPUTING THE COST OF CREDIT

Determining the cost of credit is easy using the formula for simple interest. The formula for calculating the total cost of installment credit is somewhat more complicated. The cost of a revolving charge account can be calculated using the previous balance method, the adjusted balance method, or the average daily balance method.

Simple Interest Formula

In Chapter 10, you learned that *interest* is money paid for the use of someone else's money. In the case of savings, interest is the amount the financial institution pays you for the use of your deposit. In the case of a loan, interest is the money you pay the business or financial institution for the use of its money. **Simple interest** is interest computed on the amount borrowed (or saved) only, without compounding. The simple interest method of calculating interest assumes one payment at the end of the loan period. The cost is based on three elements: the amount borrowed (or principal), the interest rate, and the amount of time for which the principal is borrowed. The formula for computing simple interest is as follows:

$$\text{Interest (I)} = \text{Principal (P)} \times \text{Rate (R)} \times \text{Time (T)}$$

PRINCIPAL

In Chapter 10, you learned that *principal* is an amount in a savings account on which interest accrues. The term has a similar meaning when referring to a loan. A loan's **principal** is the amount borrowed, or the unpaid portion of the amount borrowed, on which the borrower pays interest. For example, if you borrow $10,000 to buy a car, that $10,000 is the principal, or amount of the loan. Part of each payment you make goes toward paying down the principal. The rest of the payment is interest. After a number of payments, the principal on your car loan may drop to $8,000, which is the unpaid portion of the amount you borrowed.

RATE

The *interest rate* is expressed as a percentage. The higher the rate, the higher the cost of the loan.

TIME

The length of time the borrower will take to repay a loan is expressed as a fraction of a year: 12 months, 52 weeks, or 360 days. (In most transactions, the standard practice is to use 360 as the number of days in a year for computing simple interest.) For example, for a six-month loan, the time is expressed as $\frac{1}{2}$, because 6 months is half a year. If money is borrowed for three months, the time is expressed as $\frac{1}{4}$. When a loan is for a certain number of days, such as 90, the time is expressed as 90/360, or $\frac{1}{4}$.

Figure 18-1 contains a simple interest problem showing the dollar cost of borrowing. In this problem, a person has borrowed $500 and will pay interest at the rate of 12 percent a year. The loan will be paid back in four months.

The simple interest formula also can be used to find principal, rate, or time when any one of these factors is unknown. For example, in Figure 18-2, the interest rate is 18 percent. The borrower paid a total of $26 in interest and repaid the loan in 18 months. What was the principal?

To find the missing rate, you can use the same formula. See Figure 18-3 (page 438) for an illustration. In simple-interest problems, the rate stated—in this case, 9 percent—is also the *annual percentage rate (APR)*. As you learned in Chapter 16, the APR is the cost of credit stated as a yearly percentage.

SIMPLE INTEREST

figure 18-1 ◄◄

$I = P \times R \times T$

To multiply by a percent, first change it to a decimal: drop the percent sign, then move the decimal point two places to the left.

$I = ?$
$P = \$500$
$R = 12\%$
$T = 4$ months

$I = 500 \times .12 \times {}^4/_{12}$
$= 500 \times .12 \times {}^1/_3$ (Four months is ${}^4/_{12}$ or ${}^1/_3$ of a year.)
$= 60 \times .3333$
$= \$20$

SIMPLE INTEREST (COMPUTING PRINCIPAL)

figure 18-2 ◄◄

$I = P \times R \times T$

Or change the formula to read:

$I = \$26$
$P = ?$
$R = 18\%$
$T = 18$ months

$$P = \frac{I}{R \times T}$$

$26 = P \times .18 \times {}^{18}/_{12}$
$= P \times .18 \times {}^3/_2 (1.50)$
$= P \times .27$

$$= \frac{\$26}{.18 \times 1.50}$$

$P = 26 \div .27$
$= \$96.30$

$$= \frac{\$26}{.27}$$

$$= \$96.30$$

As shown in Figures 18-2 and 18-3, you can either plug the numbers into the existing formula or rearrange the formula. Either way, you can find the unknown amount by simple mathematics.

Annual Percentage Rate Formula

Consumers often use an installment plan to pay for major items such as boats, cars, and furniture, making regular payments over time. To determine the APR for installment plans, in which the borrower repays the loan with more than one payment, use the formula in Figure 18-4 (page 438). Work through the problem in the Math Minute to see how to apply the formula.

$I = P \times R \times T$

$I = \$18$
$P = \$300$
$R = ?$
$T = 240 \text{ days}$

$18 = 300 \times R \times {}^{240}/_{360}$
$ = 300 \times {}^{2}/_{3} \times R$
$ = 200 \times R$

$R = 18 \div 200$
$ = .09 \text{ or } 9\%$

Or change the formula to read:

$$R = \frac{I}{P \times T}$$

$$= \frac{18}{300 \times {}^{2}/_{3}}$$

$$= \frac{18}{200}$$

$$= .09 \text{ or } 9\%$$

To calculate the finance charge, use the following formula:

Finance Charge = Total Price Paid – Cash Price

Where:
Total Price Paid = (number of payments x amount of each payment) + down payment
Cash Price = the total price you would have paid if you had paid in cash rather than with a loan

Then use the finance charge in the following formula to calculate the approximate annual percentage rate:

$$APR = \frac{2 \times n \times f}{P(N+1)}$$

Where:
n = number of payment periods in one year
f = finance charge
P = principal or amount borrowed
N = total number of payments to pay off amount borrowed

An installment contract requires a **down payment**, or part of the purchase price paid in cash up front, reducing the amount of the loan. When you buy a car, you will probably have to pay at least 10 percent of the purchase price in cash. If you trade in your old car, the dealer will likely use the value of your trade-in as your down payment rather than give you cash for your old car.

In Figure 18-4, notice that the total price paid is more than the cash price. The total price includes all installment payments plus the down payment. Each payment includes principal and interest. The difference between the total price and the cash price is the finance charge.

By law, installment contracts must reveal the finance charge and the annual percentage rate. There are two ways to calculate APR: an APR formula and the APR tables. The APR tables are more precise; the formula only approximates the APR.

Math Minute

Computing the Finance Charge and APR

The Perezes are buying a new sofa. The cash price is $800. They decide to pay for it with an installment loan rather than pay cash. They put $100 down and borrow $700. They will pay off the loan principal in 12 monthly payments of $66 each. To determine their APR, you must first use the formula in Figure 18-4 to calculate their finance charge:

Total Price = (12 payments $\times$ $66) + $100 down payment = $892

Finance Charge = $892 total price − $800 cash price = $92

Then use the finance charge in the APR formula from Figure 18-4:

$$APR = \frac{2 \times 12 \text{ payments} \times \$92 \text{ finance charge}}{\$700 \text{ principal} (12 \text{ payments} + 1)} = \frac{2,208}{9,100} =$$

.2426 = 24.26%

Based on the above example, solve for finance charge and APR in the following case:

Mark and Dian bought a new refrigerator. The cash price was $1,200. They paid down $49, borrowing $1,151, which they will repay in payments of $49 per month for the next 27 months.

Solution:

Total price = (27 payments $\times$ $49) + $49 down payment = $1,372

Finance charge = $1,372 total price − $1,200 cash price = $172

$$APR = \frac{2 \times 12 \times 172}{1,151 (27 + 1)} = \frac{4,128}{32,228} = .1281 = 12.81\%$$

Credit Card Billing Statements

The cost of using an open-ended (revolving) credit account varies with the method the creditor uses to compute the finance charge. Creditors must tell you the method of calculating the finance charge. Finance charges are usually calculated based on the monthly billing cycle. Purchases made up to the closing date are included in the monthly bill. Finance charges are computed on the unpaid balance after the billing date. Creditors must tell you when finance charges begin on your account, so you will know how much time you have to pay your bills before the finance charge is added. Most creditors offering revolving credit give you a 20- to 25-day grace period to pay your balance in full before imposing a finance charge. Creditors may calculate finance charges on open-ended credit accounts using the adjusted balance method, the previous balance method, or the average daily balance method. The way the creditor determines the finance charge can make a big difference in the size of your credit card bills.

ADJUSTED BALANCE METHOD

When creditors use the adjusted balance method, they apply the finance charge only to the amount owed after you've paid your bill each month. For example, suppose your previous month's balance was $400. When the bill comes, you pay $300. If the creditor uses the adjusted balance method, you will pay a finance charge only on the unpaid balance ($400 – $300 = $100). As you can see in Figure 18-5, the adjusted balance method has the lowest finance charge.

To calculate the finance charge for this month, first determine the monthly rate by dividing the annual rate (18 percent) by 12 months. In this case, the monthly rate is 1.5 percent. Then multiply the balance due of $100 by 1.5 percent or .015 to determine the finance charge of $1.50. Then add the finance charge to the balance to determine the new account balance for the next billing cycle.

PREVIOUS BALANCE METHOD

When creditors use the previous balance method, they impose the finance charge on the entire amount owed from the previous month. This method allows no deductions for payments made. As shown in Figure 18-5, this method applies the monthly rate to the entire $400 (that month's balance). This is the most expensive way to figure the finance charge for the credit user.

AVERAGE DAILY BALANCE METHOD

Most creditors use the average daily balance method for computing finance charges. Using this method, creditors calculate your balance on each day of the billing cycle. They then compute average daily balance by adding together all daily balances and dividing by the number of days in the cycle (usually 25 or 30). Payments made during the billing cycle are used in figuring the average daily balance. Because payments made during the period reduce the average daily balance, this method often results in a lower finance charge than does the

The adjusted balance method, the previous balance method, and the average daily balance method produce different results. This example is based on a billing period of 30 days:

	Adjusted Balance Method	Previous Balance Method	Average Daily Balance
Monthly Interest Rate	1.5%	1.5%	1.5%
Previous Balance	$400	$400	$400
Payments	$300	$300	$300 (on the 15th day)
Interest Charge	$1.50	$6.00	$3.75
	($100 × 1.5%)	($400 × 1.5%)	(average balance of $250 × 1.5%)*

*To figure average daily balance:

$$\frac{(\$400 \times 15\ days) + (\$100 \times 15\ days)}{30\ days} = \$250$$

previous balance method. The example in Figure 18-5 assumes a billing cycle of 30 days.

Some credit card companies are using a new, more costly method of calculating average daily balance called *two-cycle billing*. This method calculates the finance charge on the average daily balance over the last two billing periods (typically 2 months) rather than just one. For example, suppose you start with a zero balance. You make a credit purchase on March 10. When the bill arrives on March 30, you make a partial payment. On April 30, you pay it off. With two-cycle billing, even though you paid off the balance, on your May bill you would still owe interest on the balance you carried in March and April. The result is higher interest and no grace period. You are paying interest from the date of purchase. Avoid credit cards that use two-cycle billing.

✓ Check Your Understanding

1. Explain how economic conditions affect the cost of credit.
2. Why is a grace period important to you?

CHAPTER 18 • Responsibilities and Costs of Credit

441

Chapter Assessment

SUMMARY

18.1

* Your credit responsibilities to yourself include not going into debt beyond what you can comfortably repay, checking out businesses before you buy, comparison shopping, and using credit with the attitude that you will meet your obligations.

* Your responsibilities to creditors involve limiting your spending to amounts you can repay, understanding the terms, and contacting the creditor if an emergency prevents you from making a payment.

* Creditors are responsible for assisting consumers in making purchases, applying fair credit policies and informing them of the rules, and dealing fairly with credit problems.

* Protect your credit card. Keep account information in a safe place. Notify creditors immediately of a lost or stolen card. Do not lend your card.

* To protect your cards online, deal only with companies you trust, enter personal information only if you see the browser's symbol of a secure site, check the site's privacy policy, and don't respond to e-mail or pop-up requests for personal information.

* To reduce your credit costs, accept only the credit you need and make more than the minimum payment each month. Do not increase spending when income increases. Keep no more than two credit cards and pay cash for small purchases.

18.2

* Factors that determine the cost of credit include the source, amount and length of time, ability to repay, type of credit, prime rate, collateral, economic conditions, and the business's costs of providing credit.

* The simple interest formula ($I = P \times R \times T$) does not involve compounding.

* The annual percentage rate (APR) formula calculates the costs of installment credit. It includes the down payment and all monthly payments in the total price. The difference between the total price and the cash price is the finance charge.

* Most creditors calculate finance charges by the adjusted balance method, the previous balance method, or the average daily balance method. Costs vary depending on the method used.

REVIEW TERMS

Directions

Can you find the definition for each of the following terms used in Chapter 18?

down payment	**principal (loan)**
fixed-rate loans	**rebate**
garnishment	**simple interest**
prime rate	**unused credit**

1. The total amount borrowed, or the unpaid portion of the amount borrowed, on which the borrower pays interest.

2. The remaining credit available to you—that is, your credit limit minus the amount you have already spent.

3. Interest computed on the amount borrowed (or saved) only, without compounding.

4. The interest rate that banks offer to their best business customers.

5. Partial refund of an amount spent.

6. Part of the purchase price paid in cash up front, reducing the amount of the loan.

7. Loans for which the interest rate does not change over the life of the loan.

8. Legal process that allows part of your paycheck to be withheld for payment of a debt.

REVIEW FACTS AND IDEAS

1. Describe some consequences of excessive debt.

2. What responsibilities do creditors have toward consumers?

3. What is your liability and responsibility if your credit card is lost or stolen?

4. What can you do to protect your credit cards from unauthorized use?

5. What can you do to help protect your credit card and personal information when making online transactions?

6. List several things you can do to avoid unnecessary credit costs.

7. Why is it important to make more than the minimum payment on your credit card debt?

8. Explain why a $1,000 installment loan at 8 percent for two years would result in a higher cost of credit than the same loan over one year.

9. How can unused credit work against you when you apply for a new loan?

10. List several factors that affect the cost or interest rate you will have to pay to get a loan.

11. What is the formula for computing simple interest?

12. What is the formula for computing the APR on installment credit?

13. In calculating the finance charge in the APR formula, what makes up the total price?

14. Explain the three methods for determining the finance charge on revolving credit.

1. Search the Internet for current articles about online privacy. You might find an article about "phishing," about efforts to enhance online security, or about how to shop safely online. Read one of the articles you find. Then write a bulleted list of the key points in the article. Be prepared to share your findings with your class.

2. Visit an online shopping site and follow links to the company's privacy policy. Write a one-page paper, analyzing the key points of the policy. In what ways does the company safeguard privacy? In what ways will customers give up some privacy if they buy from this company? Would you feel comfortable buying from this site? Why or why not?

3. Visit the Federal Reserve System online at www.federalreserve.gov and click on "consumer information." Select an article about consumer credit and read it. In one page or less, summarize in your own words the tips in this article you found most useful.

4. Suppose you want to buy a new jacket for $100. You can choose to pay for it with cash or by check, debit card, or credit card. Which method is the least expensive? What possible costs might be associated with the other methods of payment?

5. Using the formula for simple interest, solve the following problems, rounding to the nearest penny.
   a. I = ?
      P = $500
      R = 18 percent
      T = 6 months
   b. I = ?
      P = $1,000
      R = 13.5 percent
      T = 8 months
   c. I = ?
      P = $108
      R = 15 percent
      T = 3 months
   d. I = ?
      P = $89.50
      R = 8 percent
      T = 9 months

6. The following simple interest problems have different elements missing. Solve for the missing elements, using the formula shown in this chapter. Round to the nearest penny.

    a. I = $8
        P = ?
        R = 12 percent
        T = 60 days ($^{60}/_{360}$)

    b. I = $54
        P = ?
        R = 18 percent
        T = 18 months ($^{18}/_{12}$)

    c. I = $510
        P = $2,100
        R = ?
        T = 2 years ($^{24}/_{12}$)

    d. I = $36
        P = $108
        R = ?
        T = 18 months ($^{18}/_{12}$)

7. Using the process illustrated in Figure 18-4 and the Math Minute, determine the APR for the following problems:

    a. The purchase price of an item requires a down payment of $60, with the balance to be paid in 12 monthly payments of $60 each. The cash price is $700.

    b. The purchase price of an item requires a down payment of $100 and 24 monthly payments of $90. The cash price is $2,000.

    c. The cash price of an item is $200. The down payment is $20, and 10 monthly payments of $22 each are to be made.

    d. The cash price of an item is $895. With $95 down, the balance is payable in 15 monthly payments of $60 each.

8. With the previous balance method, the finance charge is calculated on the balance first, and then the monthly payment is subtracted to determine the new balance. On a separate sheet of paper, complete the following chart, using a calculator and rounding to the nearest penny. The APR is 12 percent. What is the total finance charge paid?

Balance	+	Finance Charge	=	Balance	−	Payment	=	New Balance
$100		_____		_____		$20.00		_____
_____		_____		_____		20.00		_____
_____		_____		_____		20.00		_____

Total Finance Charge $_____

9. Suppose you decide to pay off your $100 credit card debt by making only the minimum payment of $10 each month. Your APR is 12 percent and your lender uses the previous balance method. On a separate sheet of paper, complete a chart like the one in question 7 above. Extend the chart until the debt is completely paid off. How many months would it take to pay off the debt if you make only the minimum payment? What total finance charge would you pay?

10. With the adjusted balance method, the monthly payment is subtracted before the finance charge is calculated. The amount of the finance charge is then added to obtain the new balance. On a separate sheet of paper, complete the following chart, using a calculator and rounding to the nearest penny. The APR is 18 percent. What is the total finance charge paid?

Balance	−	Payment	=	Balance	+	Finance Charge	=	New Balance
$500		$50.00		_____		_____		_____
_____		$50.00		_____		_____		_____
_____		$50.00		_____		_____		_____
Total Finance Charge						$_____		

11. Suppose you want to borrow $1,000 to make a purchase, and you want to pay it back with equal monthly payments over one year. Divide the class into three groups. Each group is responsible for contacting one type of lender in your area: bank, finance company, or retail store. Contact several lenders in your group's category. Find out the APR and the total finance charge for the loan from the lenders you contact. With your group, report your findings to the class.

Solve Problems ⊕ Explore Issues

1. Your friend Salma is proud of her ability to have and use credit. She buys lunch every day on credit, and at the end of the month she pays only the minimum balance due. When one credit card is at its limit, she switches to another credit card. She figures she can just go on charging forever because she can just make minimum payments. Do you see any problems with this behavior? Explain to Salma how she is incurring finance charges.

2. Your cousin is considering whether to buy a new sound system. She can use installment credit at the store (18% APR), or she can put the purchase on her credit card. Her credit card has a variable rate, which is 9.9% right now, but is likely to increase in the next few months. What is your advice?

3. Arturo's aunt gave him a loan for $200 and asked him to repay it in 9 months at 5 percent annual interest. On the Internet, locate a notes and interest planner tool to calculate how much Arturo will owe his aunt 9 months from now.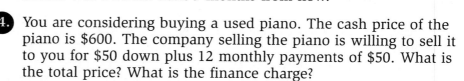

4. You are considering buying a used piano. The cash price of the piano is $600. The company selling the piano is willing to sell it to you for $50 down plus 12 monthly payments of $50. What is the total price? What is the finance charge?

5. If you were to purchase a major appliance and pay for it this year, borrowing $800 at 18 percent for 8 months, how much would you pay to finance this purchase?

6. You buy a new car that sells for $14,000 by trading in your car and using the trade-in allowance of $2,000 as a down payment. You pay the balance at $295 a month for 48 months. What is the APR?

7. Logan ran up a credit card debt of $1,000. He decided that he would not put any more purchases on the card until he had paid off the debt. He can pay $50 a month, and the interest rate is 18 percent. On the Internet, locate a loan planner tool to find out how many monthly payments Logan will have to make to pay off his debt. How many years will he be paying on the debt?

For related activities and links, point your browser to **www.mypf.swlearning.com**

Problems with Credit

20/10 Rule
debtor
bankruptcy
unsecured debt
involuntary
  bankruptcy

voluntary
  bankruptcy
discharged debts
Chapter 11
  bankruptcy
Chapter 7
  bankruptcy

exempted
  property
Chapter 13
  bankruptcy
reaffirmation

Consider This. . .

Jadeyn has income of $1,500 per month, but when she totals her expenses, she has over $2,100 per month in bills to pay.

"I'm ready for some type of debt relief," Jadeyn told her credit counselor. "My income just doesn't cover my expenses. I didn't overspend, either. Last year I had to have extensive dental work. I had to get a different car because my old one was costing too much in repairs each month. And then my dog had to have surgery. The end result is that I'm buried. I have more expenses than income!"

Getting Unstuck

Goals
- **Explain methods for solving credit problems.**
- **Outline bankruptcy laws and choices.**

◢ SOLVING CREDIT PROBLEMS

One major disadvantage of credit is that it can lead to overextension (overspending). Many people get into trouble with credit every year, and they represent all levels of income and social standing.

Credit problems usually do not happen suddenly. Certainly, emergencies can and do occur, causing people to get buried in debt. Typically, however, credit problems arise after months and years of poor planning, impulse buying, and careless budgeting. If you recognize early enough that you are falling into an excessive debt problem, you can cure it before it becomes disastrous.

The 20/10 Rule

Credit counselors often suggest use of the **20/10 Rule** to people beginning to use credit: Your total borrowing should not exceed 20 percent of your yearly take-home pay, and you should not take on monthly payments that total more than 10 percent of your monthly take-home pay. The 20/10 Rule does not apply to mortgage loans for housing. However, it does apply to all other types of closed-ended as well as open-ended credit.

Suppose that your yearly take-home pay is $21,000 and your monthly take-home pay is $1,750. Your total borrowing should not exceed $4,200 (20 percent of your yearly take-home pay). Your monthly credit payments should not be more than $175 (10 percent of your monthly take-home pay). Following the 20/10 Rule can help you keep your debt within your means to repay.

Credit Counseling

If you get into serious problems with credit, you can seek counseling from a private or government-sponsored counseling service. Sometimes the service charges a small fee. A counselor will help you set up a realistic budget and will give advice about how to stay within your budget. You cannot get a loan from a credit counseling service, but a counselor will work with your creditors to reduce interest rates and set up a payment plan that you can afford.

You can find consumer credit counseling services in the Yellow Pages or online. A local nonprofit organization affiliated with the National Foundation for Consumer Credit (NFCC) is the Consumer Credit Counseling Service (CCCS). Anyone overwhelmed by credit obligations can contact a CCCS office. The NFCC Web site at www.nfcc.org will help you find a CCCS office near you. You may even be able to work with a CCCS counselor over the Internet. Some churches, private foundations, universities, military bases, credit unions, and state and federal housing authorities provide similar services.

Debt Adjustment

People who are in deeper credit trouble than advice can solve often go to a finance company for debt adjustment. There are two types of debt adjustment. One is a *debt-adjustment service plan*. The finance company takes over your checkbook, including your paycheck and your bills. The company uses your checkbook to make the payments on your nonsecured and revolving credit accounts for a period of three to five years, after which your checkbook will be returned to you. To be eligible for a debt-adjustment plan, you need to maintain a monthly income and that income must be sufficient to pay off your bills in three to five years. Typically, the services include a four-step plan, similar to the one shown in Figure 19-1.

The second type of debt adjustment is a *debt consolidation loan*. This plan is similar to the debt-adjustment service plan, except that the finance company loans you money to pay off your debts. You then

DEBT-ADJUSTMENT SERVICE PLAN   figure 19-1 ◄

1. Take your paycheck and checkbook and make debt payments for you. You are given an allowance until all bills have been paid off. This arrangement can take three to five years if you are in deep trouble.
2. Counsel you so that you understand how you got so far into debt and how to avoid doing so again in the future.
3. Work with you to create a reasonable budget that you can live with. Credit cards are taken away and given back slowly as the advisor becomes certain that you understand how to use them wisely.
4. Supervise your budget and help you make any needed changes or adjustments.

make one payment a month to the finance company until the debt is repaid. The main difference here is that in order to get the consolidation loan, you must have some type of collateral, such as a house, that secures the payment of the debt. If you make payments as agreed, the second mortgage on your house is released. If you fail to make payments as agreed, the house is *foreclosed* and sold to pay off the debt.

Credit Repair

After the damage is done and your credit rating is poor, you can take steps to repair it. You can obtain copies of your credit reports, challenge incorrect information, and respond to disputes. Or, for a fee, a credit-repair company will do these things for you.

If your credit rating is poor for good reasons, you can begin to repair your record by using credit responsibly from this point on. Start by paying off your debts through credit counseling or debt adjustment. Then begin the repair process by making small purchases on your credit card and paying off the balance in full each month. Credit repair is a slow process. It may take several years of responsible credit management to raise your rating enough to enable you to get a loan when you need one.

For people who become addicted to credit and are not able to control their credit use, the only wise course is to live debt-free. People who fall into this category should pay cash for all purchases and use credit only for emergencies, and then pay off the debt as quickly as possible.

©GETTY IMAGES/PHOTODISC

What are some ways in which people can deal with credit problems?

Credit Scams

Credit counseling, adjustment, and repair scams abound. You may receive e-mail or pop-up messages, see TV ads, or get calls from telemarketers, promising to repair your credit record "instantly." They may offer to reduce your debt if you pay a fee up front or you sign your house over to them. Such promises are warning signs of a scam. Paying off a large debt and repairing a poor credit record take time—often several years of responsible credit management. Beware of offers that do the following:

1. Require you to pay a fee before performing any service.
2. Do not tell you your legal rights.
3. Suggest that you start a "new" credit report by applying for a new social security number or employer identification number (EIN).
4. Recommend that you not contact the credit bureau yourself.

By law, finance companies may not charge you until they have performed the promised services. They must give you a copy of the "Consumer Credit File Rights Under State and Federal Law" before you sign a contract. They must provide a written contract that shows the organization's name and address and spells out the payments, total cost, and services to be performed. Every state has legitimate nonprofit credit counseling services that charge little or no fee. Your local bank or government consumer protection office can supply a list of reputable organizations.

Net Nuggets

Consumer Credit Counseling Services (CCCS) provides budget counseling, educational programs, debt management assistance, and housing counseling. The organization's Web site has resources and information on consumer education and rights, debt counseling, credit fraud, obtaining your credit report, loan calculators, and even an account balancer to balance your checkbook. Check out the CCCS Web site at cccsintl.org.

▶ BANKRUPTCY

A **debtor** is a person who owes money to others. When debtors are in severe debt trouble and cannot meet their bills, the final and most serious step is bankruptcy. **Bankruptcy** is a legal process that relieves debtors of the responsibility of paying their debts or protects them while they try to repay. Bankrupt debtors are said to be *insolvent*. They have insufficient income and assets to pay their debts. Bankruptcy is a second chance, but it carries serious consequences.

Bankruptcy Laws and Their Purpose

Bankruptcy law in the United States has two goals. The first is to protect debtors by giving them a fresh start, free from creditors' claims. The second is to give fair treatment to creditors competing for debtors' assets. Many creditors complain that the bankruptcy code requires them to tighten credit because it is too easy for people to give up their debts rather than accept responsibility for them. On the other hand, bankruptcy casts a shadow over an individual's credit record.

Since the original federal Bankruptcy Act of 1898, various laws have been passed that have made it either easier or harder to file for bankruptcy. The Bankruptcy Reform Act of 1994 tightened the rules for bankruptcy but allowed insolvent debtors to keep more of their assets. Congress is considering ways to tighten bankruptcy laws and make it more difficult for people to use bankruptcy to avoid paying their credit card debts. The idea behind new legislation is to prevent people from abusing the protections provided by the laws. However, for debtors, the legislation would mean much less debt relief.

Bankruptcy laws treat two general classes of debt: secured and unsecured. As you learned in Chapter 18, *secured loans* are loans backed by specific assets that the debtor pledged as collateral to assure repayment. If the debtor does not pay, the creditor can take possession of the pledged asset. **Unsecured debt** is a loan that is not backed by pledged assets. In bankruptcy, most of the debtor's resources may be used to repay this kind of debt.

Types of Bankruptcy

Bankruptcy can be voluntary or involuntary. **Involuntary bankruptcy** occurs when creditors file a petition with the court, asking the court to declare you, the debtor, bankrupt. If the court decides to declare you bankrupt, it takes over your property and other assets to pay off as much of your debt as possible. Involuntary bankruptcy does not occur very often because most creditors prefer to be repaid in full over a period of time rather than settle only for a portion of your remaining assets.

Voluntary bankruptcy, the most common kind, occurs when you file a petition with a federal court asking to be declared bankrupt. The court notifies local newspapers and your creditors of your pending bankruptcy. Once notice is given, creditors may file claims. The court collects your assets and sells your property to pay your debts. Usually the value of all the bankrupt debtor's assets is not enough to pay off all the debts. The court sells the assets and gives each creditor a share.

©GETTY IMAGES/PHOTODISC

Discharged debts are debts erased by the court during bankruptcy proceedings. Creditors can no longer seek payment for these debts. However, some debts cannot be discharged.

Although bankruptcy provides debtors with a second chance, why is it such a serious issue to consider?

The bankruptcy process deals with debtors in one of two ways: liquidation or reorganization. Under *liquidation*, the court sells the debtors' assets and uses the proceeds to pay as much of the debts as possible. The remaining debt is then discharged. Under *reorganization*, debtors may keep their property but must submit a plan to the court for repaying a substantial portion of their debts.

The types of bankruptcy can be distinguished by which of these methods they use. **Chapter 11 bankruptcy** is a reorganization form of bankruptcy for businesses that allows them to continue operating under court supervision as they repay their restructured debts. The two kinds of bankruptcy available to individuals are Chapter 7 and Chapter 13.

CHAPTER 7 BANKRUPTCY

Commonly called *straight bankruptcy*, **Chapter 7 bankruptcy** is a liquidation form of bankruptcy for individuals that wipes out most debts in exchange for giving up most assets. To get debts discharged, debtors must give up all their property except for certain exempted items. **Exempted property** is the possessions that the bankrupt debtor is allowed to keep because they are considered necessary for survival. Federal laws exempt a number of items, as shown in Figure 19-2.

Some debts are not discharged and must still be paid. These include child support, alimony, income taxes and penalties, student loans, and court-ordered damages due to malicious or illegal acts. Once declared bankrupt, an individual cannot file for bankruptcy again for six years.

CHAPTER 13 BANKRUPTCY

Chapter 13 bankruptcy is a reorganization form of bankruptcy for individuals that allows debtors to keep their property and use their income to pay a portion of their debts over three to five years. Debtors work out a court-enforced repayment plan. Under Chapter 13, often referred to as the *wage-earner's plan*, some debts are totally discharged, but family obligations still remain for child support and alimony.

Chapter 13 bankruptcy may seem better for the debtor in terms of reestablishing credit. However, the blemish on the debtor's credit record caused by any form of bankruptcy is hard to overcome for many years.

Legal Advice

A person considering bankruptcy should seek good legal advice. In most states it is possible to file for bankruptcy without an attorney. But the law is complicated, and a good bankruptcy attorney can tell you which of your assets will be protected and which exempted items

FEDERALLY EXEMPTED ITEMS FOR AN INDIVIDUAL* (ADJUSTED FOR INFLATION ANNUALLY)

figure **19-2**

1. $17,425 equity in a home.
2. $2,775 interest in a motor vehicle.
3. Items worth up to $450 for a single item for household goods and furnishings, appliances, clothing and personal items, for a total of not more than $9,300.
4. $1,150 in jewelry.
5. $1,750 in tools, books, and other items used in a trade or business.
6. Other property worth up to $925, plus up to $8,725 of the unused part of the $17,425 exemption for equity in a home.

* Exempted amounts vary from state to state, based on state bankruptcy laws. Exempted items should be doubled for joint filing.

you can claim. The attorney can also assist you in deciding which bankruptcy plan will work best to help you solve your credit problems.

Reaffirmation of Debts

Creditors may ask debtors to agree to pay their debts, even after bankruptcy has discharged them. The agreement to repay discharged debts is called **reaffirmation**. You may choose to reaffirm a particular debt if a friend or family member co-signed the loan and you don't want to saddle this person with the debt. Also, you may choose to reaffirm rather than allow the collateral, such as a car, to be repossessed. Reaffirmation requires a court hearing, and debtors have 30 days to change their minds about promising to repay. A creditor is prohibited from harassing debtors to reaffirm after the court proceedings are over.

✓Check Your Understanding

1. Does the 20/10 Rule apply to open-ended credit or closed-ended credit?
2. What is credit repair?
3. When you can't seem to control your purchases, what can you do?

Lesson 19.2

Reconsidering Bankruptcy

Goals
- Discuss the major causes of bankruptcy.
- Describe the advantages and disadvantages of declaring bankruptcy.

▶ MAJOR CAUSES OF BANKRUPTCY

Bankruptcy is a last-resort solution to credit problems. Common reasons why individuals file for bankruptcy are job loss, emotional spending, failure to budget and develop a good financial plan, and catastrophic injury or illness.

Job Loss

According to Consumers Union, two thirds of people in bankruptcy have been unemployed for a period of time before the filing. While you cannot control unexpected events in life, such as a layoff, you can plan and save for them. Rather than spend all your income, save a portion each month to help you get through rough financial times. Avoid overuse of credit, locking you into high payments. If unemployment causes your income to fall, these payments could tip you into bankruptcy.

Emotional Spending

Consumers often get into trouble through purchases based on emotion rather than reason. Buy what you need, not to impress people or for recreation. Impulse purchases can quickly add up to more debt than you can afford.

 **Communication Connection**

Talk with several friends or relatives about their buying patterns. Do they tend to make purchases based on need or emotion? Do they feel comfortable with their approaches or would they like to change them? Write a one-page summary of your discussions.

Failure to Budget and Plan

Many people who go bankrupt neither have nor follow a budget. Many do not know how to set up a budget and are not willing to ask for help in solving their credit problems.

Bankruptcy is not a condition limited to poor people. Poor planning can occur at any income level. No matter what your financial position, you must keep your spending and borrowing in proportion to your income. Most causes of bankruptcy can be avoided by careful planning and decision making, based on good financial judgment, advice, and goals.

©GETTY IMAGES/PHOTODISC

How could serious injury or illness lead to bankruptcy?

Catastrophic Injury or Illness

Medical care costs a great deal. Some insurance policies have dollar limits for major illnesses. While not all catastrophic injuries or illnesses result in bankruptcy, they often damage a person's finances for many years. For example, a person hospitalized for a long time with a critical illness could easily owe $100,000 a month for medical care, drugs, room charges, and other fees. If the person has no insurance, his or her savings can be wiped out in the first month. Many people with this type of debt try to pay it back at a rate they can afford. It may be years, even decades, before this type of debt can possibly be repaid, if ever.

◣ ADVANTAGES OF BANKRUPTCY

For individuals whose debt situation seems hopeless, bankruptcy offers a solution. While this solution is not without a price, bankruptcy does offer the following advantages:

1. *Debts are erased.* Bankruptcy offers a fresh start. It reduces or eliminates overwhelming bills, and the debtors can start over. With good financial planning and counseling, they can avoid future credit problems. However, future credit may be more difficult to obtain and much more costly for anyone who has filed bankruptcy.

2. *Exempted assets are retained.* While Chapter 7 bankruptcy requires debtors to give up most of their assets in order to erase their debts, they can keep certain amounts and types of properties. With these exempted items, they can start over. When a husband and wife file joint bankruptcy, the cushion for a new start becomes softer because the dollar amounts for exempted items are doubled.

3. *Certain incomes are unaffected.* Bankruptcy will not affect certain types of income a debtor may have, such as social security, veterans' benefits, unemployment compensation, alimony, child support, disability payments, and payments from pension, profit-sharing, and annuity plans. These sources of income need not be considered even in a Chapter 13 bankruptcy, in which a required payment plan is established.

4. *The cost is small.* Attorneys' fees and court costs in bankruptcy are relatively small in comparison to the amount of financial relief provided. On the first visit to an attorney's office, a debtor will be given total cost estimates and information about the options available in bankruptcy proceedings.

▶ DISADVANTAGES OF BANKRUPTCY

While bankruptcy offers debt relief, it carries serious consequences. Bankruptcy should be considered a last resort. Some of the disadvantages of bankruptcy are:

1. *Credit is damaged.* A bankruptcy judgment destroys your credit record for a long time. This judgment cannot be wiped off your credit records for 10 years. During that time, you could find it very difficult or impossible to obtain credit. You would have to pay cash for everything. If you did get credit, it would be at a very high interest rate because you would be considered a very high risk. For example, credit card interest rates often exceed 25% for people who have filed bankruptcy. Bankruptcy is a notice to creditors and others that, at one time, you were unable or unwilling to meet your financial responsibilities. Depending on the circumstances that caused the bankruptcy, people may continue to mistrust you in business affairs for well beyond the 10 years.

2. *Property is lost.* Most of your property will be taken away and sold to pay your debts. You may not even be able to keep exempt assets. Assume that you own a house worth $120,000 that has a mortgage of $90,000 against it. Your equity is $30,000. While the bankruptcy code allows you to keep the first $17,425 of equity in your home, you may be required to sell the home. You will be allowed to keep $17,425 and the remaining amount must be used to pay off creditors. Or, if you own a car valued at $5,000 and you owe $2,800 on the car, your equity is $2,200. Since this amount is less than the allowance for a car, you will not have to sell the car. However, if you have a car valued at $8,000 with a loan of $5,000, your equity is $3,000. You are allowed only equity of

$2,775. In this case, you will probably have to sell the car and use all proceeds over $2,775 to help pay off your creditors.

3. *Some obligations remain.* Regardless of the type of bankruptcy selected, all debt is not erased. Certain obligations, such as child support, must be paid in full. Other debts also remain: income taxes and penalties that are less than three years old, student loans, and other debts at the discretion of the bankruptcy court. If a lender can prove that there was any type of false representation on the debtor's part in connection with a debt, the debt will not be discharged.

4. *Some debts can be reaffirmed.* You may feel the need to reaffirm some debts to protect your co-signers or avoid losing an important asset. However, by reaffirming, you will not get the fresh start that you probably need.

5. *Co-signers must pay.* After you have been declared bankrupt under Chapter 7, your co-signers must repay the loans they co-signed. Co-signers are likely to be your close friends or family members. Leaving them saddled with the debt can damage your personal relationships.

✅ Check Your Understanding

1. What kinds of spending are most likely to get you into credit trouble? What can you do to avoid these dangers?
2. Do you believe that advantages of bankruptcy outweigh the disadvantages? Discuss.

When Bankruptcy Is the Best Choice

Ben and Michelle were married less than two years when she became pregnant with their first child. He was working full time and had good health insurance that paid 80 percent of all charges that were reasonable and necessary. The pregnancy appeared to be normal until shortly before the expected delivery date. At that time, it was discovered that the baby would be born with serious health problems, including a hole in her heart, birth defects that would leave her deaf, and underdeveloped organs that would require considerable medical attention.

Six months later, the baby came home, having survived six weeks in the hospital, three surgeries, and a poor prognosis. She would have to undergo several more surgeries in order to repair the damage and birth defects. Already the cost of medical services was more than $1 million, with the couple's share more than $100,000.

But medical technology has come a long way, and when the baby was a year old, she had her last operation, which repaired her hearing loss and removed feeding tubes so that she could for the first time eat on her own. The final medical bills were in and the couple owed more than $300,000 to hospitals, doctors, labs, and surgeons.

Faced with payments that were overwhelming, the couple elected bankruptcy. It was the best choice for several reasons. First, even making payments spread out over ten years, they were unable to meet other financial obligations. Second, the debt would prevent them from moving forward with a financial plan for the future of their child as well as their own financial security. Third, bankruptcy allowed them the debt relief they needed to avoid the stress of overwhelming debt.

Think Critically
1. Do you know someone who has faced a financial disaster for which bankruptcy might be the best choice? Describe the situation.
2. Do you know someone who is facing bankruptcy because of overspending, careless planning, or greed? What advice would you give this person?

Chapter
Assessment

SUMMARY

* The 20/10 Rule suggests that your total debt not exceed 20 percent of yearly take-home pay and your monthly payments not exceed 10 percent of your monthly take-home pay.
* Credit counseling services give budget advice and work with your creditors to make a payment plan you can afford.
* Debt adjustment involves either a debt-adjustment service plan or a debt consolidation loan.
* Bankruptcy laws are designed to help people under severe debt get a fresh start.
* Bankruptcy deals with debt through liquidation or reorganization.
* Chapter 7 bankruptcy is a liquidation form in which debtors must give up most of their assets in exchange for debt relief.
* Chapter 13 bankruptcy is a reorganization form in which debtors may keep their property but must follow a court-enforced repayment plan.

* Common causes of bankruptcy are job loss, emotional spending, failure to budget, and catastrophic injury or illness.
* Bankruptcy offers the advantages of erasing some debts, exempting some possessions, allowing certain sources of income to remain unaffected, and low cost.
* Bankruptcy carries serious consequences: Your credit is damaged for 10 years. You lose much of your property. Some debts are not discharged. Your co-signers are saddled with your debt.

Directions

Can you find the definition for each of the following terms used in Chapter 19?

20/10 Rule	discharged debts
bankruptcy	exempted property
Chapter 7 bankruptcy	involuntary bankruptcy
Chapter 11 bankruptcy	reaffirmation
Chapter 13 bankruptcy	unsecured debt
debtor	voluntary bankruptcy

1. A legal process that relieves debtors of the responsibility of paying their debts or protects them while they try to repay.

2. Credit guideline stating that total borrowing should not exceed 20 percent of yearly take-home pay and monthly payments should not exceed 10 percent of monthly take-home pay.

3. A type of bankruptcy in which creditors file a petition with the court, asking the court to declare the debtor bankrupt.

4. A type of bankruptcy in which the debtor files a bankruptcy petition with the court, asking to be declared bankrupt.

5. Possessions that the bankrupt debtor is allowed to keep because they are considered necessary for survival.

6. A liquidation form of bankruptcy for individuals that wipes out most debts in exchange for giving up most assets.

7. A reorganization form of bankruptcy for individuals that allows the debtors to keep their property and use their income to pay a portion of their debts over three to five years.

8. An agreement to repay discharged debts.

9. A loan that is not backed by pledged assets.

10. A reorganization form of bankruptcy for businesses that allows the businesses to continue operating under court supervision as they repay their restructured debts.

11. A person who owes money to others.

12. Debt erased by the court as a result of bankruptcy proceedings.

REVIEW FACTS AND IDEAS

1. What sources of help in solving credit problems are available to you?

2. Where can you find out about nonprofit credit counseling services in your area?

3. What is a debt consolidation loan and what is required to qualify?

4. What are some warning signs that a credit counseling, adjustment, or repair deal is a scam?

5. What is the purpose of bankruptcy?

6. What are two ways that a debtor may be declared bankrupt?

7. What are two ways that the bankruptcy process deals with debtors?

8. Under Chapter 7 bankruptcy, what must a debtor give up in exchange for debt relief?

9. Which types of family obligations are not discharged by bankruptcy?

10. Why are some possessions exempted during bankruptcy?

11. Once you are declared bankrupt, how much time must pass before you can again file for bankruptcy?

12. How long does a bankruptcy judgment remain on your credit record?

13. How does Chapter 13 bankruptcy differ from Chapter 7 bankruptcy?

14. Why is it a good idea to seek advice from an attorney before filing for bankruptcy?

15. Why might a debtor choose to reaffirm a debt after the bankruptcy process has discharged it?

16. List four common reasons for filing bankruptcy.

17. List the advantages and disadvantages of filing bankruptcy.

APPLY YOUR KNOWLEDGE

1. Search through the Yellow Pages, business directories, or online, and list several of the following:
   a. Nonprofit credit counseling services
   b. Finance companies that offer debt-adjustment services
   c. Attorneys specializing in bankruptcy
   d. Classes or other credit counseling services provided in the community, either for a fee or free
   Visit the Web site of one business of each type and write a brief summary of the kinds of information and services each provides.

2. Search the Internet for advice on staying out of credit trouble. Make a list of at least five tips that you found most helpful. Note the URL where you found each tip.

3. Read the classified section of your newspaper every day for one week, checking for bankruptcy notices. Most newspaper classified sections are available online. Collect the legal notices section and answer these questions:
   a. How many total bankruptcies were filed in the seven-day period?
   b. How many of the bankruptcies were joint bankruptcies (husband and wife)?
   c. What is the lowest amount of debt claimed?
   d. What is the highest amount of debt claimed?
   e. How many of those filers represented themselves? How many used an attorney?
   f. What was the lowest amount of property claimed as exempt?
   g. What was the highest amount of property claimed as exempt?

4. Look up the original federal Bankruptcy Act of 1898 in a reference book or online, and write a report covering the following:
   a. Provisions of the law (in outline form)
   b. Exempted items allowed and types of income excluded
   c. Procedures or steps involved in filing bankruptcy

5. Search for articles online or in print publications for information on bankruptcy reform legislation that Congress recently passed or is considering. Answer these questions:
   a. What key changes would this law make?
   b. How would these changes affect consumers and creditors?
   c. How would the law likely influence the availability of credit? Explain.

6. Is it possible in your area to file bankruptcy without the aid of an attorney? What is the procedure for filing bankruptcy, with or without an attorney? (You can find out by calling your local legal aid society or by asking at a courthouse.)

Solve Problems ⊕ Explore Issues

1. Your friend Yu-lan has trouble paying his bills. He has taken a second job in order to make all his payments, but the long hours and hard work are causing him health problems. What suggestions do you have in helping him manage his credit problems?

2. Nathan and Daisy have decided to get help with their credit problems rather than declare bankruptcy. They want to extend the time for repaying loans, but they don't want to hand over their checkbook and credit cards to a finance company. What other options do they have?

3. Beatriz owns a small store. The store has been losing money for some time. Beatriz is the sole owner of the store, and her personal assets are the store's assets as well. Explain to Beatriz the differences among Chapters 7, 11, and 13 bankruptcy.

4. Shamar and Ronette Churchwell are considering bankruptcy. They have the following assets. How much (total) will they be allowed in exempted items?
   a. $34,000 equity in home
   b. $5,000 equity in motor vehicle

    c. $500 in household goods and furnishings, $2,000 in appliances, $1,000 in personal items and clothing, and $2,000 in musical instruments

    d. $8,000 in jewelry

5. M. J. Majesky has filed for bankruptcy and has the following debts. After the bankruptcy, which debts will remain?

    a. $500 owed to a chiropractor

    b. $300 owed in child support

    c. $870 owed in student loans

    d. $1,200 owed in back taxes

    e. $530 owed to a department store

    f. $650 owed to an automobile repair shop

    g. $950 owed to a jewelry store

6. Rodrigo Soto has the following assets. What amounts would be considered exempted items?

    a. $3,500 equity in a home

    b. $3,000 interest in a motor vehicle

    c. $150 in household furnishings

    d. $300 in appliances

    e. $150 in personal items

    f. $300 in a pet parrot

    g. $1,500 in musical instruments

    h. $300 in jewelry

    i. $600 in tools

    j. $15,000 life insurance proceeds

    k. $300 a month in unemployment insurance benefits

For related activities and links, point your browser to **www.mypf.swlearning.com**

PROJECT

Managing Credit and Debt

Previous unit projects concentrated on examining your financial position, building and protecting your savings and investments, and planning your retirement and estate. In this project, you will learn more about credit and debt load and how to protect yourself from fraudulent use of your credit cards.

▶ YOUR USE OF CREDIT

Credit will enable you to enjoy a standard of living that otherwise would not be possible. Nearly everyone uses credit. Wise consumers analyze their use of credit annually, comparing sources, interest rates, minimum payments, and other features (such as rebates) of accounts. Figure U4-1, on page 470, illustrates a worksheet for analyzing your creditworthiness. Complete this analysis with Worksheet 1 in the *Student Activity Guide* to give you an idea of how you are handling credit in your life.

When examining your use of credit, you may want to keep control sheets for tracking your progress in paying off debts. A sample control sheet is shown in Figure U4-2, on page 471. You can make similar sheets for each credit card or account to track each monthly payment. At the end of the year, you can total the finance charges. Keeping the control sheets will also help you see the cost of your credit card purchases. The amount of the finance charge is shown on the monthly statement from the creditor, along with the previous balance, payments and returns (credits), new charges (debits), and the new monthly balance.

▶ YOUR DEBT LOAD

A *debt load* is the amount of outstanding debt at a particular time. Whether your debt load is acceptable to you will depend on your ability to meet the regular payments, your ability to pay off the debt quickly if necessary, and your level of comfort with the amount of debt you owe.

Credit Analysis

Directions: List each type of credit you have and its features. Then complete the analysis to determine what action can and should be taken.

	Monthly Payment	No. of Payments Left	Outstanding Balance	APR	Special Features	Ranking
Installment credit:						
Personal loans:						
Automobile	___	___	___	___	___	___
Home improvement	___	___	___	___	___	___
Other: ___	___	___	___	___	___	___
	___	___	___	___	___	___
Charge accounts:						
1. ___	___		___	___	___	___
2. ___	___		___	___	___	___
3. ___	___		___	___	___	___

Total debt outstanding . . . .$ ___

Average APR . . . . ___

How long will it take to pay off the outstanding debt? (Total outstanding debt divided by total monthly payments) ___

Which debts do you feel comfortable with? ___

Which debts do you feel uncomfortable with? ___

Which debts will you pay off first (those with lowest ranking)? ___

What are some anticipated future debt needs? ___

Which credit sources will you use for future debt (those with highest ranking)?

___

Control Sheet:
VISA Account

(1) Date	(2) Previous Balance	(3) Payments (Credits)	(4) New Charges (Debits)	(5) Finance Charge	(6) New Balance (2 − 3 + 4 + 5)
1/1	$280.63	$35.00	$20.00	$7.22	$272.85
2/3	272.85	35.00	0	7.01	244.86
3/2	244.86	35.00	15.00	6.88	231.74
3/4	231.74	35.00	0	6.55	203.29

Figure U4-3, on page 472, shows a worksheet for determining whether you have a comfortable debt load. One rule says that installment debt should not exceed 20 percent of yearly take-home pay. Another holds that you should be able to pay off all installment debts in one year at your current monthly payments. Still another says that you should be able to pay off your debts within 30 days if absolutely necessary (with all the cash you can raise).

Complete your debt-load analysis, using Worksheet 2 in the *Student Activity Guide*. Compute your self-score. If you sense trouble with debt, the solution is to pay off old debts before taking on new ones. Assessing your debt load will help you determine the severity of your debt problem so that you can take corrective action before it is too late. Debts are future earnings already spent. Unfortunately, many people never assess how much future income they have already committed to debt and whether the types and sources of credit they use are most advantageous to them.

► PROTECTION FROM CREDIT FRAUD

The cost of credit card fraud exceeds $3 billion a year. Maybe you will never be a victim, but everyone pays for credit card fraud through higher interest charges, membership fees, and other costs that are passed along to customers.

To protect yourself, do the following:

1. Shred receipts and carbons or carbonless copies so that numbers cannot be read.

2. Do not allow store clerks to write your credit card numbers and expiration dates on checks.

Your Debt Load

Directions: Answer the following statements with a "Yes" or "No." Then read the information following the statements to make an assessment of your debt load.

1. You pay only the minimum amount due each month on charge and credit accounts.   YES   NO

2. You make so many credit purchases that your debt load (total debts outstanding) never shrinks.   YES   NO

3. You are usually not able to make it until the end of the month and must borrow from savings.   YES   NO

4. You have borrowed from parents or others and do not have plans to repay the debt.   YES   NO

5. You are behind on one or more of your payments.   YES   NO

6. You worry about money often and are discouraged.   YES   NO

7. Money is a source of arguments and disagreements in your family.   YES   NO

8. You often juggle payments, paying one creditor while giving excuses to another.   YES   NO

9. You really don't know how much money you owe.   YES   NO

10. Your savings are slowly disappearing, and you are unable to save regularly.   YES   NO

11. You've taken out loans to pay off debts, or have debt consolidation loans.   YES   NO

12. You are at or near the limit of your credit lines on credit and charge accounts.   YES   NO

13. You worry more about the amount of the payment than the amount of interest (interest rate) you are paying on loans.   YES   NO

ASSESSMENT: Total number of "Yes" answers _____

If you answered yes to 8 or more statements, you need immediate action to correct your debt load. If you answered yes to 4–7 statements, you should seek to remedy the defects in your debt load soon. If you answered yes to 1–3 statements, you are in pretty good shape and can solve your debt problems. If you answered no to all the statements, congratulations—keep up the good work!

3. Pay cash in cases where you suspect your credit information may not be secure.

4. Never give credit information over the telephone or on the Internet to a person or company you do not know.

5. When shopping online, check for your browser's security icon to make sure your transaction will be encrypted.

6. Never sign blank credit slips, and draw a line through blank spaces when you sign.

7. Verify your monthly statements to be sure you have been properly charged.

8. Notify creditors in advance of an address change.

9. Never lend your credit cards to anyone.

10. Never put your account number on the outside of an envelope or on a postcard.

11. Use a separate credit card with a low credit limit for purchases from merchants you don't know, for use on the Internet, and for times when you feel uncomfortable with the situation. This way you minimize the fraud that could occur.

You can probably think of many more ways to protect yourself from credit fraud. One bad experience will convince you that it's worth your time to take precautions. After reading the description of the following credit practices that mislead many consumers every year, ask yourself how you can avoid becoming a victim.

◀ CREDIT REPAIR FRAUD

Phony credit repair companies guarantee that they can fix your credit history instantly, get you out of debt, or get credit cards for you. They often use 900 numbers so you can contact them. These services cost you a large fee even though they are often provided at no charge by credit bureaus, nonprofit credit counseling services, and legitimate organizations that counsel you and help you reestablish your credit responsibly.

In reality, credit repair companies do not magically "fix" your credit history. Once you have a poor credit history, bankruptcy, or other negative information in your record, it cannot be removed or changed. Instead, these companies find other sources of credit you can apply for. They sell you a list of companies that will issue credit cards to people with poor or no credit ratings. You could do this research yourself. For example, you can buy a book that contains a list of reputable card issuers that offer reasonable interest and no annual fees.

ADVANCE-FEE LOANS

These advertisements guarantee you a loan after you have paid a fee in advance, claiming bad credit or no credit is not a problem. You may hear on television or radio a claim that "no applicant is ever turned down." But what really happens is this: The applicant fills out an application and pays the advance fee. The fee is often substantial—from $25 to $200. Then credit is arranged and all payments are closely monitored. The borrower is not allowed to get even one day behind on payments, or aggressive debt-collection practices begin.

A legitimate lender does not charge a fee for applying for open-ended credit, nor will the lender guarantee that you will qualify for credit. Whenever it seems too easy, there is likely a good reason to be suspicious.

ETHICAL DECISIONS

Ethics are principles of morality or rules of conduct. Ethical behavior conforms to these rules; unethical behavior violates them. You may have many opportunities to take advantage of other people. When these opportunities come your way, stop and think how you might feel if you were victimized. Figure U4-4, on page 475, lists some circumstances involving credit. Think about how you might react to each circumstance. Complete the situational analysis in Worksheet 3 in the *Student Activity Guide* to develop skill in analyzing ethical issues.

Situational Analysis

For each situation described below, explain how you would respond and why. What are the ethical issues involved in each decision?

1. You walk by an ATM in a mall. You see a bank debit card that was left there by a previous user. You look around and there is no one nearby to claim the card. If you leave it there, someone else may find it. What would you do?

2. You make a payment on your credit account at a customer service center. The worker, who is new and in training, accidentally credits your account for more than you paid. For example, you gave her $25 and she credited your account for $50. What would you do?

3. Someone you know returns merchandise to a store and gets a credit on his charge account, knowing that he purchased the merchandise elsewhere. What would you do?

4. Your friend frequently buys clothing on credit, wears it to a special event, and returns it to the store before the account is due, claiming the garment is damaged or dirty. She then receives a credit or a refund for the merchandise. What would you do?

Resource Management

Project: **Managing Your Resources**

nit 5 begins with personal decision making, where you will learn how to make good decisions based on your needs and wants.

When you leave home for the first time, you will have many housing options from which to choose. But there's also a lot to learn about renting and buying a residence.

Buying a car takes thought and preparation. You'll consider all the costs—from depreciation to accessories—and you'll learn ways to maintain your car's resale value.

The chapter on family decisions covers a wide range of topics. You will begin with marriage. From there you will examine family financial responsibility, divorce, and the financial aspects related to the death of a family member.

Personal Decision Making

TERMS TO KNOW

opportunity cost
basic needs
values
collective values
innovations
custom
economy

product
 advertising
target market
company
 advertising
industry
 advertising

odd-number
 pricing
loss leader
cherry picker
micromarketing

Consider This. . .

Masami is preparing to go to college in the fall and isn't sure what he'll do with his summer. He can work full time and save more money, or he can go out with his friends and enjoy the break between high school and college.

"Making this decision is really tough," Masami thought. "I'd like to have a fun summer with my friends. On the other hand, if I work, I can set aside more money. This would help reduce my student loans and make college less stressful in terms of financing. For me, it's a toss-up. Most of my friends are taking the summer off, and I could join them for one last time. Part of me says that's the right thing to do, but then part of me says it would be more responsible to set money aside for the future."

Making Better Decisions

Goals
- Apply the decision-making process to solve consumer problems.
- Explain economic needs and wants that influence consumer decision making.

▶ THE DECISION-MAKING PROCESS

Buying decisions play an important role in managing your personal finances. Each buying decision involves a trade-off. When you buy something, you give up the opportunity to use the money for something else, such as to make a different purchase or to save. To help you make good purchase decisions, approach your decisions with a rational, step-by-step process that leads you through defining your needs and evaluating alternatives before making a final choice. This rational decision-making process will help you decide how to use your money in ways that will benefit you most.

Step 1: Define the Problem

The first step in the decision-making process is to define the problem to be solved. Once you have identified it, you can look for ways to solve the problem in a manner that fits your financial resources.

©GETTY IMAGES/PHOTODISC

Defining the problem is not as easy as it sounds. For example, let's say you need a computer to do schoolwork. But what *specific* needs does this computer have to fulfill? Do you need to be able to use your computer at home and at school? Will your schoolwork require the use of a DVD drive, or would you just like to have this feature if you can afford it? To truly define the problem to be solved, you must identify all the specific functions you need this product to perform now and in the foreseeable future. You must also distinguish between "wants" and "needs." Since your resources are limited, you may have to give up some wants in order to fulfill your needs.

Why should you approach your purchase decisions with a step-by-step process?

If you can't define the problem, then perhaps you should think more carefully about spending your money. Would you be buying on impulse? How badly do you really need this item?

Once you have defined the problem, you must then gather information on possible solutions. List all alternative solutions and the cost of each. In the computer problem example, you might list these possible solutions:

1. Use a computer at school (on campus) or at a public library.
2. Rent a computer at a copy center or technology store.
3. Buy a new computer and printer.
4. Buy a used computer and printer.

To make a wise decision, you need to know what products and services are available that will meet your needs and how much each will cost to use or purchase. For instance, you need to know where computer labs are located on the school campus. The cost of use will include a lab fee as well as mileage to and from campus and the time involved. Most libraries have computers available for students or the public to use, and these machines also provide Internet access for research purposes. Or, you could go to a full-service copy center or technology store that rents the use of computers. There is usually an hourly fee, plus a charge for printed pages. Most also offer Internet access.

For the possible purchase of a new or used computer, you need to list desired features and then visit various computer stores, department stores, and discount stores in person or online for comparative shopping. At each location, you should make a note of the brands available, features, costs, and warranties. The classified ads and the Internet are good sources for used computers and printers.

The Internet makes comparison shopping easy. With the click of the mouse, you can go quickly from store to store without the time and expense of traveling. Plus, many sites offer price comparisons among merchants selling the same product. For example, if you want to compare computer prices, you could go to a site such as My Simon at www.mysimon.com. Enter "computer" in the search engine and have immediate access to product and price comparisons for all kinds of computer equipment. Online product reviews can also help you compare features and prices. For example, some computer publications such as *PC World* at www.pcworld.com constantly review computers and related equipment. *Consumer Reports Online* at www.consumerreports.org offers reviews of all kinds of products for the price of a subscription. Since *Consumer Reports* accepts no advertising, its product reviews lack the bias that could creep into reviews offered by commercial publications.

Keep a written record of the information you collect on choices of products and services. By doing so, you can compare alternatives and costs more easily. Figure 20-1 shows information collected for comparison in the computer problem.

figure 20-1 ◄

	Per Month	Per Year
Option 1. Use a public/school computer lab		
Time: 5 hours each weekend	20 hours	240 hours
Gas: 6-mile round-trip each weekend	$3.00	$36.00
Lab Fee: $15 per year	1.25	15.00
Paper (1 ream per month)	3.00	36.00
	$7.25	$87.00
Option 2. Rent a machine at a copy center		
Time: 5 hours each weekend	20 hours	240 hours
Gas: 20-mile round-trip each weekend	$ 10.00	$ 120.00
Fee: $6 per hour	120.00	1,440.00
Cost of printing: $.10 per page	50.00	600.00
	$180.00	$2,160.00
Option 3. Buy a new computer and printer		
With student discount, laptop and printer	$800 cash or $900 financed	
Payments on one-year loan at 9%	$ 75.00	$ 900.00
Internet service provider charge	21.95	263.40
Paper (1 ream per month)	3.00	36.00
Toner for printer (2 per year at $30 each)	5.00	60.00
	$104.95	$1,259.40
Option 4. Buy a used computer and printer		
From private individual ($300 one-time cost)		$300.00
Internet service provider charge	$21.95	$263.40
Paper (1 ream per month)	3.00	36.00
Toner for printer (2 per year at $30 each)	5.00	60.00
	$29.95	$659.40
	(plus cost of repairs or maintenance if needed—no warranty)	

Step 3: Compare Choices

Your resources—time as well as money—are limited. Each choice to do or buy something involves a *trade-off*. Buying one thing means giving up the opportunity to buy something else with the money or saving it for a future purchase. Whenever you make a choice, the value of your next best alternative is the **opportunity cost** of that choice. For example, in the chapter-opening situation, suppose Masami could earn $1,000 by working over the summer. If he decides to spend the summer with his friends, the opportunity cost of his choice is the

$1,000 income he gives up. If he decides instead to work, the opportunity cost of that choice is the value to him of the time he could have spent with his friends. Part of comparing choices is considering the value to you of the options you would have to give up.

When comparing total costs, consider time and convenience as well as dollar costs. In some cases, convenience may be more important than cost, as long as the cost is reasonable. Using the computer example, you may decide that the convenience of having your own computer is worth the extra dollar cost. You may also decide that even though the cost of owning a new computer will be greater, you prefer to avoid the uncertainty of possible repairs on used equipment. Purchasing used computers and printers is riskier because previous owners may not have maintained them properly.

Also, as your computer skills increase, you may find home as well as school uses for a computer. If so, buying may be a better decision for you than renting. You must weigh these kinds of factors along with dollar costs when comparing choices.

Modern technology services offer many advantages to consumers, but consumers should first make sure they can afford them. Check for hidden fees. Installation, monthly hardware rental fees, and cancellation fees can mount up. Often providers offer an incentive discount for signing up, but the real rate starts a few months later. Know what the total costs will be before you make a financial commitment.

Step 4: Make a Decision

If you follow the steps outlined in the preceding paragraphs, the decision you make will be based on a careful analysis of the problem, thorough information gathering, and analysis of that information. The wise decision in any situation is the one that best meets your needs, is within your budget, and gives you the most value for your dollar investment. Take the time you need to carefully evaluate the information you gathered about each choice before you make a decision, especially for expensive or complex products.

Step 5: Take Action

After you make a decision, you must take action to implement your chosen solution. Because you have made a thorough analysis of choices for solving your problem, you can be sure that you have made the best decision you could with the available information.

Step 6: Re-evaluate

After several months have passed, revisit your decision. Are you happy with the choice you made? If not, what could you do differently next time to make a better decision? Should you do something different now? If your needs have changed or your initial decision isn't working out, go through the decision-making process again to decide whether to make a change.

Reflect on decisions you have made in the past. Do you now regret some of your decisions? If so, did you use the decision-making process or did you buy the first model you saw? While using a decision-making process won't make every decision perfect, it will help you make better decisions in the important aspects of your life.

◢ ECONOMIC WANTS AND NEEDS

Basic needs are the ingredients necessary for maintaining physical life. They include food and water, shelter, and clothing. Some people would add safety and security to this list. Until people have met their basic needs, they have little need for anything else life has to offer.

Life-enhancing wants include, but are not limited to, the following:

1. Food, clothing, and shelter beyond what is necessary for biological survival.

2. Medical care to improve the quality and length of life.

3. Education to achieve personal goals, both social and economic.

4. Travel, vacations, and recreation to improve personal enjoyment of life.

5. Gadgetry or luxuries to make life more fun or comfortable.

You may have decided that many life-improving items are necessary for your happiness. But you must admit that they are really *wants*, not *needs*. You do not *need* them for your physical survival.

What is the difference between your basic needs and your wants?

Individual Wants

Beyond the basics, you decide what you "want" based on factors such as your values, personal preferences, income, and leisure time. Your wants, in turn, drive your buying decisions. The "best" choice is not the same for everyone. These factors vary among individuals and societies. They also change throughout your life.

1. *Values.* Each person has his or her own set of values. **Values** are the principles by which a person lives. Different people value things differently. One person may highly value education. Someone else may highly value time with family. You make economic choices based on your values. For example, if you highly

value education, you will probably decide to save a large portion of your income for college. The person who highly values time with family may choose to save toward a family vacation.

2. *Personal Preferences.* Personal preferences or *tastes* are your likes and dislikes. One person may enjoy a weekend alone in the mountains hiking, while another would choose a visit to Disneyland. Based on personal preferences, you make economic choices. You spend your money for things consistent with your personal tastes.

3. *Income.* The amount you earn will influence the choices you make. As you learned in Chapter 10, *discretionary income* is the money left over after you have paid your expenses. This is the money you can spend or save as you wish. The more discretionary income you have, the higher the quality and quantity of products you can consider. The ability to afford goods and services to fulfill the wants you consider important will affect your satisfaction with employment, your personal life, your goals, and other personal factors such as self-esteem. For example, if owning a lot of expensive "things" is important to you, then you may pursue educational goals that will likely land you a high-paying job.

4. *Leisure Time.* The amount of free time you have and the kinds of activities you enjoy also affect how you choose to spend your discretionary income. Retired people have a large amount of leisure time, so their wants are likely to include recreational spending for such things as travel and sportswear. If you enjoy skiing in your spare time, you will likely choose to spend your money on skis, lift passes, and ski apparel.

Prepare a list of the five top "wants" in your life today and briefly describe each one. How might your list be different ten years from now?

Collective Values

Collective values are things that are important to society as a whole; all citizens share in their costs and in their benefits. The society in which you live influences your values, goals, and choices because it demands responsibility and accountability from citizens.

1. *Legal Protection.* One of the collective values a society shares is the desire for preserving legal and personal rights and being protected from others who would violate those rights. Law enforcement is the result of society's collective value for protection of citizens and property.

2. *Employment.* Most people who are able will work because it is expected and demanded in order to survive in this society. Most of us are aware of this subtle, yet very real, pressure to perform in the work arena. Therefore, we strive to do the best we can and to get a job that pays well for the effort we put forth. In this way, we can be personally satisfied with our productivity and at the same time satisfy society's demand for citizens who contribute.

3. *Progress.* The relative state of progress of the country in which you live (its technological advances and perceptions about the importance of those advances) will affect your purchase decisions. United States society is technologically advanced and places a high value on innovations. **Innovations** are new ideas, methods, or devices that bring about changes in the way we live. If you are like most Americans, you will likely buy products that offer the latest innovations.

©GETTY IMAGES/PHOTODISC

What are collective values?

4. *Quality of Environment.* Natural resources are of great value and concern to society as a whole because they are very limited, and some cannot be replaced. Because of our collective priority of preserving a quality environment for ourselves and future generations, our society supports activities such as land-use planning, preserving natural beauty and wildlife, and establishing air pollution standards. We also expect producers to minimize the environmental damage caused by the production of their products and services. Environmental quality is important to society as a whole, and individuals respond to this concern by acting and purchasing accordingly.

5. *Public and Government Services.* Our country is organized to be "of the people, by the people, and for the people." We have a highly advanced and intricate system of government made up of the people, performing services for the people, with money contributed (through taxes) by the people. Our system of taxation takes money from those who have it and redistributes it to those who need it. Americans place high value on government-provided services for all citizens, from police protection to public parks.

✓ Check Your Understanding

1. How can the Internet help you gather information about different purchase options?

2. What should you consider in addition to dollar cost when comparing the total costs of alternative solutions?

Lesson 20.2

Spending Habits

Goals
- List and describe factors that influence spending decisions.
- Analyze marketing strategies that influence spending decisions.

▶ FACTORS THAT INFLUENCE SPENDING

Consumer purchasing decisions are influenced by personal factors and outside factors that encourage or discourage spending. When you plan a major purchase, examine your motives to make sure you are buying for your own reasons and not because of outside influences that are not in your best interest.

Personal Factors

Many personal factors influence consumer spending decisions. Personal factors include such things as personal resources; position in life; customs, background, and religion; and values and goals.

1. *Personal Resources.* Your personal resources include your time, money, energy, skills and abilities, and available credit. The more you possess of any one of these factors, the greater your purchasing power. For example, the amount of time you have available to compare prices and options before purchasing a product will

affect your ability to make wise buying decisions. The job skills you possess will affect the amount of money you can earn and, consequently, your purchasing power.

2. *Position in Life.* Your position in life includes such factors as age, marital status, gender, employment status, living arrangements, and lifestyle. Spending patterns of single people are different from those of married couples and families. For example, a new parent will spend on baby products. Women will buy different kinds of clothes than do men.

3. *Customs, Background, and Religion.* A **custom** is a long-established practice that takes on the force of an unwritten law. Families may be faithful to customs that their members have followed for generations. Cultures as well as religious and other groups share common customs. For example, people of a cultural or religious group may observe special holidays that are not observed nationally. The customs of the groups to which you belong will influence your buying patterns.

4. *Values and Goals.* Values are deep-seated and slow to change, but they do change over time. Goals change often. You accomplish one goal and then move on to others. Your value system may change as your goals in life are met or not met. Individual and family values and goals are expressed through choices of entertainment, literature, sports, luxuries, and so on. These choices are reflected in decisions to purchase goods and services, use of time, and attitudes toward accumulating possessions.

How do customs influence spending decisions?

Outside Factors

Factors outside yourself also affect your spending patterns. These include the economy, technological advances, the environment, and social pressures.

1. *The Economy.* The **economy** refers to all activities related to production and distribution of goods and services in a geographic area. Economists measure economic activity in different ways to describe the financial well-being of the nation. The general condition of the economy affects every one of us, and we react to it accordingly. For example, when interest rates on car loans are high, fewer people buy new cars. Consequently, older cars are kept longer. When the economy is strong and growing, people are more optimistic and willing to spend money more freely. When the economy is slowing down or in a recession, people hold back on buying items that can be postponed, such as luxury goods.

2. *Technological Advances.* You may be fascinated with new electronic games. Or you may be interested in the world's first

mass-market electric-powered car. Perhaps you want to add a new solar heating device to your home to make it more energy efficient. Many Americans place a high value on new technological advances. Many people want to have the newest, most convenient, and interesting gadgets. As new goods and services are created to raise our standard of living, many people willingly purchase them.

3. *The Environment.* Concern for the environment can affect buying decisions. Citizens are concerned with home projects, community activities, and statewide programs to beautify and preserve, recycle, and protect existing resources and the environment. Thus, this interest in the environment affects consumers' actions and also their product preferences. People are buying more products that are ecologically safe, biodegradable, or recyclable.

4. *Social Pressures.* Social pressures often induce consumers to buy goods and services beyond their ability to pay. Your friends, relatives, and co-workers all influence your buying decisions. The media (radio, television, newspapers) also act as sources of social pressure for consumers. Through advertising, the media convince consumers to buy goods and services designed to keep them young, good-looking, and healthy.

 Global View

In 1996, more than 40% of elementary school children and 77% of junior high students in Tokyo, Japan attended cram schools, known as "juku." Parents spent a great deal of money to send their children to these schools. Japanese children started to attend cram schools mainly to keep up with school classes; to prepare for entrance examinations into Japan's prestigious and competitive schools and universities; and to accompany friends who also attended the juku.

Think Critically: In this situation, how are personal factors and outside factors affecting the spending decisions of these Japanese children's parents?

▶ PLANNING MAJOR PURCHASES

Because major purchases generally tie up future income or take a big bite out of accumulated savings, carefully consider your needs and wants before committing to a large purchase. Ask yourself these questions, take time to reflect on your answers, and then make a final decision based on a rational—not emotional—perspective.

1. Why do I want this product?

2. How long will this product last?

3. What substitutes are available and at what cost?

4. By postponing this purchase, is it likely that I will choose not to buy it later?

5. What types of additional costs are involved, such as supplies, maintenance, insurance, and financial risks?

6. What is the opportunity cost of this purchase? That is, what next-best alternative would I have to give up to make this purchase? Do I want this item more than any other choice I could make?

7. What is the total cost of this product (cash price, deferred price, interest, shipping charges, and so on)?

Once you have made a purchase decision, you need to determine whether to pay cash or use credit. Even though you may have the cash available, you should not automatically pay cash for all purchases. If you do, your cash reserves will dwindle, or you may have to do without many conveniences you could have now with wise use of credit. Figure 20-2 (page 490) shows a comparison of various options available for buying a refrigerator, with positive and negative consequences.

Comparison shopping will allow you to determine whether you are getting the best quality for the price. The same brand often sells at considerably different prices at different retailers, depending on the seller's markups. By shopping various retail outlets you may be able to save money. In addition, many stores offer sale prices at various times of the year or at regular intervals. Before making a major purchase, monitor prices for a while to see if it goes on sale.

Take advantage of store policies that will refund part of your purchase price if the item you bought goes on sale within the next two weeks or month. This policy, together with a liberal return policy, should affect your choice of merchants. For example, a store that allows you to return a purchase within a reasonable period of time (a month or more) is much better than a store that will not accept returns or give refunds.

The fact that you are paying a high price does not necessarily mean you are getting the best quality merchandise. It pays to be aware of what is good quality and what you should expect from the merchandise. The nonprofit Consumers Union tests the quality of many

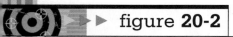 figure 20-2

CASH OR CREDIT PURCHASE?

Item	Cash	Credit
Refrigerator		
Price	$800 + $15 delivery charge	$50/month ($900 total) + $15 delivery charge
Total cost	$815	$915
Substitute Used refrigerator		
Price	$400 + $15 delivery charge	$30/month for 15 months + $15 delivery charge
Total cost	$415	$465
Considerations	Ties up cash; cannot make other purchases. No monthly payments. Reduces savings balance. No interest charges.	Allows for budgeting; ties up future income. Can make other purchases. Establishes credit. Interest charged.

products and compares different brands. It publishes the results in its *Consumer Reports* print and online magazine. You can also find product reviews in specialty magazines and Web sites. For example, *Backpacker* magazine reviews outdoor equipment. However, keep in mind that reviews by for-profit organizations could be influenced by the manufacturers who advertise in the magazine or Web site. Especially for major purchases, check reviews in several sources before making your choice.

▶ MARKETING STRATEGIES THAT INFLUENCE SPENDING

Numerous marketing strategies lure us into stores to buy goods and services. Many of these strategies are subtle, and we are often unaware of their impact on our buying patterns.

VIEWPOINTS

When does the gathering and use of information about individuals constitute an invasion of privacy? For example, the main purpose of an Internet "cookie" is to identify a Web site's users and possibly prepare customized Web pages for them. The Web site may gather and store information about you such as your name, address, interests, and spending patterns; where you go on the Web site; and other personal aspects.

Think Critically: Do you object to information being gathered about you by Web sites? If so, why? Do you feel that consumers should have control over how personal information about them is collected and used? Do you think that new privacy protection laws are needed to regulate the use of information in the computer age?

Advertising

The primary goal of all advertising is to create within the consumer the desire to purchase a product or service. Some advertising is false and misleading; other advertising is informational and valuable.

Advertising appears in a variety of media (billboards, television, radio, Internet, newspapers, magazines, leaflets, balloons, and t-shirts), all carefully coordinated to reach specific consumer groups. Advertising agencies create colorful and attractive campaigns, often appealing to emotions rather than reason. They hire celebrities, compose catchy jingles, develop slogans, design colorful logos, and choose mascots to identify their products. There are three basic types of advertising: product, company, and industry.

1. *Product Advertising.* Advertising intended to convince consumers to buy a specific good or service is called **product advertising**. Advertisers often repeat the product name several times during commercials to help consumers remember it. Many ads feature famous athletes, actors, or other celebrities. Advertisers hope that your positive feelings for the celebrity will carry over to the product. Testimonials from people who have used the product, giveaways, and other promotional gimmicks are used to persuade consumers to buy. Ads are carefully planned to appeal to certain types of consumers. A **target market** is the specific consumer group to which the advertisements are designed to appeal. Television advertisers consider the day of the week, time of day, and type of program when placing their product ads. Products advertised during football games differ from products advertised during daytime television because the target markets are different.

2. *Company Advertising.* Advertising intended to promote the image of a store, company, or retail chain is known as **company advertising**. This type of advertising usually does not mention specific products or prices. Instead, it emphasizes the overall quality and reliability of the company and its products. For example, a company ad might feature company-sponsored community projects. A store ad might talk about the store's friendly employees or wide selection. These ads are designed to promote a favorable attitude toward the company so that you develop a loyalty to the store and shop there frequently.

3. *Industry Advertising.* Advertising intended to promote a general product group without regard to where these products are purchased is called **industry advertising**. For example, the dairy industry emphasizes the nutritional value of milk and other dairy products. Consequently, the whole dairy industry benefits when people drink more milk and eat more dairy products. Often, industry ads stress concern about energy conservation or environmental protection. General health and safety ads are often presented in industry campaigns, such as ads by the tobacco industry that discourage teen smoking.

Pricing

The price of merchandise depends on several factors. Supply and demand determine what will be produced and the general price range. The cost of raw materials and labor, competitive pressures, and the seller's need to make a reasonable profit are some of the factors that determine the price of a product. But there is more to pricing than adding up the production costs and including a profit. Retailers understand the psychological aspects of selling goods and services and use pricing devices to persuade consumers to buy. For example, if buyers believe they are getting a bargain or think they are paying a lower price than they really are, they are more inclined to buy the product or service. **Odd-number pricing** is the practice of setting prices at uneven amounts rather than whole dollars to make them seem lower. For example, the price tag might read 99 cents instead of $1.00. Because the price is under a dollar, it seems lower. Consumers perceive a price of $5.98 to be significantly lower than $6.00. As a result, they are more likely to buy the product at $5.98 than at $6.00.

Discounts are often available for buying in large quantities. However, you cannot assume that because you are buying the large economy size you are actually paying less per ounce than if you bought a small size. Compare unit prices on all sizes.

Sales

Stores advertise end-of-month sales, anniversary sales, clearance sales, inventory sales, holiday sales, pre-season sales, and so on. They may mark down merchandise substantially, slightly, or not at all. To be sure that you are actually saving money by buying sale items, you must practice comparison shopping and know the usual prices. When an ad states that everything in the store is marked down, check carefully for items that only appear to be marked down.

A **loss leader** is an item of merchandise marked down to an unusually low price, sometimes below the store's cost. The store may actually lose money on every sale of this item because the cost of producing the item is higher than the retail price. However, they use the loss leader to get customers into the store in the hope that they will buy other products as well. Profits from the sale of other items are expected to make up for the loss on the loss leader. There is nothing illegal or unethical about a loss leader as long as the product advertised is available to the customer on demand. A customer who buys only loss leaders is called a **cherry picker**. Retailers rely on customers to buy other products to make up for the loss on loss leaders, so they are not fond of cherry pickers.

©GETTY IMAGES/PHOTODISC

How can you ensure that you are actually saving money by buying sale items?

Promotional Techniques

To lure customers into their stores, retailers may use promotional techniques, such as displays, contests and games, frequent-buyer cards, coupons, packaging, sampling, and micromarketing.

1. *Displays.* Retail stores often use window displays and special racks of new items to entice customers. Products are arranged attractively, and the promotion may carry a theme centered on the nearest holiday—Halloween, Thanksgiving, or Christmas, for example. Color schemes, decorations, music, and special effects often set off the products in a way that will attract attention.

2. *Contests and Games.* Grocery stores, department stores, fast-food restaurants, and other retail stores that depend on repeat customers often use contests and games to bring customers into the store. Individual product packages, such as cereal boxes, may contain game cards. The possibility of winning something or getting something for nothing appeals to many people. Large and small prizes are offered with the intention of getting customers to come back and buy more so they can get more game cards, have more chances to win, and receive some of the minor prizes. Careful reading of the rules on the game card or other token reveals the customer's chances of winning. Usually, the chances of winning a major prize are small.

3. *Coupons. Manufacturer coupons* offer cents off on specific products from a particular manufacturer and may be redeemed wherever the product is sold. *Store coupons* offer discounts on specific products, usually for a short period of time, and only at a specific store. Manufacturer and store coupons may be inside or outside the package, in newspapers or magazines, on a store shelf, or even online. Coupons may not be redeemed for cash but do reduce the price of the product when purchased, encouraging customers to buy this product over a competitor's. Stores that accept manufacturer coupons return the coupons to the manufacturer for a refund of the amount given to the customer.

4. *Frequent-Buyer Cards.* Some stores use frequent-buyer cards that they punch with each purchase. The cards can also be computerized with each purchase being recorded electronically. Customers who accumulate enough punches, purchases, or points may receive some type of reward, such as gift certificates or merchandise. Frequent-buyer cards are used to build customer loyalty and repeat business for future purchases. *Customer-loyalty cards* are another version. Customers enroll in the program and receive a card. Each time they buy at the store, an electronic reader scans their card, and they receive lower prices on certain items they buy. The card enables the store to track what individual consumers buy. The store can then use this information to target advertising to individual preferences.

5. *Packaging.* Packages do more than just protect the product inside. They are also promotional tools. Manufacturers design packaging to appeal to the eye as well as provide the necessary consumer information. Distinctively designed packages attract the customer's attention away from competitive products. Company logos, brightly colored designs, pictures of people happily using the product, and other attention-getters appear on product boxes. Packaging emphasizes special features, such as "sugar free," "no preservatives," "new and improved," and many others. Size and shape of packages also attract attention. Containers that appear to hold more of the product or are reusable as storage devices appeal to consumers. Boxes that contain a game or prize inside will say so prominently on the outside of the box. Coupons may be included inside or on the package.

6. *Sampling.* Many companies promote their products through sampling. Small sample-size free packages of a product may be sent directly to households, included with newspapers delivered to homes, or distributed within a store or shopping center. When a new product is first introduced, sampling enables potential customers to try it. Some companies advertise in magazines and newspapers, with offers for free samples by mail.

7. *Micromarketing.* Many companies buy information about consumers in order to target promotions to those who are most likely to buy their products. Information about a person's lifestyle, marital status, family, age, and buying habits is known as *psychographics*. Micromarketers gather this information from previous purchases using credit cards or checks, customer-loyalty cards, public information, and other sources provided by government, post office, banks, and credit bureaus. Internet stores can also discover your preferences by electronically tracking your progress around the site. The product pages you view give the store a sense of the kinds of products that interest you. The purpose of gathering this kind of information is to target you with promotions for specific products and services that you are likely to buy.

While mass marketing is designed to reach millions at once through television ads, coupons, and other techniques, **micromarketing** is a marketing strategy designed to target specific people or small groups with products that they are likely to want. For example, when a couple has their first child, they are likely to receive ads, samples, and coupons for baby products. The birth record of the child is public information, and micromarketers gather it to find out who is most likely to want baby products. Targeted promotions make marketing more efficient. Rather than pay the cost of mailing samples of baby products to everyone, baby-product manufacturers can send samples only to consumers with babies.

✓Check Your Understanding

1. How do social pressures affect your buying habits?
2. Why do companies use micromarketing?

Issues in Your World

When you purchase a product from an online retailer, you likely register with the site and provide some information about yourself. The next time you visit, the site may present you with suggestions for products. The products may be companions to your previous purchase or products similar to items you are currently browsing at the site. How does the Web site know who you are and what you like?

When you register with an online retailer—and sometimes even when you don't—the site places a cookie, or small data file, on your computer. The next time you visit the site, the cookie sends the stored information about you back to the site. This way, the site can recognize its returning customer. As you travel around the site, the cookie keeps track of the product pages you visit. The online retailer is building a database of your preferences. This is micromarketing, Internet-style. The advertising targets you, a target market of one customer. This custom tailoring benefits you in that the ads you see really might interest you. It benefits the retailer by increasing the chances of making another sale to you.

With your e-mail address provided in your registration, the retailer can also send you advertising by e-mail. By knowing your product interests, the retailer can inform you of special offers on related products.

Internet micromarketing has its dark side—privacy concerns. Many companies that collect customer information online sell their customer databases to other companies. Also, the same technology that allows legitimate retailers to personalize their site for you can be used to steal information from you. Cookies can contain *spyware*. This is a program installed on your computer without your knowledge that constantly collects data about you and uses your Internet connection to send it to advertisers. Although spyware is not illegal, the potential for abuse is cause for concern. Consumers have no control over the data collected or its use.

Think Critically

1. Suppose you bought a music CD at an online music store. The next time you visited, the site popped up a list of similar music CDs for your consideration, including some at a special low price. Is this kind of service worth the possible loss of privacy to you? Explain.

2. Would you like to receive e-mail advertising? How is this kind of advertising like or unlike advertising delivered by U.S. mail?

Chapter
Assessment

SUMMARY

20.1

* The decision-making process typically involves six steps: define the problem, gather information, compare alternatives, select an alternative, take action, and reevaluate.
* Basic survival needs include food, clothing, and shelter. Everything else is a "want."
* Your wants are shaped by such factors as your values, personal preferences, income, and leisure time.
* Collective values that affect spending habits include the desire for legal protection, employment, progress (innovations), preserving the environment, and public services.

20.2

* Personal factors that influence individual spending habits include personal resources; position in life; customs, religion, and background; and values and goals.
* Factors outside yourself that affect your spending habits include the financial health of the economy, advances in technology, the environment, and social pressures.
* When planning major purchases, make sure you want the product for rational rather than emotional reasons. Research and compare before you buy.
* Advertising seeks to create a desire to purchase goods and services.
* Product advertising promotes a specific product to its target market.
* Company advertising promotes a positive company image.
* Industry advertising promotes a general product group to benefit all sellers in that industry.
* Consumers perceive prices stated in uneven amounts as lower than they really are.

* Loss leaders lure customers to the store, hoping they will buy other more profitable products.
* Promotional techniques to increase spending include displays, contests and games, coupons, frequent-buyer cards, attractive packaging, sampling, and micromarketing.

REVIEW TERMS

Directions

Can you find the definition for each of the following terms used in Chapter 20?

opportunity cost	innovations
basic needs	loss leader
cherry picker	micromarketing
collective values	odd-number pricing
company advertising	product advertising
custom	target market
economy	values
industry advertising	

1. Ingredients necessary for maintaining physical life.

2. Things that are important to society as a whole; all citizens share in their benefit and in their cost.

3. Merchandise marked down to a very low price, often below the store's cost.

4. The practice of setting prices at uneven amounts rather than whole dollars to make them seem lower.

5. New ideas, methods, or devices that bring about changes in a society's way of life.

6. A long-established practice that takes on the force of an unwritten law.

7. All activities related to production and distribution of goods and services in a geographic area.

8. Advertising that attempts to convince consumers to buy a specific good or service.

9. Advertising intended to promote the image of a store, company, or retail chain.

10. The specific consumer group to whom an advertisement is designed to appeal.

11. Advertising that attempts to sell a general product group without regard to where these products are purchased.

12. A person who buys only the store's loss leaders.

13. The principles by which a person lives.

14. A marketing strategy designed to target specific people or small groups with products that they are likely to want.

15. The value of your next best alternative whenever you make a choice.

REVIEW FACTS AND IDEAS

1. List and describe the six steps in the decision-making process.

2. How can the Internet help you comparison shop?

3. What is opportunity cost and why is it important in decision making?

4. What is the difference between basic needs and wants?

5. Why is it important to distinguish between wants and needs when defining the problem in a buying decision?

6. Explain how factors such as peer pressure and living arrangements affect spending patterns.

7. What are some personal factors that influence a person's or a family's spending patterns?

8. How do your values affect your use of money?

9. What are some outside factors that determine a person's or family's spending patterns?

10. For major purchases, why should you check reviews from more than one source before making a decision?

11. List six different advertising media. Which are mass media?

12. Why do companies use odd-number pricing?

13. Why aren't retailers fond of cherry pickers?

14. On what theme do promotional displays often center?

15. What is the purpose of frequent-buyer cards?

16. What are two functions of a product's package?

17. What is the purpose of micromarketing?

APPLY YOUR KNOWLEDGE

1. Using the steps in the decision-making process, make a decision that will satisfy your desire for a CD player.

2. Use key words to search the Internet for a price comparison site. Go to one of the sites you find. Then request a price comparison for a product you are interested in. What range of prices did the search engine find for the same product? What other features does the price comparison site offer to help you research and select products?

3. What community-centered and national environmental concerns do you have? What can you do as a single concerned citizen to help preserve the quality of the environment?

4. How do your spending patterns differ from those of your parents? What things do you buy that your parents also purchase? Can you trace any of these purchases to a strong family custom, background, or religion?

5. How are you or the members of your family affected when interest rates are very high? Do you benefit, or are you hurt? How? Can you think of anyone who is affected in the opposite way from you? Why is this so?

6. Spend an evening viewing television. List the jingles, key words, and slogans used in each commercial. How many commercials can you automatically sing along with? Also list the celebrities you saw in the ads and the products they promoted. Why do you think each celebrity was chosen for that particular product? Explain the emotional appeal behind each advertising slogan or campaign.

7. Log onto the Internet. What advertisements appear on your home page? Do they seem targeted to you? Next, surf around a well-known online store. What products are advertised on each page you visit? Why do you think the retailer chose to advertise those particular products in those places?

8. Look around at some different types of Internet advertising. What kinds of things can advertisers do with their ads online that they cannot do in a print magazine? Do you think Internet advertising is as effective at getting customers to buy as advertising on television? Why or why not?

Solve Problems ⊕ Explore Issues

1. Think of a major purchase that you would like to make if you could. Then follow the steps in the decision-making process up to the point of taking action. Write a description of what you did at each step. Include cost and feature comparisons where appropriate. What specific model and brand would you buy? Why?

2. Decide on a product or service you would like to buy. Do comparison shopping by checking with at least three different retailers. Use the Internet, phone, store visits, ads, or other means to find out information about features, total price, warranties, etc. Which seller offers the best value for your money? Support your conclusion.

3. Using Figure 20-1 as a guide, comparison shop for a computer with options of cash or credit purchase. Include the purchase price and credit terms. Analyze all options in a report.

4. Watch a television program for one hour anytime during the day. Determine the program's target audience (teenagers, children, homemakers, sports fans, families). Pay close attention to all commercials shown during the hour. Write your answers to the following questions on a separate piece of paper:
   a. List all the commercials. Categorize them as product, company, or industry advertising. (Public-service advertisements and political campaigns are industry advertisements.)
   b. Rate each commercial as good, fair, or poor, depending upon how well it is directed to the television program's target audience.
   c. Rate each commercial according to tastefulness (either good taste or poor taste). Do you find it offensive, degrading, or insulting? Explain why you liked or disliked the commercial.
   d. Which ads do you think were most effective? Why?

5. Bring to class an advertising insert from a newspaper. It should be from a department store, local discount store, or grocery store. Write your answers to these questions on a separate piece of paper:
   a. How many individual ads show odd-number pricing?
   b. How many mention how much money the buyer will save or what the regular price is?
   c. How many contained coupons or references to coupons?
   d. Which ones mentioned frequent-buyer cards, games, or special incentives?

e. Is the insert attractively presented? Rate each ad for attractiveness and readability.

   f. Identify any loss leaders.

   Attach the advertising insert to your answers. On the insert, write comments next to the items to identify them as examples of loss leaders, odd-number pricing, and so on.

6. Describe a store display built around the theme of the most recent major holiday. Describe colors used, products displayed, product arrangement, location in the store, and other aspects. Were there any actual price reductions?

7. List any stores in your area that use one or more of the following promotional techniques. Beside each store name, describe the specific techniques used.

   a. Contests and games

   b. Frequent-buyer or customer-loyalty cards

   c. Coupons

   d. Sampling

   e. Other

8. Find an appealing advertisement on the Internet and click on it. Then answer the following questions:

   a. What product or service is the advertiser selling?

   b. How does the arrangement of the advertiser's site help you learn more about the product or service?

   c. How can you order the product or service?

   d. Did the site give you a way to contact the company for additional information?

   e. Would you buy this product or service? Why or why not?

Renting a Residence

TERMS TO KNOW

dormitory	security deposit	tenant
efficiency	fee	lease
apartment	landlord	eviction

Consider This. . .

Doria was finishing her sophomore year in college, and at age 20, she was able to make housing choices. During her first two years, she had lived in university housing.

"We have lots of important decisions to make," she told her roommate. "We could stay right here in the dorm, but that may not be our best bet. Living off-campus has advantages, but there are also some variables that we haven't been concerned about living here. For example, we'll have to pay separate utility bills, and we'll need transportation to get to class. Parking is limited on campus, too. To afford to rent a house, we'd have to take in a few more people. But this is also pretty exciting, and I'm looking forward to the change."

Housing Decisions

Goals
- Describe several housing rental alternatives.
- Discuss potential living arrangements and moving choices.

▶ HOUSING ALTERNATIVES

You will soon have many important choices to make. One is where to live. You may choose to attend a nearby college and live at home with your parents. This would lower your costs so you can save toward a place of your own. Even when parents charge rent to help with costs, it is usually less expensive to commute than to live on your own.

Communication Connection

Would you consider renting an apartment after you finish high school? Write a one-page report on what you see as the advantages and disadvantages of this living arrangement. Would your parents agree with you?

Once you reach the age of adulthood, what are some different housing alternatives open to you?

On-Campus Housing

Many college students prefer to live on campus. A **dormitory** is an on-campus building that contains many small rooms that colleges rent to students. The rooms usually contain needed furniture such as beds, dressers, closets, and study tables. You might have a roommate, or for an extra charge, you might be able to have your own private room. Most dormitories have centrally located lounges for watching television and facilities for doing laundry. Dormitories provide a convenient location, plus eating facilities, with the meals included in the cost. Although individual rooms are small, with

©GETTY IMAGES/PHOTODISC

limited space for living and studying, the cost per school term may be less than for other housing alternatives.

Many colleges have sororities and fraternities that provide on-campus housing. To live in one of their buildings, you would have to become a member in a process called *pledging*. Typically, sororities and fraternities seek new members with goals, abilities, and ideals similar to those of the organization. For example, some require a certain grade point average. Others look for an interest in community service.

Housing cooperatives are also available on many larger campuses. When you live in a cooperative, you get a room similar to one in a dormitory. But the difference is in your responsibilities. In addition to keeping your room clean and usable, you share in cooking, cleaning, and maintaining the building. In exchange, your monthly rent is less because you help provide services for yourself and the group.

Major advantages of on-campus housing include closeness to classes and campus activities, access to campus resources such as the library and health center, and a feeling of being part of campus life. On the other hand, students often pay a flat fee for housing and meals, which includes services you may or may not use.

Apartments

If you don't attend college, or if you choose to live off campus, then your first residence away from home will likely be an apartment. At this stage of your life, your resources will probably be tight. The rent amount is usually based on the size and quality of the apartment and facilities provided, as well as distance to downtown jobs, college campuses, and shopping centers. You can find apartments in your chosen area in brochures, newspaper ads, and online.

An **efficiency apartment**, or *studio apartment*, is an apartment with one large room that serves as the kitchen, living room, and bedroom, plus a bathroom. Efficiencies have less living space than other apartments, but they are the least expensive. Larger apartments with separate living and dining areas are available in a variety of floor plans, including two-story models, called *townhouses*.

Apartments are often located in multi-unit buildings in which the number of units may be as few as two or as many as several hundred. Facilities provided may include a laundry room, storage area, swimming pool, tennis courts, and clubhouse. In addition, all or part of the utilities (heat, light, and garbage service) may be included in the rent payment.

Apartments provide independence and flexibility but also require responsibility and good judgment. Most apartment buildings have rules that make close living more enjoyable for all, such as no pets, no music or noise after 11 p.m., and restricted hours for use of some facilities, such as the pool.

Duplexes

As you learned in Chapter 14, a *duplex* is a building with two separate living units. Usually both living areas of the house are exactly the same, but there are separate entrances for each. Duplexes usually offer more space than apartments and more privacy, with only one close neighbor. They may include a garage or carport, private laundry facilities, and other privileges and responsibilities similar to a house. For example, an apartment renter is not expected to perform maintenance activities. A duplex renter, however, may be expected to mow the grass and maintain the landscaping around the unit.

Condominiums

As you recall from Chapter 14, a *condominium* is an individually owned unit in an apartment-style complex with shared ownership of common areas. The condominium owner, upon purchase of a unit, becomes a member of the homeowners' association, which is responsible for the property management. Each owner pays a monthly fee to cover the cost of maintaining the common areas and the outside portion of the units. The individual owners are responsible for maintaining the interior of the units. Common areas may include a variety of athletic and recreational facilities. If you are renting a condominium, you will have the same responsibilities for upkeep as the owner.

Houses

Rental houses offer many attractive features. However, they are often considerably more expensive to rent than apartments. You are paying for neighborhood living, often garage space and more living area, privacy, and the other comforts of home ownership. But you are also likely to find many of the same restrictions as with other rentals, such as no pets allowed. Because rented houses are investment properties that people buy and sell, the property may be shown to prospective new owners while you are living there. You may be asked to move if a new owner is purchasing it for private use rather than as a rental.

▶ LIVING ARRANGEMENTS

Choosing a roommate can be difficult. Just because you like someone doesn't mean that you can successfully live together. Your living habits may be very different. Be sure you are compatible with your potential roommate before you move in together. Discuss possible areas of disagreement that may cause trouble if not settled in advance. Some questions that you should answer for each other include:

    1. Do you smoke or drink? How do you feel about others who do?

2. Do you like a clean living area at all times, or are you easygoing and casual about your environment?

3. Do you have steady employment or another source of income to ensure that you can pay your share of expenses?

4. What are some of your goals? Do you want to continue your education, work full-time, or travel?

5. What are your leisure activities? What activities will you share with (or impose on) your roommate?

6. What type of transportation do you have? Will you share transportation? If so, what are the costs and how will you divide them?

You might also consider having more than one roommate. The more personalities involved, however, the more difficult it becomes to have problem-free relationships. Matching similar personality types will increase the chances for a successful living arrangement.

The more you know about each potential roommate, the better you will be able to get along and work out problems. It is a good idea to get to know each person before moving in together. Roommates need not be completely alike to get along. However, they do need to be aware of, and be able to accept, each other's personality traits and differences.

Where to Live

The decision of where to live will depend largely on finances. For college students who choose on-campus housing, many of the decisions discussed in this chapter will be predetermined. Renting in the community involves more planning. You must determine how much rent you can comfortably pay. Then you can begin shopping for the housing option that best meets your needs. Here are some considerations to think about as you decide where to live:

1. *Deposits and fees.* A **security deposit** is a refundable amount paid in advance to protect the owner against damage or non-payment. If you take care of the property and pay your rent on time, you should get the security deposit back when you move. Utility companies (such as the power company) may require you to make a security deposit when you first open an account. A **fee**, on the other hand, is a non-refundable charge for a service. For example, the owner may charge a fee for cleaning the apartment for the next renter.

2. *Length of time you plan to live in the residence.* If you sign a lease for six months, you have made a commitment to remain for that length of time. You may face penalties if you wish to move sooner.

3. *Distance from work or school.*

4. *Distance from a laundry, shopping, gas stations, and other frequently used services.*

5. *Repairs and maintenance you are expected to perform.*

Most financial experts advise allotting 30 percent of your total budget for housing. At first, you may need a roommate to share costs. Later, you may be able financially to carry the burden of living alone.

What to Take

Rental housing can come furnished or unfurnished. *Furnished* means that the basics are provided—bed, dresser, sofa, chairs, lamps, dining table and chairs, and essential appliances. An *unfurnished* rental residence may or may not include basic kitchen appliances such as stove and refrigerator. Usually the fewer the items furnished, the lower the rent. If you have enough furnishings or can acquire the essentials for an unfurnished residence, you can save a considerable amount in rent.

On what factors does the decision of where to live depend?

You can buy or rent furnishings. Compare purchase and rental payments carefully before you make a decision. Many companies rent furniture with an option to buy. For example, at the end of the rental period, you would have the option to buy the furniture at a price reduced by the portion of each rental payment made during that time. However, rent-to-own options are usually very expensive. Be sure to compute total costs and compare them to other financing options for purchasing furniture.

Basic household and personal items necessary for setting up housekeeping include the following:

1. Towels, wash cloths, sheets, cleaning cloths
2. Cleaning supplies (mops, brooms, buckets, vacuum cleaner, detergent, and cleansers)
3. Personal items (shampoo, cosmetics, soap, and other personal hygiene items)
4. Clothing, shoes, and other apparel
5. Dishes, silverware, pots, and pans
6. Lamps, clothes hangers, clocks, radio, television, and decorations

You may also need to provide rugs, draperies, shower curtain, and mirrors. You or your roommates may be able to contribute some of these items. Or, you may decide to buy jointly. Make a list of things to be purchased jointly. If you buy some things jointly and one of you decides to move, you must then divide the purchases. Before moving in, you and your roommates should agree on who will get what joint items when you dissolve the living arrangement. To avoid arguments later, keep a written record of these agreements.

► PLANNING YOUR MOVE

Begin planning your move several months in advance. Others who have experienced a similar move can help you with advice and contributions of household items. Here are some ways to prepare:

1. Set aside savings to cover the security deposit, first and last months' rent, fees, and initial expenses and purchases. If you have a pet, you may have to pay an additional security deposit or fee.

2. Have a reliable source of income to pay rent, utility bills, and shared expenses. Expect that your potential landlord will run a credit report to verify your ability to pay the rent. You will have to fill out an application that requires considerable personal and financial information.

3. Accumulate over time what you need to live independently, such as clothing, towels, sheets, pillows, small appliances, and dishes to minimize the items you need to buy when you move.

4. Plan the move with your career goals in mind. If your goal is to finish college, then your living plan should help you achieve this goal. For example, if you are planning to go to college in September and live on campus, it would probably not be wise to go out on your own for the three summer months. The expenses would be too high, and you would be better off saving your money to help meet college expenses.

5. Make arrangements for transporting furnishings. Professional movers can be expensive and must be reserved in advance. If you instead enlist friends to help you move, you may need to rent a truck that you reserve in advance. Also, plan to provide refreshments or a meal for your friends if the move will take several hours.

A good way to organize your preparations is to make a household needs inventory, such as the one shown in Figure 21-1. Decide with your roommates what you will need and check off each item as you fulfill the need.

Why is it wise to plan your move several months in advance?

@GETTY IMAGES/PHOTODISC

Group Financial Decisions

All roommates are responsible for meeting the obligations they agree upon. For example, each person must pay his or her share of the rent, so that the total rent is paid on time. You will probably share utilities equally, as well as garbage service, cable TV, Internet access charges, monthly telephone charges, and group activity expenses. Long-distance telephone calls and cell phone charges should be paid for individually. But expenses such as gasoline or groceries might be divided according to percentage of use. Laundry services usually are an individual expense.

figure **21-1**

What Is Needed	Date Needed	Cost	Date Completed
1. Dishes/towels	October 1	$100	_____
2. First and last months' rent	October 1	$1,400	_____
3. Security deposit	October 1	$100	_____
4. Moving-in fees	October 1	$250	_____
5. Car (share of expenses)	September 1	$150	_____
6. Job (part-time)	August 1		_____
7. Prepare household budget	September 1		_____
8. Plan with roommates	June 1		_____
9. Plan with parents	May 1		_____

Group budgeting allows for the careful allocation of expenses, so that each person pays his or her share. The budget should be prepared and put into writing following a good discussion. Figure 21-2 (page 512) is an example of a group budget.

As one method of paying these expenses, each person could have a separate account for individual expenses, and the group could have a joint account from which shared expenses are paid. You and your roommates should decide how much each person must deposit into the joint account by a certain date each month. Then you can decide who will write checks from the joint account to pay for rent, utilities, and other expenses incurred throughout the month. Individual roommates should be responsible for paying their own individual expenses on time.

Any plan for taking care of expenses should be agreed upon by all roommates so that everyone is satisfied. Put your agreements in writing so that no misunderstandings occur.

Moving Costs

Moving costs include the time and money spent in packing, storing, transporting, loading and unloading, and unpacking. Professional movers charge according to the amount you have to move, the distance to your new residence, and whether or not you want them to do the packing. You can save a lot of money by doing your own packing.

You can save even more by renting a truck or trailer and using your own labor for loading, driving, and unloading. If you are just moving

 figure 21-2

Expense	Monthly Cost	Robin's Share	Carmen's Share	Kendra's Share
Rent	$900	$300	$300	$300
Utilities (average)	150	50	50	50
Cable TV and Internet access	45	15	15	15
Gasoline/insurance /repairs	120	40	40	40
Groceries	600	200	200	200
Household supplies	90	30	30	30
TOTALS	$1,905	$635	$635	$635

across town, the rental will likely be cheaper if you can return the vehicle to the place where you rented it. However, for a longer move, you can rent a truck or trailer one way and return it to the rental agency's branch in the new city. One-way rental fees are usually a flat rate, plus mileage and gasoline, and a refundable security deposit. The rates vary, so compare before renting.

Installation Charges

When you move into a new residence, you will pay some installation charges, such as a telephone and cable TV. You must also arrange to turn on the electricity and other utilities. Many utility companies charge new customers a refundable security deposit.

Other companies, such as the telephone company, charge a one-time non-refundable fee. The installation charge is added to your first bill. Monthly service rates vary according to the kinds of services you select. For example, you will pay more for services such as call-waiting or caller ID. You will need to buy your own telephone and other attachments, such as caller ID or a messaging machine.

✓ Check Your Understanding

1. The decision of where to live will depend largely on what?
2. What questions should you and your potential roommate ask each other before deciding to live together?

The Rental Process

Goals
- List the advantages and disadvantages of renting a place to live.
- Describe the elements of a rental application, rental inventory, and lease.
- Discuss landlord and tenant responsibilities.

◣ ADVANTAGES OF RENTING

A **landlord** is the owner of rental property. A **tenant** is the person who rents property from a landlord. Because renting offers many advantages, it is a popular choice, especially among young people just getting started on their own. Some of the advantages renters enjoy are:

1. *Mobility.* Many people prefer to rent because of the ease and speed with which they can move when a good job opportunity comes along elsewhere. If you are unsure about whether or not you will stay in the same location for a long period, then renting a residence is wise.

2. *Convenience.* Many landlords provide a number of conveniences for their tenants. For example, rental properties often have laundry and recreational facilities. Also, rental units are often conveniently located near major shopping areas, downtown, or business centers.

3. *Minimal Responsibilities.* Renting usually relieves you of many of the responsibilities of home ownership. The landlord bears most responsibility for repairs, maintenance of the grounds, and property management.

4. *Social Life.* Apartments located in multi-unit buildings offer the opportunity to meet others and socialize informally, especially those that provide recreational facilities.

5. *Lower Living Expenses.* Apartment rent is usually lower than the cost of buying a house. Sharing expenses with roommates lowers individual costs even more.

▶ DISADVANTAGES OF RENTING

Renting has drawbacks as well. Some frequently mentioned disadvantages are:

1. *Noise.* Residents of apartments, duplexes, or condominiums share common walls with neighbors above, below, or beside them. Consequently, music, conversations, and other activities of neighbors can be overheard. Strange hours or unusual habits of neighbors can be very irritating.

2. *Lack of Privacy.* Because conversations and other activities can be overheard through common walls, tenants often feel that their neighbors know too much about their private lives. Problems associated with shared facilities—laundry and recreation, for example—also become annoying to some tenants.

3. *Small Quarters.* The typical apartment is smaller than some other housing alternatives. Five hundred to 1,000 square feet of living space is average for an apartment. A house may have 1,200 or more square feet of living space.

4. *Lack of Storage Area.* The small size of many apartments means less cabinet and closet space. Also, few rental properties offer more than a small amount of additional storage space for rarely used items.

5. *Lack of Parking.* Many rental properties do not provide garages or off-street parking, especially in city centers. Tenants' cars are subjected to the hazards of the weather and those associated with parking on busy streets. In complexes that provide parking lots, visitor parking is often very limited.

▶ RENTAL AGREEMENTS

Whenever you rent a place to live, you will have to fill out an application similar to the one shown in Figure 21-3. The purpose of the application is to allow the landlord to check your employment (income), previous rental experience, credit rating, and so on. The landlord does this type of checking to assure that you are a good risk—that you will likely pay your rent and be a good tenant. The landlord may refuse to rent you property because of your past rental history, employment record, or credit rating. Rental may not be denied, however, solely on the basis of race, religion, national origin, sex, or marital status. Some states have passed laws to prohibit denial of rental to tenants with small children.

figure **21-3** ◄

RENTAL APPLICATION

Date _____

Section 1. Personal Information

Applicant:
Name _____
Current Address_____
_____
Phone_____
Landlord _____
Landlord's Phone_____
Previous Address _____
_____
Previous Landlord _____
Landlord's Phone_____

Co-Applicant:
Name _____
Current Address_____
_____
Phone_____
Landlord _____
Landlord's Phone_____
Previous Address _____
_____
Previous Landlord_____
Landlord's Phone_____

Section 2. Employment

Employer _____
Address_____
_____
Phone_____
Monthly take-home pay $_____
Years employed at this job _____

Employer _____
Address_____
_____
Phone_____
Monthly take-home pay $_____
Years employed at this job _____

Section 3. Credit

Bank _____
___ Checking ___ Savings/Investment

Companies through which you have credit
cards or charge accounts:
_____
_____
_____

Bank _____
___ Checking ___ Savings/Investment

Companies through which you have credit
cards or charge accounts:
_____
_____
_____

Section 4. Personal References

Name _____
Phone_____
Relationship to applicant_____

Name_____
Phone_____
Relationship to applicant_____

I hereby swear that the above information is true and complete. I understand that incomplete or
inaccurate information on this application may result in denial and/or eviction.

Applicant Signature:
_____ *Date:* _____

Co-Applicant Signature:
_____ *Date:* _____

VIEWPOINTS

Choosing tenants is a critical decision for landlords. They need to avoid tenants who will pay their rent late, damage the rental unit, or cause legal or practical problems. However, the tenant selection process also needs to be nondiscriminatory.

Think Critically: Assume that you are a prospective tenant filling out a landlord's rental application. What questions do you think are fair for the landlord to ask? What questions would be considered discriminatory?

Leases and Month-to-Month Agreements

Basically there are two types of rental agreements: leases and month-to-month tenancy agreements. A **lease** is a written agreement that allows a tenant to use property for a specified time period and rent. You may sign a lease for six months, one year, two years, or any period agreed upon. The landlord cannot raise the rent until the lease expires, except as agreed upon in the lease. But if you decide to move before the lease expires, you are still responsible for the remaining rent payments. At least 30 days prior to the end of your lease, the landlord should inform you of any rent increase. If you do not wish to stay longer than the time of your lease, you must notify the landlord in writing in advance, as specified in the lease. Often leases require 30-days' notice prior to departure. Figure 21-4 is an example of a lease agreement.

If you rent month-to-month, you can leave anytime, as long as you give the required notice. The agreement does not bind you to pay rent for a period of time longer than a month, as a lease does. However, renting by the month also does not establish the rent amount for more than a month. The landlord can raise the rent anytime or ask you to leave anytime. Still, the ease of moving in and out is an advantage of renting month-to-month. If your plans are very uncertain and you need maximum flexibility, then month-to-month rental may be a good option for you.

Both a lease and a month-to-month rental agreement will include provisions for deposits and their return, termination of rental, rent payments, tenant and landlord responsibilities, and various other matters. If you do not understand any part of the agreement, ask the landlord to explain. If the answer is not satisfactory, get a legal interpretation or refuse to sign the agreement and go elsewhere. Both a lease and a month-to-month rental agreement are legally binding when you sign them.

figure **21-4**

RESIDENTIAL LEASE AGREEMENT
AND SECURITY DEPOSIT RECEIPT

THIS INDENTURE, made this ___29th___ day of ___October___ , 20 _ _ , between

___Brendan Martin___ , hereinafter designated the Lessor

or Landlord, and ___Teresa Thomas___ , hereinafter designated the Lessee,

WITNESSETH: That the said Lessor/Landlord does by these presents lease and demise the residence

situated at ___614 Dundas Street___ in ___Cincinnati___ City,

___Hamilton___ County, ___Ohio___ State,

of which the real estate is described as follows:

614 Dundas Street, Cincinnati, Ohio,

upon the following terms and conditions:

1. **Term:** The premises are leased for a term of ___one (1)___ years, commencing the ___1st___ day of ___November___ , 20 _ _ , and terminating the ___31st___ day of ___October___ , 20 _ _ .

2. **Rent:** The Lessee shall pay rent in the amount of $ ___$600.00___ per month for the above premises on the ___1st___ day of each month in advance to Landlord.

3. **Utilities:** Lessee shall pay for service and utilities supplied to the premises, except ___None___ which will be furnished by Landlord.

4. **Sublet:** The Lessee agrees not to sublet said premises nor assign this agreement nor any part thereof without the prior written consent of Landlord.

5. **Inspection of Premises:** Lessee agrees that he has made inspection of the premises and accepts the condition of the premises in its present state, and that there are no repairs, changes, or modifications to said premises to be made by the Landlord other than as listed herein.

6. **Lessee Agrees:**
   (1) To keep said premises in a clean and sanitary condition;
   (2) To properly dispose of rubbish, garbage, and waste in a clean and sanitary manner at reasonable and regular intervals and to assume all costs of extermination and fumigation for infestation caused by Lessee;
   (3) To properly use and operate all electrical, gas, heating, plumbing facilities, fixtures and appliances;
   (4) To not intentionally or negligently destroy, deface, damage, impair, or remove any part of the premises, their appurtenances, facilities, equipment, furniture, furnishings, and appliances, nor to permit any member of his family, invitee, licensee or other person acting under his control to do so;
   (5) Not to permit a nuisance or common waste.

7. **Maintenance of Premises:** Lessee agrees to mow and water the grass and lawn, and keep the grass, lawn, flowers, and shrubbery thereon in good order and condition, and to keep the sidewalk surrounding said premises free and clear of all obstructions; to replace in a neat and workmanlike manner all glass and doors broken during occupancy thereof; to use due precaution against freezing of water or waste pipes and stoppage of same in and about said premises and that in case water or waste pipes are frozen or become clogged by reason of neglect of Lessee, the Lessee shall repair the same at his own expense as well as all damage caused thereby.

8. **Alterations:** Lessee agrees not to make alterations or do or cause to be done any painting or wallpapering to said premises without the prior written consent of Landlord.

9. **Use of Premises:** Lessee shall not use said premises for any purpose other than that of a residence and shall not use said premises or any part thereof for any illegal purpose. Lessee agrees to conform to municipal, county and state codes, statutes, ordinances, and regulations concerning the use and occupation of said premises.

10. **Pets and Animals:** Lessee shall not maintain any pets or animals upon the premises without the prior written consent of Landlord.

11. **Access:** Landlord shall have the right to place and maintain "for rent" signs in a conspicuous place on said premises for thirty days prior to the vacation of said premises. Landlord reserves the right of access to the premises for the purpose of:
   (a) Inspection;
   (b) Repairs, alterations or improvements;
   (c) To supply services; or
   (d) To exhibit or display the premises to prospective or actual purchasers, mortgagees, tenants, workmen, or contractors. Access shall be at reasonable times except in case of emergency or abandonment.

12. **Surrender of Premises:** In the event of default in payment of any installation of rent or at the expiration of said term of this lease, Lessee will quit and surrender the said premises to Landlord.

13. **Security Deposit:** The Lessee has deposited the sum of $ ___600.00___ , receipt of which is hereby acknowledged, which sum shall be deposited by Landlord in a trust account with ___Citizens___ bank; savings and loan association, or licensed escrow, ___Cincinnati___ branch, whose address is ___201 Main Street, Cincinnati, Ohio___
All or a portion of such deposit may be retained by Landlord and a refund of any portion of such deposit is conditioned as follows:
   (1) Lessee shall fully perform obligations hereunder and those pursuant to Chapter 207, Laws of 1973, 1st Ex Session or as may be subsequently amended.
   (2) Lessee shall occupy said premises for ___one (1)___ months or longer from date hereof.
   (3) Lessee shall clean and restore said residence and return the same to Landlord in its initial condition, except for reasonable wear and tear, upon the termination of this tenancy and vacation of apartment.
   (4) Lessee shall have remedied or repaired any damage to apartment premises;
   (5) Lessee shall surrender to Landlord the keys to premises;
Any refund from security deposit, as by itemized statement shown to be due to Lessee, shall be returned to Lessee within fourteen (14) days after termination of this tenancy and vacation of the premises.

IN WITNESS WHEREOF, the Lessee has hereunto set his hand and seal the day and year first above written.

___/s/ Brendan Martin___   ___/s/ Teresa Thomas___
LANDLORD   LESSEE
___610 Dundas Street___
___Cincinnati, Ohio___
ADDRESS

(Acknowledgment)

If you live in a rental property, you are expected to leave it as you found it. Normal wear and tear is expected and accepted. However, anything broken or misplaced is not acceptable. Therefore, to assure that you are not accused of such acts as breaking, damaging, or taking furnishings, prepare an inventory of the premises at the time you move in.

The inventory should list and describe the conditions of the property. Note such things as broken windows, missing window screens, holes in walls, torn carpeting, plumbing problems, and appliance problems. You and your landlord should tour the property together to take the inventory, so that you both agree on its contents. Then you or the landlord should make a copy for each of you. When you move out, you and your landlord should once again take an inventory. The comparison between this inventory and the initial one will often determine whether or not you get your security deposit back. Figure 21-5 shows an inventory and condition report that can be used in a variety of rental situations.

▶ LANDLORD/TENANT RESPONSIBILITIES

Although most states have passed landlord/tenant laws, there are no national laws. However, laws concerning residential rental units generally include similarly worded landlord and tenant obligations.

Landlord Obligations

Housing laws in most states require that landlords provide a dwelling that is habitable (livable) at all times. A dwelling is considered habitable if the following conditions are met:

1. The exterior (including roof, walls, doors, and windows) is weatherproof and waterproof.

2. Floors, walls, ceilings, stairs, and railings are in good repair.

3. Elevators, halls, and stairwells meet fire and safety regulations. (Smoke detectors are required in each unit in most states. Tenants are responsible for testing the alarms, replacing batteries, and reporting any defects.)

4. Adequate locks are provided for all outside doors, working latches are provided for all windows, and exits meet fire and safety regulations.

5. Plumbing facilities comply with local and state laws and are in good working condition.

figure **21-5**

INVENTORY AND CONDITION REPORT

Use this report to record the contents and condition of your unit when you move in and before moving out. If you mark anything as being either dirty or damaged, describe it fully on an additional sheet. Use the blank before each item to indicate how many there are. Ask the landlord to sign your copy.

		Dirty Yes*	No	Damaged Yes*	No
Living Room					
___ Couch	1	☐	☐	☐	☐
___ Chair.	2	☐	☐	☐	☐
___ End table	3	☐	☐	☐	☐
___ Easy chair	4	☐	☐	☐	☐
___ Floor lamp	5	☐	☐	☐	☐
___ Table lamp	6	☐	☐	☐	☐
___ Coffee table	7	☐	☐	☐	☐
___ Light fixture	8	☐	☐	☐	☐
___ Rug or carpet	9	☐	☐	☐	☐
___ Floor	10	☐	☐	☐	☐
___ Walls	11	☐	☐	☐	☐
___ Ceiling	12	☐	☐	☐	☐
Bedroom					
___ Bed frame(s)	13	☐	☐	☐	☐
___ Headboard(s)	14	☐	☐	☐	☐
___ Mattress	15	☐	☐	☐	☐
___ Mattress cover	16	☐	☐	☐	☐
___ Bed springs	17	☐	☐	☐	☐
___ Dresser	18	☐	☐	☐	☐
___ Nightstand	19	☐	☐	☐	☐
___ Drapes or curtains	20	☐	☐	☐	☐
___ Mirror	21	☐	☐	☐	☐
___ Light fixture	22	☐	☐	☐	☐
___ Rug or carpet	23	☐	☐	☐	☐
___ Floor	24	☐	☐	☐	☐
___ Walls	25	☐	☐	☐	☐
___ Ceiling	26	☐	☐	☐	☐
Bedroom					
___ Bed frame(s)	27	☐	☐	☐	☐
___ Headboard(s)	28	☐	☐	☐	☐
___ Mattress	29	☐	☐	☐	☐
___ Mattress cover	30	☐	☐	☐	☐
___ Bed springs	31	☐	☐	☐	☐
___ Dresser	32	☐	☐	☐	☐
___ Nightstand	33	☐	☐	☐	☐
___ Drapes or curtains	34	☐	☐	☐	☐
___ Mirror	35	☐	☐	☐	☐
___ Light fixture	36	☐	☐	☐	☐
___ Rug or carpet	37	☐	☐	☐	☐
___ Floor	38	☐	☐	☐	☐
___ Walls	39	☐	☐	☐	☐
___ Ceiling	40	☐	☐	☐	☐
Kitchen					
___ Working stove	41	☐	☐	☐	☐
___ Working oven	42	☐	☐	☐	☐

		Dirty Yes*	No	Damaged Yes*	No
___ Oven racks	43	☐	☐	☐	☐
___ Broiler pan	44	☐	☐	☐	☐
___ Working refrigerator	45	☐	☐	☐	☐
___ Ice trays	46	☐	☐	☐	☐
___ Working sink	47	☐	☐	☐	☐
___ Working garbage disposal	48	☐	☐	☐	☐
___ Counter tops	49	☐	☐	☐	☐
___ Range hood w/working fan	50	☐	☐	☐	☐
___ Working dishwasher	51	☐	☐	☐	☐
___ Hot and cold running water	52	☐	☐	☐	☐
___ Drawers	53	☐	☐	☐	☐
___ Dinette table	54	☐	☐	☐	☐
___ Dinette chairs	55	☐	☐	☐	☐
___ Light fixture	56	☐	☐	☐	☐
___ Floor	57	☐	☐	☐	☐
___ Walls	58	☐	☐	☐	☐
___ Ceiling	59	☐	☐	☐	☐
Bathroom					
___ Towel racks	60	☐	☐	☐	☐
___ Tissue holder	61	☐	☐	☐	☐
___ Mirror	62	☐	☐	☐	☐
___ Medicine cabinet	63	☐	☐	☐	☐
___ Counter top	64	☐	☐	☐	☐
___ Working sink	65	☐	☐	☐	☐
___ Working tub	66	☐	☐	☐	☐
___ Working shower	67	☐	☐	☐	☐
___ Working toilet	68	☐	☐	☐	☐
___ Toilet seat	69	☐	☐	☐	☐
___ Shower curtain	70	☐	☐	☐	☐
___ Cabinet	71	☐	☐	☐	☐
___ Light fixture	72	☐	☐	☐	☐
___ Hot and cold running water	73	☐	☐	☐	☐
___ Floor	74	☐	☐	☐	☐
___ Walls	75	☐	☐	☐	☐
___ Ceiling	76	☐	☐	☐	☐
Miscellaneous					
___ Door key	77	☐	☐	☐	☐
___ Windows	78	☐	☐	☐	☐
___ Window screens	79	☐	☐	☐	☐
___ Mailbox	80	☐	☐	☐	☐
___ Mailbox key	81	☐	☐	☐	☐
___ Thermostat	82	☐	☐	☐	☐
___ Other	83	☐	☐	☐	☐
___	84	☐	☐	☐	☐

Do all the windows work? ....
Does the heat work properly? ....

_____ Tenant

_____ Witness

_____ Date

_____ Landlord

_____ Date

*Describe fully on an additional sheet.

6. Water supply provided is adequate.

7. Lighting, wiring, heating, air conditioning, and appliances are in good condition and comply with local and state building and safety codes.

8. Buildings and grounds are clean and sanitary; garbage receptacles are adequate. (Tenants may be responsible for garbage removal charges.)

Tenant Obligations

Tenant obligations usually are stated specifically in the lease or month-to-month agreement. If they are not stated, the following tenant responsibilities are implied:

1. To read, understand, and abide by the terms of the rental agreement.

2. To pay the rent on or before the due date. Failure to make a rent payment as stated in the rental agreement may result in late fees, termination of the agreement, or eviction. **Eviction** is the legal process of removing a tenant from rental property.

3. To give 30- to 60-days' notice of intent to move. This notice will prevent the loss of security deposits and allow the landlord time to rent the unit before you move.

4. To keep the premises in good, clean condition and to prevent unnecessary wear and tear or damage to the unit.

5. To use a dwelling unit only for the purposes for which it is intended. For example, you should treat appliances and other furnishings in a reasonable manner. If the landlord pays for utilities, you should use them in a reasonable manner.

What are some obligations owed by tenants to their landlords?

6. To allow the landlord access to the living unit to make repairs or improvements.

7. To obey the rules of the apartment complex or other community living area covering such things as quiet hours, use of recreational facilities, use of laundry facilities, and parking regulations.

✔Check Your Understanding

1. How is a lease different from a month-to-month rental agreement?

2. Explain the purpose of a rental inventory prepared when you first move into rental property and when you move out.

Issues in Your World

Before You Sign the Lease

Many owners of rental property would rather lease space to you than rent it to you month-to-month. A lease gives both the *lessor* (the landlord) and the *lessee* (the tenant) the security of knowing the property is committed for a fixed period of time. But the lease can be a trap if you don't understand its provisions before you agree.

For example, many lessors offer "specials" to those who sign leases for a year or more. These specials may include reduced monthly rent, reduced deposits and fees, and other concessions. But in most cases, if you need to terminate the lease before the agreed-upon time, there can be enormous consequences.

In a typical "special" lease offer, the lessor states that regular monthly rent is $600 per month. If the lessee signs a one-year lease, the rent is reduced to $550 and the move-in fee is also reduced from $300 to $100. The savings are significant. But the lease also states that if the lessee terminates the agreement prior to one year, he or she must repay the entire rent reduction and the balance of the reduced fee.

Suppose you are the lessee and you must move out early, say at the beginning of the eighth month. You would have to pay back seven months' worth of reduced rent ($50 × 7) plus the additional $200 move-in fee, for a total of $550. In addition, you are still obligated to pay the remaining five months' rent (at the higher rate) unless the lessor can find another tenant to take your place. This type of "deal" can be very, very expensive.

Before you sign the lease, be sure to read it carefully and understand your commitments. You may be able to negotiate better terms at the beginning, before you sign the lease.

Think Critically

1. Check your newspaper or online listings for rental housing in your area. Do you see any lease specials? Describe them.

2. Do you know someone who is leasing property? Ask to see the person's lease agreement. What potentially expensive provisions does it contain?

Chapter Assessment

SUMMARY

21.1
- Living with your parents and commuting to school or work will help you save toward a place of your own.
- On-campus housing options include dormitories, fraternity or sorority houses, and housing cooperatives.
- Generally, the more facilities and conveniences an apartment offers, the higher the rent.
- Duplexes, condominiums, and rental houses offer more space than apartments, but are usually more expensive and require tenants to do some maintenance.
- To live together successfully, roommates must have compatible living habits and work out responsibilities in advance.
- When deciding where to live, consider deposits and fees, length of time you plan to live there, distance from work or school, nearby shopping and services, and maintenance costs.
- Prepare to move by accumulating needed items over time and saving to cover initial expenses.
- Professional movers charge according to amount to be moved, distance, and extent of packing services desired. Moving yourself saves money.
- When you move in, you will have to pay fees to have utilities installed or turned on.

21.2
- Advantages of renting include mobility, convenience to shopping and work, minimal responsibilities for maintenance, opportunity for social interaction, and lower expenses.
- Disadvantages of renting include noise from close neighbors, lack of privacy, small living space, lack of storage, and scarce parking.
- Landlords use the rental application to determine if you are a good risk as a tenant.

* If you lease, you agree to rent the space for a specified time and rent. During this time the landlord cannot raise the rent, but you must pay for the entire term if you move out early.

* If you rent month-to-month, you can leave anytime, but the landlord can raise the rent anytime.

* Landlords are responsible for providing a safe and habitable place for tenants to live.

* Tenants are responsible for paying rent on time, obeying the rules, and taking reasonable care of the property.

REVIEW TERMS

Directions

Can you find the definition for each of the following terms used in Chapter 21?

dormitory	landlord
efficiency apartment	lease
eviction	security deposit
fee	tenant

1. The legal process of removing a tenant from rental property.

2. A non-refundable charge for a service.

3. A refundable amount paid in advance to protect the owner against damage or non-payment.

4. A person who rents property from a landlord.

5. An on-campus building that contains small rooms that colleges rent to students.

6. The owner of rental property.

7. A written agreement that allows a tenant to use property for a specified time period and rent.

8. An apartment with one large room that serves as the kitchen, living room, and bedroom, plus a bathroom.

REVIEW FACTS AND IDEAS

1. If you go to college, what are some advantages of living on campus?

2. How do landlords protect themselves against damage tenants do to the property?

3. What kinds of responsibilities should roommates share jointly?

4. List four advantages of renting a residence.

5. List four disadvantages of renting a residence.

6. What is the purpose of a rental application?

7. How does a lease differ from a month-to-month rental agreement?

8. Why should you take an inventory of your rental unit and have the landlord sign it before you move in?

9. List several conditions a landlord must meet in order to make rental property habitable.

10. List several tenant obligations when renting.

APPLY YOUR KNOWLEDGE

1. Ask two people separately to answer the questions in the "Living Arrangements" section on pages 507–508. Based on the answers, would the three of you be a compatible living group? List the problems you would have to work out to live together successfully. Then get together and role-play a discussion in which you work out these problems. Record your agreements in writing.

2. What possessions have you accumulated that you would need in order to set up housekeeping in an apartment?

3. What basics would you have to acquire to live independently? Which of these would you have to buy and which could you borrow to save money?

4. Make a list of things you should do before moving out on your own.

5. To move your possessions from your present home to a new residence, what types of transportation are available to you? What is the best and least expensive for you?

1. Prepare a report comparing the rental prices and availability of apartments, duplexes, condominiums, and houses in your area. To compare prices, living conditions must be comparable—compare two-bedroom unfurnished apartments to two-bedroom unfurnished duplexes, and so forth. Also, note how many are presently available in each category, the high and low prices, and the average rental prices. (Hint: You can look up this information on the Internet. Your local newspaper's classified section will probably be available online.)

2. Select a large city in another state. Search the Internet for apartments to rent in that city. (Hint: Include the city name as well as "rent" and "apartment" as key words in your search engine.) Select a moderately priced apartment there and print out or write down the description of it. Be sure to note the rent. Then find a similar apartment in a smaller town. What is the rent for this apartment? What can you conclude about the cost of living between these two locations, based on apartment rents?

3. Using the community resources in your area, find out the installation deposits and fees for the following services:
   a. Telephone
   b. Electricity
   c. Cable TV
   d. Water or garbage services
   Are any of these fees partially or fully refundable? If so, under what conditions?

4. Find out the rates or prices for the following telephone services in your area:
   a. Standard phone
   b. Pager
   c. Voice messaging
   d. Caller ID
   e. Wireless communications
   f. Call forwarding
   g. Call waiting
   h. Unlisted telephone number
   i. Additional phone jack installed

For related activities and links, point your browser to **www.mypf.swlearning.com**

Buying a Home

market value
  (real estate)
equity
points
closing costs
Multiple Listing
  Service (MLS)

offer
earnest money
acceptance
counteroffer
fixed-rate
  mortgage

adjustable-rate
  mortgage (ARM)
title
deed
lien

Consider This. . .

Coley and Donika have been married for five years, and they have managed to save money toward buying their own home.

"I think we have enough down payment money saved to buy a home with four bedrooms, though we really need only two bedrooms right now," Coley said to his wife.

"I'm not sure we have as large a down payment as you think," Donika replied. "We'll have to pay other costs as well, such as closing costs and moving expenses."

"Okay," Coley agreed. "Let's start out with a smaller house that meets our needs and has potential for improvement. We can sell and move to another house when we start our family. By then we'll have built up some equity."

Why Buy a Home?

Goals
- Discuss the advantages of home ownership.
- Describe the costs and responsibilities of home ownership.

▶ ADVANTAGES OF HOME OWNERSHIP

Because the purchase of a home may be the most expensive decision you ever make, you should carefully weigh the advantages, costs, and responsibilities. Although many single people own their own homes, marriage and family usually create the greatest need for home ownership. The need for room to expand as the family grows is often the main reason that families buy a home.

Home ownership offers financial advantages, but owning a home is more than a financial decision. Your own home also offers advantages that improve your quality of life. These personal advantages are important factors in your decision to buy a home.

Equity Increases

In Chapter 12, you learned that the market value of a stock is the price for which it is bought and sold on the market. Similarly, the **market value** of a home is the highest price that the property will bring on the market. In other words, it is the price at which the property could be bought and sold on the market. Real estate agents and professional appraisers from a bank can *appraise* or estimate the market value of your home by comparing it to similar homes that have sold recently. The typical price for which these similar homes sold is a good estimate of the current market value of your home. Real estate agents appraise homes to help the owners establish a selling price. Banks appraise homes to determine how much they can safely loan to the buyers.

The market value of homes tends to increase or *appreciate* over time. For example, if you buy a home for $100,000 and two years later you could sell it for $110,000, then your property has appreciated by $10,000. Appreciation is one way that your equity in your home increases. **Equity** is the difference between the market value of property and the amount owed on it.

Your equity also increases because each loan payment you make decreases your debt. When you sell your home years later, the increased market value and the lower remaining debt owed will result in greater equity. Equity turns to cash when you sell the home. For example, if you purchase a home valued at $150,000 and have a loan of $120,000, your initial equity is $30,000. Suppose that when you decide to sell, the market value has increased to $170,000 and your loan debt is down to $100,000. Your equity would be the $170,000 selling price minus $100,000 owed, or $70,000. The cash you receive from the sale would be the $70,000 equity minus selling expenses. The Math Minute shows the step-by-step calculations in determining the current equity in a home.

©GETTY IMAGES/PHOTODISC

What kinds of quality-of-life advantages do homeowners enjoy?

Tax Savings

The interest you pay on your home loan, along with the property taxes, are tax deductible. These deductions lower the cost of home ownership. Because of these tax savings, owning real estate is a *tax shelter*. Renters cannot deduct any part of their rent payments from their income taxes. Even though your equity in your home may be increasing each year, you do not pay tax on it until you sell your home, and even then you can avoid taxes on the gains.

Quality-of-Life Advantages

Home ownership offers privacy and personal freedom not available to renters. In your own home you make all the decisions and have free use of all facilities. Owning a home also provides a feeling of security and independence. Knowing that the home is yours to do with as you wish and when you wish can be very satisfying. You also get a sense of stability and belonging to your community. You have "put down roots," so you care about what happens in your neighborhood.

⏱ Math Minute

Suppose you bought a home for $200,000. Your lender required a 20 percent down payment. Therefore, your down payment amount was:

$$\$200,000 \times .2 = \$40,000$$

Your initial loan amount (ignoring other costs) was:

$$\$200,000 - \$40,000 = \$160,000$$

Now let's say that you have been making payments on your house for two years, reducing your debt by $8,000. Therefore, you now owe $160,000 − $8,000 = $152,000.

Your house has been appreciating at 5 percent per year for two years. As a result, the current market value is:

$$\$200,000 \times .05 = \$10,000$$
$$\$200,000 + \$10,000 = \$210,000 \text{ after year 1}$$
$$\$210,000 \times .05 = \$10,500$$
$$\$210,000 + \$10,500 = \$220,500 \text{ after year 2}$$

Your equity is now:

$$\$220,500 \text{ market value} - \$152,000 \text{ remaining debt} = \$68,500$$

Problem: Felipe and Concepcion bought a house two years ago for $175,000. They put 15 percent down. Their payments over the last two years reduced their debt by $6,000. Houses in their area have been appreciating at 4 percent per year. Find the following:
1. The amount of their down payment.
2. The amount of their initial loan.
3. The amount of their current debt.
4. The current market value.
5. Their current equity.

Solution:
1. Down payment = $26,250
2. Initial loan = $148,750
3. Current debt = $142,750
4. Current market value = $189,280
5. Current equity = $46,530

▶ COSTS AND RESPONSIBILITIES OF HOME OWNERSHIP

Home ownership carries significant costs and responsibilities. Before deciding to buy a home, you must make sure that you can financially handle the costs and that you are personally ready to accept the responsibilities.

Down Payment

Most conventional (not government-backed) loans require a 10 to 30 percent down payment. For example, if you are purchasing a home for $150,000, you will need $15,000 (10 percent) to $45,000 (30 percent) for the down payment. For many people, saving enough money for the down payment takes a number of years.

Mortgage

Home buyers usually borrow the rest of the purchase price, after the down payment, from a bank or other financial institution. A loan to purchase real estate is called a *mortgage*. Payments on a mortgage are made over an extended period—for example, 15 or 30 years. The larger your down payment, the lower your monthly mortgage payments. Property taxes and the cost of property insurance are often included with the mortgage payments.

Mortgage lenders often add a finance charge in the form of **points**. Each point equals 1 percent of the loan amount. For example, 3 points on a $100,000 loan would be $3,000. Points are essentially extra interest that borrowers must pay at closing (time of purchase). The amount is tax deductible. However, points increase the cost of the loan. When you compare loan rates, be sure to consider the points. Lenders usually offer lower interest rates in exchange for higher points. Whether or not this trade-off is a good deal depends on how long you plan to keep your house. A lower interest rate will result in lower monthly payments. Over many years, the lower payments may make up for the cost of the points and save you money. But since points are paid up front, you could lose money if you keep your house for only a few years.

Closing

Closing costs, also referred to as *settlement costs*, are the expenses incurred in transferring ownership from buyer to seller in a real estate transaction. Closing costs may add another $3,000 to $5,000 to the purchase of your home. The buyer usually pays for a title search to make sure the seller is the legal owner and that no one else has claims on the property. The buyer may also pay for a personal credit report, loan fees, assumption fees (to take over someone else's mortgage), closing fees (fees for preparing the paperwork), recording fees, some portion of taxes and interest owed, and property insurance.

Property Taxes

The real estate property tax is a major source of funding for local governments. Homeowners pay property taxes based on the assessed value of land and buildings. A local taxing authority determines the assessed value of your property, usually a percentage of the market value. A home worth $100,000 might have an assessed value of $90,000 (or 90 percent of its market value). If the property tax rate is $24 per thousand of assessed value, you will pay 90 times $24, or $2,160 a year in property taxes. Your annual property taxes are tax deductible.

Insurance

A homeowner must have property insurance covering the structure as well as the contents of a home. A more detailed explanation of homeowners insurance is presented in Chapter 26.

Utilities

Because most homes are larger than apartments or other rental units, the utility bills are usually larger. The homeowner pays for all utilities and garbage services, whereas a renter may pay for some but not all of these services. In addition, when repairs are needed to water or sewer lines, the homeowner is fully responsible for the costs.

Maintenance and Repairs

As a homeowner, you will be responsible for maintenance and repairs inside and outside your home. Before you choose to buy, make sure you are willing to spend the time and money needed to keep your home in good condition.

Ongoing maintenance includes such tasks as painting, mowing, landscaping, weeding, and fixing things that break or wear out from normal use. You would incur not only the costs but also the responsibility for doing these tasks or arranging to have them done.

In addition to ongoing maintenance, you will occasionally have to make very expensive repairs or improvements to your home. For example, a roof lasts only about 15 years. The furnace and water heater will also need replacing in about that length of time. You must save to cover these future major expenses.

Once you have purchased a house, what kinds of financial obligations can you expect?

©GETTY IMAGES/PHOTODISC

Net Nuggets

The Web site http://homebuying.about.com/ contains articles and other resources for the first-time homebuyer. Essential information covers the 11 steps to buying a home; mortgages; credit reports; surveys and deeds; preventing foreclosure; working with real estate agents; home inspections; and other key topics.

✔ Check Your Understanding

1. Why do people choose to buy a house rather than rent a residence?
2. What responsibilities go with home ownership?

Lesson 22.2

The Home-Buying Process

Goals
- Describe the steps in the home-buying process.
- Discuss how to obtain financing and the closing process.

▶ FINDING AND SELECTING A HOME

In buying a home, you should consider such factors as location, accessibility, nearness to employment, type and quality of construction, cost and effort of maintenance, and personal likes and dislikes. Before starting your search, make a list of the features you want your home and neighborhood to have and the price range you can afford. Prioritize the list according to each feature's importance to you. No house will meet all your desires. You will have to make trade-offs. Therefore, you should have a clear understanding of what you want most before you begin to look.

Working with a Real Estate Agent

Before selecting a home to buy, look at many houses. You can look by yourself or work with a real estate agent. Agents are trained to know the market, help you find the right home, and assist you with the purchase, financing, and closing.

Real estate agents earn a commission for their work. The commission is a percentage of the sale price, usually around 5 percent to

7 percent. The seller pays the commission, and the agents working for the buyer and seller split it. As the purchaser, you do not pay the agent's commission. However, be aware that because the seller pays the commission, the agents representing both the buyer and the seller really work for the seller. The more you spend for the home, the more money your agent earns.

Career Focus

Real estate agents have a thorough knowledge of the real estate market in their community. They know which neighborhoods are best suited to fit their clients' needs and budgets. Agents also act as middlemen in price negotiations between buyers and sellers. Real estate agents must have a high school degree, be 18 years old, and pass a written test, which includes questions on basic real estate transactions and laws. Agents must have a license, which is renewed every two years. Maturity, tact, trustworthiness, and enthusiasm for the job are required in order to motivate prospective customers.

For more information, refer to the *Occupational Outlook Handbook* at www.bls.gov or search the Internet using such key words as "careers," "jobs," and "real estate."

You can find homes for sale online or in the newspaper classified ads, including those that the owners are selling themselves, without a real estate agent. A big advantage of having an agent, however, is to gain access to the multiple listings. The **Multiple Listing Service (MLS)** is a real estate marketing service in which agents from many real estate agencies pool their home listings and agree to share commissions on the sales. Home sellers contract with a particular agency to have their homes listed. Agents from all participating real estate agencies can then show all properties in the listings to their potential buyers. Sellers gain wide exposure for their property. Buyers can sift through the large pool of property descriptions to select those they want to visit.

In some locations, the complete MLS is available to everyone online. In other locations, only real estate agencies that pay a subscription fee have access to the complete listings. In most places, individual agencies post some of their listings on their Web site for anyone to see. Listings include detailed descriptions of the homes, including number of rooms, total square footage, special features such as a fireplace and garage, and amount of land included. Most listings also include photographs of the homes. Some online listings include virtual tours in which you can see a video presentation that goes from room to room. When viewing properties online, you have the advantage of being able to compare prices while viewing numerous homes without having to be there in person.

After you have narrowed your choices to a small number of homes that are in your price range and match your needs fairly well, you should visit the homes with your agent. Take notes, both pro and con, on the features of each house and neighborhood. Do not make a decision on the spot. After touring your list of finalists, use the decision-making process to make your final selection.

Making an Offer

To let the homeowner know of your interest in buying the home and the price you are willing to pay, you sign an agreement called an offer. An **offer** is a formal document that expresses interest in entering into a contract with someone else. A real estate offer explains the terms of the purchase, including the price you are offering, the down payment, the mortgage amount, and the dates when you will close the deal and take possession. You will have to include earnest money with your offer. **Earnest money** is a portion of the purchase price that the buyer deposits as evidence of good faith to show that the purchase offer is serious. This money is set aside in an account until the transaction is completed.

Earnest money protects the seller in case you fail to meet the terms of the agreement. If you and the seller have agreed on the transaction, the seller will take the house off the market until the deal is completed. During that time, the house cannot be sold to anyone else. If you then back out of the deal, you will likely forfeit your earnest money to the seller. One way to avoid losing your money is to make your offer *contingent* (dependent) on obtaining financing and the property passing an inspection. That way, if you do not qualify for a mortgage on this property, or an inspection reveals major flaws in the house, you will not have violated the contract and you will get your earnest money back.

The seller may or may not accept your initial offer. When the seller agrees to your offer exactly as stated, you have an acceptance. An **acceptance** is a formal agreement to the terms of an offer, forming a contract between the parties. You may withdraw your offer only until the seller accepts it. Once accepted, the offer is a contract.

If the seller wants to change any part of the offer, he or she makes a **counteroffer**, or an offer in response to another offer. For example, if you offered to buy at a lower price than the seller was willing to accept, the seller may make a counteroffer with a different price. Often a buyer's initial offer is lower than the price for which the house is listed. The seller then counteroffers a price below the initial listing but higher than the buyer's first offer. Buyer and seller negotiate until they either agree on a mutually acceptable selling price or decide not to make the transaction. You have the choice of accepting or rejecting each counteroffer.

▶ OBTAINING FINANCING

After you have come to an agreement with the seller, you will have to arrange for your loan. To finance your purchase, you must have funds for a down payment and closing costs, meet certain requirements of your lending institution, and select the type of mortgage you want.

Down Payment Sources

The most common sources of down payment money are personal savings and informal loans from parents or relatives. Most lending institutions will not allow mortgage applicants to formally borrow their down payment. In other words, you must invest a substantial amount of your own cash in the property. Because the down payment can be $5,000 to $10,000 or more, many first-time home buyers have difficulty saving the money and must "borrow" it informally from parents or relatives.

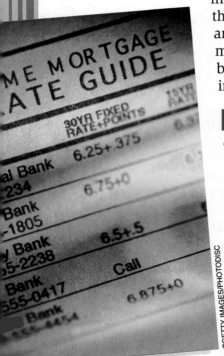

©GETTY IMAGES/PHOTODISC

What are the two basic types of mortgages?

Qualifying for a Mortgage

To qualify for a mortgage, you must complete an extensive loan application. The financial institution will check your credit history, employment, and references. You must prove to the lender that you are capable of meeting the monthly payment. The lender will look for evidence that you can meet your current bills. The lender will also look at the type and amount of your current debts, the amount and source of your income, and your creditworthiness. Generally, the lender will judge that you can handle monthly mortgage payments that do not exceed 30 to 40 percent of your take-home pay.

The lender will also appraise the house you intend to buy. Since the house is the collateral for the loan, the lender must be assured that it is worth enough to cover the loan. If you default, the lender will have to repossess and sell the house to recover the loan amount.

Types of Mortgages

There are two basic types of mortgages: fixed-rate mortgages and adjustable-rate mortgages. A **fixed-rate mortgage** is a mortgage on which the interest rate does not change during the term of the loan. An **adjustable-rate mortgage (ARM)** is a mortgage for which the interest rate changes in response to the movement of interest rates in the economy as a whole.

The rate for an ARM usually starts lower than the current rates for a fixed-rate mortgage. The lender then adjusts the ARM rate based on the ups and downs of the economy. The lender may decrease the ARM's rate, but usually the rate goes up. For example, at a given time, fixed-rate loans may be offered at 8 percent. This rate would remain unchanged for the 30-year term of the loan. At the same time, adjustable-rate mortgages may be offered at 5 percent. The trade-off for this low initial rate is its variability. The lender may raise the rate over time to 10 or 12 percent as interest rates go up in the economy. Most adjustable-rate mortgages specify maximum rate increases (such as 2 or 3 percent a year) and ceilings (such as a top of 12 percent) to which the interest rate can rise.

▶ TAKING TITLE TO PROPERTY

After you and the seller have reached an agreement, and you have arranged your financing, the next step is the *closing*. At this meeting, title to the property will be transferred to you. The **title** is a legal document that establishes ownership. The **deed** is a legal document that transfers title of real property from one party to another.

Before you take ownership, you will want to make sure that the title is *clear*—that is, free of any liens. A **lien** is a financial claim on property. For example, if the previous owner used the home as collateral for a loan other than the mortgage, then that lender has a financial claim or lien. This claim must be paid before ownership of the property can be transferred. To ensure a clear title, you should order a *title search*. For a fee, a title insurance company will search public records and issue a report. If the company discovers that the title is clear, it will issue you a title insurance policy that protects you from any claims arising from a defective title. Most lenders require that the borrower buy title insurance.

Before the closing, the lending institution prepares the loan papers. If any problems arise, the lender will notify you and the seller. For example, some deeds may carry restrictions that limit the kind of building that can be erected and the use of the property. Inspections, such as termite examinations, must be carried out. Any repairs required by the terms of the sale must be completed.

©GETTY IMAGES/PHOTODISC

What is the difference between the title and the deed?

When all these procedures are completed, you and the seller will be notified of the closing date. In this meeting, you and the seller sign the papers and pay all related closing costs, such as those shown in Figure 22-1. If you have a real estate agent, the agent will attend the meeting with you and help you through the process. At the closing, the home becomes yours.

✓ Check Your Understanding

1. What are the advantages of the Multiple Listing Service?
2. What is the difference between a fixed-rate loan and an ARM?

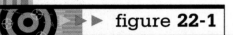 figure **22-1**

TYPICAL CLOSING COSTS

REAL ESTATE CLOSING COSTS

Type of Cost	Typical Amount	Who Pays
Credit Report (on buyer)	$50	Buyer
Property Appraisal Fee	$300 to $500	Buyer
Pest/Damage Inspection	$150 to $300	Buyer
Electrical/Plumbing/Water Inspection Report	$150 to $300	Buyer
Mortgage Loan Fee	Varies	Buyer
Mortgage Loan Assumption Fee	Varies	Buyer
Document Preparation (Escrow Closing Fee)	$150 to $750 depending on selling price of property	Buyer and Seller
Notary Fees and Filing Fees	$25 to $100	Buyer and Seller
Title Search; Title Insurance	$300 to $750 depending on selling price of property	Seller
Survey	$250 to $750	Seller
Real Estate Sales Commission	A percentage of price of home, from 5% to 7% of sale price	Seller
Attorney's Fees	Varies	Buyer and Seller
Interest and Taxes Owed	Varies	Buyer and Seller
Transfer Taxes and Fees	Varies	Seller

A 15-Year or 30-Year Mortgage?

Lenders typically offer mortgages that run for a term of 15 years or 30 years. Before choosing a loan term, consider the differences. A 15-year mortgage has significant advantages:

1. Fifteen-year loans have lower interest rates than 30-year loans. For example, if a 30-year fixed-rate mortgage has a rate of 6.375%, you could get a 15-year fixed-rate mortgage for 5% or less. Thus, you will pay much less total interest over the life of the loan.

2. You will pay off a 15-year mortgage in half the time of a 30-year mortgage, enabling you to enjoy the payment-free status sooner.

3. Because the loan term is shorter, lenders consider a 15-year mortgage less risky. Thus, the borrower may receive more favorable loan costs, such as lower loan origination fees, lower closing costs, and easier loan qualification requirements.

But 15-year loans also have disadvantages that make a 30-year loan more attractive to many home buyers:

1. Because the loan will be paid off in 15 years rather than 30, the monthly payment will be significantly higher. Many home buyers do not earn enough income to qualify for a 15-year loan because of the payment size.

2. The 15-year loan will often require a much higher down payment at closing. In other words, the home buyer must have more cash up front, such as 20% or more of the cost of the property.

3. The 15-year loan payment may put a strain on your budget, even though you are paying off the house at a faster rate. The payment may take such a large bite out of your paycheck that you would not have enough left over to live comfortably. If so, choose a 30-year loan instead.

The loan term is an important consideration for home buyers. Your choice will affect your budget in a major way.

Think Critically

1. Which mortgage term (15 or 30 years) sounds better to you? How does your choice relate to your age?

2. Do you know someone with a 15-year mortgage? If so, ask why he or she chose the shorter term.

Chapter Assessment

SUMMARY

22.1

* Financial advantages of home ownership include increasing equity and tax savings from deductible mortgage interest and property taxes.
* Quality-of-life advantages of home ownership include privacy, freedom, and a sense of belonging to a community.
* Home ownership involves costs such as a down payment, mortgage payments, closing costs, property taxes, property insurance, and utilities.
* As a homeowner, you are responsible for ongoing repairs and maintenance plus any major expenses required to keep your home in good condition.

22.2

* Before starting your house search, prioritize a list of the features you want and determine the price range you can afford.
* Real estate agents' commission is a percentage of the sale price, paid by the seller.
* Search the multiple listings for homes that meet your criteria. Once you have narrowed your choices, visit these homes and note their good and bad points.
* Make an offer on your selected home and put up earnest money. The seller may accept your offer or make a counteroffer.
* Once you have agreed on a price and terms of the sale, the offer becomes a contract.
* To obtain financing, you must fill out an application and meet the lender's requirements. You can get a fixed-rate or an adjustable-rate mortgage.
* At the closing, you will sign papers and money will exchange hands. Then, the title will be transferred to you.

Directions

Can you find the definition for each of the following terms used in Chapter 22?

acceptance	fixed-rate mortgage
adjustable-rate mortgage (ARM)	lien
	market value (real estate)
closing costs	Multiple Listing Service (MLS)
counteroffer	
deed	offer
earnest money	points
equity	title

1. A legal document that establishes ownership.

2. The expenses incurred in transferring ownership from buyer to seller in a real estate transaction.

3. A real estate marketing service in which agents from many real estate agencies pool their home listings and agree to share commissions on the sales.

4. The highest price that a property will bring on the market.

5. A mortgage on which the interest rate does not change during the term of the loan.

6. A formal agreement to the terms of an offer, forming a contract between the parties.

7. A legal document that transfers title of real property from one party to another.

8. A formal document that expresses interest in entering into a contract with someone else.

9. The difference between the market value of property and the amount owed on it.

10. An offer in response to another offer.

11. A portion of the purchase price that the buyer deposits as evidence of good faith to show that the purchase offer is serious.

12. A financial claim on property.

13. A mortgage for which the interest rate changes in response to the movement of interest rates in the economy as a whole.

14. A mortgage finance charge paid by the borrower at closing, with each point being equal to 1 percent of the loan amount.

REVIEW FACTS AND IDEAS

1. What are some financial advantages of owning your home?

2. What two factors increase a homeowner's equity?

3. When do you pay taxes on home equity?

4. What are some non-financial advantages of owning your home?

5. What would be the typical down payment range on a $100,000 home?

6. Under what circumstances should you consider paying higher points in exchange for a lower interest rate on a mortgage?

7. What do closing costs pay for?

8. On what are property taxes based?

9. As a homeowner, what are your responsibilities for maintenance and repairs?

10. Summarize the steps in the home-buying process.

11. How can a real estate agent help you in buying a home?

12. Why does earnest money usually accompany an offer?

13. Describe the negotiation process between the buyer and seller of a home.

14. Why are the initial interest rates offered for ARMs usually less than the rates offered for fixed-rate loans?

15. What is the purpose of a title search and title insurance?

1. Go to the library or search the Internet to find out the annual rate that houses are appreciating in your area. If you bought a house for $150,000 now, how much would it be worth a year from now, at the current rate of appreciation?

2. With your instructor's permission, arrange to visit a real estate agent at work. Discuss with the agent the process of purchasing a house, including the steps, length of time, and costs involved. Ask the agent to show you what the multiple listings look like. If possible, ask the agent if you can go along when the agent shows a house to a prospective buyer. Write a brief paper summarizing what you have learned.

3. You might ask, "Why should I go to the expense of hiring someone to sell my property for me?" Because of the complexities of real estate ownership today, it is often wise to engage the services of a professional real estate agent. Find out through research or an interview with one or more real estate agents at least five services that a professional can provide in selling your home.

4. Search the Internet for the multiple listings in your area. If you cannot gain access without a subscription, go to the Web site of a large real estate agency that operates in your area. Write a bulleted list of the types of information supplied in the house listings. Look at the listings for several houses in your neighborhood. Write a brief summary of the kinds of houses available near you, including their price range, house styles, internal features, and amount of land included.

5. With your instructor's permission, visit a title insurance company in your area and ask people there what they do, how they gather information, and how they are able to insure titles. Briefly summarize your notes in one page or less.

6. Obtain the home mortgage rates from a local bank, savings and loan association, credit union and, if possible, online lenders. Compare these rates and such terms as the down payment, loan costs (points), loan length, and maximum amount available in order to determine which of them offers the best financing rates.

1. You bought your home last year for $130,000. You made a down payment of 20 percent. Through your mortgage payments, you have reduced your debt by $2,000. The annual appreciation rate for homes in your area has averaged 3 percent.
   a. What was the amount of your down payment?
   b. What was your initial loan amount?
   c. How much do you owe now?
   d. What is the current market value of your home?
   e. What is your equity in the home now?

2. If you buy a house for $125,000, how much down payment will you have to make if the lender requires a down payment of (a) 10%, (b) 15%, (c) 20%, and (d) 25%?

3. Suppose you accept a mortgage for $150,000. What finance charge will you have to pay at closing if the lender charges (a) 1 point, (b) 2 points, or (c) 3 points?

4. Suppose your local taxing authority requires you to pay property taxes at the rate of $16 per thousand. Your house is assessed at $210,000. How much property tax will you owe each year?

5. Make a list of the features you want in a home. Include features of the location where you would like to live as well as features of the house and property. Then prioritize your list in order of importance to you. Select a moderate price range for homes in your area. Then search the newspaper classified ads or online listings for houses in that price range that meet your criteria. Clip or print out the listings for three houses that you would like to tour if you were in the market for a home. Which of your criteria do these houses meet and which do they not meet?

6. Using just the closing costs specifically stated in Figure 22-1, what range of costs should the buyer expect to pay (minimum and maximum)? What range of costs should the seller expect to pay? Assume that the house sold for $180,000.

7. Search the Internet for an electronic loan planner tool to solve this problem To buy a home, you will have to borrow $100,000 at 7% interest for 30 years for 360 monthly payments. What will your monthly payment be?

For related activities and links, point your browser to **www.mypf.swlearning.com**

Buying and Caring for a Vehicle

TERMS TO KNOW

pre-approval
vehicle
  identification
  number (VIN)
vehicle emission
  test

sticker price
dealer add-ons
lemon
oxidize

polishing
  compound
abrasives
upholstery

Consider This. . .

Hee-Jan works part-time and attends school full-time. He lives at home with his parents, and his take-home pay is over $600 a month.

"I'm ready to buy a car," he told his parents. "It says here in the paper that with just $100 down, I can finance the purchase of a brand-new car. I'd have to make 60 payments of $350 each. I make nearly twice that much each month, so I can afford the car. How can I get the best deal?"

Buying a Vehicle

Goals
- **Describe the process of buying a car.**
- **Explain automobile leasing costs, processes, advantages, and disadvantages.**
- **Discuss consumer protection available for new- and used-car buyers.**

▶ STEPS IN THE CAR-BUYING PROCESS

What is your dream car? You might long to drive a small, red sports car, a convertible with two seats and a high-powered engine. Unfortunately, for most people this type of car is not very practical. The high purchase price of the car is only one factor. You must also consider the cost of insurance, licensing and registration, gas, maintenance, and repairs.

Identify Your Needs and Wants

Buying a car starts with identifying your needs (not just your wants). What do you need to do with your car? Will you drive a lot of miles? (Gas mileage might be a major factor in your buying decision.) Do you plan to haul a lot of people or gear? Will you take the car off-road? What features would you like to have if you could afford them? After you have made your list of wants and needs, prioritize them. You may have to trade off some of the wants for a lower price.

Determine What You Can Afford

Before you start shopping for a car, determine how much you can afford to spend. One general guideline is that you can afford monthly payments of no more than 20 percent of the money you have left after paying all your regular monthly expenses, such as rent, utilities, credit card payments, etc. Also figure into your budget the costs of maintaining your car and putting gas in it.

Identify and Research Your Choices

Select several types of cars that would meet your needs. In the library or online, research the features of each possibility. Print and online magazines such as *Consumer Reports, Edmunds.com,* and *Car and Driver* offer an abundance of information on different car models. Look for articles about performance, repair records, safety records, gas mileage, and prices.

Compare the features of the models you are considering against your list of wants and needs. Note the pros and cons for each model. Use your list and price range to narrow your choices to just a few that best fit you. When comparing prices, be sure to compare models with the same options.

Decide Whether to Buy New or Used

A primary decision is whether to buy a new car or a used one. Cost is a major factor in this decision. A new car is much more expensive than the same model bought used. Can you afford the high price of a new car? Also, a new car loses much of its market value as soon as you drive it off the lot. A car can lose as much as 20 percent of its value in its first year. By buying a well-maintained used car, you can get more car for your money.

On the other hand, a used car is likely to need more repairs. Even if you have a mechanic check the car's overall health before you buy, a used car is still a bit of an unknown, especially if you are buying from an individual rather than a dealer. You could be buying someone else's problems. A dealer may offer a warranty that you would not get from an individual, but a dealer will typically charge more for the used car.

©GETTY IMAGES/PHOTODISC

Why is it important to research your car choices?

Net Nuggets

The cars.com Web site guides the buyer in every aspect of buying and selling used or new cars. Shopping advice covers vehicle history reports, financing, warranties, and insurance. The extensive research section provides photos, prices, specifications, buying guides, and vehicle reviews for all makes and models of cars. There are even links to loan payment calculators and Kelley Blue Book values. Check out the Web site at www.cars.com.

Get Credit Pre-Approval

Find out how much money you will be qualified to borrow *before* visiting car dealers. This process is called **pre-approval**. Pre-approval separates financing from the process of negotiating the price of the car.

It also allows you to compare total costs of buying, including credit rates. You may or may not actually take the loan from the financial institution that pre-approved you, but at least you will know how much you can spend and a credit rate you can get before you shop for a car.

To get pre-approved, visit your credit union or bank and fill out an application. Based on the information you supply, the loan officer will determine how much the institution would be willing to lend you. The loan officer will then give you a form stating this pre-approved amount and rate. Typically, the pre-approval will expire in 30 or 60 days, after which you must reapply if you want the loan.

Research Insurance Rates

Check out the insurance rates on your vehicle choices. If a car is rated as a "sports car," the cost of insurance may be much higher than vehicles rated higher for safety and other features. A call to your insurance agent to get this information helps to rule out choices when insurance is too high.

Search for Available Vehicles

Search your newspaper's classified ads and the Internet for cars available in your area from dealers and from individual sellers. Many areas offer a free print publication, such as *Auto Trader*, dedicated to used-vehicle listings. If your area has such a publication, you can probably find it in the lobby of car parts stores and various other neighborhood stores and restaurants. Many Web sites, such as http://autotrader.com, www.autobytel.com, www.edmunds.com, and http://autos.msn.com, allow you to search electronically for specific models, both new and used. Most will even get price quotes for you.

Make a list of the available cars that match your specifications, including their features and prices. These are your finalists—the cars that you think are worth your time to investigate further.

Test Drive Each Vehicle

Sometimes descriptions are quite different from the actual car. Test drive the cars of interest to you. Compare ride, handling, braking, features, and cost. Try all the features to see how well they work. Play the radio to judge the sound, but then turn it off so that you can hear the sounds of the car as you drive. Is the engine quiet? Especially when evaluating used cars, listen for noises that might indicate a problem. When you accelerate, look for dark smoke from the exhaust. This is a sign that the car is burning oil, which would require an expensive repair. Look for rust and mismatched paint that might mean the car has been in an accident.

Take your time. Don't be in a hurry when shopping for a car. Some salespeople will try to pressure you into buying right away. Resist that temptation. You will enhance your bargaining position with patience and knowledge of the car you are planning to buy. Experts recommend never buying a vehicle on your first visit to a dealership, and before buying, check the dealer's reputation. A call to the Better Business Bureau will give you valuable information about the number and types of complaints consumers have made about this dealer.

Check the History of a Used Vehicle

You can learn the history of any used vehicle if you have its **vehicle identification number (VIN)**. Each vehicle has a unique VIN that identifies it. This number is available on vehicle documents and on the dashboard in front of the driver, and is visible through the front windshield.

Get the VIN from the used vehicle you are considering, and enter it into the online search tool at Carfax (www.carfax.com). A detailed history for one vehicle costs approximately $20, and you can get reports on several vehicles for around $25. The full report provides information such as whether the vehicle has been in a serious accident, how many times the vehicle has been sold, and the mileage readings each time it was sold, so that you can check for odometer rollbacks.

Get the Vehicle Checked Mechanically

After the used vehicle has passed the VIN check and you've decided you'd like to buy it, have it checked out by a mechanic to make sure it is sound. You'll want to know whether the engine is in good shape. A compression test can tell you if the head gasket is about to go out. You'll also want to be sure the transmission is okay. If the vehicle passes these two critical tests, then ask for a complete check to see what might need to be done and how much the repairs would cost. For example, you'll want to know if it needs a tune-up, how much longer the brakes will last, whether it needs new tires, and so on. A vehicle inspection may cost around $150. Be sure to ask how much the inspection will cost before you have the vehicle checked.

Many states require vehicles to pass a **vehicle emission test**, which is a test to verify that a vehicle meets the minimum clean-air standards. The fee for the test is usually about $15 to $30. However, repairs needed to meet the test requirements may cost much more. Before deciding to buy a car, ask the seller for the record showing that it passed the most recent vehicle emission test. If the seller cannot produce the record, ask the seller to have the vehicle tested before you buy.

Determine a Fair Price

Decide what price you feel is fair before you make any offer for a car. Kelley Blue Book publishes a popular pricing guide for all models and years. You can find the publication in the library or online at www.kbb.com. By looking up the model and year of the car you are considering, you can find an estimated fair price for it. You can also get a feel for a fair price by checking other ads for cars of the same model and year to see what other sellers are charging.

For a new car, the **sticker price** or *manufacturer's suggested retail price (MSRP)* is the price shown on the tag in the car's window. A fair price for a new car usually lies somewhere between the sticker price and the price the dealer paid for it (the *invoice price*). Many car-buying Web sites, such as www.edmunds.com and http://autos.msn.com, can tell you the dealer's invoice price. According to the Automobile Association of America (AAA), the dealer's invoice is approximately 90 percent of sticker for compact and subcompact vehicles. It is approximately 84 to 87 percent of sticker for luxury vehicles. Depending on the vehicle's popularity and the number currently on the market, a fair price is likely to be 3 to 6 percent above invoice. Arm yourself with this knowledge before making an offer.

Negotiate the Price

Make up your mind that you will not be pressured into paying more than you feel is fair. Stick to facts and don't reveal emotions to sellers. For example, don't make statements like, "This car is just what I want." This type of information can weaken your bargaining position. Make your initial offer lower than your top price. Then be prepared to negotiate.

To prevent confusion in determining the true price of the new car, negotiate the price of the new car separately from the price for your trade-in. After you have settled on a fair price for the new car, ask how much the dealer will give you for your old car. If the dealer does not offer an amount close to the trade-in value quoted for your car in the Kelley Blue Book, then plan to sell your old car yourself rather than trade it in. Selling the car yourself is a hassle, but you will likely get more money for it that way.

Some car-buying sites, such as www.edmunds.com, will contact dealers in your area and ask them to send you a free price quote by e-mail for the car you want. You can use these quotes as the starting point for negotiations.

If you are uncomfortable negotiating the price of a vehicle, you may wish to use the services of a professional. Through your automobile club, a wholesale membership such as Costco, your credit union, or an online car-buying service, you can get a price based on cost to the dealer. Once you know exactly what car you want, the service will locate the car, negotiate the price, and arrange for its delivery. This service may not be free, but it can potentially save you money.

If you do your own negotiating, be aware of common dealer negotiating practices. For example, the salesperson might say that he or she needs approval from the sales manager. The salesperson leaves you for several minutes and then returns to say your low offer just isn't acceptable. Be polite but don't be intimidated. If the price you are discussing is still below the maximum you set for yourself as the fair price, then make a counteroffer that is a little higher but still no higher than your top price. Walk away from the deal if you feel you are being pressured or the dealer won't come down to a price you feel is fair.

©GETTY IMAGES/PHOTODISC

What are some tips in successfully negotiating the price of the car?

Dealer Add-Ons

After you have agreed on the price, the dealer may try to increase the purchase price by the use of dealer add-ons—high-priced, high-profit dealer services that add little or no value. For example, dealer preparation is nothing more than cleaning the car and checking the air in the tires and the oil in the engine. These services should be provided without extra charge. Other common dealer add-ons include protective wax or polish, rust-proofing, and extended warranties. Rarely are these special services worth the cost. Just say no!

▶ FINANCING YOUR CAR

The best way to buy a car is with cash. You won't have to pay any interest that way. Unfortunately, most people don't have enough money to buy a car for cash. Therefore, you will probably have to get a loan.

Financial Institutions

Banks, credit unions, and even insurance companies offer vehicle loans for 36, 48, 60, or 72 months. Longer terms mean lower monthly payments but higher total interest paid because you are using the money for a longer period of time. In many cases, your local credit union will offer the best car loan. Often, a credit union will finance more of your purchase (requiring less of your own cash), have lower interest rates, and require smaller monthly payments. Compare rates and terms before selecting a loan.

Most new car dealers offer financing. On particular models and at particular times of the year, they may offer you better terms than those available from other sources. These special deals are sponsored by the manufacturers or their financing agencies to stimulate sales or to promote a particular model. GMAC (General Motors Acceptance Corporation) is an example of a finance company that makes loans on cars through dealerships. Ford, Chrysler, and most other manufacturers offer similar programs. You would make your payments to the finance company—not the dealer. You will have to qualify for the credit just as if you were applying for credit at a financial institution. Use caution with this type of financing. Don't allow a special promotional loan rate to influence you to buy a more expensive car.

► LEASING A CAR

Rather than purchasing a new car, you might consider leasing. A car lease is similar to an apartment lease. It is a written agreement that allows you to use the property (in this case, a car) for a specified time period and monthly payment. You do not own the car. You are simply renting its use. However, at the end of the lease period, you usually have an option to buy the car for the price specified in the lease agreement. For example, you may lease a car for two years. At the end of two years, you can turn it in and lease a new one, or you can buy the car. The selling price specified in the lease is based on the expected value of the car at the end of the two-year lease term.

Because interest on car loans is not tax deductible, auto leasing is a popular option. Individuals can afford to lease a more expensive car than they could buy on credit. In 2003, slightly more than one third of all cars and trucks were leased rather than sold. The reason is that many people cannot afford the big price tag on new cars. Leasing provides an alternative—no large down payment or trade-in to worry about. Just drive away for a set monthly payment! On the other hand, remember that after making all of the payments, you still own nothing.

► CONSUMER PROTECTION FOR CAR BUYERS

As you learned in Chapter 8, a *warranty* is a written statement about a product's qualities or performance that the seller assures the buyer are true. A warranty clearly states what the manufacturer will do if the product does not perform as it should. A new car warranty provides a buyer with some assurance of quality. Car warranties vary in the time and mileage of the protection they offer and in the parts they cover. The main aspects of a warranty are the coverage of basic parts against manufacturer's defects; the power train coverage for the engine, transmission, and drive train; and the corrosion warranty that usually applies to holes due to rust, not to surface rust.

Sometimes, however, being aware of warranty provisions is not enough. Some cars have so many problems (or such hard-to-fix problems) that warranty coverage is of little comfort to their owners. As a result of consumer frustration, many states have enacted lemon laws.

Lemon Laws

Even the most careful purchases can turn out to be lemons. A **lemon** is a car with substantial defects that the manufacturer has been unable to fix after repeated attempts. Because some vehicles just seem to lead from one repair to another, many states have lemon laws. According to most state laws, you have a lemon if, in the first year of ownership or 12,000 miles, (a) you've taken the car into the dealer for four unsuccessful attempts to repair the same substantial defect or (b) your car has been out of service for a total of at least 30 days. Lemon laws allow you to get a new car or your money back. Unfortunately, this protection is not automatic. You need to have good documentation and be prepared for a long process. A proceeding called arbitration and a possible lawsuit may be necessary to enforce your state's law. Figure 23-1 (page 554) indicates what to do if you have a lemon.

The FTC Used-Car Rule

People who buy a used car must be concerned about whether it has some hidden defects or potentially expensive repairs ahead. The Federal Trade Commission "Used-Car Rule" is designed to protect used-car buyers. This rule does not guarantee that the car has no problems. However, it does require used-car dealers to inform consumers ahead of purchase about who will be responsible for paying for certain repairs if they occur after the sale.

The rule requires dealers to place a sticker, called the "Buyer's Guide," on all used cars they offer. Figure 23-2 (page 555) illustrates this sticker. If the "As is" box is checked, the buyer must pay all repair costs. If the "Warranty" box is checked, the dealer will pay to repair the items listed as under warranty for the specified period of time. Cars bought from a private seller do not carry a warranty. While you may save money by buying directly from the previous owner, you cannot expect the previous owner to make repairs or stand by the condition of the vehicle. For this reason, a pre-purchase mechanical check is crucial when buying from an individual or with an "as is" sticker.

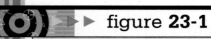 figure 23-1   WHAT TO DO IF YOU HAVE A LEMON

Here are some things you can do to protect yourself in the event you end up with a lemon:

1. When you take the car in for repair, give the dealer a written list of problems. Make sure these problems are in the dealer's repair records. Keep copies of each list and the repair receipts you are given.

2. Any time you are returning to have the same item repaired, point it out to the dealer. Make the dealer aware that the problem is continuing and not new. Again, keep copies of each list and their attempted repairs.

3. If your car qualifies as a lemon, tell the car dealer. Bring copies of your records. If the dealer is not responsive, contact the manufacturer's zone office. Talk to the consumer relations office, or go all the way to their national headquarters if necessary. Follow up the conversation with a letter and copies of your records. Be sure you keep your own copy of the letter and the original documentation.

4. If the defect is serious and the car is dangerous to drive, file for arbitration immediately. Make sure you fill out all necessary forms. State the problem clearly and, once again, provide copies of your documentation.

5. Demand a quick hearing date. Remind the arbitrators that under Section 703 of the Magnuson-Moss Warranty Act you are entitled to an arbitration decision within forty days of filing.

6. You are under no obligation to accept a prolonged hearing. You can demand that the arbitration panel meet and make a decision.

7. If you are not satisfied with the arbitrator's decision or the process, you might want to contact a lawyer who specializes in lemon-law cases. The Center for Auto Safety in Washington, D.C., may be able to help you.

✅Check Your Understanding

1. Why should you not play the radio the whole time you are test driving a car?

2. Why is it important to know the dealer invoice price before making an offer on a new car?

figure **23-2** ◄

BUYERS GUIDE

IMPORTANT: Spoken promises are difficult to enforce. Ask the dealer to put all promises in writing. Keep this form.

Chrysler	New Yorker	1993	A0A085C147961
VEHICLE MAKE	MODEL	YEAR	VIN NUMBER

T6204B

DEALER STOCK NUMBER (Optional)

WARRANTIES FOR THIS VEHICLE:

☒ AS IS – NO WARRANTY

YOU WILL PAY ALL COSTS FOR ANY REPAIRS. The dealer assumes no responsibility for any repairs regardless of any oral statements about the vehicle.

☐ WARRANTY

☐ **FULL** ☐ **LIMITED WARRANTY.** The dealer will pay ____% of the labor and ____% of the parts for the covered systems that fail during the warranty period. Ask the dealer for a copy of the warranty document for a full explanation of warranty coverage, exclusions, and the dealer's repair obligations. Under state law, "implied warranties" may give you even more rights.

SYSTEMS COVERED: **DURATION:**

_____   _____
_____   _____
_____   _____
_____   _____

☒ **SERVICE CONTRACT.** A service contract is available at an extra charge on this vehicle. Ask for details as to coverage, deductible, price, and exclusions. If you buy a service contract within 90 days of the time of sale, state law "implied warranties" may give you additional rights.

PRE PURCHASE INSPECTION: ASK THE DEALER IF YOU MAY HAVE THIS VEHICLE INSPECTED BY YOUR MECHANIC EITHER ON OR OFF THE LOT.

SEE THE BACK OF THIS FORM for important additional information, including a list of some major defects that may occur in used motor vehicles.

Issues in Your World

How to Sell a Used Car

If you sell your old car yourself, here are some steps that will help you make a quicker sale:

1. Wash and polish the outside, vacuum and clean the inside, and shampoo the upholstery. Check fluid levels and tire pressure, and make certain all lights are functioning. A car that appears well-cared-for will bring a higher price.

2. Set a reasonable price. Check a recent National Automobile Dealers Association (NADA) or Kelley Blue Book in print or online for estimates of fair market value. Check the classified ads in your newspaper to be sure this price is within the range advertised by other people selling the same model and year as your car.

3. Advertise your vehicle in local newspapers. Weekend ads are usually most effective. If possible, also advertise in a used-car listing publication in print and online.

4. Present the truth to prospective buyers—what's good about the car as well as its weaknesses. Disclose the last time you had a tune-up, and allow prospective buyers to check maintenance records.

5. Go along when the potential buyer test-drives your car. Give the buyer a chance to think about and evaluate your car. Observe any inspections performed by a mechanic.

6. Always ask for cash or a cashier's check in payment. Remove the license plates if they cannot be transferred.

7. Make sure that you have the title, registration, and other documents that are required to sell the car. Meet the buyer at the motor vehicles division and transfer title when you receive the cash or cashier's check. Never let a new owner drive away with a car that is still in your name.

8. Notify your insurance company immediately that you have sold the car. During the time you are attempting to sell your car, be sure to maintain at least the minimum coverage (usually liability) required in your state.

Think Critically

1. Why should you tell the truth about your car?
2. Why should you go along on a potential buyer's test drive?
3. Why should you insist on cash or a cashier's check in payment for your car?

Maintaining Your Vehicle

Goals
- **Identify the costs of owning and operating a car.**
- **Describe methods for extending the life of your car and maintaining its resale value.**

▶ COST OF OPERATING A CAR

Most people spend more of their income on a car and related expenses than on any other item except housing and food. The initial outlay for the vehicle (down payment, taxes, title registration, and other fees) plus ongoing loan and insurance payments are just part of the cost of ownership. Costs associated with operating your car add considerably to the overall cost of ownership.

Gas and Oil

The cost of gasoline depends on the fuel efficiency of your car's engine and the number of miles you drive. Larger vehicles and more powerful engines often require more fuel. Gasoline and oil are variable operating expenses. This means that your cost varies with the number of miles you drive and with the constantly fluctuating price of gas.

In an effort to improve gas mileage and reduce air pollution from exhaust fumes, car manufacturers are starting to introduce hybrid vehicles. A *hybrid* is a type of vehicle that uses alternate energy sources, such as natural gas or battery power, in addition to or in place of gasoline. They can get high miles per gallon while cutting the cost of operation substantially.

Depreciation

As you learned in Chapter 14, *depreciation* is a decline in the value of property due to normal wear and tear. As a car ages, the number of miles driven increases, the physical condition begins to deteriorate, and mechanical difficulties arise. Also, styles and consumer tastes change over time. All these factors usually cause cars to lose market value. However, not all cars depreciate. Very old vehicles in excellent condition may *appreciate*, or increase in value, if people value them as collectors' items.

Depreciation is the single greatest cost of owning a car. The cost of gasoline comes second. In most cases, the age of a car is the most important factor in determining its resale or trade-in value. Other factors include mileage, mechanical condition, model popularity, size, and color. A car will retain more of its value over time if it is well-maintained and has fewer miles on it at the time of sale. Popular models depreciate more slowly than other models.

Registration and Title

All states charge a fee to register a car title. As you learned in the last chapter, a *title* is a legal document that establishes ownership. A car title lists the legal owner (usually the lending institution) and the registered owner (you). You must pay title fees and sales taxes only at the time you buy the car. However, you must pay a license tag fee each year and pay for emissions testing in some states typically every two years.

Maintenance and Repairs

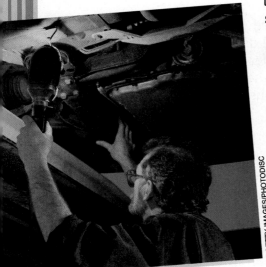

What kinds of costs are involved in operating a car?

The owner's manual will tell you what services your car needs and how often. Typically, you can expect to change the oil every few thousand miles, have a major engine tune-up every 20,000 to 30,000 miles, and perform other maintenance at scheduled intervals. Car systems that you should monitor and maintain include emissions control, air-conditioning, brakes, and transmission.

You also should plan for unscheduled repairs. Such things as flat tires, broken belts, and leaky hoses happen from time to time, and the repairs can be costly. Saving money for car repairs should be part of your monthly budget. As your car gets older, repair costs will increase. You should expect to replace relatively inexpensive parts such as fan belts, hoses, the battery, and the muffler, but also plan for occasional expensive repairs such as replacing the alternator. You will also need new tires at some point. Tires can cost from $50 to $200 apiece (or much more for specialty tires).

Accessories

Many people choose to add certain features to make their vehicles safer, more functional and attractive, or more efficient. These items include snow tires, floor mats, seat covers, wheel covers, striping and paint features, alarm systems, and sound systems. In some cases, these costs will add to the value of the vehicle; in other cases, they will subtract from it.

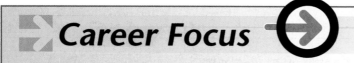

Career Focus

Automobile salespersons generally work for new or used car dealers. Salespersons usually are the first to greet customers and determine their interests. They then explain and demonstrate a vehicle's features in the showroom and on the road. Finally, they negotiate the terms and price of the sale. Automotive salespersons must be tactful, well-groomed, and able to express themselves well. Their success in sales depends upon their ability to win the respect and trust of prospective customers. A high-school diploma is typically the minimum requirement. Most new salespersons receive extensive on-the-job training, including mentoring by sales managers and experienced salespeople.

For more information, refer to the *Occupational Outlook Handbook* at www.bls.gov or search the Internet using such key words as "careers," "jobs," and "automobiles."

EXTENDING THE LIFE OF YOUR CAR

Because a car is expensive, you will get your best value (cost versus benefit) if you take care of your investment. By performing routine maintenance, taking care of the interior and exterior, and practicing good driving habits, you can keep your car running well and looking good.

Maintain Fluid Levels

Many newer cars claim to run 7,000 or more miles between oil changes. But changing oil more frequently can add years of life to a car. Oil lubricates the moving parts of the engine and keeps it clean. Oil must be changed to eliminate accumulated dirt and sludge. Your individual driving habits will dictate how often you should change the oil. For example, the frequent starting and stopping of city driving wear oil out sooner than do long expressway trips.

Experts advise changing oil every 3,000 miles, or every three months, whichever comes first, for city driving. You should replace the oil filter when you change the oil. The filter helps clean the oil circulating through the engine. Lubrication, oil change, and oil filter replacement (called "lube, oil, and filter") should cost from $20 to $35, depending on the size of the engine. Figure 23-3 points out differences in engine oil and helps you decide which one is right for your vehicle.

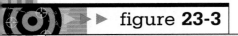 figure **23-3**

ALL OIL IS NOT THE SAME

ENGINE OIL GRADES AND VISCOSITY

All engine oils are not the same. There are various service grades, depending on additives that are mixed in.

Service Grade
Service SF is the highest grade of engine oil for gasoline-powered vehicles. If you drive a late model car, the owner's manual will specify service grade, or may simply say "heavy duty." Service SF will work in these cars.

Viscosity
Oil thickness requirements vary with temperature ranges in your area. Viscosity is indicated by the letters "SAE." The higher the number, the thicker the oil. For example, SAE 40 means the oil is thicker than SAE 30. If your area has great variations in temperature, you will likely want a multigrade oil for changes in temperature.

Multigrade oil is marked with two numbers, such as 10W-40. In this example, the 10 applies to cold weather and the 40 applies to hot weather. If, for example, the rating is 5W-30, then the car needs more viscosity to get started, and then evens out once it is warm. Usually a 10W-30 or 10W-40 can be used year-round.

You should also regularly check and maintain the proper fluid levels for your transmission, power-steering, and brakes. These car functions must have fluid to work properly.

Perform Routine Maintenance

Don't wait for trouble before checking fluid levels and inspecting belts, hoses, and tire pressure. Inspect tires for wear and replace them before tread wear puts you in danger of a blowout. Most car owners find that by replacing parts periodically, they can avoid major problems. These ongoing routine checks and fixes should cost $150 to $300 a year but will save you major repairs in the long run. The owner's manual will tell you mileage or time intervals for certain servicing.

Keep Your Car in a Garage

If possible, keep your vehicle in a garage. Using a garage protects the vehicle from theft and vandalism. It also protects from weather, which can damage or destroy the vehicle's finish and even affect its mechanical condition. Low temperatures, for example, affect almost every component. The engine is harder to start, and the battery is weaker. Thus the starter has to work harder, and the charging system is stressed.

Preserve the Exterior

It's important to keep your vehicle clean. When water sits on the surface of metal, it can cause rust. Cleaning off road grime occasionally will protect the shiny finish. Apply protective wax to guard your paint from the damaging rays of the sun and from snow-melting chemicals spread on streets in cold climates. If you live near the coast, wax is essential for protecting from the salty air.

Wax the paint twice a year—before the cold and rainy winter and before the hot and dry summer. Once the paint has begun to **oxidize** (permanently lose its color and shine because of chemical reaction with the air), it is very difficult to restore the original gloss. In most cases, a vehicle with oxidized paint must be repainted to restore its shine. A **polishing compound** is a substance that can smooth out surface scratches, scuffs, and stains. Polishing compounds, often called cleaners or pre-waxes, can be tricky to use. They often contain **abrasives**, which are coarse materials that scour or rub away a surface. Used gently, an abrasive can remove the top layer of paint. An abrasive will expose the shiny paint underneath. But rubbed too vigorously or too often, an abrasive will strip the paint right down to the primer.

©GETTY IMAGES/PHOTODISC

Why is it important to keep your car clean?

Just as important as washing and waxing is repairing dents and paint chips before rust has a chance to take hold. You can get a small amount of vehicle paint that matches your car's color from a dealer that sells your make of car. When something nicks your paint, such as a rock that hits your car when you drive, you should touch up the ding. First clean the area with mild soap and dry it. Then apply the touch-up paint in very small amounts.

Preserve the Interior

The condition of the inside of your vehicle is also very important for good resale value. The **upholstery** is the seat-covering material. Generally, cloth upholstery is more durable than vinyl. Although spills and dirt are more difficult to clean off of cloth upholstery, vinyl can crack and tear when it gets too hot or cold and can be punctured by sharp objects. Leather upholstery holds up best, but it is more expensive and requires regular cleaning and lubricating to keep it soft.

Floor mats will protect the carpeting and are a good investment. You can cover the interior of your trunk with an old blanket to protect it. Avoid eating messy foods in the car and vacuum frequently to keep your car's interior in good condition. Products are available to rub on vinyl dashboards and plastic interior surfaces to protect them from fading and cracking from exposure to the sun's rays. If you must park your car in the sun for long periods of time, you might consider covering the inside of your windshield with an inexpensive cardboard shade made for the purpose.

Follow Wise Driving Habits

Good driving habits can keep your vehicle running efficiently for years. New vehicles have a "break-in period." You will need to drive differently during this period than later in your vehicle's life.

When the vehicle is new:

1. Don't drive for long stretches at a constant speed. Vary speed as driving conditions permit.
2. During the first thousand miles, drive progressively faster, accelerating gradually.
3. Avoid fast starts, sudden stops, sharp turns, and rapid gear changes to help your brakes get broken in.
4. Drive at moderate speeds and around town, avoiding long trips so your tires can get adjusted. You may need additional wheel balancing and front-end alignment.

For all vehicles:

1. Don't race a cold engine. Give it 10 to 15 seconds to warm up to allow the oil to start circulating. Then drive off gently as soon as the engine is running smoothly.
2. Keep coolants in the radiator during hot weather and antifreezes in it during very cold weather.
3. When driving a vehicle with a manual transmission, shift deliberately, pausing as you move through the neutral position.
4. Don't shift into a forward gear when your vehicle is rolling backward, or vice versa.
5. When stopped in traffic, hold the vehicle in place with the brakes rather than engaging the clutch, to avoid excessive wear on the clutch.
6. Don't turn the steering wheel when the vehicle is motionless. This strains the front-end components. Turn the wheel only when the vehicle is moving.
7. Keep the windshield and back window free of ice, using a scraper rather than your wiper blades. Running wipers over a dry surface can scratch the glass and tear the blades.

8. Glance at gauges and warning lights as you drive. When your vehicle signals you to stop or to get something checked, do it right away. For example, if the oil pressure gauge or warning light shows, it could mean your engine is about to self-destruct. When your engine shows it's too hot, turn off the air-conditioner and drive slower. If overheating is severe, pull over and stop the engine quickly. Open the hood, but do not unscrew the radiator cap.

9. Finally, always wear your seat belt. It can save your life!

✓ Check Your Understanding

1. Why do vehicles usually depreciate? What might cause a particular vehicle to appreciate?

2. Why should you avoid turning the steering wheel while the vehicle is not in motion?

Chapter Assessment

23.1
* Buying a car starts with identifying and prioritizing your needs and wants. Then determine what you can afford.
* Identify models that would meet your needs. Research them, compare features, and narrow your choices to a few.
* Decide whether to buy new or used.
* Get a loan pre-approved. Then test drive your top choices. Before buying a used vehicle, check its history by looking up its VIN and have a mechanic check it.
* Determine a fair price before you make an offer.
* Make your initial offer below your top price. Then negotiate, but be prepared to walk away if the seller pressures you or will not come down to a fair price.
* Banks, credit unions, insurance companies, or the car dealer offer car loans.
* Leasing is renting the use of a vehicle, often with an option to buy at the end of the lease term.
* Lemon laws help consumers get a new car or their money back if the car they purchased has substantial, unfixable defects.

23.2
* Costs of operating a vehicle include the down payment, title registration, sales taxes, loan and insurance payments, and annual license fees.
* The amount you spend for gasoline depends on the fuel efficiency of your engine, the number of miles you drive, and gas prices.
* Most vehicles depreciate as they get older, wear out, and go out of style.
* Perform regular maintenance, such as oil changes and tune-ups, according to the schedule in your owner's manual.

* Protect your vehicle's exterior by cleaning, waxing, touching-up paint chips, and keeping it in a garage, if possible.
* Protect your vehicle's interior by vacuuming, applying protective products to vinyl and leather surfaces, and buying protective coverings such as floor mats.
* During the break-in period on a new vehicle, vary your speed, accelerate gradually, and drive at moderate speeds.
* Wise driving habits include allowing the vehicle to warm up, keeping coolants and fluid levels up, acting on early warning signs announced by gauges and noises, and wearing your seat belt.

REVIEW TERMS

Directions

Can you find the definition for each of the following terms used in Chapter 23?

abrasives	sticker price
dealer add-ons	upholstery
lemon	vehicle emission test
oxidize	vehicle identification number (VIN)
polishing compound	
pre-approval	

1. A car with substantial defects that the manufacturer has been unable to fix after repeated attempts.

2. The process of qualifying for a loan before you begin looking for a car.

3. A number unique to a car that serves to identify it.

4. High-priced, high-profit dealer services that add little of value to your car purchase.

5. A test to verify that a vehicle meets the minimum clean-air standards.

6. A substance that can smooth out surface scratches, scuffs, and stains.

7. Coarse materials that scour or rub away a surface.

8. Seat-covering material.

9. The price shown on the tag in a new car's window.

10. To permanently lose color and shine because of chemical reaction with the air.

REVIEW FACTS AND IDEAS

1. What is the first step in the car-buying process?

2. How can you determine how much you can afford to spend for a car?

3. What are some sources of information about cars—their safety, repair record, reliability, and so on?

4. What are the advantages and disadvantages of buying a used car?

5. What should you do to evaluate a car during a test drive?

6. How can you find out if the mileage shown on a used car's odometer has been rolled back?

7. What should you do to assure that the used car you are considering is mechanically sound?

8. How can you determine a fair price for a new or used car?

9. How is leasing different from buying a car?

10. What are some costs of operating a car?

11. What are some factors that cause a car to depreciate?

12. What are some steps you can take to extend the life of your car?

13. Why is it important to change the oil regularly?

14. List three things you can do to protect your car's interior.

15. Explain five wise driving strategies.

APPLY YOUR KNOWLEDGE

1. Make a list of car dealers in your area. Divide into groups. Each group should visit one dealer. Collect brochures on various car models and look at sticker prices. As a group, report your findings—characteristics of the cars in the dealer's product line, price ranges, how you were treated, and so on.

2. Choose a car topic that you would like to learn more about, such as which is the best car stereo or which motor oil works best for a particular kind of car. Find articles about this topic in current issues of *Consumer Reports* and *Car and Driver* magazine in print or online. Write a one-page summary of your findings.

3. Choose a particular model of used car. Find listings for this model for sale in your area, using an Internet car-buying site or your newspaper's classified ads in print or online. Write a paragraph about the cars you found. How many are for sale? What are their years and prices? What options do they include? How do the prices offered by dealers compare to those of private sellers?

4. Visit Kelley Blue Book at www.kbb.com and look up the trade-in value of your car or your family's car. This is the estimated amount a dealer would give you for your car in trade for a new one. Now look up the used-car retail price for the same car. This is an estimate of a fair price that a buyer could expect to pay for the car. Now subtract the two figures. What is the difference? What does this number represent?

5. Talk to a loan officer about the process of pre-approval for a car loan. Ask to see application forms and discuss qualifications. Based on the information gathered, prepare a summary of income requirements for an auto loan. For example, what monthly income would it take to be able to afford a particular model of Ford? What would the monthly payments be?

6. In groups, prepare a list of options that you feel are important to have in a car. Then research the price of each option. For example, if you want a six-CD changer, then what would it cost to add this feature to the base price of a car? You will find prices for these items in consumer magazines in your library or at online car-buying sites, or visit dealerships and study the sticker prices on cars of your choice. Are the prices of options different for different car models?

7. Divide into groups. Each group should make an appointment to visit a different car dealer that offers leasing as well as purchase financing. Select a vehicle on the lot. Ask the finance manager to describe the terms for leasing this vehicle. Also ask the manager to show you the payments and total cost for leasing and for purchasing the vehicle using the company's credit terms. Which option is least expensive for this vehicle—lease or buy? Each group should report its findings to the class.

8. Prepare a budget that lists potential costs a car owner may face. Ask someone who has owned a car for a long time to help you complete the list. For example, in computing the year's depreciation, check the classified ads to see what that year and model of car is selling for. Deduct this from the purchase price of the car and divide by the years of age. Keep in mind that a vehicle depreciates more in the first few years than it does later. Determine a total cost and summarize in a paragraph your findings about the costs of operating a vehicle.

9. Find out the costs of registration and license fees in your state. You can get this information by calling or visiting the Web site of your state's motor vehicles division. Or, you can visit the division's local office.

10. Borrow a vehicle owner's manual and read through it. In the section that discusses regular maintenance schedules, find out how often the oil needs to be changed, how often a major tune-up is required, and what things must be checked, repaired, or replaced at regular intervals. Based on this information, prepare a cost summary for a year of regular maintenance.

11. Research different types of waxes and cleaning compounds that you might use on a vehicle. Compare their features, what they will do, and the costs, together with possible hazards. Estimate the cost of keeping a car clean, waxed, and touched up for a year.

12. For a week, observe drivers as you are riding to and from school or at other times of the day. Keep a list of things drivers do to avoid injuries and accidents. Also keep a list of things drivers do that could potentially cause harm to themselves and others. Write a summary of what you have learned.

Solve Problems ⊕ Explore Issues

1. Your friend Leonard is considering buying a small older car. He works part-time after school and on holidays. In the summer, he makes good wages but is saving for college. He visits a local dealer who suggests that buying an older car is not a good idea. The dealer points out that the car may break down, will likely cost a lot to maintain, and wouldn't be dependable. Do you agree? What advice would you give Leonard?

2. Your friend Arethea has decided to buy a car. Because she is working at a regular job, she thinks she can afford a new car. She isn't sure how much she can afford to pay for monthly car payments, and she doesn't know how much of a down payment she might need to make. How would you advise her to get started in the car-buying process?

3. To buy the new car Arethea selected, she would need a loan for $20,000. The dealer would finance the loan at 6.5 percent for 60 months. Use an online car loan calculator to determine: (a) the monthly payment, (b) total payments, and (c) total interest.

4. Ralph Ginzberg has already purchased two cars. He is ready to buy a third car but frankly, he tells you, the experience is so negative that he's putting it off for as long as possible. When you talk to him, you discover that the problem lies in the buying process itself. When Ralph gets into a dealership, he feels pressured. He then buys something that he later regrets. What advice can you give him to have a more positive experience?

5. Consuela Chavez just purchased a new car. Now she faces a decision: Should she add to the cost of her purchase with undercoating and rust protection, a polish shine application, and a three-year extended warranty? Altogether, these items will add almost $1,000 to the price of the car. She's concerned because the dealer told her that these will add to the life of the car, and she plans to keep it for a long time. What is your advice?

6. You are buying a new car and are considering whether to trade in your old vehicle. The dealer tells you that you are paying $1,500 less on the new car because of your trade-in. But you find that in reality you would get a $1,500 reduction in price for having no trade-in and for paying cash. Discuss the pro's and con's of trading in your car versus selling it yourself.

7. Your friend Vijay has a car that has been fixed four times for the same problem—a faulty starter. Advise him about lemon laws.

8. You are looking at a vehicle for possible purchase. A sticker on the window called the "Buyer's Guide" says this vehicle is sold strictly "As Is." What does this mean?

9. Your friend Courtney is excited about buying her first car. She is paying cash for the car. This purchase will deplete her savings, but she has a part-time job that pays $100 a week. Explain to her the costs of operating a car.

10. Kyle Okihiro just purchased a new car. He plans to drive the car at least 100,000 miles and then get as much money as he can for it. What advice can you give him about extending the life of the car and improving its resale value?

For related activities and links, point your browser to **www.mypf.swlearning.com**

Family Decisions

TERMS TO KNOW

wedding party
civil ceremony
itinerary
reservation
travel agency

overbook
dissolution of
  marriage
property
  settlement
  agreement

alimony
cremation

Consider This. . .

Akira and Emi have announced their engagement and plans to be married. They both have large families and want a formal wedding with all the trimmings.

"By waiting a year, we'll be able to plan this wedding thoroughly, and we'll both be finished with college," Akira said to Emi. "It also gives us time to save money, since we can't expect our parents to pay for the type of wedding we'd like to have."

"You're right," replied Emi. "There are a million details, and I'd like to enjoy this period of time. I think a year is just the right amount of time between the announcement and the wedding. We also need to plan the honeymoon. Do you want to hike in the mountains or relax on the beach?"

Family Plans and Goals

Goals
- Describe the steps, costs, and planning involved in getting married.
- Discuss important family living decisions.
- Outline the steps needed to plan a successful vacation.

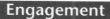

► MARRIAGE AND COMMITMENT

Statistics show that people are waiting until later to get married and start families, and that more are choosing to remain single. For those who choose to have a long and committed relationship, the process can be vastly rewarding and surprisingly complex.

Assuming that a couple has the legal capacity to get married (age 18 in most states), many honest discussions about goals and values should precede the decision to legalize their commitment. For example, if one person feels that having children is a vital part of the couple's lives together while the other does not want children, this difference could present an insurmountable obstacle. It's also important to discuss issues such as working, political and religious beliefs, where to live, roles (such as who pays the bills), hobbies, vacations, and living styles (from perfectionist to slob).

Engagement

When a couple decides to commit to a life together, they become *engaged*, or formally pledged to each other. An engagement or commitment ring, a symbol of this pledge, can cost between a few hundred and a few thousand dollars.

An engagement period of six months to a year allows the couple time to prepare for the wedding, make plans for the future, and set joint goals. Once the couple announces their engagement to friends and family, they are ready to begin planning the many steps to ensure a smooth and memorable wedding.

Premarital Counseling

Some religions require pre-marriage counseling sessions. The couple meets with a member of the clergy or designated counselor, together and separately, to discuss issues that will be vital to the success of the

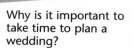

Why is it important to take time to plan a wedding?

©GETTY IMAGES/PHOTODISC

marriage and family life. Topics most often discussed include money and budgeting, the meaning of the marriage commitment, in-laws and other potential problems, and religious aspects of marriage that are unique to each faith. The counseling sessions should be planned early, well before making final preparations for the wedding.

Ceremony Plans and Costs

Planning for the wedding ceremony should begin at least six months in advance. Figure 24-1 (page 574) is a bride's budget worksheet, which shows the many preparations to consider. (A groom may use a similar worksheet.) This worksheet should be completed in rough-draft form as the wedding plans progress. As costs begin to add up, the bride and groom may decide to adjust their preferences to reduce expenses.

A number of print magazines and Web sites offer helpful information for planning a wedding. At www.brideandgroom.com and www.modernbride.com, you can find the latest ideas on making the wedding memorable and seamless. The site www.wedalert.com offers checklists and a budget worksheet to help you plan your wedding. At www.Americanbride.com, brides can register to receive special offers and information about all types of products and services, from engraved invitations to caterers.

The bride and groom and each set of parents should prepare guest lists and then combine them. The number of guests and the size of the wedding party will determine the number of invitations needed, size of the church, cost of the reception, and so forth. The **wedding party** consists of the people who are active participants in the wedding ceremony: the bride and groom, best man, maid or matron of honor, bridesmaids, ushers, flower girl, and ring bearer.

In the past, wedding expenses were paid by the bride's family. Today, the couple pays for more of the expenses, along with the groom's family, who usually pays for items such as the rehearsal dinner or reception or maybe splits the expenses with the bride's family.

Typically, the following expenses belong solely to the groom:
1. Bride's ring(s)
2. Marriage license
3. Wedding gift for the bride
4. Gifts for the best man, groomsmen, and ring bearer
5. The bride's bouquet and going-away corsage, corsages for mothers and grandmothers, and boutonnieres for the men in the wedding party
6. Cleric's or judge's fee
7. Bachelor dinner (unless given and paid for by the best man)
8. Lodging (if necessary) for out-of-town groomsmen

BRIDE'S BUDGET WORKSHEET

Engagement Party

Invitations . . . . $_____
Food. . . . . _____
Beverages . . . . _____
Music. . . . . _____
Rental fees . . . . _____
Decorations. . . . . _____
Professional services. . . . _____
Gratuities . . . . _____

Total. . . . . $_____

Stationery

Invitations . . . . $_____
Announcements . . . . _____
At-home cards . . . . _____
Personal stationery. . . . . _____
Stamps . . . . _____

Total. . . . . $_____

Clothing

Wedding dress. . . . . $_____
Headpiece/veil . . . . _____
Shoes. . . . . _____
Accessories. . . . . _____
Personal trousseau . . . . . _____

Total. . . . . $_____

*Denotes expenses usually
shared by both families

Bridesmaids' Luncheon

Invitations and
    place cards . . . . $_____
Food. . . . . _____
Beverages . . . . _____
Rental fees . . . . _____
Decorations. . . . . _____
Professional services. . . . _____
*Gratuities . . . . _____

Total. . . . . $_____

Photographs

Engagement portrait. . . . $_____
Wedding portrait . . . . . . _____
Formal photos . . . . _____
Reprints . . . . _____

Total. . . . . $_____

Wedding Ceremony

Sanctuary rental . . . . $_____
Music. . . . . _____
Decorations . . . . _____
Flowers for attendants. . . _____
Aisle runner . . . . _____
Transportation
    to/from ceremony. . . . _____
*Gratuities. . . . . _____
Miscellaneous . . . . _____

Total. . . . . $_____

Reception

Hall rental . . . . $_____
Decorations . . . . _____
Music. . . . . _____
Food . . . . _____
Beverages . . . . _____
Wedding cake . . . . _____
Favors . . . . _____
Professional services. . . . _____
*Gratuities . . . . _____

Total. . . . . $_____

Other

Bridal consultant fees . . . $_____
Accommodations for
    out-of-town
    attendants . . . . _____
*Security guard . . . . _____
Sound recording of
    ceremony . . . . _____
*Insurance for
    wedding gifts . . . . _____
Bride's blood test
    (if required). . . . . _____
Groom's ring . . . . _____
Gift for groom . . . . _____
Gift for attendants . . . . . _____
Special effects. . . . . _____
Other fees . . . . _____
                                _____
                                _____
                                _____

Total. . . . . $_____

GRAND TOTAL . . . . $_____

9. Groom's special clothing, including clothing for rehearsal dinner, wedding, and honeymoon

10. Delivery of wedding presents to new home

The bride and groom usually plan the wedding jointly, giving much consideration to cost. The size of the wedding, time of day, location, and formality of the bride's dress determine the style of the wedding.

A *formal wedding* may be held in the daytime or in the evening, and all guests and participants wear formal attire (which, for evening, includes long gowns and tuxedos). A *semiformal wedding* usually is held during the afternoon or early evening, with less formal wear required of guests. While the wedding party may still dress as formally or informally as they choose, guests generally wear suits and dresses normally chosen for special occasions. An *informal wedding* may be held outside, in a church, or almost anywhere. No special clothing is required for the wedding party or guests.

Some couples prefer a **civil ceremony**, which is a wedding performed by a public official, such as a judge or justice-of-the-peace, rather than a member of the clergy. This is a quick, inexpensive ceremony and requires the presence of two witnesses in most states.

The Honeymoon

Immediately following the wedding reception, the newly married couple often takes a honeymoon trip. Resorts and places that provide different types of entertainment are popular. Honeymoons may be inexpensive car trips, elaborate cruises, or flights to exotic islands. It may last from several days to several weeks and cost several thousand dollars. A couple generally plans the honeymoon together, carefully considering preferences and sharing costs.

▶ FAMILY FINANCIAL DECISIONS

When people live together in a committed relationship, they form a new family unit. The family should make major decisions together, based on each person's needs and wants. Ideally, decisions regarding goals, the budget, and division of responsibilities are open to discussion at any time.

Family Goals

Couples should examine their needs and set goals for the future together. Short-term goals involve decisions about the near term, such as where to live for now, whether both partners will work, what major purchases to make this year and next, and what leisure activities they will participate in, jointly and separately. Intermediate goals are goals the couple wants to pursue in the next five to ten years: whether they want children, where the couple will live in the foreseeable future, and whether either partner should consider a career change. Long-term goals are goals for the distant future. They include decisions about children's education (savings and investments), special events, and retirement.

Financial goals should:

1. Be realistic and based on your income and life situation. An annual vacation in the Caribbean might not be realistic on a modest income.

2. Be listed in specific measurable terms. The goal of "accumulating $10,000 in a mutual fund within five years" is a clearer goal than "saving money for future expenses."

3. Specify the action you plan to take and serve as the basis for various financial activities.

As you learned in Chapter **8**, a *financial plan* is a set of goals for spending, saving, and investing the money you earn. It summarizes your current financial situation, analyzes your financial needs, and suggests a direction for your financial activities. You can create this document yourself or use the assistance of a professional financial planner.

The Family Budget

In Chapter 8, you learned the steps in creating a budget. You can follow these same steps in creating a budget for your family. But unlike an individual budget, a family budget should consider the needs and goals of each family member in allocating resources. Since family resources are limited, family members will need to negotiate and make compromises to prepare a plan that works best for the family as a whole.

A family budget allocates spending, saving, borrowing, and investing of the family's pooled resources to meet future goals. Joint decisions are often difficult because more people are involved in the decision making. Nevertheless, family budgeting and communicating are essential parts of a successful marriage.

Dividing Responsibilities

Maintaining a household entails many ongoing responsibilities, many of them financial. For example, a couple may choose to have individual as well as joint checking accounts. If the family unit has only one checking account, managing the account will be easier if only one person writes the checks. Otherwise, accidental overdrawing can easily result.

Many couples choose to have individual checking accounts, and each partner is responsible for part of the income and part of the bills. For example, the couple may decide that one partner will pay utilities, groceries and household expenses, and the car payment, and the other will pay the rent, entertainment expenses, insurance premiums, and miscellaneous expenses. Then each partner is responsible for balancing his or her checking account each month and meeting his or her part of the budget.

Couples must divide other ongoing household tasks as well. Perhaps one partner might take charge of preparing tax returns and doing the family grocery shopping. The other partner might take responsibility for making vacation arrangements, planning social engagements, and arranging to have home repairs done. Housecleaning can be less distasteful if partners do the tasks they like best and share equally the tasks that neither likes to do. By agreeing on how to divide up household responsibilities, both partners can do their fair share and avoid the resentment that may result from an unequal division of labor.

Global View

Arranged marriages are common in the Indian subcontinent (India, Pakistan, and Bangladesh), even among those in the educated middle class. Many people believe that arranged marriages are more successful than marriages in Europe and the U.S. They assert that romantic love does not necessarily lead to a good marriage and that real love comes from a properly arranged union between two individuals and their families.

Think Critically: How might family decision making be different in the Indian subcontinent from the way it is in Western societies?

▶ VACATION PLANNING

Vacations are an important part of life. Well-planned vacations maximize the time available for fun.

Kind of Vacation

Apply the decision-making process to help you choose a vacation. First, define the problem: What does your family want most from a vacation—relaxation, excitement, travel, adventure, special events, visiting relatives, or a combination? Based on these goals for the vacation and the time and money available, identify your alternatives, as shown in Figure 24-2. Then gather information about each alternative, weigh the pros and cons of each, and make a final decision. A successful vacation depends on selecting the trip that will best satisfy family members, saving for it, and planning it carefully.

©GETTY IMAGES/PHOTODISC

Why should you plan vacations ahead of time?

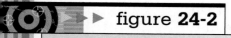
VACATION ANALYSIS		
$500 or less	**$500 – $1,500 to spend**	**More than $1,500**
Camping	Car trip	Car or plane trip
Visiting relatives	Sports (skiing, other adventure)	Tours/group travel
Sports events	Amusement parks	Varied entertainment options
Three days or less	Three to five days	Five days or more

Itineraries

If you plan your vacation activities ahead of time, then you can use your vacation time to do them rather than waste time finding hotels, figuring out transportation, and other practical details. Start your planning by writing out what will happen, when, at what cost, and what needs to be done. An **itinerary** is a detailed schedule of events, times, and places. List each day's activities, as shown in Figure 24-3, and build in flexibility. Bad weather or unexpected problems may require you to change your plans. Plan a few alternative activities that you can do if you need to make a change.

You may want to list on your itinerary the time it takes to do certain activities, distances to get to and from activities, methods of transportation, and special notes, such as "bring camera." When designing your itinerary, be sure to leave enough time to do the planned activities in a relaxed way. Check on seasonal adjustments that may change operating days, fees, and opening or closing times. Before going on vacation, leave a copy of your itinerary with a neighbor or friend in case of emergency.

Reservations

Make reservations whenever possible. A **reservation** is an advance commitment to receive a service at a specified later date. A room reservation guarantees that a hotel or motel room will be waiting for you when you arrive. Hotels and motels may be booked up, or full, well in advance of your vacation date. Therefore, make reservations early; a month or more before your vacation is not too soon. You can make reservations for airlines, buses, trains, boats, and car rentals. You can get airline boarding passes and seat assignments a few days before your trip, even with ticketless travel. Confirm your flight reservations at least 24 hours before you leave, because flights are often canceled or changed at the last minute.

figure 24-3 ◄

ITINERARY

Date	Time	Activity
Monday	8:00 A.M.	Arrive at airport (Flight 739 leaves at 9:05 A.M.).
	10:00 A.M.	Arrive at Los Angeles airport. Take hotel shuttle service; arrive at hotel by 10:45 A.M.
	12:00 noon	Lunch at hotel restaurant.
	1:30 P.M.	Disneyland for remainder of day. Dinner at Disneyland.
Tuesday	8:00 A.M.	Breakfast at Howard Johnson's.
	9:00 A.M.	Knott's Berry Farm (20 minute ride by tour bus). Spend day there; eat lunch there.
	7:00 P.M.	Leave Knott's Berry Farm; go to dinner at Bob's Big Boy.
	8:00 P.M.	Return to hotel.
Wednesday	8:00 A.M.	Breakfast at Pancake House.
	9:00 A.M.	Universal Studios. Tour begins at 10:00 A.M., lasts until noon.
	12:00 noon	Lunch at nearby restaurant. Catch tour bus at 1:30 P.M. to return to hotel.

You may choose to use a **travel agency**, which is a business that arranges transportation, accommodations, and itineraries for customers. The agent can make plane and hotel reservations for you, and can help you plan the whole trip if you like. Agents get their fee from the airlines and hotels you book. However, if you want itinerary planning, you will likely have to pay a fee for the service.

You can book your flights and accommodations online by going to the Web sites of specific airlines, hotels, car rental agencies, and entertainment centers, or make all the reservations through a full-service travel site such as Expedia (www.expedia.com) or Travelocity (www.travelocity.com). If you enter your travel times and preferences at a full-service site, the search tool will present you with a list of available flights that meet your criteria. You can even have them listed in order of price. You can select a flight and pay for it online with your credit card number.

At the Airport

Flights today are often ticketless. You receive a reservation number when you book your flight. At the airport, you check in, often at a computerized kiosk, and receive your boarding pass. This process is often quicker than waiting in line to check in, especially if you are traveling light—with just carry-on bags. Ticketless flying protects you from lost or stolen tickets, which would cost $50 or more to replace.

Bring a photo ID, such as your driver's license or passport. You will need it to get through security. Do not carry any sharp objects, such as a pocket knife or toenail clippers. A security officer will confiscate anything that could be used as a weapon. Pack such items in your checked luggage.

Arrive at the airport at least an hour and a half before your flight's departure time. This gives you time to check in and pass through security. Often, airlines **overbook** flights, which means that they sell more reservations than they can fulfill. Airlines overbook flights because some people do not show up for a scheduled flight, and the airlines make more money if their flights are full. If more people show up for the flight than the plane can accommodate, the airline will ask people to give up their seats voluntarily in exchange for a future free ticket and a later flight. Passengers "bumped" (forced to miss a flight involuntarily) are usually entitled to compensation, often in the form of cash, a coupon, or a free flight. By arriving early to check in, you can decrease your risk of an overbooking problem.

By signing up for an airline's free frequent-flyer program, you can earn credit toward a free ticket. You receive credit for miles traveled each time you fly with that airline. You may also receive frequent-flyer miles for staying at a participating hotel, renting from a participating car rental agency, booking online, or whatever the airline defines in its program. After you accumulate enough miles, you earn a free flight or an upgrade (to first class), though the airlines often limit your flight options.

At-Home Preparations

Before leaving on your vacation, you should take care of a few things at home. Ask a neighbor to pick up your newspaper, or call the paper to stop delivery while you are gone. Fill out a form at the post office to have your mail held there rather than delivered. By stopping these deliveries, you avoid a buildup of mail and newspapers that may tip off burglars that you are away from home.

Arrange for someone to feed your pets, care for your plants, mow the lawn, and do other household duties that cannot wait for your return. Use an automatic timer for lights so that they come on in the evening and go off a few hours later, giving the appearance that you are home. Lock all doors and windows and close the curtains. It is also a good idea to ask a neighbor to keep an eye on things while you are away. Finally, you might wish to alert the local police, so that an officer can check the security of your home while you are on vacation.

Last-Minute Details

Plan your packing so that you have everything you need, but don't overpack. Remember, you have to carry that heavy suitcase from place to place. Make a list of things you will need, such as cameras, special clothing, and personal items. Take only what you need in the smallest possible containers. Be sure to pack enough clothing to last the entire vacation without laundering (unless it is a very long vacation). Close all bottles and other containers tightly to avoid leaks. Do not forget medications you might need. Put important medications and break-ables in your carry-on baggage. Be sure the carry-on case meets airline requirements in size and weight.

You may wish to take major credit cards. However, leave at home in a safe place all the cards you do not need. Take enough cash to pay the expenses that require cash only. Charge other expenses on a credit card. Because of the availability of ATMs across the country and around the world, you can obtain cash easily while on vacation.

✓Check Your Understanding

1. Why is it important to have at least six months' time between the engagement and wedding?
2. What is an advantage of booking a flight online through a full-service travel site?

Online Travel Planning

Have you ever considered doing all of your travel planning online? The Net offers a number of travel-planning sites; and while there are some risks, the savings can be substantial.

At some Web sites, you can do fare searches, check seat availability, book flights, and even book cruises, car rentals, and hotel rooms. For example, www.cheaptickets.com offers discount fares and rates on reservations, once you register online. You will need to give personal information including your credit card number to use this service.

At www.priceline.com, you can check the availability of flights that are inexpensive and underbooked because they are often scheduled at less desirable flight times—after 10 P.M. or before 8 A.M. Using this Web site you can also get substantial discounts on flights to "hot destinations." The downside is that you must be able to take the openings on short notice, and this requires flexibility in travel plans.

Another popular site, www.travel.com, offers special advisories, airport locations and gate locations, ATM locations, embassy locations, flight information, and weather reports. This type of information can be very important when traveling to foreign countries or when time between flights is extremely tight.

Many sites, such as www.travel-for-less.com, provide discount airfares and discount cruises. This type of site offers tickets on an auction basis. You bid on the tickets that are available, and the airline or cruiseline will take the highest bid.

Internet research when planning trips can save you both time and money. Even if you book your tickets by telephone, you can still benefit from the information and search-and-compare features of the Internet.

Think Critically

1. What distant vacation destination appeals to you most? Use the Internet to find the best airfare and motel rate for this destination.

2. What is the downside of using the Internet to make reservations and pay for flights?

Dealing with Life's Uncertainties

Goals
- **Describe the steps and costs in a divorce.**
- **Discuss preparations for death, life's final plans.**

▶ DIVORCE

In all but a few states, a *divorce* is now called a **dissolution of marriage** or *no-fault divorce*, which means that irreconcilable differences have led to the breakdown of the marriage. One partner does not have to prove fault by the other to be granted a divorce. If one partner wants the marriage to be dissolved, it can be done. The only time fault is considered is when the issue of child custody arises.

Cost of Divorce

Expenses involved in divorce are high. They may include attorneys' fees (one attorney for each party), court costs and filing fees, child support and alimony, division of property, expenses for a child-custody hearing, and settlement costs. The more issues there are to settle, the higher the attorneys' fees will be.

Often the divorcing couple can agree outside of court and enter into a **property settlement agreement**. This is a document specifying the division of assets agreed to by both parties and entered in court for the judge's approval. The more that the divorcing couple can settle out of court, the less the divorce proceedings will cost.

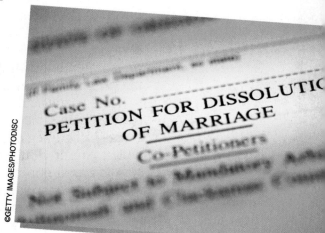

©GETTY IMAGES/PHOTODISC

In divorce, the law assumes that both parents are responsible for supporting the children to the best of their ability. The *custodial parent*, or the parent with whom the children will live, fulfills most support obligations by taking care of the children every day. In most cases, the parent who is not granted custody will be required to pay *child support*—monthly payments to the custodial parent to help provide food, clothing, and shelter for the children. The amount of the payments will depend on the income of both parents and their ability

What is the value in a divorcing couple settling issues out of court?

to pay. Sometimes both parents share custody, and the children live part of the year with each parent.

Alimony is money paid by one former spouse to support the other. The money may be paid as one lump sum or monthly payments, usually for a set number of years, until the former spouse can become self-supporting. Alimony is awarded in some cases when one spouse has been dependent on the other for a number of years and has little means of self-support. Child support and alimony are at the discretion of the judge and become binding on the parties under the divorce decree. Amounts of child support and alimony can be modified only by another court order.

Steps in Divorce

Dissolving a marriage is often a lengthy and unpleasant process. One party goes to an attorney, and the attorney prepares the documents and files them with the court. The other party is served with copies of the papers, called Petition for Dissolution of Marriage, and given a short time to appear (file papers) if there is a disagreement with the proposals set forth in the petition. The petition specifies how the first party proposes to divide property and award custody, amounts desired for any child support, visitation rights, and so on. If the second party fails to appear (defaults), then the first party is awarded whatever is asked in the petition. In most cases, the second party does appear, and a court date is set to decide the issues that cannot be settled between the parties.

Often it takes many months, even a year or more, for the case to be heard in court. Consequently, a hearing will be held to establish temporary custody, child support, visitation rights of the non-custodial parent, and other matters. Many of the temporary provisions tend to become permanent. Often both parties agree in writing to property settlement and other matters prior to the court date. When the judge approves the agreement, it is entered as part of the *decree*, which is a final statement of the dissolution decisions. A decree is final and binding on both parties until modified by the court.

If the parties cannot agree on a settlement, the case then goes to court. There is no jury in divorce cases. Both parties present their cases. In child-custody cases, witnesses may be called to determine which parent would be the better custodial parent. The judge's decision is based entirely on the best interests of the children. All other matters—property, alimony, amount of child support, visitation rights—are also decided in court. Once the decree is entered, the court usually imposes a waiting period before either party may remarry.

▶ DEATH: A FINAL PLAN

Aging and death are part of living and need planning to make the process easier for loved ones left behind. All adults should prepare for death, not just people who are about to die.

Survivors' Benefits

The surviving spouse and children are usually provided with some kind of death benefits. Survivors need to check to see what benefits have accrued through the years.

Life insurance benefits are not taxable to the recipients. Benefits from a life insurance policy can be obtained by mailing a copy of the death certificate, the original life insurance policy, and a claim form to the life insurance company. (Life insurance is described in detail in Chapter 27.)

The Veterans Administration pays a benefit to survivors of armed-service veterans. The benefit may include a grave marker, funeral service, and small amount of cash. Children of veterans may also be entitled to scholarships and educational grant benefits.

The Social Security Administration also pays a death benefit to surviving families. The more the deceased person earned over his or her lifetime, the larger the payment. An estimated death benefit will appear on your annual Social Security statement. The administration also pays a one-time death benefit of $255 to the surviving spouse or minor children who qualify.

Many employer pension plans pay lump-sum or monthly benefits to the surviving families. The family will probably have to apply to receive these benefits.

Why should all adults plan their final arrangements and expenses?

Last Expenses

The costs involved when a person dies can range from a few hundred dollars to many thousands. These expenses include final medical and hospital charges, funeral expenses, casket, and burial. By preparing instructions and making provisions for these costs in advance, you spare survivors the emotional decision-making process at a time of vulnerability. Survivors who are grieving the loss of a loved one are often unprepared to make the many decisions involved in planning a funeral and burial. At such an emotional time, a family may incur elaborate final expenses that they or the estate cannot afford.

FUNERALS

The cost of a funeral can range from $2,500 to $10,000 or more, depending on type of casket and burial. Typical funeral charges include moving the body (to funeral home, church or synagogue, and cemetery), embalming and preparation for public viewing, casket, use of facilities, and funeral staff fees. They may also include the hearse; family limousine; escort to cemetery; obituary (newspaper death notice); clergy fees; printed memorial folders, memorial book, and thank-you cards; death certificate; and all necessary permits. The cost of a burial plot and marker are additional expenses.

Many funeral homes have prearranged plans available at guaranteed costs. Payments made in advance for the funeral are placed in trust and earn interest. You should be able to get a full refund if you cancel the plan. Look over any "pre-need" or prepayment plan you consider. It may lock you into using the services of a particular funeral home at uncertain future prices. If you move away or the home goes out of business, you may have trouble getting your money back.

CREMATION

Cremation is a process of reducing a body to ashes in a high- temperature oven. The ashes are placed in an urn. The urn is presented to the family for safekeeping or burial. Cremation is a less expensive alternative to embalming and "cosmetizing" the body for public viewing. When a body is not cremated within a certain time span, usually two days, it must be embalmed or otherwise prepared for burial. Cremation, like immediate burial without a funeral, permits the survivors to hold a memorial service at any time or place, without having the body present. This procedure is less expensive and may be more comfortable for families and other mourners.

Communication Connection

Select an older adult, such as a parent, grandparent, or friend, with whom you feel comfortable speaking. Ask the person if he or she has made any plans covering last expenses, such as funeral arrangements. Discuss why the person has or hasn't made such plans. Then write a one-page report, covering your conversation. Did the discussion change your mind about any such arrangements you might make?

✓ Check Your Understanding

1. What is the particular circumstance that causes the court to consider "fault" in a divorce proceeding?

2. What are some costs involved in a funeral?

Chapter Assessment

SUMMARY

24.1

* The engagement marks the time to begin planning the marriage ceremony, honeymoon, and living arrangements.
* Some religions require premarital counseling to prepare couples for a successful marriage.
* Weddings can be formal, semiformal, or informal, or you can choose a civil ceremony.
* Family financial decisions should be based on common goals and a family budget agreed to by all family members.
* Families should divide up household responsibilities so that all members do their fair share.
* Vacation planning is based on time and money available, along with interests of all family members.
* Plan your itinerary and make reservations ahead of time, so that you can relax and enjoy your vacation.
* You can gather vacation information, compare prices, and make most reservations online.
* Make arrangements for care of your home and pets while you are away.

24.2

* In most states, divorce laws are no-fault.
* Divorce can be expensive. Former spouses must decide how to divide property and which parent will have custody of children and which will pay child support. If they cannot agree, the court will decide.
* Steps in getting a divorce include filing a petition, agreeing to a property settlement, attending a court hearing, and obtaining a divorce decree.
* Death is part of life, and all adults must prepare in order to make the process easier for their loved ones left behind.

* Families are often eligible for survivors' benefits from life insurance policies, veterans' or social security benefits, and employer pension plans.
* Last expenses include the costs of hospital and medical care, a funeral, possibly cremation, and burial.

REVIEW TERMS

Directions

Can you find the definition for each of the following terms used in Chapter 24?

alimony	property settlement agreement
civil ceremony	reservation
cremation	travel agency
dissolution of marriage	wedding party
itinerary	
overbook	

1. An advance commitment to receive a service at a specified later date.

2. The people who are active participants in the wedding ceremony.

3. A detailed list of events, times, and places planned for a trip.

4. To sell more reservations than can be fulfilled.

5. Another term for divorce, meaning irreconcilable differences have led to the breakdown of the marriage.

6. A document specifying the division of assets agreed to by both parties in a divorce.

7. Money paid by one former spouse to support the other.

8. The process of reducing a body to ashes in a high-temperature oven.

9. A business that arranges transportation, accommodations, and itineraries for customers.

10. A wedding performed by a public official, such as a judge or justice-of-the-peace, rather than a member of the clergy.

REVIEW FACTS AND IDEAS

1. What is the purpose of premarital counseling?

2. How long before the wedding should a couple begin making preparations?

3. List some expenses that are traditionally handled by the bride and her family.

4. List some expenses that are traditionally handled by the groom and his family.

5. What are the differences among a formal wedding, a semiformal wedding, an informal wedding, and a civil ceremony?

6. What are some household responsibilities that families should divide among family members?

7. How can your family go about choosing a family vacation?

8. What types of things should you list on your vacation itinerary?

9. Why should you build flexibility into your itinerary?

10. How can the Internet help you with your vacation plans?

11. How can frequent-flyer programs benefit you, and how do you earn credit toward the benefit?

12. List some preparations that you need to make before leaving on vacation. Include preparations designed to keep burglars from realizing that you are gone.

13. What are some costs involved in getting a divorce?

14. What are the steps in getting a divorce?

15. What types of survivors' benefits are available when a person dies?

16. What are some costs of death and burial?

APPLY YOUR KNOWLEDGE

1. Describe a wedding that you have attended in the last year or two (include wedding party, dress, flowers, reception, and so on).

2. Describe the wedding you would choose for yourself, including setting, type of ceremony, wedding party, total cost, number of guests, honeymoon plans, and so on.

3. Use three Web sites to obtain information about wedding costs and planning. List the site addresses and summarize the kinds of assistance they provide to couples who are planning to get married.

4. How does a family budget differ from an individual budget?

5. Design a three-day itinerary for a trip to a resort area within about 1,000 miles of where you live. Include all necessary information. Use the Internet to determine prices and availability of transportation, accommodations, and entertainment tickets.

Solve Problems ⊕ Explore Issues

1. Write a report describing different engagement ring options:
   a. Diamond solitaire with matching bands. Compare costs of different sizes of diamonds.
   b. Gold and silver bands. Compare quality, width, and costs.
   c. Costs of stones other than diamonds: rubies, emeralds, and sapphires. Compare different sizes of each.
   d. Financing plans available.

2. Squire Alexander and Latasha Williams will be married in a month. Both are working now and plan to work at least five years before having children. They have asked for your opinion on how they should divide household duties, because both of them work eight hours a day, five days a week. Devise a plan for dividing financial responsibilities, including checkbook balancing and financial planning, along with non-financial duties.

3. You and a friend have decided to take a trip. For each of the following situations, describe a trip you would take and list all of the costs that would be involved in each trip.
   a. You each have $100 to contribute and could get away for a three-day weekend. You have one car that does not need maintenance or repairs.
   b. You each have $500 to spend and could get away for three to five days.
   c. You each have $1,500 to spend and could be away for 10 days.

4. What types of divorce/dissolution laws are in effect in your state? Are they no-fault or fault laws? What are the waiting periods? Describe the procedures for dissolution. [Hint: This information is probably available online through your state government Web site.]

5. Divide into groups. With your instructor's permission, each group should arrange to visit a local funeral home. Ask someone there to walk you through preparations for a funeral, including the costs and decisions you would have to make. Each group should present an oral report to the class.

*For related activities and links, point your browser to **www.mypf.swlearning.com***

Managing Your Resources

Unit 5 presented personal decision making (Chapter 20), renting or buying a home (Chapters 21 and 22), owning a car (Chapter 23), and family decisions (Chapter 24). This project will extend your knowledge into related areas.

▶ PERSONAL DECISION MAKING

Home improvement, car purchases, and other major expenses are common ways for criminals to take advantage of unsuspecting consumers. Let's look at some situations you may face in the future.

Don't Call Me, I'll Call You

A typical home-improvement fraud might work like this: Someone knocks on your door and compliments you on your well-maintained yard. The person notices that your house needs painting. The person assures you that he or she is qualified to perform the work and could do the job more quickly and cheaply than a large company. But because the company is small, he or she will need payment up front to buy materials and cover expenses. After getting your money, the person may never do the work or may do such a poor job that you would have been better off without it. Figure U5-1, on page 594, lists some tips for handling this type of pitch.

Promises, Promises

An "unconditional, lifetime, money-back guarantee" is only as good as the person or company that offers it. When the company goes out of business, the guarantee goes with it. Another common guarantee says, "Good as long as you own this car." The dealer offering this guarantee is counting on the fact that you won't keep the car more than a few years. When things start to go wrong, you will no longer be the owner.

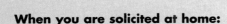
When you are solicited at home:

1. Don't sign today. Any agreement that is worthwhile can wait until you have time to think about it.

2. Don't give cash. When you give a check, you may have the option of stopping payment. But you must act quickly. It is better to avoid giving cash or check until you have had time to reconsider. Many states have laws (called "green river laws") that allow you three business days after a purchase over $25 with a check or credit card to change your mind and revoke the transaction.

3. Check it out. Ask the Better Business Bureau or your state attorney general's office for consumer complaints about the individual or company. Are they authorized to do business in your state? Are there consumer complaints on file against them?

4. Compare prices. Compare the prices for labor and materials with other sources. This may take several days but is worth it.

5. Don't hurry. If you didn't originate the sale, don't allow others to "create demand" for a product. Don't allow others to talk you into something you don't want.

6. When in doubt, don't. Make this your motto. As the saying goes, "If something seems too good to be true, it probably is." Get all the information you need, then evaluate it carefully. If you still have doubts, wait.

All That Glitters

This investment scheme capitalizes on the desire to get rich quick, coupled with an attraction to beautiful and rare objects (from gold to diamonds). Thousands of counterfeit Krugerrands (gold coins) circulate across the nation. Investors have no idea they are fake until they try to sell them. By then the seller has vanished. Gold-painted lead also appears to be the real thing—gold bullion. Investors who pay up front, before verifying true value, get stuck with worthless lead. Junk gems are passed off as valuable rubies, sapphires, emeralds, and diamonds. They are advertised as rough stones that need polishing, but they are junk. When you purchase these items by mail, you may have little recourse.

Complete Worksheet 1 in the *Student Activity Guide* to analyze situations involving possible rip-offs. (This worksheet also appears on page 599 of this project.)

▶ MORTGAGE LOANS

First-time homebuyers need to know the anticipated monthly payment when they purchase a house. The monthly payment will depend on the type of mortgage: fixed rate or variable rate.

Computing the Payment Amount

The largest cost of homeownership is the house payment. The total payment is based on the (a) amount of the loan, (b) interest rate, and (c) length of time to repay the loan. As you learned in Chapter 22, the interest rate on a *fixed-rate mortgage* remains constant over the life of the loan. Under a fixed-rate mortgage, a $50,000 loan at 8 percent spread over 15 or 30 years would result in the following payment:

	30-Year Loan	15-Year Loan
Monthly payment:		
Principal and interest	$366.85	$477.68
Property taxes (based on		
assessed value of $70,000		
and tax rate of $15 per thousand)	87.50	87.50
Homeowners insurance premium	10.00	10.00
Total monthly payment	$464.35	$575.18

Note, however, that while monthly payments are higher on the 15-year loan, your total interest would be lower over the life of the loan. For example, under the 30-year term, you would repay $132,066 ($366.85 × 12 payments per year × 30 years). Under the 15-year term, you would repay $85,982 ($477.68 × 12 payments per year × 15 years). This is a savings of $46,084!

The interest rate on an *adjustable rate mortgage (ARM)* starts low but changes as the loan progresses. For example, for the first three or five years, the rate may be several percentage points below a similar fixed-rate loan. After that initial time period, the lender can raise the rate as much as two or three percent a year, with a cap or maximum rate that can be charged. Typically, when fixed mortgage rates are 8 percent, an ARM might start at 5 percent for three years but increase to as much as 12 percent, if interest rates continue to rise. This type of loan is ideal for someone who plans to move frequently and can sell the house and move when it is time for a mortgage rate increase.

Loan Fees

When financial institutions loan money to homebuyers, they charge *loan fees* that pay the costs of setting up the loan. Loan fees may range from $100 to $2,500 or more, depending on the loan. In most cases, if the loan does not go through for some reason, the borrower forfeits the loan fees.

Mortgage lenders often charge *points*, or finance charges that the borrower must pay at the beginning of the loan. One point is 1 percent of the loan amount. Three points charged for a $50,000 loan would be a 3 percent fee, or $1,500 ($50,000 $\times$ 3% = $1,500).

Mortgage Payment Amount

The chart below provides a simple way to estimate what your mortgage payment amount would be. The higher the interest rate, the higher your monthly payment. To estimate your monthly mortgage payment (for principal and interest only), complete these steps:

1. In the chart, find your mortgage interest rate in the first column.

2. Run your finger across that row until you reach the column for the length of your loan. This number is your monthly mortgage payment factor. For example, for a 7 percent, 30-year mortgage, the factor is 6.64.

3. Multiply this factor by the number of thousands in the mortgage principal. For example, in $50,000, there are 50 thousands. Multiply 6.64 times 50. Your monthly payment for a $50,000 loan at 7 percent for 30 years would be $332.

Monthly Mortgage Payment Factors (per $1,000 of loan amount)	Loan Rate	30 Yrs.	25 Yrs.	20 Yrs.	15 Yrs.
	6.0%	5.94	6.40	7.16	8.40
	6.5%	6.29	6.73	7.46	8.69
	7.0%	6.64	7.06	7.76	8.98
	7.5%	6.99	7.39	8.06	9.27
	8.0%	7.34	7.72	8.36	9.56
	8.5%	7.69	8.05	8.68	9.85
	9.0%	8.05	8.39	9.00	10.14
	9.5%	8.41	8.74	9.32	10.44
	10.0%	8.78	9.09	9.65	10.75

Complete Worksheet 2 in the *Student Activity Guide* to estimate mortgage payments for different mortgage rates and amounts. (This worksheet also appears on page 599 of this project.)

▶ HOUSING OPTION: BUILDING A HOME

When you decide to build a new home rather than buy an existing one, you hire a builder and the process begins. First, you must choose house plans for the size and style of the house you want. Often the builder has lots for sale, and you must select a lot from the builder's inventory. In other cases, you may own a vacant lot or purchase a lot and contract with the builder for only the house itself.

The first cost of building a house is the *architect's fee* for drawing up the house plans. Based on your desires and what you can afford, the architect prepares a house plan. The architect's fee ranges from $1,500 to $3,000 or more, depending on house size and value. The more complicated the floor plans, the higher the fee.

Once you and the builder (often called a *building contractor*) agree on the house specifications and price, the builder will have a building contract drawn. It specifies what is to be done, what materials are to be used, and a timetable for completion. You would probably have to make a large down payment so that the builder can purchase materials. Your loan will generally be approved only after the house is completed. Therefore, the builder may provide a *construction loan* that finances construction and is paid off when the house is completed. While you do not pay for the construction loan, the interest costs on the loan are a part of the builder's costs of operation and are included in the price of the house.

Any changes in the original plans will increase your costs. Such a change requires a separate agreement to account for the added costs of this construction.

The government requires inspections of new construction at regular intervals for electricity, plumbing, and so on to make sure it meets building codes. While the builder is responsible for any required charges (as a part of the total price), delays can result when construction must wait for inspectors to arrive. Closing costs are similar to those for buying a previously owned home, except that the builder replaces the seller. At closing, all subcontractors (companies working for the contractor, such as plumbers and electricians) and all expenses of construction will be paid.

Complete Worksheet 3 in the *Student Activity Guide* to get an idea of the type of house you would like to build. (This worksheet also appears on page 600 of this project.)

▶ AUTO REPAIR RIP-OFFS

Overcharging and needless repairs cost motorists billions of dollars each year. Some states require repair shops to give written estimates. The final bill cannot be increased by more than 10 percent without your prior authorization. Many states require that the repair shop return replaced parts to you rather than discard them. This practice allows you to examine the part that has been replaced.

You should be wary when allowing others to check your car's engine, tires, belts, fluid levels, and the like. For example, you go in for an oil change and the mechanic reports that you should replace your water pump, hoses, valve covers, and other parts. These repairs may be needed, or maybe not. If the mechanic finds a number of problems, or one very expensive problem, be suspicious. Ask for evidence of the problem.

Figure U5-2 shows a list of tips from New York City's Department of Consumer Affairs to help you know what to do when you experience car trouble. Complete Worksheet 4 in the *Student Activity Guide* about suspicious situations related to car repairs. (This worksheet also appears on page 601 of this project.)

figure **U5-2**

WHEN YOU RUN INTO CAR TROUBLE

Tips from New York City's Department of Consumer Affairs

- Look for a reliable mechanic before you are faced with an emergency. Ask friends for references.

- If you suspect your car needs repairs, have it checked before it becomes a big repair.

- For large repairs, get two estimates and compare the charges. Let the shops know you are comparison shopping.

- List all symptoms so you won't forget anything when you are talking to a mechanic. Give a copy of the list to the mechanic and keep a copy for yourself. Make sure all of the symptoms are taken care of before you accept the work for full payment.

- Don't authorize work unless you understand what is being done. Add-on work that does not apply to the reason for your repair should be suspect.

- Don't tell a mechanic to "get this car in good running order." This is a blanket opportunity for them to do anything whether or not it is essential.

- Don't sign a repair order unless you understand what is being done to your car. Question each line item.

- Keep itemized bills. Good records will help you in the event work is not satisfactory. Mechanics should stand behind their work. Be able to tell the mechanic, "I had this fuel pump replaced by you two months ago. It should be working." Have the documentation with you to prove it.

- If you suspect you are being overcharged, ask to see the supplier's parts price list.

- Find out which local and state government agencies have jurisdiction over auto-repair complaints. Use the agency if necessary to get satisfaction.

WORKSHEET 1

Before You Buy: Ripoffs and Warning Signals

BEFORE YOU BUY...

Directions: Analyze the following situations and determine what might be wrong.

Situation 1. You receive an e-mail that says you qualify for a new mortgage. You can get a $300,000 loan for as little as $600 a month. Bad credit is no problem. You can refinance at any time. Just click the link for a free consultation.

Situation 2. You receive a telephone call that offers you free products for answering a few simple questions. All you have to do is give them your name, social security number, address, and other personal information, and they will send you free samples of merchandise that you use or would like to try based on your lifestyle.

Situation 3. You see an ad in the classified pages where a desperate investor is seeking to unload his collection of rare baseball cards and comic books at lower-than-market prices. He needs the money right away and will sell to the highest bidder. You call to get the address, and when you show up, there are several others there who are interested in the merchandise and are bidding on it.

WORKSHEET 2

Computing Mortgage Payments

Directions: Compute the following estimated mortgage amounts, using the chart supplied on page 596.

What is your estimated mortgage payment for:

30-year mortgage		25-year mortgage		15-year mortgage	
1. $50,000	8%	2. $70,000	6%	3. $80,000	7.5%
4. $100,000	6%	5. $100,000	7%	6. $100,000	8%
7. $150,000	7.5%	8. $150,000	9%	9. $150,000	10%

WORKSHEET 3

Building Your Dream Home

Directions: Answer the following questions and complete the research suggested to specify your dream home. Be sure to list your sources of information.

1. What style of house do you prefer? (two-story, ranch, Victorian, Tudor, and so on)

2. Attach a picture of a house that closely resembles the home of your dreams.

3. Prepare a floor plan that details the rooms and configuration, along with windows, doors, and so on.

4. What is the total square footage of your home?

    How many bedrooms?

    Bathrooms?

    Describe the kitchen and eating area(s).

    Describe the general layout of the house, starting at the front door and ending at the back door or on the second floor.

5. Describe the lot and landscaping, including lot size and shape.

6. Describe the block—what part of town, city or country, the neighborhood or region.

7. Based on today's costs of building real estate, what would it cost to build this house? (Hint: You need to consult newspaper or online ads that describe similar new properties or interview a builder or other reliable source.)

8. Prepare a report of your findings, including a cover page, drawings or exhibits, narrative of information, and list of sources of information.

WORKSHEET 4

Ripoffs and Warning Signals (Your Car)

Directions: Read each of the following statements that could be a potential ripoff. Write the warning signal (a point that makes you uncomfortable) and what you would do about it.

1. Your car is making pinging noises every time you accelerate to pass another car or go up a hill. You stop by a service station and while your car is being filled with gas, you casually ask what could be wrong. The attendant replies that he would be happy to take a look at it when he gets off work, and that he could probably fix it in his spare time. Repairs could cost as little as $50 or as much as $250.

2. You are on vacation and driving the family car. You had it tuned up before you left, and your tires are fairly new. Along the way, you stop for gas. While checking the oil, the attendant notices that one of your hoses is loose. He fixes it (no charge) but then sees that you have an oil leak. He offers to make the repair within an hour for $100 plus parts.

3. You take your car in for its regular tune-up and maintenance. You take a list of things that need to be done. An hour later, you receive a telephone call and are asked to authorize extra repairs that total $500. These repairs are not related to the tune-up or regular maintenance. But when the car is up on the rack, the mechanic sees that the work needs to be done.

unit

Risk Management

CHAPTERS

25 **Introduction to Risk Management**

26 **Property and Liability Insurance**

27 **Health and Life Insurance**

Project: **Managing Personal Risks**

Unit 6 begins with risk—what it is and how to manage it. In Chapter 25, you will examine different types of risks along with strategies to manage risks.

In Chapter 26, you will learn the specifics of property insurance—how to protect your residence and personal possessions and how to protect yourself from liability as a result of your negligence or errors in judgment.

In Chapter 27, you will learn about rising health costs and the need for health insurance. Finally, you will learn about life insurance: who needs it, how it works, and the types available.

Introduction to Risk Management

TERMS TO KNOW

risk (insurance)	indemnification	speculative risk
insurance	probability	insurable interest
insurer	personal risks	risk management
policy	property risks	risk avoidance
premium	liability risks	risk reduction
policyholder	pure risk	risk assumption

Consider This. . .

Karen was visiting with her financial planner and discussing plans for purchases and investments in the future. Her planner asked about Karen's current insurance coverage.

"I have basic insurance on my car," she answered, "but I don't really know whether it's adequate or too much. I hear a lot about life insurance, but I haven't bought a policy. At this point in my life, I can't afford a lot of money going for payments. Still, I don't want to take chances that could drain my savings. You've mentioned risk management. What is that? Is that the same thing as insurance?"

What is Insurance?

Goals
- **Explain the concept of insurance.**
- **Define insurance terminology and types of risk.**

▶ SPREADING THE RISK

Chapter 11 described *risk* as the chance of financial loss from a decline in an investment's value. In terms of insurance, **risk** is the chance of financial loss from perils to people or property. Perils to people include declining health, injury, and death. Perils to property include damage or loss from fire, vandalism, car accidents, and theft, among many others. **Insurance** is a method for spreading individual risk among a large group of people to make losses more affordable for all. There are many types of insurance, including life, health, homeowners, and automobile. They all provide one important thing: relief from fear of severe financial loss due to events beyond your control.

Here's an example of how insurance works. Suppose your textbook for this class costs $60. If you lose it, you will have to pay that amount to replace it. An average of 10 out of every 100 textbooks (or 1 out of every 10) are lost each school year. Based on this statistic, the expected losses in a class of 30 students would come to 3 books, at a total cost of $180 (3 × $60). The class could establish an insurance company to help lower the cost of these expected losses to individual students. Every student would contribute $6 to the company. The total of $180 collected would be used to replace the books. The cost to each student would be relatively low ($6), and no one student would have to pay the full $60.

An insurance company, or **insurer**, is a business that agrees to pay the cost of potential future losses in exchange for regular fee payments. When people buy insurance, they join a risk-sharing group (the insurer) by purchasing a written insurance contract (a **policy**). Under the policy, the insurer agrees to assume an identified risk for a fee (the **premium**), usually paid at regular intervals by the owner of the policy (the **policyholder**). The insurer collects insurance premiums from policyholders under the assumption that only a few policyholders will have financial losses at any given time. To make a profit, the insurer must collect more in premiums than it pays out for losses and operating expenses. In years when a major disaster occurs, such as a hurricane, flood, or earthquake, an insurer may pay out more in benefits than it receives in premiums.

Insurance is not meant to enrich—only to compensate for actual losses incurred. This principle is called indemnification. **Indemnification** means putting the policyholder back in the same financial condition he or she was in before the loss occurred.

Probability is the mathematics of chance and the root of indemnification. Every event can be described in terms of probability or likelihood that something will happen.

Insurers set premiums based on statistical probability. In other words, they estimate the likelihood of potential losses. They gather and analyze large amounts of historical data to determine how many of a particular loss occurred, on average, in a population over a given time period. From this analysis they can predict approximately how many such losses to expect among their policyholders over a similar future time period, such as a year. For example, in a sample of 100,000 drivers under the age of 18, an insurer can predict approximately how many will have accidents in a given year. The higher the probability of a loss occurring, the higher the premium for insuring against it. Remember that insurers deal in averages. They cannot predict which individuals will suffer losses.

How can a major disaster affect an insurer financially?

©GETTY IMAGES/PHOTODISC

VIEWPOINTS

Experts believe that in order to reduce teen-driving accidents, the most effective policies limit teens' driving exposure—for example, night driving and passenger restrictions for beginning drivers and higher ages for initial licensure. Curfews that apply to late-night activities for 13–17 year-olds also reduce crashes and crash injuries.

Think Critically: Do you think that such policies are effective? Do they infringe on teens' rights?

▶ INSURANCE TERMINOLOGY

To understand all types of insurance, let's begin with some basic vocabulary. In addition to the terms defined above, here are some typical words that relate to insurance:

1. *Actuarial table*—a table of premium rates based on ages and life expectancies.

2. *Actuary*—a specialist in insurance calculations and statistics.

3. *Beneficiary*—a person named on an insurance policy to receive the benefits from the policy.

4. *Benefits*—sums of money to be paid for specific types of losses under the terms of an insurance policy.

5. *Cash value*—the amount of money payable to a policyholder upon discontinuation of a life insurance policy.

6. *Claim*—a policyholder's request for reimbursement for a loss under the terms of an insurance policy.

7. *Coverage*—protection provided by the terms of an insurance policy.

8. *Deductible*—the specified amount of a loss that the policyholder pays before the insurer is obligated to pay anything. The insurance company pays only the amount in excess of the deductible.

9. *Exclusions*—specified losses that the insurance policy does not cover.

10. *Face amount*—the amount stated in a life insurance policy to be paid upon death.

11. *Grace period*—the additional time after the premium due date that the insurer allows the policyholder to make the payment without penalty (usually 30 days).

12. *Hazard*—a condition that creates or increases the likelihood of some loss. For example, lightning can create a fire and defective house wiring can increase the likelihood of a fire.

13. *Insurance agent*—a professional insurance salesperson who acts for the insurer in negotiating, servicing, or writing an insurance policy.

14. *Insured*—the person or company protected against loss (not always the owner of the policy).

15. *Loss*—an unexpected reduction in value of the insured's property caused by a covered peril; the basis of a valid claim for reimbursement under the terms of an insurance policy.

16. *Peril*—an event whose occurrence can cause a loss; people buy policies for protection against such perils as a fire, storm, explosion, accident, or robbery.

17. *Proof of loss*—the written verification of the amount of a loss that must be provided by the insured to the insurer before a claim can be settled.

18. *Standard policy*—the contract form that has been adopted by many insurers, approved by state insurance divisions, or prescribed by law (modifications are made to suit the needs of the individual).

19. *Unearned premium*—the portion of a paid premium that the insurer has not yet earned because the policy term has not ended. The unearned premium is returned to the policyholder when a policy is canceled.

▶ INSURABLE RISKS

You face risks every day. From the moment you get out of bed, you take chances. You could slip and fall. You could have an accident in the kitchen. You could have your stereo stolen or injure another person or property while driving your car. Insurance gives you financial protection from the losses associated with these types of risks. To be *insurable*, the risk must have the potential to result in serious financial loss not under the control of the insured.

There are three major insurable risks: personal, property, and liability. You should consider each of these risks as you make plans to protect your financial interests. Figure 25-1 gives examples of common risks and ways to protect yourself from their occurrence or to reduce their impact on you financially.

Personal Risks

Personal risks are the chances of loss involving your income and standard of living. You can protect yourself from personal risks by buying life, health, and disability insurance. Besides protecting yourself, insurance against personal risks protects others who are depending on your income to provide food, clothing, shelter, and the comforts of life. As you will learn in Chapter 27, this type of insurance can be very expensive. You will be faced with many choices in coverage, costs, and potential benefits.

Property Risks

The chances of loss or harm to personal or real property are called **property risks**. For example, your home, car, or other possessions could be damaged or destroyed by fire, theft, wind, rain, accident, and other hazards. To protect from such losses, you purchase property insurance. As you will learn in Chapter 26, insurance for your home and car requires many decisions that will affect premiums and coverage.

How is an insurable risk defined?

©GETTY IMAGES/PHOTODISC

figure **25-1** ◄◄

Risks	Causes (Perils)	Ways to Protect Yourself
1. Losing job (income)	Poor economy Company's financial condition Job-skills obsolescence	Learn new skills; make yourself more valuable
2. Illness or injury	On-the-job accident Chronic health condition or handicap	Health insurance Disability insurance Retraining programs
3. Death of wage earner	Dangerous activities including sports or job; illness	Life insurance Get training/lessons Take safety precautions
4. Liability for others' injuries	Careless driving Hazard at home/place of work	Liability insurance Signs, warnings, supervised uses
5. Loss of property to theft	Vehicle stolen Robbery	Locks/security devices Park in well-lit and secure places

Liability Risks

Liability risks are the chances of loss that may occur when your errors or inappropriate actions result in bodily injury to someone else or damage to someone else's property. For example, you could accidentally cause injury or damage to others or their property by your conduct while driving a car. Or a person could fall because of your home's crumbling front steps and break an arm. Liability insurance will protect you when others sue you for injuring them or damaging their property.

✓Check Your Understanding

1. What is the purpose of insurance?
2. Explain the concept of an insurable risk.

Risk Management

Goals
- Discuss the risk-management process.
- Explain how to create a risk-management plan.
- Discuss ways to reduce the costs of insurance.

▶ RISK-MANAGEMENT PROCESS

Personal, property, and liability risks are all types of pure risk. A **pure risk** is a chance of loss with no chance for gain. Because pure risks are accidental and result in loss (not gain), they are generally insurable. In contrast, a **speculative risk** is a risk that may result in either gain or loss. When you buy stock, you could either make or lose money. Because speculative risks are not accidental and may result in gain or loss, they are uninsurable.

In order for you to buy insurance, the risk must be insurable and you must have an insurable interest to protect. An **insurable interest** is any financial interest in life or property such that, if the life or property were lost or harmed, the insured would suffer financially. For example, you cannot buy insurance on someone else's house. Unless you own the house, you would not suffer a financial loss if it burned down. However, if you depend on your spouse's income to live, then you have an insurable interest in your spouse and can buy insurance on his or her life.

While you cannot eliminate risk, you can manage it so that a loss does not become financially devastating. **Risk management** is an organized strategy for controlling financial loss from pure risks. As shown in Figure 25-2 on page 611, the risk-management process involves three steps: (1) identify risks of loss, (2) assess the seriousness of their financial impact, and (3) select the best ways to handle the risks.

Risk management is more than buying insurance for every possible peril that could occur. Some risks are not serious enough to insure. Others are better handled by taking steps to avoid the risk or reduce the chances that the risk will occur.

figure 25-2

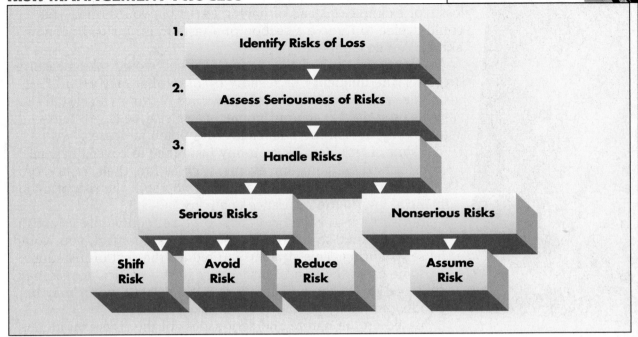

1. **Identify Risks of Loss**

2. **Assess Seriousness of Risks**

3. **Handle Risks**

Serious Risks

Nonserious Risks

| Shift Risk | Avoid Risk | Reduce Risk | Assume Risk |

Step 1: Identify Risks of Loss

Ask yourself what financial risks you take daily, such as when you drive a car, own a house, or plan a party. As you will see in later chapters, many potential losses could occur. Even though they may not happen as a result of your error or fault, you still can be responsible for damages to others and to property.

Step 2: Assess Seriousness of Risks

Human activities and the ownership of property reflect a certain amount of risk. Some risks are high priority because they could have serious financial consequences. For example, when driving your car, you could destroy the property of others, injure others, or even kill someone. Because potential losses are very great, driving is a high-priority risk. Other types of risk may have a relatively low financial consequence or may have only a very small chance of occurring. These types of risk are therefore of a lower priority.

Step 3: Handle Risks

There are four risk-management techniques: avoid, reduce, assume, or shift. A good risk-management plan uses a combination of these strategies to balance risks, costs of insurance, and potential losses.

What are some means by which risks can be reduced?

To *avoid* risk, called **risk avoidance**, you would eliminate the chance for loss by not doing the activity that could result in the loss. For example, instead of having a party at your house, you could decide to reserve a section of a restaurant. Instead of snow skiing, you go camping.

To *reduce* risk, called **risk reduction**, you would take measures to lessen the frequency or severity of losses that may occur. For example, you may put studded snow tires on your car, install fire alarms or sprinklers in your home, or use seat belts. All these steps would lessen the financial risk of potential losses.

To *shift* or *transfer* risk, you buy insurance to cover financial losses caused by damaging events, such as fire, theft, injury, or death. By making premium payments, you shift the risk of major financial loss to the insurance company.

To *assume* risk, called **risk assumption**, you would establish a monetary fund to cover the cost of a loss. In effect, you would be self-insuring. This strategy can reduce the cost of insurance. In some cases the cost of insuring against a particular risk may be too great, or the probability that the risk will occur may be too low to justify paying an insurance premium.

Based on the nature and seriousness of the risks you identified, you should select the risk-management techniques that best handle each risk. For example, you just purchased a car. Because driving a car is a serious risk, you buy auto insurance to shift some of the risk. (It's also required in most states.) You like bungee-jumping, but since engaging in this activity would make your health insurance premium extremely high, you decide to avoid the risk and not do the activity. You know that your old house will probably need major repairs soon. You decide to assume this risk by starting a home-maintenance fund and contributing regularly to it.

Global View

In December 1999, a tremendous flood and mudslide in Caracas, Venezuela, killed some 30,000 people who lived in shacks on the surrounding hillsides. As a result of this disaster, the government relocated 150,000 refugees to towns in the country's empty interior. The promise of jobs and homes lured the homeless families to relocate. The project was expected to cost the government billions of dollars.

Think Critically: Is it possible to protect yourself against all types of risks? If you choose to do nothing, what costs can result? How do those costs compare with the cost of risk management?

► MAKING A RISK-MANAGEMENT PLAN

Everyone faces risks and the potential losses they bring. Some people choose to do nothing—but this is in fact a choice. When you allow events to control your life, they also drain your finances in unpredictable and expensive ways. To avoid possible financial disaster, create a risk-management plan, listing the risks you identified, your assessment of their financial impact, and the techniques that you plan to use to manage each risk.

Figure 25-3 (page 614) outlines a risk-management plan that a young person might develop. As you progress through different life stages, your priorities will change, and you will need to adjust your plan accordingly. For example, life insurance may become a higher priority when you have children who depend on your income. You can use the model presented as Figure 25-3 for developing a risk-management plan for any stage in life.

Insurance is an important part of any risk-management plan. In general, financial advisers say that a basic insurance plan should help reduce the following:

1. Potential loss of income due to the premature death, illness, accident, or unemployment of a wage earner.
2. Potential loss of income and extra expense resulting from the illness, disability, or death of a spouse or other family member.
3. Potential loss of real or personal property due to fire, theft, or other hazards.
4. Potential loss of income, savings, and property resulting from personal liability (injuring a person or damaging the property of others).

For each risk that you will face, you can find ways to reduce, avoid, or assume part of the risk yourself. However, when a risk is significant and can have drastic consequences, then shifting the risk by purchasing insurance is a good idea. In Chapters 26 and 27, you will learn more about specific types of insurance.

► REDUCING INSURANCE COSTS

As you consider an insurance plan, think about the following ways to save on insurance costs:

- *Increase Deductibles.* A deductible is the specified amount of a loss that you must pay. The insurer's obligation to pay begins only after you have paid your full deductible. Generally, the

Risk	Seriousness of Financial Impact	Method for Handling
1. Auto accidents	High	Collision and liability insurance Reduce risk—driver's education class
2. Theft or damage to personal property in apartment	Medium	Renter's insurance Reduce risk—add bolt lock to door
3. Theft or damage to personal property at work or in my car	Medium	Renter's/homeowner's standard policy Floater policy (for higher priced items) Reduce risk—alarm in vehicle; keep items locked and out of sight
4. Injury to apartment visitors	Medium	Renter's insurance Low probability of occurring—assume risk above renter's insurance coverage
5. Personal illness and sports injuries	High	Health insurance Avoid some risk—stop bungee-jumping Reduce some risk—wear a helmet for mountain biking Reduce risk—get special training
6. Vision and dental needs	Low	Assume risk—contribute $10 a month to a fund to pay for new glasses and dental work, when needed (self-insure).
7. Income protection	Medium/low (depending on life situation)	Life insurance (to protect dependents) Disability insurance (to provide income if I can't work) Insurance to make minimum payments when I am unemployed

higher the deductible, the lower the insurance premium. For example, premiums for a policy with a $100 deductible will be considerably higher than for a policy with a $500 deductible. To reduce your premiums, you can accept a higher deductible.

- *Purchase Group Insurance.* The premiums for group plans are usually considerably lower than for an individual plan, especially for health insurance. If group plans are available to you through your job, credit union, a social or professional organization, or other similar group, you will likely save money by enrolling in them.

- *Consider Payment Options.* How you pay premiums can save you considerable money over a short period of time. Monthly payments usually contain an extra charge, while semiannual payments do not. Typically, premiums are paid annually or semi-annually. Agreeing to have your premiums automatically deducted from your checking account or paying electronically may also reduce your costs. Always compare payment options and weigh the differences in costs.

- *Look for Discount Opportunities.* Many insurance companies offer discounts for special conditions. For example, non-smokers can get lower premiums on fire and health insurance. Taking driver's education and getting good grades can reduce automobile insurance costs for teenagers. Having more than one vehicle or more than one insurance policy with a company can result in multiple-policy discounts.

- *Comparison Shop.* Like many other things you buy, it pays to shop around for insurance. Get quotes from several insurers. Be sure to give each one the same information so you can compare exact coverage and costs. When getting cost estimates for many types of insurance, you need to know what your property is worth. Also, maintaining a good driving record is important when getting price quotes for automobile insurance. It's also important to know exactly what coverage you need—and don't need—before talking to insurers.

The financial strength of the insurer may be a major factor in keeping down insurance costs. You can find ratings for different insurers in print and online publications of the A.M. Best Company and Standard & Poor's. Ask people you know for recommendations about insurers they have used. Check with your state insurance commissioner to see what companies are legally doing business in the state, and which companies have had complaints filed against them. You can access your state insurance commissioner at your state government Web site.

✅ Check Your Understanding

1. What is a "pure risk"?
2. How can changing your deductible reduce your insurance premium?

Issues in Your World

 Softening the Blow

Since the Great Depression, the United States has had many programs designed to protect people from the harsh realities of risk in their lives. *Transfer payments* are government grants to some citizens paid with taxes collected from other citizens. Essentially, the government uses taxes to transfer some wealth from those who have it to those who do not. Some transfer payments are made in cash. Others are made "in kind." That is, the government provides the needed item rather than cash. These programs are available to U.S. citizens:

Payments in Cash

1. *Unemployment Compensation.* When workers are laid off, they are eligible to receive a percentage of their pay for a specified number of weeks, or until they get a new job (whichever comes first).
2. *Disability Payments.* For injured workers, the disability portion of social security pays a monthly benefit until the workers recover, or for the rest of their lives if they remain disabled.
3. *Temporary Assistance for Needy Families (TANF).* Low-income families with children can receive a monthly payment for a maximum of 4 years. To receive the benefit, adults in the family must work to gain the experience needed to become self-sufficient.

Payments in Kind:

1. *Food Stamps.* People with insufficient money to buy food may qualify to receive food stamps, which are government vouchers that can be exchanged for food items.
2. *National School Lunch Program.* Children from low-income families may receive free or low-cost lunches at school. The schools receive cash subsidies and donated food from the government
3. *Medicaid.* Medicaid is government-sponsored health insurance for people living in poverty who cannot afford private health insurance.

These programs are temporary. They are designed to help sustain people while they are re-training, recovering, or working to get back on their feet financially. They are not permanent solutions.

Think Critically

1. What would you do if you lost your job and had no immediate source of cash for food and other necessities? How would you cope?
2. Visit your state government Web site and list resources that are available to people in need.

Chapter Assessment

SUMMARY

25.1
* Insurance is a method of spreading risk across a large group, so that no one member must endure the full cost of a devastating loss.
* Insurers make a profit by collecting more in premiums than they pay out in losses and operating expenses.
* Insurance is not meant to enrich, but to return the policyholder to the same financial condition as before the loss occurred.
* Insurers analyze historical data to help predict how many losses to expect among their policyholders over a given time period. They base premiums on these statistical averages.
* To be insurable, a risk must have the potential to result in serious financial loss not under the control of the insured.
* Insurable risks include personal risks (life and health), property risks (home and car), and liability risks (causing injury to others or their property).

25.2
* To buy insurance, a risk must be insurable and you must have an insurable interest to protect. You have an insurable interest in a life or property if its loss or damage would cause you financial harm.
* Risk management is an organized strategy for controlling financial loss from pure, not speculative, risks.
* The risk-management process begins with identifying risks, then assessing their financial impact, and finally devising a plan to handle them.
* You can choose to transfer serious risks by buying insurance, assume nonserious risks yourself, and take steps to avoid or reduce other risks.

* Based on your assessment of the risks you identified, select the best risk-management options for handling each one, and combine these into a plan.
* To reduce insurance costs, you can increase deductibles, buy group plans, change payment options, take advantage of discounts, and comparison shop.

REVIEW TERMS

Directions

Can you find the definition for each of the following terms used in Chapter 25?

indemnification	**probability**
insurable interest	**property risks**
insurance	**pure risk**
insurer	**risk (insurance)**
liability risks	**risk assumption**
personal risks	**risk avoidance**
policy	**risk management**
policyholder	**risk reduction**
premium	**speculative risk**

1. A method of spreading individual risk among a large group of people to make losses more affordable for all.

2. The chances of loss involving your income and standard of living.

3. A chance of loss with no chance for gain.

4. An organized strategy for controlling financial loss from pure risks.

5. The risk-management technique that involves taking measures to lessen the frequency or severity of losses.

6. The mathematics of chance; the likelihood that something will happen.

7. The chance of financial loss from perils to people or property.

8. The chances of loss or harm to personal property or real estate.

9. The chances of loss that may occur when your errors or inappropriate actions result in bodily injury to someone else or damage to someone else's property.

10. A risk that may result in either gain or loss.

11. The risk-management technique of eliminating the chance for loss by not doing the activity that could result in the loss.

12. The risk-management technique of establishing a monetary fund to cover the cost of a loss.

13. Putting the insured back in the same financial condition as before the loss occurred.

14. Any financial interest in life or property such that, if the life or property were lost or harmed, the insured would suffer financially.

15. A business that agrees to pay the cost of potential future losses in exchange for regular fee payments.

16. A written insurance contract.

17. A fee usually paid at regular intervals to an insurer for an insurance policy.

18. The person who owns an insurance policy.

REVIEW FACTS AND IDEAS

1. Why do people buy insurance?

2. Explain how insurance works.

3. How do insurers make a profit?

4. Explain the concepts of probability and indemnification.

5. How do insurers decide how much to charge in premiums?

6. Define the words *deductible, peril,* and *loss.*

7. List the three major types of insurable risks.

8. What type of risk is not insurable?

9. Why can't you buy insurance on your neighbor's house?

10. Explain the three-step risk-management process.

11. Explain the concepts of risk avoidance, risk reduction, risk assumption, and risk transfer.

12. What should you include in a risk-management plan?

13. How can you reduce your insurance costs?

14. Explain why the National School Lunch Program is a "transfer payment in kind."

1. Prepare a list of insurers in your area. Include the types of insurance sold by each company. For each insurance agency, list the insurance companies represented. (Hint: The Yellow Pages of your telephone directory should have all these listed under "Insurance.")

2. Based on Figure 25-1, list any current or anticipated risks you or your family face or will face in the near future. You might include risks for recreation and travel opportunities, injuries on the job, and so on.

3. Based on your personal situation, analyze your current personal, property, and liability risks. Then assume that you are now 10 years older. Based on being where you would like to be and doing what your current goals dictate, analyze your personal, property, and liability risks for this stage in your life.

4. Using Figure 25-2 as a guide, identify your most significant risks and the perils that cause them. Then list ways that you can protect yourself by either reducing the financial impact of the risk or reducing its chances of occurring.

5. Visit your state insurance commissioner online. Download and print the complaint form if one is available, and write a paragraph about what recourse you may have when you feel an insurer is treating you unfairly.

6. Find *Standard & Poor's* in your library. Look up the financial strength ratings for particular insurance companies until you find two with different ratings. Then look up the meaning of these ratings. Which company did *Standard & Poor's* judge to be financially stronger? How did the two ratings differ?

7. Using Figure 25-3 as a guide, prepare a risk-management plan for yourself. You may need assistance from parents to determine your current insurance coverage. As an alternative, interview a person at a different life stage and ask for advice on an appropriate risk-management plan.

Solve Problems ⊕ Explore Issues

1. Carmen and Jose are planning to get married next summer. They don't own a car and plan to rent an apartment. They intend to have children in the next few years. What advice can you give them about risk and risk management? When should they consider purchasing insurance?

2. Your cousin LaMarr has decided to take up snow skiing. He has asked you how he can avoid paying for high medical bills if he gets injured. Currently, he is under his parents' group health insurance policy, but his parents have informed him that he will be responsible for all costs of learning to ski, including any costs not paid by insurance. How can he maximize his opportunities while minimizing his risks and costs?

3. A neighbor has asked for your advice regarding insurance. She is single, owns her own car, and works full time. She is buying a home and has student loans and other debts to pay. She would like to know what risks she is facing and what she might do about them. Help her identify and assess her risks, and develop a plan to manage them, based on her situation.

4. Julia Jimenez made this statement: "I don't take any chances. Everything I own is insured, including my life and ability to provide money for my family. In fact, I pay so much in insurance premiums that there isn't much money left for doing fun things. Am I doing something wrong?" Discuss how handling risk does not always mean buying insurance.

5. Kate Ito is single and under age 25. She just started her first full-time job with group health insurance. She has a car. She has had no accidents or traffic tickets. She has an apartment that contains furnishings and personal belongings. Prepare a list of the risks she may face. What types of insurance coverage may she need?

6. Interview an insurance agent. Find out what an agent can do to help you purchase various types of protection.

For related activities and links, point your browser to **www.mypf.swlearning.com**

Property and Liability Insurance

TERMS TO KNOW

renter's policy
homeowner's policy
endorsement
co-insurance clause
personal property floater

liability coverage
attractive nuisance
collision coverage
comprehensive coverage
personal injury protection (PIP)

uninsured/ underinsured motorist coverage
no-fault insurance
umbrella liability insurance

Consider This. . .

Helen attends college full time and shares a rented house with two housemates.

"As renters, we have to insure our personal possessions, and we're responsible for what happens on the property, even though we're only renting," she told her housemates. "We need to talk to an agent about renter's insurance to protect us in case of theft, fire, or freezing pipes. The good news is that we won't have to pay very much—probably between $150 and $300 a year."

Property Insurance

Goals
- **Explain the purpose of renter's and homeowner's insurance.**
- **Describe fire, theft, and other forms of property insurance policies.**

▶ RENTER'S INSURANCE

If you rent your residence, you don't have to worry about insuring the building. That is the landlord's responsibility. However, if your apartment burned down, you could still suffer a significant financial loss. Your personal possessions that you keep in your rented home are your responsibility to protect—not the landlord's. You are also responsible for personal injuries that occur inside your home.

A **renter's policy** is insurance that protects renters from property and liability risks. A renter's policy will protect your personal possessions inside the rental property from loss due to fire, smoke, and other types of damage such as water or moisture, freezing, or heat. For example, if you rent an apartment and there is a fire in the building, your personal property (couch, chairs, bed, clothing, and so on) may suffer damage. A renter's policy will cover the costs of repairing or replacing damaged or destroyed property.

If someone is injured while in your rented home, you may be *liable*, or legally obligated to pay the expenses that result from the injury. Your renter's policy will pay for medical costs incurred by your guests. A renter's policy will also protect your personal possessions while they are in your car or at work. If you have particularly valuable possessions at your home, in storage, or with you as you travel, you might have to buy special coverage for the items. For example, a standard renter's or homeowner's policy often does not cover a notebook computer. Tell your insurance agent about your most valuable possessions to find out if you need extra coverage.

▶ HOMEOWNER'S INSURANCE

A **homeowner's policy** is insurance that protects property owners from property and liability risks. It is similar to renter's insurance, except that it includes coverage for the building as well as personal possessions inside the building. All homeowner's policies cover property owners' losses from these three types of risks:

1. Hazards such as fire, water, wind, and smoke that may physically damage the house or its contents.

2. Criminal activity, such as robbery, burglary, arson, and vandalism.

3. Liability—the legal responsibility to pay the cost of another person's losses or injuries. Doing something careless, such as improperly supervising a swimming pool or not removing items from a staircase, may be classified as negligence in a lawsuit.

Homeowner's policies may be very basic or very broad in their coverage. Figure 26-1 (page 626) lists common types of homeowner's policies. *Package policies* that include several types of coverage in a single contract usually carry a lower premium than you would pay for each coverage separately.

What are some types of hazards that cause losses for property owners?

How Much Coverage Do You Need?

Generally, people insure the contents of their house for at least half the value of the building. For example, a building insured for $150,000 is likely to have contents covered for at least $75,000. This includes all types of personal possessions, from furniture and furnishings to clothing, appliances, utensils, artwork, and other personal property.

To be sure you are reimbursed for all damaged or destroyed property, you should complete a household inventory, as shown in Figure 26-2 on page 629. This inventory is similar to the personal property inventory you prepared in Chapter 8, except that a homeowner's inventory usually needs to be more comprehensive. Your household inventory should include documentation that shows proof of ownership and value. Some people keep receipts and take pictures or a home video. Keep this documentation in a safe place (such as a safe deposit box). Most insurance agents provide household inventory forms to their customers. However, some things are not covered by property insurance. Figure 26-3 (page 628) lists items that generally are excluded (not covered).

Avoid overinsuring property—that is, buying more insurance than is necessary to cover the value. An insurer will pay no more than the actual replacement value of the home. For example, if your home valued at $150,000 with contents worth $75,000 were totally destroyed, the insurer would pay no more than $225,000 ($150,000 + $75,000). If you owned a $300,000 homeowner's policy, you would still receive reimbursement of no more than $225,000. As you learned in Chapter 25,

HO-1	**Basic Coverage**	Fire, lightning, windstorm, hail, explosion, riot, civil commotion, aircraft, nonowned vehicles, smoke, vandalism, malicious mischief, theft, and glass breakage. Limits apply, such as $500 or 5 percent of policy value, whichever is less.
HO-2	**Broad Form**	Broader list of perils; broader definitions; still has restrictions and limits, such as fire from fireplaces being excluded; limit of $1,000 or 10 percent of policy value, whichever is less.
HO-3	**Special Form**	All-risk coverage on dwelling itself; a loss not specifically excluded (such as flood) is covered.
HO-4	**Renter's**	Insuring personal property on a broad-form basis with advantages of homeowner's policy (such as special coverage in event of flood or water damage).
HO-5	**Comprehensive**	Most comprehensive policy available; dwelling and contents are covered on all-risk basis.
HO-6	**Condominium Owner's**	HO-4 coverage for condominium owners (wording is adjusted to fit legal status of condominium owner).
HO-7	**Older Homes**	Meets special needs of owners of older buildings that have been remodeled and would have high replacement costs (actual cash value basis rather than replacement cost basis).

insurance follows the legal principal of indemnification. It will reimburse either the actual cash value of a loss or the amount needed to restore you to your pre-loss financial position, whichever is less. You cannot "make" money from an insurance claim.

Claims adjustors, also known as *insurance adjustors*, determine the value of the property destroyed or damaged by a covered hazard. Also, insurers employ *insurance investigators* who look for evidence of destroyed or damaged property. They also look into cases where people try to claim damages that did not occur. Fraudulent insurance claims can result in criminal charges, fines, or both.

An **endorsement** is a written amendment to an insurance policy. Policyholders often use endorsements to add coverages to their policy for an additional premium. For example, you can add flood or earthquake insurance as an endorsement to your homeowner's policy.

figure **26-2** ◀ ◀

HOUSEHOLD INVENTORY

Room	Type of Property	Replacement Cost	Receipt/Proof
Kitchen	Appliances:		
	Stove/oven	$ 600	Sears, 7/02
	Microwave	400	Penneys, 9/01
	Toaster	25	Gift
	Mixer/blender	125	Shaleys, 1/03
	Bread maker	250	K-Mart, 6/03
	Cabinets and contents:		
	Dishes	500	
	Pots and pans	500	
	Silverware	800	Oneida, 2/00
	Clock on wall	100	Gift
	Table and chairs	1,200	Dixons, 5/03
	Curtains	500	Wards, 8/02
Family Room	Bookcase, books	2,000	
	Couch and chair	1,000	Dixons, 2/03
	End tables/lamps	800	Dixons, 2/03
	Television	1,000	Mel's, 3/04
	Stereo	1,200	Mel's, 3/04
	Paintings	700	Dixons, 2/03
Bedroom	Antique bedroom set	5,000	Appraisal
	Clothing	2,000	
	Jewelry	500	
	Picture/mirrors	800	Dixons, 2/03
Garage	Lawn mower	900	Swath's, 3/02
	Garden tools	300	
	Camping equipment	800	Mel's, 3/04
	Bicycles	1,800	Jon's, 3/04
Utility Room	Washer/dryer	1,200	Sears, 3/03
	Cleaning supplies	100	

Coverage added to the existing policy by endorsement is often called *extended coverage*. Instead of adding coverages to existing policies, some homeowners save money by purchasing a more comprehensive form of homeowner's policy.

Most property insurance policies contain a **co-insurance clause**, a provision requiring policyholders to insure their building for a stated percentage of its replacement value in order to receive full reimbursement for a loss. The percentage is usually at least 80 percent. Insurers do not require 100 percent coverage because even if your property is

Items Not Covered by Most Homeowner's Insurance Policies:

- Articles insured separately (floater) such as jewelry, collections, and portable computers

- Animals, birds, fish, and other pets

- Motorized land vehicles (licensed for use), except for lawn mowers and things used on the property exclusively

- Stereos, radios, CBs, cellular phones, or CD players in vehicles

- Aircraft and parts of aircraft

- Property of renters, boarders, and other tenants (unless they are related to the owner and not paying rent)

- Business property in storage, such as samples

- Business property pertaining to a business that is conducted at the residence (separate insurance is required)

- Business property away from the residence

completely destroyed, the land and the building foundation will probably still be usable. If you do not meet the co-insurance minimum coverage, then you will receive less than the full amount of the damages.

Physical Damage Coverage

Hazards such as fire, wind, water, and smoke may damage or destroy your home, or cause you to temporarily lose use of it. The main component of homeowner's insurance is protection against financial loss due to damage or destruction to a house or other structures. Detached structures on the property, such as a garage or shed, as well as trees, plants, shrubs, and fences are also included in the coverage. If damage from a covered hazard prevents you from using your property while it is being repaired or replaced, your homeowner's policy will pay for temporary housing for a limited time.

Theft and Vandalism Coverage

Theft and vandalism coverage protects your personal belongings against loss from criminal activity, such as robbery and criminal damaging. It covers your property when it is in your home or with you when you are away from home. Common types of homeowner's and renter's policies include this coverage.

Calculating Insurance Reimbursement for a Loss

The co-insurance clause in a homeowner's policy requires that you buy coverage equal to a stated percentage of the property's replacement value in order to receive full reimbursement for a loss. For example, an 80 percent co-insurance clause would require the following coverage on a $150,000 house:

$$\$150,000 \times .8 = \$120,000 \text{ coverage required}$$

Many homeowners believe they can save money by underinsuring. Say the owners of the home in our example decide to buy only $100,000 of insurance instead of the required $120,000, thinking that $100,000 will cover most losses. Then they have a fire that results in a loss valued at $50,000. They think their $100,000 policy will cover the loss. But that isn't the case. Because they did not meet the $120,000 requirement, the insurer will reimburse based on the percentage of coverage they do have:

$$\$100,000/\$120,000 = .833 \text{ or } 83\ 1/3\%$$

To determine the reimbursement, the insurer will multiply the value of the loss by this percentage:

$$\$50,000 \times .833 = \$41,650$$

Thus, for a $50,000 loss, the homeowners will receive only $41,650, or 83 1/3% of the loss.

Problem: Najib bought a house for $200,000. His co-insurance requirement is 85 percent. Najib bought insurance for $120,000 to save money on insurance premiums. Last month, a storm caused $50,000 damage to his house. How much will the insurer reimburse?

Solution:
$200,000 × .85 = $170,000 required coverage
$120,000/$170,000 = .7059, or 70.59%
$50,000 × .7059 = $35,295 reimbursement Najib will receive

Communication Connection

Study your room at home and make a list of the major items in it. How difficult or costly would it be to replace these items if they were stolen? Can you place a replacement cost on each item? What about items of "sentimental" value?

A **personal property floater** is insurance coverage for the insured's moveable property wherever it may be located. People often buy it to protect specific items of high value, such as jewelry, coin and stamp collections, fine art, musical instruments, and the like. A standard homeowner's policy has limits on coverage of personal property. For example, your policy may pay up to $1,500 for computers and related technology, $5,000 for jewelry, and $2,000 for collections. If, in fact, you have personal property worth more than these minimum amounts, you can protect it with a floater.

A floater protects property without regard to its location at the time of loss. If you have a floater to cover your jewelry, then you would receive compensation if your jewelry were stolen from your motel room while you were on vacation. A floater requires a detailed description of the item and periodic appraisals to verify its current value.

©GETTY IMAGES/PHOTODISC

Why might someone take out a personal property floater?

Liability Coverage

Liability coverage is insurance to protect against claims for bodily injury to another person or damage to another person's property. For instance, if a guest in your home falls and breaks a leg, you may be held liable for medical expenses. If you own a dog, you are responsible for acts of the dog. If the dog bites someone, you are covered for the medical expenses of treating the injury. If your child hits a baseball through a neighbor's window, you are covered for the physical damage caused.

Lawsuits can be very expensive, so all homeowners and landlords should carry liability insurance. Most common homeowner's and renter's policies include liability coverage. Homeowners are responsible for acts occurring on their property, even acts involving *uninvited* people, such as door-to-door solicitors or delivery people. In most cases, homeowners will not be held liable for damages by a trespasser (unlawful intruder) unless they set a trap with the intent to harm the trespasser.

An **attractive nuisance** is a dangerous place, condition, or object that is particularly attractive to children, such as a swimming pool. If a child sneaks into a private pool without permission and is hurt, the homeowner will be held liable for the child's injuries. The owner is usually responsible, even if he or she takes steps to prevent entry into the pool.

▶ SHOPPING ONLINE FOR INSURANCE

Most large insurers have Web sites where you can get information about the policies and premiums they offer. To compare the offerings of many companies, the Internet is a good resource. Searching on the keyword "insurance" will lead you to many consumer-oriented sites, such as InsuranceMachine.com, NetQuote.com, and Insure.com. At these sites you can get insurance quotes for all types of insurance policies, along with a wealth of information to help you evaluate insurance options.

✅ Check Your Understanding

1. Why do renters need insurance?

2. Why is it important not to overinsure your property?

Lesson 26.2

Automobile and Umbrella Insurance

Goals
- Discuss common types of automobile insurance coverage.
- Explain the concept of liability insurance and an umbrella policy.

▶ AUTOMOBILE INSURANCE

Most states require minimum automobile insurance for registration of a motor vehicle. Automobile insurance covers costs of damage to the vehicle, its owner, and any passengers. It also covers costs of repairs to other vehicles, medical expenses of occupants in other vehicles involved in an accident, and property damage (shrubs, trees, and fences) caused by vehicle operation. Standard policies also cover theft.

Cost of Automobile Insurance

Automobile insurance is expensive. Premiums are based on a number of factors, such as:
1. Model, style, and age of car

2. Driver classification (age, sex, marital status, driving record)

3. Location (city, county) of driver and car

4. Distances driven

5. Purpose of driving (such as work)

6. Age and sex of other regular drivers of the car

Premium discounts are available for certain conditions, such as more than one vehicle insured with the same company, driver's education training, and good grades in high school and college (usually a B average or better).

Your driving record includes the number and type of traffic tickets, called *infractions*, along with your accident record. An infraction might be a parking ticket, failure to come to a complete stop at a stop sign, or an improper left-hand turn. More serious offenses, called *misdemeanors*, include speeding, driving without a license, or reckless driving. Very serious traffic violations, such as drunk driving, hit and run, or leaving the scene of an accident, are *felonies* in most states. Felonies and misdemeanors increase your insurance premiums. Also, felonies often result in loss of license for a period of time and remain part of your driving record for at least three years.

Except for vintage (antique) cars, older cars require less insurance than newer cars, because older cars are worth less. New and expensive cars cost more to insure because they are worth more and would therefore be more expensive to repair or replace.

As you learned in Chapter 25, insurers base their premiums on statistical probabilities calculated from historical data. From their analyses, insurers have determined that some classes of drivers have a higher probability of getting into accidents than others. For example, young, single drivers are statistically more likely to be involved in an accident than are married drivers over 25. As a result, insurers charge higher premiums to young, single drivers.

Net Nuggets

Teenagers drive less than all but the oldest people, but their numbers of crashes and crash deaths are disproportionately high. The risk of crash involvement per mile driven among 16-19 year-olds is four times the risk among older drivers. The Web site www.carsafety.org, which is co-sponsored by the Insurance Institute for Highway Safety, provides detailed statistics about the problem. Also included are stories of teenagers involved in car accidents, along with practical tips on what teens and their parents can do to promote safe driving.

Similar statistics may cause insurers to charge higher premiums on sports cars than on family cars and on young, male drivers than on their female counterparts. Certain geographic locations (such as large cities) have had higher accident rates than others over the years. As a result, insurers charge higher rates to drivers in these hazardous areas.

The farther you drive on a regular basis (such as to work), the higher your insurance premiums. Who will be driving, primarily and occasionally, will also be a factor in determining cost. Adding a teenage driver to an existing policy will increase premiums. Another important consideration is the number of claims filed. When you file too many claims, your premiums increase. Also, when you are in an accident that is your fault, and your insurance company has to pay money to another person, you are likely to see a *surcharge*, or increased premium for one to three years.

Types of Automobile Insurance Coverage

There are five basic types of automobile insurance: liability, collision, comprehensive, personal injury protection (PIP), and uninsured/underinsured motorist. All types of insurance purchased in a single policy are known as *full coverage*. Figure 26-4 (page 634) shows a comparison of coverages for automobile insurance.

LIABILITY COVERAGE
Most states require all drivers to carry liability insurance. The purpose of liability coverage in auto insurance is the same as in homeowner's insurance: it protects the insured against claims for bodily injury to another person or damage to another person's property. It pays nothing toward the insured's own losses, either personal injury or damage to the vehicle. However, if an accident is legally not your fault, the other driver's liability coverage will pay for damages to your car. If the accident is your fault and all you have is liability coverage, your insurance will not pay for the damages to your car.

Liability insurance coverage is usually described using a series of numbers, such as 100/300/50. These numbers mean that the insurer will pay up to $100,000 for injury to one person, $300,000 total for all people, and $50,000 for property damage in an accident. Premiums charged for liability insurance vary according to the amount of coverage.

COLLISION COVERAGE
Collision coverage is automobile insurance that protects your own car against damage from accidents or vehicle overturning. This coverage will pay for the damage to your car in the event you are at fault and the other driver's liability insurance does not have to pay. Most collision coverage has a deductible. For example, you may pay the first $500 (as specified by your policy) for repairs, and the insurer pays the

AUTOMOBILE INSURANCE

	Who Is Protected:	
	Policyholder	**Other Persons**
Liability coverage:		
Personal injuries	No	Yes
Property damage	No	Yes
Collision coverage:		
Damage to insured vehicle	Yes	No
No-fault provision	Yes	No
Comprehensive coverage:		
Damage to insured vehicle	Yes	No
Personal injury protection:		
Medical payments	Yes	Yes
Pedestrian coverage	Yes	No
Uninsured/underinsured motorist coverage:		
Bodily injury	Yes	Yes

rest. Because many minor traffic accidents involve damage that costs less than many deductibles, it is wise to have a larger deductible and pay lower premiums. In other words, paying the first $1,000 for each accident would be less expensive than having a $500 deductible and paying higher premiums.

©GETTY IMAGES/PHOTODISC

COMPREHENSIVE COVERAGE

Damage to your car from causes other than collision or vehicle overturning is covered by **comprehensive coverage**. The causes might be fire, theft, tornado, hail, water, falling objects, natural disasters, and acts of vandalism. For example, if your car is scratched while parked in a mall lot, your comprehensive insurance pays for the damage. Usually, there is a very small or no deductible for comprehensive coverage.

PERSONAL INJURY PROTECTION (PIP)

Also known as *medical coverage insurance*, **personal injury protection (PIP)** is automobile insurance that pays for medical, hospital, and funeral costs of the insured and his or her family and passengers,

What is the difference between collision coverage and comprehensive coverage?

regardless of fault. If the insured is injured as a pedestrian or bicyclist, this insurance will pay the medical costs. To reduce costs for this kind of insurance, buy a car with airbags, antilock brakes, and other safety devices that lower the risk of injury.

UNINSURED/UNDERINSURED MOTORIST COVERAGE

Uninsured/underinsured motorist coverage is automobile insurance that pays for your injuries when the other driver is legally liable but unable to pay. In other words, if the other driver is legally at fault for the accident but has no insurance or insurance that is insufficient to cover the costs, your insurer will pay your medical costs. This coverage also protects you as a pedestrian if you are hit by an uninsured vehicle.

No-Fault Insurance

Many states have passed *no-fault insurance laws*. These laws set up a system of compensation for auto accidents that does not require a legal determination of who was at fault. **No-fault insurance** is automobile insurance in which drivers involved in an accident receive reimbursement for their medical and repair expenses from their own insurer.

The basic idea behind no-fault insurance is to avoid the years of legal battling required to settle a case and determine fault. Even then, drivers with no assets and no insurance will not be able to fix the other driver's car or pay for damages resulting from their negligence. It was also hoped that by reducing the number of lawsuits, more money could go to injured people and get to them faster.

Assigned-Risk Policies

If you have an accident that costs your insurer large sums of money, the insurer may cancel your insurance. The number of traffic citations and fines on your record may also cause your insurer to cancel your policy. If so, you may not be able to find another insurer willing to insure you.

Every state has an *assigned-risk pool* that consists of people who are unable to obtain automobile insurance. The state assigns these people to different insurers in the state. The insurers must then provide coverage. However, the insurance would cost you several times the normal rate for insurance premiums until you were able to establish a good driving record.

▶ UMBRELLA LIABILITY INSURANCE

People who maintain minimum liability coverage on their automobile and residence can also purchase an umbrella liability policy to pick up where the other coverage left off. **Umbrella liability insurance**, also called a *personal catastrophe policy*, supplements your basic auto and property liability coverage by expanding reimbursement limits and including some risks that were excluded in the basic coverage.

Umbrella liability insurance would generally pay up to $1 million or $2 million for any accidental injuries caused to another person while you are driving, for an accident that occurred on your property, or in the course of your employment. This type of policy protects you from extraordinary losses, which are extremely high claims because of unusual circumstances. For example, you may be involved in an automobile accident in which a person receives a permanent injury. Medical costs may exceed $500,000 with additional costs for many years to come. As long as you carry minimum liability requirements on your automobile insurance, the umbrella policy would cover the rest.

✓Check Your Understanding

1. Why do young, single drivers generally pay higher automobile insurance premiums than do married drivers over 25?

2. What is the purpose of no-fault insurance laws?

Driving Uninsured

In most states, drivers are legally required to have liability insurance. This insurance protects others from loss when the accident is not their fault. Still, many people drive uninsured, even though it is against the law. For uninsured drivers, the following are some likely consequences:

1. They may be cited for failure to have insurance. The fine for this offense can be severe.

2. Their citation may subject them to state *financial responsibility laws*. These laws would require them to file special forms with the state each year, proving they have insurance or the ability to pay for damage they may cause. Filing these forms will cause them to have even higher insurance rates.

3. Because they do not have insurance, an accident may be deemed their fault automatically, requiring them to pay for damages.

4. Continued lack of insurance, following a citation, can result in jail, loss of driving privileges, and large fines.

Uninsured motorists also cause consequences to others on the road:

1. Because people drive without insurance, or without enough insurance, other drivers must carry uninsured/underinsured motorist coverage. This raises the cost of insurance for everyone.

2. When insured drivers file claims that their insurance company must pay because the other driver was uninsured, this loss goes against the policyholders. Thus, another person's failure to have insurance can result in your premiums being increased.

3. It may take longer to process claims and get your car repaired when an uninsured driver is at fault.

So, obey the law and carry the required insurance. You as well as everyone else will benefit.

Think Critically

1. Have you read about an accident where a person had no insurance? What were the consequences?

2. What are the requirements for car insurance in your state? What is the penalty for those who disobey that law?

Chapter Assessment

26.1

* Renter's insurance protects your possessions at home, in the car, and at work, and pays medical costs if someone is injured in your rented home.
* Homeowner's insurance includes property and liability protections plus coverage for the building itself.
* Homeowner's insurance protects against three risks: physical damage from natural perils, losses resulting from theft or vandalism, and liability.
* Insurers will reimburse no more than replacement value, so overinsuring will result in higher premiums with no additional benefits.
* The co-insurance clause requires you to insure your building for a stated percentage of its replacement value to receive full reimbursement for a loss.
* A personal property floater covers valuable moveable property generally not covered by basic policies.
* Liability coverage protects you in the event someone is injured in your residence.
* You can shop for insurance online at insurers' Web sites, or compare quotes from many insurers at consumer-oriented insurance search sites.

26.2

* All states require minimum liability insurance coverage for motor vehicles.
* Factors such as type of car, driving record, coverage desired, and deductibles affect auto insurance premiums.
* Insurers charge more to drivers in categories that statistics reveal as having a higher probability of getting into accidents.
* Liability auto coverage protects others who may be injured or have property damage as a result of your negligence.

- Collision auto coverage repairs damage to your vehicle when you are at fault in an accident.
- Comprehensive auto coverage protects your vehicle from non-collision losses, such as from theft, storms, and falling objects.
- Uninsured/underinsured motorist coverage protects you in the event the other driver, who is at fault, is uninsured or does not have enough insurance.
- No-fault insurance laws require insurers to pay the losses of their own insureds rather than requiring the at-fault driver's insurer to pay.
- People who own basic liability coverage on their car and home can buy umbrella liability insurance to expand coverage and reimbursement limits.

REVIEW TERMS

Directions

Can you find the definition for each of the following terms used in Chapter 26?

attractive nuisance
co-insurance clause
collision coverage
comprehensive coverage
endorsement
homeowner's policy
liability coverage
no-fault insurance

personal injury protection (PIP)
personal property floater
renter's policy
umbrella liability insurance
uninsured/underinsured motorist coverage

1. Insurance coverage for the insured's moveable property wherever it may be located.

2. An insurance policy provision requiring policyholders to insure their building for a stated percentage of its replacement value in order to receive full reimbursement for a loss.

3. Insurance to protect against claims for bodily injury to another person or damage to another person's property.

4. Automobile insurance in which drivers involved in an accident receive reimbursement for their medical and repair expenses from their own insurer.

5. Automobile insurance that pays for medical, hospital, and funeral costs of the insured and passengers involved in an accident, regardless of fault.

6. Insurance that supplements basic auto and property liability coverage by expanding reimbursement limits and including some risks that were excluded in the basic coverage.

7. Insurance that protects renters from property and liability risks.

8. Insurance that protects property owners from property and liability risks.

9. A written amendment to an insurance policy.

10. A dangerous place, condition, or object particularly attractive to children.

11. Automobile insurance that protects the insured's own car against damages from accidents or vehicle overturning.

12. Automobile insurance that protects the insured's own car against damages from causes other than collision or vehicle overturning.

13. Automobile insurance that pays for the insured's injuries when the other driver is legally liable but unable to pay.

REVIEW FACTS AND IDEAS

1. Explain the differences between a renter's policy and a homeowner's policy.

2. All homeowner's policies cover property owners' losses from what three types of risks?

3. As a general guideline, how much coverage should you buy for the contents of your house?

4. What are some items typically excluded from property insurance?

5. What do insurance adjustors and insurance investigators do?

6. Explain the concept of co-insurance.

7. What kind of coverage should you buy to insure your expensive guitar collection?

8. Give several examples of an attractive nuisance.

9. List several factors that affect the cost of automobile insurance.

10. How are infractions different from misdemeanors?

11. What is the purpose of automobile liability insurance?

12. Explain the difference between comprehensive physical damage coverage and collision coverage.

13. Why should a person carry uninsured/underinsured motorist protection?

14. Explain the concept of no-fault insurance.

15. What is the purpose of an assigned-risk pool?

16. Why might someone purchase an umbrella liability policy?

APPLY YOUR KNOWLEDGE

1. Prepare a household inventory, listing only the contents of your room or one room in your home. Follow Figure 26-2 as an example. Next to each item, record its approximate value, and indicate whether or not you have a receipt to prove its cost and a photo of each item.

2. Write a few paragraphs discussing the perils of overinsuring or underinsuring property. Be specific in the consequences that may result in either case. How can you be sure that you are insuring property for its appropriate replacement value? (Hint: Ask people who have property insurance how they determined value, such as the assessed valuation as provided on property tax rolls.)

3. Outline ways you can protect valuables from being stolen from your home or automobile. Research the cost of protection devices or services.

4. Get a price quote for full-coverage automobile insurance on the car of your choice. Determine ways to reduce premium costs through discounts or other methods. Write a paper reporting your results.

5. Visit your state government Web site and gather information to answer these questions: What type and how much liability coverage does your state require for drivers? How are financial responsibility laws enforced? For example, is vehicle insurance tied to vehicle registration? What are the fines or penalties if a driver is caught without insurance? You can get information on this subject from a driver's manual, or look in the library or online for relevant laws.

6. Visit the Web sites of two insurers and list the features of each insurer's basic automobile policy. How are their coverages alike or different? If possible, get a price quote from both companies for their auto policy. Which do you think provides the best coverage for your premium dollar? Why?

7. Interview an insurance agent about the need for umbrella liability insurance in your state. Ask questions about coverage availability, maximum policy limits, and premium costs. Also ask about exclusions. What situations would not be covered by the policy?

Solve Problems ⊕ Explore Issues

1. Your friend Aruna is renting an apartment. She has nice furniture that she inherited from her grandparents. One day while you are having lunch, she mentions to you that last year the pipes burst in her apartment building and she was lucky that her valuable furnishings were not damaged. You ask if she has renter's insurance, and she says no. The landlord has insurance, though. How would you advise her?

2. As a first-time house buyer, your friend Tarlton is considering what type of insurance to buy. Describe the types of insurance that Tarlton might consider. (Refer to Figure 26-1.)

3. Your friend Serafina owns a home that has a value of $180,000. Her insurance policy has an 80 percent co-insurance clause. She has the property insured for $140,000. Later that year, a tree falls on her house during a storm, causing damages of $25,000. How much reimbursement will she be able to collect?

4. Your neighbor owns a particularly valuable collection of antique plates. She estimates their value at more than $10,000. When talking about the plates, you learn that she has homeowner's insurance but no personal property floater for the plates. Explain to her the reason for a floater.

5. Your friend Luis is complaining about the high cost of automobile insurance. He really would like to own his own car but, at age 19, he feels he can't afford the insurance premiums. Discuss with him ways he can reduce the amount of insurance premiums.

6. Loucresha Jordan carried the following insurance on her car at the annual costs shown:

Comprehensive physical damage	$ 80
Property damage liability ($25,000)	70
Bodily injury liability (100/200)	175
Collision ($250 deductible)	150
Total Premium	$475

As a result of an accident in which Loucresha was negligent, the driver of the other car was awarded $9,800 for injuries to himself and $2,100 in damages to his car. Loucresha's auto was damaged at a cost of $820. Her medical bills were $135.

a. How much did the insurer have to pay in claims as a result of the accident?

b. What is the maximum the policy would pay for injuries to the other driver?

c. Provided the premiums stayed the same, how many years' premiums would be required to equal the total paid by the insurer as a result of this one accident?

Health and Life Insurance

TERMS TO KNOW

health insurance
group health insurance
COBRA
coordination of benefits
preferred provider
  organization (PPO)
health maintenance
  organization (HMO)
Medicare

Medicaid
disability insurance
life insurance
incontestable clause
rider
term life insurance
permanent life insurance
cash value

Consider This. . .

Ramona wasn't feeling well and was sure it was strep throat. She had had it before and knew the symptoms.

"I need a doctor's appointment," she told her friend. "I'm insured under my mother's policy at work. I have an insurance card that allows me to see the doctor, but I have to pay a $30 co-payment at the time I go to the clinic. The doctor will give me a test called a 'lab culture' to be sure that I have strep. I'll have to pay 20 percent of the cost of that test. Then I'll get a prescription, and I have a $20 co-payment for that. Even with insurance, this illness will cost me $75 plus another $80 for time lost from work. Healthcare sure is expensive!"

Health Insurance

Goals
- Describe group and individual health insurance plans.
- Discuss common types of health insurance coverage and plans.
- Explain Medicare and Medicaid coverage.

▶ GROUP AND INDIVIDUAL HEALTH PLANS

The cost of medical care has escalated dramatically. People with no health insurance provided through employment often cannot afford individual policies. Tens of millions of Americans do not receive proper medical care because they have no insurance. Many states have implemented healthcare reform to meet the needs of vast numbers of uninsured people. Also, rising premiums have forced employers who provide health insurance for their employees to search for ways to control costs. Most are requiring employees to pay a larger share of the cost.

Health insurance is a plan for sharing the risk of high medical costs resulting from injury or illness. Like other forms of insurance, health insurance reduces risk by spreading it among many people. In exchange for regular premiums, the insurer promises to pay medical expenses for the treatments covered by the policy.

©GETTY IMAGES/PHOTODISC

How has the rising cost of healthcare affected Americans?

Group Policies

The most common type of health insurance is **group health insurance**. This is health insurance issued to a group, such as an employer or trade association, to cover individuals in the group and sometimes their dependents. All those insured have the same coverage and pay a set premium. Because a group represents a large portion of potential business for an insurer, a group can usually negotiate better coverage and lower premiums than individuals can get on their own.

Some groups pay the premiums as a benefit to their members. More commonly, however, as in the case of employer and employee, the two share the premium costs. Group plans make up over 70 percent of all health insurance issued. The insurer may not cancel the insurance of any group member unless the person leaves the group or the group plan itself is terminated.

The *Consolidated Omnibus Reconciliation Act*, or **COBRA**, allows people who leave employment to continue their health insurance under the company plan for a limited period of time (usually 18 months). During this period, former employees pay premiums individually for the same group coverage they had while employed. The purpose of this law is to give former employees time to obtain other insurance, either on their own or through a new employer.

The *Health Insurance Portability and Accountability Act of 1996 (HIPAA)* limits the pre-existing conditions that group plans may exclude. It also makes it illegal for an insurer to deny coverage based on health status, though it does not limit the amount the insurer may charge for coverage. The purpose of the law is to increase your ability to obtain insurance when you start a new job and lower your chances of losing your current health insurance.

If a family has more than one group insurance plan, the insurers will share the costs of a claim. **Coordination of benefits** is a group health insurance provision that specifies how the insurers will share the cost when more than one policy covers a claim. This provision assures that reimbursement will not exceed 100 percent of allowable expenses. For example, if a couple has two policies—one through the husband's employer and one through the wife's employer—then one policy may pay 80 percent of the medical expenses and the other the remaining 20 percent. The couple would not be reimbursed for more than 100 percent of the expenses incurred.

Individual Policies

People can also buy individual health insurance policies. The premiums are usually high. Unlike group plans, most individual policies require a physical exam, and insurers may refuse to cover individuals with health problems. Moreover, individuals may have to wait 90 days before coverage begins. Members of group plans receive immediate coverage.

Most states require insurers to make some type of individual policy available for purchase by people who do not have group policies. States have high-risk insurance pools whereby people with pre-existing conditions (such as diabetes) can buy insurance. Unfortunately, the premiums are very high and placement on a waiting list can exclude people from coverage when they need it.

Sometimes medical costs can exceed the limits of a standard health policy. To protect against this risk, people can buy *supplemental health insurance*. This type of policy is designed to pay high deductibles and co-payments as well as medical fees that are higher than the insured's standard policy allows. For example, a standard plan may pay up to $450 a day for a hospital room, but the actual charges may come to $500 per day. A supplemental policy would pay the difference of $50 per day.

TYPES OF HEALTH INSURANCE COVERAGE

Health insurance policies typically cover basic health (medical, hospital, and surgical) and major medical. Some cover dental and vision needs for a higher premium. The main purpose of these kinds of coverage is to protect consumers from doctor and hospital bills that could ruin them financially.

Basic Health Insurance

Basic health coverage includes medical, hospital, and surgical costs. Medical coverage helps pay for physician care that does not involve surgery. This type of coverage pays for office visits and routine services, such as X-rays and laboratory tests. When the policy covers prescriptions, it generally requires the use of generic rather than name-brand drugs. Hospital coverage pays hospital bills for room, board, and drugs. Surgical coverage pays for part or all of a surgeon's fees for an operation. Usually the insurance covers only necessary (not cosmetic or elective) surgery and excludes some types of surgery.

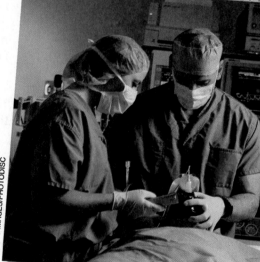

Major Medical Expense Insurance

Major medical coverage provides protection against the catastrophic expenses of a serious injury or illness. Coverage is beyond basic health insurance and usually specifies a lifetime maximum, such as $1 million. For example, when a patient is admitted to the hospital for an organ transplant or some other major surgery, the cost can be $500,000 or more.

The major medical coverage often has a *co-insurance provision* requiring the insured to pay some portion (often 20 percent) of all bills. For a higher premium, a *stop-loss provision* could be included. It would provide that after the insured has paid some specified amount in deductibles and co-insurance, the insurer would fully pay the rest.

Why is major medical coverage so important?

Dental and Vision Insurance

Some group plans also provide dental and vision coverage for an additional cost. Most dental plans have low deductibles and co-insurance requirements of 20 percent or more. They also state upper limits, such as $1,500 per year per person, and cover only certain types of services, such as exams, X-rays, and fillings. Insurers often pay for some services, such as crowns or bridges, at a much lower rate (such as 50 percent).

In some cases, insurers cover only certain types of services. For example, the cost of an amalgam filling (metal) is far less than a porcelain filling. Most dental policies will pay only for amalgams except when the filling is in the front teeth. If you want a porcelain filling for a back tooth, you would have to pay the cost difference. For instance, if your dentist charges $180 for a porcelain filling, and your insurance allows only $90, then insurance will pay 80 percent and you must pay 20 percent of the $90. In addition, you must pay the $90 difference between the dentist's fee and the allowable amount.

Math Minute — Calculating Costs of Services Not Fully Paid by Insurance

George decided to have a porcelain crown rather than a gold crown. His dental insurance will pay 80 percent of the cost of a gold crown. The policy sets the allowable amount for a gold crown at $800. George's dentist billed his insurer for $900, the cost of the porcelain crown. How much will insurance pay? How much does George have to pay?

First, compute how much insurance will pay on the gold crown:

$$\$800 \times .8 = \$640 \text{ will be paid by insurance}$$

Then subtract the amount paid by insurance from the total for the porcelain crown:

$$\$900 \times 640 = \$260 \text{ due from George}$$

Problem: Saburo is considering having special dental work done for a total of $1,200. His dental insurance policy sets $1,000 as the allowable amount for the procedure and covers the procedure at 90 percent. How much will insurance pay? How much will Saburo have to pay?

Solution:
The insurer will pay $900 ($1,000 × .9).
Saburo must pay $300 ($1,200 − 900).

Vision insurance often pays for exams for eye disease as well as for prescription adjustments and lenses. Policies usually cover an eye examination on a regular basis—once every year or two—and the purchase of single-vision corrective lenses. Some policies offer limited coverage for prescription sunglasses and contact lenses.

▶ PRIVATE HEALTH PLANS

Employee health plans are grouped into two categories: unmanaged and managed. *Unmanaged (traditional fee-for-service) plans* allow employees to choose any doctor and to be reimbursed for usually 80 percent of the expenses incurred after a deductible. Deductibles often range from $100 to $1,000 per patient, or $300 or more per family. This plan is the most expensive because there is less strict control on costs or services.

Managed-care plans rely on a network of contracts with healthcare providers. To receive maximum reimbursement, employees covered by a managed-care plan must select doctors who belong to the network. The policy requires employees to obtain pre-approval for any surgery or hospital admission and two or three doctors' opinions before allowing a major procedure to be done. The insurer exercises significant control over the types of services provided and the maximum benefits allowed for those services. Preferred provider organizations and health maintenance organizations are the two most common types of managed-care plans.

A **preferred provider organization (PPO)** is a group of healthcare providers (doctors and hospitals, for example) who band together to provide health services for set fees. Patients must choose doctors from an approved list. There are limits on types of services that can be provided and fees that can be charged. Patients usually must pay a *co-payment*, or an amount in addition to premiums. The co-payment is a set amount per office visit or per prescription.

A **health maintenance organization (HMO)** is a group plan offering prepaid medical care to its members. An HMO often has its own facilities and provides a full range of medical services. Patients must choose doctors on the HMO staff, including one doctor to be their *primary-care physician (PCP)*, or main provider. To see a specialist, patients must get a referral from their PCP first. Otherwise, the insurance will not cover the visit to the specialist. In this way, the PCP acts as a "gatekeeper."

An advantage of belonging to an HMO is that preventive care, such as routine physical exams, is generally covered. The idea of an HMO is to encourage people to come in for treatment before a minor ailment becomes a major problem. HMO patients may have

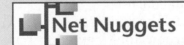

Net Nuggets

Healthfinder® serves as a gateway consumer health information Web site, developed by the United States Department of Health and Human Services. The site contains links to carefully selected information and Web sites from over 1,700 health-related organizations. Among the site's many offerings is a section for teenagers with a wide variety of topics, including athletics, car and bike safety, first aid, nutrition, babysitter's training, healthy lifestyles, and weight control. Check out the site at www.healthfinder.gov.

to pay a co-payment of around $15 to $30. HMOs that are *capitated* (meaning "per person") receive a fixed monthly premium for each patient, regardless of whether the patient seeks medical care. Thus, while an HMO plan is generally less expensive for employees, people sometimes feel that their choices of doctors and treatment options are limited.

Hybrid plans are also available today. They strongly resemble an HMO, but they allow you to choose your own doctor or allow you to go to specialists without seeing your primary-care physician first. Many people prefer these plans because they have more choice and control over medical services.

▶ HEALTH SAVINGS ACCOUNTS

If you have insurance with a $1,000 or higher deductible, you are eligible to participate in a *Health Savings Account (HSA)*. You can set aside money in an HSA to pay medical expenses not paid by your insurance, including your deductible. Your contributions to the account are tax deductible. Your employer may contribute to your account as well. Money withdrawn from an HSA to pay medical expenses is tax free. The remaining money in the account grows on a tax-deferred basis, like an IRA.

▶ MEDICARE AND MEDICAID

Medicare is government-sponsored health insurance for people currently age 65 or older. For people born after 1960, the age for full benefits is 67. Medicare is run by the Social Security Administration and funded by employee payroll deductions. Like other plans, there are maximum benefits, exclusions, and other requirements. Retired people pay a monthly premium for Medicare insurance. For an additional premium, people can buy *Medigap* insurance (a supplemental private insurance policy) to pay the deductibles and co-payments not covered by Medicare.

Medicaid is government-sponsored health insurance for people with low incomes and limited resources. This program is designed to help families who live in poverty and are unable to afford private health insurance or medical care. Like Medicare, there are limitations and exclusions.

✓ Check Your Understanding

1. Why is group insurance generally less expensive than individual policies?
2. What is the purpose of COBRA?

Issues in
Your World

All people need adequate healthcare to maintain a high quality of life. To have access to the quality of healthcare available in this country, health insurance is essential to help pay the high and rising costs. Yet Census Bureau statistics show that nearly 44 million Americans were uninsured in 2002, with some sources citing close to 50 million uninsured in 2004. Of these, nearly 10 million were children. This is an estimated 15.2% of the population and 11.6% of all children.

According to the U.S. Census (2003) and the Kaiser Commission on Medicaid and the Uninsured:

- Eight out of ten people who are uninsured are in working families. In other words, they work part-time jobs or in fields where no health insurance benefits are provided.

- Non-Hispanic whites make up three quarters of the uninsured.

- About 18,000 Americans die each year of treatable diseases because they don't have health coverage (Institute of Medicine, 2004).

Lack of insurance results in poor health and shorter lives for many Americans. There are costs to society as well, such as: (1) Developmental deficiencies from insufficient healthcare during infancy; (2) Expenses for chronic health conditions not treated until they become emergencies; (3) Lost income due to reduced job productivity and employment; (4) Diminished overall health in the country due to low immunization and lack of access to preventive healthcare; (5) Healthcare expenses paid by taxpayers for uninsured patients; (6) Higher program costs (such as social security, criminal justice, and Medicare); (7) Social inequality (with lower income Americans being at a definite disadvantage).

Some say a single-payer, government-sponsored health plan is the answer. This is the type of system that exists in many other countries, such as Canada, and most western European countries. Others say we can reform the system we have so that health insurance becomes portable—that is, you can take it with you from job to job. Whatever the answer, we as a country must find a way to provide access to affordable healthcare for all Americans.

Think Critically

1. Suppose you had no health insurance. How would this fact affect the decisions you make about your healthcare?

2. Conduct some Internet research about the problem of uninsured Americans. Is the problem getting better or worse? Explain.

Disability and Life Insurance

Goals • Discuss different types of disability insurance.
• Describe the characteristics of different life insurance plans.

▶ DISABILITY INSURANCE

Disability insurance is an insurance plan that makes regular payments (usually monthly) to replace income lost when illness or injury prevents the insured from working. This type of insurance is frequently referred to as *income protection* because coverage compensates workers for loss of income resulting from serious illness or injury. Generally there are two types of disability insurance: short-term and long-term. Short-term disability insurance provides benefits for up to two years. For periods over two years and up to retirement, people need long-term disability insurance.

Of all types of insurance, disability insurance is the most overlooked. People think nothing can happen to them that will interrupt their earning power. Unfortunately, recovery from an accident or an illness can extend for weeks or even months. Yet while you are disabled (unable to perform your job), your regular living expenses go on.

Disability coverage requires a *waiting period*. Benefits don't begin the day you become disabled. The waiting period may be from 30 to 180 days. (The longer the waiting period, the lower the premium.) During this time, you would likely be on sick leave from work and would be collecting regular pay. Disability benefits begin after the waiting period and end as soon as you can return to work.

Why is disability insurance the most overlooked type of insurance?

©GETTY IMAGES/PHOTODISC

The maximum *duration of benefits* under most disability policies would be until age 65 or early retirement if you qualify. A few policies pay benefits for life if you become permanently disabled. In addition, the maximum amount you can collect is usually 50 to 75 percent of your regular pay. (The lesser the percentage, the lower the premium.)

Guaranteed renewability of coverage will protect you against cancellation if your health declines. Without this provision, an insurer could

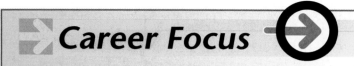

Career Focus

Insurance underwriters identify and calculate the risk of loss from policyholders, establish appropriate premium rates, and write policies that cover these risks. With the aid of computers, they analyze information in insurance applications to determine if a risk is acceptable and will not result in a loss. A bachelor's degree in almost any field—plus courses in business law and accounting—provides a good general background and may be sufficient to qualify as an entry-level underwriter. Because computers are an integral part of most underwriters' jobs, computer skills are essential, along with an interest in analyzing information and paying attention to detail. Underwriters must possess good judgment in order to make sound decisions.

For more information, refer to the *Occupational Outlook Handbook* at www.bls.gov or search the Internet using such key words as "careers," "jobs," and "insurance."

refuse to renew your insurance. The premium for renewability is higher, but the coverage may be worth the extra cost.

Group Disability Insurance

Group disability insurance plans are generally the least expensive option. In many cases, the employer pays for part or all of the plan. However, the insurance is good only as long as you work for the employer. When you leave, you lose all policy rights.

Social Security Disability Insurance

Most workers in the United States participate in the social security program. As you learned in Chapter 5, social security is more than retirement income. Social security is OASDI (old age, survivors, and disability insurance) as well as HI (health insurance—Medicare). Because you have social security taxes deducted from your paycheck, you are entitled to disability payments from social security in the event you become disabled and cannot work. To qualify, you will have to prove the extent of your disability, fill out forms, and have medical exams as required by the Social Security Administration. Workers are considered disabled if they have a physical or mental condition that prevents them from doing any gainful work, and the condition is expected to last for at least 12 months or result in death. Your benefits are determined by your pay and by the number of years you have been covered under social security.

You learned in Chapter 5 that workers' compensation is insurance that covers your expenses if your injury or illness resulted from your job. If you are partially or totally permanently disabled, workers' compensation will pay monthly benefits. This insurance also carries a death benefit. It provides a burial payment and an allowance for living expenses for survivors of people killed on the job. Like social security benefits, these benefits are determined by your earnings and your work history.

▶ LIFE INSURANCE

Life insurance is insurance that provides funds to the beneficiaries when the insured dies. Consider the financial needs that a family will face after the death of a wage earner—and how much income will be needed to pay the ongoing expenses of daily living. The purpose of life insurance, then, is to protect others who depend on you as a source of income. Figure 27-1 shows a list of purposes that life insurance can fulfill. As you can see, some types of life insurance provide savings as well as death benefits.

Like all types of insurance, life insurance is based on risk sharing and probability. To predict the probability of death at different ages, insurers use *mortality tables*. These are based on statistics gathered about life expectancy and death rates among various types of people. Insurers set premiums based on these tables. For example, older people have a higher probability of dying while the policy is in effect than do younger

 **figure 27-1**

PURPOSES OF LIFE INSURANCE

Why You Should Purchase Life Insurance:

- to pay off a home mortgage and other debts at the time of death
- to provide lump-sum payment to children when they reach a specified age
- to provide an education or income for children
- to make charitable bequests after death
- to provide for retirement income
- to accumulate savings
- to make estate and inheritance tax payments
- to take care of children's needs as they are growing up
- to provide cash value that can be borrowed

people. As a result, insurers generally charge older people higher premiums. Other factors enter the calculation as well. For example, people who smoke tend to die sooner than people who don't, and premiums reflect this. Someone with a serious health problem, such as heart disease, may not be able to buy life insurance at all.

To obtain life insurance, you will have to supply a detailed medical history. You may be required to have a medical examination, especially for large policies.

You may be able to buy inexpensive group life insurance through your employer. A *group life insurance plan* insures a large number of people under the terms of a single policy without a medical examination. Employers often provide group life insurance as an employee benefit. However, when you leave your job, you cannot take the coverage with you.

Why are younger people generally charged lower life insurance premiums?

Provisions of Life Insurance Policies

An important provision in every life insurance policy is the right to name your beneficiary. As you learned in Chapter 25, *beneficiaries* are the people named in an insurance policy to receive the benefits of the policy. The beneficiaries of a life insurance policy will receive the amount specified in the policy at the death of the insured. Beneficiaries can be anyone, but married couples often name each other or their children as beneficiaries. If the children are minors, parents may name a trustee to handle the money on behalf of the children.

An **incontestable clause** is a provision of a life or health insurance policy that once the policy has been in effect for a stated period of time (usually two years), the insurer may no longer question items on the application in order to deny coverage. After the specified period, the insurer cannot dispute the policy's validity during the lifetime of the insured for any reason, including fraud. A reason for this provision is that the beneficiaries should not be made to suffer because of acts of the insured.

A life insurance **rider** is a small insurance policy that modifies the coverage of the main policy. A rider usually adds or excludes various coverages or alters benefits. Insurers offer many riders, and the costs can add up. Be sure you need the extra coverage before agreeing to the added premium.

Guaranteed insurability riders give you the right to buy a new policy or additional coverage without showing evidence of good health. Many insurers offer *accidental death* riders. In the case of accidental death, some riders allow *double indemnity*. This means that the beneficiary is paid twice the face amount of the insurance. For your beneficiaries to collect this benefit, you would have to die within a certain time after the injury (and death must be directly related to the injury), and death must occur before you reach age 60 or 65. A *waiver of premium* rider allows you to stop paying premiums and keep your coverage in force if you become disabled and cannot work. This rider usually does not kick in until you've been disabled at least six months.

Types of Life Insurance

There are two main types of life insurance: temporary and permanent. Temporary life insurance lasts for a specified period and contains no savings or cash value. Permanent insurance, however, lasts for life. It also includes a residual or cash value and is therefore a form of savings plan.

TEMPORARY LIFE INSURANCE

The most common form of temporary life insurance is term insurance. **Term life insurance** is a life insurance policy that remains in effect for a specified period of time. If the insured survives beyond that time, coverage ceases with no remaining value. Term policies are sometimes called "pure" insurance because they have value only if the covered risk occurs (death) while the policy is in effect. They have no savings component, as permanent life policies do. Parents often buy 15- or 20-year term policies to protect their children in case the parents should die while the children are still young. By the time the term policy ends, the children will be grown and out on their own, so the parents no longer need the policy.

Term insurance policies can have additional features, such as optional conversion to a permanent life policy. Additional features generally raise premiums, however, and beyond a certain age, term insurance may not be renewable. The main advantage of term insurance is its low cost.

With *decreasing term insurance*, the amount of coverage decreases each year while the premium remains the same. A 20-year decreasing term policy decreases in coverage each year until the value reaches zero at the end of 20 years. If the insured dies during the first year of the policy, it pays the full benefit (let's say $100,000). If the insured dies during the second year, death benefits decrease to, say, $95,000. So, the coverage of the policy decreases by a specified amount each year. In contrast, the death benefit on *level term insurance* remains constant from beginning to end.

Renewable term insurance gives the policyholder the right to renew each year, without having to pass a physical exam. Premiums increase with each renewal because the policyholder is older (and the risk of death greater), but the death benefits remain the same.

Another type of temporary life insurance is *credit life* or some version of it, such as mortgage life insurance. Credit life insurance will repay a debt should the borrower die before doing so. You can obtain this type of coverage from the lender. However, in most cases it would be cheaper to buy term insurance.

PERMANENT LIFE INSURANCE

Permanent life insurance is life insurance that remains in effect for the insured's lifetime and builds a cash value. **Cash value** is the savings accumulated in a permanent life insurance policy that you would receive if you canceled your policy. You could also borrow using your policy's cash value as collateral. If you do not repay the loan, the policy will repay it out of the death benefit when you die. Four common types of permanent life policies are straight life, limited-pay life, universal life, and variable life.

Straight life (also known as *whole* or *ordinary life*) is a policy for which you pay premiums throughout your life, and the policy pays a stated sum at death to your beneficiary. The amount of your premium depends primarily on the age at which you purchase the policy. The premiums are high enough to pay for the death benefit plus contribute to the policy's cash value.

Limited-pay life is a policy on which premiums are limited to a specific number of years (such as 20 years) or until age 65. At the end of the payment period, the policy is considered "paid up." However, you remain insured for life, and the company will pay the face value of the policy at your death.

Like all permanent life policies, *universal life* combines a savings plan with a death benefit. However, unlike the others, the premium and death benefit on a universal life policy are not fixed. The policyholder can choose to change the death benefit and the amount or timing of premiums during the life of the policy. Thus, the face value of the policy can be reduced or raised without rewriting the policy. The interest rate earned on the cash value varies with short-term rates in the economy.

Variable life combines a death benefit with investment options. Variable life policyholders pay fixed regular premiums. The insurer invests part of the premiums in securities chosen by the policyholder. Policyholders designate what portion of the net premium (the amount left over after paying for the death benefits) is to be invested in stocks, bonds, or short-term money market instruments. Both the death benefit and the cash value rise (or fall) with the investment results. While a minimum death benefit is guaranteed, there is no guaranteed cash value.

✓Check Your Understanding

1. Why do insurers use mortality tables?

2. How is universal life insurance different from other permanent life policies?

Chapter Assessment

SUMMARY

27.1

* Group health insurance provides broad coverage at lower rates than do individual policies.
* COBRA allows people who leave their jobs to keep the company health insurance for a limited time.
* HIPAA limits exclusions for pre-existing conditions and makes it illegal to deny coverage based on health status.
* People without a group plan can buy individual health insurance, but they may have to pass a physical exam.
* Typical health insurance includes basic medical and major medical. Some offer dental and vision coverage for a higher premium.
* Managed-care plans contract with a network of healthcare providers, and patients must choose providers from the network.
* PPOs and HMOs are types of managed-care plans.
* If you have high-deductible health insurance, you can make tax-deductible contributions to an HSA to pay medical expenses not paid by your insurer.
* Medicare and Medicaid are government-sponsored health plans. Medicare covers people age 65 or older. Medicaid covers people with low incomes and limited resources.

27.2

* Disability insurance replaces your income if you are injured or ill and cannot work.
* Social security offers disability insurance for workers who become disabled and cannot work for at least 12 months.
* Workers' compensation covers workers who are injured or killed on the job.
* Life insurance provides funds to beneficiaries when the insured dies.

* Insurers set life insurance premiums based on life expectancy and death rates compiled in mortality tables.

* Term life insurance remains in effect for a specified time. If the insured survives beyond that time, coverage ceases with no remaining value.

* Permanent life insurance remains in effect for the insured's lifetime and has a savings component (cash value) as well as a death benefit.

* Common types of permanent life policies are straight life, limited-pay life, universal life, and variable life.

REVIEW TERMS

Directions

Can you find the definition for each of the following terms used in Chapter 27?

cash value
COBRA
coordination of benefits
disability insurance
group health insurance
health insurance
health maintenance
    organization (HMO)
incontestable clause

life insurance
Medicaid
Medicare
permanent life insurance
preferred provider
    organization (PPO)
rider
term life insurance

1. A group health insurance provision that specifies how the insurers will share the cost when more than one policy covers a claim.

2. An insurance plan that makes regular payments to replace income lost when illness or injury prevents the insured from working.

3. A small insurance policy that modifies the coverage of the main policy.

4. A plan for sharing the risk of high medical costs resulting from injury or illness.

5. Insurance that provides funds to the beneficiaries when the insured dies.

6. A provision of a life or health insurance policy that once the policy has been in effect for a stated period of time, the insurer may no longer question items on the application in order to deny coverage.

7. Government-sponsored health insurance for people currently age 65 or older.

8. Health insurance issued to a group, such as an employer or trade association, to cover individuals in the group and sometimes their dependents.

9. A group of healthcare providers who band together to provide health services for set fees.

10. Life insurance that remains in effect for the insured's lifetime and builds a cash value.

11. A group health insurance plan offering prepaid medical care to its members.

12. The savings accumulated in a permanent life insurance policy that you would receive if you canceled your policy.

13. Law that allows people who leave employment to continue their health insurance under the company plan for a limited period of time.

14. Government-sponsored health insurance for people with low incomes and limited resources.

15. A life insurance policy that remains in effect for a specified period of time, after which coverage ceases with no remaining value.

REVIEW FACTS AND IDEAS

1. What are many employers doing to help control their costs for providing health insurance for their employees?

2. Why do group health insurance plans usually have better coverage and lower premiums than individual plans?

3. What does HIPAA do and not do to help people obtain health insurance?

4. What is supplemental health insurance? Who should buy it?

5. What does basic health insurance cover?

6. What does major medical insurance cover?

7. How is a managed-care plan different from an unmanaged health insurance plan?

8. What is the difference between an HMO and a PPO?

9. In what way does a primary-care physician in an HMO act as a gatekeeper?

10. What are some advantages of a health savings account?

11. How is Medicare different from Medicaid?

12. What is the purpose of disability insurance?

13. Why would a person need life insurance?

14. How is permanent life insurance different from term life insurance?

15. Identify and describe three types of term insurance.

16. What is credit life insurance?

17. Identify and describe four types of permanent life insurance.

APPLY YOUR KNOWLEDGE

1. Gather information about the costs of healthcare in the last decade. Magazines, newspapers, the Internet, and books report the costs and trends. Write a paper describing what has been happening and who is to blame. (You will note that various sources blame each other.) Make your own determination based upon your findings.

2. Interview a person who has recently had surgery or been in the hospital for several days or longer. Ask this person about the type of services provided and the approximate cost per day of those services. Ask him or her how much of the cost was paid by insurance and how much (percentage or dollar amount) he or she will have to pay. Write a report on your findings.

3. Obtain a brochure describing the benefits of a group health insurance plan. If you don't know someone who belongs to this type of plan, your local library and the Internet will have information about group plans. Write a paper summarizing your findings—types of coverages, deductibles, co-payments, exclusions, and so on.

4. Search the Internet for information on Medicare. A good place to start is the government site for Medicare at www.medicare.gov. Find out what types of medical/hospital/surgical and major medical coverages it provides and how much of these costs the patients must pay. Then look into Medigap insurance. Based on your findings, do you feel that Medigap insurance is a good value for a person on Medicare?

5. Prepare an analysis of your disability needs, assuming that you are working full-time, are married, and have one child. Pick a career that you would like to have and use a realistic amount of income for a beginning worker (with 1 to 3 years of experience).

6. Examine the list of life insurance needs shown in Figure 27-1. Can you add anything to this list? Can you delete anything? Prepare a list of life insurance needs based on your personal situation as you imagine it will be in 10 years.

Solve Problems ⊕ Explore Issues

1. Your friend is considering two career opportunities—one in which she would be an independent contractor and have no benefits provided, and one in which she would work as an employee of a company and have full health insurance as well as other benefits. Explain to her the importance of having health insurance and how her options for insurance might differ, depending on which of the two career choices she makes.

2. A young couple is a dual-income family. Both have full medical coverage provided through their employers. They figure that this "double coverage" will pay off if they get injured or become ill because they can claim benefits twice. Explain to them the concept of coordination of benefits for group health insurance policies such as theirs.

3. Your cousin is working but cannot afford to buy an individual health insurance policy. His employer does not provide a group plan. Explain to him the importance of major medical coverage.

4. Your friend Darnell is working full time at two jobs in order to make house payments and buy a new car. His wife Kara is working nights so she can care for the children during the day. Darnell can purchase both short-term and long-term disability insurance for a small premium ($10 a month) through his employer's group insurance plan. Explain to them the importance of disability insurance.

5. As a young, unmarried person, you are contemplating college next year and the pursuit of a professional degree that will take six years or more to complete. A neighbor sells life insurance and wants you to buy a universal life policy with a $100,000 face value. Explain to him what type of policy, if any, you would consider purchasing.

6. You and your spouse are in your mid-twenties. You are expecting your first child. Both of you are presently working. You hope to buy your first house in the next few years. Discuss your need for life insurance and the type of life insurance you would purchase now and five years from now.

For related activities and links, point your browser to **www.mypf.swlearning.com**

Managing Personal Risks

In this project, you will apply risk and insurance concepts. You will also do some further exploring and assessing of your insurance needs. You'll learn how to compute the true cost of insurance, how to file an insurance claim, what to do if you have an accident, what you can do to reduce health insurance costs, how to use mortality tables, and how to build a good lifetime insurance plan.

▶ THE TRUE COST OF INSURANCE

People buy insurance for protection against the risks of financial uncertainty and unexpected losses. The alternative—being uninsured—represents large and undefined risks that can leave you feeling uncomfortable. Since the alternative of not being insured is often unacceptable, most people are covered by some type of insurance most of their lives.

Auto Insurance

Let's look at automobile insurance first. Your full-coverage policy might offer these coverages and annual costs:

Liability coverage, 100/300/50	$560
Collision coverage, $50 deductible	180
Comprehensive coverage, $50 deductible	90
Personal injury protection	80
Uninsured/underinsured motorist	60
Towing	15
Total annual cost	$985

If you were willing to increase the deductibles, your savings could be considerable. Let's assume that a $500 collision deductible would reduce the cost of the coverage in our example by $100 a year. Over a five-year period, your total insurance costs would be:

Full coverage, $50 deductible:
$985 × 5 = $4,925

Full coverage, $500 deductible
$885 × 5 = $4,425
Savings: $500

In five years, you would have saved enough in premiums to pay a $500 loss, should it occur. Check your options for saving on insurance premiums. Calculate the savings over time, and decide whether you would likely save more in premium reductions than you would likely pay out in losses.

You can also lower your premiums by reducing the limits of liability coverage from 100/300/50 to your state's minimum. This method of sharing the risk will save premium dollars, but you risk greater loss if you are at fault in an accident.

Figure U6-1 illustrates another way to save on premiums. It will help you decide when it would be wise to save by reducing or dropping collision coverage on your car.

Life Insurance

Let's now compute the cost of a whole life insurance policy and compare the results to the purchase of term insurance. To do this, we must use the time value of money concept—the fact that money will grow over time because it is earning interest.

Suppose you are age 25 and purchased a $100,000 face value whole life policy. The annual premium for this policy is $250. The policy will pay a guaranteed rate of 6 percent (on the policy's cash value) after

▶ figure **U6-1**

DETERMINING WHEN TO REDUCE OR DROP COLLISION INSURANCE

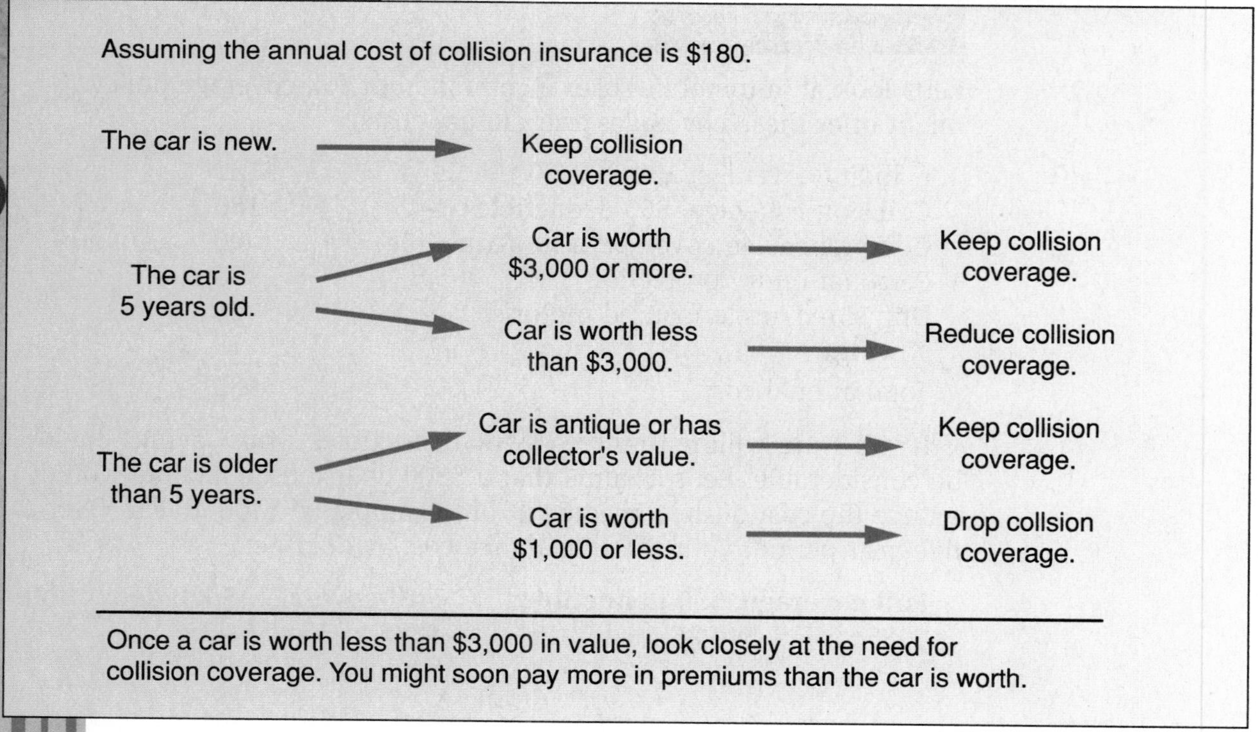

Assuming the annual cost of collision insurance is $180.

The car is new. ⟶ Keep collision coverage.

The car is 5 years old.

Car is worth $3,000 or more. ⟶ Keep collision coverage.

Car is worth less than $3,000. ⟶ Reduce collision coverage.

The car is older than 5 years.

Car is antique or has collector's value. ⟶ Keep collision coverage.

Car is worth $1,000 or less. ⟶ Drop collsion coverage.

Once a car is worth less than $3,000 in value, look closely at the need for collision coverage. You might soon pay more in premiums than the car is worth.

UNIT 6 PROJECT

the first year. At the end of the first year, there is no cash value. The entire premium is used to cover commissions and policy costs. After the first year, a portion of the premium covers the cost of insurance and the rest is deposited in a savings plan. The amount deposited accumulates as cash value.

In the example below, the death benefit remains at $100,000 over a five-year period. During this time, the cost of insurance rises slightly each year, leaving a smaller amount of the premium for savings. Assuming the 6 percent rate holds, the cash value of the policy after five years would be $634.95. (See the table that follows.)

Year	Premium	Insurance Cost	Savings Plan Deposit + Interest			Cash Value at Beg. Year
1	$250.00	$100.00	$0			$0
2	250.00	102.00	148	+	0	148
3	250.00	104.00	146	+	$8.88	302.88*
4	250.00	106.00	144	+	18.17	465.05
5	250.00	108.00	142	+	27.90	634.95
Totals	$1,250.00	$520.00	$580		$54.95	$634.95

*Assume the full premium is paid at the beginning of each year. To compute the interest earned at the end of Year 2, multiply $148 by 6 percent. Then add the deposits of $148 and $146 to interest earned of $8.88 to derive the Year 3 cash balance of $302.88.

As an alternative, you could purchase term life insurance. Assume the term premiums are the same as the cost of the insurance alone in the whole life example: $100 (Year 1), $102 (Year 2), $104 (Year 3), $106 (Year 4), and $108 (Year 5). You deposit the difference between the whole life premium ($250) and the term premium at the beginning of each year in a 6 percent savings account. That is, you invest $150 in Year 1 ($250 − $100); $148 in Year 2 ($250 − $102); $146 in Year 3; $144 in Year 4; $142 in Year 5. With whole life insurance, the cash value is $634.95. With term insurance, the accumulated value of the savings account at the end of five years would be $873.79. The difference is $238.84 ($873.79 − $634.95). (See the table that follows.) In this case, you can achieve a higher savings balance through buying term insurance and saving on your own.

Year	Beginning Balance	Deposit	Interest	Ending Balance
1	$ 0	$150	$ 9.00	$159.00
2	159.00	148	18.42	325.42
3	325.42	146	28.29	499.71
4	499.71	144	38.62	682.33
5	682.33	142	49.46	873.79**

**The total saved at the end of five years is $873.79.

Complete Worksheet 1 in the *Student Activity Guide* to compute the future value of savings between different life insurance policies. (This worksheet also appears on page 675 of this project.)

► HOW TO FILE A CLAIM

When you have sustained a loss, such as fire damage to your home, you must file a claim. To receive compensation for the insured property, you must be organized before you file the claim. First, you should know your policy and its coverages, limitations, and exclusions.

Keep receipts and other documentation of value. If you own antiques, collectibles, or other items for which you have no receipt, have the items appraised so that you will have a certificate of authenticated value. Such an appraisal may cost $100 or more, but it will help you receive the full reimbursement due you when you file a claim.

If property is stolen, call the police and fill out a report. Without evidence of a break-in or a police report as documentation, the insurance company has no way to verify that the incident took place. Also, you must take ordinary precautions against break-in and theft. If, for example, you leave your car unlocked, the insurer may not pay benefits for stolen property. You should have good notes about what was taken, witnesses, time of day, what you observed, and so on.

If property is damaged, you will need to get repair estimates—usually more than one. Contact your insurer right away, and have documentation and notes ready. The insurance adjustor will take your report and ask you questions. It's important to be clear and accurate when supplying information. You must also take reasonable precautions to avoid further damage. For example, if a storm creates a hole in your roof, you must cover the hole as soon as possible with plastic or some other protective covering to avoid rain damage to your home's contents. If you do not act quickly to protect your property, the insurer may not pay for the extra damage.

Worksheet 2 on page 676 shows a sample claim form that your insurer would require you to complete to report property damage. Fill out Worksheet 2 in the *Student Activity Guide* based on the hypothetical information provided.

► WHAT TO DO IF YOU HAVE AN AUTOMOBILE ACCIDENT

Sooner or later, it is likely to happen to you. Either as a driver or as a passenger, you may be involved in an automobile accident. Most accidents are the result of human error. The higher the speed, the higher the likelihood of a serious injury and damage to property.

If you are involved in an accident, there are several things you must do. Figure U6-2 below lists standard procedures to follow. Your state may have additional things you should do, or not do, following an accident. You will find this information in your state's driver's manual or a similar publication from the motor vehicles division or licensing department. You should be familiar with this information before an accident occurs.

Your state has accident reporting forms. Get one and fill it out for a fictional situation. In most cases, you have only three days (72 hours) to fill out an accident report once you are in an accident.

◢ HOW TO REDUCE HEALTH CARE COSTS

The best way to avoid high medical costs is to stay well. Corporations across America are realizing the importance of "wellness" programs in an attempt to keep their employees healthy. Here are some fundamental ways you can stay healthy:

1. Eat a balanced diet and keep your weight within reasonable limits.

2. Avoid smoking.

WHAT TO DO IF YOU'RE IN AN ACCIDENT figure **U6-2** ◄◄ (⊙)

If you are involved in a motor vehicle accident, standard requirements are as follows:

1. Stop your vehicle, turn off the ignition, and remain at the scene of the accident. If feasible, pull your car to the side of the road so you won't impede traffic.

2. Get the names and addresses of other drivers, passengers, and witnesses. Make notes of what happened, including time of day, weather conditions, roadway location, signal lights, and so on. Write down vehicle license numbers.

3. Fill out the necessary accident report forms within the time requirements in your state (usually 3 days). Give a copy of the report to your insurance company. Also obtain a copy of the police report, if any.

4. Provide assistance to persons who are injured; seek medical help if needed. Stay at the scene of the accident until all needed information is exchanged and all involved parties leave the scene.

5. Always have your insurance and vehicle registration information with you. Get insurance and vehicle registration information from the other driver; copy it from the documentation rather than taking it down orally.

6. Know the laws of your state. There may be additional requirements where you live.

3. Don't drink to excess.

4. Get sufficient rest and relaxation.

5. Drive carefully; avoid and reduce risks where possible.

When you do use health care services, there are additional ways to minimize your costs and your insurer's costs. Figure U6-3 lists some methods of reducing health care costs and maximizing the benefit from services that you can use.

Complete Worksheet 3 in the *Student Activity Guide* to answer questions about reducing health care costs. (This worksheet also appears on page 677 of this project.)

▶▶ figure U6-3   HOW TO CUT HEALTH CARE COSTS

When you are the patient, whether or not insurance is involved, you can maximize your health care dollars by:

1. Knowing your insurance coverage, limitations, and exclusions.

2. Taking insurance information with you when visiting a hospital or doctor's office and when picking up prescriptions.

3. Taking a list of questions with you to the doctor. Take notes so you will remember specific answers.

4. Giving your doctor information needed to make correct diagnoses. Write down symptoms, relevant past history, what you have done or taken so far, and related information.

5. Asking the doctor about short- and long-term side effects of prescriptions. Read prescription directions and information supplied by a pharmacist and/or the manufacturer.

6. Getting second (and third) opinions for any type of surgery or medication with serious risks or potential for side effects.

7. Predetermining fees and services that will be provided for treatments, surgeries, and lab work. Exclude tests or costs that you can cover in less expensive ways. For example, you can go to a local clinic and have a cholesterol test for $10 to $15. At a doctor's office, it can cost you five to ten times that amount.

8. Using generic medicines.

9. Being cautious and asking lots of questions. Remember: You are in charge of your health care and the doctor is assisting you, not the other way around! Take charge of your own life, nutrition, and lifestyle and know what it takes to stay healthy and strong.

LIFE EXPECTANCY AND MORTALITY TABLES

In a current edition of an almanac, you will find both life expectancy tables and mortality tables. For example, a person born in 2000 was expected to live 76.0 years if a man or 80.8 years if a woman. For a person who was 45 in 2000, life expectancy was another 34.8 years for men or 42.0 years for women.

Another table shows life expectancies over time. For example, in 1920, the average life span was 54.1 years (53.6 for men and 54.6 for women). By 1970, the average life span had risen to 70.8 (67.1 for men and 74.7 for women).

Life expectancy and mortality tables are used by insurance actuaries in setting life insurance premiums. A mortality table matches age with a mortality rate and sets a premium accordingly. Figure U6-4 is part of a mortality table from the American Council of Life Insurance. Use this table to complete Worksheet 4 in the *Student Activity Guide*. (This worksheet also appears on page 678 of this project.)

MORTALITY TABLE (PARTIAL)

figure **U6-4**

Age	Deaths per 1,000	Life Expectancy (Years)
25	1.11	59
30	2.33	48
40	3.21	37
45	4.58	33
50	5.86	28
55	8.44	21
60	12.88	18
65	17.22	15
70	26.10	13

▶ BUILDING A PERSONAL INSURANCE PLAN

As you make choices about the type and amount of insurance you will buy, keep the following guidelines in mind:

1. To avoid billing fees, you can have premiums deducted automatically from your checking account, or pay them quarterly or semiannually. You may also be able to pay online.

2. Read the policy carefully. If you discover a clause you do not understand, call your agent for clarification.

3. Review your policies regularly to see if the coverage meets your needs. As your family situation changes, you might wish to modify your life insurance coverage. As your car gets older, you should consider dropping collision insurance.

4. Consider carefully the outcome of switching insurers or changing policies. If you do, be sure you are approved for the new insurance—and that it is correct as represented—before dropping your old insurance.

5. Get to know your insurance agent. Use his or her expertise. Ask lots of questions and be sure you understand all coverages, limitations, exclusions, and so on. Discuss your changing needs and get his or her recommendations, but make your own decisions.

6. Don't hold onto policies or companies for sentimental reasons. Be a wise comparison shopper. When you are certain you can do better with another company, and have taken proper precautions, move forward to secure a new policy.

7. Don't keep overlapping policies with the hope of making a quick profit off insurance claims. Group policies require coordination of benefits. Private policies that overlap coverage in a group policy can be very expensive.

8. Use deductibles wisely! By paying the first part of an expense yourself, you can save a bundle on insurance rates.

9. Keep your insurance up-to-date. Pay premiums promptly and take advantage of any discounts. Ask regularly about what new discounts, such as for nonsmokers, are available to reduce premiums.

Complete Worksheet 5 in the *Student Activity Guide* to review what you have learned about preparing a personal insurance plan. (This worksheet also appears on page 679 of this project.)

WORKSHEET 1

Computing Future Value

Assume that you purchased a whole life policy for $100,000 and your premiums were $300 a year, with $150 covering insurance and $150 directed to your savings plan. The insurance cost increases by $3 every year. You are guaranteed 5 percent interest on your savings for the first five years, but will not earn interest until the end of the second year.

Required:

1. Prepare a table that lists how much total premium you will have paid in five years, total insurance cost for five years, and the balance in your savings portion at the end of five years for the whole life policy. (See page 669.)

2. How much would you have had in savings if you had bought a term policy for $150/year (for 5 years) and put the remainder in a savings account at your bank with interest compounding at the rate of 4 percent a year?

WORKSHEET 2
Insurance Claim Form

Directions: Fill out the claim form below based on the following information. The insured is Mary B. Ownbey, who lives at 845 Oak Street, Wellington, Ohio 45887. Her phone number is (202) 555-0180. Her policy number is KN338-44-2281, and her agent is G. Smiley. Her home was broken into sometime between 8 p.m. and 2 a.m. (Friday evening) while she was away. The kitchen was vandalized (spray paint on the walls and eggs thrown on the floor); the carpeting in the dining room was stained as well. A police report was filed (Case 95-2288) by Officer K. Bridges. There were no witnesses. The walls in the kitchen must be scraped and painted; the carpeting must be cleaned or replaced if the stain cannot be removed. The value of the damage is estimated at $500. The house was painted last year ($100 for the kitchen walls); the carpet was new a year ago ($2,000 for the damaged carpeting). Both were purchased at Excel Interiors and she has a receipt. The property is located in the home at the above address. Use today's date.

Claim No. _____

Name of Insured _____

Address _____

_____ Phone _____

Policy No. _____ Agent _____

Describe what happened: _____

_____

_____

_____

Was a police report filed? _____ Case No. _____
(Attach copy)

Police officer taking report _____

Were there any witnesses? _____ List their names and addresses:

_____

_____

Description of property damaged _____

Value of property _____

Date purchased _____ Purchase price _____

Where purchased _____ Receipt? _____

Where is property now located (for inspection)? _____

_____

_____   _____
Date   Signature of Insured

WORKSHEET 3

Reducing Health Care Costs

Directions: Answer the following questions about ways you can reduce health care costs.

1. Do you eat well-balanced meals and exercise regularly?

2. Do you get sufficient rest and relaxation?

3. Do you know your health insurance coverages, limitations, and exclusions?

4. Do you use generic prescriptions where possible? (Generic drugs are less expensive versions of brand-name drugs. Because there is no advertising or other expenses of mass marketing, the cost is lower.)

5. Do you shop around for the best prices in (a) dental work, (b) vision care and glasses, (c) prescriptions, (d) charges for office visits, and (e) supplies, vitamins, and other health care purchases?

6. List some things you and your family can do to reduce health care costs.

7. Explain why it is important to ask questions when you visit your doctor.

WORKSHEET 4

Interpreting a Mortality Table

Directions: Based on the mortality table on text page 671, answer the following questions.

1. At the bottom of the Life Expectancy column, what does the number 13 mean?

2. On average, people who are 50 years old now could be expected to live to be what age?

3. In the Deaths per 1,000 column, what does the number 1.11 mean?

4. In a group of 10,000 people, all age 40, an average of how many could be expected to die in the next year?

WORKSHEET 5
Your Personal Insurance Plan

1. Explain the purpose of each of the following types of insurance.

    a. Homeowner's insurance:

    b. Automobile insurance:

    c. Liability insurance:

    d. Health insurance:

    e. Disability insurance:

    f. Life insurance:

2. Based on your current situation, what types of insurance do you currently purchase?

    a. Homeowner's insurance:

    b. Automobile insurance:

    c. Liability insurance:

    d. Health insurance:

    e. Disability insurance:

    f. Life insurance:

3. How do you anticipate your need for each of these insurance coverages will change in the next five years?

    a. Homeowner's insurance:

    b. Automobile insurance:

    c. Liability insurance:

    d. Health insurance:

    e. Disability insurance:

    f. Life insurance:

4. List several guidelines for building a plan for purchasing all types of insurance.

7

Consumer Rights and Responsibilities

Project: **Exploring Ethical Issues**

Unit Seven focuses on the role of consumers in determining what is produced and sold. In Chapter 28, you will examine the market economy in which you live. You will explore wise buying practices and discover both your rights and your responsibilities.

In Chapter 29, you will take a look at federal laws and agencies that have been formed

to help protect you. In Chapter 30, you will find out about the legal system of the United States. You'll learn about how a trial happens—the personnel, the process, and the results. You will also discover other methods of reaching redress, from negotiating to small-claims courts and governmental assistance.

Role of Consumers in a Free Enterprise System

TERMS TO KNOW

free enterprise	equilibrium price	bait and switch
producers	competition	fake sale
consumers	monopoly	low-balling
scarcity	price-fixing	pyramid schemes
supply	purchasing power	redress
demand	transfer payments	

Consider This. . .

Mei-ling is a full-time student. She does side jobs to earn money during the school year and works full-time in the summer.

"I don't have a lot of money," she told her best friend, "so I have to spend carefully. There are just so many things I'd like to have. Yesterday, I saw an ad on TV about a hammock that would be perfect for my room. It really looks comfortable, and I could use it outside, too. I'm not sure whether it's a good buy or not. How can I find out about products like this one?"

Our Free Enterprise System

Goals	• Discuss the basic characteristics of the marketplace.
	• List and describe the three basic components of a free enterprise system.

▶ CHARACTERISTICS OF THE MARKETPLACE

In the United States, we live in a free enterprise system. **Free enterprise**, also called a *market economy* or *capitalism*, is an economic system in which producers and consumers are free to engage in business transactions with minimal government interference. Both producers and consumers play an active role in the operation of the system. **Producers** are the manufacturers or makers of goods and services for sale. **Consumers** are the buyers and users of goods and services. Everyone is a consumer because everyone must consume at least some goods and services produced by others in order to live. Many consumers are also producers—that is, they provide goods and services for others to consume.

©GETTY IMAGES/PHOTODISC

Why is every person a consumer?

Scarcity

In any economy, consumers' wants are unlimited. However, the resources for producing the products to satisfy these wants are limited. This basic economic problem is called **scarcity**. A country's economic system determines what products its businesses will produce with its limited resources. In our free enterprise system, consumers play a key role in determining what businesses will produce. Consumers' purchasing decisions act as votes. When consumers buy a particular product, they are casting their dollar votes for that product. After the "votes" are counted, producers know what consumers want. To make a profit, producers must provide goods and services that consumers will buy.

As an individual consumer, you have limited resources as well. You must decide what to buy with your limited money to achieve the greatest satisfaction or *utility*. As you make your individual buying decisions, other consumers are doing the same. Together, your spending decisions and those of other consumers determine which products will succeed and which will fail and leave the market. Producers want to maximize their profits. Therefore, they will heed these cues from the marketplace and produce more of the products that are selling and less of those that aren't.

Supply and Demand

A free enterprise system determines what goods and services businesses will produce, in what quantities, and at what prices through the interaction of supply and demand. **Supply** is the quantity of goods and services that producers are willing and able to provide. **Demand** is the willingness and ability of consumers to purchase goods and services at certain prices. You, along with other consumers, create demand for a product with your purchasing "votes."

Generally, if enough consumers demand a product (are willing and able to buy it at a certain price), producers will make it. The system works like this:

1. Increased demand creates a situation in which the supply of the product is not sufficient to satisfy all consumers who want to buy it. As a result, producers can raise their prices.

2. The high prices bring large profits to the producers.

3. Large profits prompt current producers to make more of the product and attract other producers to start providing the product, increasing the supply.

4. Supply then exceeds demand, and consumers can pick and choose. In order to entice consumers to buy their product instead of their competitors', producers reduce their prices.

5. Reducing prices, in turn, lowers profits, and producers begin to produce less.

6. Eventually, the product reaches the **equilibrium price**. This is the price at which the quantity supplied equals the quantity demanded of the product. At this price, there is just enough of the product available for all consumers who want to buy it.

Consumer Power

Consumers have the ultimate power in a free enterprise system. Consumers determine what is produced and at what price. Collectively, consumer buying decisions direct the production of goods and services. When consumers purchase a good or service, they are casting dollar votes for its continued production. If consumers refuse to buy a good or service, the price will drop. When the good or service still does not sell, producers will no longer provide it. Producers will supply only those goods and services that people want and are able to buy. Thus, in our free enterprise system, consumers actually exercise the power to determine what will be produced and at what price. This power is called *consumer sovereignty*.

Global View

Some protest organizations have been conducting boycotts against Morocco because of its occupation of Western Sahara since 1978 and human rights abuses of the Saharawi people. Tourists are encouraged not to visit Morocco. Boycott supporters believe that this economic pressure against Morocco will persuade the country's government to change its political policies.

Think Critically: Do you believe that consumer boycotts are effective? Would you participate in a consumer boycott?

Producer Power

Producers also have power in a free enterprise system, because they can employ various techniques to influence consumer buying decisions. They use advertising and other marketing strategies to try to increase demand for their products. Advertising can be informative and give important facts about the quality and features of products. It can also be false and misleading and, unfortunately, damaging to the consumer's personal financial situation. To manage your personal finances successfully, you must understand the role of advertising and other marketing strategies in our economic system and become a careful consumer.

▶ PARTS OF A FREE ENTERPRISE SYSTEM

Three basic conditions must exist for a free enterprise system to function smoothly: (1) competition, (2) purchasing power, and (3) informed consumers. If one of these conditions is missing or not functioning properly, the system begins to fail. The free enterprise system gains strength when each part of this triangle functions properly. Figure 28-1 (page 684) illustrates the interplay of the three parts.

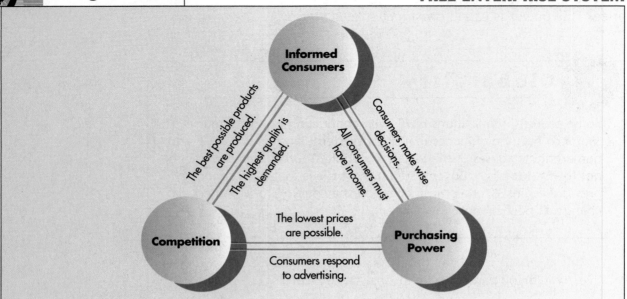

Competition

In order for prices to rise and fall with changes in supply and demand, competition must exist. **Competition** is the rivalry among sellers in the same market to win customers. It occurs when there is more than one seller of a good or service. All businesses selling the same or similar products must compete for the same customers. A **monopoly** is a market with many buyers but only one seller. Without competition, the one seller has no incentive to improve quality or lower prices. However, when a market has many sellers, the competition results in improved quality and lower prices.

VIEWPOINTS

In a global economy, products and services are available from around the world. What you purchase will determine who will have jobs—and who won't. Many persons believe that if you don't buy American-produced products, American workers will suffer. However, if you as a consumer buy a product that is not of highest quality and the most economical, you are not using your purchasing power wisely.

Think Critically: Do you buy American products first? Why or why not? Do you agree that consumers have the right to purchase the best value, regardless of who makes the product? Why or why not?

Illegal business practices can reduce competition and result in higher prices. **Price-fixing** is an illegal agreement among competitors to sell a good or service for a set price. There is no real competition because prices have been predetermined, or fixed. Because price-fixing prevents the forces of supply and demand from determining prices freely in the marketplace, it impedes free enterprise, and the government has made it illegal.

Purchasing Power

For free enterprise to operate, citizens must have the ability to buy. In the United States, most adults have income from their jobs that they can spend on goods and services. However, the purchasing power of the dollar goes up or down with the economy. **Purchasing power** is the value of money, measured in the amount of goods and services that it can buy.

In a period of *inflation*, when prices are generally rising in the economy, purchasing power decreases. For example, if the price of a soft drink rises from $1.50 to $2.00, then your income won't buy as many soft drinks. Your purchasing power has decreased. Purchasing power also declines during periods of *recession*, when production, employment, and income are declining. People who lose their jobs or have their wages reduced cannot buy as many goods. The result is an overall loss of purchasing power in the economy.

The government also shifts purchasing power among citizens by making transfer payments. **Transfer payments** are government grants to some citizens paid with money collected from other citizens, generally through taxes. For the receivers, transfer payments are *unearned income*. They did not earn the income by working at a job. However, transfer payments provide purchasing power for needy people. Welfare, social security, and veterans benefits are all transfer payments. So are food stamps, reduced-price school lunches, and housing assistance.

©GETTY IMAGES/PHOTODISC

What role does purchasing power play in a free enterprise system?

Informed Consumers

A free enterprise system must have informed consumers who know their rights and responsibilities in the marketplace. When consumers make wise decisions, the system works to weed out inferior products and keep prices at acceptable levels. When consumers do not act in a responsible manner, prices increase.

✓ Check Your Understanding

1. What group, as a whole, has the ultimate power to determine what will be produced and at what prices in a free enterprise system?
2. What happens when supply of a product exceeds demand?

Lesson 28.2

Consumer Problems

Goals
- **Describe deceptive practices used to defraud consumers.**
- **Discuss how to be a responsible consumer.**

▶ FRAUDULENT AND DECEPTIVE MARKETING PRACTICES

The marketplace is full of deceptive and misleading ways to induce consumers to buy goods and services of inferior quality or things they do not really need or want. In many cases, little can be done once the consumer has been duped into making a purchase. Dishonest sellers quickly disappear or deny wrongdoing. Therefore, consumers must educate themselves to recognize a potential fraud before they become victims. Prevention is still the best safeguard against financial misfortune.

Bait and Switch

Bait and switch is an illegal sales technique in which a seller advertises a product with the intention of persuading consumers to buy a more expensive product. The "bait" is the bargain product that gets customers into the store. When they arrive to purchase the advertised product, however, the salesperson then switches their interest to a more expensive product. In some cases, the bait is a poor-quality product that is placed next to high-quality merchandise. The poor-quality bait is advertised to be of better quality than it is, giving customers the idea that they are really getting a bargain. In other cases, when customers ask for the bait merchandise, they are told that it is sold out, but that comparable merchandise is available—for more money.

To avoid the bait-and-switch trap, educate yourself about products and prices. When a product is advertised at a special price, find out its quality and regular price. Shop around before making major purchases.

Fake Sales

Probably the most common of all consumer frauds is the **fake sale**. A merchant advertises a big sale but keeps the items at regular price or makes the price tags look like a price reduction when there actually is none. Often the merchant increases the prices just prior to the sale and alters the price tags to show the so-called markdowns. The only way consumers can protect themselves from fake sales is to know products and prices and to plan purchases. Just because a flashy sign shouts "SUPER SAVINGS" does not mean that prices have been reduced. Only product and price knowledge can help you distinguish a real bargain from a fake sale.

Low-Balling

Repair shops sometimes use a deceptive practice called "low-balling." **Low-balling** is advertising a service at an unusually low price to lure customers, and then attempting to persuade them that they need additional services. For example, when repairers dismantle appliances, they discover other "necessary" repairs. If the consumers refuse the offer of additional repairs, the repairers then charge an extra fee for reassembly.

Another form of low-balling is applying pressure, either bluntly or subtly, to convince car owners that their cars need additional work for safe operation. For example, a repair shop may offer a special on brake relining. But when the mechanics inspect the brakes, they find several other "necessary" repairs. Customers may wind up with a front-end alignment, wheel balancing, or other repairs that are not really as urgent as they are led to believe.

To protect yourself from this type of low-balling, state that you want no repairs other than those agreed upon unless the repair shop informs you of the additional cost ahead of time and you choose to authorize the extra repairs. You should not pay for unauthorized work. Before having major work done, get a second opinion. Discuss major car repairs with someone you trust who knows about the mechanical aspects of cars.

Pyramid Schemes

Pyramid schemes are mostly illegal multilevel marketing plans that promise distributors commissions from their own sales and those of other distributors they recruit. A cash investment of some kind is usually required to become a distributor. The pyramid consists of managers at the top and a lot of middle and lower distributors arranging parties, recruiting new distributors, and selling products to friends and acquaintances. The managers at the top make big profits by selling the products to the distributors below them in the pyramid—not to the general public. However, most distributors lower in the pyramid never make a profit or recover their initial investment. Instead, they are left with a lot of low-quality products that their friends won't buy.

The best defense against pyramid sales schemes is to remember that you cannot expect to make big profits without hard work. Before committing to such a plan, investigate it. Talk to people who have purchased the products. Check with local consumer protection agencies. Think it through. What is the company's track record? Does the company have evidence to back up its claims? Who will buy this product? Will your commission depend on recruiting other distributors? Be skeptical if the company requires you to buy a "starter kit" of sales brochures and product inventory.

Pigeon Drop

The term *pigeon drop* refers to any method used by experienced con artists to convince vulnerable people to invest in phony investments, swampland real estate, or other swindles. The pigeon is the unsuspecting consumer. Con artists often target trusting people who know little of such scams but do have a source of money. For example, senior citizens become the targets of fast-talking "financial experts." The con artist may ask them to deposit their savings in an investment fund. These funds are then to be loaned out at high interest rates. The con artist promises the victims monthly payments for the use of their money. In some cases the trusted adviser immediately disappears with the money. In other cases the swindler maintains an outwardly healthy business and pays dividends to the victims until it is no longer advantageous to do so. Then the swindler disappears with the investments. By maintaining a supposedly legitimate business for a period of time, the swindler can gain additional victims—friends eager to get in on the deal at the recommendation of the original victims.

The best protection against this type of swindle is the local Better Business Bureau. The Bureau is equipped to investigate questionable schemes, so-called investment experts, and unsound businesses. If someone approaches you with a suspicious deal, insist upon seeing credentials, annual financial reports, and proof of past dealings. Invest only in established firms with a proven track record. Deposit your money only in financial institutions that are insured by the government.

Fraudulent Representation

Telephone or door-to-door solicitations made by people who claim to represent well-known companies or charities are another type of swindle. Consumers buy products and then learn that the products have been rebuilt or stolen, or are inferior merchandise with the reputable name on it. In some cases the product is worthless or unusable. One such scam is the sale of discount coupons to be used in numerous restaurants and businesses. When the buyers present the coupons for a discount or free merchandise, they discover that the merchant has not authorized the coupon.

Before giving money to someone claiming to represent a major company or charity, check with the organization to verify the person's identity. The local Better Business Bureau will have a record of solicitors who repeatedly engage in questionable practices.

Health and Medical Product Frauds

A common type of swindle involves deceptive advertising for expensive "miracle" pills, creams, and devices to enhance the consumer's health and beauty. The ads are designed to appeal to the typical consumer's desire to be healthy and attractive. Usually, deceptive health and medical advertisements carry endorsements and pictures of people who have found success using the product. Magazines, newspapers, Web sites, e-mail, and flashy tabloids often carry these advertisements. The manufacturers ask you to mail money to a post office box to receive the miracle product. Often you pay your money but never receive the product. If you do receive the product, it is totally ineffective.

Infomercials

An *infomercial* is a lengthy paid commercial TV advertisement that includes testimonials, product demonstrations, and presentation of product features. These programs usually last 15 to 30 minutes and target people with specific needs that are usually emotional—from weight loss to hair growth. While the product may be reputable, there is no guarantee, and claims about results may be greatly exaggerated. With infomercials, it is important to find out before you buy whether the business is reputable and the product works. Be cautious about giving credit card numbers over the telephone. Don't expect that because something "worked" for the paid actors describing the product on television that you will receive the same results.

Internet Fraud

When you are online, you will be bombarded by advertisements, from banners to e-mail. Some of these are legitimate; others are not. On the Internet, fraudulent businesses can appear genuine. Don't assume that a professional-looking Web site means that the company is legitimate. You may order and pay for goods and never receive them. When you give credit card numbers and other personal information to these scam artists, you can be a victim of theft—of your money and even your identity. When shopping online, it is safest to stick to businesses you know.

Telemarketing Fraud

Consumers lose billions of dollars each year to telemarketing fraud. One warning sign is the offer of a "free" prize if you pay shipping and handling. A truly free prize never requires that you pay a fee. Foreign lotteries are illegal, and sweepstakes requiring you to pay any money are not legitimate. Fake charities frequently ask for money around holidays and after disasters. Fraudulent telemarketers will ask you to courier money to them or give a credit card number to claim your prize. Unsolicited calls from people who know a lot about you should ring an alarm. Promises of big prizes, wonderful vacations, and no-risk investments usually turn out to be fraud. They collect the tax, fees, delivery charges, and other "costs" from you, and that's the last you ever hear.

What kinds of telemarketing fraud might you experience?

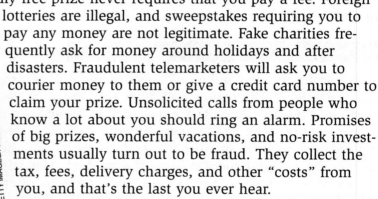

©GETTY IMAGES/PHOTODISC

Many reputable companies use telemarketing to sell existing customers more products they do not need. You can protect yourself from these calls by saying "no, thank you" and hanging up. You can greatly reduce the number of unwanted telemarketing calls you receive by signing up with the government's *National Do Not Call Registry*. You can register online at www.donotcall.gov. If your name is on the list, you can file a complaint at the site if a telemarketer calls you. Registration is free and effective for 5 years.

◤ BEING A RESPONSIBLE CONSUMER

Learning to identify various deceptive marketing tactics is the first step toward consumer responsibility. Prevention is your best protection. After you have been swindled, it is difficult to undo the financial damage. To protect yourself, be alert for the warning signs of a scam. Educate yourself on products and prices, and seek redress when necessary.

Identify Deceptive Practices

When you hear unrealistic claims, be suspicious. Watch for warning signals in claims or offers made through advertising and by salespeople. Figure 28-2 lists common warning signals of possible deception that should catch your attention.

Shop Smart, Including Online

Our economy produces a large assortment of products from which to choose. Many products are complex, and the methods used to sell them are sometimes misleading. Internet shopping has added new dangers as well as helpful shopping tools. To make wise buying decisions, consider these ideas:

1. *Be aware of prices.* Know regular or "list" prices of common items. Terms often used in advertising, such as "manufacturer's list price" and "suggested retail price," and phrases such as "comparable value" or "value $40, you pay only $35," attract your attention, but the prices actually may not be reduced.

2. *Shop at several stores. Comparative shopping* means comparing quality, price, and guarantees for the same products at several different stores. Use online price-comparison search tools to help you find the best deal.

WARNING SIGNALS

figure 28-2

**WARNING SIGNALS
Watch Out When You Hear This:**

1. You can get something for nothing.

2. You will receive a free gift if you reply now.

3. You or your home has been specially selected.

4. You can make high earnings with no exerience or little effort.

5. You have been selected to complete an advertising questionnaire.

6. You may attend a demonstration with no obligation to buy.

7. If you don't decide now, you will lose a golden opportunity.

8. You may buy a high-quality product for an incredibly low price.

9. To receive a product or service, you must first send money.

10. To receive your prize, you must supply your credit card or checking account number.

3. *Understand sale terminology. Sale* means that goods are being offered for sale but not necessarily at reduced prices. *Clearance* means that the merchant wants to clear out all the advertised merchandise but not necessarily at a reduced price. *Liquidation* means that the merchant wants to sell immediately to turn the inventory into cash. Again, prices may not be reduced.

4. *Avoid impulse buying.* Take a list with you when you shop, and buy only what is on the list. Watch for displays of merchandise that attract your attention but are expensive and unnecessary. When shopping online, don't let an attractive Web site or the ease of entering a credit card number lure you into buying something you don't need.

5. *Plan your purchases.* Thoroughly research major purchases before making your choice. Read online and printed product information and comparative reviews. Do not make major purchases during periods of emotional stress or when your judgment is impaired. Ask questions so you are sure that you understand claims, features, prices, and terms. For example, the product may show net price after a mail-in rebate. You may not qualify for the rebate or it may have expired.

6. *Compute unit prices. Unit pricing* is the cost for one unit of an item sold in packages of more than one unit. For example, to compare the price of a 15-ounce box with the price of a 24-ounce box, divide the total price of each box by the number of ounces in it. The result is the price per ounce of each box. The lowest unit price for products of comparable quality is the best buy.

7. *Read labels.* Know ingredients and what they mean. For example, a shirt that is 100 percent cotton may shrink, or if it is a dress shirt, it will probably have to be pressed each time you wear it. A product that says, "Dry Clean Only" will be more expensive to maintain.

8. *Check containers carefully.* Be sure packages have not been opened or damaged. Occasionally harmful substances have been injected into products. Report any suspicious openings in packages to the store manager.

9. *Read contracts.* Read and understand contracts and agreements before signing.

10. *Keep receipts and warranties.* Print out warranty statements and sales receipts from online purchases. For all major purchases, keep receipts along with warranties, guarantees, or other written promises for possible enforcement later.

11. *Compute total cost.* Check the total cost of an item, including supplementary items (such as batteries), delivery charges, finance charges, and other add-on costs. In some cases, the base price may be lower than for similar products, but once you add

up all the related charges, you will find that the total cost exceeds other choices.

12. *Ask for references.* Ask for references from company representatives to be sure they really do represent the company. Call the company to check.

13. *Be loyal.* Patronize online and bricks-and-mortar businesses that have good reputations and have served you well in the past. Tell others when you have a good experience, and ask others for recommendations of doctors, accountants, repair shops, and other service businesses.

14. *Check up on businesses.* Check for valid certifications, licenses, bonding, and endorsements. Use your local Better Business Bureau and state records divisions to be sure you are getting service from qualified and reputable professionals.

15. *Wait a day for major purchases.* Always wait at least 24 hours before making a major purchase. Be sure that you would not be making the purchase on impulse and that you were not coerced into wanting the item. Many people change their minds after a "cooling-off" period before making a major buying decision.

Math Minute   Computing Unit Prices

Which is better: 24 ounces for $2.59 or 15 ounces for $1.89? To determine which is better, you'll need to know the cost per unit. To compute cost per unit, divide the total cost by total units:

$2.59/24 ounces = 10.8 cents per ounce
$1.89/15 ounces = 12.6 cents per ounce

In this case, the 24-ounce container is the better buy.

Problem: Which is better, 3 for $.89 or 6 for $1.99?

Solution:

$.89/3 = 29.7 cents each
$1.99/6 = 33.2 cents each

Thus, 3 for $.89 is the better buy.

Stay Informed

You are responsible for educating yourself about products and services before you buy. To protect yourself, actively seek consumer information in the following ways:
  1. Become familiar with sources of information on goods and services, such as *Consumer Reports*, consumer-oriented Web sites, and local agencies.

2. Read warranties and guarantees. Ask questions so that you can fully understand performance claims. Get written guarantees and warranties whenever possible.

3. Read and understand care instructions before using a product.

4. Analyze advertisements about products before buying.

5. Know the protections offered by consumer protection laws, and know how to seek a remedy to consumer problems.

6. Inform appropriate consumer protection agencies of fraudulent or unsafe performance of products and services. Do not hesitate to make your dissatisfaction known to help others avoid the problem and to prompt producers to improve their product or service.

7. Report wants, likes, and dislikes as well as suggested improvements and complaints to retailers and manufacturers.

Why should you educate yourself about products and services?

Seek Redress

When you have a complaint or need to solve a problem about a product or service, you have a right to seek redress. **Redress** is a remedy to a problem. When you have a consumer problem, you have a right to expect the business to work with you to resolve the problem. The remedy might be your money back, a repair, or some other compensation. Here are some suggestions for filing a complaint and resolving problems.

First, take the product back to the store where you bought it. Calmly explain the problem to a salesperson there. If necessary, talk to a manager. If you bought the item online, then talk to a customer service representative on the phone. Explain the specifics about the problem and give evidence. Retain all warranties, sales receipts, and related material. If necessary, provide photocopies of necessary information to explain and support your position. Be firm but not angry. Say that you are dissatisfied and explain why. Indicate the type of adjustment you want: refund, repair, replacement, or other action. Many consumer problems can be resolved simply by discussing them reasonably with the retailer.

If you are not satisfied with the manager's remedy, then put your complaint in writing to the store's owner or headquarters. If you do not receive satisfaction, write to the manufacturer or distributor and state your complaint. In any written correspondence, describe your previous interactions with store personnel and explain why you are dissatisfied with the result. Be specific. Send photocopies of evidence, such as sales receipts, warranties, or anything else that will help you

UNIT 7 • Consumer Rights and Responsibilities

support your position. Be firm and again state the type of adjustment you want. Specify a reasonable time limit in which to resolve the problem.

If you are still dissatisfied with the result, file a complaint with the appropriate government agency for consumer protection. There may be more than one private or public agency to assist you in solving the problem.

A last resort is to seek legal recourse. For claims involving relatively small sums (usually a maximum between $2,000 and $5,000, as specified by the state), small-claims court offers a much faster process than a full court procedure. It is also less expensive because attorneys are not required. You must pay a filing fee and appear on the assigned court date. Small-claims courts are discussed in detail in Chapter 30.

✔Check Your Understanding

1. What makes a sale a "fake sale"?
2. What is the first step toward consumer responsibility?

Issues in Your World

When you explore different Web sites, be aware that you are not always anonymous. Some sites can immediately determine certain information about you when you visit that site, such as the type of computer system you use, the company you use to access the Internet, and the last Web page you visited. You can find out what information your computer automatically transmits by visiting the Center for Democracy and Technology's privacy demonstration at http://snoop.cdt.org/.

At some Web sites you must log in, register, and/or give information about yourself. This information is saved and often shared with others. These *mouse tracks* enable others to determine whether you are a potential customer and what types of interests you have.

Some Web sites electronically record information about your visit to their site by depositing a piece of information called a *cookie* onto your computer. Once a cookie is saved on your computer, that Web site can keep track of information about your visit, such as which parts of the site you visit. This helps site operators determine the most popular areas of their site and it helps them improve what they offer. Cookies also allow for more efficiency when revisiting a site because:

- Your preferences for visiting certain areas of the site are stored in your cookie file. The next time you return, the section you like best may already be displayed for you.

- You may be alerted to new areas of interest based on sites you have previously visited.

- Your past activity may be recorded in the cookie file so the site knows what you like, and thus offer you products and services tailored to your interests.

Some versions of browser software can be set to notify you before a Web site places a cookie on your computer. Then you can choose to accept or reject the cookie. Some browsers will allow you to deactivate a cookie. You can also delete cookie files, but you would then lose the customizing offered by the sites.

Think Critically
1. What Web sites do you visit regularly? What information have you given them about yourself?
2. How could you benefit from having cookies on your computer?

Chapter Assessment

28.1
* All economies face the problem of scarcity, because resources are limited but consumer wants are not. A country's economic system determines what the limited resources will be used to produce.
* In a free enterprise system, consumers determine what products will be produced and at what prices. To make a profit, producers must provide products consumers will buy.
* The interaction of supply and demand determine what will be produced, in what quantities, and at what prices.
* Prices rise and fall with demand and supply until they eventually reach an equilibrium price at which quantity supplied equals quantity demanded.
* Producers have the power to influence buying decisions through advertising and other marketing strategies.
* To function smoothly, a free enterprise economy needs competition, purchasing power, and informed consumers.
* Competition among sellers to win customers leads to better quality products and lower prices.
* Inflation and recession reduce consumer purchasing power. Government transfer payments shift purchasing power from some citizens to others.

28.2
* Bait-and-switch schemes lure customers into the store with advertised bargains. Then salespeople try to switch customers to a more expensive product.
* Fake sales make customers think prices are reduced when they really aren't.
* Low-balling repair shops offer a repair at a low price, and then discover several other "necessary" services.
* Pyramid schemes depend on recruiting multiple levels of distributors.

- Pigeon drops lure trusting people into making phony investments with promises of extraordinary returns.
- Some telephone and door-to-door solicitors claim to represent a reputable company or charity.
- Health and medical product frauds appeal to the emotions with promises of enhanced beauty and health.
- Infomercials are lengthy TV ads with emotional appeals that often do not meet expectations.
- A professional-looking Web site can lead consumers to believe that the business is legitimate when it is not.
- To be a responsible consumer, learn to identify deceptive practices, follow wise buying habits, stay informed, and seek redress for consumer problems.

REVIEW TERMS

Directions

Can you find the definition for each of the following terms used in Chapter 28?

bait and switch	price-fixing
competition	producers
consumers	purchasing power
demand	pyramid schemes
equilibrium price	redress
fake sale	scarcity
free enterprise	supply
low-balling	transfer payments
monopoly	

1. A remedy to a problem.

2. Mostly illegal multilevel marketing plans that promise distributors commissions from their own sales and those of other distributors they recruit.

3. Advertising a service at an unusually low price to lure customers, and then attempting to persuade them that they need additional services.

4. An advertised "big sale" that really offers merchandise at regular prices.

5. A market with many buyers but only one seller.

6. An illegal sales technique in which a seller advertises a product with the intention of persuading consumers to buy a more expensive product.

7. Government grants to some citizens paid with money collected from other citizens, generally through taxes.

8. The value of money, measured in the amount of goods and services that it can buy.

9. The rivalry among producers in the same market to win customers.

10. Willingness and ability of consumers to purchase goods and services at certain prices.

11. The quantity of goods and services that producers are willing and able to provide.

12. An economic system in which producers and consumers are free to engage in business transactions with minimal government interference.

13. The buyers and users of goods and services.

14. Manufacturers or makers of goods and services for sale.

15. The basic economic problem of unlimited consumer wants but limited resources to satisfy those wants.

16. The price at which the quantity supplied equals the quantity demanded of a product.

17. An illegal agreement among competitors to sell a good or service for a set price.

REVIEW FACTS AND IDEAS

1. The United States operates under what economic system?

2. What causes the basic economic problem of scarcity?

3. As the supply of a product increases, what happens to the price?

4. Why do producers heed the cues of the marketplace?

5. How do consumers have the power to determine what is produced and at what price?

6. What power do producers have in a free enterprise system?

7. What are the three basic conditions that must exist in a free enterprise system?

8. How does competition affect prices and product quality?

9. What economic conditions cause purchasing power to decrease?

10. How can you protect yourself from bait-and-switch tactics?

11. Why do people at the top in a pyramid scheme make big profits while those lower in the pyramid do not?

12. List five warning signals that alert consumers to the possibility of deceptive marketing practices.

13. What are some wise buying practices that can help you shop smart?

14. What are some ways that you can stay informed in the marketplace?

15. What procedures should you follow to seek redress for a consumer problem?

16. Under what circumstances should you consider using a small-claims court to resolve a consumer complaint?

APPLY YOUR KNOWLEDGE

1. Give an example of a new product that has succeeded and one that has failed because of consumers' influence.

2. Watch one hour of television in the early evening and record the number and types of commercials. What do the advertisements tell you about products and their target consumers? Make a chart on a piece of paper listing each commercial and describing it as shown in the following example:

Time of Commercial	Product Advertised	Length of Commercial	Product Information Featured
7 P.M.	Toothpaste (NewBrite)	30 seconds	New flavor; old also available

3. Cut two product advertisements out of different magazines. Select ads that seem very different from each other in their appeal. Describe the consumers that you think each ad is targeting. How does each ad try to influence its target consumers to buy the product?

4. How is the market price of a good or service affected by:
   a. An increase in demand?
   b. A decrease in demand?
   c. An increase in supply?
   d. A decrease in supply?

5. Search through magazines, newspapers, and online for advertisements. Collect or print out and bring to class ads that offer the following:
   a. Something for nothing
   b. Bonus for early reply
   c. Offers of gifts and prizes
   d. Guarantees

6. Visit the Web site of a well-known business and check its prices and variety of products available online. Answer the following questions:
   a. Does the site show pictures of the items offered for sale?
   b. Are you able to readily determine the full price, including shipping and other charges?
   c. When can you expect to receive the goods ordered?
   d. What are your payment options?
   e. What types of personal information do you have to supply?
   f. Does the site offer secure ordering (look for the closed-lock icon at checkout)?
   g. What is the return policy?
   h. Does the business have a privacy policy?

Solve Problems ⊕ Explore Issues

1. Compute unit prices for the following pairs and determine which of the two is the better deal:
a. 3 for 98 cents or 8 for $2.99
b. 4 for $1.00 or 12 for $3.39
c. 24 oz. for $1.98 or 36 oz. for $2.49
d. 2 lbs. for $2.19 or 5 lbs. for $5.89

2. Copy the ingredients from the labels of the following products:
a. Pain pills
b. Breakfast cereal
c. Liquid cleaning product
d. Bug spray
Do any of the labels carry warnings? What types of precautions are suggested?

3. Read the warranty or guarantee for a household product that your family has purchased. What does the manufacturer agree to do? What exceptions are stated? What actions does the manufacturer state it will not agree to do?

4. Visit *Consumer Reports* online or obtain an issue from your library, and answer the following questions:
a. Who publishes the magazine?
b. Who advertises in the magazine?
c. How are products tested and compared for quality?
Select a tested product and summarize three key findings that would most influence your buying decision.

5. Assume that you bought a new hair dryer at a local department store last week. Write a letter of complaint because the hair dryer makes a strange rattling noise. Give factual information concerning the dryer. Make up information for the sales receipt and warranty that you will enclose with the letter. Refer to key facts from these documents to support your position. Request a refund or other adjustment.

For related activities and links, point your browser to **www.mypf.swlearning.com**

Consumer Protection

TERMS TO KNOW

flammability
recall
generic drugs

childproof devices
care labels
fraud

consumer
advocate

Consider This. . .

Madhu bought a computer at an online auction Web site. He gave his credit card number and expiration date, along with his name and home address for shipping.

"I think you can get a pretty good deal when you buy online," he told his instructor, "but at the same time, I worry about giving personal information to a company that I don't know. When I checked with the Better Business Bureau online, I learned that this company meets its criteria and that there are no complaints filed against it. That makes me feel a little better."

Laws to Protect Consumers

Goals
- Describe your rights as set forth in the Consumer Bill of Rights.
- Describe the protections provided by major federal consumer protection laws.

▶ THE CONSUMER BILL OF RIGHTS

For many years the consumer's position in the marketplace was characterized by the phrase "buyer beware." The consumer had little protection against unfair business practices. Since 1960, however, Congress has passed a number of major consumer-protection laws. One of the most important steps in the direction of consumer protection was the adoption of the Consumer Bill of Rights. This was proposed by President John F. Kennedy during his 1962 State of the Union Address, and later was expanded by Presidents Richard Nixon and Gerald Ford. It outlines the following consumer rights:

1. The right to safety: protection against products that are hazardous to life or health.

2. The right to be informed: protection against fraudulent, deceitful, or grossly misleading practices and assurance of receiving facts necessary to make informed choices.

3. The right to choose: access to a variety of quality products and services offered at competitive prices.

4. The right to be heard: assurance of representation of consumer interests in formulating government policy and of fair and prompt treatment in enforcement of the laws.

5. The right to redress (remedy): assurance that buyers have ways to register their dissatisfaction and to receive appropriate compensation for valid complaints.

6. The right to consumer education: assurance that consumers have the necessary assistance to plan and use their resources to their maximum potential.

FEDERAL CONSUMER PROTECTION LAWS

Since the 1930s, Congress has passed many laws to protect consumers from unsafe products and unfair or deceptive business practices. These laws help ensure that consumers get quality goods and services for their hard-earned dollars. We may be on the verge of another wave of consumer legislation as Congress considers consumer privacy rights in the Information Age.

Food, Drug, and Cosmetic Act of 1938

The Food, Drug, and Cosmetic Act of 1938 requires that foods be safe, pure, and wholesome; that drugs and medical devices be safe and effective; and that cosmetics be safe. The law also requires truthful labeling on these products. The weight or volume of the contents and name and address of the manufacturer must be on the label. The law prohibits use of containers that are misleading because of size, thickness, or false bottoms.

The FDA approves drugs before they can be sold. Requirements for salability include years of research, testing, and proof of effectiveness and safety. While this process takes time and slows down the availability of drugs to consumers, it assures them that products meet standards of safety, purity, and usefulness.

Flammable Fabrics Act of 1953

The Flammable Fabrics Act enabled the Consumer Product Safety Commission to set flammability standards for clothing, children's sleepwear, carpets, rugs, and mattresses. **Flammability** is the capacity for catching on fire. The law prohibits the selling of wearing apparel made of easily ignited material. The flammability standard for children's sleepwear requires that the garment will not catch fire when exposed to a match or small fire. The flame-retardant finish must last for 50 washings and dryings. Proper care instructions to protect sleepwear from agents or treatments known to cause deterioration of the flame-retardant finish must be on all labels.

©GETTY IMAGES/PHOTODISC

What are the advantages and disadvantages of the FDA's testing of drugs?

Meat Inspection Laws

The Poultry Products Inspection Act of 1957 requires poultry to be inspected for harmful contaminants. Passed in 1967, the Wholesome Meat Act updated the Meat Inspection Act of 1906 and provided for stricter standards for slaughtering facilities of red-meat animals. Both of these acts protect consumers in the purchase of chicken and beef by standardizing inspection procedures.

Hazardous Substances Labeling Act of 1960

The Hazardous Substances Labeling Act, passed in 1960, requires that warning labels appear on all household products that are potentially dangerous to the consumer. In most cases, products found to be unacceptably hazardous must be recalled. A **recall** is a request for consumers to return a defective product to the manufacturer. The manufacturer will either refund the consumers' money or fix the product so that it is no longer hazardous. Before producing more of the product, the manufacturer will fix the flaw in its design.

Kefauver-Harris Drug Amendment of 1962

As a result of the Kefauver-Harris Drug Amendment of 1962, drug manufacturers are required to file notices of all new drugs, which must be tested for safety and effectiveness before being sold to consumers. This amendment also provides for the manufacture and sale of generic drugs. **Generic drugs** are medications with the same composition as the equivalent brand-name drugs, but they are generally less expensive. National brand names are usually more expensive than generic products because of the added costs of development, advertising, and marketing. To compensate drug companies for the costs of developing new drugs, the law offers the developing companies patent protection. Patents give the companies the sole right to sell their new drugs for a certain number of years before other companies may produce and sell the generic equivalents.

Cigarette Labeling and Advertising Act of 1965

The Cigarette Labeling and Advertising Act of 1965 requires warning labels of possible health hazards from smoking. Today these warning labels are even more specific. For example, original labels read: "Warning—Cigarette smoking may be hazardous to your health." Current labels read: "Surgeon General's Warning: Quitting smoking now greatly reduces serious risks to your health."

National Traffic and Motor Vehicle Safety Act of 1966

The National Traffic and Motor Vehicle Safety Act of 1966 established national safety standards for automobiles and for new and used tires. The National Highway Traffic Safety Administration of the Department of Transportation is charged with supporting and enforcing provisions of the act. Its responsibilities include increasing public awareness of the need for safety devices, testing for safety, and inspecting vehicles for proper safety equipment.

Child Protection and Toy Safety Act of 1966

As a precaution against accidents to children, the Child Protection and Toy Safety Act was passed in 1966. This act bans the sale of toys and children's articles containing hazardous substances and those that pose electrical, mechanical, or thermal dangers. These products can be inspected and removed from the marketplace.

The act requires special labeling for children's products, along with devices that make potentially dangerous products childproof. **Childproof devices** are devices designed to resist tampering by young children. For example, childproof caps on medications are designed so that children cannot open them.

Fair Packaging and Labeling Act of 1966

The Fair Packaging and Labeling Act requires product labels to contain accurate names, quantities, and weights. The labeling rules apply to all types of consumer products, such as groceries, cosmetics, cleaners, and chemicals. It is the responsibility of the consumer to compare weights and sizes of products available—a much easier job when accurate, standard information is available for comparison.

Permanent Care Labeling Rule of 1972

Effective since 1972, the care labeling rule specifies that clothing and fabrics must be labeled permanently with laundering and care instructions. **Care labels** give instructions for cleaning, wash and dry temperature, and other care needed to preserve the product. The labels must stay attached and be easy to read for the life of the garment.

©GETTY IMAGES/PHOTODISC

What is the value of having care labels in clothing and fabrics?

Toy Safety Act/Generic Drug Act (1984)

The Toy Safety Act of 1984 permits the Consumer Product Safety Commission to quickly recall toys and other articles intended for use by children that might present a substantial risk of injury. Similarly, the Generic Drug Act of 1984 speeds up the Food and Drug Administration approval process of generic versions of drugs whose patents have expired. These two laws attempt to protect the consumer more quickly than in the past by reducing roadblocks that would slow down safety recalls or keep drug prices high for consumers.

Children's Online Privacy Protection Act of 1998

The Children's Online Privacy Act applies to the online collection of personal information from children under 13. Rules spell out what a Web site operator must include in a privacy policy, when and how to seek verifiable consent from a parent, and what responsibilities an operator has to protect children's privacy and safety online.

Global View

In the early 1990s, legislation was introduced by the Brazilian government to update consumer protection laws and regulations. Although the new code represented a huge step for Brazil, consumer protection still lacks the necessary efficiency. The majority of the population is unaware of consumers' rights. To address this issue, an Internet site—the Santa Catarina Consumers Portal—has been developed to globalize consumer assistance services and to spread knowledge over the entire country. It brings together scientific and academic research, e-government services, software, and free virtual legal assistance in matters concerning consumer rights.

Think Critically: How can technology help consumers understand their rights and achieve redress? What responsibility does each consumer have in this process?

Family and Educational Rights and Privacy Act (FERPA)

FERPA is a federal law that protects the privacy of student records. Parents and students over 18 have the right to inspect and review the student's education records maintained by the school. Any errors or misleading information may be corrected. Schools must obtain written permission from the parent or student over 18 before releasing any information from the student's record. Only directory-type information, such as name, address, and phone number, may be disclosed without consent. Parents and students may request that even this information not be disclosed. One important feature is the requirement of student identification numbers that are not social security numbers.

Health Insurance Portability and Accountability Act (HIPAA)

In Chapter 27, you learned about provisions of HIPAA intended to help people get and keep health insurance coverage. HIPAA also sets rules about who can see your health information. The law applies to doctors, nurses, pharmacies, hospitals, health insurance companies, employer group health plans, and government programs such as Medicare and Medicaid. Protected information includes medical records, conversations, information about you in the computer system, and billing information. Consumers are allowed to have a copy of all their health records, make corrections, know how information is being used, and decide whether to give permission to share this information. One important feature is the elimination of the social security number as a personal identifier for patients.

✓ Check Your Understanding

1. What are some ways that consumer laws protect you as a consumer?

2. Why should the online safety of young children be a consumer concern?

Lesson 29.2

Agencies to Protect Consumers

Goals
- **Identify national sources of consumer information and assistance.**
- **List and describe state and local agencies and private consumer assistance.**
- **Explain how to contact public officials to express opinions.**

▶ SOURCES OF CONSUMER PROTECTION

When you need assistance with a consumer problem, numerous federal, state, local, and private organizations are available to help you. These sources also offer an abundance of helpful consumer information at their Web sites. You can even file a consumer complaint online.

Many federal government agencies provide information of interest to consumers. Some of these agencies handle consumer complaints, and others direct complaints to agencies or sources that address consumer issues. Most agencies can be easily located through the Internet.

DEPARTMENT OF AGRICULTURE

Within the Department of Agriculture (USDA), there are a number of agencies that exist to meet various consumer needs. The Agricultural Marketing Service inspects food to ensure wholesomeness and truthful labeling, develops official grade standards, and provides grading services. For example, eggs must meet specific standards to be classified as extra large, jumbo, large, medium, or small. The Food and Nutrition Service provides food assistance programs, such as the food stamp and school lunch programs, and information on diets, nutrition, and menu preparation. The Cooperative Extension Services provides consumer education materials (pamphlets and booklets) on such topics as budgeting, money management, food preparation and storage, gardening, credit counseling, and many more. Most of the materials are free. You can find the USDA online at www.usda.gov.

NATIONAL INSTITUTE OF STANDARDS AND TECHNOLOGY

The National Institute of Standards and Technology (NIST) (www.nist.gov) is an agency within the Department of Commerce. Its mission is to promote economic growth by working with industry to develop and apply technology, measurements, and standards. NIST sponsors the *Malcolm Baldrige National Quality Award* given each year to U.S. businesses that achieve high standards of quality in their business practices.

NIST serves an important purpose for consumers. It sets uniform standards of weights and measures. NIST is the reason that you don't have to shop with a tape measure or scale to make sure you get what you pay for. NIST sponsors a network of state and local agencies that set performance standards for measuring devices used to determine the costs and amounts of products sold to consumers. For example, agencies of the NIST network would determine the amount of error that is acceptable for a gas pump or grocer's scale and establishes testing procedures for enforcing the standards.

FOOD AND DRUG ADMINISTRATION

One of the many agencies within the Department of Health and Human Services (www.os.dhhs.gov) is the Food and Drug Administration (FDA) (www.fda.gov). The FDA enforces laws and regulations preventing distribution of mislabeled foods, drugs, cosmetics, and medical devices. The FDA does the following:

1. Requires testing and approval of all new drugs.
2. Tests new and existing products for health and safety standards.
3. Provides standards and guidelines for poisonous substances.
4. Controls the standards for identification, quality, and volume of food containers.
5. Establishes guidelines for labels and proper identification of product contents, ingredients, nutrients, and directions for use.
6. Investigates complaints.
7. Conducts research and issues reports, guidelines, and warnings about substances found to be dangerous or potentially hazardous to health.

CONSUMER PRODUCT SAFETY COMMISSION

The Consumer Product Safety Commission (CPSC) (www.cpsc.gov) protects consumers from unreasonable risk of injury or death from potentially hazardous consumer products. The commission enforces standards for consumer products, bans products that are too dangerous, arranges recalls, and researches potential product hazards.

©GETTY IMAGES/PHOTODISC

FEDERAL COMMUNICATIONS COMMISSION

The Federal Communications Commission (FCC) (www.fcc.gov) regulates interstate and international communications by radio, television, wire, satellite, and cable. The FCC's Consumer Information Bureau (www.fcc.gov/cib) is the consumer's one-stop source of information, forms, applications, complaints, and current issues before the FCC.

What government agency protects consumers from hazardous products?

FEDERAL TRADE COMMISSION

The Federal Trade Commission (FTC) regulates unfair methods of competition, false or deceptive advertising, deceptive product labeling, inaccurate or obsolete information on credit reports, and concealment of the true cost of credit. The FTC is also the federal clearinghouse for complaints of identity theft. The FTC refers victims to the appropriate agencies for action.

Net Nuggets

The Federal Trade Commission's Web site provides valuable consumer protection information. The area dedicated to e-commerce and the Internet offers tips on how to protect your privacy online; Net-based business opportunities; "dot cons"; unsolicited e-mail; shopping safely online; online scams; and many other related topics. Check out this site at www.ftc.gov/ftc/consumer.htm.

UNITED STATES POSTAL INSPECTION SERVICE

The United States Postal Inspection Service (USPSIS) (www.usps.gov/websites/depart/inspect) is a federal law enforcement agency that investigates consumer problems pertaining to illegal use of the mail. The USPSIS enforces postal laws, protecting consumers from dangerous articles, contraband, fraud, pornography, and identity theft involving the mail. Through its Consumer Protection Program, USPSIS resolves unsatisfactory mail-order transactions, even in cases where no fraud has occurred. **Fraud** is the intentional misrepresentation of information with the intent to deceive or mislead.

FEDERAL AVIATION ADMINISTRATION

The Federal Aviation Administration (FAA) (www.faa.gov) is an agency of the U.S. Department of Transportation. It controls air traffic and certifies aircraft, airports, pilots, and other personnel. The FAA writes and enforces air safety regulations and air traffic procedures.

SECURITIES AND EXCHANGE COMMISSION

The main purpose of the Securities and Exchange Commission (SEC) (www.sec.gov) is to protect investors and maintain the integrity of the securities markets. The SEC requires companies to disclose certain financial and other information, so that investors can research investment options before buying. The SEC also oversees stock exchanges, brokers, and investment advisors to protect investors in their dealings with securities professionals. SEC's Office of Investor Education and Assistance serves investors who complain to the SEC about investment fraud or the mishandling of their investments by securities professionals.

State and Local Assistance

Most states have a consumer protection agency, or the state attorney general may handle consumer affairs. Many county and city governments have set up consumer protection agencies or offices. Consumer leagues and public-interest research groups are also active at the state and local levels, with newsletters, pamphlets, handbooks, and Web sites on current consumer issues.

At the local level, consumers have access to legal aid societies, newspaper and broadcast action reporters, and consumer representatives on local utility or licensing boards. Independent consumer groups focusing on specific issues, such as food prices, may operate on the local level as well.

Career Focus

Consumer safety inspectors check on products used, produced, handled, stored, or marketed by various firms. They ensure that standards are maintained, respond to consumer complaints, and determine if legal action must be taken. The majority of consumer safety inspectors work for state governments. Requirements include a combination of education (often a college degree), experience, and passing scores on written examinations. People in this occupation need to be responsible and like detailed work.

For more information, refer to the *Occupational Outlook Handbook* at www.bls.gov or search the Internet using such key words as "careers," "jobs," and "consumer protection."

Private Organizations

The Better Business Bureau (BBB) (www.bbb.org) serves as a clearinghouse of information about local businesses. Complaints against local businesses may be filed with the BBB. The merchants are given an opportunity to respond to the complaint; if they do not, the Better Business Bureau may advise consumers to seek another form of redress. You can request reports regarding the nature of complaints filed against local merchants from the BBB in your area, or look up reports on specific merchants at the BBB Web site.

The BBB is not the only guardian of consumer interests in the business community. For example, the Major Appliance Consumer Action Panel (MACAP) is comprised of representatives of the home appliance industry and provides assistance in resolving or minimizing consumer problems in the purchase and use of home appliances. The automobile and furniture industries, all of which produce goods that represent significant investments for buyers, have voluntary consumer-action panels.

Consumers may also seek the support of a **consumer advocate**—a person who actively promotes consumer causes. Ralph Nader is the best-known consumer advocate. When Ralph Nader finds, through research and investigation, that an injustice or dangerous condition exists, he pursues it on behalf of all consumers. Ralph Nader may file lawsuits against companies to force them to meet safety standards, correct inequitable situations, or properly inform consumers of dangers in the use of their products.

The National Consumers League (NCL) operates the National Fraud Information Center, established in 1992 to combat fraud. In 1996, the Internet Fraud Watch was created. You can find out more about your rights and remedies at www.fraud.org. Trained counselors will help you identify danger signs of fraud as well as help law enforcement agencies get information quickly so they can respond quickly. These services are free.

The Federal Citizen Information Center (FCIC) (www.pueblo.gsa.gov) assists federal agencies in the development, promotion, and distribution of practical consumer publications. You can order free, or at very low cost, brochures on topics from how to apply for a passport to *The Consumer's Almanac*. You can order publications by mail, toll-free number, fax, or Internet.

Other consumer organizations help guide consumers in the marketplace. One such organization is Consumers Union. A not-for-profit organization, Consumers Union has the largest consumer testing facility in the world. Through its monthly magazine, *Consumer Reports*, Consumers Union gives test results and product ratings. To assure that all ratings are unbiased, Consumers Union buys all products it tests and accepts no advertising. *Consumer Reports* also prints articles dealing with insurance, credit, and other items of consumer interest. An annual buying guide is also published by Consumers Union. For a subscription fee, you can access all Consumers Union product reports online at www.consumerreports.org.

◤ PUBLIC OFFICIALS

National elected officials include the president and vice president and members of Congress. State elected officials include the governor, secretary of state, state treasurer, state attorney general, superintendent of public instruction, labor commissioner, and state senators and representatives.

Each court (federal, state, and local) has at least one judge and several clerks of court to assist in filing and information gathering. County elected officials include the county administrator, district attorney, sheriff, and tax assessor, plus a number of commissioners. Other elected local officials include the mayor, city council members, and city manager. These officials are available at county and city office buildings and meet regularly or are available to the public by appointment. The phone book lists various officials separately by state and by county, with each department listed alphabetically.

If you wish to communicate with a public official about a consumer issue, there are several ways to do so:

1. *In Person.* You can make an appointment during regular office hours as well as at meetings of government bodies, which are

generally open to the public (except for executive sessions). Almost all hearings offer citizens the opportunity to speak.

2. *By Phone.* Brief calls at reasonable hours are generally effective. Your state may supply toll-free numbers for contacting public officials.

3. *By E-mail.* Legislators receive e-mail correspondence from their constituents (people who live in the areas they represent). You can get e-mail addresses of senators and representatives from their own Web sites or from your state government Web site links.

4. *By Letter.* An effective letter written to the appropriate representative states clearly the purpose of the letter, identifies the bill by proper name and number, refers to only one issue, and arrives while the issue is current. Give reasons for your position and avoid emotionalism. Ask for specific relief—what you want the public official to do.

✔Check Your Understanding

1. What is the purpose of the CPSC?
2. Which government agency protects stock market investors?

Identity Theft: Protecting Yourself

killed identity thieves can rob you of your identity despite your best efforts at managing your personal information. For example:

1. Stolen identification cards, debit cards, and credit cards are used by thieves to call your credit card issuer and change the mailing address on your accounts. They run up charges and you don't get the bill, so you don't know what's happening. Or, they use your identification to make more false identification, have checks printed, and make purchases with your debit card.

2. Mail can be stolen from your mailbox or your garbage and used to have fake checks made up based on your bank account information. Or, new bank accounts based on your identity can be opened, with bad checks written on the accounts.

3. By posing as a landlord or employer, thieves can get a copy of your credit report. Then they open accounts and borrow large sums of money or make large purchases.

To minimize your risk, here are some things you can do:

- Do not give out personal information unless you have initiated the contact and know with whom you are dealing. Then be careful and give information on a need-to-know basis.

- Give your social security number only when absolutely necessary (when you will be receiving money). Don't carry your social security card.

- Pay attention to billing cycles; follow up when bills are late.

- Guard your mail from theft. Use post office collection boxes for outgoing mail; promptly remove mail when it arrives or get a post office box.

- Minimize the number of accounts you have and cards you carry.

- Keep personal information safe; shred discarded copies.

- Order a copy of your credit report every year; be sure it is accurate.

For more information on identity theft and what to do if it happens to you, call toll free 1-877-IDTHEFT, or visit www.consumer.gov/idtheft.

Think Critically

1. If someone stole your wallet, what could happen to the contents?

2. What should you do if your wallet or purse is lost or stolen?

3. Why should you memorize your social security number?

Chapter Assessment

SUMMARY

29.1

* The Consumer Bill of Rights outlines basic rights that consumers should expect in the marketplace.
* Some laws (such as the Food, Drug, and Cosmetic Act) set standards for product purity and safety.
* Many consumer laws (including the Fair Packaging and Labeling Act) set rules for product labeling.
* Several consumer laws (such as the Children's Online Privacy Protection Act) are designed to protect children from harm.
* FERPA and HIPAA are laws designed to protect privacy.

29.2

* The Department of Agriculture inspects and grades food.
* The Food and Drug Administration approves new drugs, tests products for safety, and sets labeling guidelines.
* The Consumer Product Safety Commission enforces product standards and bans or recalls hazardous products.
* The Federal Communications Commission regulates communications by radio, television, wire, satellite, and cable.
* The Federal Trade Commission regulates methods of competition, marketing practices, and credit reporting.
* The U.S. Postal Inspection Service investigates consumer problems pertaining to illegal use of the mail.
* The Securities and Exchange Commission requires businesses to disclose certain information for investors to evaluate and oversees the securities markets.
* Private organizations, such as the Better Business Bureau, can assist consumers with incidents of unethical and illegal practices.
* Public officials can be reached in person, by phone, by e-mail, or by letter.

REVIEW TERMS

Directions

Can you find the definition for each of the following terms used in Chapter 29?

care labels	fraud
childproof devices	generic drugs
consumer advocate	recall
flammability	

1. Medications with the same composition as the equivalent brand-name drugs but that are generally less expensive.

2. A request for consumers to return a defective product to the manufacturer for repair or a refund.

3. A person who actively promotes consumer causes.

4. Labels on clothing that give instructions for cleaning, wash and dry temperature, and other care needed to preserve the product.

5. The capacity for catching on fire.

6. The intentional misrepresentation of information with the intent to deceive or mislead.

7. Devices designed to resist tampering by young children.

1. What consumer protection action did President Kennedy propose in 1962?

2. What six consumer rights are listed in the Consumer Bill of Rights?

3. What was the purpose of the Food, Drug, and Cosmetic Act of 1938?

4. How long must a flame-retardant finish last in children's sleepwear as provided by the Flammable Fabrics Act of 1953?

5. How do patents encourage drug companies to develop new drugs?

6. What are some responsibilities of the National Highway Safety Administration?

7. What was the major purpose of the Permanent Care Labeling Rule of 1972?

8. What agency sets the standard for accuracy that your grocer's scale must meet?

9. What agency tests all new drugs that companies produce for sale in the marketplace?

10. Which agency can ban dangerous products and arrange recalls?

11. What types of communications, in addition to radio and television, are controlled by the FCC?

12. Which agency regulates false or deceptive advertising?

13. In what ways does the Securities and Exchange Commission protect investors?

14. What do the letters BBB stand for?

15. What should you include in a letter of complaint to an elected official?

1. Why should you consider buying generic products rather than brand-name products? What do you think would happen if drug development companies did not receive patent protection for a number of years before other companies could sell generic equivalents?

2. Select any garment from your closet. Read the care label. What kinds of information are on the label?

3. Cut the labels from three food products, such as soup, cereal, snacks, and processed foods. List the different types of information—such as quantity per serving, ingredients, and vitamin and mineral content—you find on the label. Are there ingredients you do not recognize? Is the nutritional value what you expected?

4. Identify the law that protects consumers from each of the following abuses:
   a. A box states that it contains 12 ounces of product when it actually contains only 6 ounces.
   b. A doctor tells an employer that an employee has a potentially expensive medical problem. Rather than risk higher health insurance premiums, the employer fires the employee.
   c. A company develops a new "miracle" drug. To get it on the market quickly, the company does not test it sufficiently.
   d. A company develops an effective new cleaning product. However, the chemicals it contains are quite dangerous. To avoid scaring potential customers, the company does not mention the dangers on the label.

5. Why are the rights protected by FERPA important to you? What could happen if these rights were not protected?

6. Visit the Federal Citizen Information Center at www.pueblo.gsa.gov and locate a news article that interests you. Write a bulleted list of the most important consumer information facts you found in the article.

7. Visit the Securities and Exchange Commission online at www.sec.gov. Follow the link to Laws and Regulations. Select one law or regulation and briefly summarize how it protects investors.

8. Go to the Better Business Bureau Web site at www.bbb.org, and look up the reports on two local companies. Write a brief summary of the kinds of information the reports give about companies.

9. Visit www.fraud.org online and answer the following questions: What services are available to consumers who have complaints? What is the process of registering a complaint?

Solve Problems ⊕ Explore Issues

1. List your state and local sources that can provide assistance with a consumer complaint.

2. Consult the *Consumer Reports Buying Guide* for the current year. Summarize the key points of three product reports that interest you.

3. Your local library contains much information about consumer problems and assistance. Visit the library and list in outline form what types of information are available for consumers.

4. Check your local newspaper for public notices of hearings by local government groups. List hearings that are scheduled. Which hearings are on issues affecting consumers? How would consumers be affected in each case?

5. Attend a public hearing on a local issue—land use or zoning, for example—and write a report on who was present, what was discussed, and the conclusion reached. Hearings are held in city hall or county buildings and are open to the public for testimony and input.

6. Check recent issues of the newspapers, news magazines, or online news sources for reports of proposed laws and regulations. Choose an issue that concerns you and investigate it. Prepare an e-mail message to the appropriate official with your comments on the proposed law or regulation.

For related activities and links, point your browser to **www.mypf.swlearning.com**

Dispute Resolution

TERMS TO KNOW

court
jurisdiction
trial court
appellate court
civil court
criminal court
statute of
  limitations

plaintiff
defendant
counterclaim
depositions
judgment
class-action
  lawsuit

alternate dispute
  resolution (ADR)
mediation
voluntary
  arbitration
binding
  arbitration

Consider This. . .

Ian wanted to paint his apartment. The landlord promised to pay for the paint if Ian provided the labor. Ian painted the apartment, as agreed, but when he asked the landlord for reimbursement, the landlord refused.

"I've tried everything," Ian told his sister. "I talked to him nicely and referred to our verbal agreement. He said that he never made such an agreement, and I have nothing in writing to prove it. Then when I moved out of the apartment, he refused to refund my deposit. He said that I painted the apartment without authorization, so he was entitled to keep my deposit. Together the paint and the deposit total $900! What can I do to get my money back?"

The Legal System

Goals
- **Describe the organization of the legal system in the United States.**
- **Explain the legal procedures from complaint to judgment.**

▶ STRUCTURE OF THE LEGAL SYSTEM

The legal system in the United States is based on common law. *Common law* is a system of laws based on decisions made in court cases. These decisions set legal *precedents*, serving as models for deciding similar cases in the future. At the base of our common law legal system are the courts. A **court** is a person or group of people whose task it is to hear and decide matters according to the law.

There are many types of courts—federal, state, and local. Each court is empowered to decide certain types or classes of cases. This power is called **jurisdiction**, which is the legal authority to hear and decide a case. A court may have original or appellate jurisdiction, or both. The court of original jurisdiction, or the first court to hear a case, is the **trial court**. An **appellate court** has appellate jurisdiction, or the authority to review the judgment of a lower court.

Courts are also classified in terms of the nature of their jurisdiction. A **civil court** has the authority to hear non-criminal cases. Civil courts typically settle matters for individuals, such as divorce or estate settlement after someone dies, or between individuals and businesses, such as contract or copyright violations and consumer complaints. Civil courts also settle disputes against a branch of the government. A **criminal court** hears cases involving punishable offenses against society. In a criminal case, the government, representing all the people, prosecutes the alleged wrongdoer.

The losing parties may appeal the decision of a civil or criminal court if they believe the court made an error in applying the law. Then an appellate court will review the decision.

Net Nuggets

Legalaid.com provides free legal tips and information for anyone involved with legal problems. It provides an attorney center, which helps users find a lawyer who is right for the case. The Web site also allows users to chat online with lawyers. There are many different topics of legal information available, including family law, immigration law, real estate law, and small business law. Legal news and updates are also available with a law video center. Check out www.legalaid.com for legal information.

Court Personnel

Our federal and state court systems require many people to operate efficiently. Some people are employees of the court. Others are called to serve temporarily on a jury.

The *judge* is the presiding officer in the court and is either elected or appointed. Attorneys are usually selected by the parties in the dispute, but are sometimes selected by the judge to present the case to the court.

The *clerk of court* enters cases on the court calendar and keeps an accurate record of the proceedings. The clerk also accepts, labels, and safeguards all items of evidence; administers the oath to witnesses and jurors; and sometimes approves bail bonds and computes the costs involved.

The *court reporter* keeps a word-by-word record of the trial, usually through the use of a special recording machine. These trial records are available to each attorney and are used for appeals.

Deputy sheriffs serve as *bailiffs* during court proceedings. Bailiffs maintain order in the courtroom at the instruction of the judge.

The *jury* is a body of citizens sworn by a court to hear the facts submitted during a trial and to render a verdict. A trial jury consists of not more than 12 people. A juror must be of legal age, a resident of the county, and able to see and hear. Jurors are chosen from a list of local citizens—usually from tax or voter rolls or from motor vehicle registration records.

The Federal Court System

The authority of federal courts comes directly from the United States Constitution and the laws enacted by Congress. The federal courts hear matters that concern the nation as a whole. These matters pertain to constitutional rights, civil rights, interstate commerce, patents and copyrights, federal taxes, currency, and foreign relations. Other matters, such as non-federal crimes, contract disputes, and divorces, are left to the states in which they occur. The federal courts may hear a dispute between citizens of two different states, but only if it involves $75,000 or more.

THE UNITED STATES SUPREME COURT

The Supreme Court is the top court of the federal court system and is located in Washington, D.C. The Supreme Court is the only federal court expressly established by the Constitution. Appeals from federal appellate courts and from state supreme courts that pertain to federal issues are heard by the Supreme Court. The Supreme Court chooses which cases it will hear. The Court sets its own *docket*, or schedule of cases, dates, and times for issues to be heard. Only cases of the greatest importance and national consequence are accepted. Thousands of actions are appealed every year, but the Supreme Court accepts only a small percentage of them.

There are nine Supreme Court justices, including a chief justice. The president appoints the justices to their positions for life. No federal judge may be dismissed or impeached for any reason other than gross misconduct.

©GETTY IMAGES/PHOTODISC

What kinds of cases are heard by the U.S. Supreme Court?

COURTS OF APPEAL

The United States is divided into 12 judicial circuits. Each circuit has a court of appeals. Each appellate court has from five to nine judges, who review final decisions of the district courts. The decisions of the courts of appeal are final in most cases.

DISTRICT TRIAL COURTS

The United States is divided into 90 federal districts, with a court assigned to each. Each district covers a state or a portion of a state. Consequently, some states may be home to more than one federal district court, while other states contain none. (These states are part of a federal district whose court is in a different state.) Each district court is a trial court, also divided into civil or criminal divisions. District courts are staffed by judges who hear cases individually, not as a panel.

Some issues are always considered federal issues, such as bankruptcy and crimes involving interstate commerce. For example, hijacking, kidnapping, bank robbery, and counterfeiting are all federal crimes and would be prosecuted in federal courts. Any criminal sentenced for a federal crime would be sent to a federal prison or penitentiary.

SPECIAL FEDERAL COURTS

Congress established special courts to hear only particular kinds of cases. These special federal courts include the Court of Claims, Customs Court, Court of International Trade, Tax Court, Court of Military Appeals, and the territorial courts. If you wanted to sue the United States, you would file a claim in a U.S. district or special federal court.

State Court Systems

The state court systems handle the greatest share of legal matters, because the Constitution sets limits on the federal system. The Tenth Amendment to the Constitution grants each state the sovereign power to enact and enforce state laws.

A state's laws are contained in its constitution and enacted by its own legislature. These laws are binding upon the citizens of the state and must not violate the U.S. Constitution. Each state has the power to run its own court system to decide issues that involve state laws. Each state establishes its own set of court procedures, determines court names, divides areas of responsibility among the various courts, and sets limits of authority among the state courts. Some issues are tried exclusively in state trial courts, such as divorce, probate, and adoption.

STATE SUPREME COURTS

In most states the highest court is the state supreme court, sometimes called the court of final appeal. Ordinarily, the state supreme court has appellate jurisdiction. The decision of a state supreme court is final, except in cases involving the federal Constitution, laws, and treaties. In many states, there are appellate courts and one supreme court.

DISTRICT AND CIRCUIT COURTS

General trial courts, often called state district courts, circuit courts, or superior courts, decide matters beyond local courts. These courts hear civil cases involving large sums of money, criminal matters with major penalties, and cases that are appealed from local courts whose decisions are questionable. Judges at this level are usually appointed by the state governor, although some may be elected for terms of four to six years. Decisions from district courts may be reviewed by the highest state court.

COUNTY AND CITY COURTS

The lowest state courts are found at the city or county level. These courts may also be called municipal or justice courts. Courts at this level have authority limited by geographic boundaries. Civil and criminal cases are heard at the local level. However, civil cases must be for small amounts only. At the local level, disputes usually are heard and decided by judges, not by juries. In very small areas, a judge may be called a justice of the peace, who is an appointed, part-time official. Justices of the peace in other areas are elected officials. Special courts at the local level may be called police courts, traffic courts, small-claims courts, and justice-of-the-peace courts.

▶ COURT PROCEEDINGS

Filing a lawsuit involves many steps, costs, and outcomes. You would need an attorney who would advise you of your chances of winning your case, explain the laws pertaining to your case, and tell you what you need to do to prepare for trial. The services of a competent attorney can cost $200 an hour or more. Some attorneys will work on a *contingency-fee* basis, which means they receive fees only if you win the case. Your state bar association can supply names of attorneys who specialize in the area of your complaint. Your attorney will appear in court on your behalf and represent your interests.

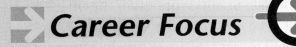

Career Focus

Paralegals help lawyers prepare for closings, hearings, trials, and meetings. They organize files, draft agreements, and coordinate law office activities. They may work in wide areas of the law or may specialize. Many paralegals use computers in their work to search or index materials. Employers usually require formal paralegal training obtained through associate or bachelor's degree programs or through a certification program. Paralegals need to have good research and investigative skills, along with computer applications knowledge.

For more information, refer to the *Occupational Outlook Handbook* at www.bls.gov or search the Internet using such key words as "careers," "jobs," and "paralegal."

All states have a **statute of limitations**, which is a legally defined time limit in which a lawsuit may be filed for various complaints. For example, in many states personal injury lawsuits must be filed within two years from the date of the injury. A lawsuit filed after the two-year limit will be dismissed.

Generally, a lawsuit involves the following steps:

1. Someone files a complaint, worded in a legally acceptable format called a *pleading*.
2. The person at whom the lawsuit is aimed is *served*, or receives notice of the suit.
3. The attorneys for both parties gather information in a period called *discovery*.
4. A trial takes place and the court makes a decision.
5. The losing party may appeal the decision to a higher court.

Plaintiff Files Complaint

The person who begins a lawsuit by filing a complaint is the **plaintiff**. The plaintiff discusses the facts of the case with an attorney. The attorney considers the matter, conducts extensive research on similar cases, and advises the client of the prospect of winning the lawsuit. If the client (plaintiff) wishes to pursue the matter, the attorney draws up the necessary papers, which the plaintiff signs. The attorney begins the action by filing the complaint with the clerk of the appropriate court. Usually the plaintiff must pay a filing fee. Generally, the complaint consists of a description of the offending acts and a request for relief.

Defendant Is Served

A certified copy of the complaint is *served* or presented to the defendant named in the lawsuit. The **defendant** is the person against whom the lawsuit is filed. The local sheriff's department or a private company may be used to serve the defendant. Because the officials must present the papers to the defendant personally, the serving process may take several days. The defendant then has a specified amount of time in which to *appear* (file a response to the complaint). The defendant must decide whether to default (not answer and automatically lose) or answer the complaint. If the defendant does not answer, the plaintiff will win the case by *default judgment*.

The defendant usually discusses the case with an attorney. Then the defendant's attorney prepares and files an answer to the complaint. The defendant may choose to file a counterclaim. A **counterclaim** is a defendant's assertion that the plaintiff is at fault and should pay damages to the defendant.

Discovery

After the defendant's attorney has filed an answer to the complaint with the appropriate court, a formal investigation called *discovery* begins. During the discovery period before trial, attorneys gather information, talk to witnesses, prepare legal arguments, take depositions, hire investigators, examine reports, and negotiate with the opposing party. The purposes of discovery are (1) to preserve evidence, (2) to eliminate surprise, and (3) to lead to settlement.

Depositions are sworn statements of witnesses taken before court appearances and recorded in writing or on videotape to preserve the memory of the issues. Many cases are settled before going to trial because both parties realize the risk involved in a trial and because information gathered by both sides is both known and shared. If the opposing parties can reach a settlement, they sign a formal agreement and the case is dropped.

Trial Takes Place

After discovery and when the parties cannot reach agreement, a trial date is set. Defendants may be entitled to a jury trial (if they could go to jail), and often juries are provided, but the right is not automatic. If there is a jury trial, the first step is choosing a jury. Citizens have a duty to serve on a jury when called by the court. The court identifies a pool of potential jurors from voting records or motor vehicle registration records. Attorneys for both sides select jurors from the pool and may *challenge* jurors (have them dismissed) if they believe the jurors are biased. Once the jury is selected, the trial begins.

The trial starts with opening statements from both sides. The plaintiff then presents evidence and witnesses, followed by the defendant. Both sides attempt to prove their claims. Both sides also attempt to discredit evidence and witnesses presented by the other side. Then the attorneys make closing arguments, and the judge instructs the jury on relevant points of law. The jury *deliberates*, or carefully considers the arguments of both sides. Then the jury reaches a decision, and the jury *foreman* (chosen leader) announces it to the court.

In deciding civil cases, one side must simply prove its position by a *preponderance*, or superiority, of the evidence. In other words, one side convinces the jury that its side is more believable. This is sometimes called "clear and convincing evidence." In deciding criminal cases, however, prosecutors must prove their case *beyond a reasonable doubt*. The defense attorneys must prove reasonable doubt of the guilt of the accused; they do not have to prove innocence.

During a trial, what role do the plaintiff and the defendant play?

The Court Enters a Judgment

Based on the decision of the jury or the judge, called the *verdict*, the court enters a judgment. A **judgment** is the final court ruling that resolves the key issues and establishes the rights and obligations of each party. In a criminal case, the judgment is the ruling of the defendant's guilt or innocence, and the consequences of guilt. In a civil case, the judgment typically establishes an amount that the losing party must pay.

The losing party has a limited time in which to appeal. A case heard in a state district court may be appealed to a circuit court. After the circuit court, the case may go to the state appeals court, and then to the state supreme court. Any matters involving national interests may be appealed to the United States Supreme Court, which may or may not choose to hear the case.

In a civil lawsuit, the losing party often must pay *court costs*. These are costs associated with a lawsuit other than attorneys' fees. They include expenses for such things as filing papers, keeping records, and paying the jury. Sometimes the losing party must also pay the winner's attorney's fee.

Check Your Understanding

1. What is common law?

2. Who serves on a jury?

Other Ways to Seek Redress

Goals
- **Define remedies available to consumers other than individual lawsuits.**
- **Explain alternative dispute resolution (ADR) options.**

▶ SELF-HELP REMEDIES

Lawsuits are lengthy, expensive, and emotionally draining. If you have a consumer problem, pursue a settlement yourself before deciding to sue. Negotiating and withholding payment are two self-help techniques that can resolve many consumer problems.

Negotiating

Negotiating is the process of finding a solution that is acceptable to both sides. The buyer must be willing to give up some things in return for the seller's changing his or her position. In most cases, when consumers complain and want some type of settlement, the seller is willing to discuss the issues to reach some type of agreement to maintain the goodwill of the customer.

Negotiating requires tactful give-and-take. You must know the specifics of the problem, what you want done about it, and what you are willing to do to make a settlement. Negotiate calmly and reasonably. Avoid emotional outbursts and confrontational statements. These only create hostility and reduce the chances of agreeing on a remedy.

Communication Connection

Assume that you purchase a television from a local retailer, using cash. When you plug it in at home, the television will not work. You want to return it, but unfortunately you didn't keep the receipt from the merchant. Role-play this situation with a classmate. What are you willing to accept or do in order to achieve a settlement?

If you buy a defective product, first seek an agreeable remedy with the merchant before pursuing legal remedies. Negotiated settlements are often much less expensive and easier to achieve than legal remedies. They are also less stressful. Begin the negotiation soon after the problem occurs. If you wait too long, you may lose your opportunity for an agreeable settlement.

Withholding Payment

As a consumer, you can withhold payment in a purchase dispute. However, you must put your complaint in a letter right away and explain the reason why you are withholding payment on the disputed amount. The law requires the seller to respond to your complaint within a reasonable time limit. You should pay all other amounts due as agreed. Your credit should not be damaged if you follow the proper procedures for questioning credit charges.

When you buy merchandise with credit, you have more leverage than if you pay cash. You can instruct the credit card company to withhold payment to the merchant. If you follow the credit card company's procedure for disputing a payment, the company will help you resolve the problem with the merchant.

▶ SMALL-CLAIMS COURT

If the disputed amount is relatively small, you might consider small-claims court. The matter will be heard quickly, but the decision is final. You must represent yourself—no attorneys are allowed—and there is no jury. A judge decides the matter. Most states set a maximum amount of $2,000 to $5,000 in damages that can be recovered in a small-claims court.

Small-claims courts are easy to use. You can get an instruction sheet from your county courthouse that explains how to file a small claim. You must know the name and address of the person with whom you have a problem. You must know the amount in contention and make a short statement of why you are entitled to the money.

Once you file your claim, the court will serve a copy of it to the defendant. The defendant has 10 days to appear. If the defendant contests (disagrees with) the claim, the court sets a hearing date. The hearing lasts about a half hour. You present your side of the case; the defendant does the same. You may bring in written statements or evidence as well as witnesses. You should summarize your position on one page and present it to the judge.

No record is made of the small-claims court hearing. It cannot be appealed. The judge's decision is final. The benefit of taking your dispute to small-claims court is financial: you pay no attorneys' fees. Court filing fees are small, typically $50 to $150. The case is heard in a few weeks at most, giving you speedy relief. If the defendant does not appear, you win by default. The judge proclaims a judgment, and the losing party is required to pay damages.

It is important in a small-claims court hearing that you be organized, calm, and specific about your complaint. If you are asking for $500 in damages, you must be prepared to show why you deserve that sum. The judge will ask questions of you and the defendant. Usually the judge will make an immediate decision or will take a 15-minute break and return with the decision.

CLASS-ACTION LAWSUITS

A **class-action lawsuit** is a legal action in which a large number of people with similar complaints against the same defendant join together to sue. Often class-action lawsuits involve products that injured many people, and the defendant is the product's manufacturer. Sometimes employees join together to sue their employer for discrimination affecting all of them. In a class-action suit, a person sues another person or a company on behalf of himself or herself and all others in the same situation. If the plaintiffs win, they split the judgment.

Why might you want to resort to small-claims court rather than a jury trial?

In some cases, you can convince a consumer protection group to file a lawsuit on your behalf. For example, the American Civil Liberties Union (ACLU) files lawsuits to protect the rights of groups of citizens. The ACLU collects money from donations to pay the costs involved in filing lawsuits. Many individuals cannot afford to pursue legal remedies without the help of such groups because of the expense involved.

GOVERNMENTAL ASSISTANCE

In addition to the sources of consumer assistance listed in Chapter 29, you may wish to seek help from a government agency to stop some objectionable practice and get your money back. In many cases, the cost to you is small, while the benefit to all consumers is great. Government agencies that can assist you with a consumer complaint include the sources shown in Figure 30-1 (page 734).

ALTERNATE DISPUTE RESOLUTION

Alternate dispute resolution (ADR) is a general term covering several methods of settling disputes without using the court system. It

figure 30-1

SOURCES OF GOVERNMENT ASSISTANCE

Automobiles	National Highway Traffic Safety Administration
Collection, Credit	State Consumer Protection Division (at your state capitol)
Drugs/Foods	Food and Drug Administration
Household	Consumer Product Safety Commission
Investment Fraud	Federal Trade Commission Securities and Exchange Commission
Medical/Dental	State Board of Medical Examiners State Department of Commerce State Board of Dental Examiners State Health Division State Board of Pharmacy
Medicare	Social Security Administration
Misrepresentation/Fraud	State Consumer Protection Division Local District Attorney Local or State Better Business Bureau
Transportation	Interstate Commerce Commission
Warranties	Federal Trade Commission

can mean negotiations (described earlier), mediation, or several forms of arbitration.

When the parties cannot reach a negotiated settlement themselves, the next step to take without involving a court is mediation. **Mediation** is a dispute resolution method in which an independent third person (a *mediator*) helps the parties come to their own solution. Mediation has no formal rules for how to proceed. The mediator listens to both sides and helps both sides sort out what is important and what they would be willing to give up to get it. The mediator has no power to impose a settlement. He or she just facilitates the negotiations between the disputing parties. Typically, the mediator charges a fee that the two parties split.

Another form of ADR is arbitration. *Arbitration* is similar to mediation, in that an independent third person, called an *arbitrator*, helps resolve the dispute. But unlike mediation, arbitration does use some rules of procedure, though they are less formal than court procedures. There are two common types of arbitration: voluntary and binding. In **voluntary arbitration**, an independent third person listens to both sides and makes a recommendation but cannot impose it. Both parties are free to accept or reject it. With **binding arbitration**, the independent third person has the power to impose a decision that both parties must accept. The parties agree before arbitration begins that they will accept the decision as final. Like mediation, the arbitrator charges a fee for this service. The two parties choose the arbitrator, who is usually a professional with expertise in the subject matter and often has a legal background.

The Yellow Pages of your telephone book has listings for mediation and arbitration services. You can also find many such resources online. Figure 30-2 lists some dispute resolution resources that you can contact.

✓Check Your Understanding

1. Why might you choose small-claims court over filing a lawsuit in regular court?

2. How is arbitration different from mediation?

DISPUTE RESOLUTION RESOURCES

figure 30-2 ◄

* **American Arbitration Association**
    Dispute Resolution Services Worldwide
    Information about ADR, articles, procedures, online services.
    www.adr.org

* **American Bar Association**
    Information about ADR choices.
    From home page, click on "public" and then "legal subject area: ADR."
    www.abanet.org

* **CPR Institute for Dispute Resolution**
    Center for Public Resources
    ADR procedures, information, training.
    www.cpradr.org

* **Divorce Mediation**
    Getting a divorce mediator; mediating online.
    www.divorceinfo.com/mediation.htm

* **Lawyer Referral and Information Service**
    How to find the right attorney, referrals, classification areas.
    www.akronbar.org

Issues in Your World

Resolving Disputes for E-Consumers

When you buy products online, you are taking a risk. If something goes wrong, you can't return the product to a physical store and talk to the manager. Online dispute resolution services include the ability to file a complaint, insurance provided through seal owners (that guarantee sites), and online dispute resolution.

If you buy from a business that displays a seal of approval, such as Square Trade (www.squaretrade.com), Webtrust (www.webtrust.org), or TRUSTe (www.truste.org), you can also find assistance in resolving disputes at these Web sites. These companies will keep track of complaints, alert members of problems, and monitor to see that disputes are resolved satisfactorily and within a reasonable period of time.

At the Better Business Bureau "BBBOnline" program (www.BBBonline.com), consumers can file complaints and view complaints filed by others, as well as see which companies have complaints filed against them. For complete alternate dispute resolution services similar to those in the traditional brick-and-mortar world, you can go to official ADR sites, such as Cyber Settle located at www.cybersettle.com. These Web sites offer arbitration for those who wish to use the service.

To file a complaint, go to the appropriate Web site and complete forms that explain the issue. The online merchant responds, and both of you can continue a dialog until all issues are "on the table." This service is often called *hosted message board negotiation*, and it is a free process for consumers.

You do have avenues for redress when shopping on the Internet. Still, it is wise to shop carefully online and buy only from known merchants.

Think Critically

1. Have you purchased something online that was poor quality or wasn't what you ordered? How did you resolve the problem?

2. In what ways is online shopping riskier than shopping in a physical store?

Chapter Assessment

30.1

* The U.S. legal system is based on common law, or decisions made in court cases that serve as models for deciding similar future cases.
* Trial courts have original jurisdiction, or the authority to hear cases first. Appellate courts review decisions of lower courts.
* Civil courts hear non-criminal cases. Criminal courts hear cases involving punishable offenses against society.
* The judge, clerk, reporter, and bailiff are court employees. The jury is a group of citizens selected to hear cases for a short time.
* The federal court system consists of district trial courts, circuit courts of appeal, and the U.S. Supreme Court. Federal courts deal with matters concerning the nation as a whole.
* State court systems typically include trial courts, appellate courts, and a state supreme court. State courts handle most legal matters.
* Court proceedings begin when a plaintiff files a complaint. If the defendant responds, a period of discovery follows. When the disputing parties do not settle, the case goes to trial.
* The attorneys select jurors from the pool of citizens called by the court. After both sides present their cases, the judge instructs the jury on relevant laws. The jury deliberates and reaches a verdict.

30.2

* Consumers can resolve most disputes themselves through negotiating or withholding payment until they reach agreement.
* Small-claims court requires no attorney and small filing fees, but the decision of the judge is final.
* A large number of people with similar complaints against the same defendant may join together in a class-action lawsuit.
* Alternate dispute resolution means settling disputes without using the court system.

* With mediation, an independent third person helps the parties come to their own solution, but the parties are not required to accept the settlement.

* In voluntary arbitration, the arbitrator makes a recommendation that the parties are free to accept or reject. In binding arbitration, the parties must accept the arbitrator's decision.

REVIEW TERMS

Directions

Can you find the definition for each of the following terms used in Chapter 30?

alternate dispute resolution (ADR)	depositions
appellate court	judgment
binding arbitration	jurisdiction
civil court	mediation
class-action lawsuit	plaintiff
counterclaim	statute of limitations
court	trial court
criminal court	voluntary arbitration
defendant	

1. A general term covering several methods of settling a dispute without using the court system.

2. A person or group of people whose task it is to hear and decide matters according to the law.

3. A court that hears cases involving punishable offenses against society.

4. A court that hears non-criminal cases.

5. The legal authority to hear and decide a case.

6. A dispute resolution method in which an independent third person has the power to impose a decision that both parties must accept.

7. A dispute resolution method in which an independent third person helps the parties come to their own solution.

8. The first court to hear a case.

9. The person who initiates a lawsuit by filing a complaint.

10. A court that has the authority to review the judgment of a lower court.

11. A legally defined time limit in which a lawsuit may be filed for various complaints.

12. The person against whom a lawsuit is filed.

13. Sworn statements of witnesses taken before court appearances and recorded in writing or on videotape to preserve the memory of the issues.

14. A defendant's assertion that the plaintiff is at fault and should pay damages to the defendant.

15. The final court ruling that resolves the key issues and establishes the rights and obligations of each party.

16. A dispute resolution method in which an independent third person listens to both sides and makes a recommendation but cannot impose it.

17. A legal action in which a large number of people with similar complaints against the same defendant join together to sue.

REVIEW FACTS AND IDEAS

1. How do court decisions affect other cases in a common law system?

2. Describe the types of matters that each of these courts hears:
   a. Trial court
   b. Appellate court
   c. Civil court
   d. Criminal court

3. On what basis may the losing party in a case appeal the decision?

4. List and briefly describe the officers of the court.

5. What is a jury and how is it selected?

6. What is the highest court of the federal court system?

7. How many federal court districts are in the United States?

8. List several "special" courts in the federal system.

9. What are the lowest state courts? Give two examples.

10. What are the steps in a lawsuit?

11. What happens during discovery?

12. What are some ways you can settle consumer problems without outside help?

13. How is a class-action lawsuit different from an individual lawsuit?

14. What are the advantages of alternate dispute resolution (ADR)?

APPLY YOUR KNOWLEDGE

1. A case that involves a dispute in a city is filed with the circuit court of a county in the same state. After a trial court hears the case, where can it be appealed?

2. A plaintiff files a lawsuit. Explain what happens until a court renders a judgment. What happens if the losing party thinks the court made a legal error in the case?

3. As a store customer, you are dissatisfied with a product purchased. Explain the self-help remedies and actions to consider in resolving the dispute.

4. Small-claims courts were set up to give the ordinary person "a say in court" for small matters otherwise not worth taking to court. Why are small-claims courts easy to use and, in some cases, more advantageous than a formal court proceeding?

5. Use the Internet to investigate government agencies that can assist you with consumer complaints. What type of complaint is each agency responsible for? Think of a past consumer complaint you or a member of your family has had. Which agency would you choose for help with this consumer problem?

6. Search the Internet for information about mediators or arbitrators. Write a one-page report on what they do, how they do it, and how consumers can employ their services.

1. Visit your local law library located at the county courthouse, a public university, or at a law school if there is one in your area. List five types of references available. Look up the statute of limitations for filing lawsuits in your state and tell how long you have to file actions in the following situations:

   a. Wrongful death or injury

   b. Real property infringement

   c. Civil action where you are the injured party in a contract

   Also in your law library, you will find books that summarize cases tried and decided in your state. Find a case that interests you and summarize the issues involved, the court's decision, and your reactions.

2. With your instructor's permission, spend a half-day at a local county courthouse. Make arrangements to observe a case being tried. Generally, you will not be allowed to leave the room until the court adjourns, nor will you be allowed to enter while court is in session. You may observe a civil or criminal case. Write a report on what you observe.

3. Examine a lawsuit that has been filed. You can look at records of cases that have been filed in your county, although you will not be given copies free of charge. Read through each case and make notes about the plaintiff, the defendant, the issue at hand, what the plaintiff was asking, and how the matter was resolved.

4. Work in groups to determine the appropriate legal remedy for each of the following situations.

   a. The plaintiff was driving his vehicle in a northerly direction when the defendant ran a stop sign going in an easterly direction and did severe damage to the plaintiff's vehicle, including personal injuries to the plaintiff.

   b. A person has paid money to a telemarketer for a product that was promised but never received. The caller said the product was high quality and that the company was a nonprofit organization to benefit disabled veterans.

   c. A local restaurant served food that caused people who ate there on a particular night to get sick. No one died, but several people were very sick for several days, causing medical bills amounting to several thousand dollars. When the cause of the illness was detected, the restaurant was required to make needed changes, and then it was allowed to reopen for business.

*For related activities and links, point your browser to **www.mypf.swlearning.com***

Exploring Ethical Issues

OVERVIEW

Ethics is the study of what is morally good and bad, right and wrong. We seek to learn what makes actions right or wrong. As you will discover, deciding the difference can be a more complex process than it might seem at first.

In this section, you will analyze situations involving ethics in the marketplace, in the workplace, and on the Internet. You will be asked to answer critical-thinking questions on each case. Record your answers in the space provided on the worksheets in the *Student Activity Guide*. In analyzing each case, you must (1) identify the problem, (2) apply relevant knowledge to the solution of the problem, and (3) draw a conclusion or reach a decision based on careful analysis of the problem. People base ethical decisions on their personal values and principles, which they develop through individual life experiences. Therefore, since everyone has different experiences, decisions about each case will probably vary.

CASE 1

Cutting It Close

Lashondra wanted to earn extra money over the summer, so she decided to start a lawn-mowing business in her neighborhood. To advertise her business, she composed a flyer to put in her neighbors' mailboxes. On the flyer she listed her services: mowing, trimming, and blowing grass clippings off the driveway and sidewalk when she finished. She offered all of these services for one low price.

Several neighbors wanted her service. In fact, more asked than she had time to serve. Not wanting to pass up the opportunity to earn so much money, Lashondra agreed to do the lawns of all who asked. She figured she would find some way to mow them all. Since she was dealing with neighbors, she did not offer any written contracts. They just agreed verbally.

For three weeks, Lashondra worked very hard but still could not finish all the lawns she had agreed to mow. She realized, though, that if she didn't trim the lawns, she could mow one additional lawn each weekend, so that's what she decided to do. Lashondra reasoned that her mower could cut grass very close to trees and walls, so the trimming didn't really seem necessary. She was giving her customers a very low price, so it was a good deal even without the trimming. Besides, she could now satisfy more customers who otherwise would have to mow their own lawns or take the time to find someone else to do them.

1. Since Lashondra and her neighbors did not sign a written contract, is Lashondra obligated to do the services she listed on her flyer? Why or why not?

2. Lashondra is 16, so she is a minor. How does this fact affect her legal and ethical obligations to her neighbors?

3. Do you agree with Lashondra's reasons for not trimming? Why or why not?

4. Are the benefits she is offering her neighbors worth giving up the trimming service to obtain?

5. If you were in Lashondra's situation, what would you do? Why?

CASE 2

I'm Anonymous

Shuet works full time and lives in an apartment with two roommates. He has met many people online, and he uses several screen names. He visits chat rooms and reads personal ads frequently, and sometimes responds to them. He never uses correct information because he wants to feel safe from anyone finding out who he really is. On several occasions, Shuet made arrangements to meet someone, but often he did not show up as agreed.

As a joke, Shuet sometimes sends insulting or vaguely threatening messages to co-workers he doesn't like. He enjoys hearing them talk about the messages at work. He doesn't mean them any real harm, so the messages don't hurt anybody. And because he's anonymous, he doesn't take any risks.

1. Do you think Shuet is acting appropriately on the Internet? Why or why not?

2. Have you ever acted in similar ways toward people on the Internet? Explain.

3. How would you feel if you received an insulting or threatening e-mail from an anonymous sender?

4. What suggestions would you make to Shuet about behaving appropriately and staying safe on the Internet?

CASE 3

Something for Nothing

Jared and Kayla work together for a fast-food restaurant. They are both good workers and have been employed for over a year. Each Christmas the company they work for has a big party for all employees. Gifts are given away to employees with outstanding service during the year.

Jared and Kayla's manager has worked for the company for over ten years. She discovered a way to falsify information in the computer to her advantage. She gets more than her fair share of gifts while others in the company do not get as much. Jared and Kayla accidentally discovered this scam. The manager encouraged Jared and Kayla to participate in the scheme.

"You two can get more gifts if you participate. If you try to turn me in, I'll have both of you fired," she said.

1. What is the ethical problem involved in this situation?

2. What are Jared and Kayla's options?

3. What would you do if you were in this situation? Why?

4. How might this case be an example of employee stealing in the workplace?

CASE 4

It's a Good Deal

When Roberto flew to see his relatives last year, he was able to earn enough air miles for a free ticket. The frequent flyer club rules are clear: The ticket is non-transferable.

Roberto bought a ticket for a flight across the country, but later discovered he couldn't go. A friend of his was planning a similar trip, so Roberto offered him the ticket for $100—much cheaper than the cost of a full fare.

When Roberto's friend tried to use the ticket on his return flight, the agent discovered that the ticket belonged to someone else. The airline refused to allow him on the plane without his paying the full price. When he told Roberto about the problem, Roberto said it wasn't his concern.

1. Discuss the pros and cons of Roberto's dilemma.

2. What's wrong with the owner of a ticket giving or selling it to someone else?

3. Would you participate in this type of a deal? Why or why not?

CASE 5

Nobody Got Hurt

Loriann bought a new dress to wear for a special occasion. During the course of the evening, she spilled some juice on the dress and was unable to remove all of the stain. The stain was small and not really visible at first glance.

The next day, Loriann decided that she would probably never wear the dress again. Anyway, the dress didn't fit as well as she would have liked, so she decided to get her money back. That afternoon she returned the dress to the store. She claimed the dress was a gift that she didn't like. The store gave her credit for the dress, and Loriann bought something else.

When asked how she could do something like that, Loriann replied, "Why not? Nobody got hurt."

1. Was there anything wrong with what Loriann did? Did anybody get hurt? Who?

2. Why do some stores have lenient return policies? Why do some stores have "no return" policies?

3. What would you do if you worked in the store and knew what Loriann had done?

4. Discuss the ethical principles involved in this case.

Glossary

A

Abrasives. Cleaning agents in car polishing compounds that contain strong chemicals or are coarse and can cause surface damage. (p. 657)

Acceptance. A formal agreement to the terms of an offer, forming a contract between the parties. (p. 535)

Adjustable rate mortgage (ARM). A mortgage for which the interest rate changes in response to the movement of interest rates in the economy as a whole. (p. 537)

Adjusted gross income. The result of adjustments subtracted from gross income. (p. 149)

Advanced degrees. Degrees earned through specialized, intensive education programs taken after the first college degree. (p. 11)

Age Discrimination in Employment Act. Law that prohibits discrimination in employment decisions against people age 40 and over. (p. 96)

Agency bond. A bond issued by a federal agency, such as the Federal Home Loan Mortgage Corporation. (p. 312)

Alimony. Money paid by one former spouse to support the other. (pp. 149, 584)

Allowances. A number that reduces the amount of tax withheld from your paycheck. (p. 89)

Alternate dispute resolution (ADR). A general term covering several methods of settling disputes without using the court system. (p. 733)

Americans with Disabilities Act. Law that prohibits discrimination on the basis of physical or mental disabilities. (p. 96)

Annual percentage rate (APR). The cost of credit expressed as a yearly percentage. (p. 394)

Annual percentage yield (APY). The actual interest rate an account pays per year, with compounding included. (p. 240)

Annual report. A summary of a corporation's financial results for the year and prospects for the future. (p. 267)

Annuity. A contract sold by an insurance company that provides an investor with a series of regular payments, usually after retirement. (p. 270)

Appellate court. A court having appellate jurisdiction (the authority to review the judgment of a lower court). (p. 723)

Application letter. A cover letter that introduces you to a potential employer and gives you a chance to sell your qualifications. (p. 42)

Aptitude. A natural physical or mental ability that allows you to do certain tasks well. (p. 23)

Assets. Items of value that a person owns. (p. 178)

Attractive nuisance. A dangerous place, condition, or object that is particularly attractive to children. (p. 630)

Audit. The examination of your tax returns by the Internal Revenue Service. (p. 145)

B

Back-end load. A sales charge paid when you sell an investment. (p. 330)

Bait and switch. An illegal sales technique in which a seller advertises a product with the intention of persuading consumers to buy a more expensive product. (p. 686)

Balanced fund. A mutual fund that invests in a mixture of stocks and bonds to minimize risk. (p. 328)

Bankruptcy. A legal process that relieves debtors of the responsibility of paying their debts or protects them while they try to repay. (p. 453)

Basic needs. The ingredients necessary for maintaining physical life, including food and water, shelter, and clothing. (p. 483)

Bear market. A prolonged period of falling prices and a general feeling of investor pessimism. (p. 288)

Benefits. Company-provided supplements to salaries, such as sick pay, vacation time, and health insurance. (pp. 7, 126)

Binding arbitration. When an independent third person has the power to impose a decision that both parties in a dispute must accept. (p. 735)

Blank endorsement. The signature of the payee written on the back of the check exactly as the name appears on the front of the check. (p. 209)

Blue chip stocks. Stocks of large, well-established corporations with a solid record of profitability. (p. 282)

Body (of a letter). The message section of a letter. (p. 47)

Bonds. Debt obligations of corporations or state or local governments. (p. 268)

Budget. A spending and saving plan based on your expected income and expenses. (p. 175)

Bull market. A prolonged period of rising stock prices and a general feeling of investor optimism. (p. 288)

C

Callable bond. A bond that the issuer has the right to pay off before its maturity date. (p. 307)

Canceled check. A check that bears the bank's stamp, indicating that it has cleared. (p. 198)

Capacity. The ability to repay a loan with present income. (p. 409)

Capital. Property possessed that is worth more than debts owed. (p. 388)

Capital gain. An increase in the value of stock above the price initially paid for it. (p. 280)

Care labels. Labels found on clothing and other products that give instructions for cleaning, wash and dry temperature, and other care needed to preserve the product. (p. 707)

Cash value. The savings accumulated in a permanent life insurance policy that you would receive if you canceled your policy. (p. 657)

Cashier's check. A check written by a bank on its own funds. (p. 214)

Certificate of deposit (CD). A deposit that earns a fixed interest rate for a specified length of time. (p. 244)

Certified check. A personal check that the bank guarantees to be good. (p. 214)

Chapter 7 bankruptcy. A liquidation form of bankruptcy for individuals that wipes out most debts in exchange for giving up most assets. (p. 455)

Chapter 11 bankruptcy. A reorganization form of bankruptcy for businesses that allows them to continue operating under court supervision as they repay their restructured debts. (p. 454)

Chapter 13 bankruptcy. A reorganization form of bankruptcy for individuals that allows debtors to keep their property and use their income to pay a portion of their debts over three to five years. (p. 455)

Character. A responsible attitude toward living up to agreements. (p. 409)

Check. A written order to a bank to pay the stated amount to the person or business (payee) named on it. (p. 198)

Checkbook register. A booklet used to record checking account transactions. (p. 205)

Cherry picker. A customer who buys only loss leaders. (p. 493)

Child support. Money paid to a former spouse for support of dependent children. (p. 149)

Childproof devices. Devices designed to resist tampering by young children. (p. 707)

Civil ceremony. A wedding performed by a public official rather than a member of the clergy. (p. 575)

Civil court. A court with the authority to hear non-criminal cases. (p. 723)

Civil Rights Act of 1964. Law that prohibits discrimination in hiring, training, and promotion on the basis of race, color, gender, religion, or national origin. (p. 95)

Class-action lawsuit. A legal action in which a large number of people with similar complaints against the same defendant join together to sue. (p. 733)

Closed-end credit. A loan for a specific amount that must be repaid, in full, including all finance charges, by a stated due date. (p. 396)

Closing costs. Expenses incurred in transferring ownership from buyer to seller in a real estate transaction. (p. 531)

COBRA. Consolidated Omnibus Reconciliation Act; federal law that allows people who leave employment to continue their health insurance under the company plan for a limited period of time. (p. 646)

Codicil. Lists small modifications to a will and then reaffirms the rest of the original will. (p. 351)

Co-insurance clause. A provision requiring policyholders to insure their building for a stated percentage of its replacement value in order to receive full reimbursement for a loss. (p. 627)

Collateral. Property pledged to a creditor to assure repayment of a loan. (p. 388)

Collective bargaining. The process of negotiating the terms of employment for union members. (p. 132)

Collective values. Things that are important to society as a whole. (p. 484)

Collision coverage. Automobile insurance that protects your own car against damage from accidents or vehicle overturning. (p. 633)

Common stock. A type of stock that pays a variable dividend and gives the holder voting rights. (p. 281)

Company advertising. Advertising intended to promote the image of a store, company, or retail chain. (p. 492)

Competition. The rivalry among sellers in the same market to win customers. (p. 684)

Complimentary close. A courteous phrase used to end a letter. (p. 47)

Compound interest. Interest computed on the original principal plus accumulated interest. (p. 239)

Comprehensive coverage. Insurance that pays for damage to your car from events other than collision or vehicle overturning. (p. 634)

Compressed workweek. A work schedule that fits the normal 40-hour workweek into less than give days; for example, four days, 10 hours each, totaling a 40-hour week. (p. 131)

Condominium. Individually owned unit in an apartment-style complex with a shared ownership of common areas. (p. 334)

Consideration. Anything of value exchanged as part of a contract. (p. 184)

Consumer advocate. A person who actively promotes consumer causes. (p. 713)

Consumers. Buyers and users of goods and services. (p. 681)

Contact. Someone you know who can provide you with inside information on job openings. (p. 30)

Contract. A legally enforceable agreement between two or more parties. (p. 182)

Convertible bond. A corporate bond that the bondholder can choose to exchange for a specified number of shares of the corporation's common stock. (p. 308)

Coordination of benefits. A group health insurance provision that specifies how the insurers will share the cost when more than one policy covers a claim. (p. 646)

Co-signer. A person who promises in writing to repay a promissory note if the maker fails to pay. (p. 187)

Counterclaim. A defendant's assertion that the plaintiff is at fault and should pay damages to the defendant. (p. 728)

Counteroffer. In a real estate transaction, a revised offer from the seller that is then accepted or rejected. (p. 535)

Court. A person or group of people whose task it is to hear and decide matters according to the law. (p. 723)

Creative listening. Listening with your mind open to new ideas. (p. 70)

Credit. Money borrowed to buy something now, with the agreement to pay for it later. (p. 387)

Credit bureau. A company that gathers, stores, and sells credit information to business subscribers. (p. 407)

Credit history. The complete record of your borrowing and repayment performance. (p. 407)

Credit rating. A measure of creditworthiness based on an analysis of a consumer's financial history. (p. 413)

Credit report. A written statement of a consumer's credit history, issued by a credit bureau to its business subscribers. (p. 408)

Cremation. A process of reducing a body to ashes in a high-temperature oven. (p. 586)

Criminal court. A court that hears cases involving punishable offenses against society. (p. 723)

Critical listening. The ability to differentiate facts from opinions. (p. 69)

Custom. A long-established practice that takes on the force of an unwritten law. (p. 487)

D

Database. A computer program that organizes data for easy search and retrieval. (p. 190)

Dealer add-ons. High-priced, high-profit car dealer services that add little or no value. (p. 551)

Debenture. A corporate bond that is not backed by collateral but only by the general credit standing of the corporation. (p. 307)

Debt collector. A person or company hired by a creditor to collect the overdue balance on an account. (p. 420)

Debtor. A person who owes money to others. (p. 453)

Deductions. 1. Amounts subtracted from gross pay. (p. 121) 2. Amounts subtracted from gross pay to arrive at take-home pay. (p. 149)

Deed. A document that transfers title of real property from one party to another. (p. 537)

Defendant. The person against whom a lawsuit is filed. (p. 728)

Deferred billing. A service available to charge customers whereby purchases are not billed to the customer until a later date. (p. 390)

Defined-benefit plan. A company-sponsored retirement plan in which employees receive, at normal retirement age, a specified monthly amount based on wages earned and number of years of service. (p. 359)

Defined-contribution plan. A company-sponsored retirement plan in which employees may choose to contribute part of their salary as a tax-deferred investment. (p. 360)

Demand. The willingness and ability of consumers to purchase goods and services at certain prices. (p. 682)

Demand deposit. An account that lets you withdraw portions of your deposited funds at any time. (p. 198)

Depositions. Sworn statements of witnesses taken before court appearances and recorded in writing or on videotape to preserve the memory of the issues. (p. 729)

Depreciation. In real estate, the decline in value of property due to normal wear and tear. (p. 337)

Direct investment. Buying stock directly from a corporation. (p. 292)

Disability insurance. An insurance plan that makes regular payments to replace income lost when illness or injury prevents the insured from working. (p. 652)

Discharged debts. Debts erased by the court during bankruptcy proceedings. (p. 454)

Discount bond. A bond purchased at less than its maturity value. (p. 268)

Discretionary income. Money that is left over when the bills have been paid. (p. 239)

Discrimination. Treating people differently based on prejudice rather than individual merit. (p. 417)

Disposable income. The money left to spend or save after taxes have been paid. (p. 174)

Dissolution of marriage. No-fault divorce; when irreconcilable differences have led to the breakdown of a marriage. (p. 583)

Diversification. The spreading of risk among many types of investments. (p. 261)

Dividend reinvestment. Using dividends previously earned on stock to buy more shares. (p. 292)

Dividends. The part of the corporation's profits paid to stockholders. (p. 280)

Dormitory. An on-campus building that contains many small rooms that colleges rent to students. (p. 505)

Downpayment. A part of the purchase price paid in cash up front, reducing the amount of a loan. (p. 438)

Downward communication. Communication that flows from higher to lower levels of an organization. (p. 72)

Duplex. A building with two separate living quarters. (p. 334)

E

Earnest money. In real estate, a portion of the purchase price that the buyer deposits as evidence of good faith to show that the purchase offer is serious. (p. 535)

Earnings per share. A corporation's after-tax earnings divided by the number of common stock shares outstanding. (p. 284)

Economy. All activities related to production and distribution of goods and services in a geographic area. (p. 487)

Efficiency apartment. An apartment with one large room that serves as the kitchen, living room, and bedroom, plus a bathroom. (p. 506)

Empathy. The ability to see others' points of view and understand their feelings. (p. 73)

Employee expenses. Any costs paid by employees and not reimbursed by employers. (p. 8)

Employment application. A preprinted form that must be filled out when applying for employment. (p. 56)

Endorsement. A written amendment to an insurance policy. (p. 625)

Entrepreneur. One who organizes, manages, and assumes the risks of a business or enterprise. (p. 9)

Equal Pay Act. Law that prohibits unequal pay for men and women doing substantially similar work. (p. 95)

Equilibrium price. The price at which the quantity supplied equals the quantity demanded of the product. (p. 682)

Equity. The difference between the market value of property and the amount owed on it. (p. 529)

Estate. All that a person owns, less debts owed, at the time of the person's death. (p. 350)

Estate planning. Preparing a plan for transferring property during one's lifetime and at one's death. (p. 350)

Estate tax. A tax levied by the federal government on property transferred from deceased people to their heirs. (p. 355)

Eviction. The legal process of removing a tenant from rental property. (p. 520)

Exempt status. A claim on Form W-4 that allows you to have no federal tax withheld from your paycheck. (p. 89)

Exempted property. The possessions that the bankrupt debtor is allowed to keep because they are considered necessary for survival. (p. 455)

Exemption. An amount you may subtract from your income for each person who depends on your income to live. (p. 148)

Experience. Knowledge and skills acquired from working in a career field. (p. 28)

F

Face value. The amount a bondholder will be repaid when the bond matures or is due. (p. 306)

Fair Labor Standards Act (Wage and Hour Act). Law that established a minimum wage and required hourly workers to be paid 1 1/2 times their hourly rate for overtime. (p. 94)

Fake sale. An advertised sale that represents regular-priced merchandise. (p. 687)

Family and Medical Leave Act. Law that allows employees to take up to 12 weeks of unpaid leave in a 12-month period for certain medical and family situations. (p. 95)

Fee. A non-refundable charge for a service. (p. 596)

Finance charge. The total dollar amount of all interest and fees you pay for the use of credit. (p. 389)

Financial advisers. Trained professional planners who give overall investment advice based on your goals, age, lifestyle, and other factors. (p. 267)

Financial plan. A set of goals for spending, saving, and investing the money you earn. (p. 174)

Fixed expenses. Costs you are obligated to pay at specific times, regardless of other events. (p. 176)

Fixed-rate loans. Loans for which the interest rate does not change (up or down) over the life of the loan. (p. 434)

Fixed-rate mortgage. A mortgage on which the interest rate does not change during the term of the loan. (p. 536)

Flammability. The capacity for catching on fire. (p. 705)

Flextime. Flexible schedules that allow employees to choose their working hours within defined limits. (p. 130)

Floating a check. The practice of writing a check on insufficient funds and hoping a deposit will clear before the check is cashed. (p. 199)

Form W-2. A form that lists income earned during the year and all amounts withheld by the employer for taxes. (p. 92)

Form W-4. A form completed for income tax withholding purposes. (p. 89)

Fraud. The intentional misrepresentation of information with the intent to deceive or mislead. (p. 712)

Free enterprise. An economic system in which producers and consumers are free to engage in business transactions with minimal government interference. (p. 681)

Front-end load. A sales charge paid when you buy an investment and sometimes when dividends are reinvested as well. (p. 330)

Futures. Contracts to buy and sell commodities or stocks for a specified price on a specified date in the future. (p. 271)

G

Garnishment. A legal process that allows part of your paycheck to be withheld for payment of a debt. (p. 427)

General obligation bond. A municipal bond backed by the power of the issuing state or local government to levy taxes to pay back the debt. (p. 310)

Generic drugs. Medications with the same composition as the equivalent brand-name drugs, but generally less expensive. (p. 706)

Gift tax. A tax on a gift of money or property, to be paid by the giver, not the receiver, of the gift. (p. 356)

Global fund. A mutual fund that purchases international stocks and bonds as well as U.S. securities. (p. 328)

Goal. A desired end toward which efforts are directed. (p. 27)

Gross income. All taxable income received, including wages, tips, salaries, interest, dividends, unemployment compensation, alimony, and so forth. (p. 148)

Gross pay. The total amount you earn before any deductions are subtracted. (p. 119)

Group health insurance. Health insurance issued to a group to cover individuals in the group and sometimes their dependents. (p. 645)

Growth and income fund. A mutual fund whose investment goal is to earn returns from both dividends and capital gains. (p. 327)

Growth fund. A mutual fund whose investment goal is to buy stocks that will increase in value over time. (p. 326)

Growth stocks. Stocks in corporations that reinvest their profits into the business so that it can grow. (p. 282)

H

Health insurance. A plan for sharing the risk of high medical costs resulting from injury or illness. (p. 645)

Health Maintenance Organization (HMO). A group health insurance plan that offers prepaid medical care to its members. (p. 649)

Hearing. The process of perceiving sound. (p. 69)

Heirs. People who receive property from someone who has died. (p. 349)

Homeowner's policy. Insurance that protects property owners from property and liability risks. (p. 624)

Horizontal communication. Communication among co-workers of equal rank. (p. 71)

Human relations. The art of getting along with others. (p. 73)

Hygiene factors. Job elements that dissatisfy when absent but do not add to satisfaction when present. (p. 79)

I

Identity. Who you are. (p. 22)

Incentive pay. Money offered to encourage employees to strive for higher levels of performance. (p. 126)

Income fund. A mutual fund whose investment goal is to buy bonds that produce current income in the form of interest. (p. 327)

Income stocks. Stocks that have a consistent history of paying high dividends. (p. 281)

Incontestable clause. A provision of a life or health insurance policy that once the policy has been in effect for a stated period of time, the insurer may no longer question items on the application in order to deny coverage. (p. 655)

Indemnification. Putting an insurance policyholder back in the same financial condition as before a loss occurred. (p. 606)

Index fund. A mutual fund that tries to match the performance of a particular securities index by investing in the companies included in that index. (p. 329)

Individual retirement account (IRA). A retirement savings plan that allows individuals to set aside money in tax-deferred savings up to a limit set by the government. (p. 357)

Industry advertising. Advertising intended to promote a general product group, without regard to where these products are purchased. (p. 492)

Inflation. A rise in the general level of prices. (p. 259)

Inheritance tax. A tax levied by a state against an heir who receives property from a deceased person's estate. (p. 356)

Innovations. New ideas, methods, or devices that bring about changes in the way we live. (p. 485)

Insurable interest. Financial interest in life or property such that, if the life or property were lost or harmed, the insured would suffer financially. (p. 610)

Insurance. A method for spreading individual risk among a large group of people to make losses more affordable for all. (p. 605)

Insurer. A business that agrees to pay the cost of potential future losses in exchange for regular fee payments. (p. 605)

Interest. Money paid for the use of money; earnings on a savings account. (p. 239)

Interests. The things you like to do. (p. 23)

Investing. The use of savings to earn a financial return. (p. 257)

Investment-grade bond. Highly rated bond that is considered safe because the issuer is stable and dependable. (p. 314)

Involuntary bankruptcy. A financial situation that occurs when creditors file a petition with the court, asking the court to declare a debtor bankrupt. (p. 454)

Itemize. To list allowable expenses on your tax return. (p. 149)

Itinerary. A detailed schedule of events, times, and places for a vacation or trip. (p. 578)

J

Job analysis. An evaluation of the positive and negative attributes of a given career choice. (p. 5)

Job interview. A face-to-face meeting with a potential employer to discuss your job qualifications. (p. 58)

Job rotation. A job design in which employees are trained to do more than one specialized task. (p. 131)

Job sharing. A job design in which two people share one full-time job, including salaries and benefits. (p. 131)

Judgment. The final court ruling that resolves key issues and establishes the rights and obligations of each party. (p. 730)

Junk bond. A bond that has a low rating, or no rating at all. (p. 315)

Jurisdiction. The legal authority of a court to hear and decide a case. (p. 723)

K

Keogh plan. A tax-deferred retirement savings plan available to self-employed individuals and their employees. (p. 358)

L

Labor union. A group of people who work in the same or similar occupations, organized for the benefit of all employees in these occupations. (p. 132)

Landlord. The owner of rental property. (p. 513)

Lease. A written agreement that allows a tenant to use property for a specified time period and rent. (p. 516)

Lemon. A car with substantial defects that the manufacturer has been unable to fix after repeated attempts. (p. 553)

Letter address. The part of a letter that contains the name and address of the person or company to whom you are writing. (p. 43)

Leverage. The use of borrowed money to buy securities. (p. 289)

Liabilities. Amounts of money owed to others. (p. 178)

Liability coverage. Insurance to protect against claims for bodily injury to another person or damage to another person's property. (p. 630)

Liability risks. The chances of loss that may occur when your errors or inappropriate actions result in bodily injury to someone else or damage to someone else's property. (p. 609)

Lien. A financial claim on property. (p. 537)

Life insurance. Insurance that provides funds to the beneficiaries when the insured dies. (p. 654)

Lifestyle. The way people choose to live their lives, based on the values they have chosen. (p. 23)

Line of credit. A pre-established amount that can be borrowed on demand with no collateral. (p. 389)

Liquidity. The ability of an asset to be converted into cash quickly without loss of value. (p. 243)

Listening. An active hearing process that requires concentration and effort. (p. 69)

Loan sharks. Unlicensed lenders who charge illegally high interest rates. (p. 399)

Lobbying. Trying to influence public officials to take political action that benefits the group the lobbyists represent. (p. 134)

Loss leader. An item of merchandise marked down to an unusually low price, sometimes below cost, to attract customers into the store. (p. 493)

Low-balling. Advertising a service at an unusually low price to lure customers, and then attempting to persuade them that they need additional services. (p. 687).

M

Market value. 1. The price for which a stock is bought and sold in the marketplace. (p. 283) 2. The highest price that a property will bring on the market. (p. 528)

Maturity date. The date on which an investment becomes due for payment. (p. 244)

Mediation. A dispute resolution method in which an independent third person helps the parties come to their own solution. (p. 734)

Medicaid. Government-sponsored health insurance for people with low incomes and limited resources. (p. 650)

Medicare. Government-sponsored health insurance for people currently age 65 or older. (p. 650)

Micromarketing. A marketing strategy designed to target specific people or small groups with products that they are likely to want. (p. 495)

Minimum wage. The legally established lower limit on wages employers may pay. (p. 94)

Minors. People under the age of legal adulthood. (p. 92)

Money market account. A combination savings-investment plan in which money deposited is used to purchase safe, liquid securities. (p. 245)

Money market fund. A mutual fund that invests in safe, liquid securities, such as Treasury bills. (p. 328)

Monopoly. A market with many buyers but only one seller. (p. 684)

Mortgage. A loan to purchase real estate. (p. 336)

Mortgage bond. A corporate bond backed by specific assets as collateral to assure repayment of the debt. (p. 307)

Motivators. Job elements that increase job satisfaction. (p. 80)

Multiple Listing Service (MLS). A real estate marketing service in which agents from many real estate agencies pool their home listings and agree to share commissions on the sales. (p. 534)

Municipal bond. A bond issued by state and local governments. (p. 310)

Mutual fund. A large, professionally managed group of investments. (p. 270)

N

Negotiable instrument. An unconditional written promise to pay a specified sum of money upon demand of the holder. (p. 186)

Net pay. The amount left after all deductions have been taken out of your gross pay. (p. 121)

Net worth. The difference between assets and liabilities. (p. 178)

Networks. Informal groups of people with common interests who interact for mutual assistance. (p. 14)

No-fault insurance. Automobile insurance in which drivers involved in an accident receive reimbursement for their medical and repair expense from their own insurer. (p. 635)

No-load fund. Mutual fund that does not charge a sales fee when you buy or sell because no salespeople are involved. (p. 330)

O

Odd-number pricing. The practice of setting prices at uneven amounts rather than whole dollars to make them seem lower. (p. 492)

Offer. A formal document that expresses interest in entering into a contract with someone else. (p. 535)

Open-ended credit. An agreement to lend the borrower an amount up to a stated limit and to allow borrowing up to that limit again, whenever the balance falls below the limit. (p. 393)

Opportunity cost. The value of your next best alternative whenever you make a choice. (p. 481)

Option. The right, but not the obligation, to buy or sell a commodity or stock for a specified price within a specified time period. (p. 271)

Overbook. When airlines have sold more reservations than they can fulfill. (p. 580)

Overdraft. A check written for more money than your account contains. (p. 199)

Overtime. The time worked beyond the regular hours; usually more than 40 hours in a five-day period. (p. 119)

Oxidize. Permanently lose color and shine in a vehicle's paint because of chemical reaction with the air. (p. 561)

P

Par value. An assigned (and often arbitrary) dollar value that is printed on a stock certificate. (p. 283)

Participation certificate. An investment in a pool of mortgages that have been purchased by a government agency. (p. 336)

Pawnbroker. A legal business that makes high-interest loans based on the value of personal possessions pledged as collateral. (p. 399)

Penny stocks. Low-priced stocks of small companies that have no track record. (p. 272)

Permanent life insurance. Life insurance that remains in effect for the insured's lifetime and builds a cash value. (p. 657)

Personal injury protection (PIP). Automobile insurance that pays for medical, hospital, and funeral costs of the insured and his or her family and passengers, regardless of fault. (p. 635)

Personal property floater. Insurance coverage for the insured's moveable property wherever it may be located; it protects property without regard to its location at the time of loss. (p. 630)

Personal risks. Chances of loss involving income and standard of living. (p. 608)

Personality. The many individual qualities that make a person unique. (p. 24)

Placement center. Source of career counseling available at a high school, college, or technical training institute. (p. 11)

Plaintiff. The person who begins a lawsuit by filing a complaint. (p. 728)

Points (Mortgage). Extra interest that borrowers must pay at closing (time of purchase), with each point being equal to 1 percent of the loan amount. (p. 531)

Policy. A written insurance contract. (p. 605)

Policyholder. The person who owns an insurance policy. (p. 605)

Polishing compound. A substance that can smooth out an automobile's surface scratches, scuffs, and stains. (p. 561)

Power of attorney. A legal document authorizing someone to act on your behalf. (p. 351)

Pre-approval. Finding out how much money you will be qualified to borrow before making a purchase. (p. 547)

Preferred Provider Organization (PPO). A group of healthcare providers who band together to provide health services for set fees. (p. 649)

Preferred stock. A type of stock that pays a fixed dividend and carries no voting rights. (p. 281)

Premium. The fee a policyholder agrees to pay to an insurance company periodically (monthly, quarterly, annually, or semiannually) for an insurance policy. (p. 605)

Price-fixing. An illegal agreement among competitors to sell a good or service for a set price. (p. 685)

Prime rate. The interest rate lenders offer to their best business customers. (p. 434)

Principal. 1. The amount borrowed, or the unpaid portion of the amount borrowed, on which the borrower pays interest. (p. 436) 2. The amount of money deposited by a saver. (p. 239)

Probability. The mathematics of chance; used by insurers to set premiums based on the statistical probability of a loss occurring. (p. 606)

Producers. Manufacturers or makers of goods and services for sale. (p. 681)

Product advertising. Advertising intended to convince consumers to buy a specific good or service. (p. 491)

Professional organization. An organization of people in a particular occupation that requires considerable training and specialized skills. (p. 134)

Progressive taxes. Taxes that take a larger share of income as the amount of income grows. (p. 142)

Promotion. The ability to advance, accept more responsibilities, and work your way up in a company. (p. 7)

Property risks. The chances of loss or harm to personal or real property. (p. 608)

Property settlement agreement. A document specifying the division of assets agreed to by both parties to a divorce and entered into court for the judge's approval. (p. 583)

Proportional taxes. Taxes for which the rate stays the same, regardless of income. (p. 143)

Prospectus. A legal document that offers securities or mutual fund shares for sale. (p. 330)

Proxy. A stockholder's written authorization to transfer voting rights to someone else, usually a company manager. (p. 281)

Purchasing power. The value of money, measured in the amount of goods and services that it can buy. (p. 685)

Pure risk. A chance of loss with no chance for gain. (p. 610)

Pyramid schemes. Mostly illegal multilevel marketing plans that promise distributors commissions from their own sales and those of other distributors they recruit. (p. 688)

R

Reaffirmation. The agreement to repay discharged debts. (p. 456)

Real estate. Land and any buildings on it. (p. 333)

Real estate investment trust (REIT). A corporation that pools the money of many individuals to invest in real estate. (p. 335)

Rebate. A partial refund of an amount spent. (p. 432)

Recall. A request for consumers to return a defective product to the manufacturer, so the manufacturer can refund the consumer's money or fix the product. (p. 706)

Reconciliation. The process of matching your checkbook register with the bank statement. (p. 207)

Redress. A remedy to a problem. (p. 694)

Reference letter. A statement attesting to your character, abilities, and experience, written by someone who can be relied upon to give a sincere report. (p. 53)

References. People over 18, not related to you, who have known you for at least one year and can provide information on your skills, character, and achievements. (p. 51)

Regressive taxes. Taxes that take a smaller share of income as the amount of income grows. (p. 142)

Renter's policy. Insurance that protects renters from property and liability risks. (p. 624)

Reservation. An advance commitment to receive a service at a specified later date. (p. 578)

Restrictive endorsement. An endorsement that restricts or limits the use of a check. (p. 210)

Resume. A summary of work experience, education, abilities, interests, and other information that may be of interest to an employer. (p. 48)

Retraining. Learning new and different skills so that an employee can retain the same level of employ-ability. (p. 11)

Return address. The part of a letter that contains the writer's complete mailing address and the date. (p. 43)

Revenue. Money collected by the government from citizens and businesses in the form of taxes. (p. 142)

Revenue bond. A municipal bond issued to raise money for a public-works project. (p. 310)

Reverse mortgage. A loan against the equity in a borrower's home in which the lender makes tax-free monthly payments to the borrower. (p. 349)

Rider. A small insurance policy that modifies the coverage of the main policy. (p. 655)

Risk. 1. The chance that an investment's value will decrease. (p. 261) 2. The chance of financial loss from perils to people or property covered by insurance. (p. 605)

Risk assumption. Self-insuring; establishing a monetary fund to cover the cost of a loss. (p. 612)

Risk avoidance. Eliminating the chance for loss by not doing the activity that could result in the loss. (p. 612)

Risk management. An organized strategy for controlling financial loss from pure risks. (p. 610)

Risk reduction. Taking measures to lessen the frequency or severity of losses that may occur. (p. 612)

Rule of 72. Technique for estimating the number of years required to double your money at a given rate of return. (p. 260)

S

Salary. The amount of monthly or annual pay that you earn for your labor. (p. 5)

Salutation. The greeting that beings a letter, using a person's name or other form of address sometimes followed by a colon. (p. 43)

Scannable resume. A resume that has been designed for easy reading by a scanner and contains key words from the applicant's career field. (p. 52)

Scarcity. A basic economic problem in which consumers' wants are unlimited, but the resources for producing the products to satisfy these wants are limited. (p. 681)

Securities. Stocks and bonds issued by corporations or by the government. (p. 242)

Security deposit. A refundable amount paid in advance to protect the owner against damage or non-payment. (p. 508)

Self-actualization. Reaching your full potential, growing, and being creative. (p. 79)

Self-assessment inventory. A listing of your strong and weak points that gives you an idea of how to prepare for a career. (p. 12)

Self-employment tax. The total social security and Medicare tax, including employer matching contributions, paid by people who work for themselves. (p. 125)

Self-esteem. Feelings of self-respect and recognition from others. (p. 79)

Seniority. The policy that the last workers hired will be the first ones laid off when jobs must be cut. (p. 132)

Service credit. An agreement to have a service performed now and pay for it later. (p. 396)

Share account. A savings account at a credit union; the shares are part ownership in the credit union. (p. 242)

Short selling. Selling stock borrowed from a broker that must be replaced at a later time. (p. 289)

Simple interest. Interest computed on the amount borrowed (or saved) only, without compounding. (p. 435)

Social Security Act. Established a national social insurance program that provides federal aid for the elderly and for disabled workers. (p. 94)

Special endorsement. An endorsement that transfers the right to cash the check to someone else. (p. 210)

Speculative risk. A risk that may result in either loss or gain and is therefore uninsurable. (p. 610)

Spreadsheet. Computer program that organizes data in columns and rows and can perform calculations using the data. (p. 189)

Standard deduction. A stated amount that you may subtract from adjusted gross income instead of itemizing your deductions. (p. 150)

Statute of limitations. A legally defined time limit in which a lawsuit may be filed for various complaints. (p. 727)

Sticker price. The manufacturer's suggested retail price of a car, appearing on the tag on the car window. (p. 550)

Stock. A unit of ownership in a corporation. (p. 270)

Stock split. An increase in the number of outstanding shares of a company's stock. (p. 291)

Stockbroker. An employee of a brokerage firm, who buys and sells securities for investors. (p. 242)

Stockholders. Shareholders; owners of a corporation. (p. 280)

Stop payment order. A request that the bank not cash a specific check. (p. 216)

Supply. The quantity of goods and services that producers are willing and able to provide. (p. 682)

Sympathetic listening. The ability to perceive from another person's point of view and to sense what the person is feeling. (p. 69)

T

Target market. A specific consumer group to which advertisements are designed to appeal. (p. 491)

Tax brackets. Income ranges to which tax rates apply. (p. 144)

Tax credit. An amount subtracted directly from the tax owed. (p. 150)

Tax evasion. Willful failure to pay taxes. (p. 144)

Taxable income. The income on which you pay tax. (p. 150)

Tenant. The person who rents property from a landlord. (p. 513)

Term life insurance. A life insurance policy that remains in effect for a specified period of time. (p. 656)

Thank-you letter. A follow-up tool to remind the interviewer of your qualifications and desire to work for the company. (p. 60)

Title. A legal document that establishes ownership. (p. 537)

Transfer payments. Government grants to some citizens paid with money collected from other citizens, generally through taxes. (p. 685)

Travel agency. A business that arranges transportation, accommodations, and itineraries for customers. (p. 579)

Trial court. The first court to hear a case or trial (a court of original jurisdiction). (p. 723)

Trust. A legal document in which an individual gives someone else control of property, for ultimate distribution to another person. (p. 352)

20/10 Rule. Your total borrowing should not exceed 20 percent of your yearly take-home pay, and you should not take on monthly payments that total more than 10 percent of your monthly take-home pay. (p. 450)

U

Umbrella policy. Insurance that supplements basic auto and property liability coverage by expanding reimbursement limits and including some risks that were excluded in the basic coverage. (p. 636)

Unemployment insurance. Insurance that provides benefits to workers who lose their jobs through no fault of their own. (p. 94)

Uninsured/underinsured motorist coverage. Automobile insurance that pays for your injuries when the other driver is legally liable but unable to pay. (p. 635)

Unsecured debt. A loan that is not back by pledged assets. (p. 454)

Unused credit. The remaining credit available to you, calculated as your credit limit minus the amount you have already spent. (p. 430)

Upgrading. Advancing to a higher level of skill to increase your usefulness to an employer. (p. 11)

Upholstery. Covering on seats, such as cloth, vinyl, or leather. (p. 561)

Upward communication. Communication that flows from lower to higher levels of an organization. (p. 72)

Usury laws. Laws setting maximum interest rates that may be charged for loans. (p. 399)

V

Values. 1. The ideals in life that are important to you. (p. 22) 2. The principles by which a person lives. (p. 483)

Variable expenses. Costs that vary in amount and type, depending on events and the choices you make. (p. 176)

Vehicle emission test. A test to verify that a vehicle meets the minimum clean-air standards. (p. 549)

Vehicle identification number (VIN). A unique number that identifies an automobile. (p. 549)

Vested. Entitled to receive a full retirement account after a specified period of time. (p. 129)

Voluntary arbitration. When an independent third person listens to both sides in a dispute and makes a recommendation but cannot impose it. (p. 734)

Voluntary bankruptcy. A financial situation that occurs when a debtor files a petition with a federal court asking to be declared bankrupt. (p. 454)

W

Warranty. A statement about a product's qualities or performance that the seller assures the buyer are true. (p. 187)

Wedding party. The active participants in a wedding ceremony—bride, groom, best man, maid of honor, and so on. (p. 573)

Will. A legal document that tells how the decedent wishes his or her property to be distributed upon death. (p. 351)

Work characteristics. Daily activities at work, such as indoor or outdoor work or working with people or alone. (p. 8)

Work history. A record of all jobs held and the length of time spent with each employer. (p. 33)

Workers' compensation. An insurance program that pays benefits to workers and their families for injury, illness, loss of income, or death that occurs as a result of a job. (p. 95)

Z

Zero-coupon bond. A bond that is sold at a deep discount, makes no interest payments, and is redeemable for its face value at maturity. (p. 312)

Index

INDEX